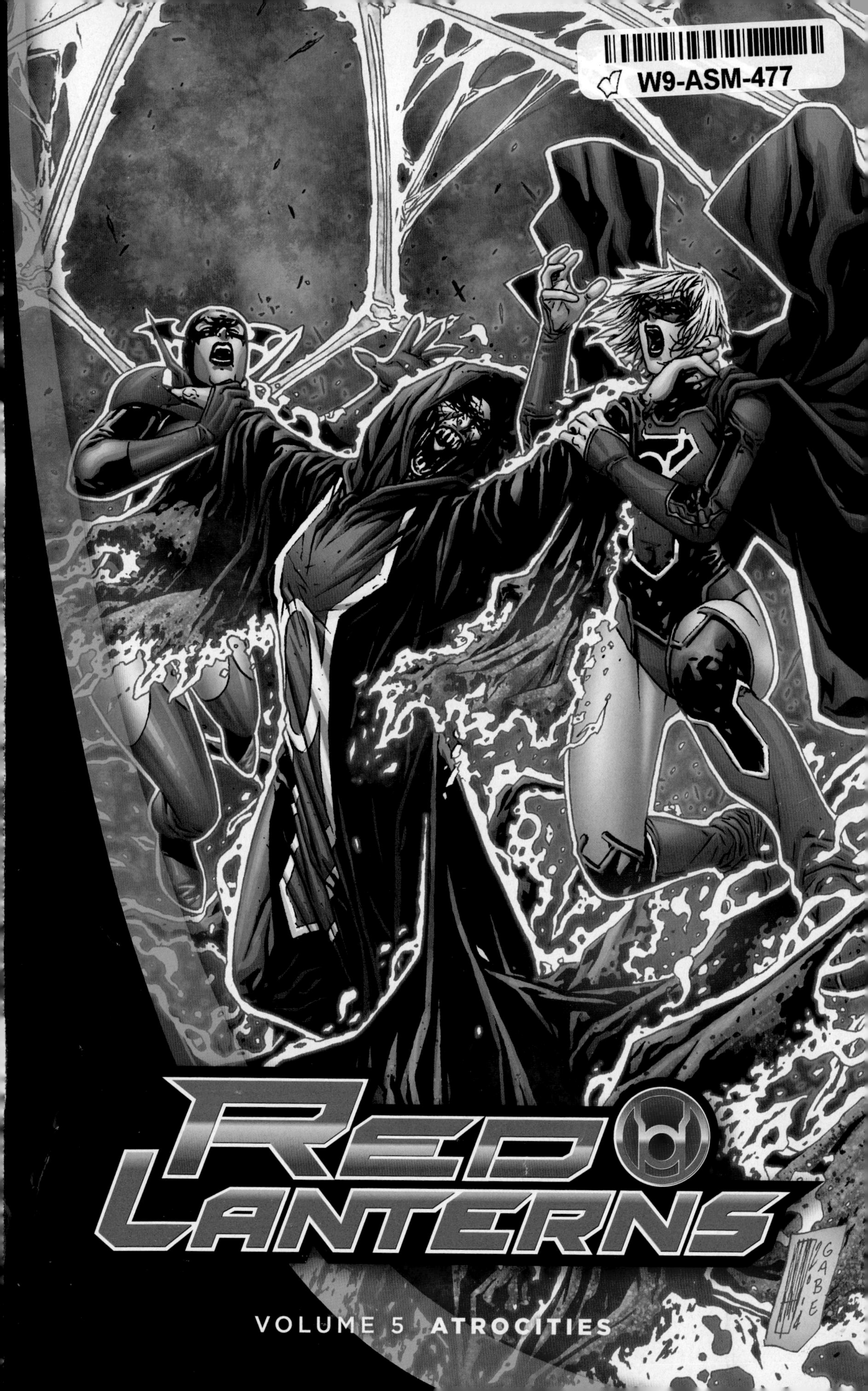
RED LANTERNS
VOLUME 5 ATROCITIES

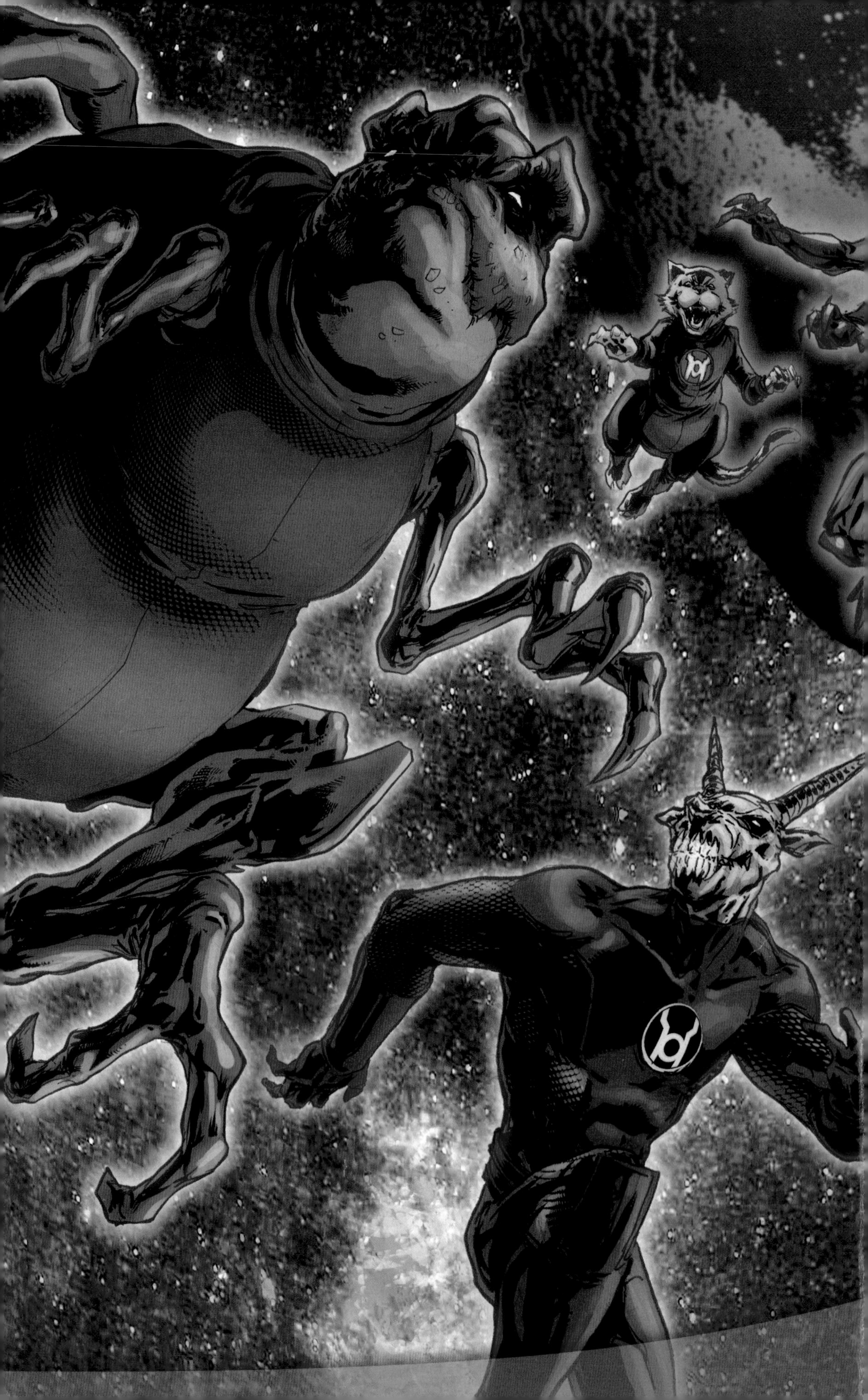

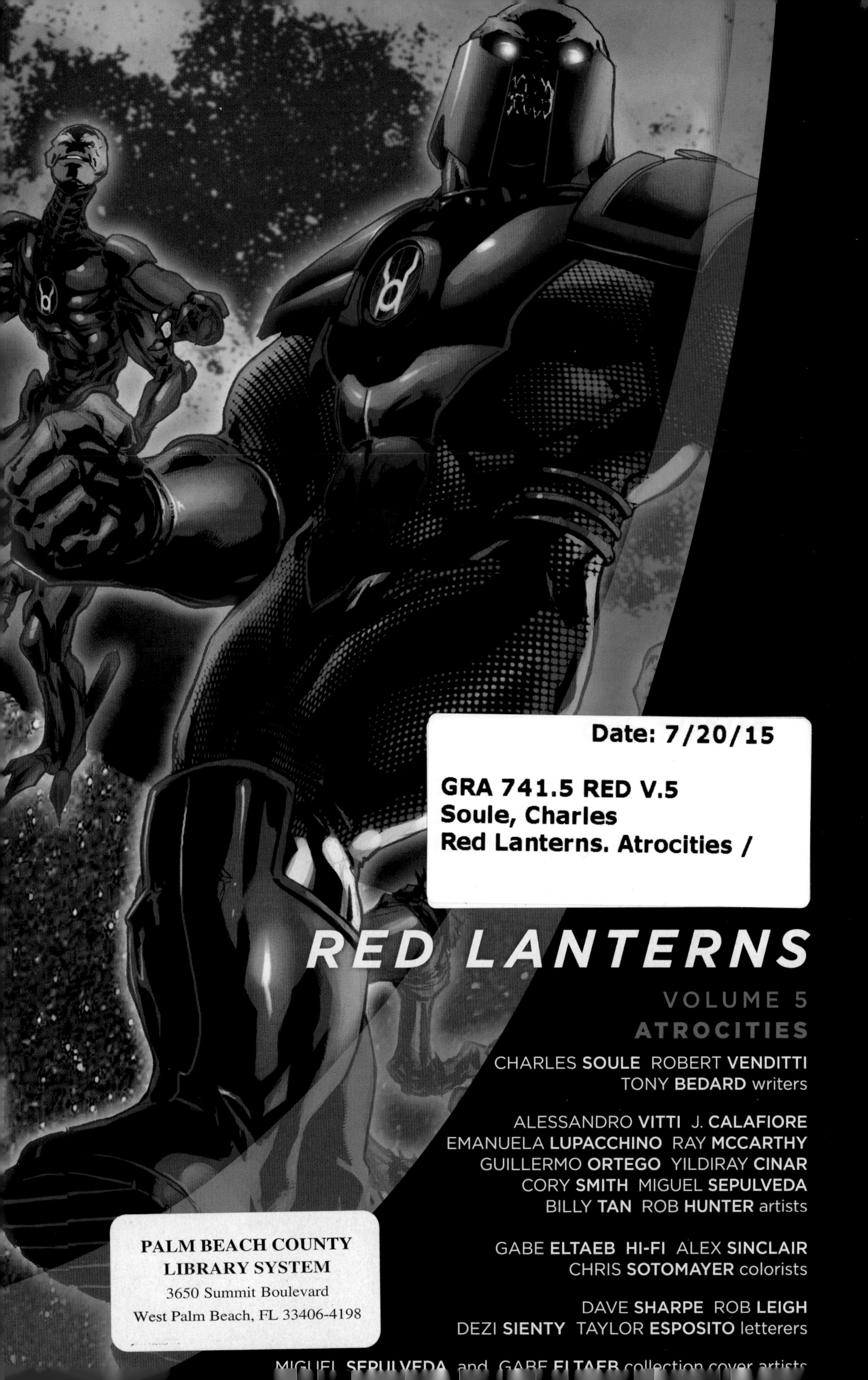

RED LANTERNS

VOLUME 5
ATROCITIES

CHARLES **SOULE** ROBERT **VENDITTI**
TONY **BEDARD** writers

ALESSANDRO **VITTI** J. **CALAFIORE**
EMANUELA **LUPACCHINO** RAY **MCCARTHY**
GUILLERMO **ORTEGO** YILDIRAY **CINAR**
CORY **SMITH** MIGUEL **SEPULVEDA**
BILLY **TAN** ROB **HUNTER** artists

GABE **ELTAEB** **HI-FI** ALEX **SINCLAIR**
CHRIS **SOTOMAYER** colorists

DAVE **SHARPE** ROB **LEIGH**
DEZI **SIENTY** TAYLOR **ESPOSITO** letterers

MIGUEL **SEPULVEDA** and GABE **ELTAEB** collection cover artists

CHRIS CONROY DARREN SHAN RICKEY PURDIN Editors – Original Series .
LIZ ERICKSON Editor ROBBIN BROSTERMAN Design Director – Books ROBBIE BIEDERMAN Publication Design

BOB HARRAS Senior VP – Editor-in-Chief, DC Comics

DIANE NELSON President DAN DIDIO and JIM LEE Co-Publishers
GEOFF JOHNS Chief Creative Officer
AMIT DESAI Senior VP – Marketing and Franchise Management
AMY GENKINS Senior VP – Business and Legal Affairs NAIRI GARDINER Senior VP – Finance
JEFF BOISON VP – Publishing Planning MARK CHIARELLO VP – Art Direction and Design
JOHN CUNNINGHAM VP – Marketing TERRI CUNNINGHAM VP – Editorial Administration
LARRY GANEM VP – Talent Relations and Services ALISON GILL Senior VP – Manufacturing and Operations
HANK KANALZ Senior VP – Vertigo and Integrated Publishing JAY KOGAN VP – Business and Legal Affairs, Publishing
JACK MAHAN VP – Business Affairs, Talent NICK NAPOLITANO VP – Manufacturing Administration
SUE POHJA VP – Book Sales FRED RUIZ VP – Manufacturing Operations
COURTNEY SIMMONS Senior VP – Publicity BOB WAYNE Senior VP – Sales

RED LANTERNS VOLUME 5: ATROCITIES

DC Comics, 1700 Broadway, New York, NY 10019
A Warner Bros. Entertainment Company.
Printed by RR Donnelley, Salem, VA, USA. 10/31/14. First Printing.

ISBN: 978-1-4012-5090-4

Soule, Charles, author.
Red Lanterns. Volume 5, Atrocities / Charles Soule, Tony Bedard, writers ; Alessandro Vitti, artist.
pages cm. — (The New 52!)
ISBN 978-1-4012-5090-4 (paperback)
1. Graphic novels. I. Bedard, Tony, author. II. Vitti, Alessandro, 1978- illustrator. III. Title. IV. Title: Atrocities.

PN6728.R439S69 2014
741.5'973 — dc23

2014027344

SUSTAINABLE
FORESTRY
INITIATIVE

Certified Chain of Custody
20% Certified Forest Content,
80% Certified Sourcing
www.sfiprogram.org
SFI-01042
APPLIES TO TEXT STOCK ONLY

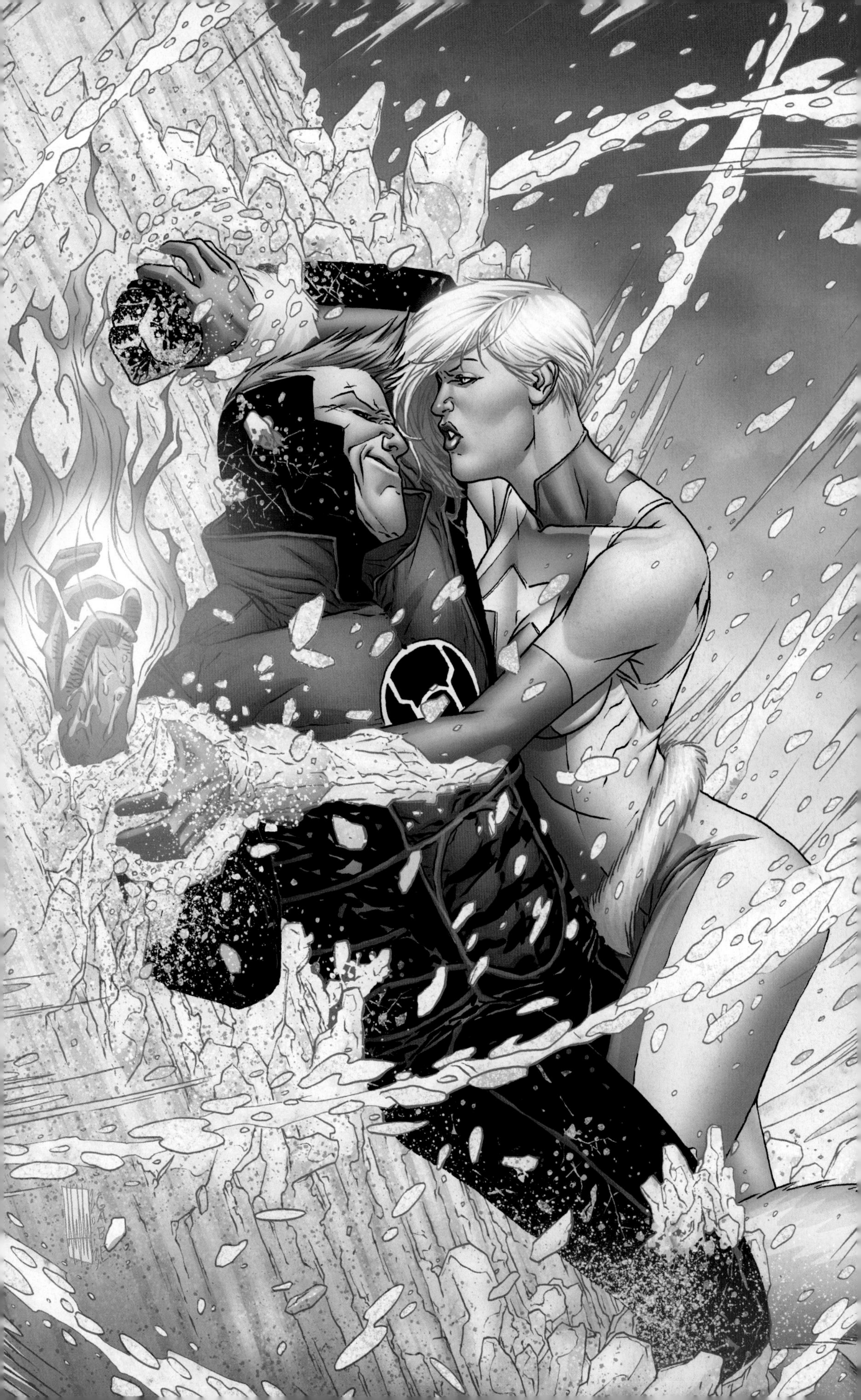

CHARLES SOULE writer **ALESSANDRO VITTI** (pages 7-11, 15, 19, 24) **J. CALAFIORE** (pages 12-14, 20-23, 25-26) artists **GABE ELTAEB** colorist
DAVE SHARPE letterer cover art by **ALESSANDRO VITTI** with **GABE ELTAEB**

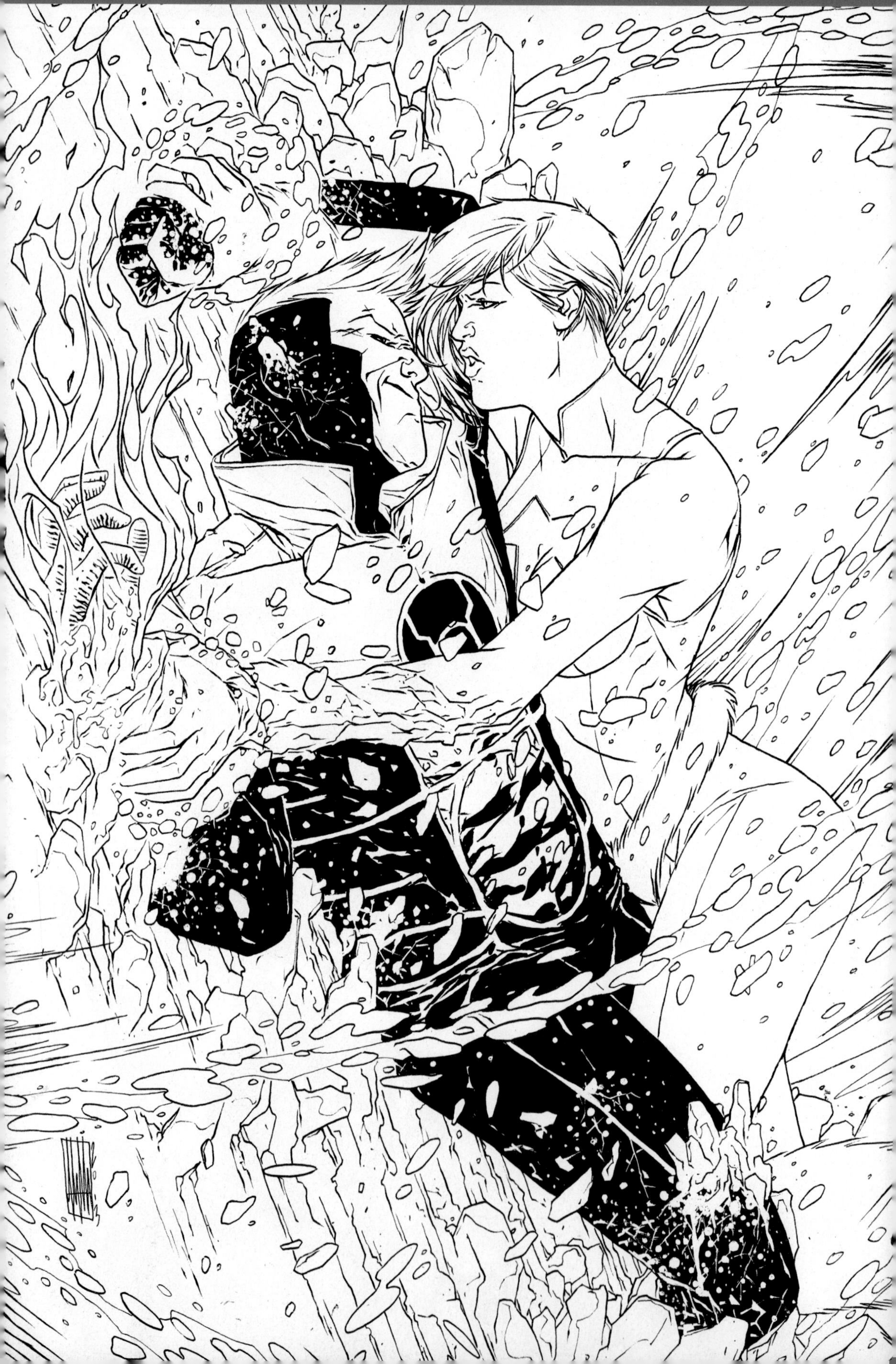

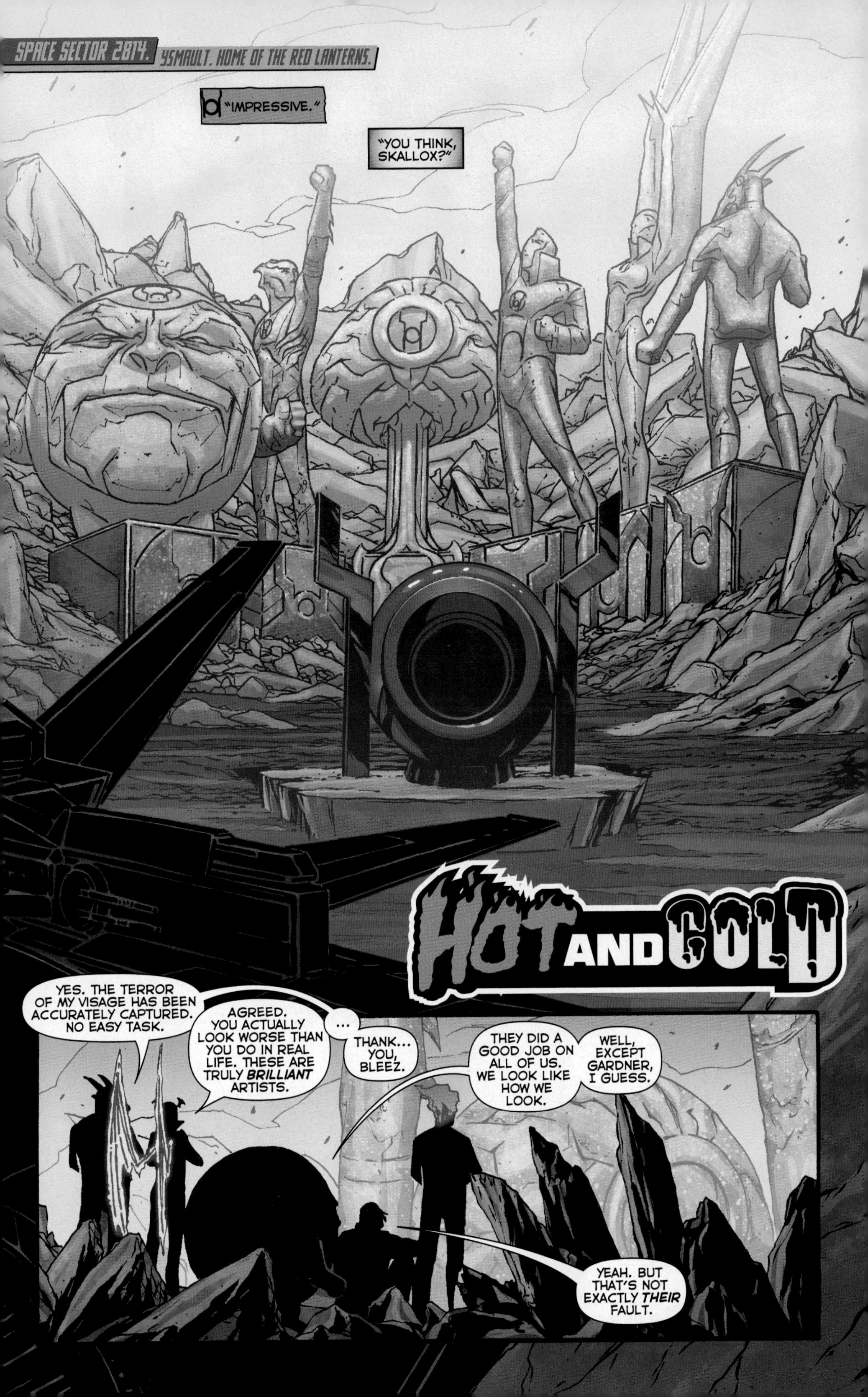
SPACE SECTOR 2814.
YSMAULT. HOME OF THE RED LANTERNS.
"IMPRESSIVE."
"YOU THINK, SKALLOX?"
HOT AND COLD
YES. THE TERROR OF MY VISAGE HAS BEEN ACCURATELY CAPTURED. NO EASY TASK.
AGREED. YOU ACTUALLY LOOK WORSE THAN YOU DO IN REAL LIFE. THESE ARE TRULY BRILLIANT ARTISTS.
...
THANK... YOU, BLEEZ.
THEY DID A GOOD JOB ON ALL OF US. WE LOOK LIKE HOW WE LOOK.
WELL, EXCEPT GARDNER, I GUESS.
YEAH. BUT THAT'S NOT EXACTLY THEIR FAULT.

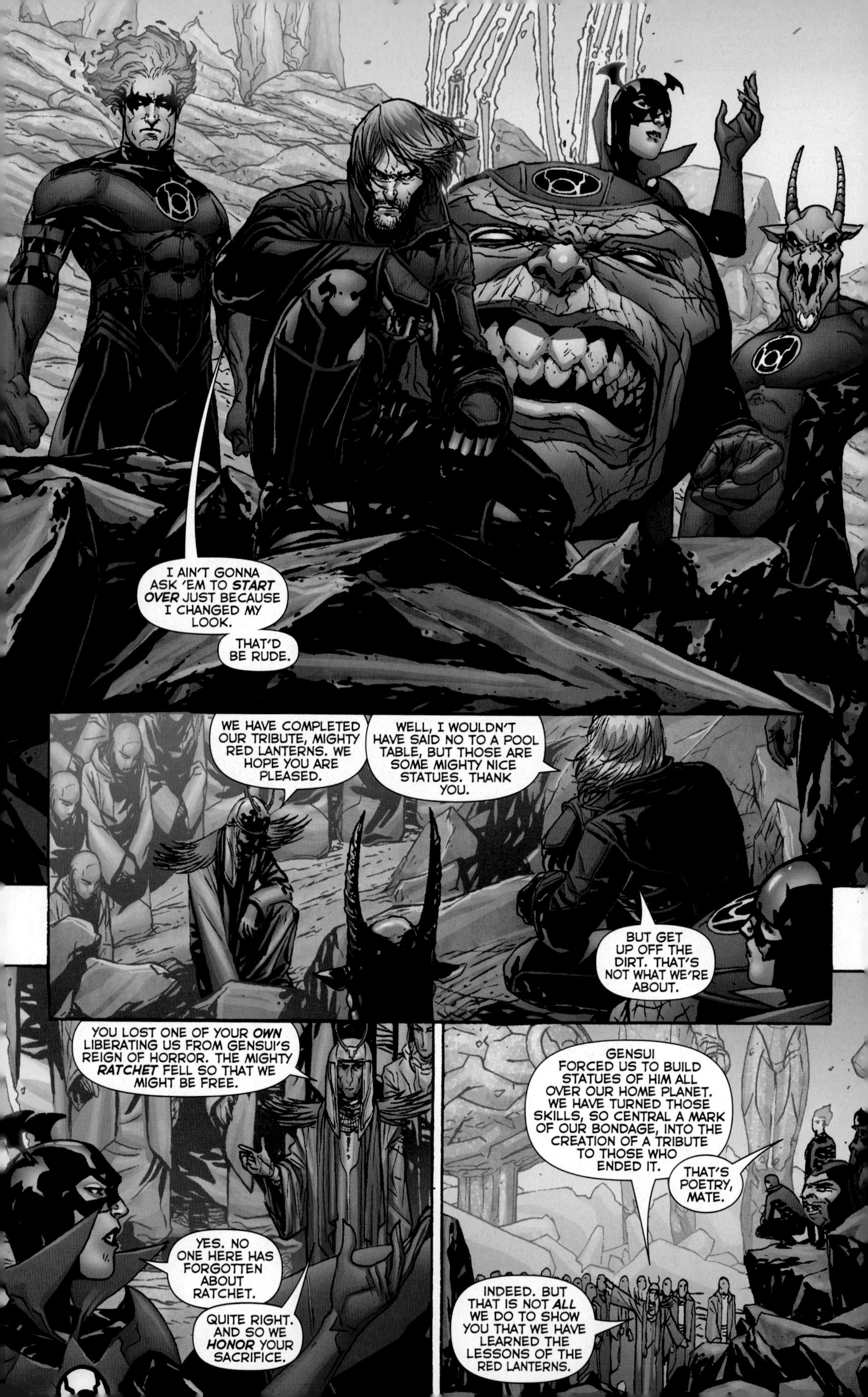

I AIN'T GONNA ASK 'EM TO START OVER JUST BECAUSE I CHANGED MY LOOK.
THAT'D BE RUDE.
WE HAVE COMPLETED OUR TRIBUTE, MIGHTY RED LANTERNS. WE HOPE YOU ARE PLEASED.
WELL, I WOULDN'T HAVE SAID NO TO A POOL TABLE, BUT THOSE ARE SOME MIGHTY NICE STATUES. THANK YOU.
BUT GET UP OFF THE DIRT. THAT'S NOT WHAT WE'RE ABOUT.
YOU LOST ONE OF YOUR OWN LIBERATING US FROM GENSUI'S REIGN OF HORROR. THE MIGHTY RATCHET FELL SO THAT WE MIGHT BE FREE.
YES. NO ONE HERE HAS FORGOTTEN ABOUT RATCHET.
QUITE RIGHT. AND SO WE HONOR YOUR SACRIFICE.
GENSUI FORCED US TO BUILD STATUES OF HIM ALL OVER OUR HOME PLANET. WE HAVE TURNED THOSE SKILLS, SO CENTRAL A MARK OF OUR BONDAGE, INTO THE CREATION OF A TRIBUTE TO THOSE WHO ENDED IT.
THAT'S POETRY, MATE.
INDEED. BUT THAT IS NOT ALL WE DO TO SHOW YOU THAT WE HAVE LEARNED THE LESSONS OF THE RED LANTERNS.

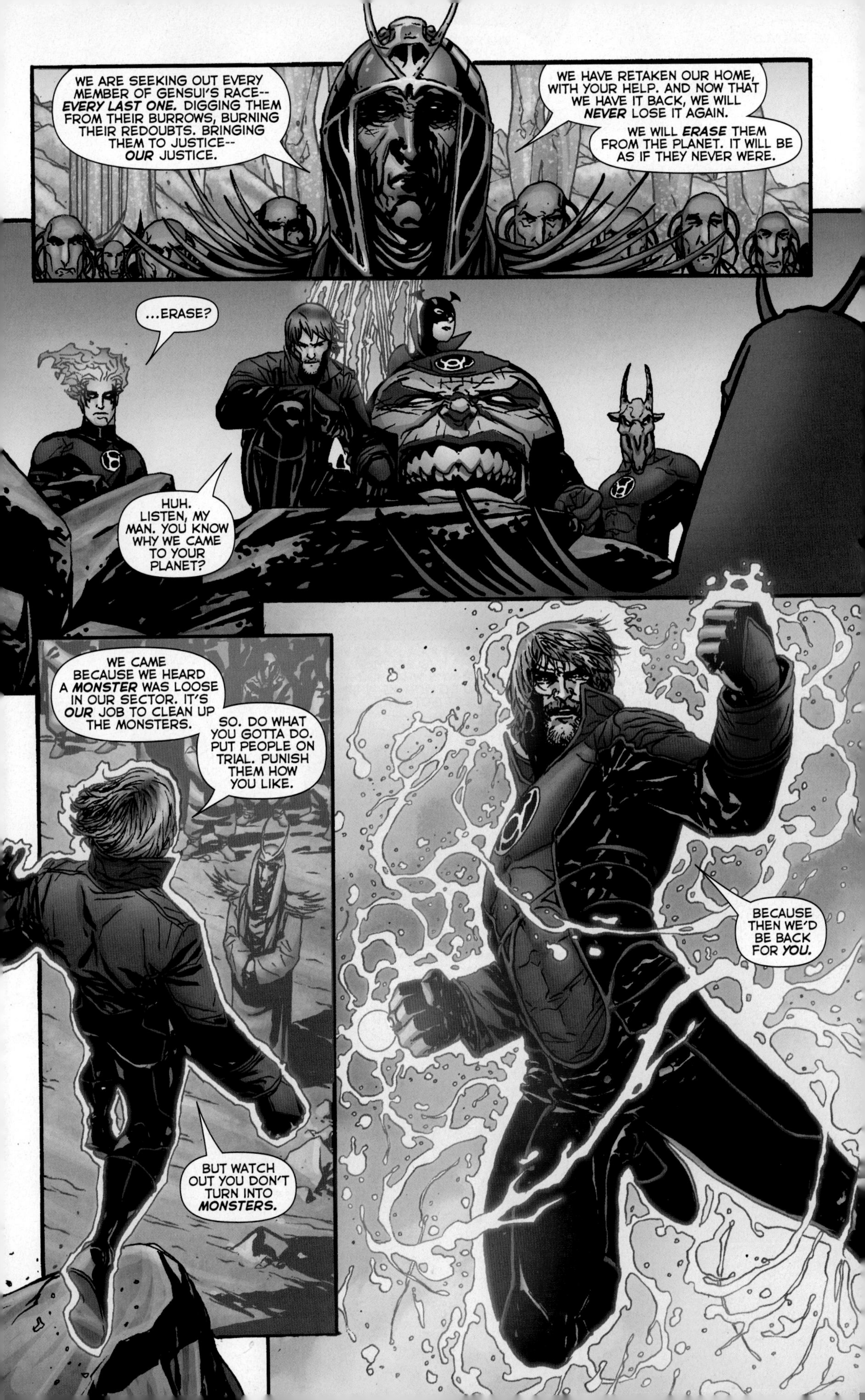

WE ARE SEEKING OUT EVERY MEMBER OF GENSUI'S RACE-- EVERY LAST ONE. DIGGING THEM FROM THEIR BURROWS, BURNING THEIR REDOUBTS. BRINGING THEM TO JUSTICE-- OUR JUSTICE.
WE HAVE RETAKEN OUR HOME, WITH YOUR HELP. AND NOW THAT WE HAVE IT BACK, WE WILL NEVER LOSE IT AGAIN.
WE WILL ERASE THEM FROM THE PLANET. IT WILL BE AS IF THEY NEVER WERE.
...ERASE?
HUH. LISTEN, MY MAN. YOU KNOW WHY WE CAME TO YOUR PLANET?
WE CAME BECAUSE WE HEARD A MONSTER WAS LOOSE IN OUR SECTOR. IT'S OUR JOB TO CLEAN UP THE MONSTERS.
SO. DO WHAT YOU GOTTA DO. PUT PEOPLE ON TRIAL. PUNISH THEM HOW YOU LIKE.
BUT WATCH OUT YOU DON'T TURN INTO MONSTERS.
BECAUSE THEN WE'D BE BACK FOR YOU.

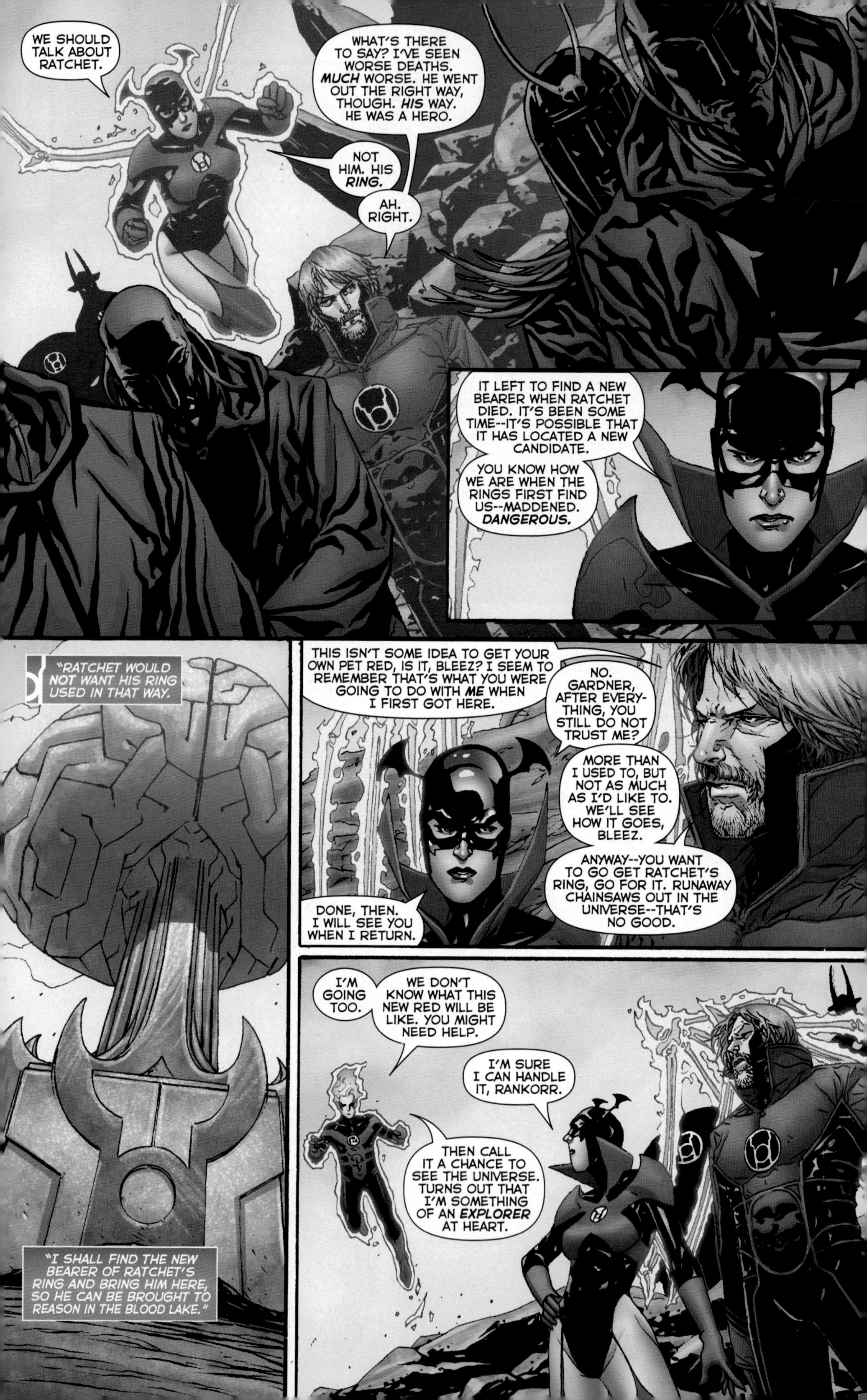
WE SHOULD TALK ABOUT RATCHET.
WHAT'S THERE TO SAY? I'VE SEEN WORSE DEATHS. MUCH WORSE. HE WENT OUT THE RIGHT WAY, THOUGH. HIS WAY. HE WAS A HERO.
NOT HIM. HIS RING.
AH. RIGHT.
IT LEFT TO FIND A NEW BEARER WHEN RATCHET DIED. IT'S BEEN SOME TIME--IT'S POSSIBLE THAT IT HAS LOCATED A NEW CANDIDATE.
YOU KNOW HOW WE ARE WHEN THE RINGS FIRST FIND US--MADDENED. DANGEROUS.
"RATCHET WOULD NOT WANT HIS RING USED IN THAT WAY.
"I SHALL FIND THE NEW BEARER OF RATCHET'S RING AND BRING HIM HERE, SO HE CAN BE BROUGHT TO REASON IN THE BLOOD LAKE."
THIS ISN'T SOME IDEA TO GET YOUR OWN PET RED, IS IT, BLEEZ? I SEEM TO REMEMBER THAT'S WHAT YOU WERE GOING TO DO WITH ME WHEN I FIRST GOT HERE.
NO. GARDNER, AFTER EVERY-THING, YOU STILL DO NOT TRUST ME?
MORE THAN I USED TO, BUT NOT AS MUCH AS I'D LIKE TO. WE'LL SEE HOW IT GOES, BLEEZ.
ANYWAY--YOU WANT TO GO GET RATCHET'S RING, GO FOR IT. RUNAWAY CHAINSAWS OUT IN THE UNIVERSE--THAT'S NO GOOD.
DONE, THEN. I WILL SEE YOU WHEN I RETURN.
I'M GOING TOO.
WE DON'T KNOW WHAT THIS NEW RED WILL BE LIKE. YOU MIGHT NEED HELP.
I'M SURE I CAN HANDLE IT, RANKORR.
THEN CALL IT A CHANCE TO SEE THE UNIVERSE. TURNS OUT THAT I'M SOMETHING OF AN EXPLORER AT HEART.

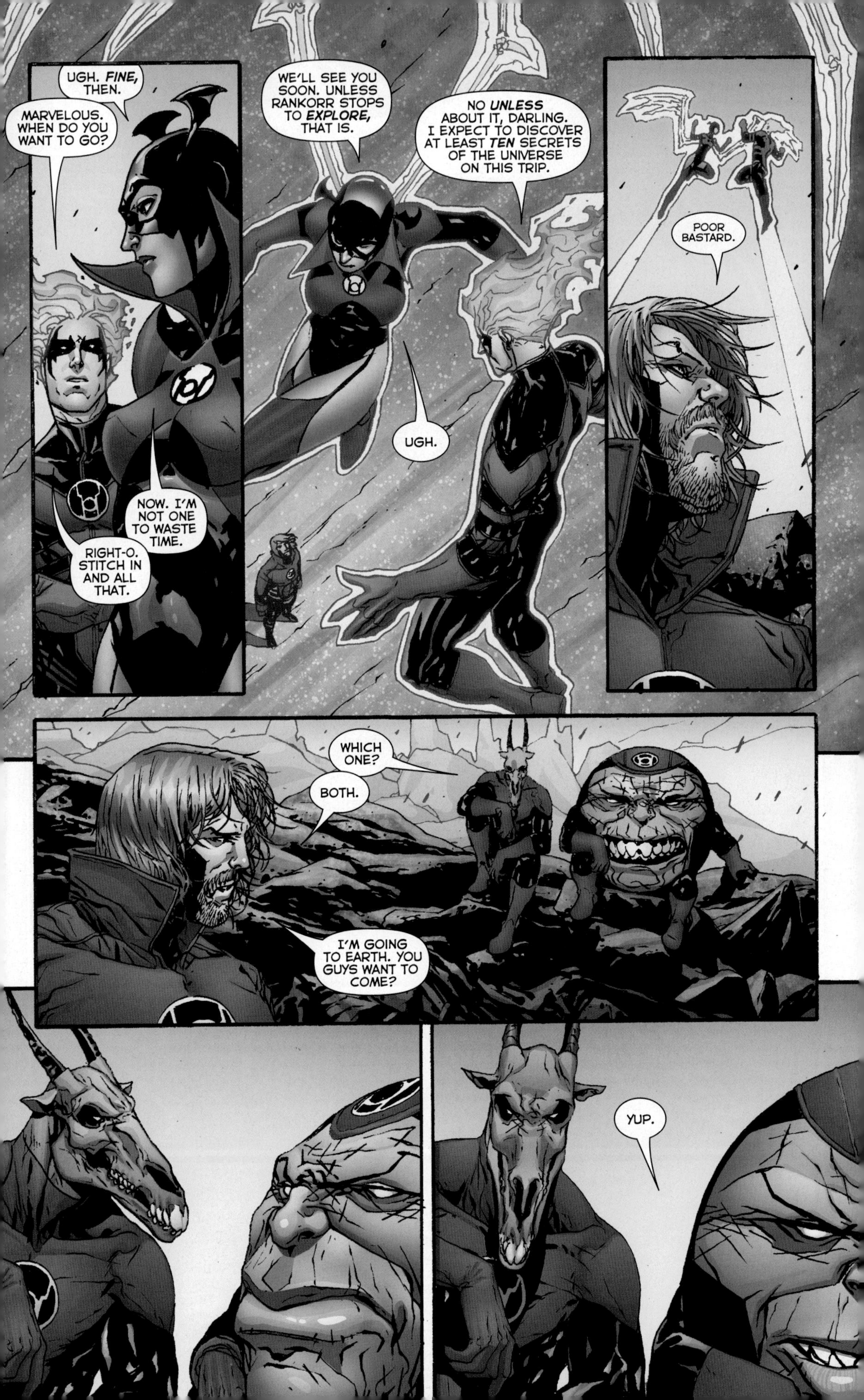
UGH. *FINE,* THEN.
MARVELOUS. WHEN DO YOU WANT TO GO?
NOW. I'M NOT ONE TO WASTE TIME.
RIGHT-O. STITCH IN AND ALL THAT.
WE'LL SEE YOU SOON. UNLESS RANKORR STOPS TO *EXPLORE,* THAT IS.
NO *UNLESS* ABOUT IT, DARLING. I EXPECT TO DISCOVER AT LEAST *TEN* SECRETS OF THE UNIVERSE ON THIS TRIP.
UGH.
POOR BASTARD.
I'M GOING TO EARTH. YOU GUYS WANT TO COME?
WHICH ONE?
BOTH.
YUP.

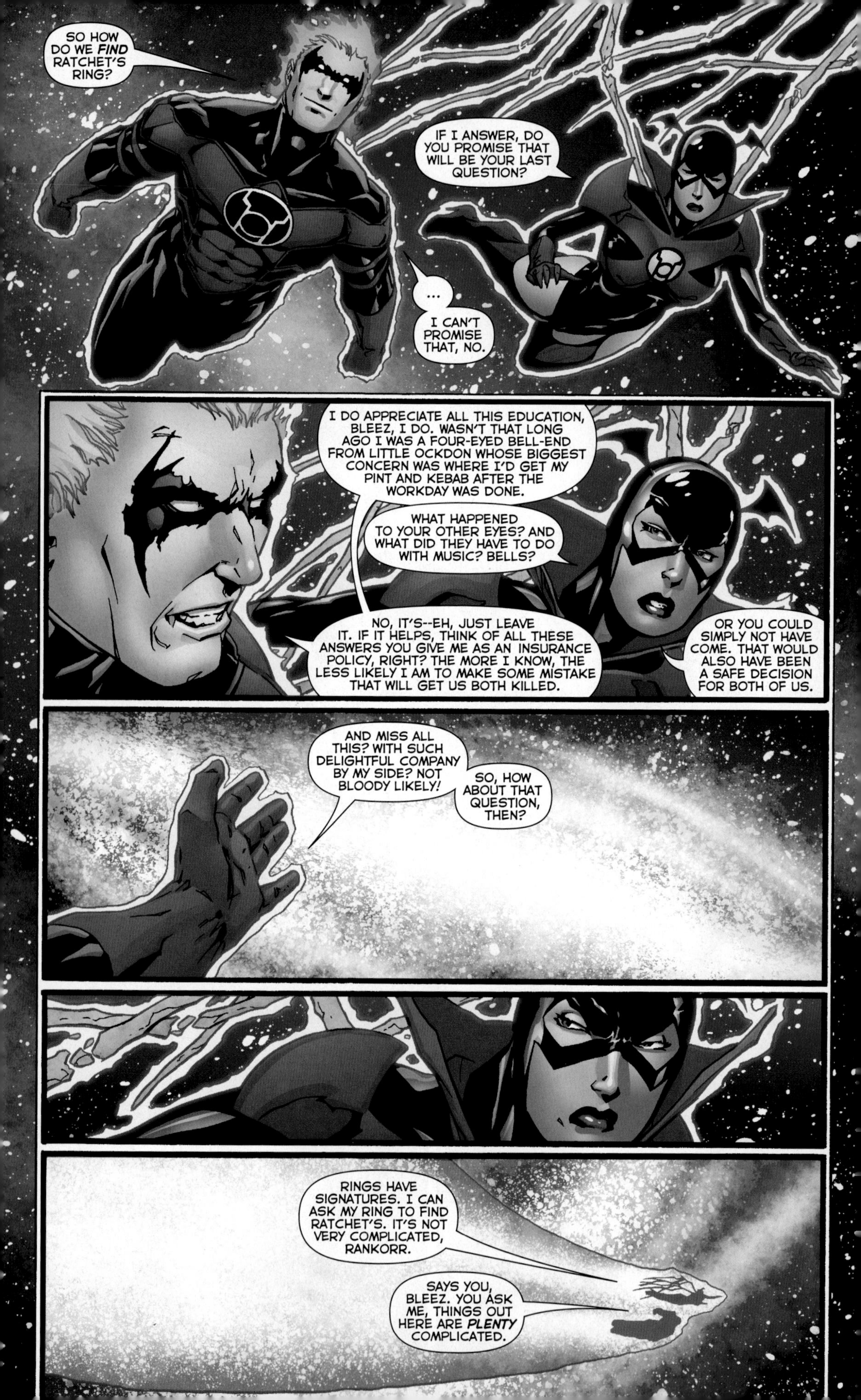
SO HOW DO WE *FIND* RATCHET'S RING?
IF I ANSWER, DO YOU PROMISE THAT WILL BE YOUR LAST QUESTION?
...
I CAN'T PROMISE THAT, NO.
I DO APPRECIATE ALL THIS EDUCATION, BLEEZ, I DO. WASN'T THAT LONG AGO I WAS A FOUR-EYED BELL-END FROM LITTLE OCKDON WHOSE BIGGEST CONCERN WAS WHERE I'D GET MY PINT AND KEBAB AFTER THE WORKDAY WAS DONE.
WHAT HAPPENED TO YOUR OTHER EYES? AND WHAT DID THEY HAVE TO DO WITH MUSIC? BELLS?
NO, IT'S--EH, JUST LEAVE IT. IF IT HELPS, THINK OF ALL THESE ANSWERS YOU GIVE ME AS AN INSURANCE POLICY, RIGHT? THE MORE I KNOW, THE LESS LIKELY I AM TO MAKE SOME MISTAKE THAT WILL GET US BOTH KILLED.
OR YOU COULD SIMPLY NOT HAVE COME. THAT WOULD ALSO HAVE BEEN A SAFE DECISION FOR BOTH OF US.
AND MISS ALL THIS? WITH SUCH DELIGHTFUL COMPANY BY MY SIDE? NOT BLOODY LIKELY!
SO, HOW ABOUT THAT QUESTION, THEN?
RINGS HAVE SIGNATURES. I CAN ASK MY RING TO FIND RATCHET'S. IT'S NOT VERY COMPLICATED, RANKORR.
SAYS YOU, BLEEZ. YOU ASK ME, THINGS OUT HERE ARE *PLENTY* COMPLICATED.

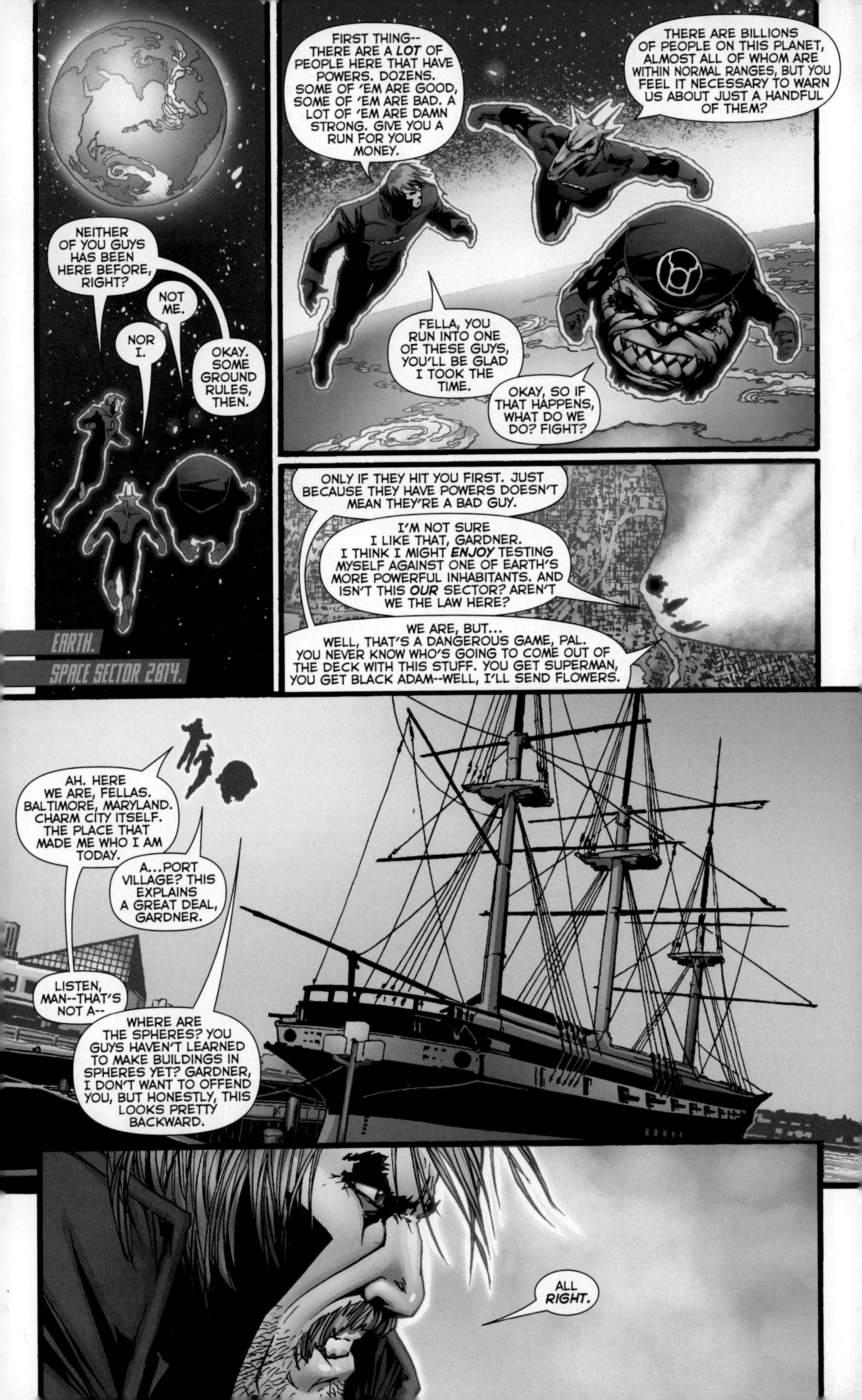
NEITHER OF YOU GUYS HAS BEEN HERE BEFORE, RIGHT?
NOT ME.
NOR I.
OKAY. SOME GROUND RULES, THEN.
EARTH.
SPACE SECTOR 2814.
FIRST THING-- THERE ARE A LOT OF PEOPLE HERE THAT HAVE POWERS. DOZENS. SOME OF 'EM ARE GOOD, SOME OF 'EM ARE BAD. A LOT OF 'EM ARE DAMN STRONG. GIVE YOU A RUN FOR YOUR MONEY.
THERE ARE BILLIONS OF PEOPLE ON THIS PLANET, ALMOST ALL OF WHOM ARE WITHIN NORMAL RANGES, BUT YOU FEEL IT NECESSARY TO WARN US ABOUT JUST A HANDFUL OF THEM?
FELLA, YOU RUN INTO ONE OF THESE GUYS, YOU'LL BE GLAD I TOOK THE TIME.
OKAY, SO IF THAT HAPPENS, WHAT DO WE DO? FIGHT?
ONLY IF THEY HIT YOU FIRST. JUST BECAUSE THEY HAVE POWERS DOESN'T MEAN THEY'RE A BAD GUY.
I'M NOT SURE I LIKE THAT, GARDNER. I THINK I MIGHT ENJOY TESTING MYSELF AGAINST ONE OF EARTH'S MORE POWERFUL INHABITANTS. AND ISN'T THIS OUR SECTOR? AREN'T WE THE LAW HERE?
WE ARE, BUT... WELL, THAT'S A DANGEROUS GAME, PAL. YOU NEVER KNOW WHO'S GOING TO COME OUT OF THE DECK WITH THIS STUFF. YOU GET SUPERMAN, YOU GET BLACK ADAM--WELL, I'LL SEND FLOWERS.
AH. HERE WE ARE, FELLAS. BALTIMORE, MARYLAND. CHARM CITY ITSELF. THE PLACE THAT MADE ME WHO I AM TODAY.
A...PORT VILLAGE? THIS EXPLAINS A GREAT DEAL, GARDNER.
LISTEN, MAN--THAT'S NOT A--
WHERE ARE THE SPHERES? YOU GUYS HAVEN'T LEARNED TO MAKE BUILDINGS IN SPHERES YET? GARDNER, I DON'T WANT TO OFFEND YOU, BUT HONESTLY, THIS LOOKS PRETTY BACKWARD.
ALL RIGHT.

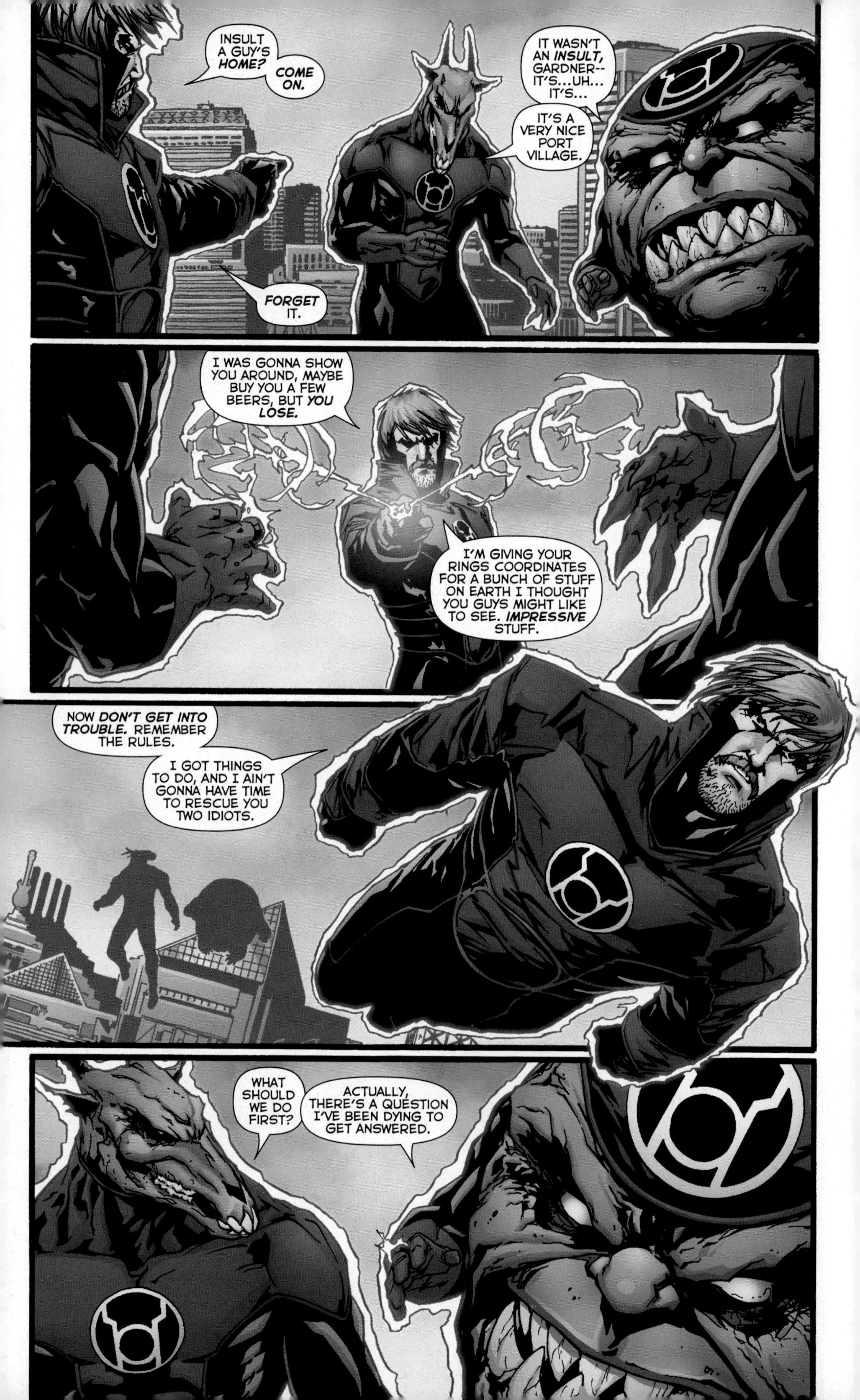
INSULT A GUY'S *HOME?*
COME ON.
IT WASN'T AN *INSULT,* GARDNER-- IT'S...UH... IT'S...
IT'S A VERY NICE PORT VILLAGE.
FORGET IT.
I WAS GONNA SHOW YOU AROUND, MAYBE BUY YOU A FEW BEERS, BUT *YOU LOSE.*
I'M GIVING YOUR RINGS COORDINATES FOR A BUNCH OF STUFF ON EARTH I THOUGHT YOU GUYS MIGHT LIKE TO SEE. *IMPRESSIVE* STUFF.
NOW *DON'T GET INTO TROUBLE.* REMEMBER THE RULES.
I GOT THINGS TO DO, AND I AIN'T GONNA HAVE TIME TO RESCUE YOU TWO IDIOTS.
WHAT SHOULD WE DO FIRST?
ACTUALLY, THERE'S A QUESTION I'VE BEEN DYING TO GET ANSWERED.

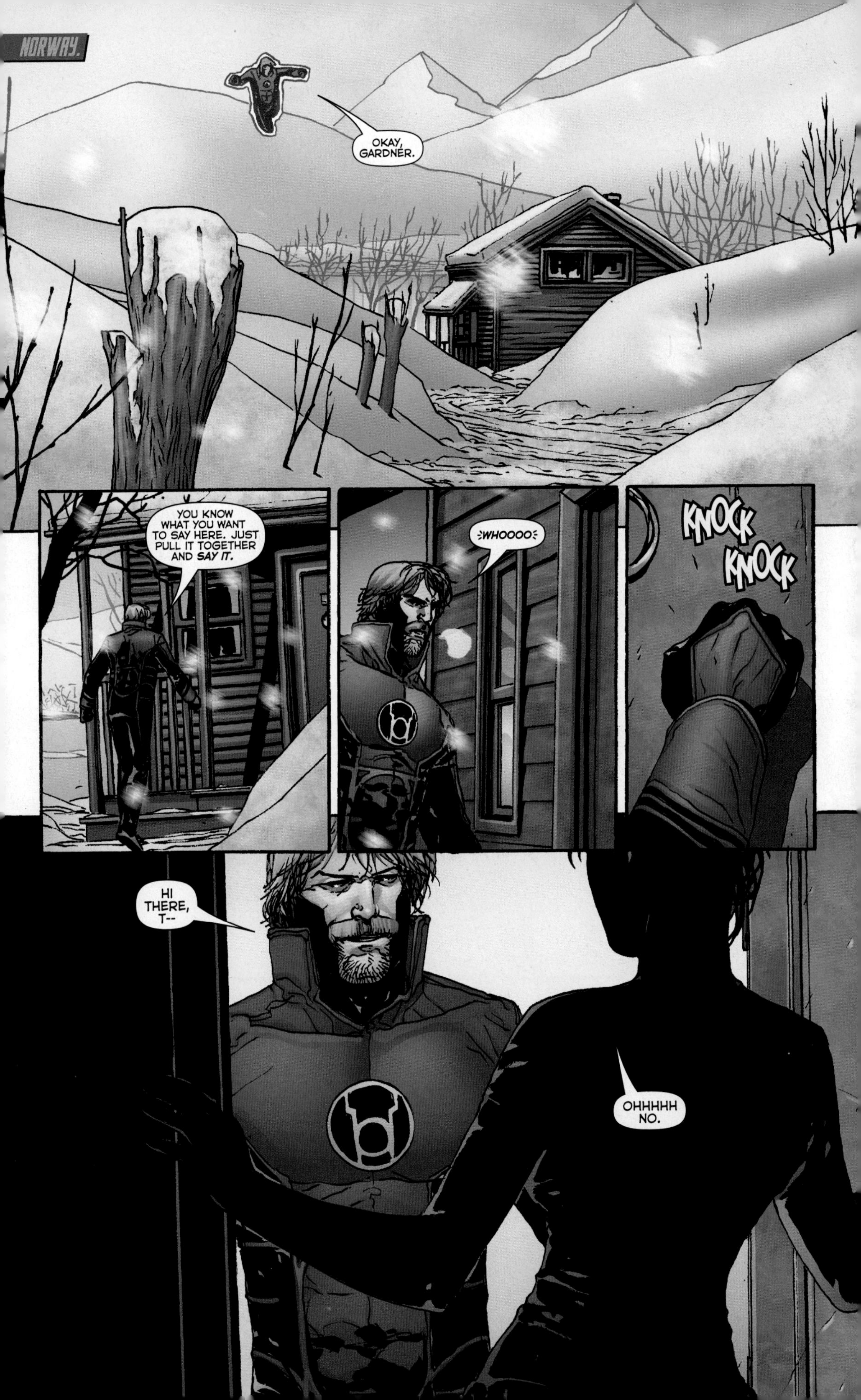
NORWAY.
OKAY, GARDNER.
YOU KNOW WHAT YOU WANT TO SAY HERE. JUST PULL IT TOGETHER AND SAY IT.
WHOOOO
KNOCK KNOCK
HI THERE, T--
OHHHHH NO.

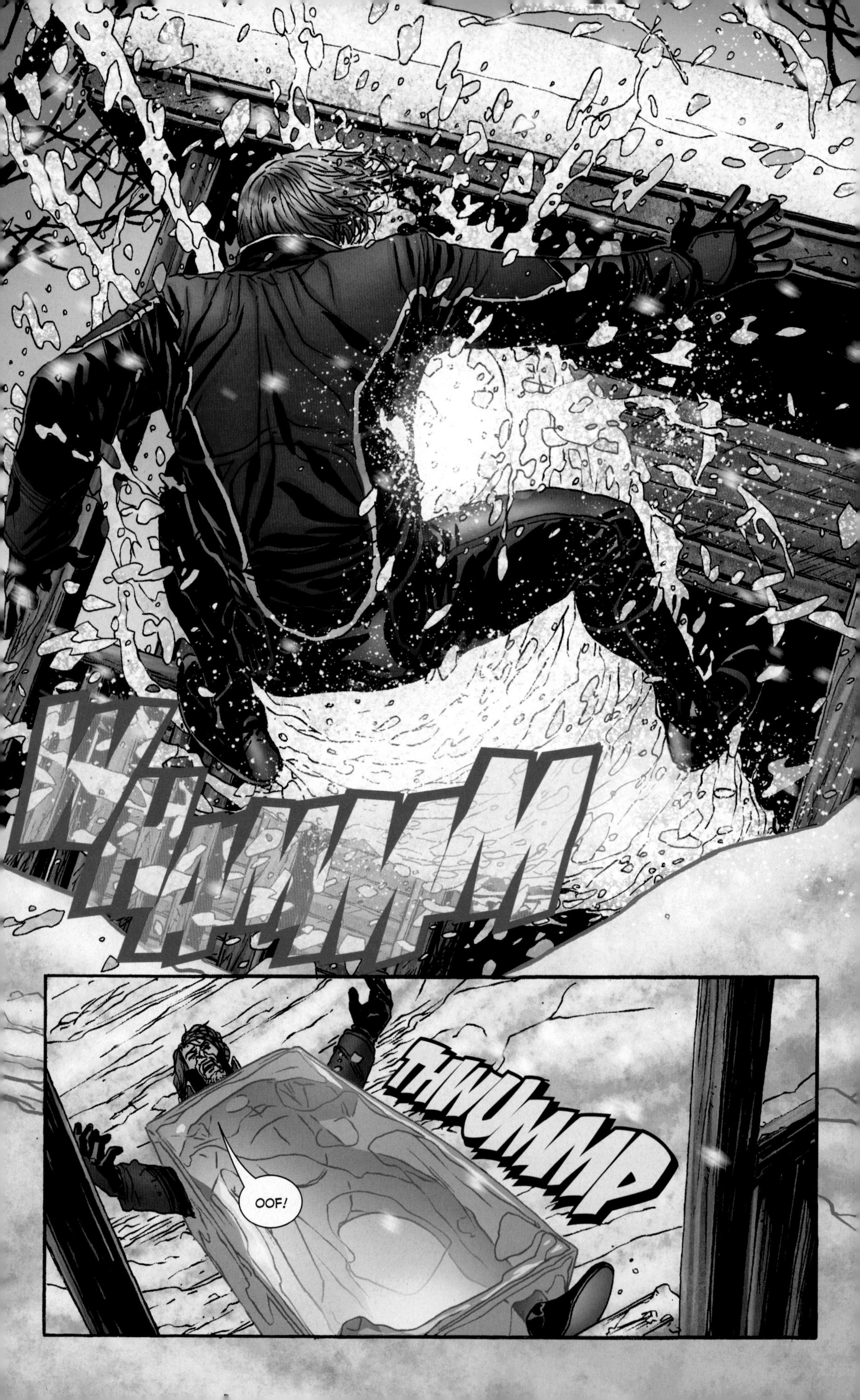
WHAMMM
THWUMMP
OOF!

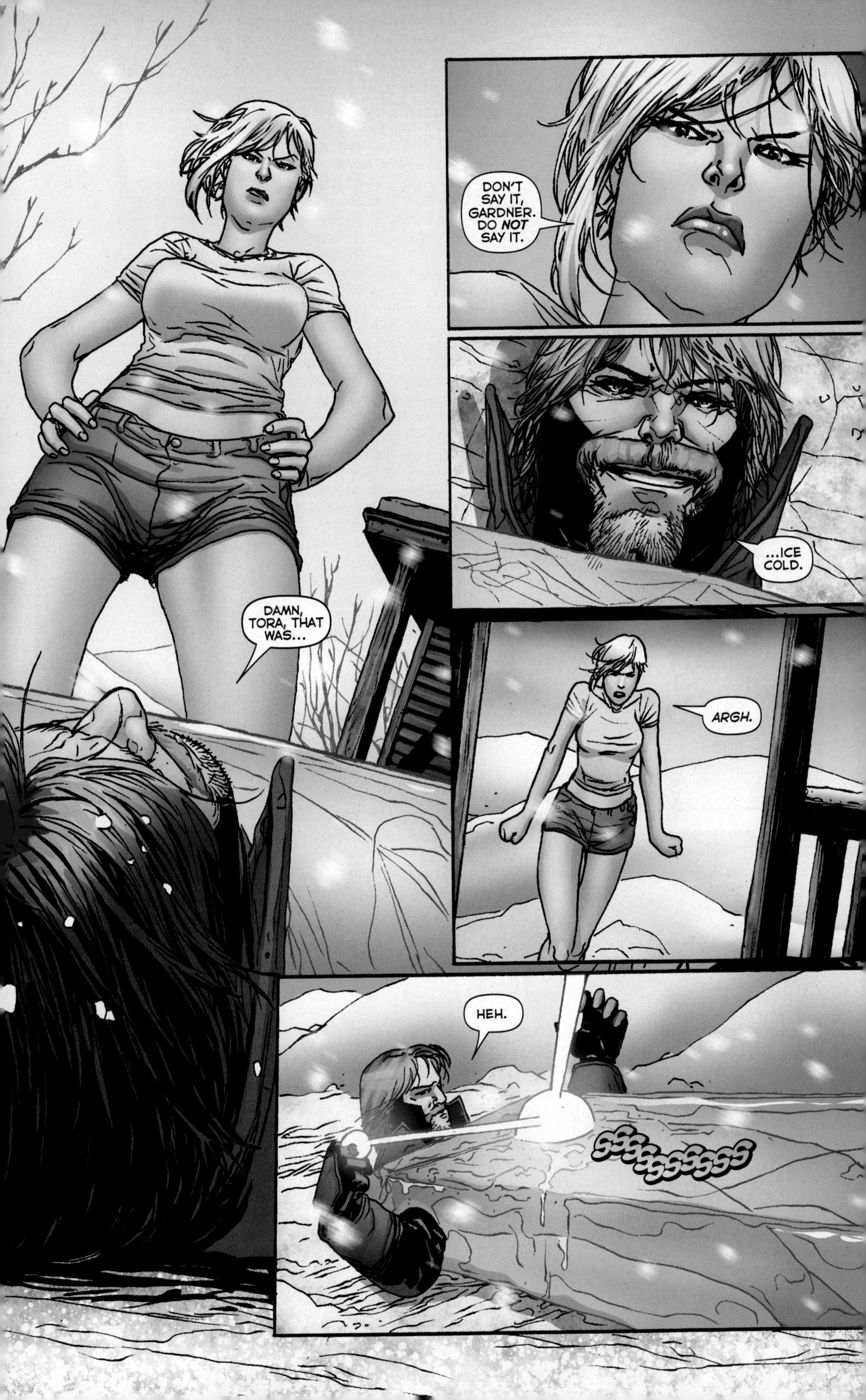
DON'T SAY IT, GARDNER. DO NOT SAY IT.
DAMN, TORA, THAT WAS...
...ICE COLD.
ARGH.
HEH.
SSSSSSSSSS

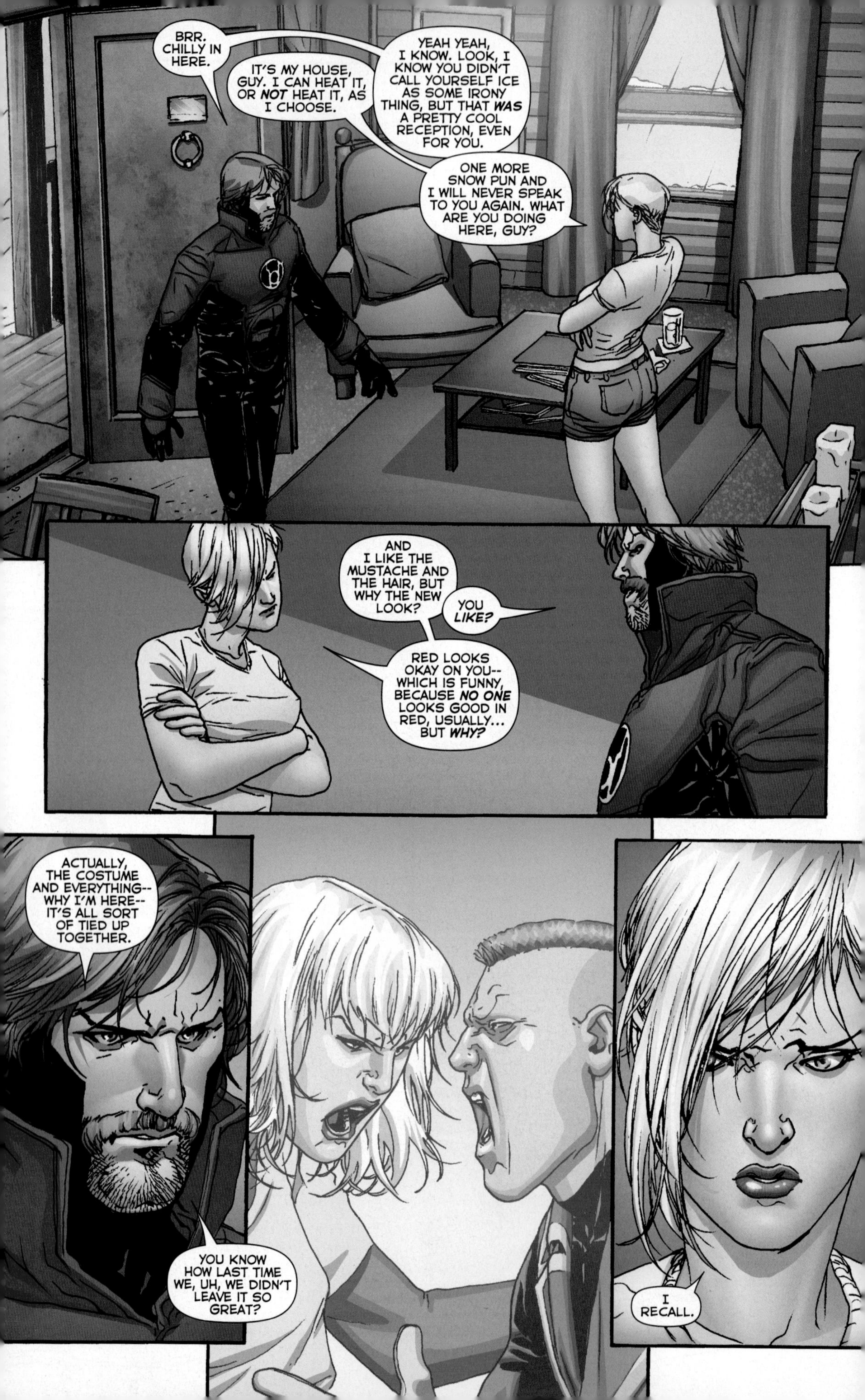
BRR. CHILLY IN HERE.
IT'S MY HOUSE, GUY. I CAN HEAT IT, OR *NOT* HEAT IT, AS I CHOOSE.
YEAH YEAH, I KNOW. LOOK, I KNOW YOU DIDN'T CALL YOURSELF ICE AS SOME IRONY THING, BUT THAT *WAS* A PRETTY COOL RECEPTION, EVEN FOR YOU.
ONE MORE SNOW PUN AND I WILL NEVER SPEAK TO YOU AGAIN. WHAT ARE YOU DOING HERE, GUY?
AND I LIKE THE MUSTACHE AND THE HAIR, BUT WHY THE NEW LOOK?
YOU *LIKE?*
RED LOOKS OKAY ON YOU-- WHICH IS FUNNY, BECAUSE *NO ONE* LOOKS GOOD IN RED, USUALLY... BUT *WHY?*
ACTUALLY, THE COSTUME AND EVERYTHING-- WHY I'M HERE-- IT'S ALL SORT OF TIED UP TOGETHER.
YOU KNOW HOW LAST TIME WE, UH, WE DIDN'T LEAVE IT SO GREAT?
I RECALL.

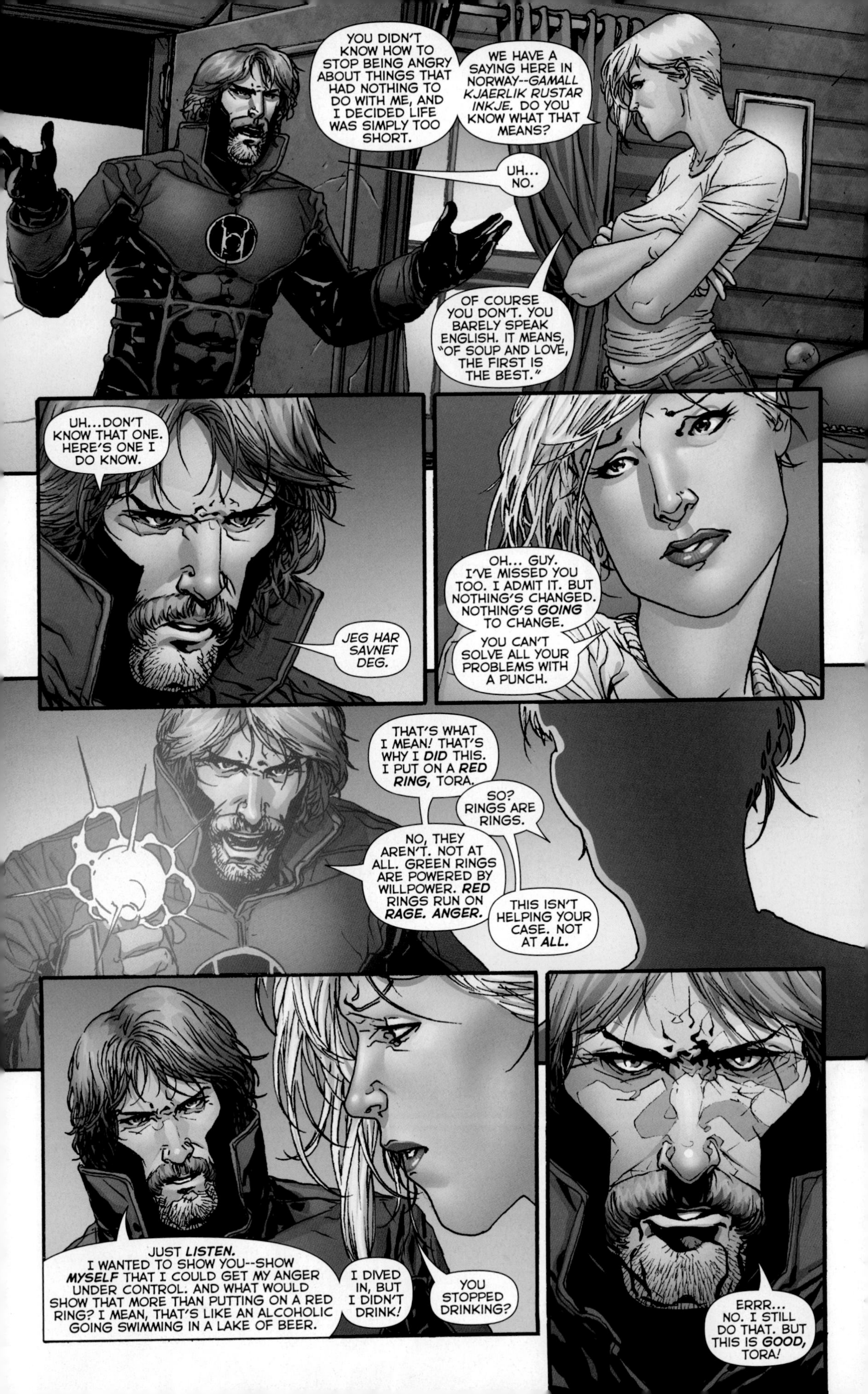

YOU DIDN'T KNOW HOW TO STOP BEING ANGRY ABOUT THINGS THAT HAD NOTHING TO DO WITH ME, AND I DECIDED LIFE WAS SIMPLY TOO SHORT.
WE HAVE A SAYING HERE IN NORWAY--GAMALL KJAERLIK RUSTAR INKJE. DO YOU KNOW WHAT THAT MEANS?
UH... NO.
OF COURSE YOU DON'T. YOU BARELY SPEAK ENGLISH. IT MEANS, "OF SOUP AND LOVE, THE FIRST IS THE BEST."
UH...DON'T KNOW THAT ONE. HERE'S ONE I DO KNOW.
JEG HAR SAVNET DEG.
OH... GUY. I'VE MISSED YOU TOO. I ADMIT IT. BUT NOTHING'S CHANGED. NOTHING'S GOING TO CHANGE.
YOU CAN'T SOLVE ALL YOUR PROBLEMS WITH A PUNCH.
THAT'S WHAT I MEAN! THAT'S WHY I DID THIS. I PUT ON A RED RING, TORA.
SO? RINGS ARE RINGS.
NO, THEY AREN'T. NOT AT ALL. GREEN RINGS ARE POWERED BY WILLPOWER. RED RINGS RUN ON RAGE. ANGER.
THIS ISN'T HELPING YOUR CASE. NOT AT ALL.
JUST LISTEN. I WANTED TO SHOW YOU--SHOW MYSELF THAT I COULD GET MY ANGER UNDER CONTROL. AND WHAT WOULD SHOW THAT MORE THAN PUTTING ON A RED RING? I MEAN, THAT'S LIKE AN ALCOHOLIC GOING SWIMMING IN A LAKE OF BEER.
I DIVED IN, BUT I DIDN'T DRINK!
YOU STOPPED DRINKING?
ERRR... NO. I STILL DO THAT. BUT THIS IS GOOD, TORA!

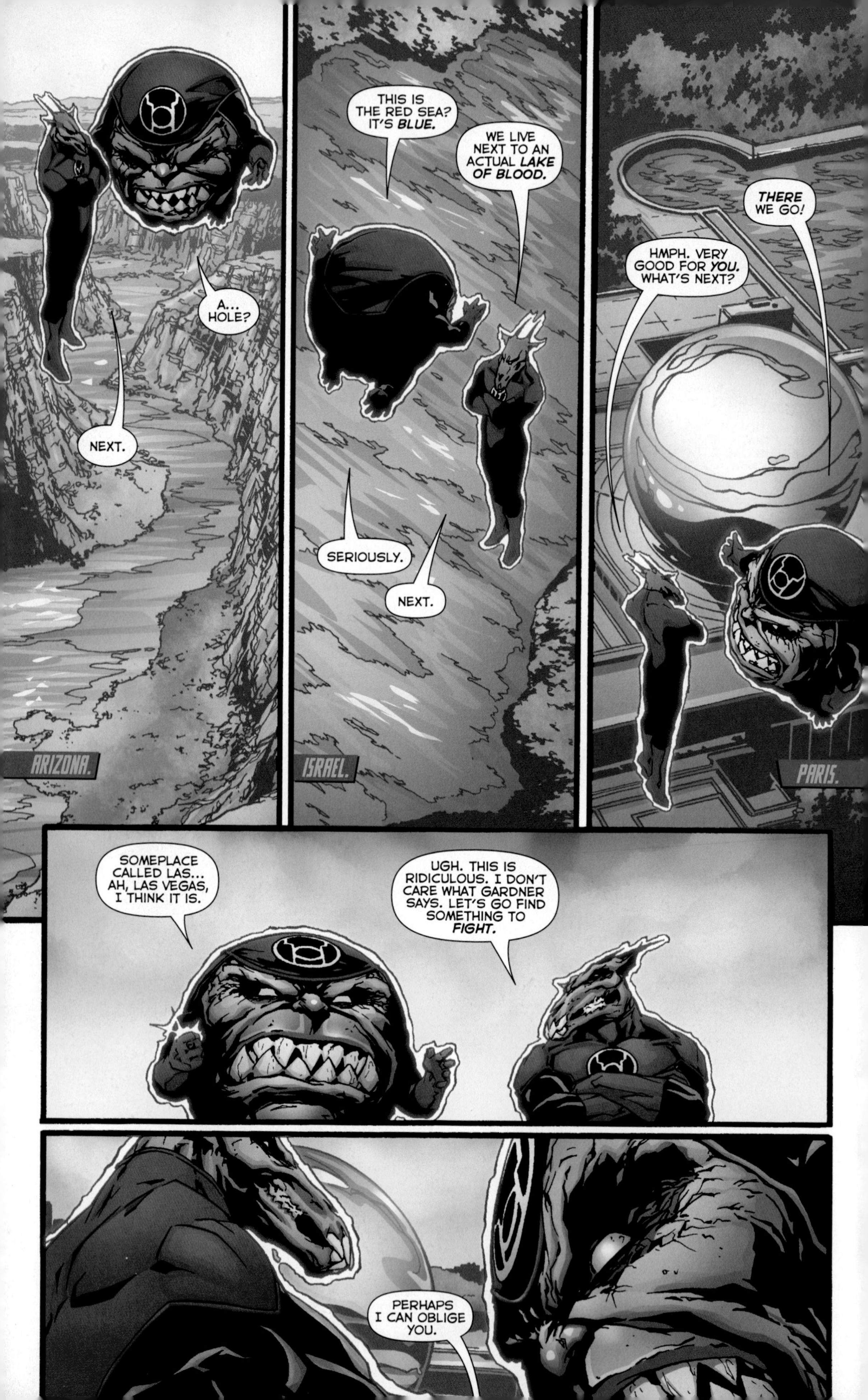
A... HOLE?
NEXT.
ARIZONA.
THIS IS THE RED SEA? IT'S BLUE.
WE LIVE NEXT TO AN ACTUAL LAKE OF BLOOD.
SERIOUSLY.
NEXT.
ISRAEL.
THERE WE GO!
HMPH. VERY GOOD FOR YOU. WHAT'S NEXT?
PARIS.
SOMEPLACE CALLED LAS... AH, LAS VEGAS, I THINK IT IS.
UGH. THIS IS RIDICULOUS. I DON'T CARE WHAT GARDNER SAYS. LET'S GO FIND SOMETHING TO FIGHT.
PERHAPS I CAN OBLIGE YOU.

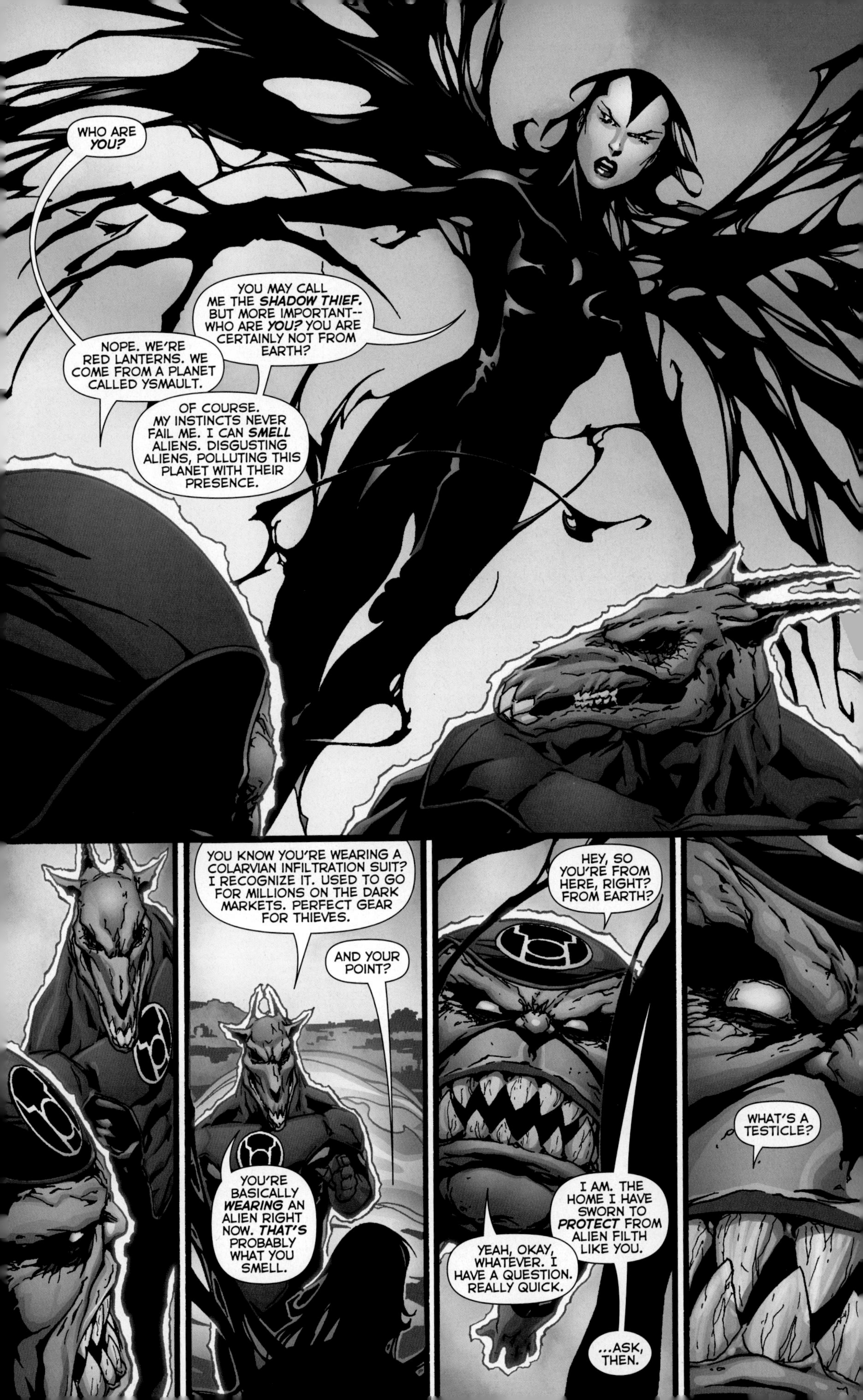
WHO ARE *YOU?*
YOU MAY CALL ME THE *SHADOW THIEF.* BUT MORE IMPORTANT-- WHO ARE *YOU?* YOU ARE CERTAINLY NOT FROM EARTH?
NOPE. WE'RE RED LANTERNS. WE COME FROM A PLANET CALLED YSMAULT.
OF COURSE. MY INSTINCTS NEVER FAIL ME. I CAN *SMELL* ALIENS. DISGUSTING ALIENS, POLLUTING THIS PLANET WITH THEIR PRESENCE.
YOU KNOW YOU'RE WEARING A COLARVIAN INFILTRATION SUIT? I RECOGNIZE IT. USED TO GO FOR MILLIONS ON THE DARK MARKETS. PERFECT GEAR FOR THIEVES.
AND YOUR POINT?
YOU'RE BASICALLY *WEARING* AN ALIEN RIGHT NOW. *THAT'S* PROBABLY WHAT YOU SMELL.
HEY, SO YOU'RE FROM HERE, RIGHT? FROM EARTH?
I AM. THE HOME I HAVE SWORN TO *PROTECT* FROM ALIEN FILTH LIKE YOU.
YEAH, OKAY, WHATEVER. I HAVE A QUESTION. REALLY QUICK.
...ASK, THEN.
WHAT'S A TESTICLE?

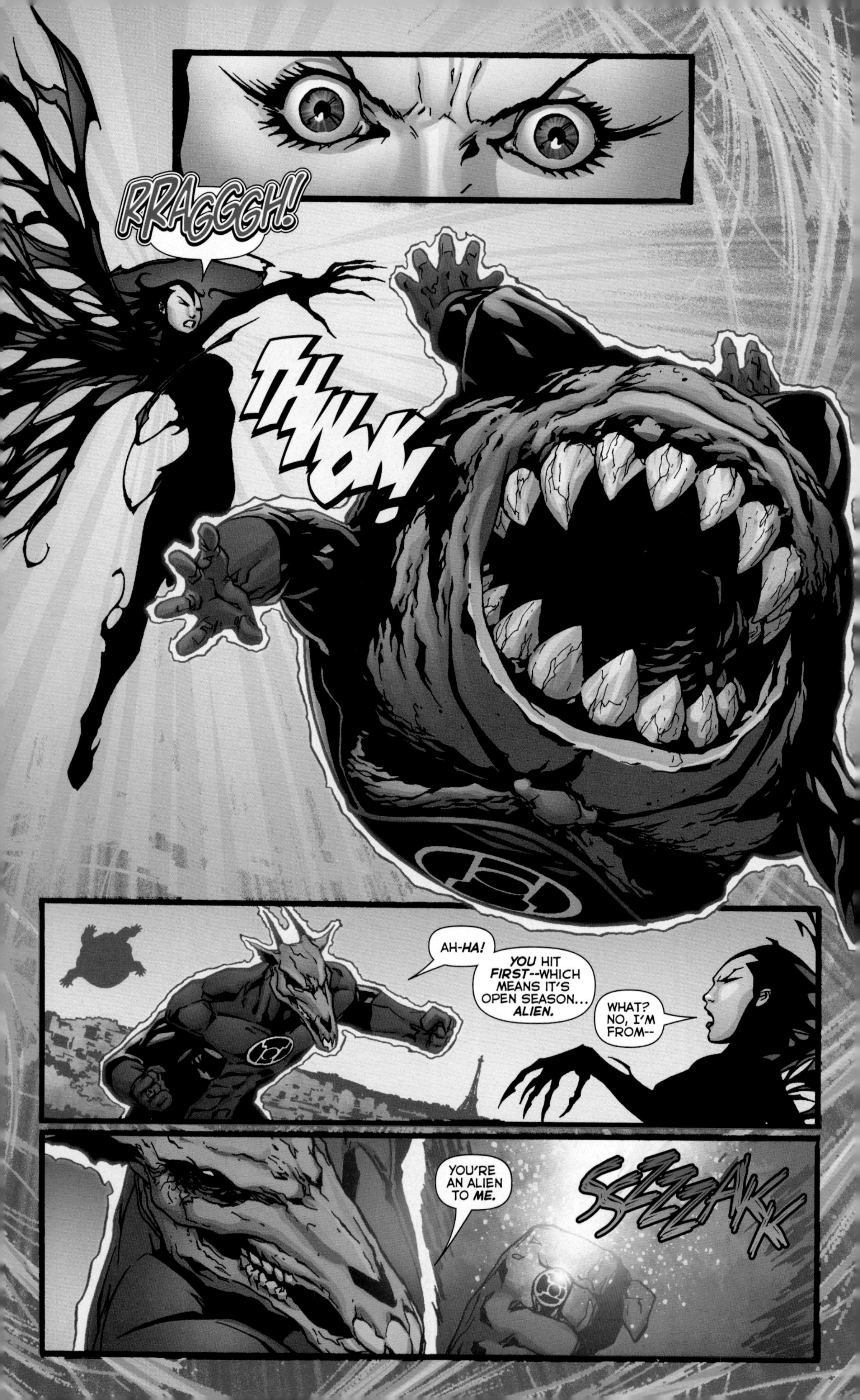
RRAGGGH!
THUNK!
AH-HA!
YOU HIT FIRST--WHICH MEANS IT'S OPEN SEASON... ALIEN.
WHAT? NO, I'M FROM--
YOU'RE AN ALIEN TO ME.
SSZZZAKK

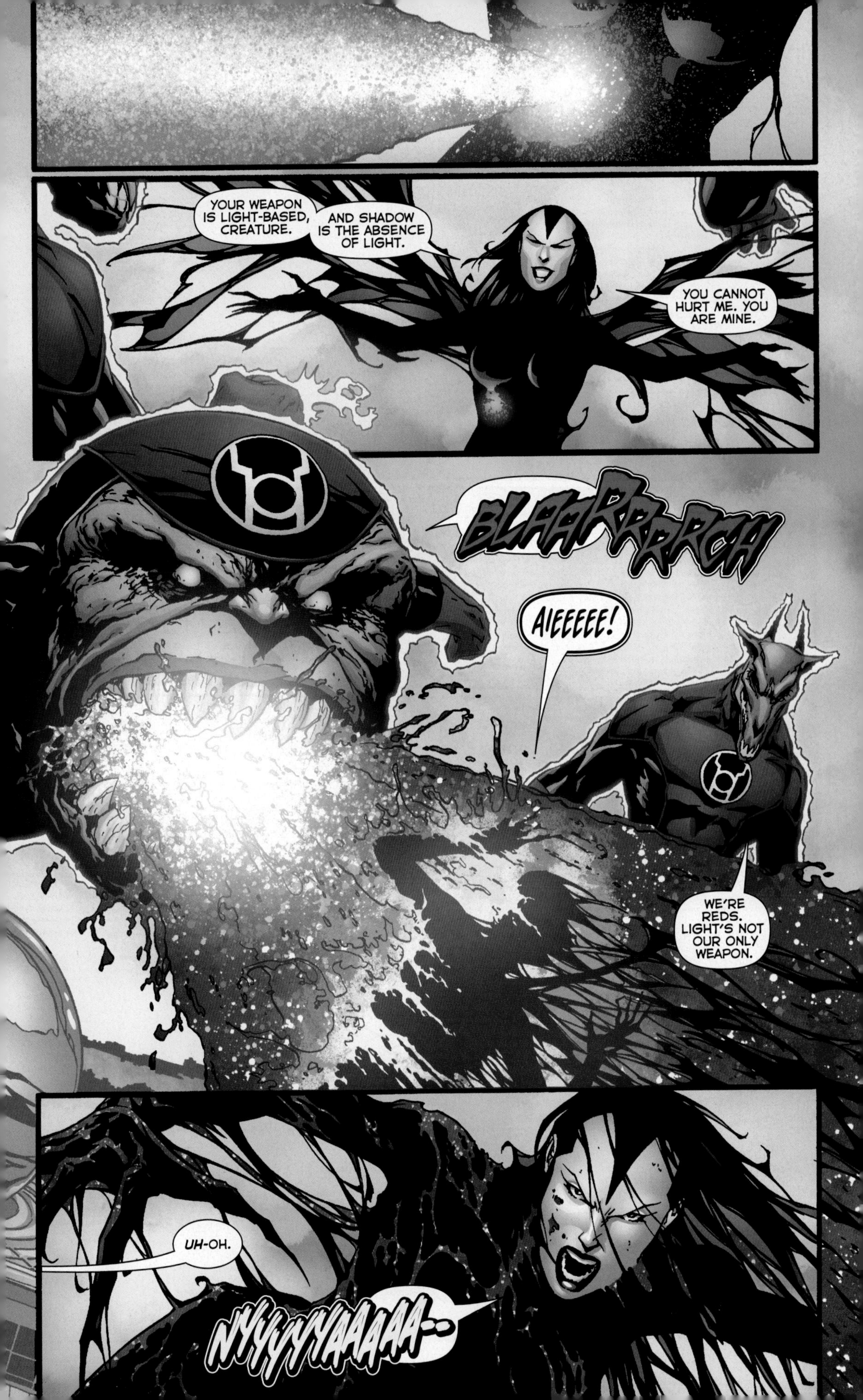

YOUR WEAPON IS LIGHT-BASED, CREATURE.
AND SHADOW IS THE ABSENCE OF LIGHT.
YOU CANNOT HURT ME. YOU ARE MINE.
BLAARRRRCH
AIEEEEE!
WE'RE REDS. LIGHT'S NOT OUR ONLY WEAPON.
UH-OH.
NYYYYAAAAA--

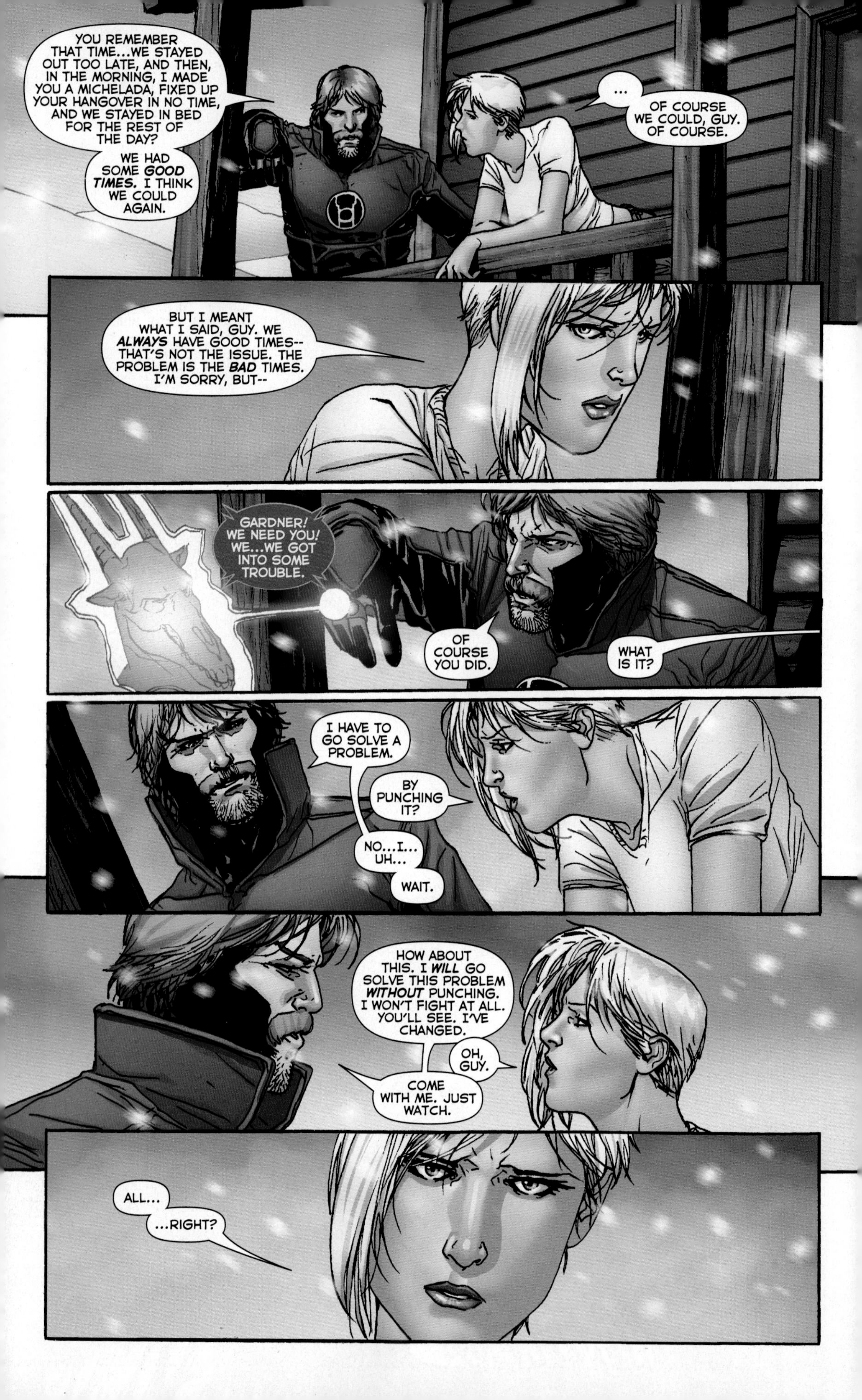
YOU REMEMBER THAT TIME...WE STAYED OUT TOO LATE, AND THEN, IN THE MORNING, I MADE YOU A MICHELADA, FIXED UP YOUR HANGOVER IN NO TIME, AND WE STAYED IN BED FOR THE REST OF THE DAY?
WE HAD SOME GOOD TIMES. I THINK WE COULD AGAIN.
...
OF COURSE WE COULD, GUY. OF COURSE.
BUT I MEANT WHAT I SAID, GUY. WE ALWAYS HAVE GOOD TIMES-- THAT'S NOT THE ISSUE. THE PROBLEM IS THE BAD TIMES. I'M SORRY, BUT--
GARDNER! WE NEED YOU! WE...WE GOT INTO SOME TROUBLE.
OF COURSE YOU DID.
WHAT IS IT?
I HAVE TO GO SOLVE A PROBLEM.
BY PUNCHING IT?
NO...I... UH...
WAIT.
HOW ABOUT THIS. I WILL GO SOLVE THIS PROBLEM WITHOUT PUNCHING. I WON'T FIGHT AT ALL. YOU'LL SEE. I'VE CHANGED.
OH, GUY.
COME WITH ME. JUST WATCH.
ALL...
...RIGHT?

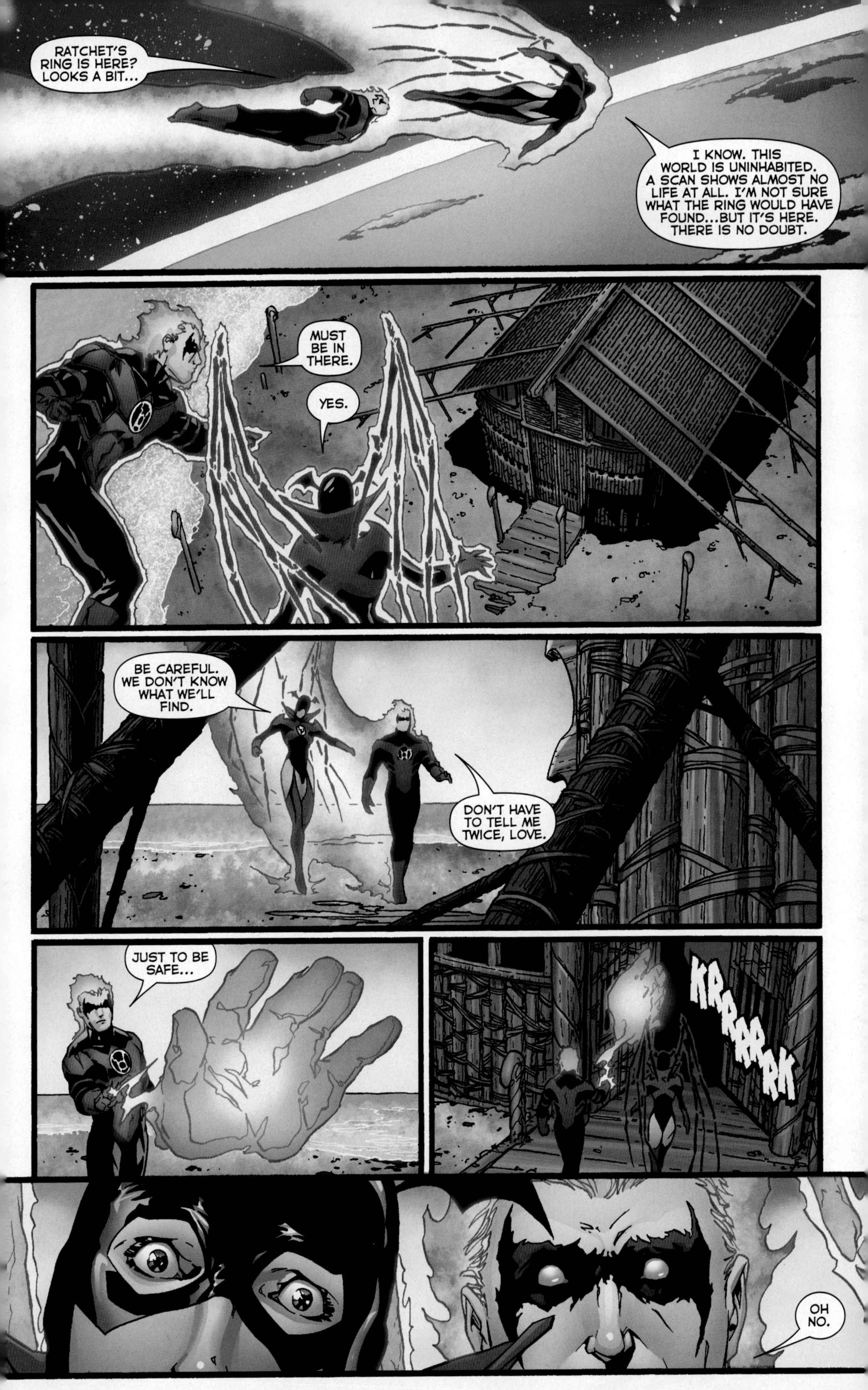
RATCHET'S RING IS HERE? LOOKS A BIT...
I KNOW. THIS WORLD IS UNINHABITED. A SCAN SHOWS ALMOST NO LIFE AT ALL. I'M NOT SURE WHAT THE RING WOULD HAVE FOUND...BUT IT'S HERE. THERE IS NO DOUBT.
MUST BE IN THERE.
YES.
BE CAREFUL. WE DON'T KNOW WHAT WE'LL FIND.
DON'T HAVE TO TELL ME TWICE, LOVE.
JUST TO BE SAFE...
KRRRRRRK
OH NO.

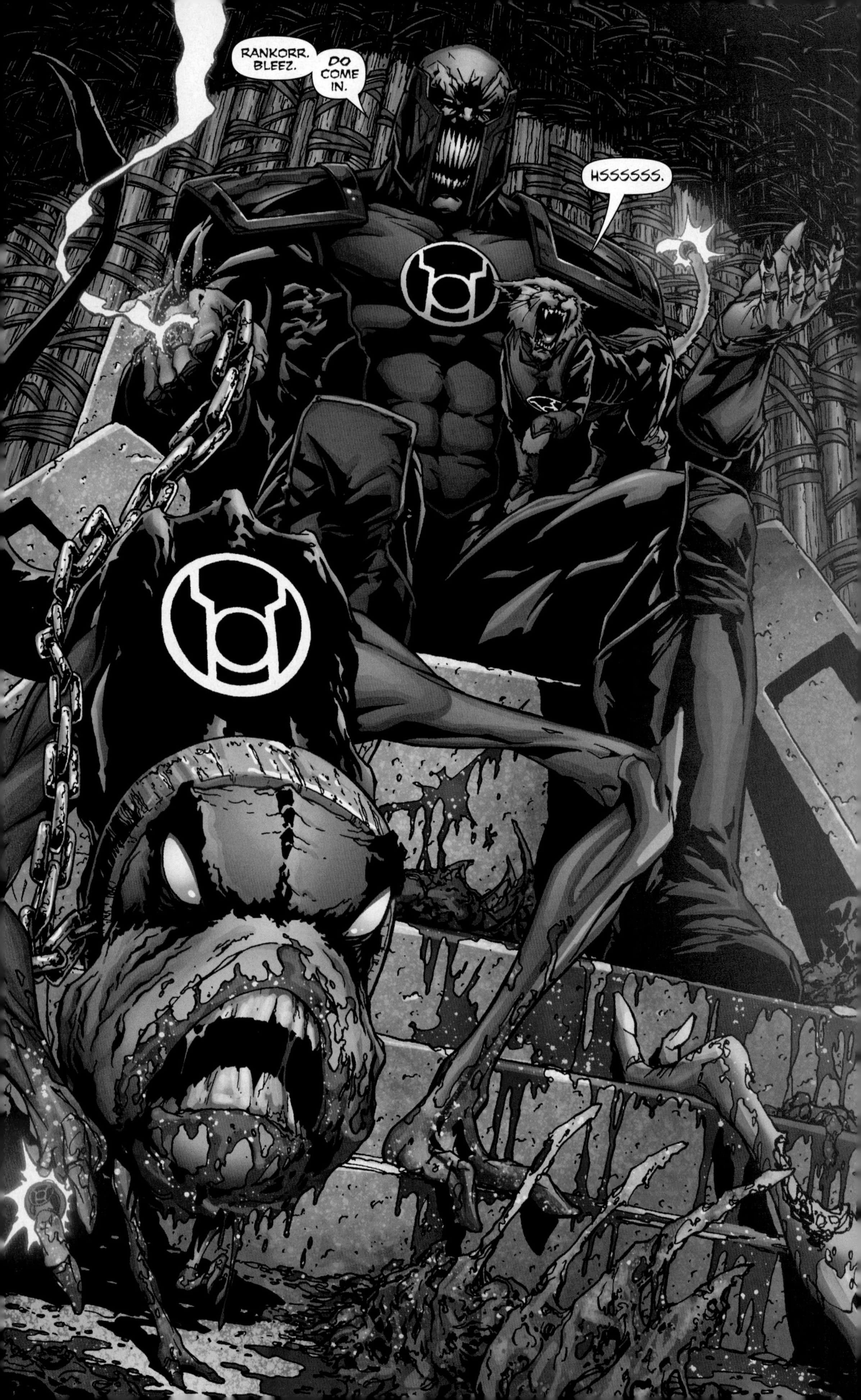
RANKORR. BLEEZ.
DO COME IN.
HSSSSSS.

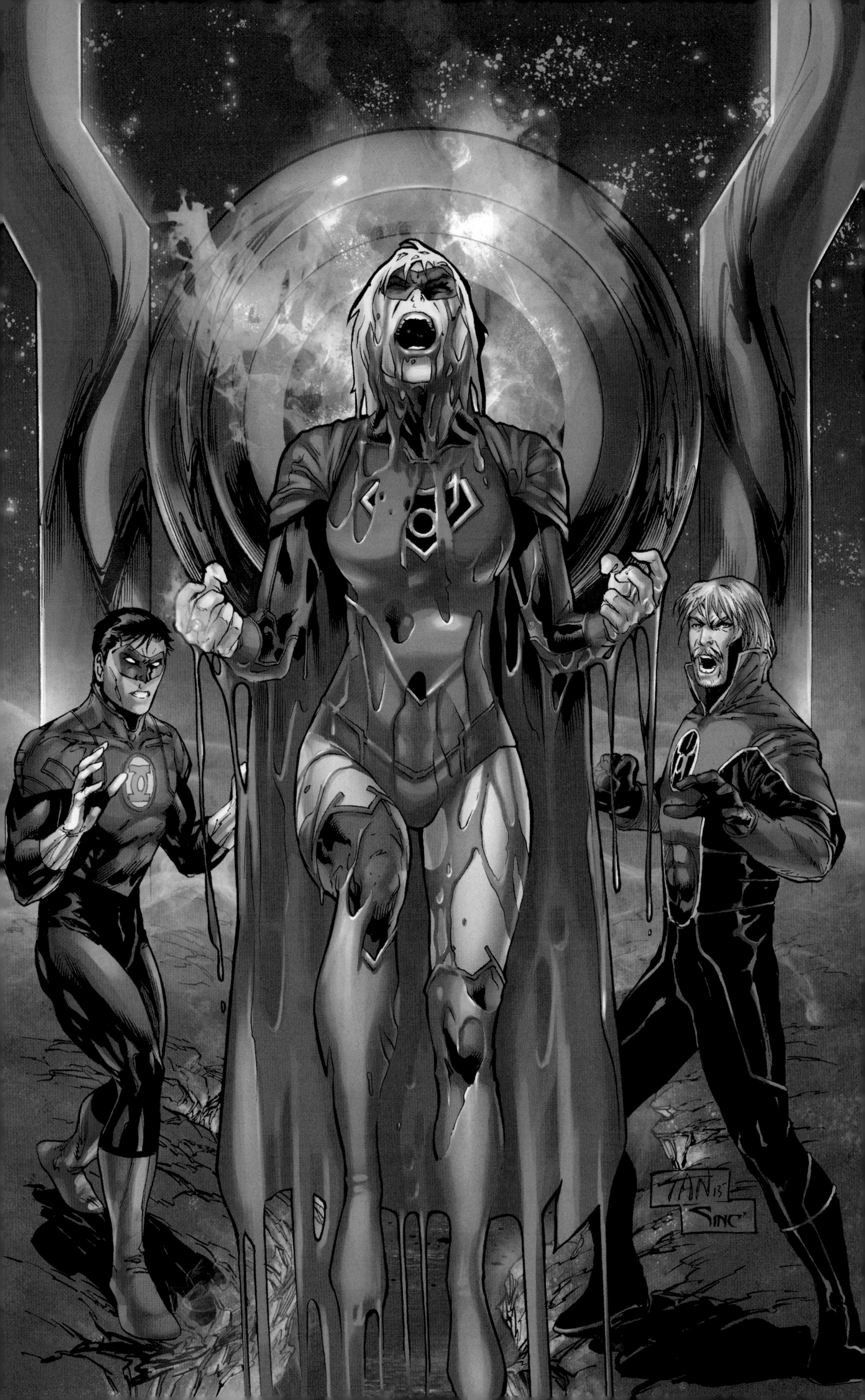
TAN 13
SINC

ROBERT VENDITTI writer **BILLY TAN** penciller **ROB HUNTER** inker **ALEX SINCLAIR** colorist **DAVE SHARPE** letterer
cover art by **BILLY TAN** and **ALEX SINCLAIR**

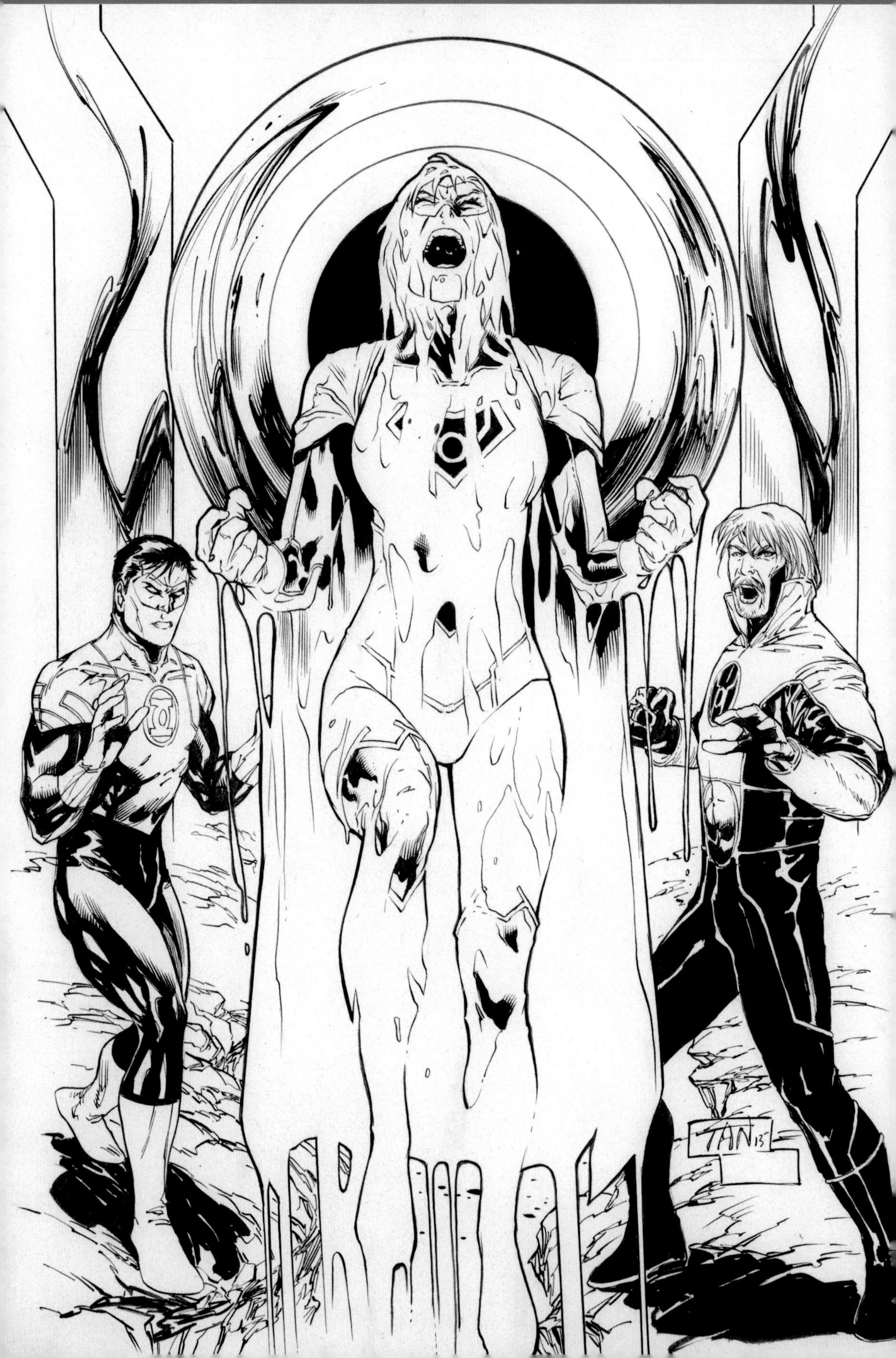

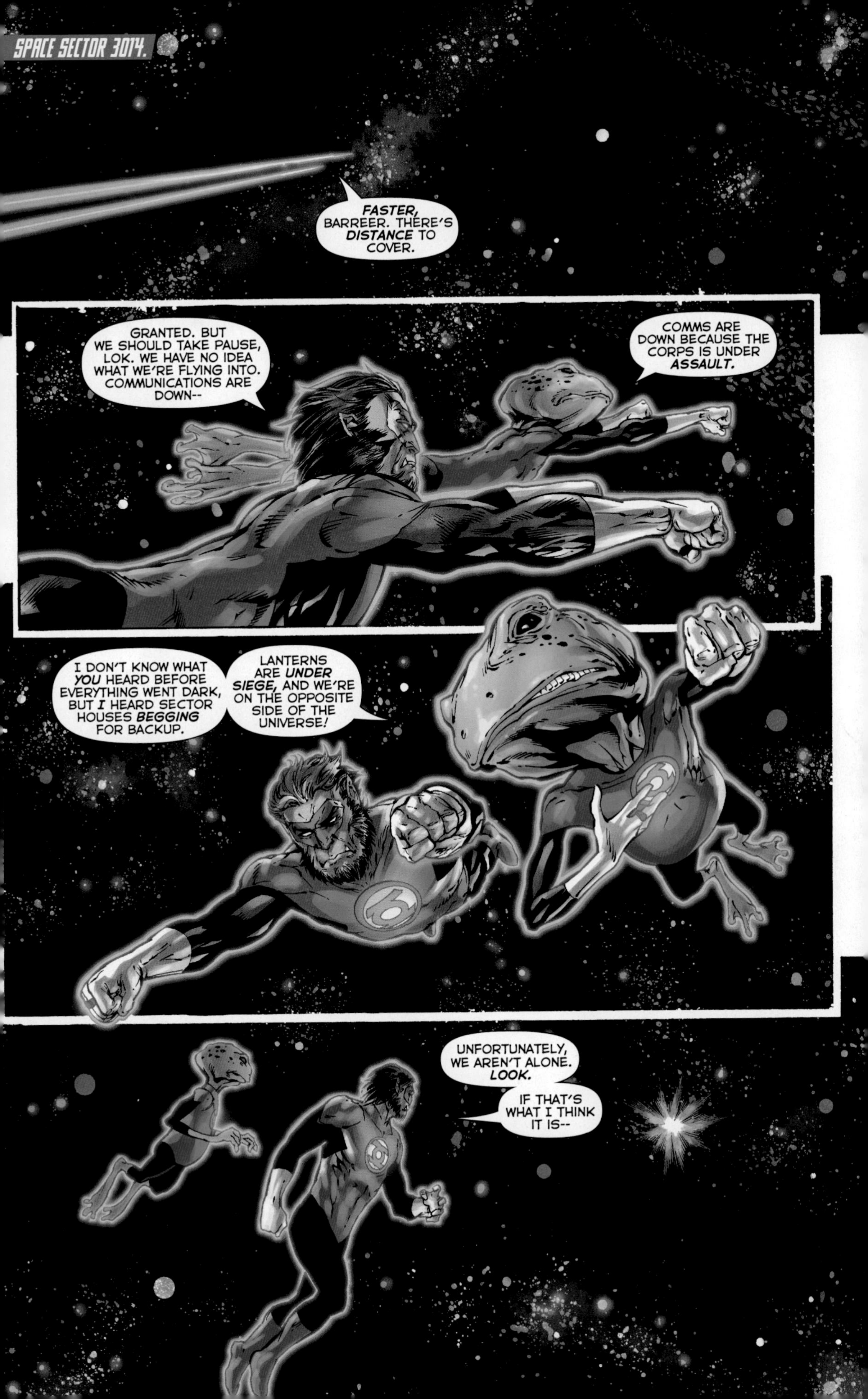
SPACE SECTOR 3014.
FASTER, BARREER. THERE'S DISTANCE TO COVER.
GRANTED. BUT WE SHOULD TAKE PAUSE, LOK. WE HAVE NO IDEA WHAT WE'RE FLYING INTO. COMMUNICATIONS ARE DOWN--
COMMS ARE DOWN BECAUSE THE CORPS IS UNDER ASSAULT.
I DON'T KNOW WHAT YOU HEARD BEFORE EVERYTHING WENT DARK, BUT I HEARD SECTOR HOUSES BEGGING FOR BACKUP.
LANTERNS ARE UNDER SIEGE, AND WE'RE ON THE OPPOSITE SIDE OF THE UNIVERSE!
UNFORTUNATELY, WE AREN'T ALONE. LOOK.
IF THAT'S WHAT I THINK IT IS--

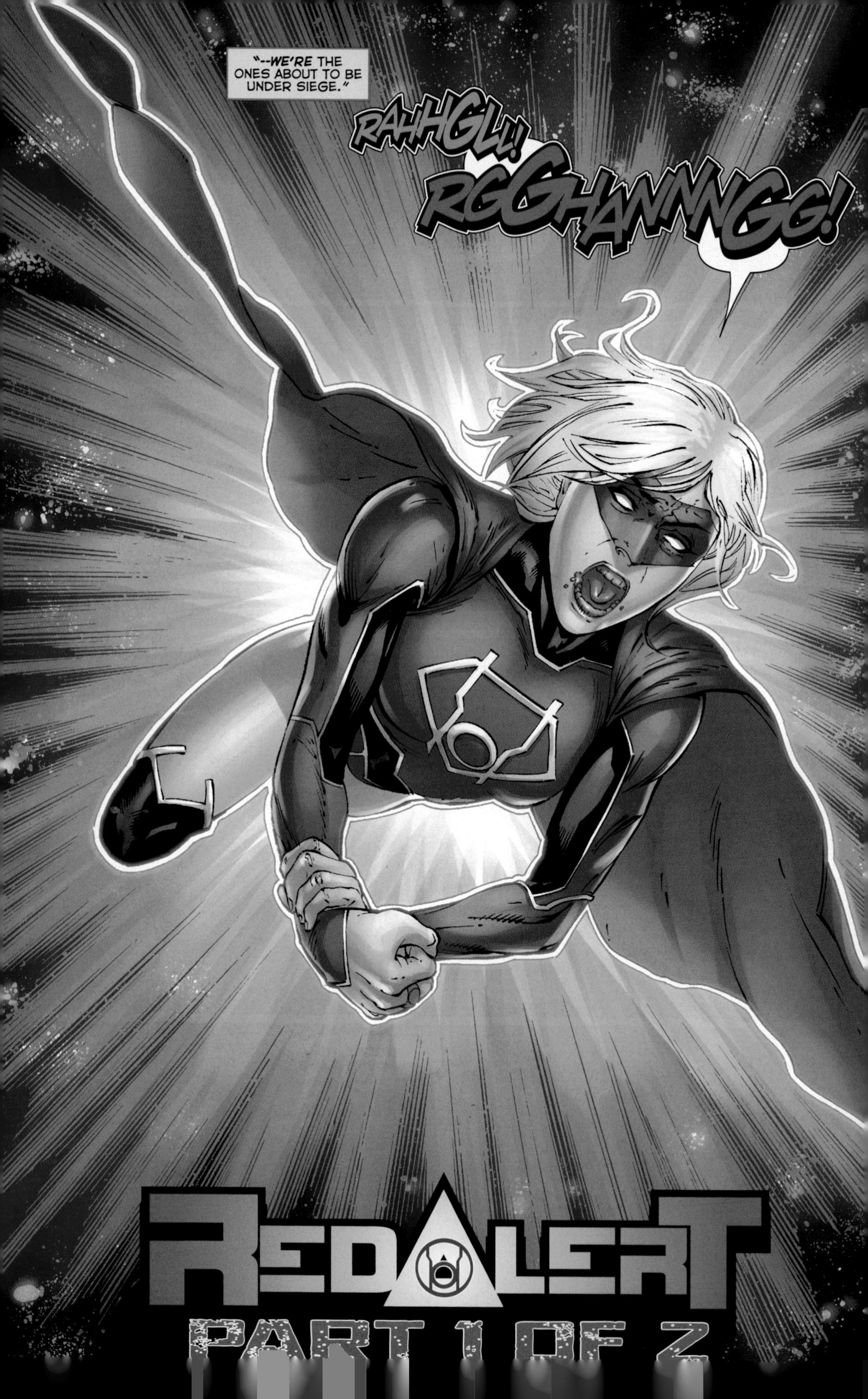
"--*WE'RE* THE ONES ABOUT TO BE UNDER SIEGE."
RAHHGLL! RGGHANNNGG!
RED ALERT
PART 1 OF 2

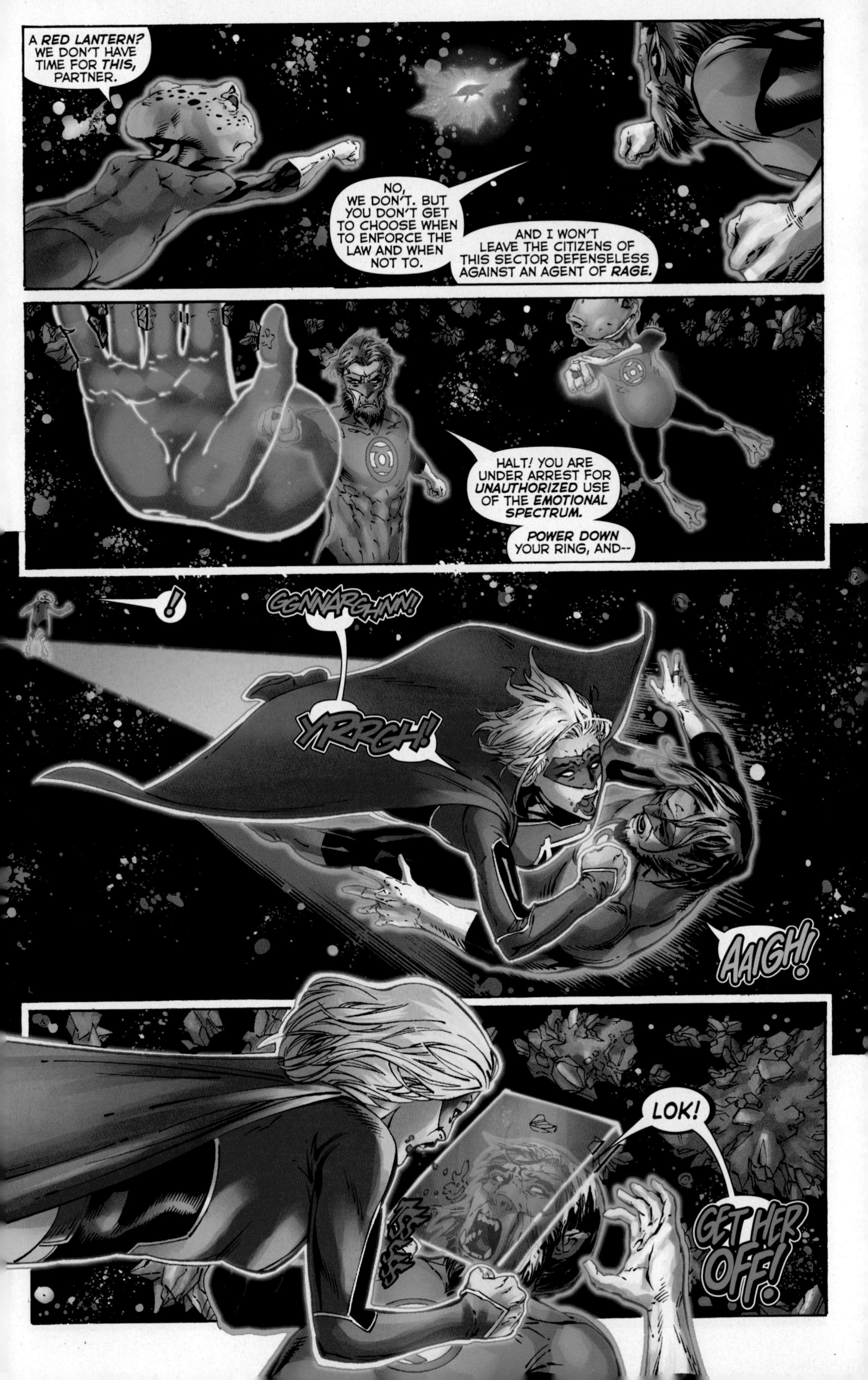
A RED LANTERN? WE DON'T HAVE TIME FOR THIS, PARTNER.
NO, WE DON'T. BUT YOU DON'T GET TO CHOOSE WHEN TO ENFORCE THE LAW AND WHEN NOT TO.
AND I WON'T LEAVE THE CITIZENS OF THIS SECTOR DEFENSELESS AGAINST AN AGENT OF RAGE.
HALT! YOU ARE UNDER ARREST FOR UNAUTHORIZED USE OF THE EMOTIONAL SPECTRUM.
POWER DOWN YOUR RING, AND--
!
GGNNARGHNN!
YRRGH!
AAIGH!
LOK!
GET HER OFF!

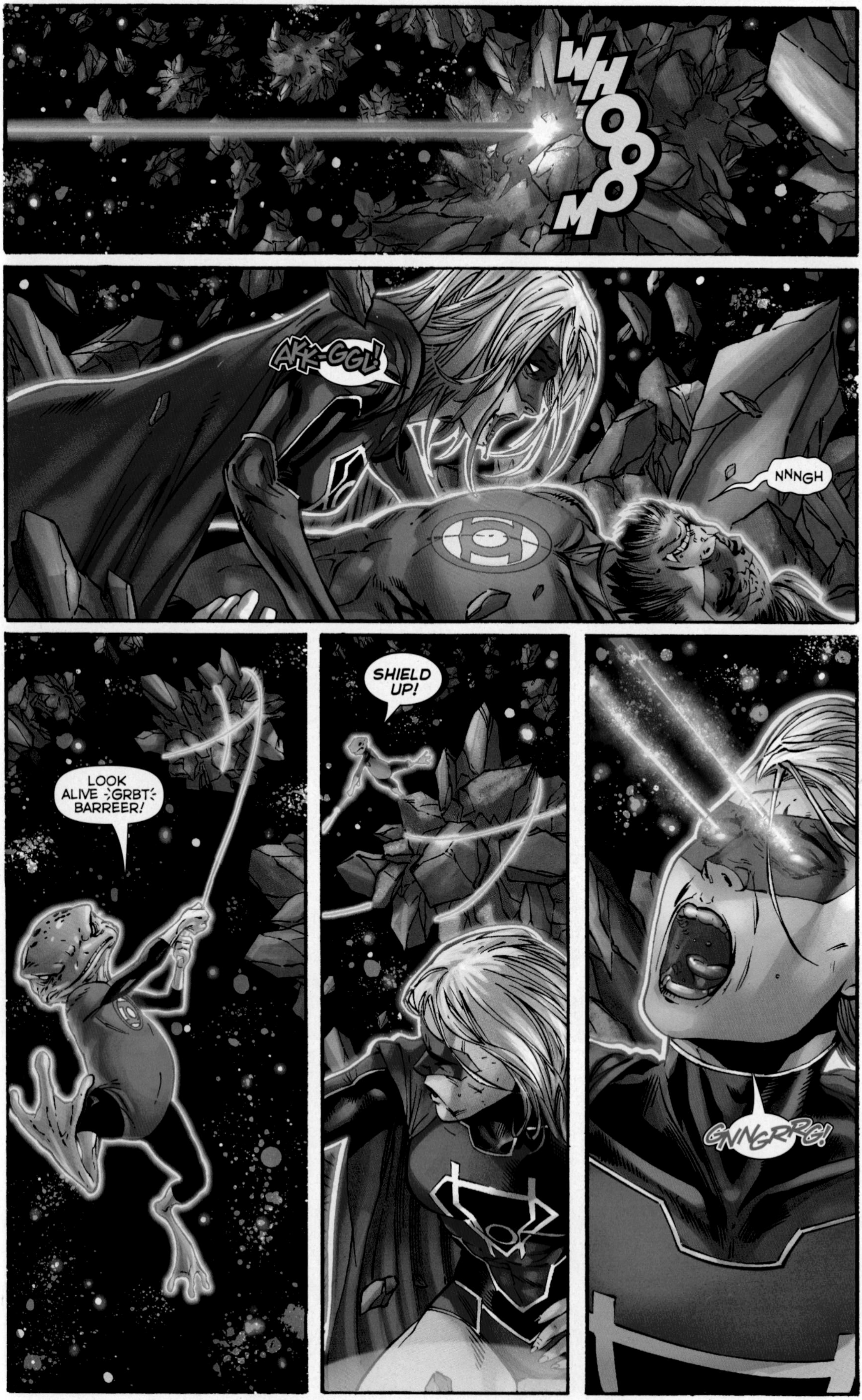
WHOOOOM
AKK-GGL!
NNNGH
LOOK ALIVE GRBT BARREER!
SHIELD UP!
GNNGRRRG!

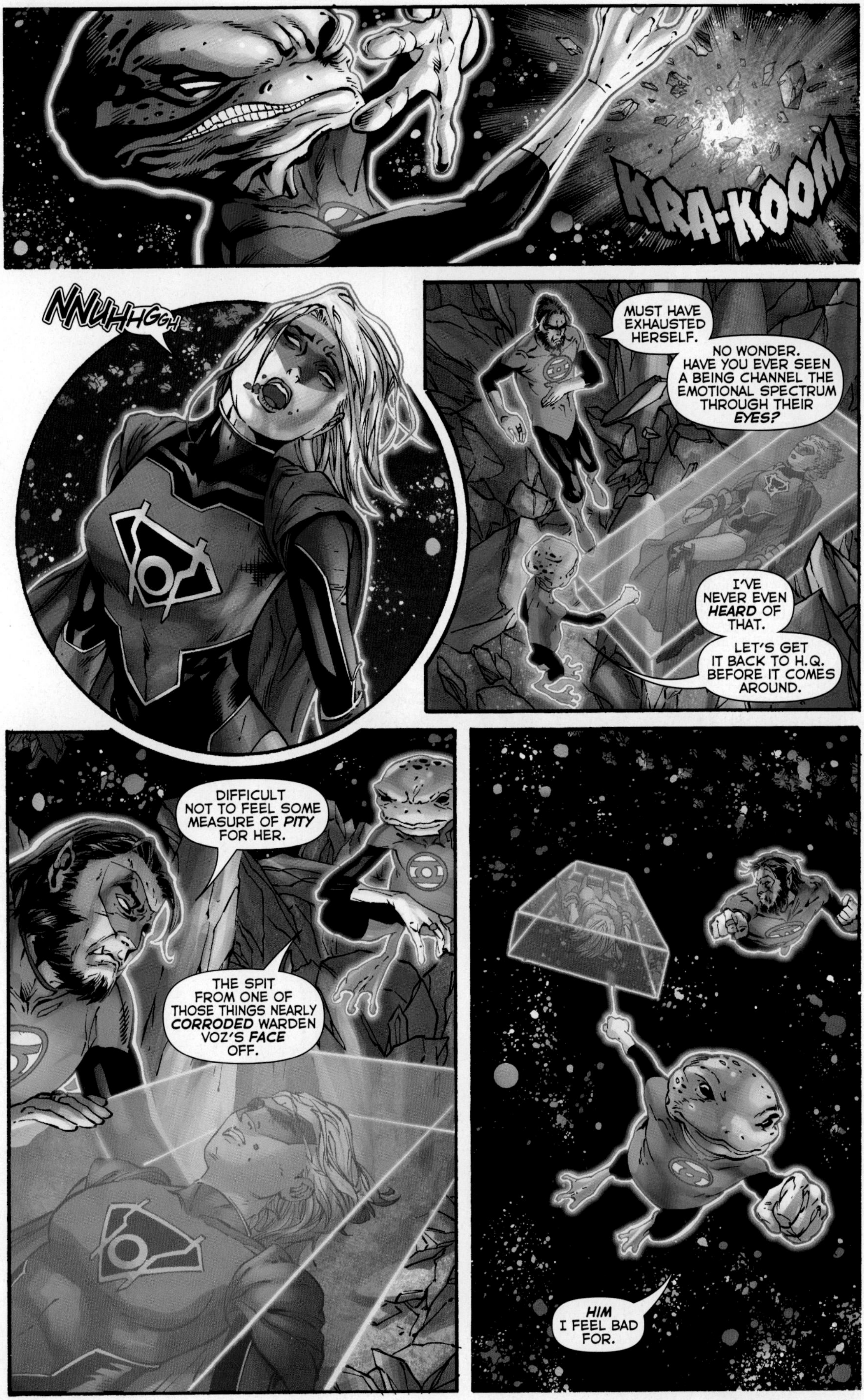
KRA-KOOM
NNUHHGGH
MUST HAVE EXHAUSTED HERSELF.
NO WONDER. HAVE YOU EVER SEEN A BEING CHANNEL THE EMOTIONAL SPECTRUM THROUGH THEIR EYES?
I'VE NEVER EVEN HEARD OF THAT.
LET'S GET IT BACK TO H.Q. BEFORE IT COMES AROUND.
DIFFICULT NOT TO FEEL SOME MEASURE OF PITY FOR HER.
THE SPIT FROM ONE OF THOSE THINGS NEARLY CORRODED WARDEN VOZ'S FACE OFF.
HIM I FEEL BAD FOR.

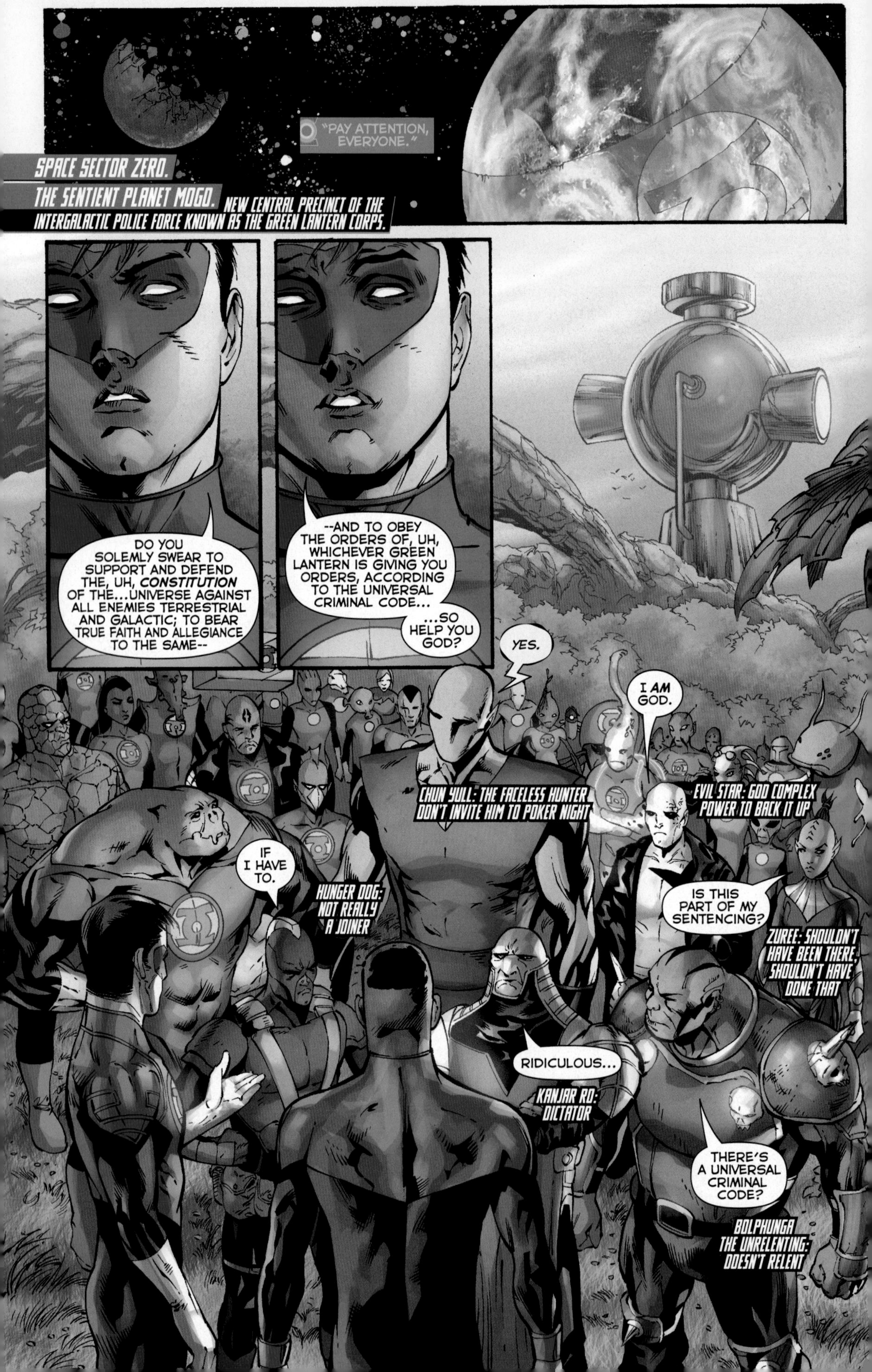
"PAY ATTENTION, EVERYONE."
SPACE SECTOR ZERO.
THE SENTIENT PLANET MOGO.
NEW CENTRAL PRECINCT OF THE INTERGALACTIC POLICE FORCE KNOWN AS THE GREEN LANTERN CORPS.
DO YOU SOLEMLY SWEAR TO SUPPORT AND DEFEND THE, UH, CONSTITUTION OF THE...UNIVERSE AGAINST ALL ENEMIES TERRESTRIAL AND GALACTIC; TO BEAR TRUE FAITH AND ALLEGIANCE TO THE SAME--
--AND TO OBEY THE ORDERS OF, UH, WHICHEVER GREEN LANTERN IS GIVING YOU ORDERS, ACCORDING TO THE UNIVERSAL CRIMINAL CODE...
...SO HELP YOU GOD?
YES.
I AM GOD.
CHUN YULL: THE FACELESS HUNTER DON'T INVITE HIM TO POKER NIGHT
EVIL STAR: GOD COMPLEX POWER TO BACK IT UP
IF I HAVE TO.
HUNGER DOG: NOT REALLY A JOINER
IS THIS PART OF MY SENTENCING?
ZUREE: SHOULDN'T HAVE BEEN THERE, SHOULDN'T HAVE DONE THAT
RIDICULOUS...
KANJAR RO: DICTATOR
THERE'S A UNIVERSAL CRIMINAL CODE?
BOLPHUNGA THE UNRELENTING: DOESN'T RELENT

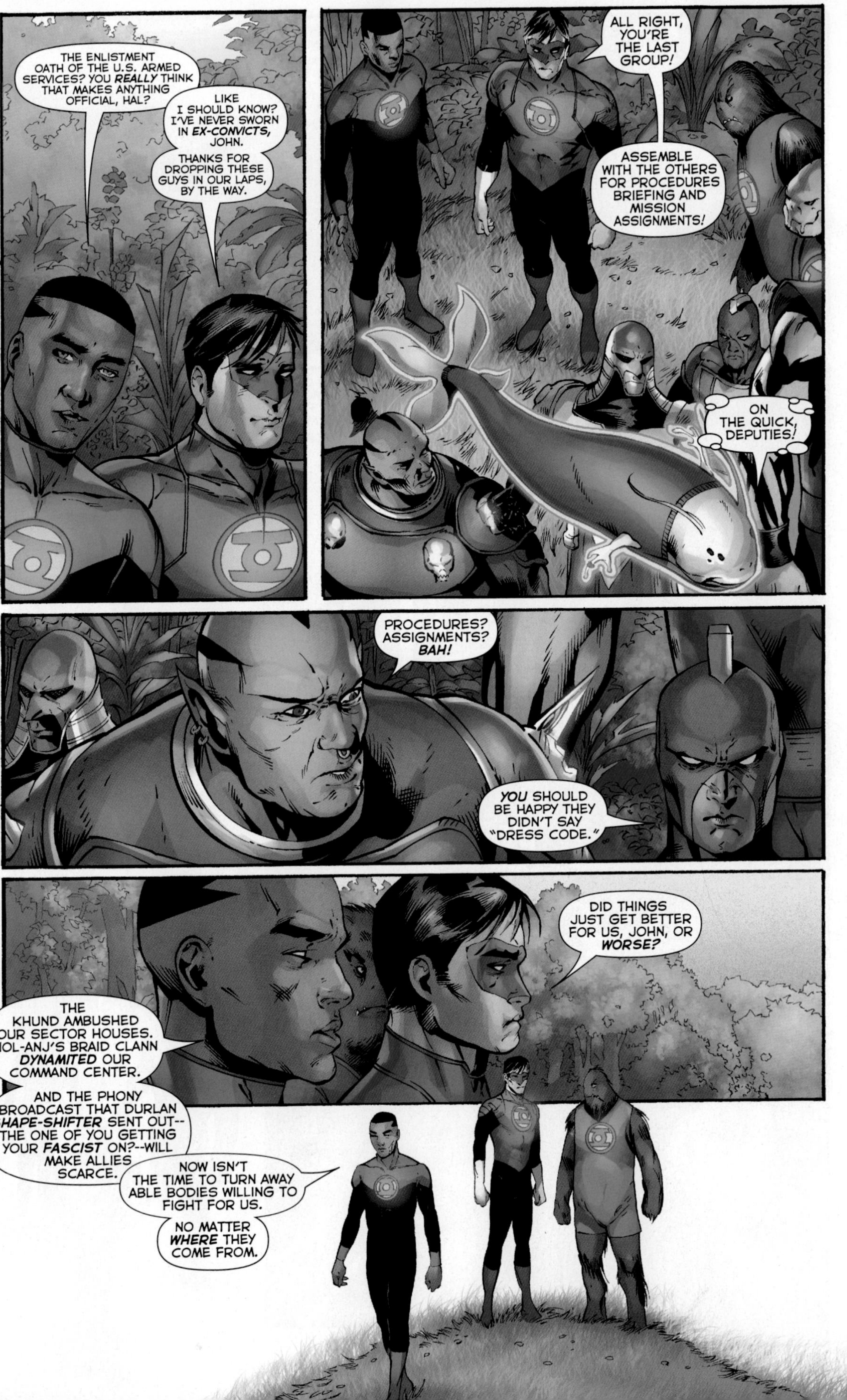
THE ENLISTMENT OATH OF THE U.S. ARMED SERVICES? YOU REALLY THINK THAT MAKES ANYTHING OFFICIAL, HAL?
LIKE I SHOULD KNOW? I'VE NEVER SWORN IN EX-CONVICTS, JOHN.
THANKS FOR DROPPING THESE GUYS IN OUR LAPS, BY THE WAY.
ALL RIGHT, YOU'RE THE LAST GROUP!
ASSEMBLE WITH THE OTHERS FOR PROCEDURES BRIEFING AND MISSION ASSIGNMENTS!
ON THE QUICK, DEPUTIES!
PROCEDURES? ASSIGNMENTS? BAH!
YOU SHOULD BE HAPPY THEY DIDN'T SAY "DRESS CODE."
DID THINGS JUST GET BETTER FOR US, JOHN, OR WORSE?
THE KHUND AMBUSHED OUR SECTOR HOUSES. NOL-ANJ'S BRAID CLANN DYNAMITED OUR COMMAND CENTER.
AND THE PHONY BROADCAST THAT DURLAN SHAPE-SHIFTER SENT OUT--THE ONE OF YOU GETTING YOUR FASCIST ON?--WILL MAKE ALLIES SCARCE.
NOW ISN'T THE TIME TO TURN AWAY ABLE BODIES WILLING TO FIGHT FOR US.
NO MATTER WHERE THEY COME FROM.

IT'S A **WRONG** DAY WHEN WE CAN COUNT ON **FELONS** OVER FELLOW LANTERNS, **EH**, GRAF?

MEANING **WHAT**, VATH? SPEAK YOUR MIND.

WHAT LITTLE THERE IS OF IT.

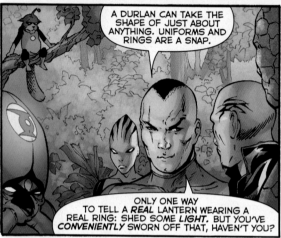

A DURLAN CAN TAKE THE SHAPE OF JUST ABOUT ANYTHING. UNIFORMS AND RINGS ARE A SNAP.

ONLY ONE WAY TO TELL A **REAL** LANTERN WEARING A REAL RING: SHED SOME **LIGHT.** BUT YOU'VE **CONVENIENTLY** SWORN OFF THAT, HAVEN'T YOU?

OUR RINGS DRAIN THE RESERVOIR OF THE EMOTIONAL SPECTRUM. I DON'T WIELD LIGHT ON **PRINCIPLE.**

SO YOU AND YOUR OBJECTORS SAY. OR MAYBE THAT'S JUST YOUR **COVER.**

ONE SPARK. GIMME JUST **ONE.**

IF YOU CAN.

WHUMP

AW, C'MON! SEE HOW **EASY** THAT WAS?

CURSE YOU, VATH.

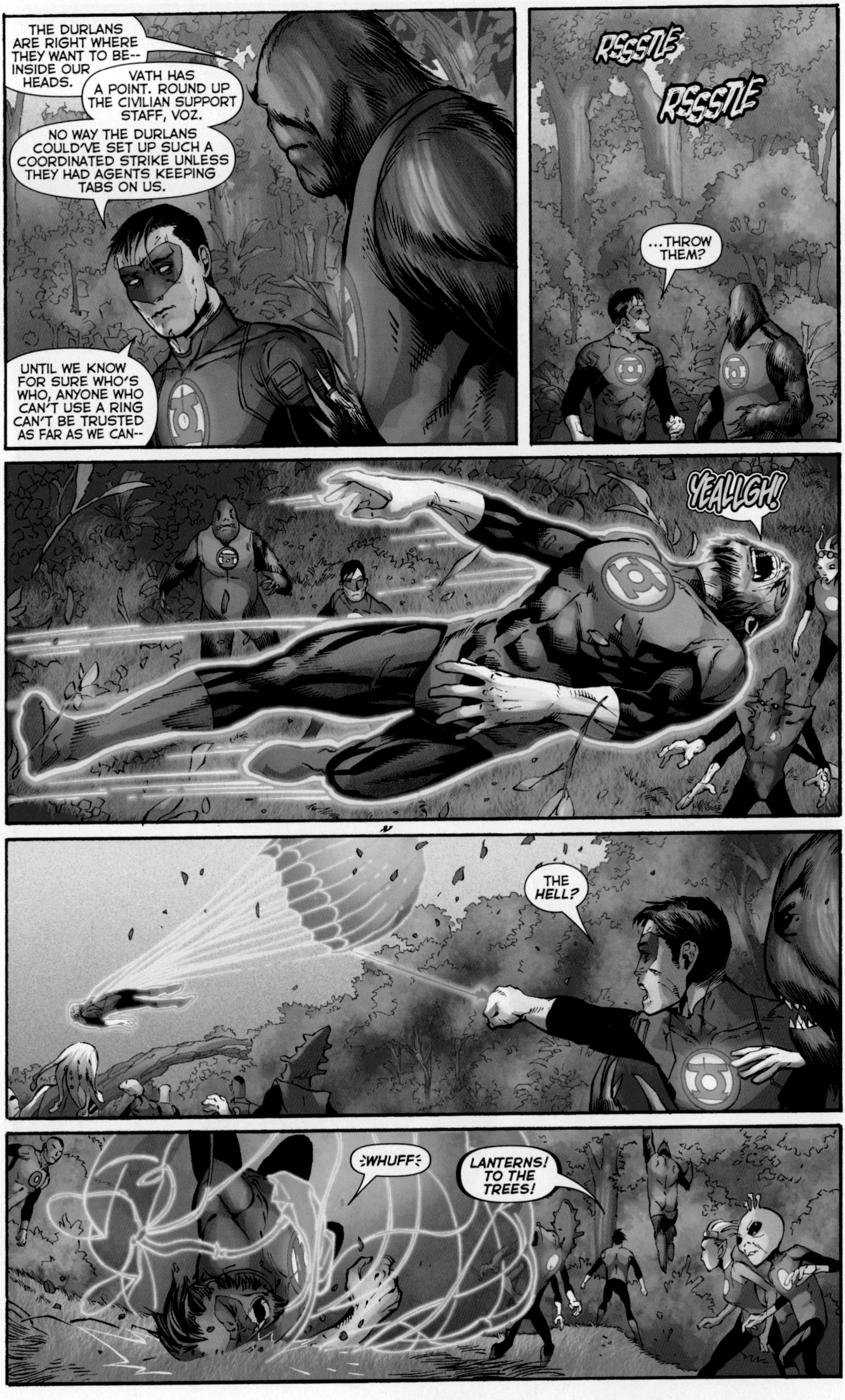
THE DURLANS ARE RIGHT WHERE THEY WANT TO BE-- INSIDE OUR HEADS.
VATH HAS A POINT. ROUND UP THE CIVILIAN SUPPORT STAFF, VOZ.
NO WAY THE DURLANS COULD'VE SET UP SUCH A COORDINATED STRIKE UNLESS THEY HAD AGENTS KEEPING TABS ON US.
UNTIL WE KNOW FOR SURE WHO'S WHO, ANYONE WHO CAN'T USE A RING CAN'T BE TRUSTED AS FAR AS WE CAN--
RSSSTLE
RSSSTLE
...THROW THEM?
YEALLGH!
THE HELL?
WHUFF
LANTERNS! TO THE TREES!

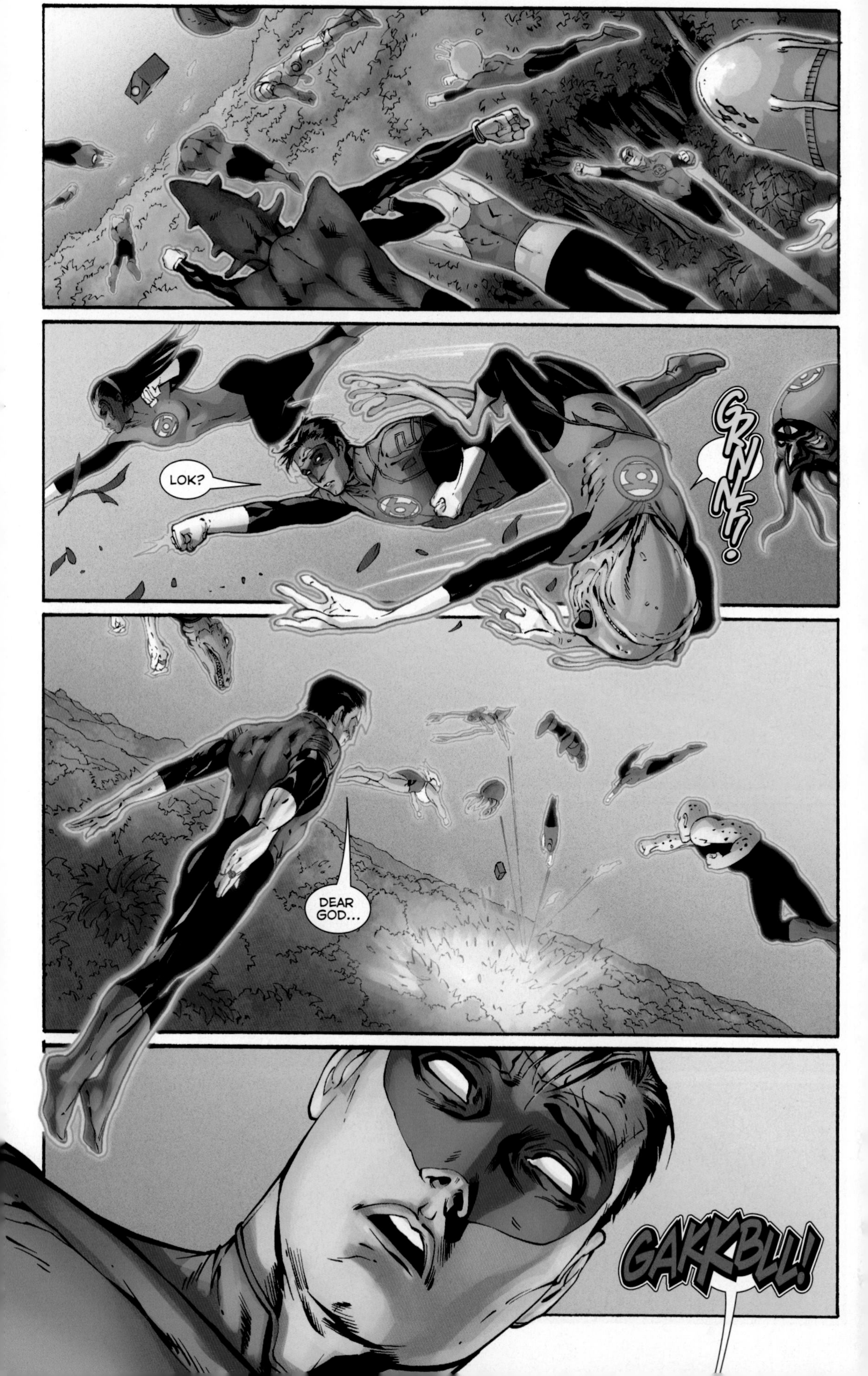
LOK?
GRNNF!
DEAR GOD...
GAKKBLL!

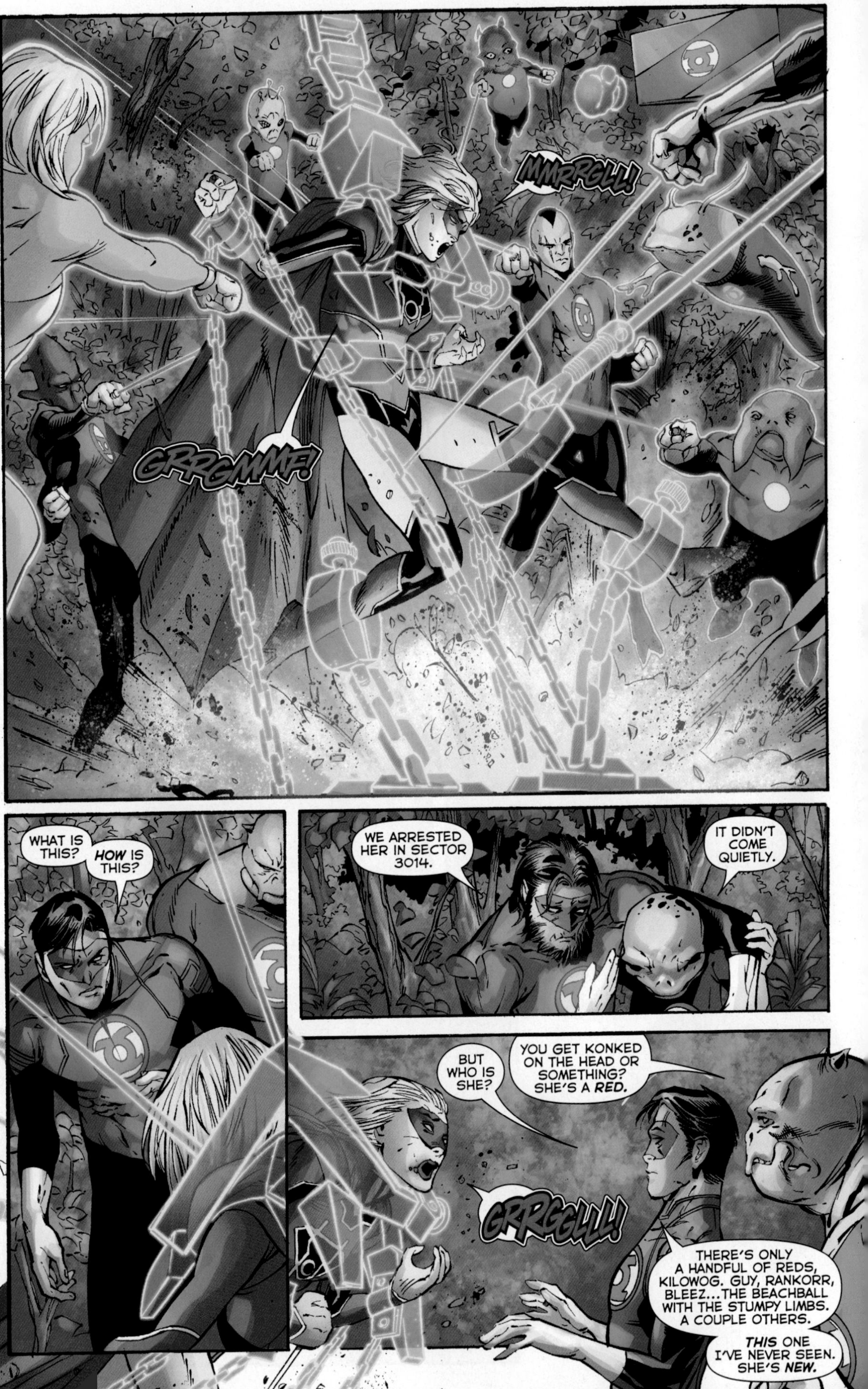
MMRRGLL!
GRRGMMF!
WHAT IS THIS? HOW IS THIS?
WE ARRESTED HER IN SECTOR 3014.
IT DIDN'T COME QUIETLY.
BUT WHO IS SHE?
YOU GET KONKED ON THE HEAD OR SOMETHING? SHE'S A RED.
GRRGGLLL!
THERE'S ONLY A HANDFUL OF REDS, KILOWOG. GUY, RANKORR, BLEEZ...THE BEACHBALL WITH THE STUMPY LIMBS. A COUPLE OTHERS.
THIS ONE I'VE NEVER SEEN. SHE'S NEW.

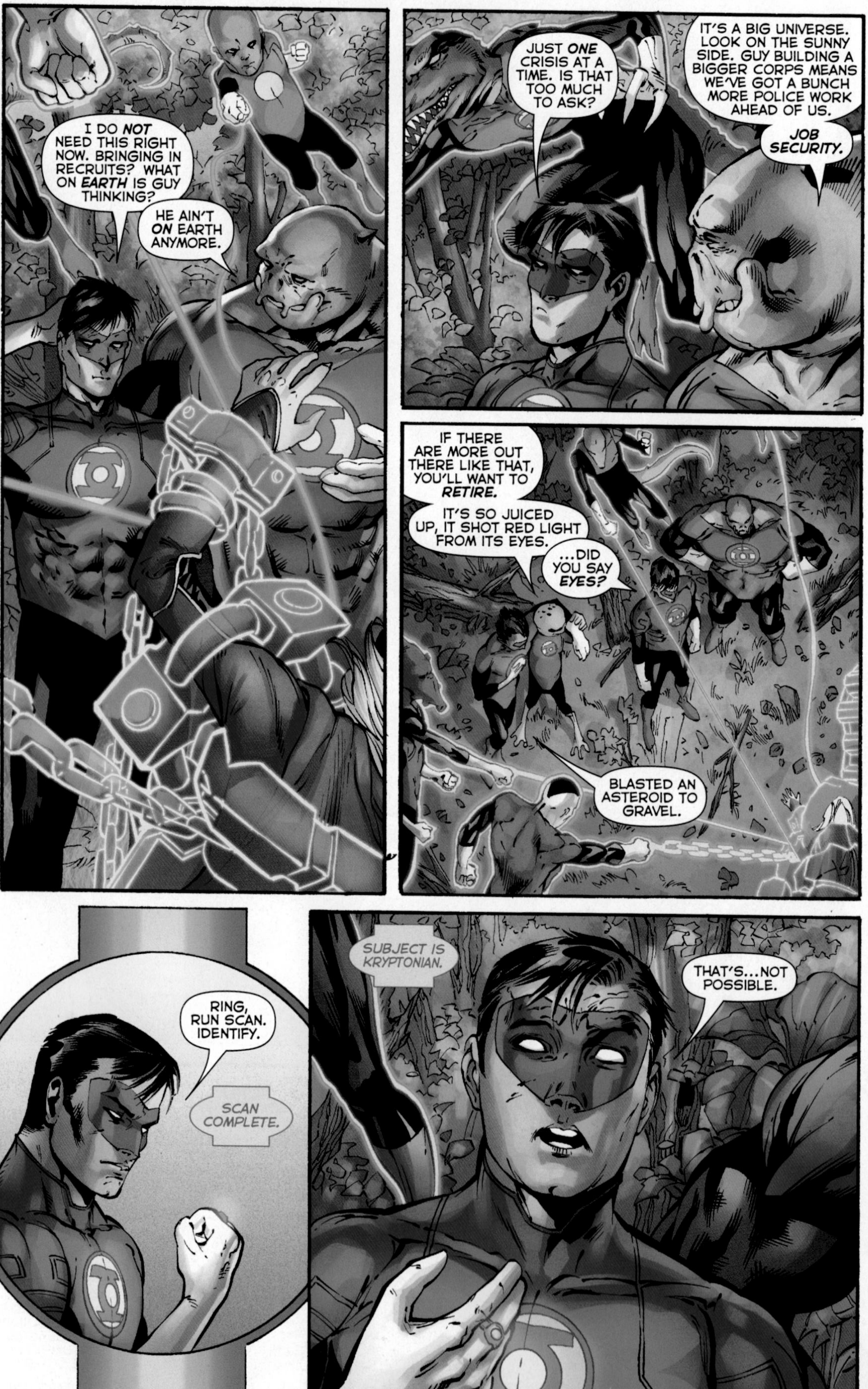
I DO NOT NEED THIS RIGHT NOW. BRINGING IN RECRUITS? WHAT ON EARTH IS GUY THINKING?
HE AIN'T ON EARTH ANYMORE.
JUST ONE CRISIS AT A TIME. IS THAT TOO MUCH TO ASK?
IT'S A BIG UNIVERSE. LOOK ON THE SUNNY SIDE. GUY BUILDING A BIGGER CORPS MEANS WE'VE GOT A BUNCH MORE POLICE WORK AHEAD OF US.
JOB SECURITY.
IF THERE ARE MORE OUT THERE LIKE THAT, YOU'LL WANT TO RETIRE.
IT'S SO JUICED UP, IT SHOT RED LIGHT FROM ITS EYES.
...DID YOU SAY EYES?
BLASTED AN ASTEROID TO GRAVEL.
RING, RUN SCAN. IDENTIFY.
SCAN COMPLETE.
SUBJECT IS KRYPTONIAN.
THAT'S...NOT POSSIBLE.

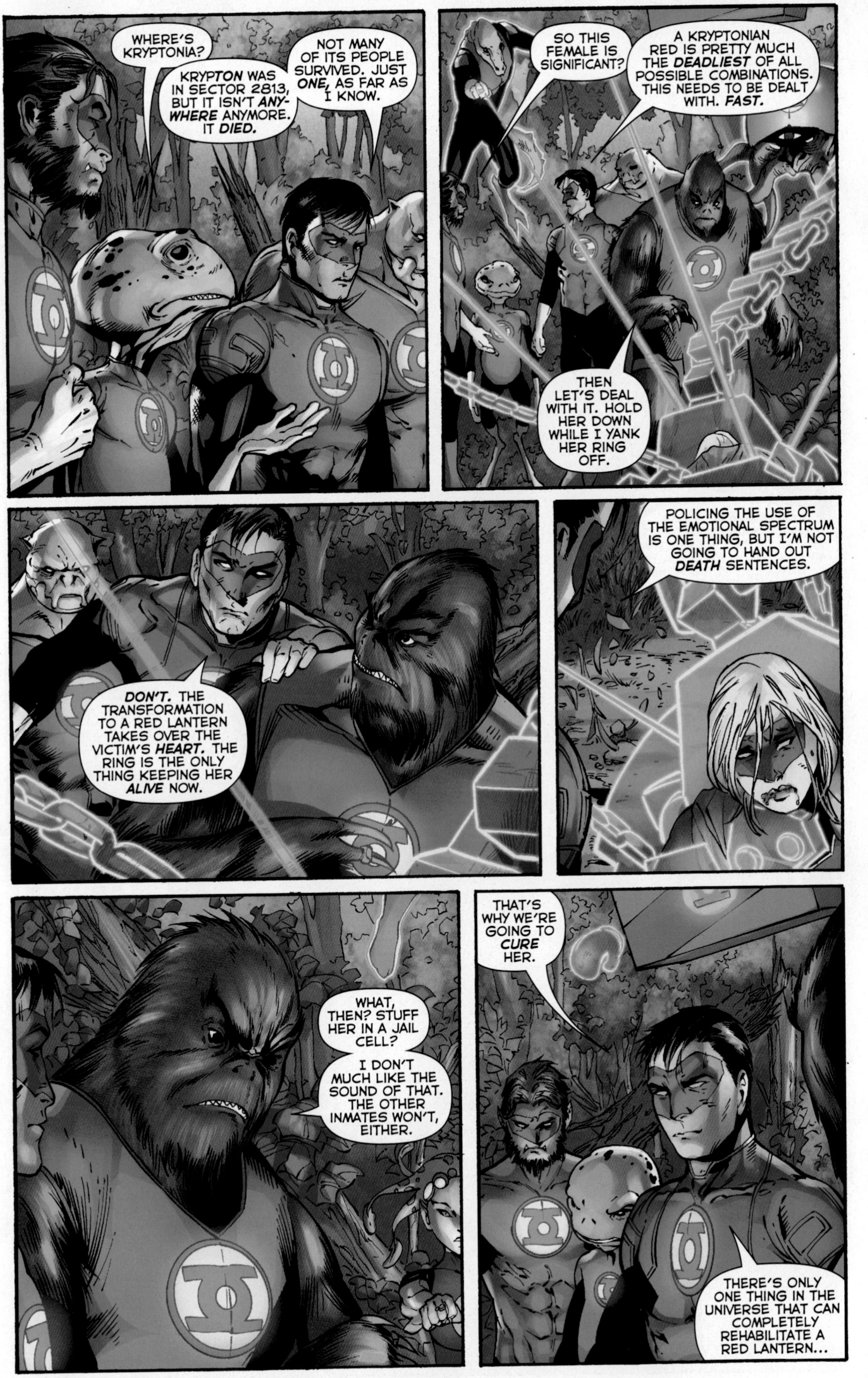
WHERE'S KRYPTONIA?
KRYPTON WAS IN SECTOR 2813, BUT IT ISN'T ANYWHERE ANYMORE. IT DIED.
NOT MANY OF ITS PEOPLE SURVIVED. JUST ONE, AS FAR AS I KNOW.
SO THIS FEMALE IS SIGNIFICANT?
A KRYPTONIAN RED IS PRETTY MUCH THE DEADLIEST OF ALL POSSIBLE COMBINATIONS. THIS NEEDS TO BE DEALT WITH. FAST.
THEN LET'S DEAL WITH IT. HOLD HER DOWN WHILE I YANK HER RING OFF.
DON'T. THE TRANSFORMATION TO A RED LANTERN TAKES OVER THE VICTIM'S HEART. THE RING IS THE ONLY THING KEEPING HER ALIVE NOW.
POLICING THE USE OF THE EMOTIONAL SPECTRUM IS ONE THING, BUT I'M NOT GOING TO HAND OUT DEATH SENTENCES.
WHAT, THEN? STUFF HER IN A JAIL CELL?
I DON'T MUCH LIKE THE SOUND OF THAT. THE OTHER INMATES WON'T, EITHER.
THAT'S WHY WE'RE GOING TO CURE HER.
THERE'S ONLY ONE THING IN THE UNIVERSE THAT CAN COMPLETELY REHABILITATE A RED LANTERN...

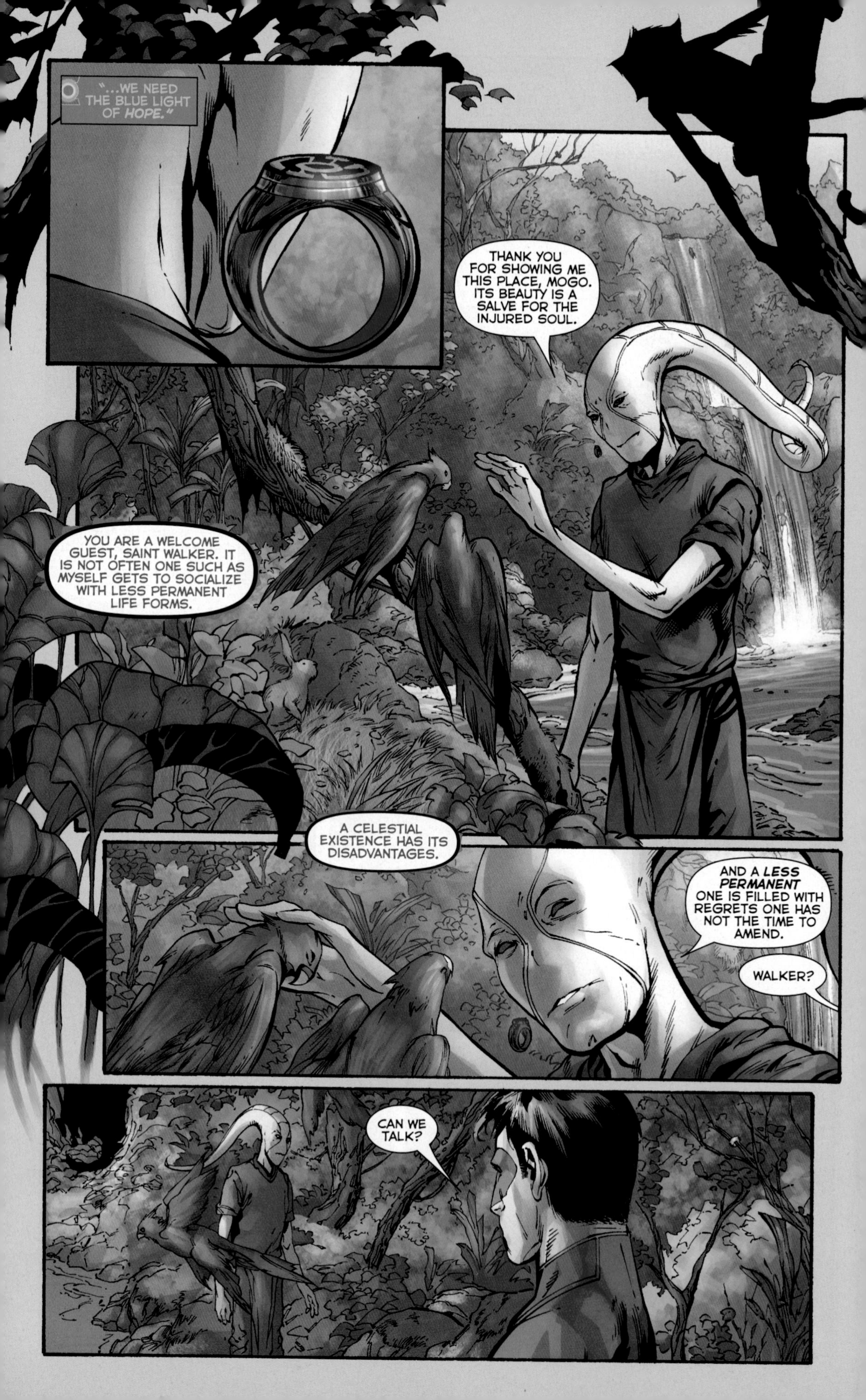
"...WE NEED THE BLUE LIGHT OF *HOPE*."
THANK YOU FOR SHOWING ME THIS PLACE, MOGO. ITS BEAUTY IS A SALVE FOR THE INJURED SOUL.
YOU ARE A WELCOME GUEST, SAINT WALKER. IT IS NOT OFTEN ONE SUCH AS MYSELF GETS TO SOCIALIZE WITH LESS PERMANENT LIFE FORMS.
A CELESTIAL EXISTENCE HAS ITS DISADVANTAGES.
AND A *LESS PERMANENT* ONE IS FILLED WITH REGRETS ONE HAS NOT THE TIME TO AMEND.
WALKER?
CAN WE TALK?

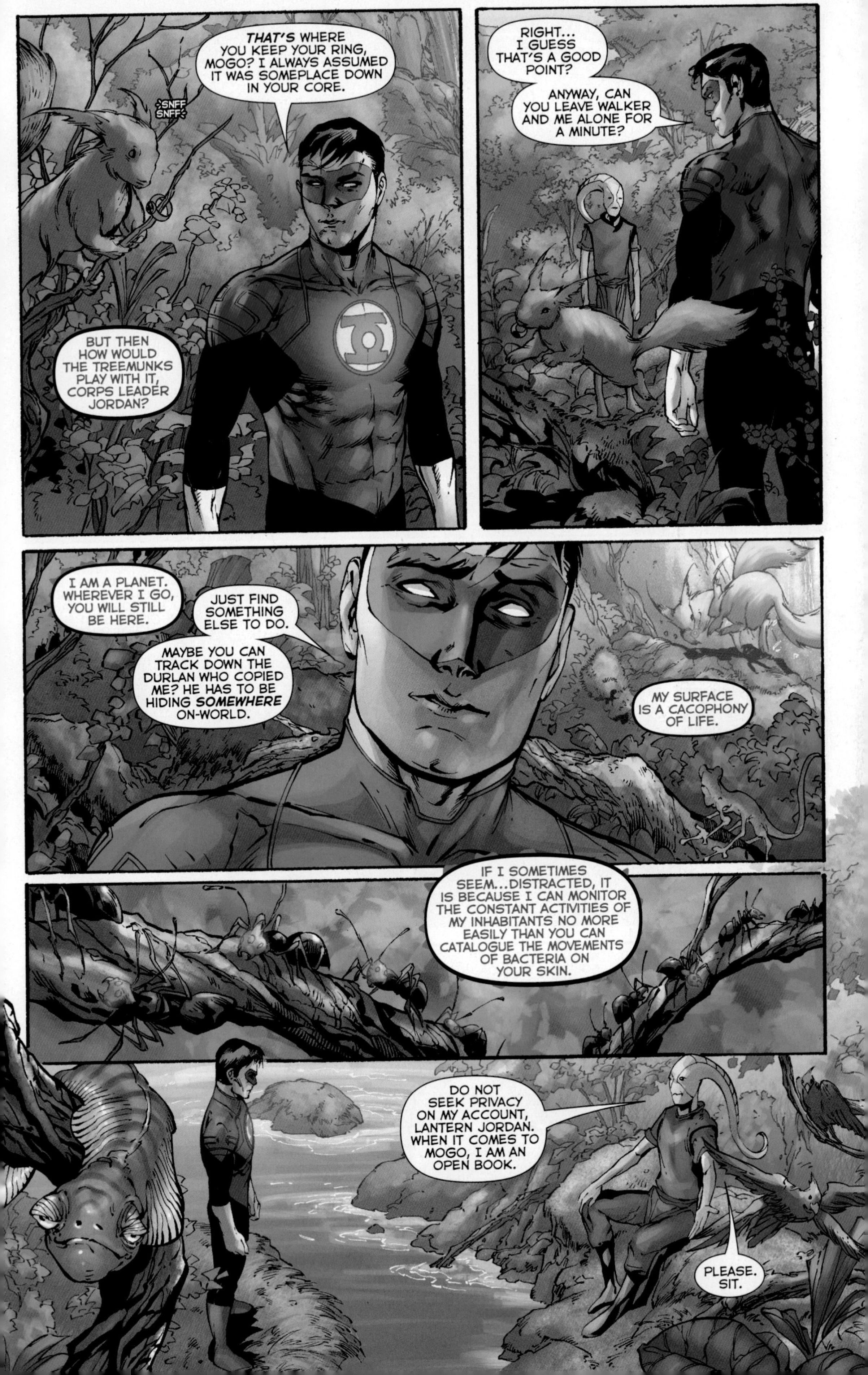
THAT'S WHERE YOU KEEP YOUR RING, MOGO? I ALWAYS ASSUMED IT WAS SOMEPLACE DOWN IN YOUR CORE.
SNFF SNFF
BUT THEN HOW WOULD THE TREEMUNKS PLAY WITH IT, CORPS LEADER JORDAN?
RIGHT... I GUESS THAT'S A GOOD POINT?
ANYWAY, CAN YOU LEAVE WALKER AND ME ALONE FOR A MINUTE?
I AM A PLANET. WHEREVER I GO, YOU WILL STILL BE HERE.
JUST FIND SOMETHING ELSE TO DO.
MAYBE YOU CAN TRACK DOWN THE DURLAN WHO COPIED ME? HE HAS TO BE HIDING SOMEWHERE ON-WORLD.
MY SURFACE IS A CACOPHONY OF LIFE.
IF I SOMETIMES SEEM...DISTRACTED, IT IS BECAUSE I CAN MONITOR THE CONSTANT ACTIVITIES OF MY INHABITANTS NO MORE EASILY THAN YOU CAN CATALOGUE THE MOVEMENTS OF BACTERIA ON YOUR SKIN.
DO NOT SEEK PRIVACY ON MY ACCOUNT, LANTERN JORDAN. WHEN IT COMES TO MOGO, I AM AN OPEN BOOK.
PLEASE. SIT.

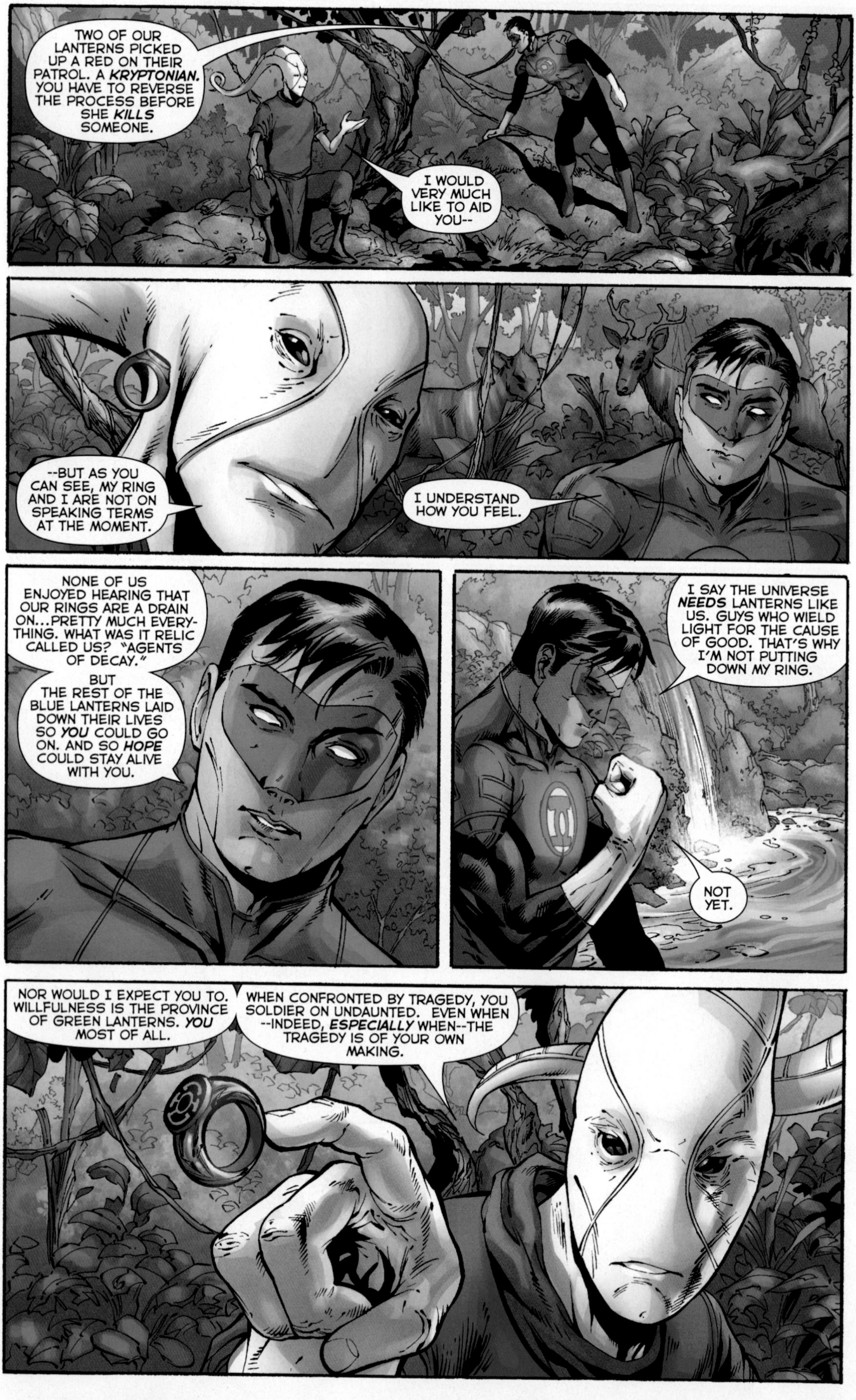
TWO OF OUR LANTERNS PICKED UP A RED ON THEIR PATROL. A KRYPTONIAN. YOU HAVE TO REVERSE THE PROCESS BEFORE SHE KILLS SOMEONE.
I WOULD VERY MUCH LIKE TO AID YOU--
--BUT AS YOU CAN SEE, MY RING AND I ARE NOT ON SPEAKING TERMS AT THE MOMENT.
I UNDERSTAND HOW YOU FEEL.
NONE OF US ENJOYED HEARING THAT OUR RINGS ARE A DRAIN ON...PRETTY MUCH EVERY-THING. WHAT WAS IT RELIC CALLED US? "AGENTS OF DECAY."
BUT THE REST OF THE BLUE LANTERNS LAID DOWN THEIR LIVES SO YOU COULD GO ON. AND SO HOPE COULD STAY ALIVE WITH YOU.
I SAY THE UNIVERSE NEEDS LANTERNS LIKE US. GUYS WHO WIELD LIGHT FOR THE CAUSE OF GOOD. THAT'S WHY I'M NOT PUTTING DOWN MY RING.
NOT YET.
NOR WOULD I EXPECT YOU TO. WILLFULNESS IS THE PROVINCE OF GREEN LANTERNS. YOU MOST OF ALL.
WHEN CONFRONTED BY TRAGEDY, YOU SOLDIER ON UNDAUNTED. EVEN WHEN --INDEED, ESPECIALLY WHEN--THE TRAGEDY IS OF YOUR OWN MAKING.

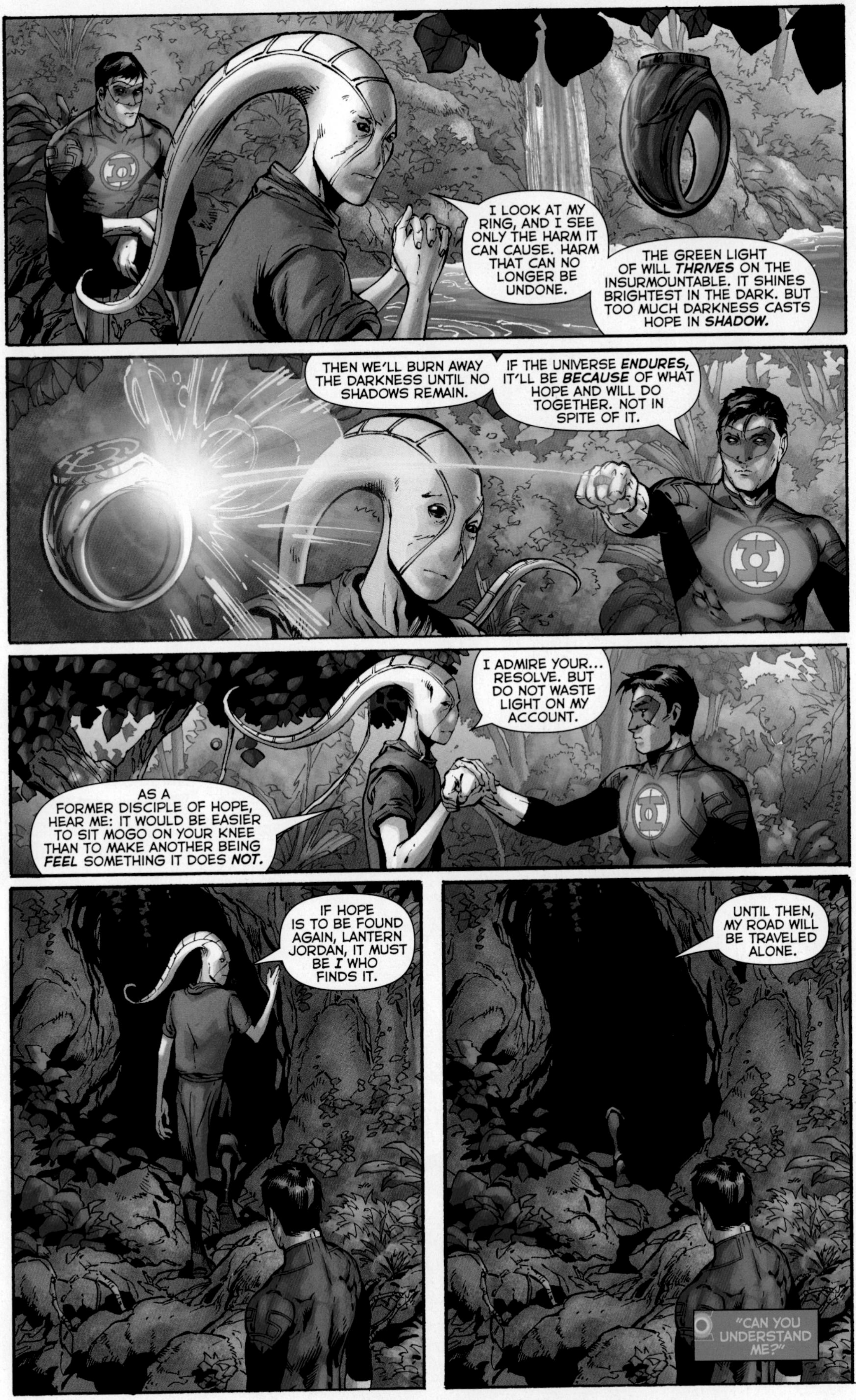
I LOOK AT MY RING, AND I SEE ONLY THE HARM IT CAN CAUSE. HARM THAT CAN NO LONGER BE UNDONE.
THE GREEN LIGHT OF WILL *THRIVES* ON THE INSURMOUNTABLE. IT SHINES BRIGHTEST IN THE DARK. BUT TOO MUCH DARKNESS CASTS HOPE IN *SHADOW.*
THEN WE'LL BURN AWAY THE DARKNESS UNTIL NO SHADOWS REMAIN.
IF THE UNIVERSE *ENDURES,* IT'LL BE *BECAUSE* OF WHAT HOPE AND WILL DO TOGETHER. NOT IN SPITE OF IT.
I ADMIRE YOUR... RESOLVE. BUT DO NOT WASTE LIGHT ON MY ACCOUNT.
AS A FORMER DISCIPLE OF HOPE, HEAR ME: IT WOULD BE EASIER TO SIT MOGO ON YOUR KNEE THAN TO MAKE ANOTHER BEING *FEEL* SOMETHING IT DOES *NOT.*
IF HOPE IS TO BE FOUND AGAIN, LANTERN JORDAN, IT MUST BE *I* WHO FINDS IT.
UNTIL THEN, MY ROAD WILL BE TRAVELED ALONE.
"CAN YOU UNDERSTAND ME?"

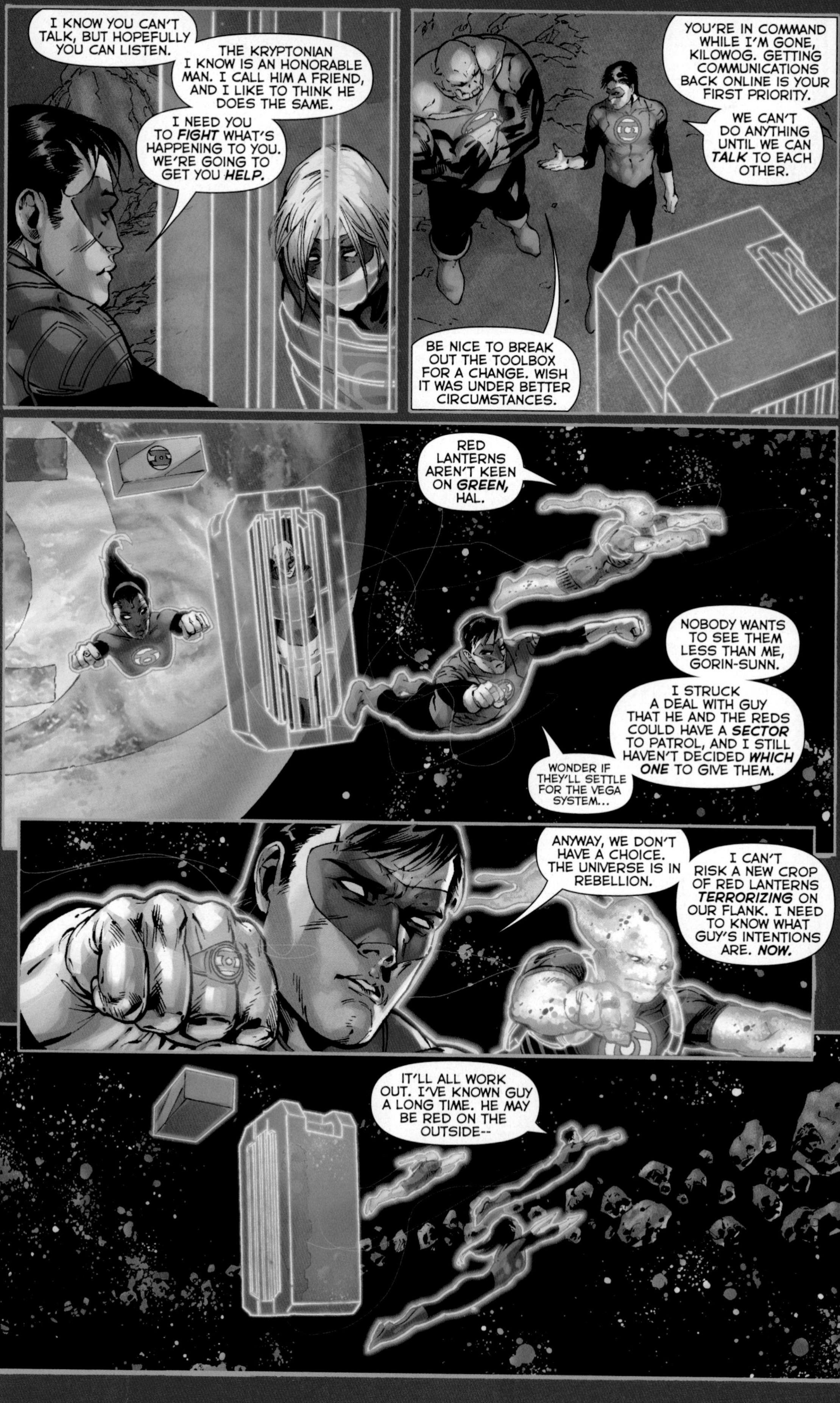
I KNOW YOU CAN'T TALK, BUT HOPEFULLY YOU CAN LISTEN.
THE KRYPTONIAN I KNOW IS AN HONORABLE MAN. I CALL HIM A FRIEND, AND I LIKE TO THINK HE DOES THE SAME.
I NEED YOU TO FIGHT WHAT'S HAPPENING TO YOU. WE'RE GOING TO GET YOU HELP.
YOU'RE IN COMMAND WHILE I'M GONE, KILOWOG. GETTING COMMUNICATIONS BACK ONLINE IS YOUR FIRST PRIORITY.
WE CAN'T DO ANYTHING UNTIL WE CAN TALK TO EACH OTHER.
BE NICE TO BREAK OUT THE TOOLBOX FOR A CHANGE. WISH IT WAS UNDER BETTER CIRCUMSTANCES.
RED LANTERNS AREN'T KEEN ON GREEN, HAL.
NOBODY WANTS TO SEE THEM LESS THAN ME, GORIN-SUNN.
I STRUCK A DEAL WITH GUY THAT HE AND THE REDS COULD HAVE A SECTOR TO PATROL, AND I STILL HAVEN'T DECIDED WHICH ONE TO GIVE THEM.
WONDER IF THEY'LL SETTLE FOR THE VEGA SYSTEM...
ANYWAY, WE DON'T HAVE A CHOICE. THE UNIVERSE IS IN REBELLION.
I CAN'T RISK A NEW CROP OF RED LANTERNS TERRORIZING ON OUR FLANK. I NEED TO KNOW WHAT GUY'S INTENTIONS ARE. NOW.
IT'LL ALL WORK OUT. I'VE KNOWN GUY A LONG TIME. HE MAY BE RED ON THE OUTSIDE--

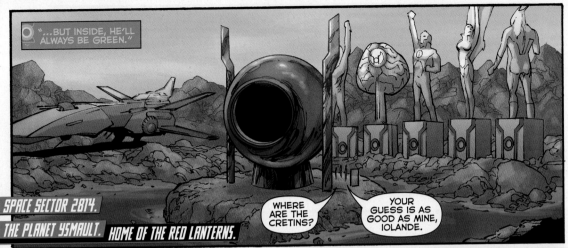

"...BUT INSIDE, HE'LL ALWAYS BE GREEN."

SPACE SECTOR 2814.

THE PLANET YSMAULT. HOME OF THE RED LANTERNS.

WHERE ARE THE CRETINS?

YOUR GUESS IS AS GOOD AS MINE, IOLANDE.

I'VE NEVER BEEN HERE WHEN THEY WEREN'T STANDING AROUND THEIR BATTERY. IT'S KIND OF WHAT THEY DO.

BUT IT'S NICE TO SEE GUY'S NEW ROLE HASN'T CHANGED HIS TENDENCY TO OVER-COMPENSATE...

SUCH PUTREFACTION. NOTHING LIKE THE SEA OF GENERATIONS MY KIND RESIDES IN.

STRANGE...

...THEIR SHIP IS JUST SITTING OUT IN THE OPEN.

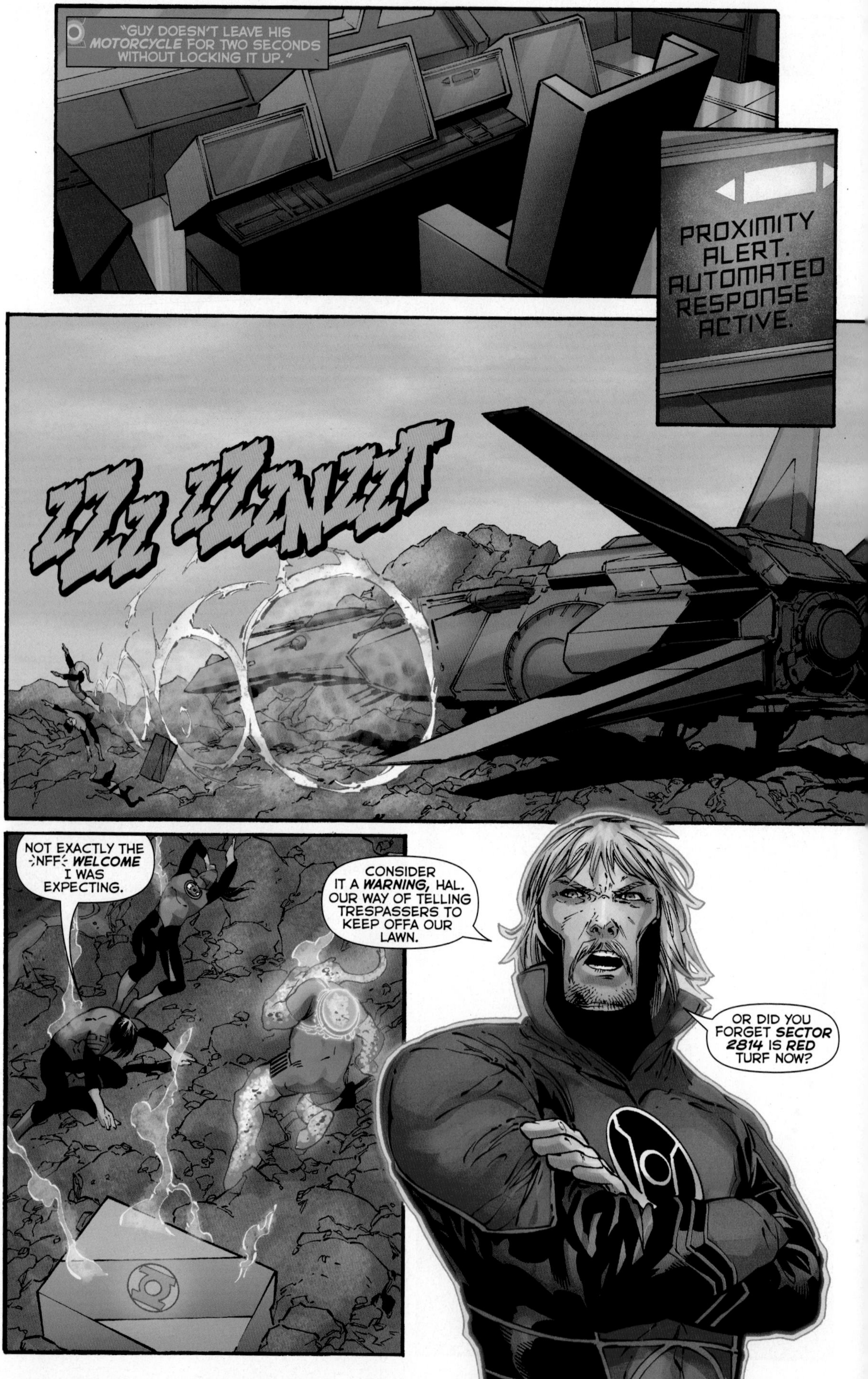

"GUY DOESN'T LEAVE HIS MOTORCYCLE FOR TWO SECONDS WITHOUT LOCKING IT UP."
PROXIMITY ALERT. AUTOMATED RESPONSE ACTIVE.
ZZZ ZZZNZZT
NOT EXACTLY THE NFF WELCOME I WAS EXPECTING.
CONSIDER IT A WARNING, HAL. OUR WAY OF TELLING TRESPASSERS TO KEEP OFFA OUR LAWN.
OR DID YOU FORGET SECTOR 2814 IS RED TURF NOW?

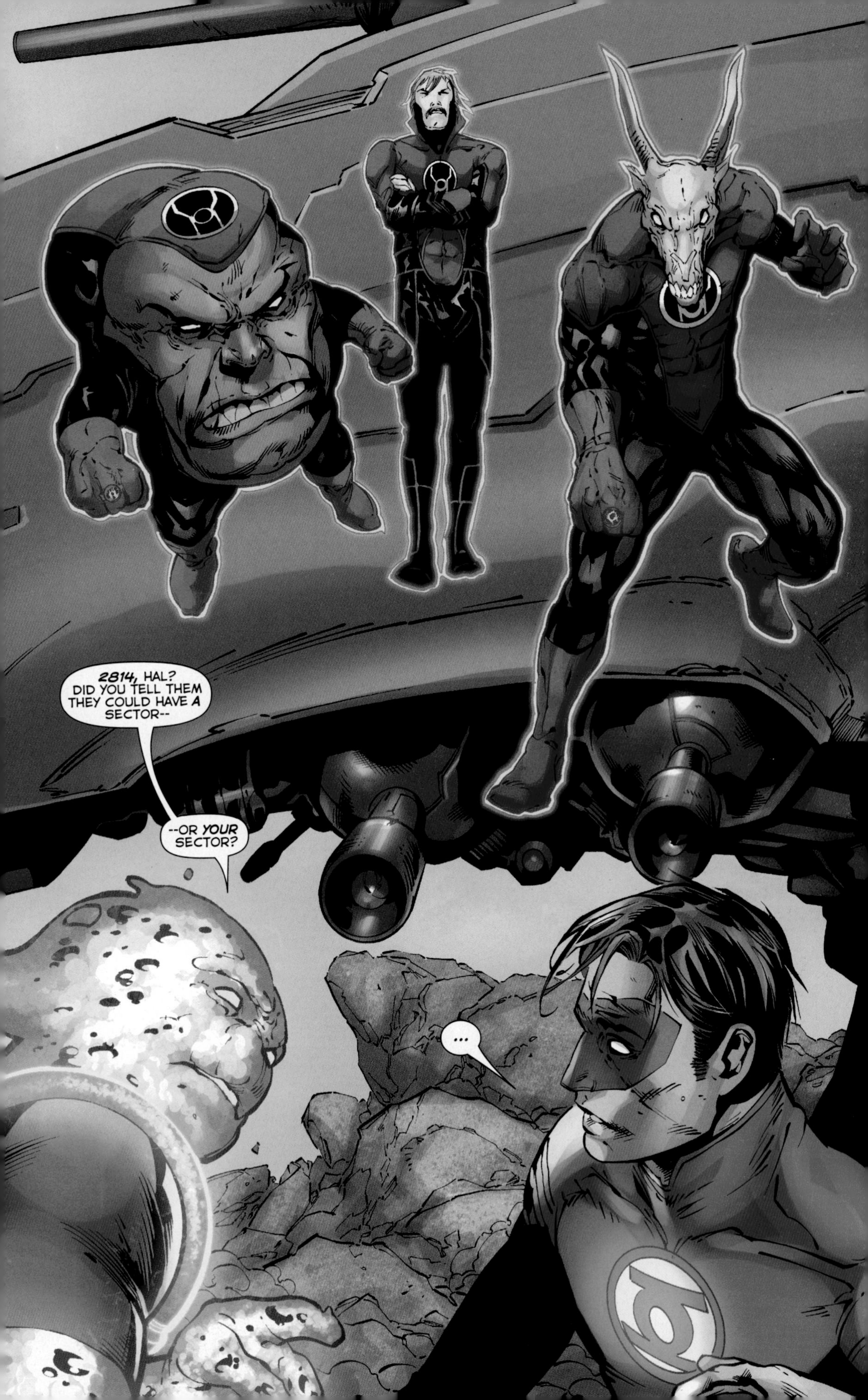
2814, HAL? DID YOU TELL THEM THEY COULD HAVE A SECTOR--
--OR YOUR SECTOR?
...

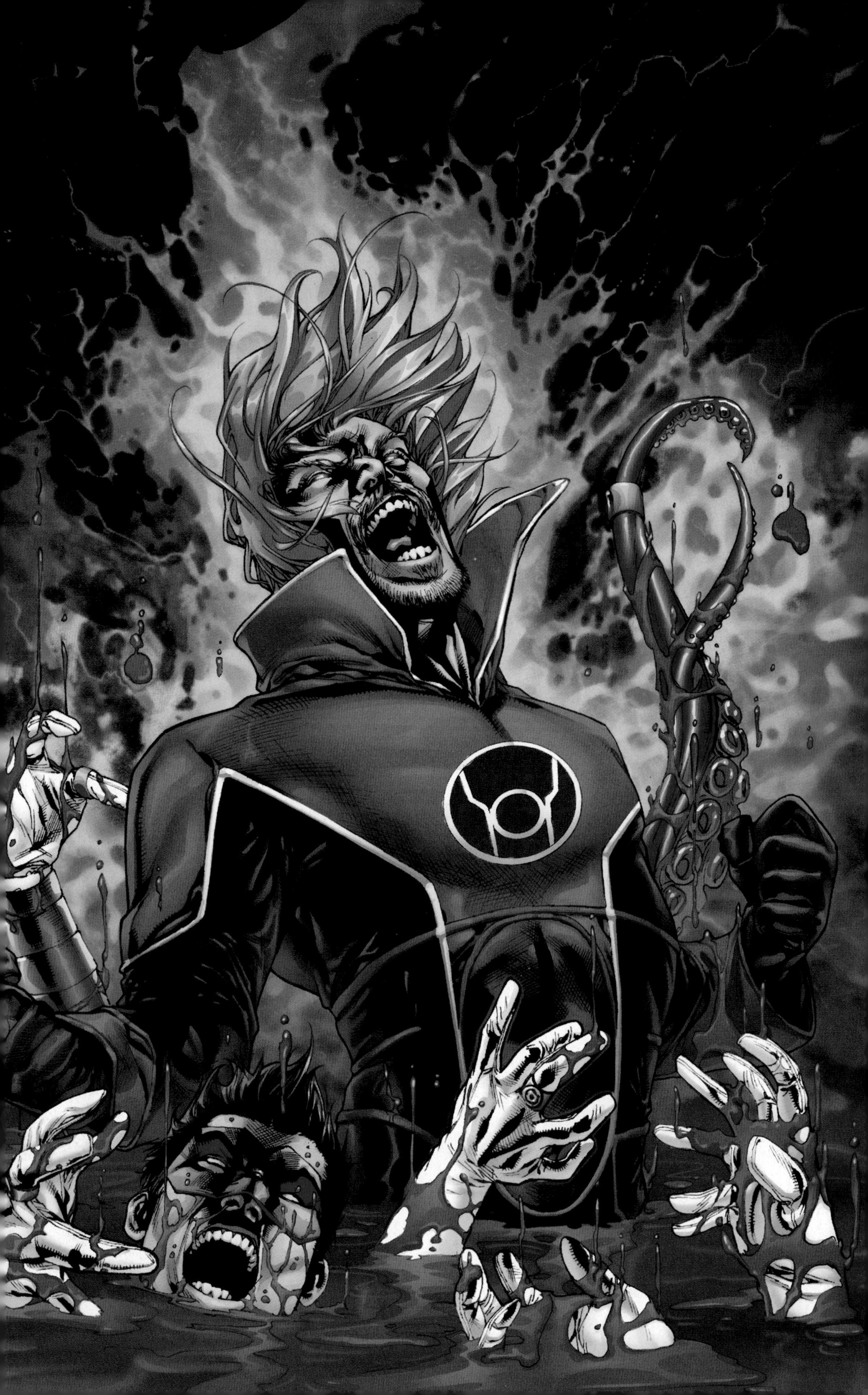

CHARLES SOULE writer ALESSANDRO VITTI artist GABE ELTAEB colorist DAVE SHARPE letterer
cover art by STEPHEN SEGOVIA with HI-FI

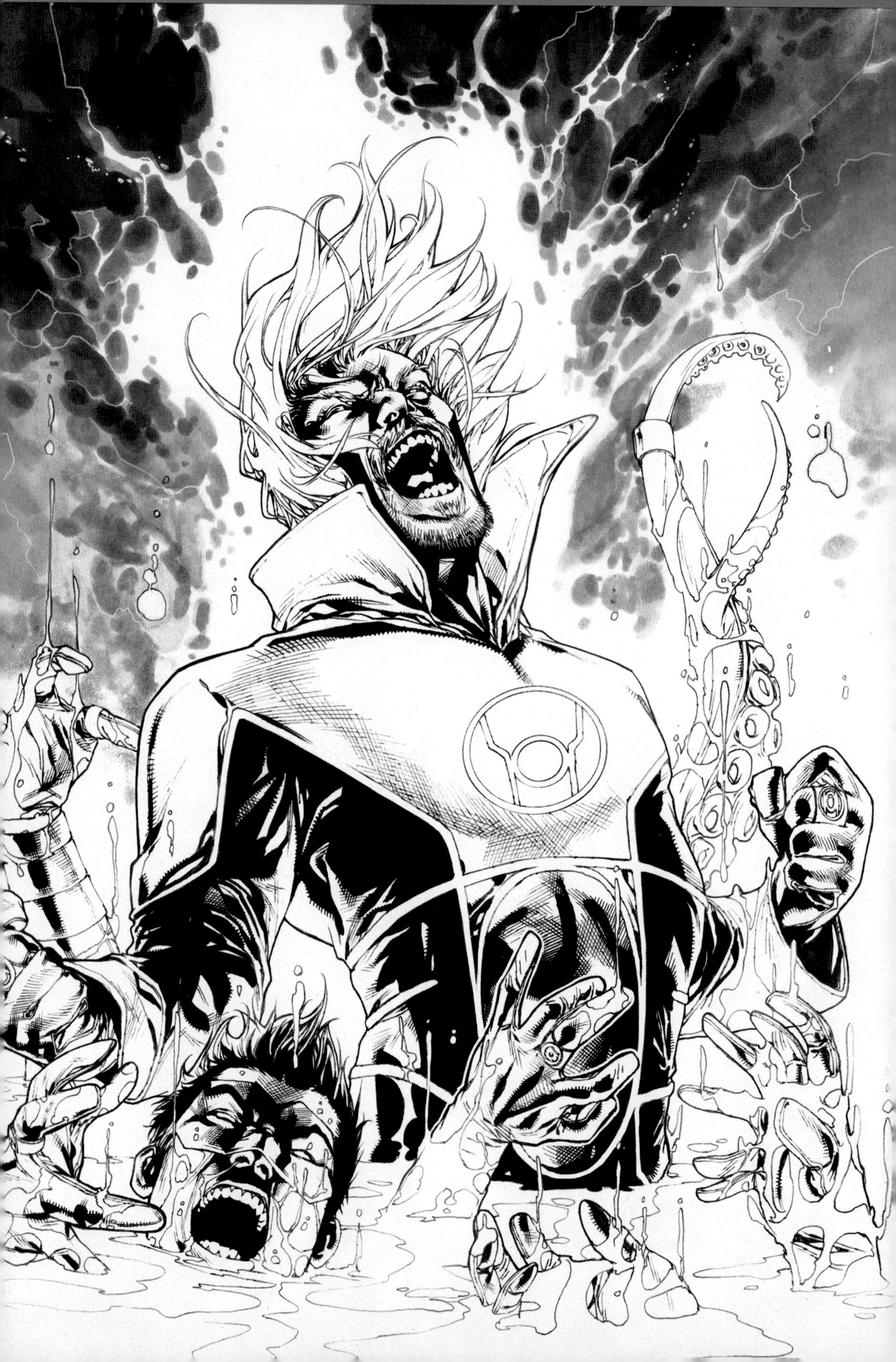

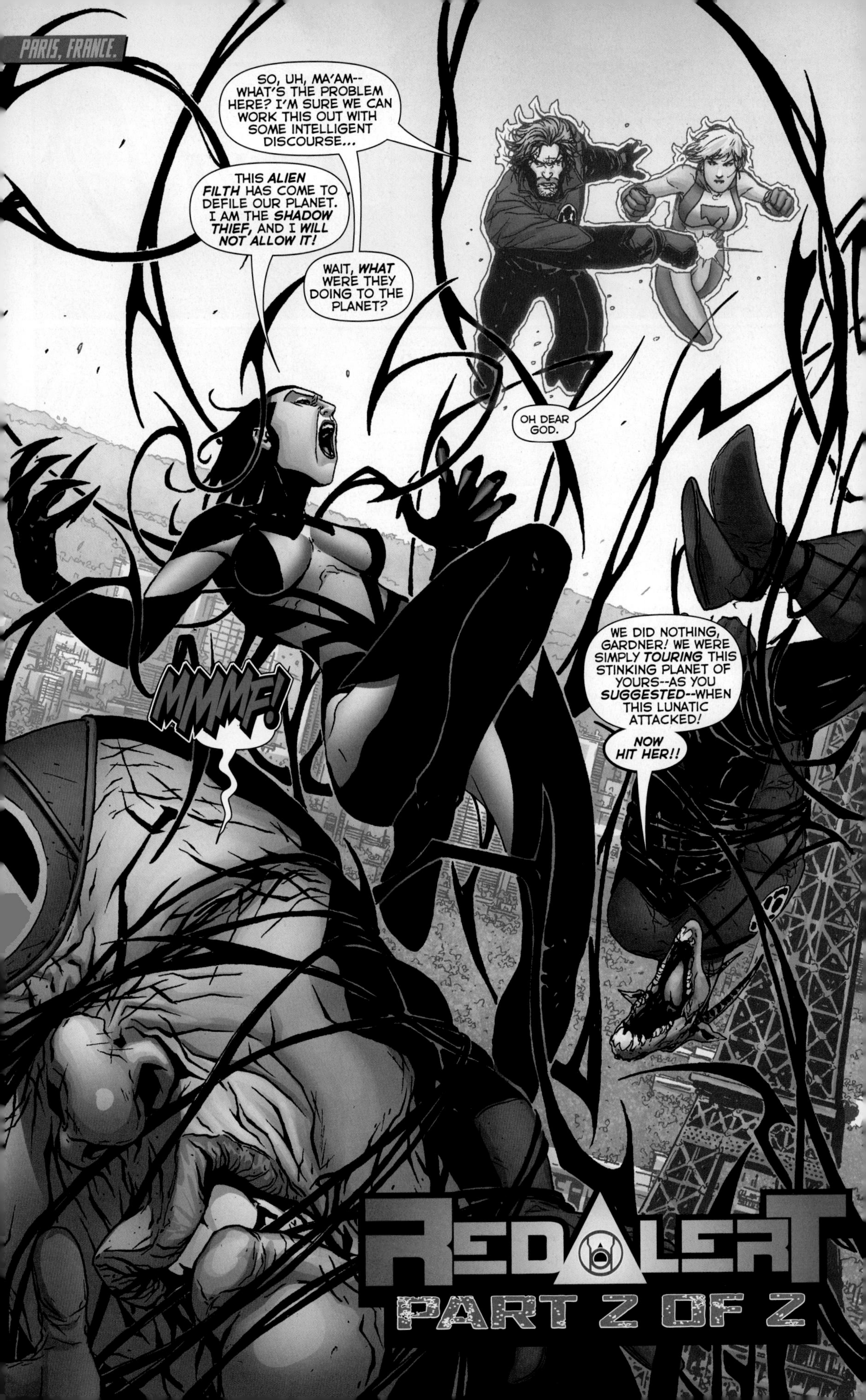

PARIS, FRANCE.
SO, UH, MA'AM--WHAT'S THE PROBLEM HERE? I'M SURE WE CAN WORK THIS OUT WITH SOME INTELLIGENT DISCOURSE...
THIS ALIEN FILTH HAS COME TO DEFILE OUR PLANET. I AM THE SHADOW THIEF, AND I WILL NOT ALLOW IT!
WAIT, WHAT WERE THEY DOING TO THE PLANET?
OH DEAR GOD.
WE DID NOTHING, GARDNER! WE WERE SIMPLY TOURING THIS STINKING PLANET OF YOURS--AS YOU SUGGESTED--WHEN THIS LUNATIC ATTACKED!
NOW HIT HER!!
MMMF!
RED ALERT
PART 2 OF 2

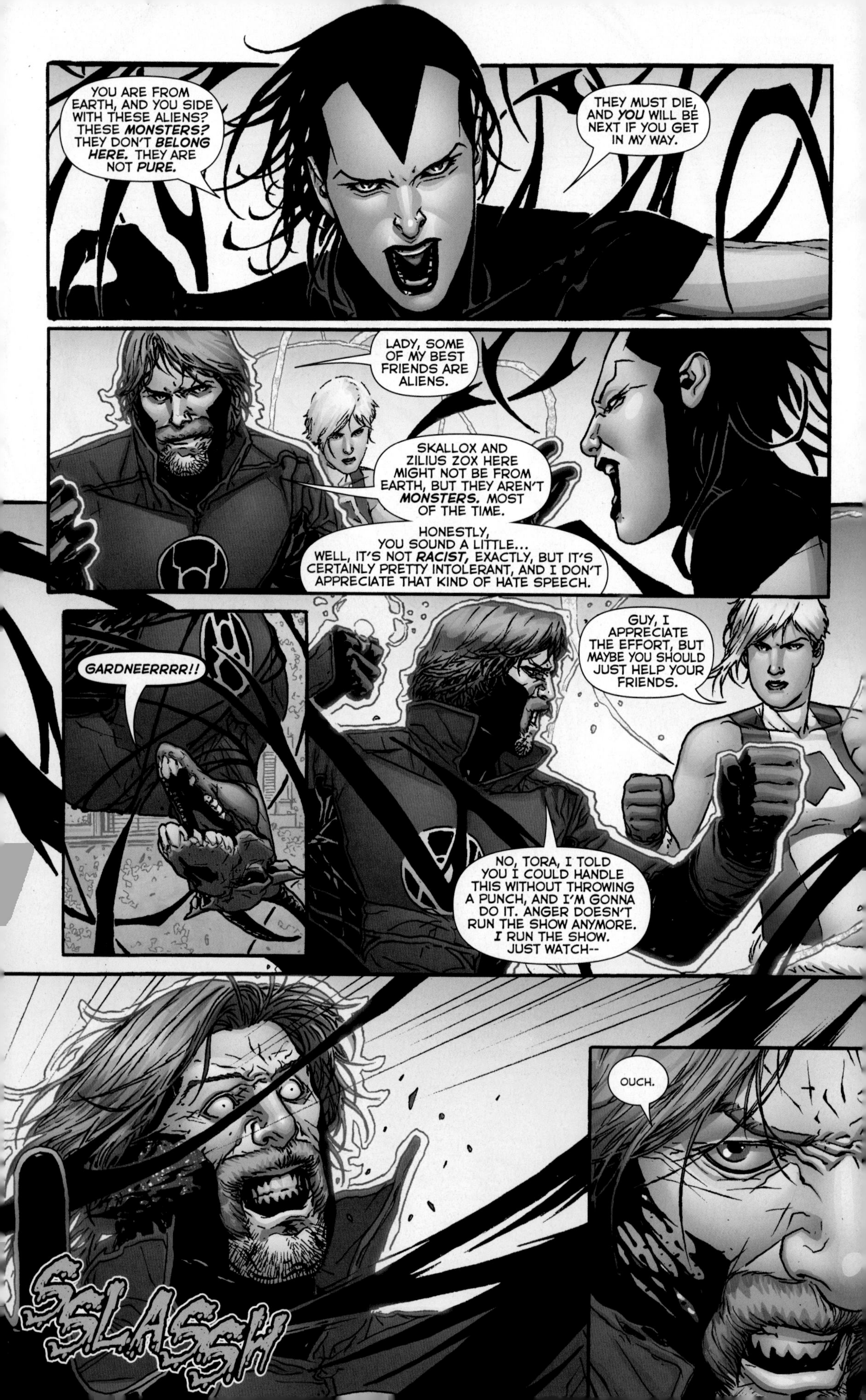
YOU ARE FROM EARTH, AND YOU SIDE WITH THESE ALIENS? THESE MONSTERS? THEY DON'T BELONG HERE. THEY ARE NOT PURE.
THEY MUST DIE, AND YOU WILL BE NEXT IF YOU GET IN MY WAY.
LADY, SOME OF MY BEST FRIENDS ARE ALIENS.
SKALLOX AND ZILIUS ZOX HERE MIGHT NOT BE FROM EARTH, BUT THEY AREN'T MONSTERS. MOST OF THE TIME.
HONESTLY, YOU SOUND A LITTLE... WELL, IT'S NOT RACIST, EXACTLY, BUT IT'S CERTAINLY PRETTY INTOLERANT, AND I DON'T APPRECIATE THAT KIND OF HATE SPEECH.
GARDNEERRRR!!
GUY, I APPRECIATE THE EFFORT, BUT MAYBE YOU SHOULD JUST HELP YOUR FRIENDS.
NO, TORA, I TOLD YOU I COULD HANDLE THIS WITHOUT THROWING A PUNCH, AND I'M GONNA DO IT. ANGER DOESN'T RUN THE SHOW ANYMORE. I RUN THE SHOW. JUST WATCH--
SSLASSH
OUCH.

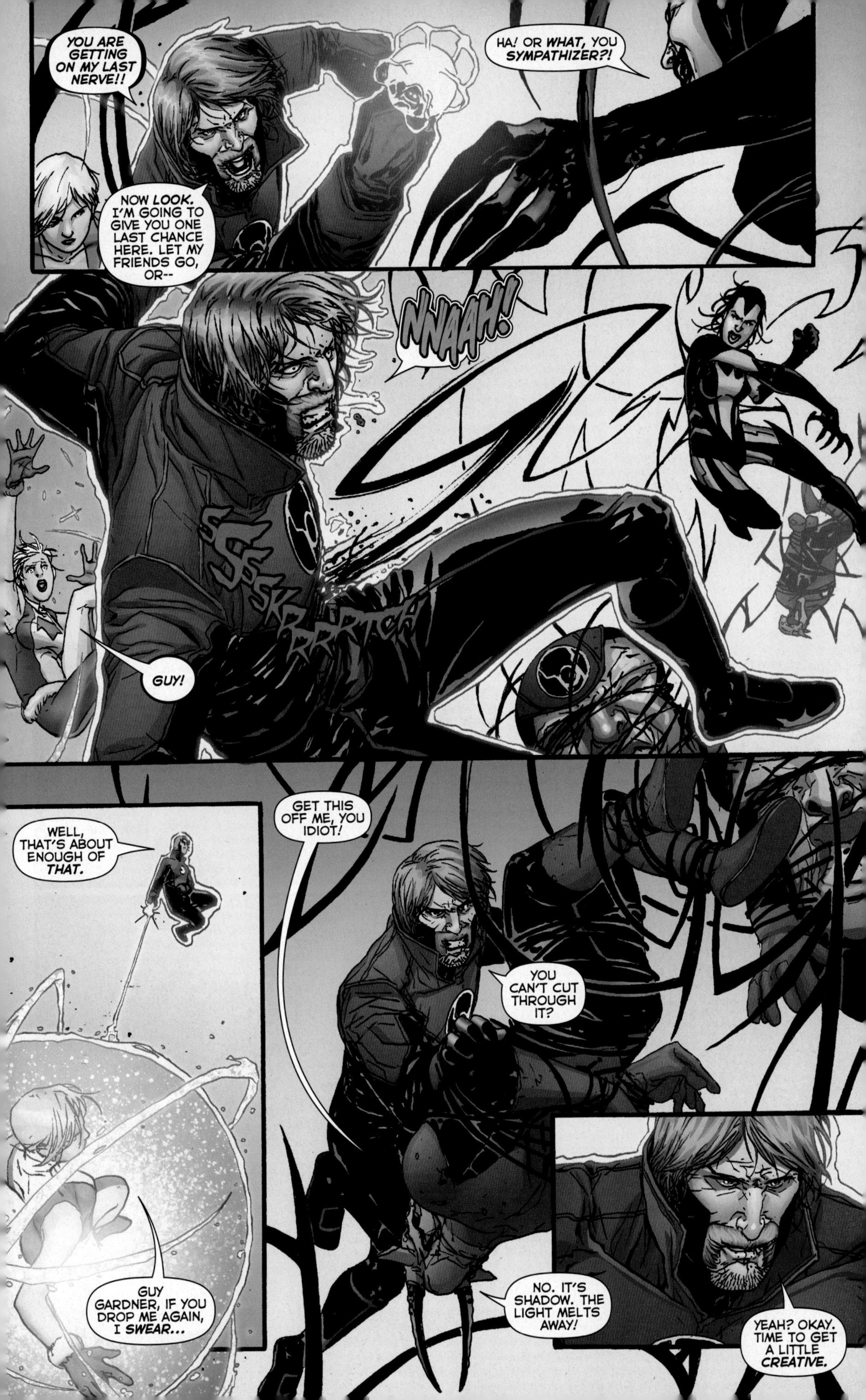

YOU ARE GETTING ON MY LAST NERVE!!
HA! OR WHAT, YOU SYMPATHIZER?!
NOW LOOK. I'M GOING TO GIVE YOU ONE LAST CHANCE HERE. LET MY FRIENDS GO, OR--
NNAAH!
SSSKRRRTCH
GUY!
WELL, THAT'S ABOUT ENOUGH OF THAT.
GUY GARDNER, IF YOU DROP ME AGAIN, I SWEAR...
GET THIS OFF ME, YOU IDIOT!
YOU CAN'T CUT THROUGH IT?
NO. IT'S SHADOW. THE LIGHT MELTS AWAY!
YEAH? OKAY. TIME TO GET A LITTLE CREATIVE.

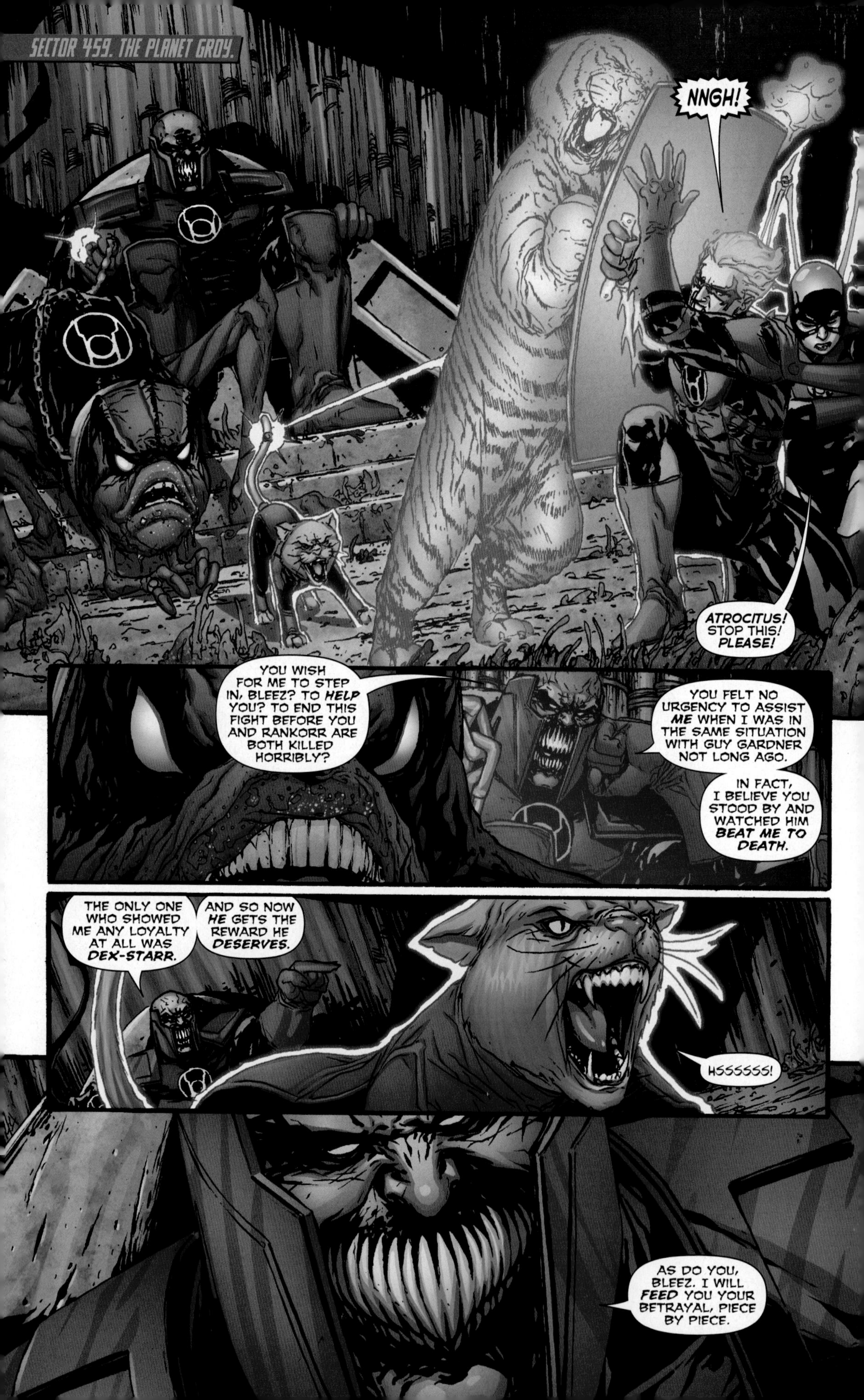
SECTOR 459. THE PLANET GROY.
NNGH!
ATROCITUS! STOP THIS! PLEASE!
YOU WISH FOR ME TO STEP IN, BLEEZ? TO HELP YOU? TO END THIS FIGHT BEFORE YOU AND RANKORR ARE BOTH KILLED HORRIBLY?
YOU FELT NO URGENCY TO ASSIST ME WHEN I WAS IN THE SAME SITUATION WITH GUY GARDNER NOT LONG AGO.
IN FACT, I BELIEVE YOU STOOD BY AND WATCHED HIM BEAT ME TO DEATH.
THE ONLY ONE WHO SHOWED ME ANY LOYALTY AT ALL WAS DEX-STARR.
AND SO NOW HE GETS THE REWARD HE DESERVES.
HSSSSSS!
AS DO YOU, BLEEZ. I WILL FEED YOU YOUR BETRAYAL, PIECE BY PIECE.

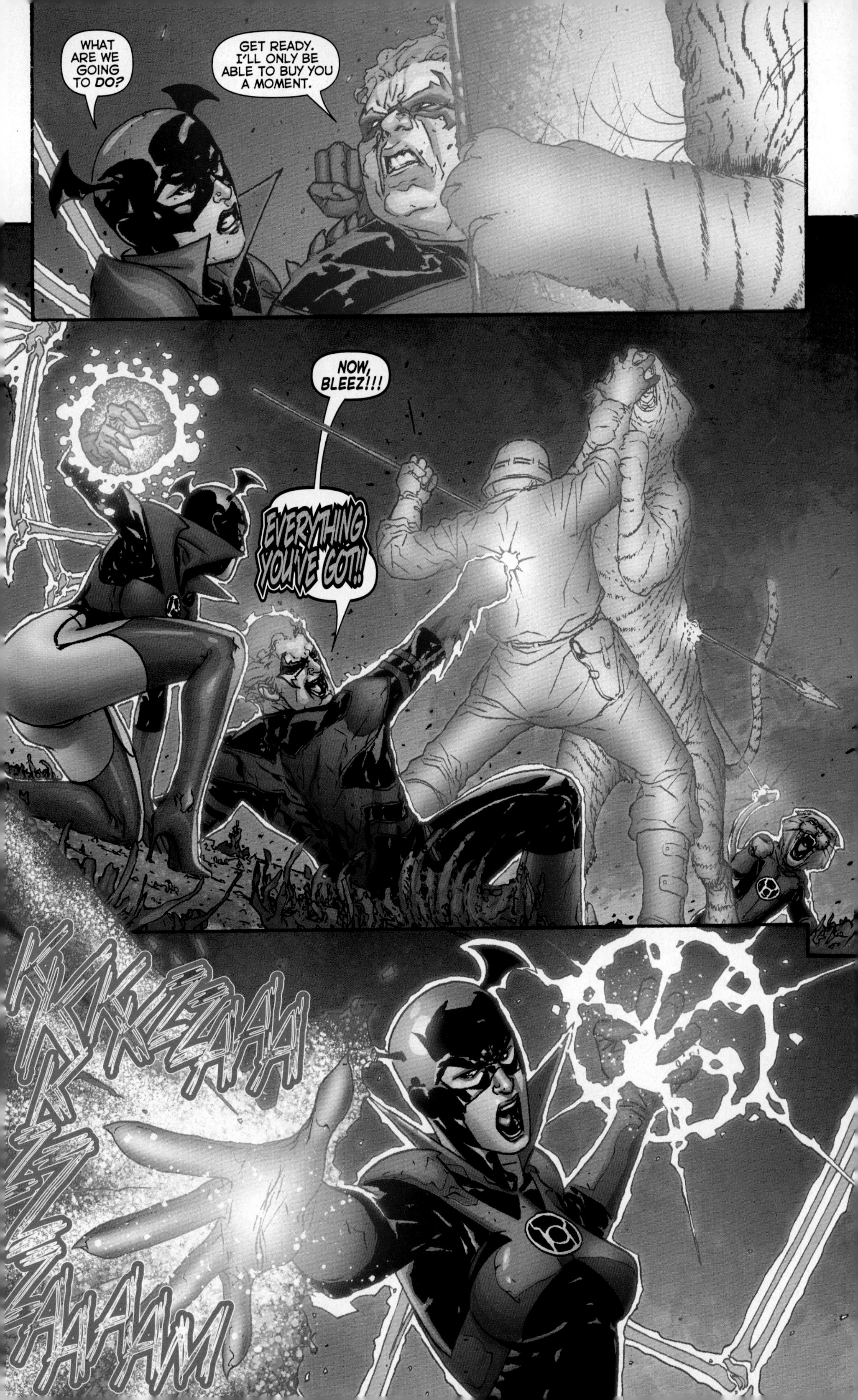
WHAT ARE WE GOING TO *DO*?
GET READY. I'LL ONLY BE ABLE TO BUY YOU A MOMENT.
NOW, BLEEZ!!!
EVERYTHING YOU'VE GOT!!
KKKKREEAAAKKKKAAAASSSHHAAAM

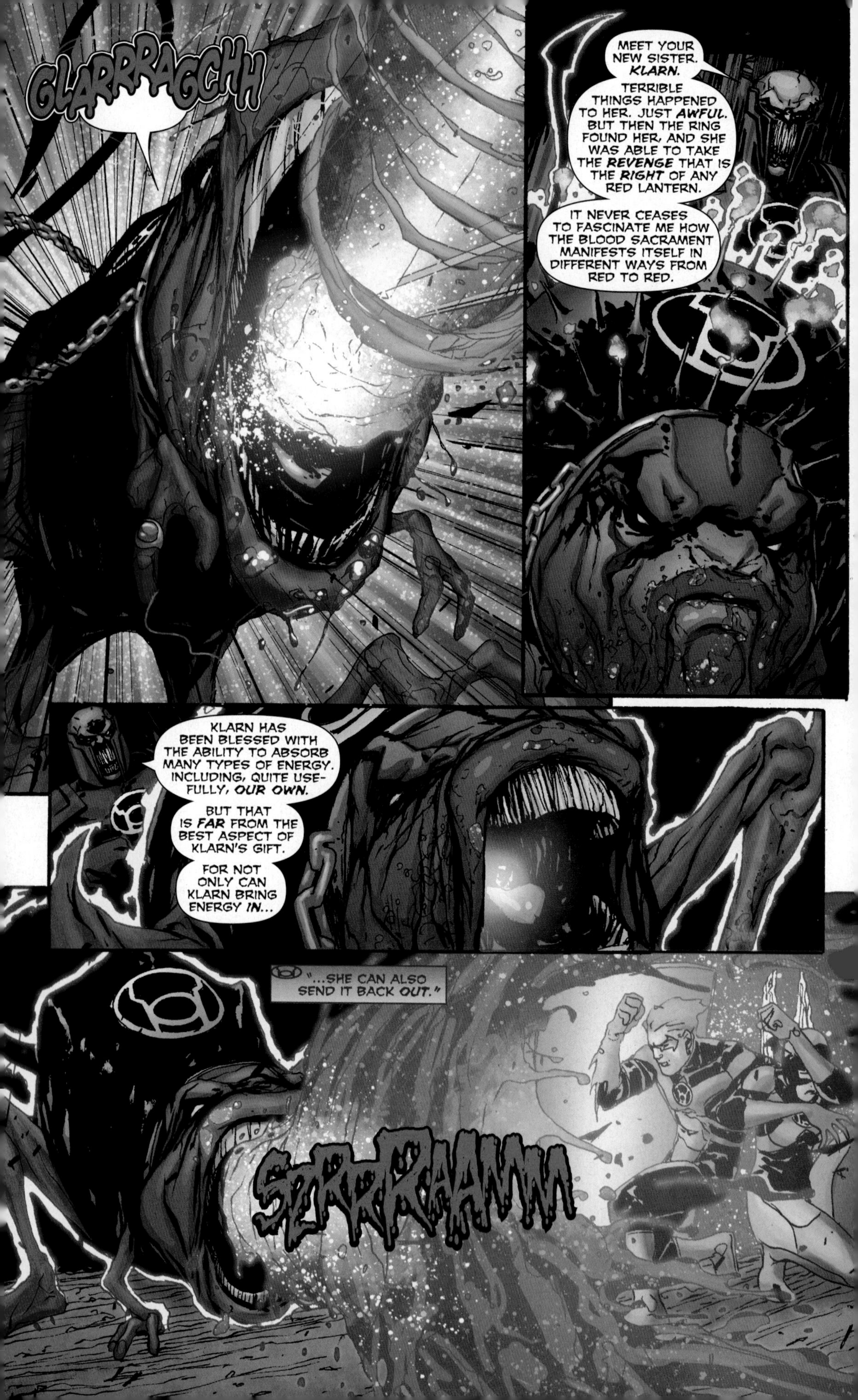
GLARRRAGCHH
MEET YOUR NEW SISTER. KLARN.
TERRIBLE THINGS HAPPENED TO HER. JUST AWFUL. BUT THEN THE RING FOUND HER, AND SHE WAS ABLE TO TAKE THE REVENGE THAT IS THE RIGHT OF ANY RED LANTERN.
IT NEVER CEASES TO FASCINATE ME HOW THE BLOOD SACRAMENT MANIFESTS ITSELF IN DIFFERENT WAYS FROM RED TO RED.
KLARN HAS BEEN BLESSED WITH THE ABILITY TO ABSORB MANY TYPES OF ENERGY. INCLUDING, QUITE USE-FULLY, OUR OWN.
BUT THAT IS FAR FROM THE BEST ASPECT OF KLARN'S GIFT.
FOR NOT ONLY CAN KLARN BRING ENERGY IN...
"...SHE CAN ALSO SEND IT BACK OUT."
SZRRAAMM

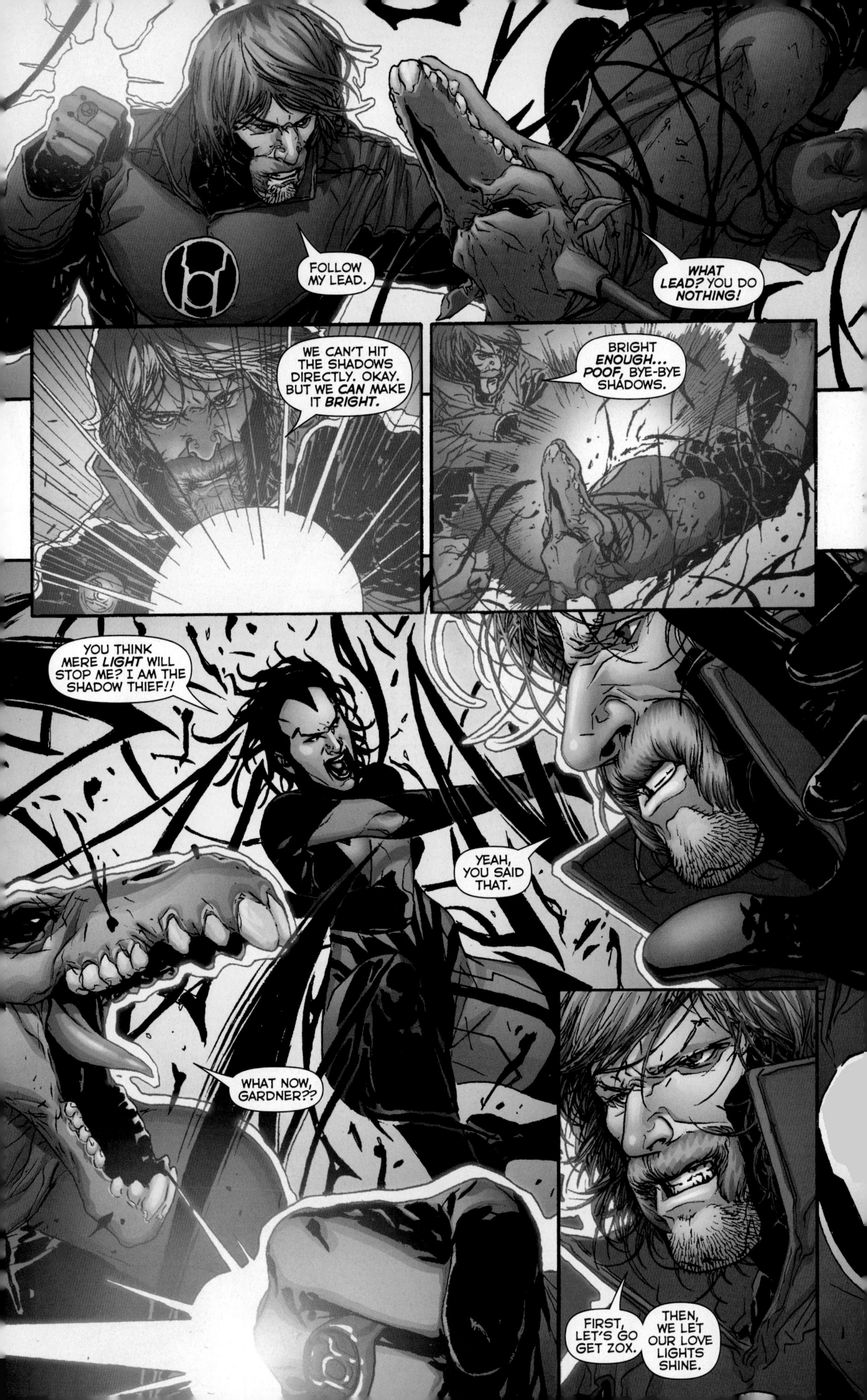
FOLLOW MY LEAD.
WHAT LEAD? YOU DO NOTHING!
WE CAN'T HIT THE SHADOWS DIRECTLY. OKAY. BUT WE CAN MAKE IT BRIGHT.
BRIGHT ENOUGH... POOF, BYE-BYE SHADOWS.
YOU THINK MERE LIGHT WILL STOP ME? I AM THE SHADOW THIEF!!
YEAH, YOU SAID THAT.
WHAT NOW, GARDNER??
FIRST, LET'S GO GET ZOX.
THEN, WE LET OUR LOVE LIGHTS SHINE.

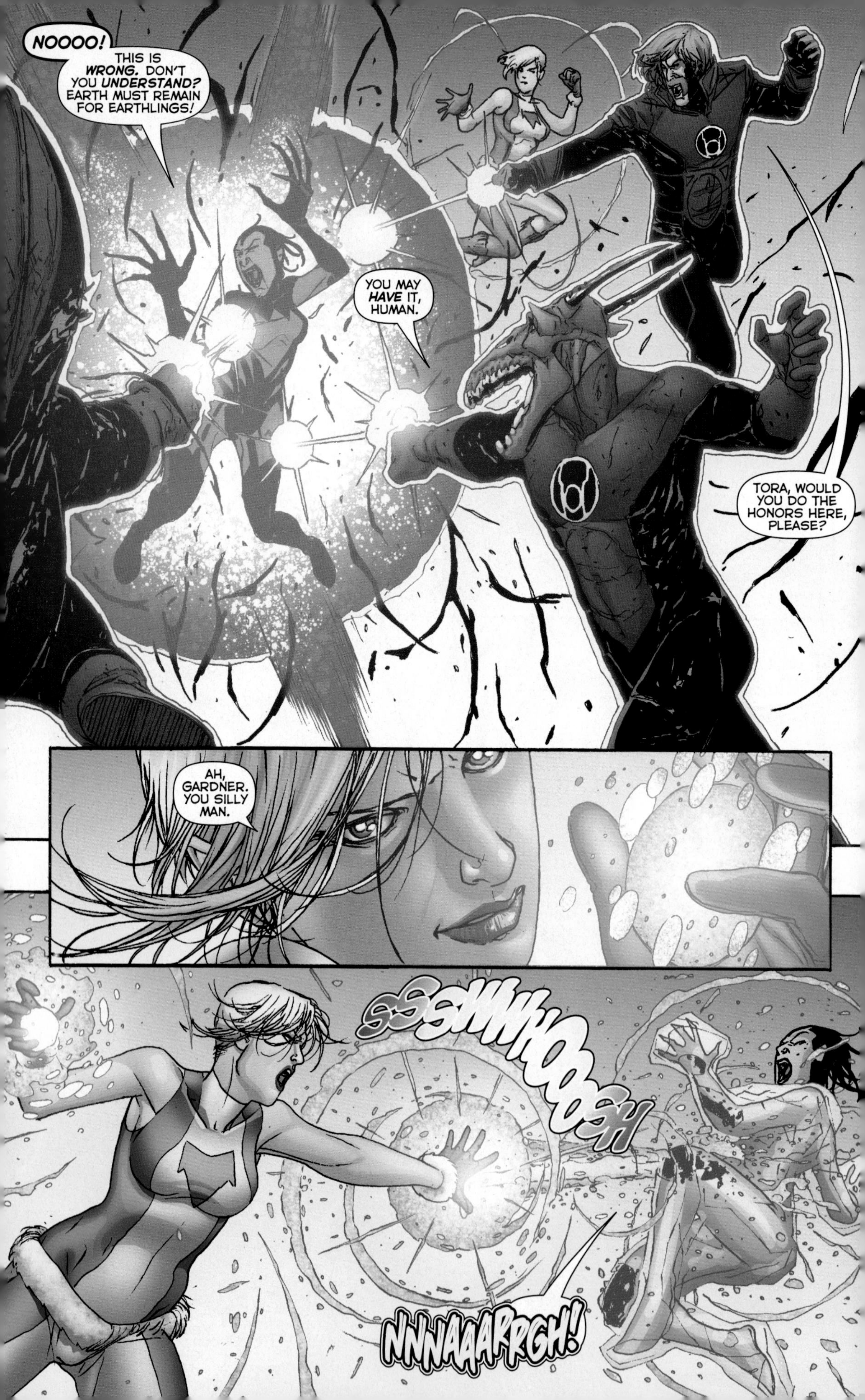
NOOOO!
THIS IS WRONG. DON'T YOU UNDERSTAND? EARTH MUST REMAIN FOR EARTHLINGS!
YOU MAY HAVE IT, HUMAN.
TORA, WOULD YOU DO THE HONORS HERE, PLEASE?
AH, GARDNER. YOU SILLY MAN.
SSSHWHOOOSH
NNNAAARRGH!

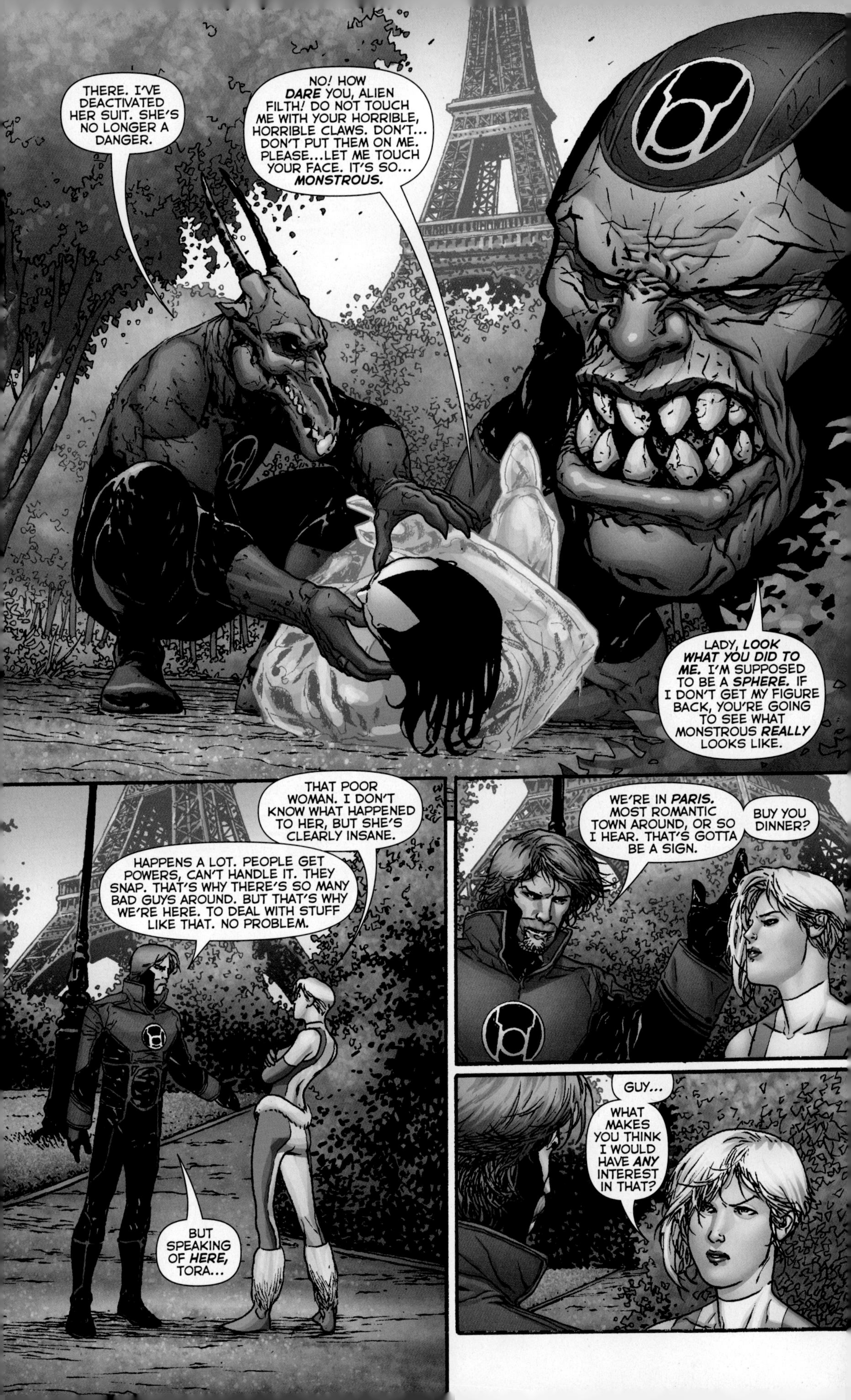
THERE. I'VE DEACTIVATED HER SUIT. SHE'S NO LONGER A DANGER.
NO! HOW **DARE** YOU, ALIEN FILTH! DO NOT TOUCH ME WITH YOUR HORRIBLE, HORRIBLE CLAWS. DON'T... DON'T PUT THEM ON ME. PLEASE...LET ME TOUCH YOUR FACE. IT'S SO... **MONSTROUS.**
LADY, **LOOK WHAT YOU DID TO ME.** I'M SUPPOSED TO BE A **SPHERE.** IF I DON'T GET MY FIGURE BACK, YOU'RE GOING TO SEE WHAT MONSTROUS **REALLY** LOOKS LIKE.
THAT POOR WOMAN. I DON'T KNOW WHAT HAPPENED TO HER, BUT SHE'S CLEARLY INSANE.
HAPPENS A LOT. PEOPLE GET POWERS, CAN'T HANDLE IT. THEY SNAP. THAT'S WHY THERE'S SO MANY BAD GUYS AROUND. BUT THAT'S WHY WE'RE HERE. TO DEAL WITH STUFF LIKE THAT. NO PROBLEM.
BUT SPEAKING OF **HERE,** TORA...
WE'RE IN **PARIS.** MOST ROMANTIC TOWN AROUND, OR SO I HEAR. THAT'S GOTTA BE A SIGN.
BUY YOU DINNER?
GUY...
WHAT MAKES YOU THINK I WOULD HAVE **ANY** INTEREST IN THAT?

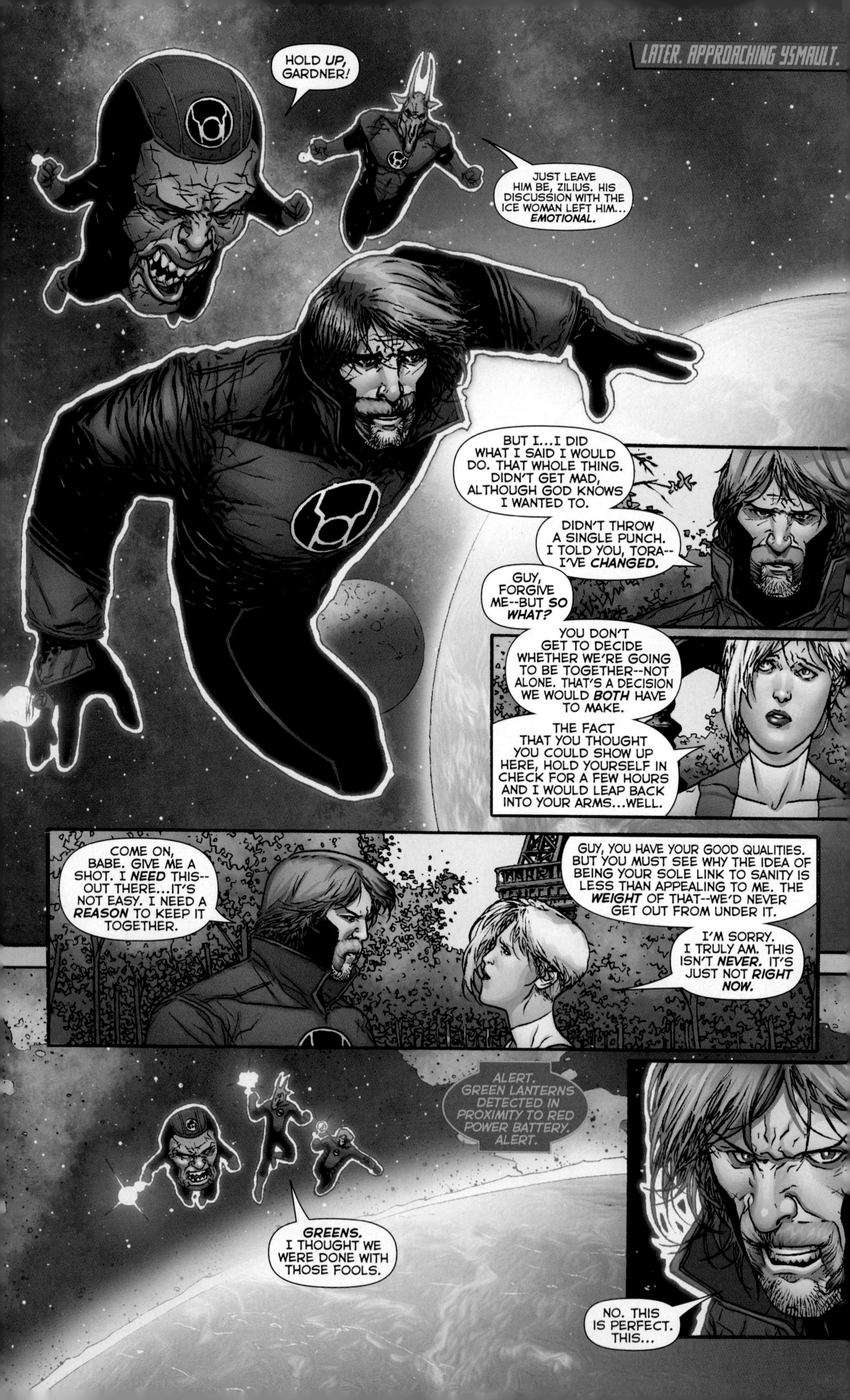
LATER. APPROACHING YSMAULT.
HOLD UP, GARDNER!
JUST LEAVE HIM BE, ZILIUS. HIS DISCUSSION WITH THE ICE WOMAN LEFT HIM... EMOTIONAL.
BUT I...I DID WHAT I SAID I WOULD DO. THAT WHOLE THING. DIDN'T GET MAD, ALTHOUGH GOD KNOWS I WANTED TO.
DIDN'T THROW A SINGLE PUNCH. I TOLD YOU, TORA-- I'VE CHANGED.
GUY, FORGIVE ME--BUT SO WHAT?
YOU DON'T GET TO DECIDE WHETHER WE'RE GOING TO BE TOGETHER--NOT ALONE. THAT'S A DECISION WE WOULD BOTH HAVE TO MAKE.
THE FACT THAT YOU THOUGHT YOU COULD SHOW UP HERE, HOLD YOURSELF IN CHECK FOR A FEW HOURS AND I WOULD LEAP BACK INTO YOUR ARMS...WELL.
COME ON, BABE. GIVE ME A SHOT. I NEED THIS-- OUT THERE...IT'S NOT EASY. I NEED A REASON TO KEEP IT TOGETHER.
GUY, YOU HAVE YOUR GOOD QUALITIES. BUT YOU MUST SEE WHY THE IDEA OF BEING YOUR SOLE LINK TO SANITY IS LESS THAN APPEALING TO ME. THE WEIGHT OF THAT--WE'D NEVER GET OUT FROM UNDER IT.
I'M SORRY. I TRULY AM. THIS ISN'T NEVER. IT'S JUST NOT RIGHT NOW.
ALERT. GREEN LANTERNS DETECTED IN PROXIMITY TO RED POWER BATTERY. ALERT.
GREENS. I THOUGHT WE WERE DONE WITH THOSE FOOLS.
NO. THIS IS PERFECT. THIS...

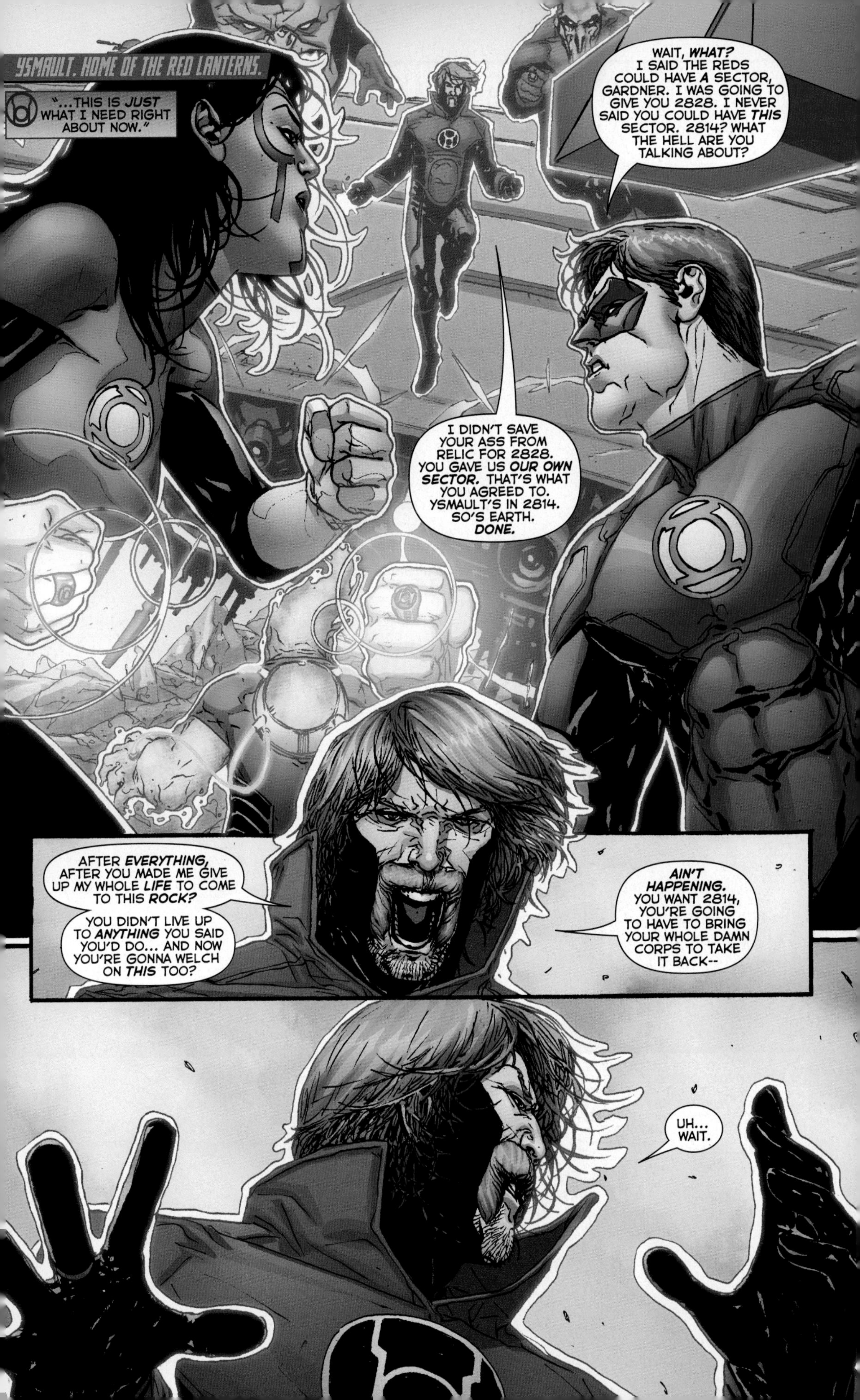
YSMAULT. HOME OF THE RED LANTERNS.
"...THIS IS JUST WHAT I NEED RIGHT ABOUT NOW."
WAIT, WHAT? I SAID THE REDS COULD HAVE A SECTOR, GARDNER. I WAS GOING TO GIVE YOU 2828. I NEVER SAID YOU COULD HAVE THIS SECTOR. 2814? WHAT THE HELL ARE YOU TALKING ABOUT?
I DIDN'T SAVE YOUR ASS FROM RELIC FOR 2828. YOU GAVE US OUR OWN SECTOR. THAT'S WHAT YOU AGREED TO. YSMAULT'S IN 2814. SO'S EARTH. DONE.
AFTER EVERYTHING, AFTER YOU MADE ME GIVE UP MY WHOLE LIFE TO COME TO THIS ROCK?
YOU DIDN'T LIVE UP TO ANYTHING YOU SAID YOU'D DO... AND NOW YOU'RE GONNA WELCH ON THIS TOO?
AIN'T HAPPENING. YOU WANT 2814, YOU'RE GOING TO HAVE TO BRING YOUR WHOLE DAMN CORPS TO TAKE IT BACK--
UH... WAIT.

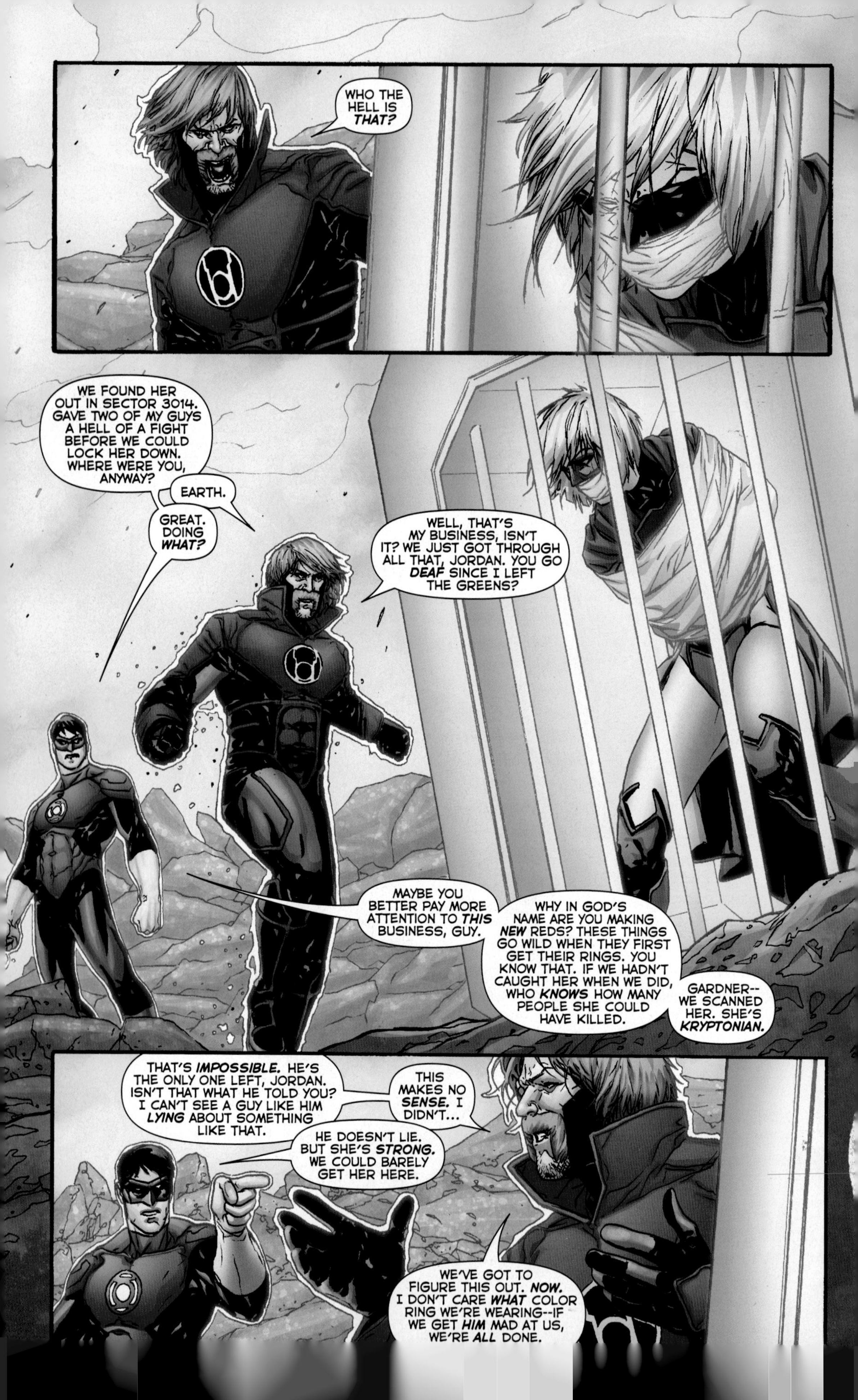
WHO THE HELL IS THAT?
WE FOUND HER OUT IN SECTOR 3014. GAVE TWO OF MY GUYS A HELL OF A FIGHT BEFORE WE COULD LOCK HER DOWN. WHERE WERE YOU, ANYWAY?
EARTH.
GREAT. DOING WHAT?
WELL, THAT'S MY BUSINESS, ISN'T IT? WE JUST GOT THROUGH ALL THAT, JORDAN. YOU GO DEAF SINCE I LEFT THE GREENS?
MAYBE YOU BETTER PAY MORE ATTENTION TO THIS BUSINESS, GUY.
WHY IN GOD'S NAME ARE YOU MAKING NEW REDS? THESE THINGS GO WILD WHEN THEY FIRST GET THEIR RINGS. YOU KNOW THAT. IF WE HADN'T CAUGHT HER WHEN WE DID, WHO KNOWS HOW MANY PEOPLE SHE COULD HAVE KILLED.
GARDNER--WE SCANNED HER. SHE'S KRYPTONIAN.
THAT'S IMPOSSIBLE. HE'S THE ONLY ONE LEFT, JORDAN. ISN'T THAT WHAT HE TOLD YOU? I CAN'T SEE A GUY LIKE HIM LYING ABOUT SOMETHING LIKE THAT.
THIS MAKES NO SENSE. I DIDN'T...
HE DOESN'T LIE. BUT SHE'S STRONG. WE COULD BARELY GET HER HERE.
WE'VE GOT TO FIGURE THIS OUT. NOW. I DON'T CARE WHAT COLOR RING WE'RE WEARING--IF WE GET HIM MAD AT US, WE'RE ALL DONE.

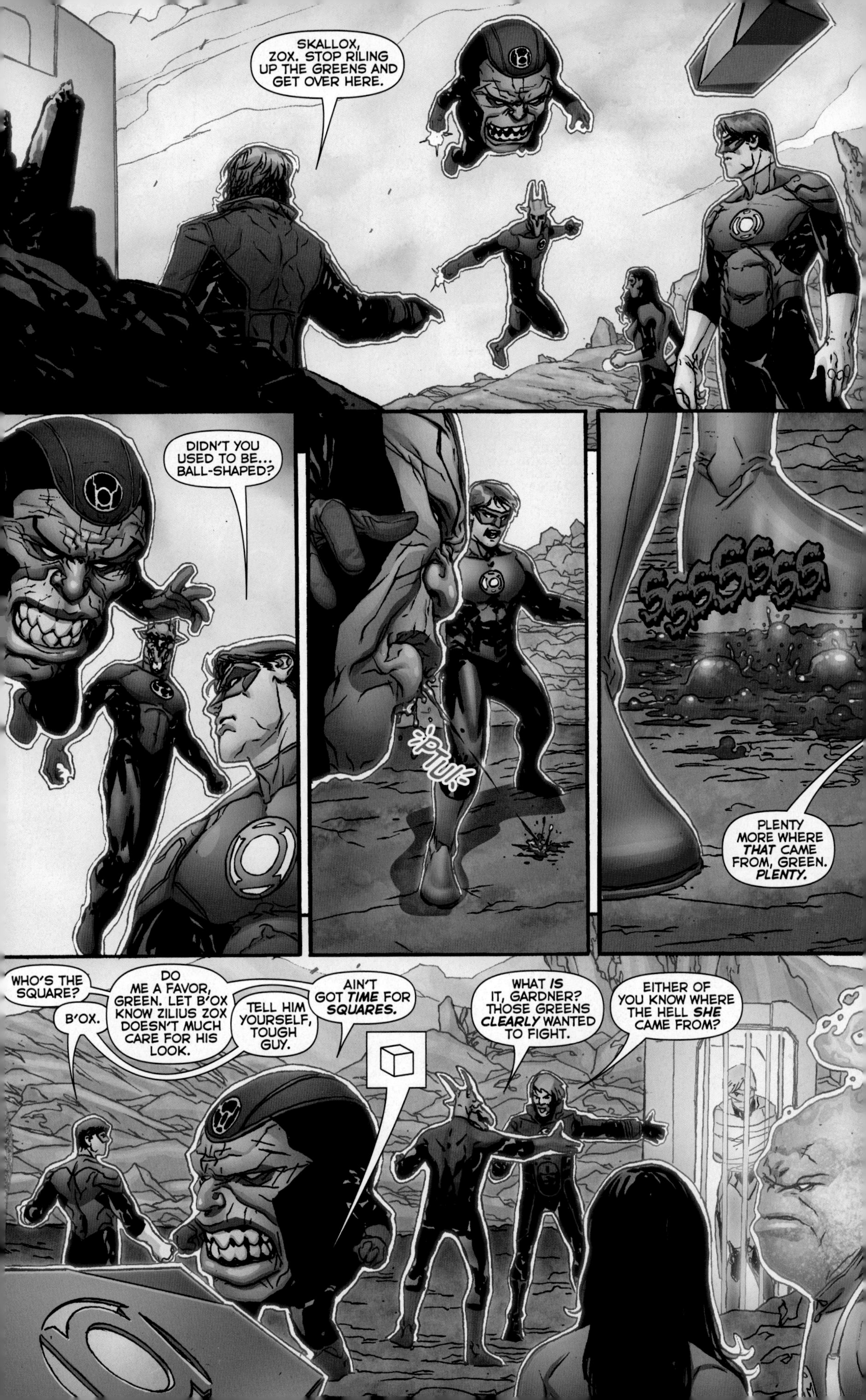
SKALLOX, ZOX. STOP RILING UP THE GREENS AND GET OVER HERE.
DIDN'T YOU USED TO BE... BALL-SHAPED?
PTUI!
SSSSSSS
PLENTY MORE WHERE THAT CAME FROM, GREEN. PLENTY.
WHO'S THE SQUARE?
B'OX.
DO ME A FAVOR, GREEN. LET B'OX KNOW ZILIUS ZOX DOESN'T MUCH CARE FOR HIS LOOK.
TELL HIM YOURSELF, TOUGH GUY.
AIN'T GOT TIME FOR SQUARES.
WHAT IS IT, GARDNER? THOSE GREENS CLEARLY WANTED TO FIGHT.
EITHER OF YOU KNOW WHERE THE HELL SHE CAME FROM?

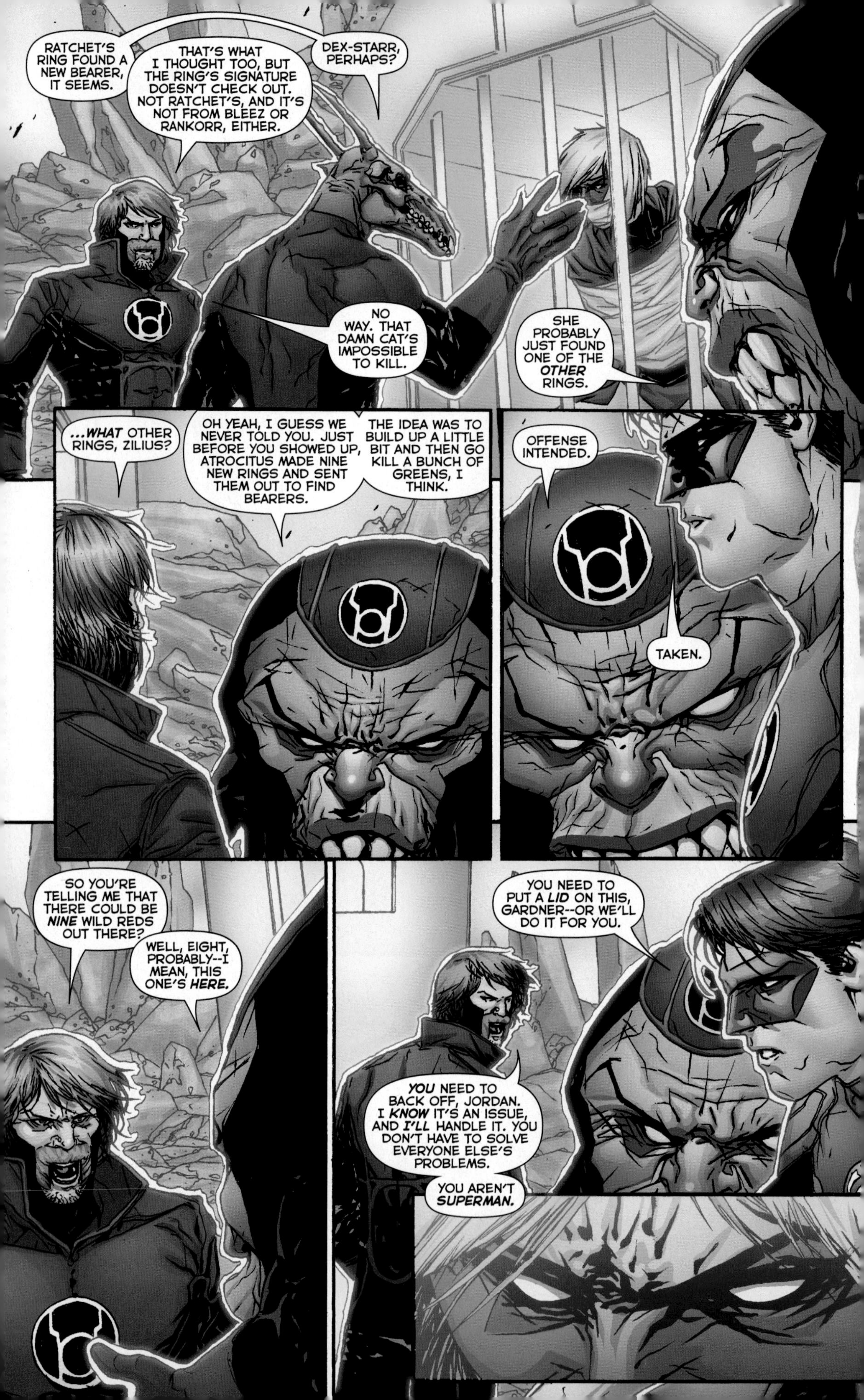
RATCHET'S RING FOUND A NEW BEARER, IT SEEMS.
THAT'S WHAT I THOUGHT TOO, BUT THE RING'S SIGNATURE DOESN'T CHECK OUT. NOT RATCHET'S, AND IT'S NOT FROM BLEEZ OR RANKORR, EITHER.
DEX-STARR, PERHAPS?
NO WAY. THAT DAMN CAT'S IMPOSSIBLE TO KILL.
SHE PROBABLY JUST FOUND ONE OF THE OTHER RINGS.
...WHAT OTHER RINGS, ZILIUS?
OH YEAH, I GUESS WE NEVER TOLD YOU. JUST BEFORE YOU SHOWED UP, ATROCITUS MADE NINE NEW RINGS AND SENT THEM OUT TO FIND BEARERS.
THE IDEA WAS TO BUILD UP A LITTLE BIT AND THEN GO KILL A BUNCH OF GREENS, I THINK.
OFFENSE INTENDED.
TAKEN.
SO YOU'RE TELLING ME THAT THERE COULD BE NINE WILD REDS OUT THERE?
WELL, EIGHT, PROBABLY--I MEAN, THIS ONE'S HERE.
YOU NEED TO PUT A LID ON THIS, GARDNER--OR WE'LL DO IT FOR YOU.
YOU NEED TO BACK OFF, JORDAN. I KNOW IT'S AN ISSUE, AND I'LL HANDLE IT. YOU DON'T HAVE TO SOLVE EVERYONE ELSE'S PROBLEMS.
YOU AREN'T SUPERMAN.

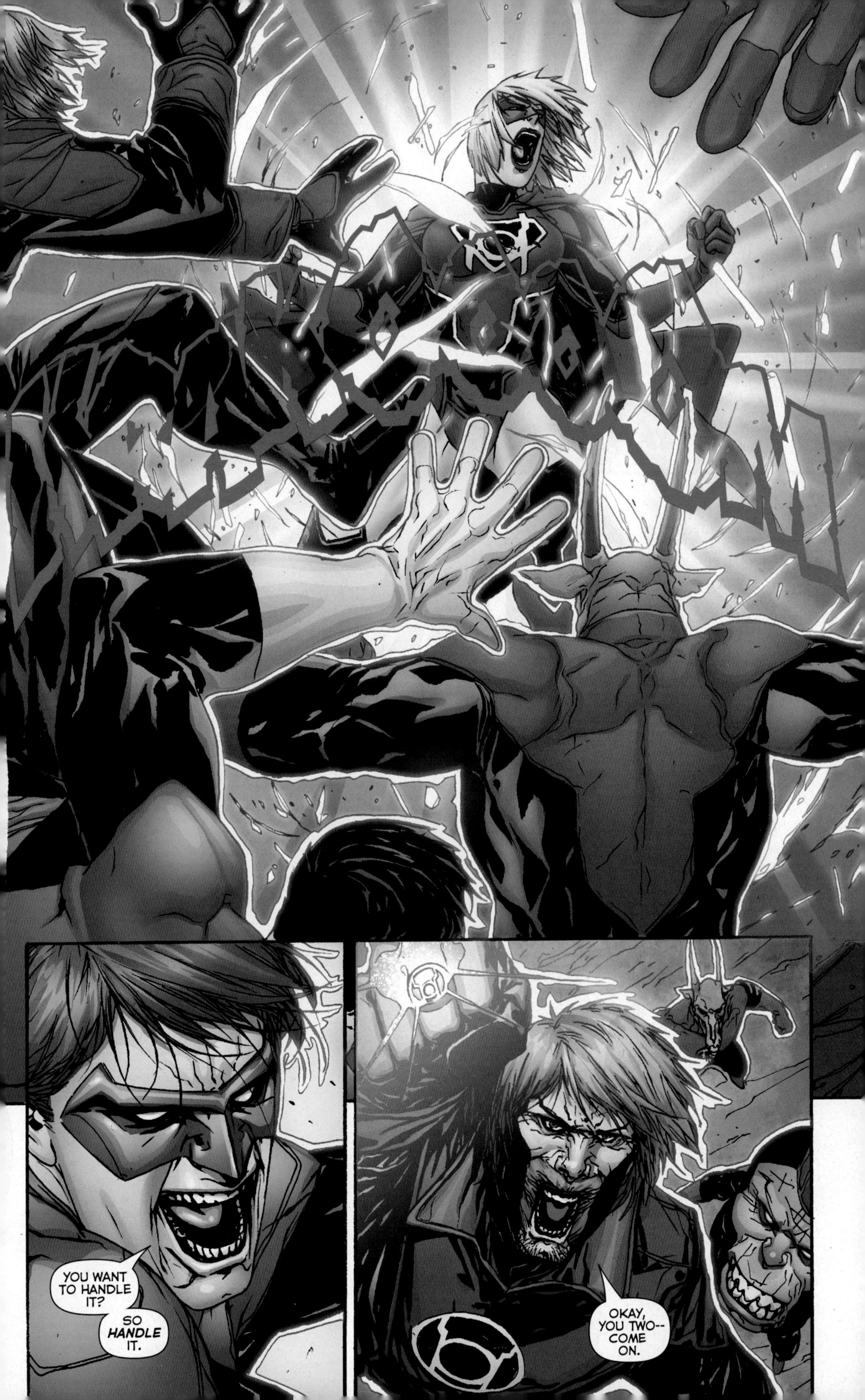
YOU WANT TO HANDLE IT?
SO HANDLE IT.
OKAY, YOU TWO-- COME ON.

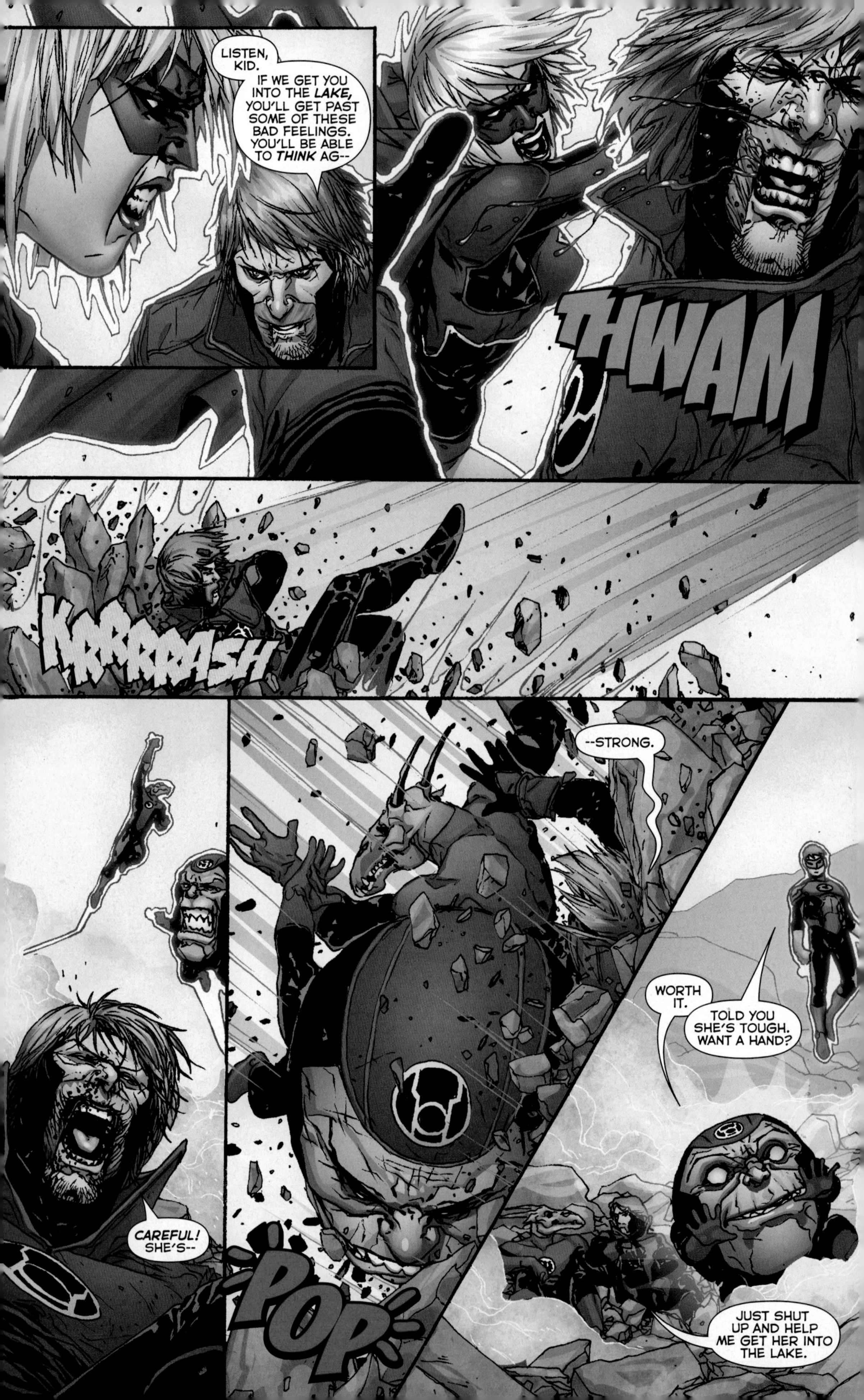
LISTEN, KID.
IF WE GET YOU INTO THE LAKE, YOU'LL GET PAST SOME OF THESE BAD FEELINGS. YOU'LL BE ABLE TO THINK AG--
THWAM
KRRRRASH
CAREFUL! SHE'S--
--STRONG.
POP
WORTH IT.
TOLD YOU SHE'S TOUGH. WANT A HAND?
JUST SHUT UP AND HELP ME GET HER INTO THE LAKE.

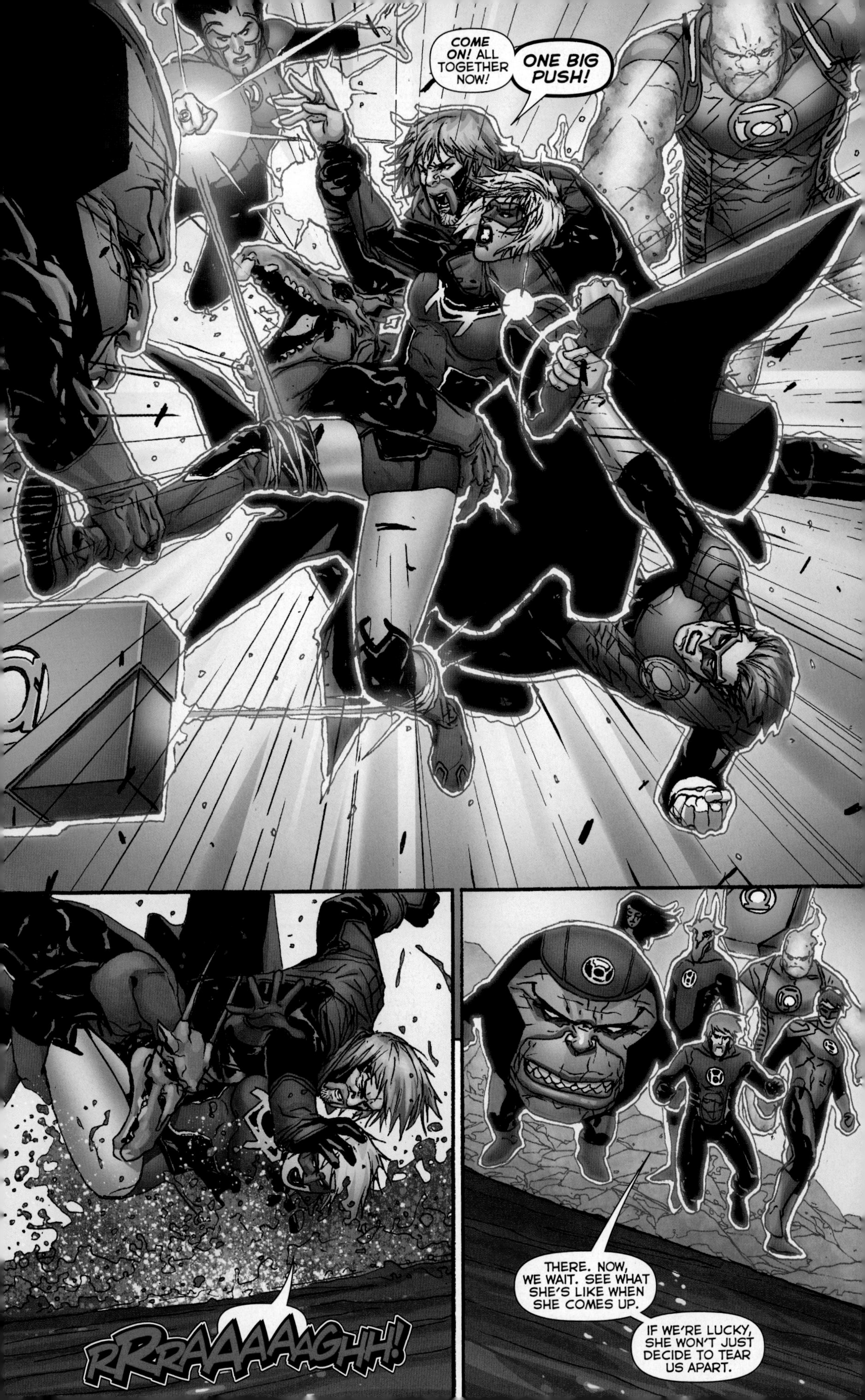
COME ON! ALL TOGETHER NOW!
ONE BIG PUSH!
RRRAAAAAAGHH!
THERE. NOW, WE WAIT. SEE WHAT SHE'S LIKE WHEN SHE COMES UP.
IF WE'RE LUCKY, SHE WON'T JUST DECIDE TO TEAR US APART.

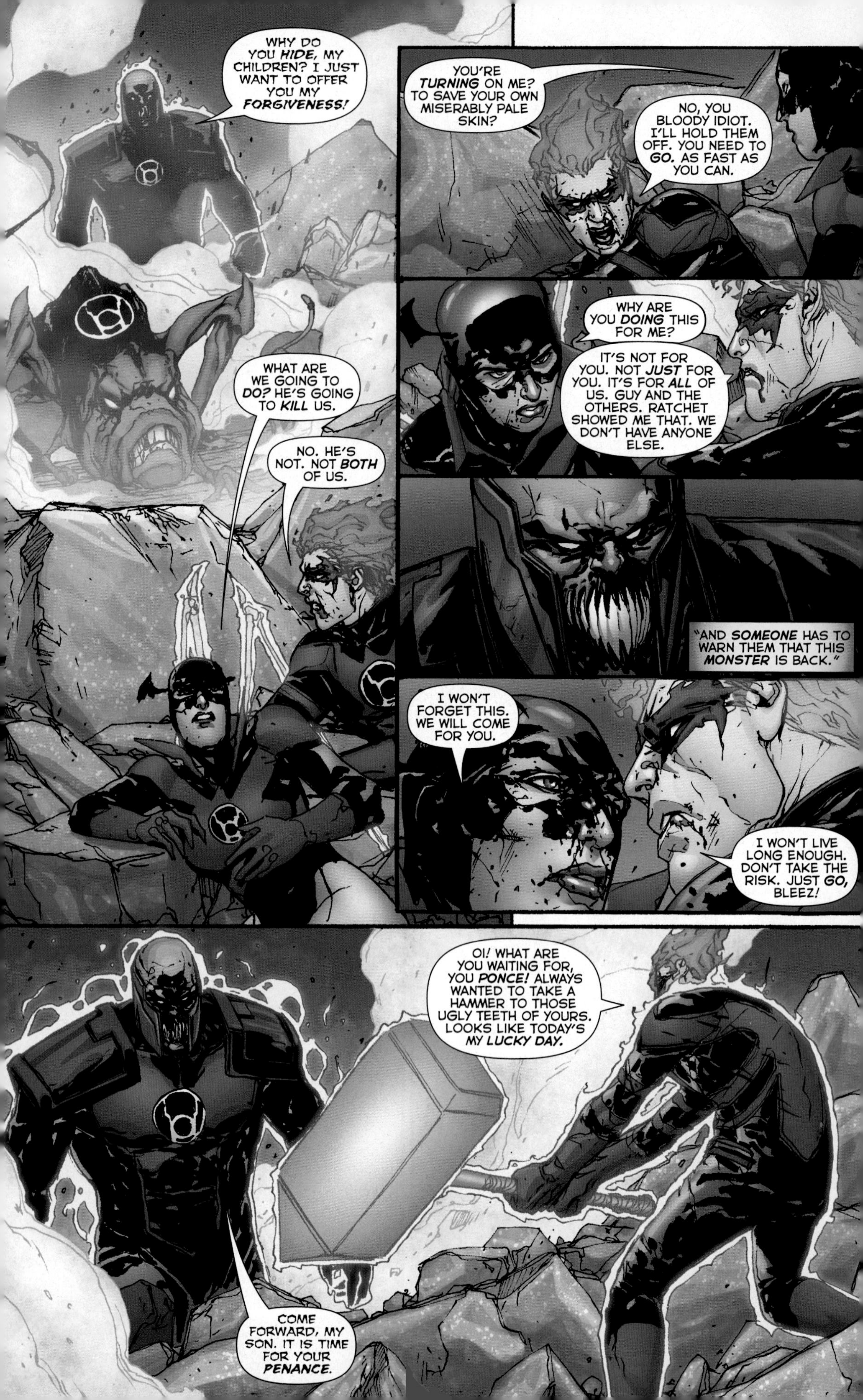
WHY DO YOU HIDE, MY CHILDREN? I JUST WANT TO OFFER YOU MY FORGIVENESS!
WHAT ARE WE GOING TO DO? HE'S GOING TO KILL US.
NO. HE'S NOT. NOT BOTH OF US.
YOU'RE TURNING ON ME? TO SAVE YOUR OWN MISERABLY PALE SKIN?
NO, YOU BLOODY IDIOT. I'LL HOLD THEM OFF. YOU NEED TO GO. AS FAST AS YOU CAN.
WHY ARE YOU DOING THIS FOR ME?
IT'S NOT FOR YOU. NOT JUST FOR YOU. IT'S FOR ALL OF US. GUY AND THE OTHERS. RATCHET SHOWED ME THAT. WE DON'T HAVE ANYONE ELSE.
"AND SOMEONE HAS TO WARN THEM THAT THIS MONSTER IS BACK."
I WON'T FORGET THIS. WE WILL COME FOR YOU.
I WON'T LIVE LONG ENOUGH. DON'T TAKE THE RISK. JUST GO, BLEEZ!
OI! WHAT ARE YOU WAITING FOR, YOU PONCE! ALWAYS WANTED TO TAKE A HAMMER TO THOSE UGLY TEETH OF YOURS. LOOKS LIKE TODAY'S MY LUCKY DAY.
COME FORWARD, MY SON. IT IS TIME FOR YOUR PENANCE.

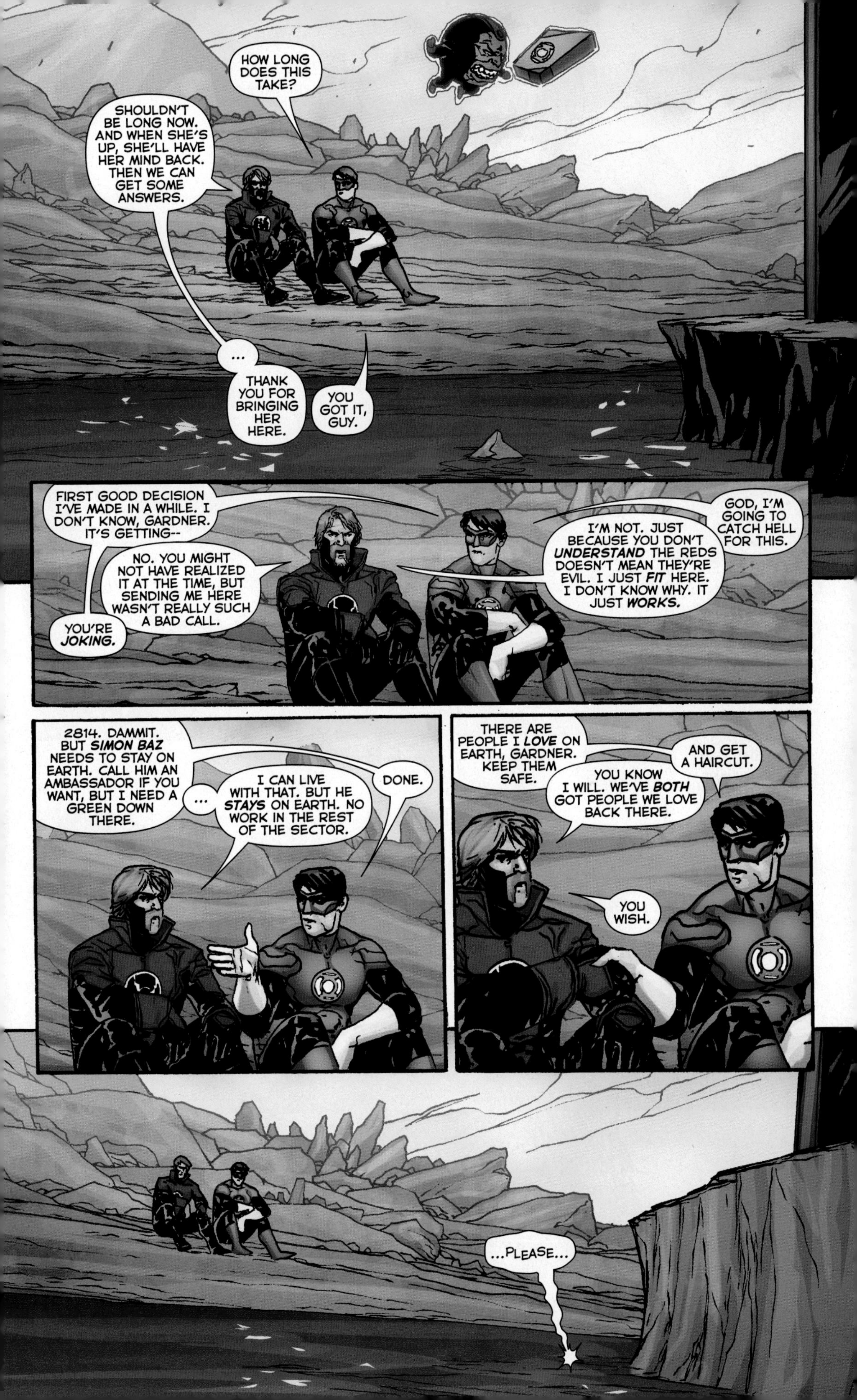

HOW LONG DOES THIS TAKE?
SHOULDN'T BE LONG NOW. AND WHEN SHE'S UP, SHE'LL HAVE HER MIND BACK. THEN WE CAN GET SOME ANSWERS.
...
THANK YOU FOR BRINGING HER HERE.
YOU GOT IT, GUY.
FIRST GOOD DECISION I'VE MADE IN A WHILE. I DON'T KNOW, GARDNER. IT'S GETTING--
NO. YOU MIGHT NOT HAVE REALIZED IT AT THE TIME, BUT SENDING ME HERE WASN'T REALLY SUCH A BAD CALL.
YOU'RE JOKING.
I'M NOT. JUST BECAUSE YOU DON'T UNDERSTAND THE REDS DOESN'T MEAN THEY'RE EVIL. I JUST FIT HERE. I DON'T KNOW WHY. IT JUST WORKS.
GOD, I'M GOING TO CATCH HELL FOR THIS.
2814. DAMMIT. BUT SIMON BAZ NEEDS TO STAY ON EARTH. CALL HIM AN AMBASSADOR IF YOU WANT, BUT I NEED A GREEN DOWN THERE.
...
I CAN LIVE WITH THAT. BUT HE STAYS ON EARTH. NO WORK IN THE REST OF THE SECTOR.
DONE.
THERE ARE PEOPLE I LOVE ON EARTH, GARDNER. KEEP THEM SAFE.
YOU KNOW I WILL. WE'VE BOTH GOT PEOPLE WE LOVE BACK THERE.
AND GET A HAIRCUT.
YOU WISH.
...PLEASE...

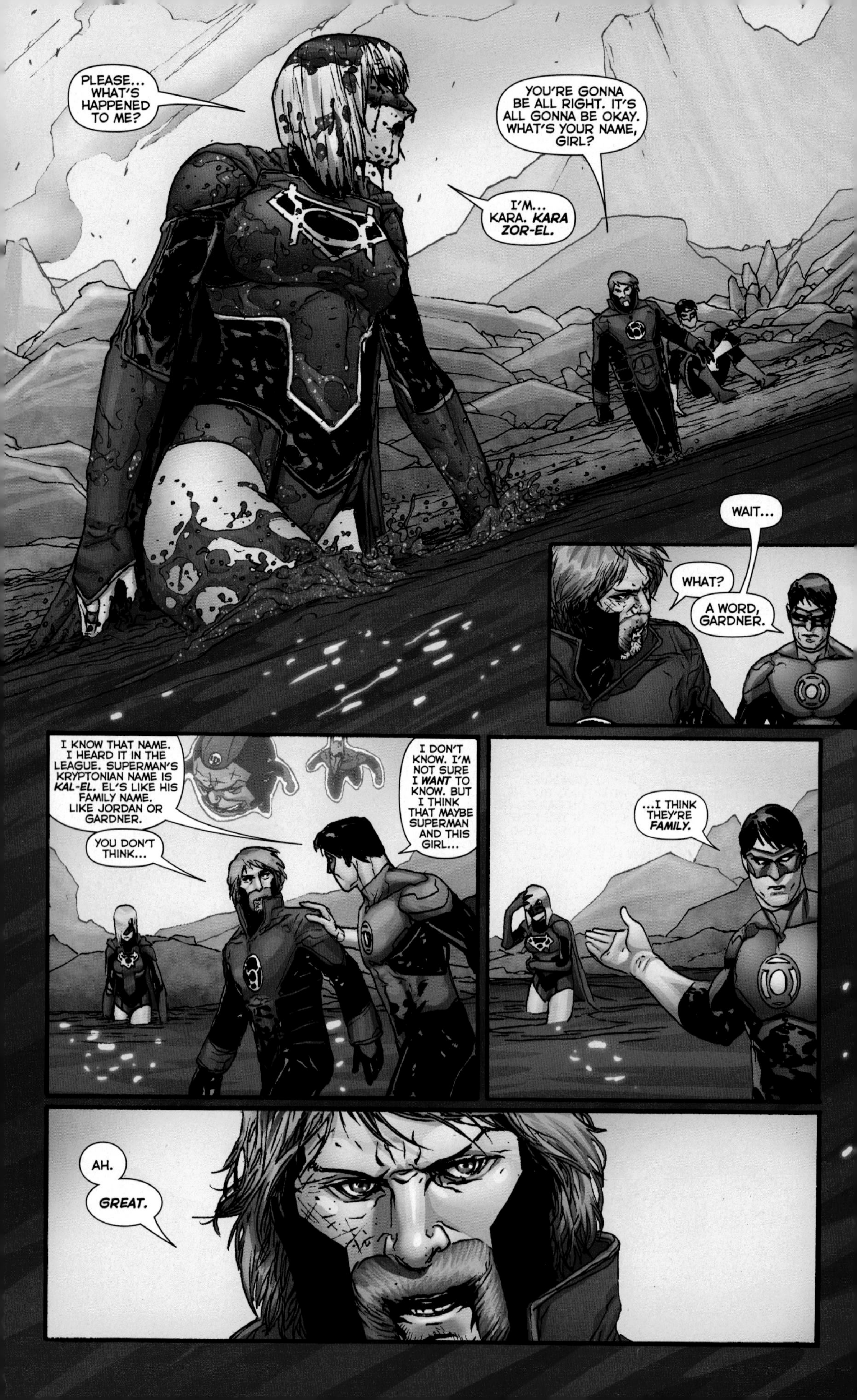
PLEASE... WHAT'S HAPPENED TO ME?
YOU'RE GONNA BE ALL RIGHT. IT'S ALL GONNA BE OKAY. WHAT'S YOUR NAME, GIRL?
I'M... KARA. *KARA ZOR-EL.*
WAIT...
WHAT?
A WORD, GARDNER.
I KNOW THAT NAME. I HEARD IT IN THE LEAGUE. SUPERMAN'S KRYPTONIAN NAME IS *KAL-EL*. EL'S LIKE HIS FAMILY NAME. LIKE JORDAN OR GARDNER.
YOU DON'T THINK...
I DON'T KNOW. I'M NOT SURE I *WANT* TO KNOW. BUT I THINK THAT MAYBE SUPERMAN AND THIS GIRL...
...I THINK THEY'RE *FAMILY.*
AH.
GREAT.

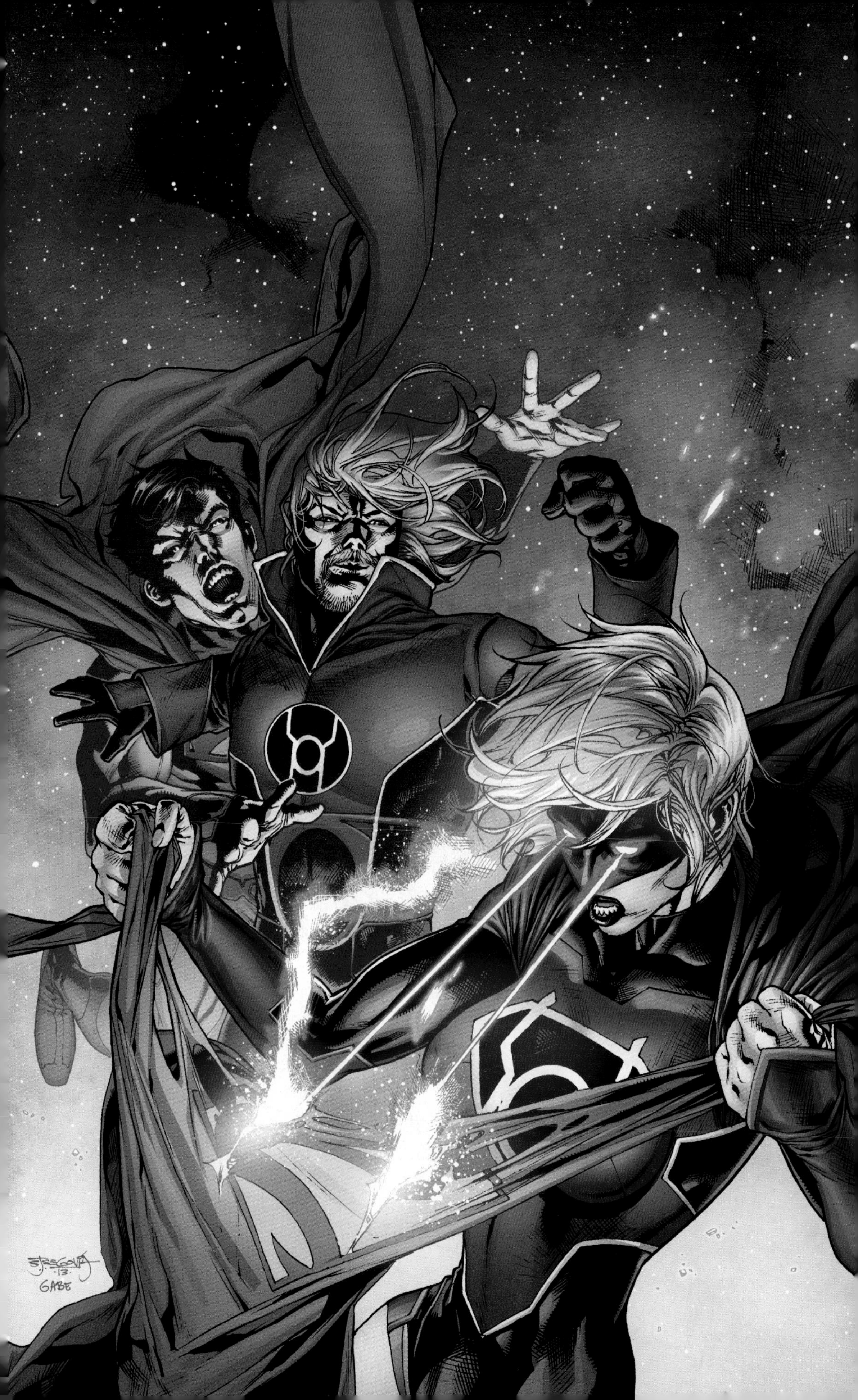
GABE

CHARLES SOULE writer **ALESSANDRO VITTI** artist **GABE ELTAEB** colorist **DAVE SHARPE** letterer
cover art by **STEPHEN SEGOVIA** with **GABE ELTAEB**

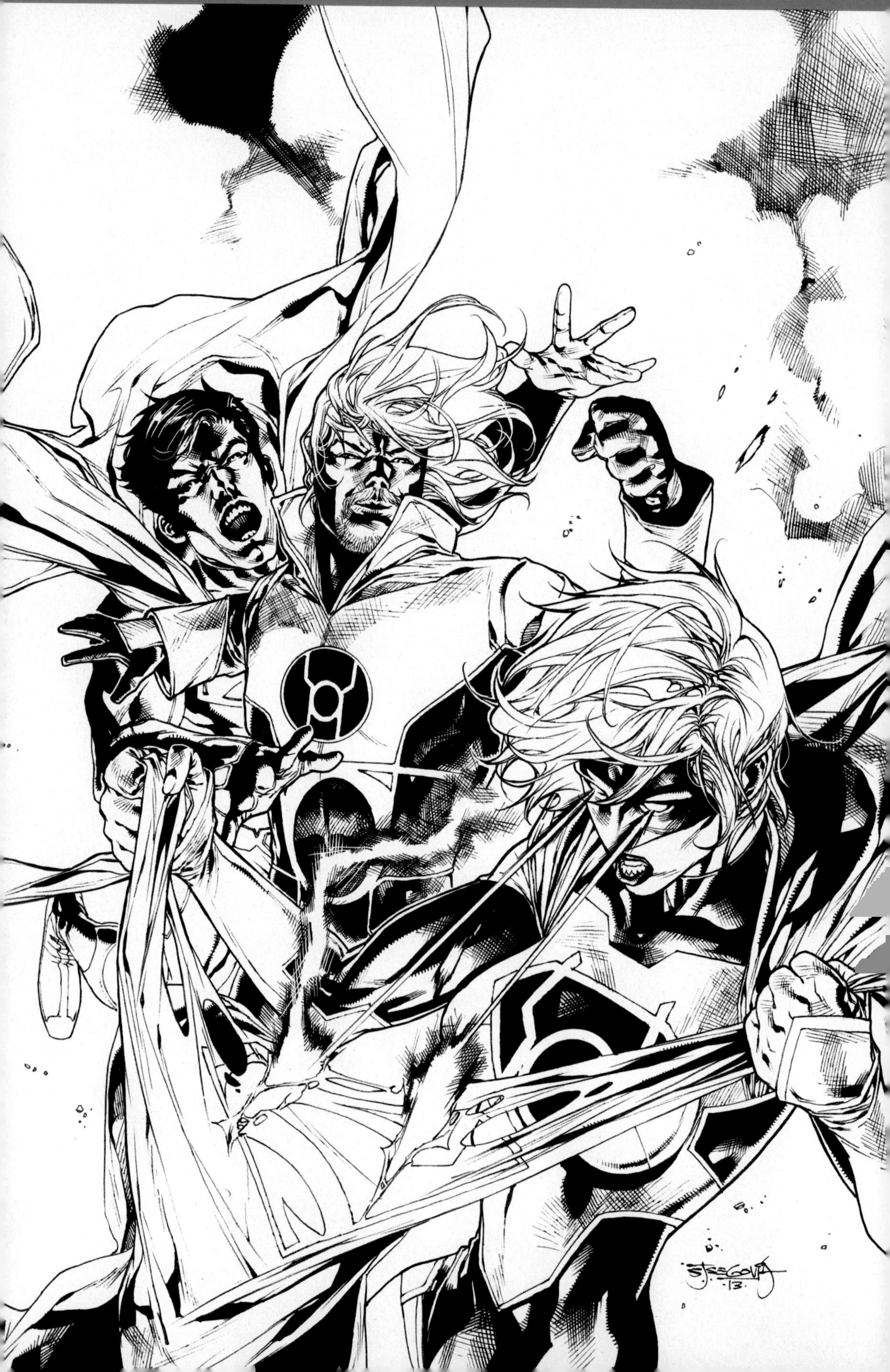

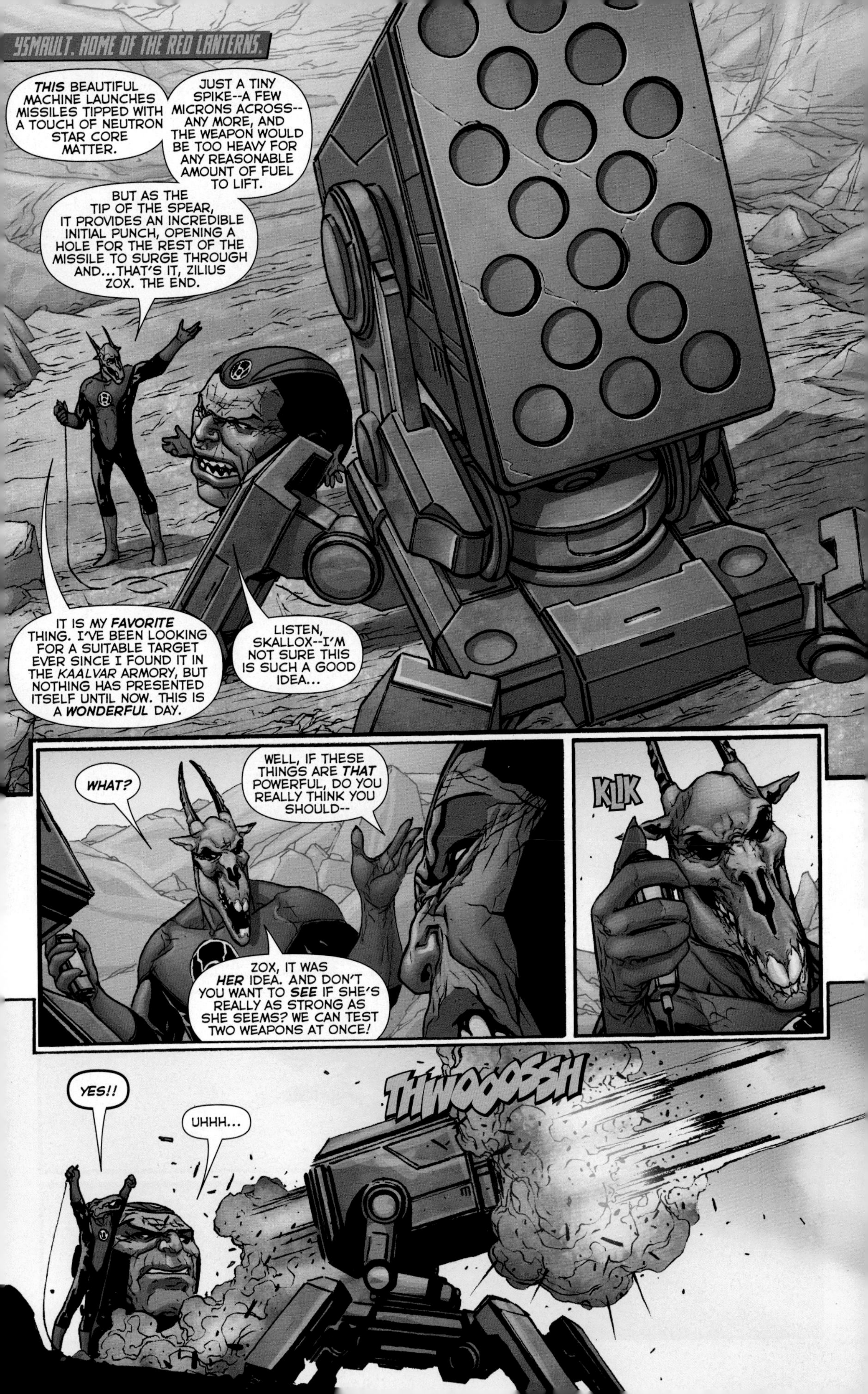
YSMAULT. HOME OF THE RED LANTERNS.
THIS BEAUTIFUL MACHINE LAUNCHES MISSILES TIPPED WITH A TOUCH OF NEUTRON STAR CORE MATTER.
JUST A TINY SPIKE--A FEW MICRONS ACROSS--ANY MORE, AND THE WEAPON WOULD BE TOO HEAVY FOR ANY REASONABLE AMOUNT OF FUEL TO LIFT.
BUT AS THE TIP OF THE SPEAR, IT PROVIDES AN INCREDIBLE INITIAL PUNCH, OPENING A HOLE FOR THE REST OF THE MISSILE TO SURGE THROUGH AND...THAT'S IT, ZILIUS ZOX. THE END.
IT IS MY FAVORITE THING. I'VE BEEN LOOKING FOR A SUITABLE TARGET EVER SINCE I FOUND IT IN THE KAALVAR ARMORY, BUT NOTHING HAS PRESENTED ITSELF UNTIL NOW. THIS IS A WONDERFUL DAY.
LISTEN, SKALLOX--I'M NOT SURE THIS IS SUCH A GOOD IDEA...
WHAT?
WELL, IF THESE THINGS ARE THAT POWERFUL, DO YOU REALLY THINK YOU SHOULD--
ZOX, IT WAS HER IDEA. AND DON'T YOU WANT TO SEE IF SHE'S REALLY AS STRONG AS SHE SEEMS? WE CAN TEST TWO WEAPONS AT ONCE!
KLIK
YES!!
UHHH...
THWOOOSSH

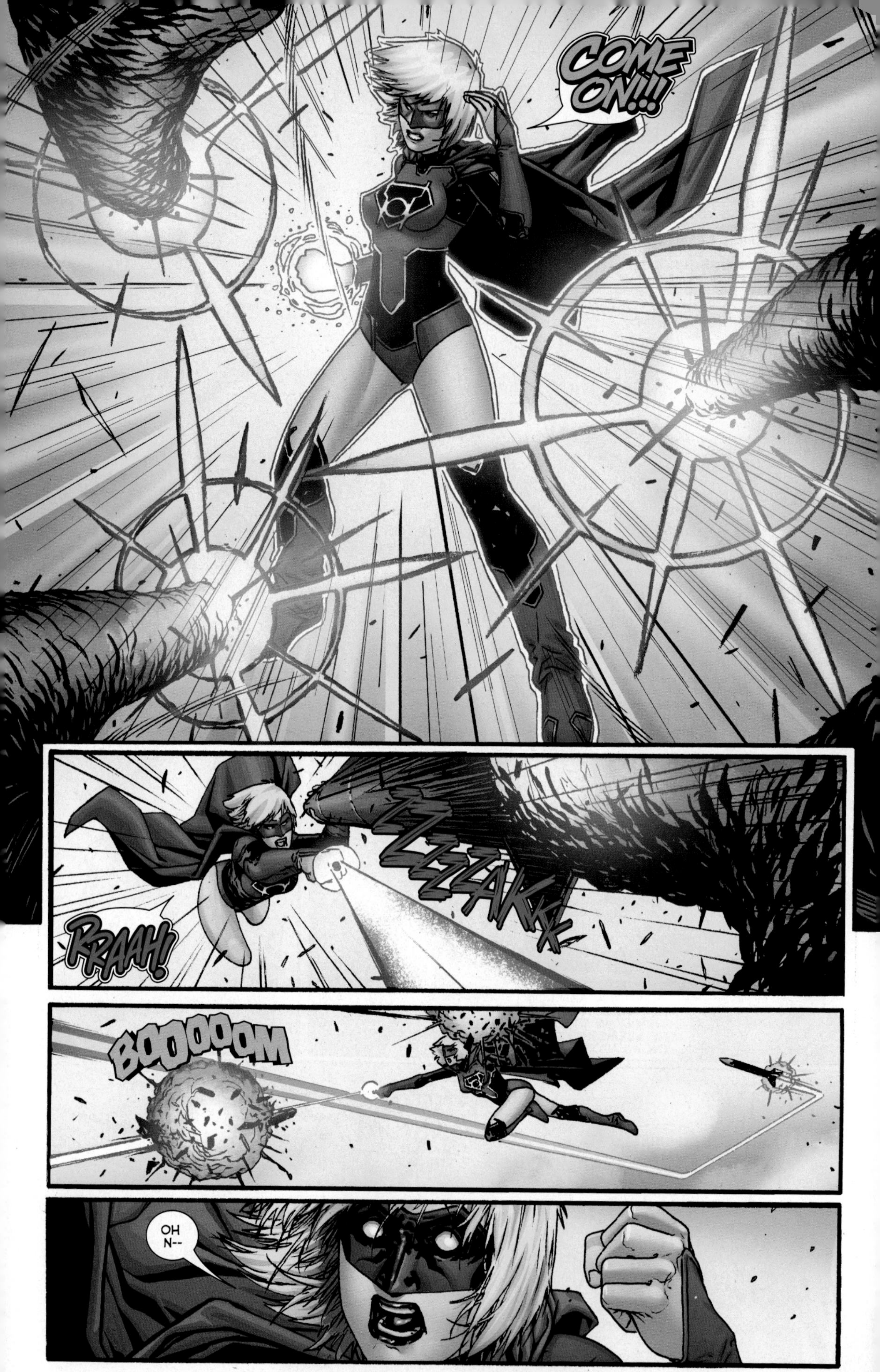
COME ON!!!
ZZZZAKKK
RRAAH!
BOOOOOM
OH N--

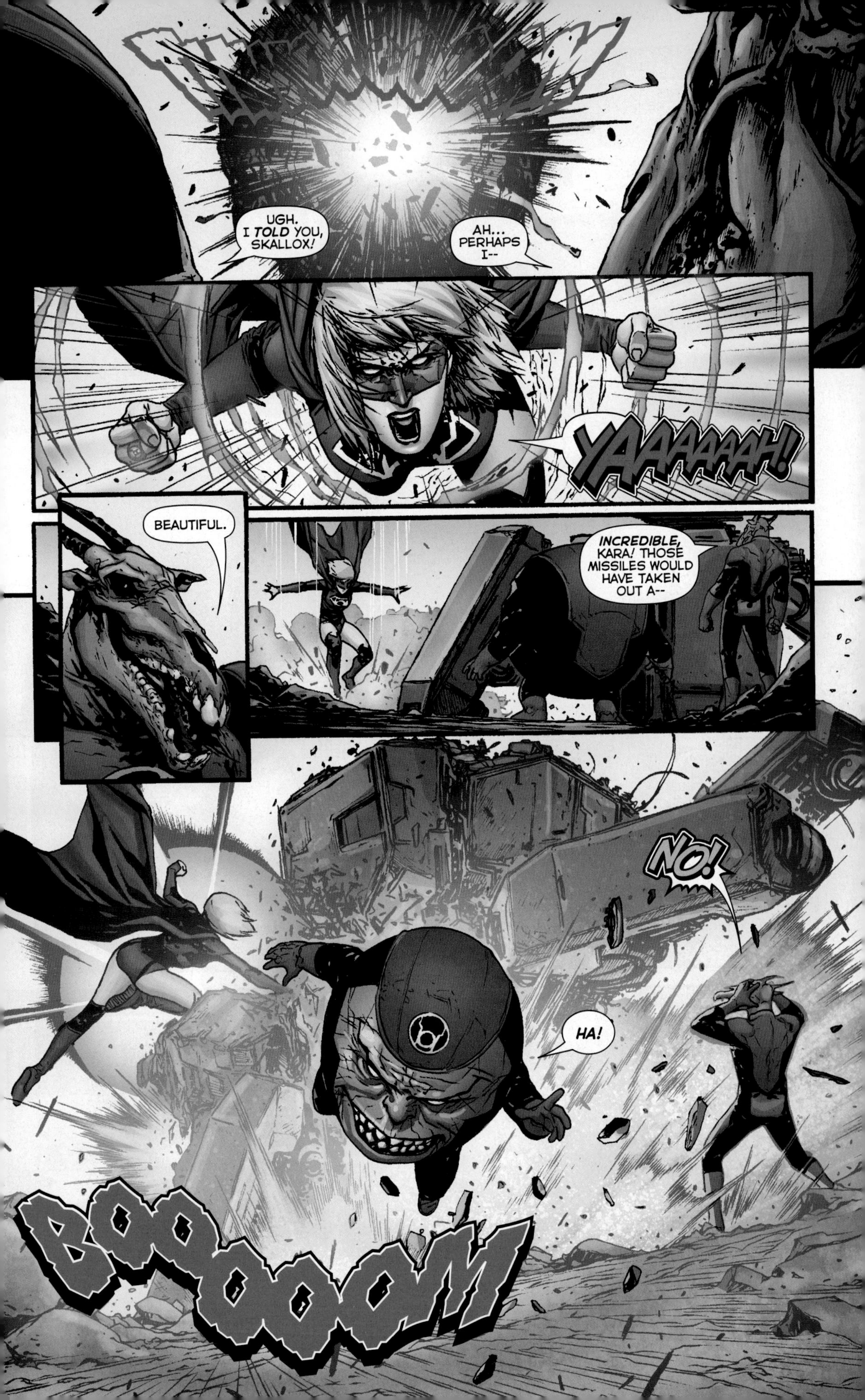
UGH. I *TOLD* YOU, SKALLOX!
AH... PERHAPS I--
YAAAAAAH!
BEAUTIFUL.
INCREDIBLE, KARA! THOSE MISSILES WOULD HAVE TAKEN OUT A--
NO!
HA!
BOOOOOM

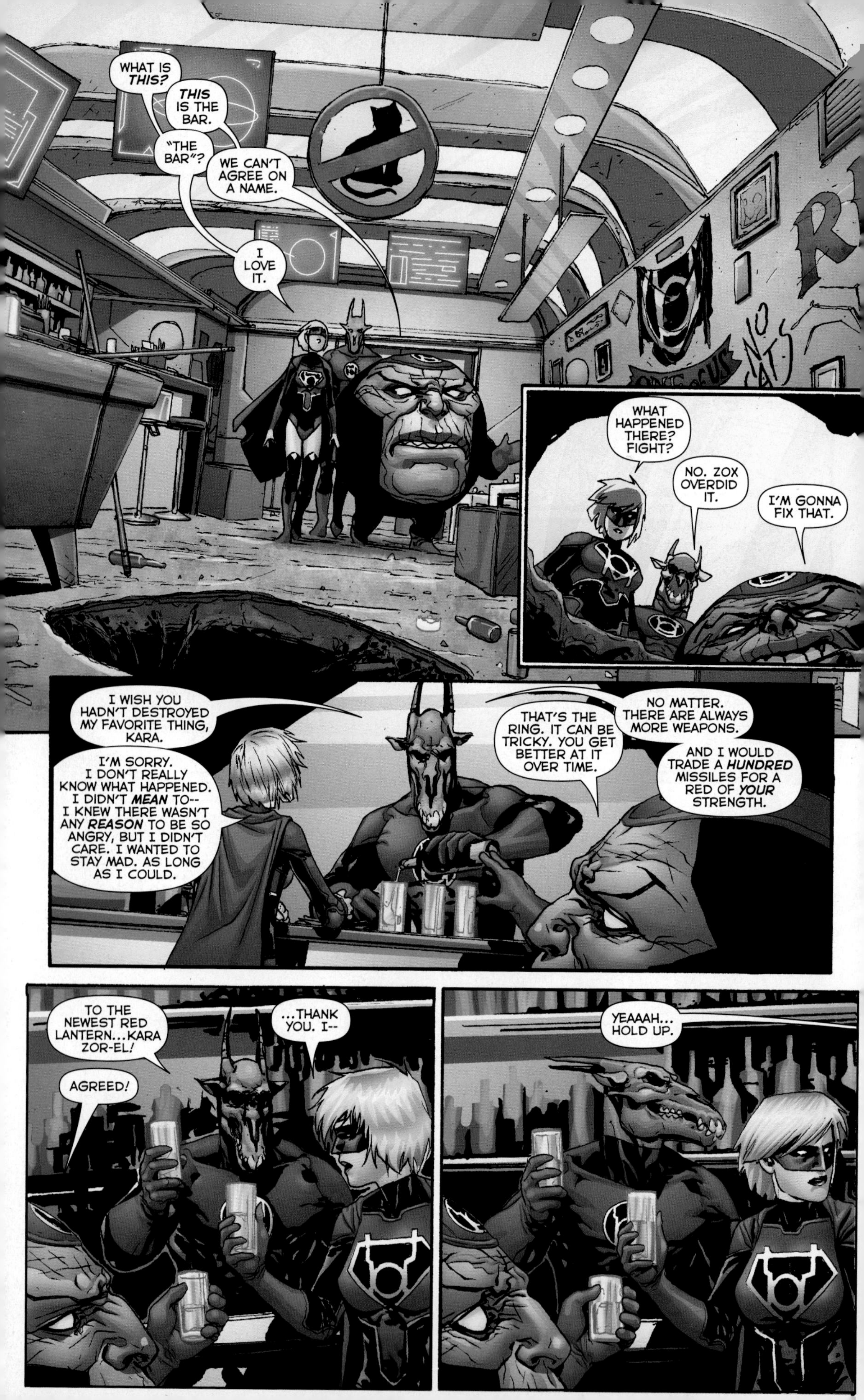

WHAT IS *THIS?*
THIS IS THE BAR.
"THE BAR"?
WE CAN'T AGREE ON A NAME.
I LOVE IT.
ONE OF US
NO CATS
WHAT HAPPENED THERE? FIGHT?
NO. ZOX OVERDID IT.
I'M GONNA FIX THAT.
I WISH YOU HADN'T DESTROYED MY FAVORITE THING, KARA.
I'M SORRY. I DON'T REALLY KNOW WHAT HAPPENED. I DIDN'T *MEAN* TO-- I KNEW THERE WASN'T ANY *REASON* TO BE SO ANGRY, BUT I DIDN'T CARE. I WANTED TO STAY MAD. AS LONG AS I COULD.
THAT'S THE RING. IT CAN BE TRICKY. YOU GET BETTER AT IT OVER TIME.
NO MATTER. THERE ARE ALWAYS MORE WEAPONS.
AND I WOULD TRADE A *HUNDRED* MISSILES FOR A RED OF *YOUR* STRENGTH.
TO THE NEWEST RED LANTERN...KARA ZOR-EL!
AGREED!
...THANK YOU. I--
YEAAAH... HOLD UP.

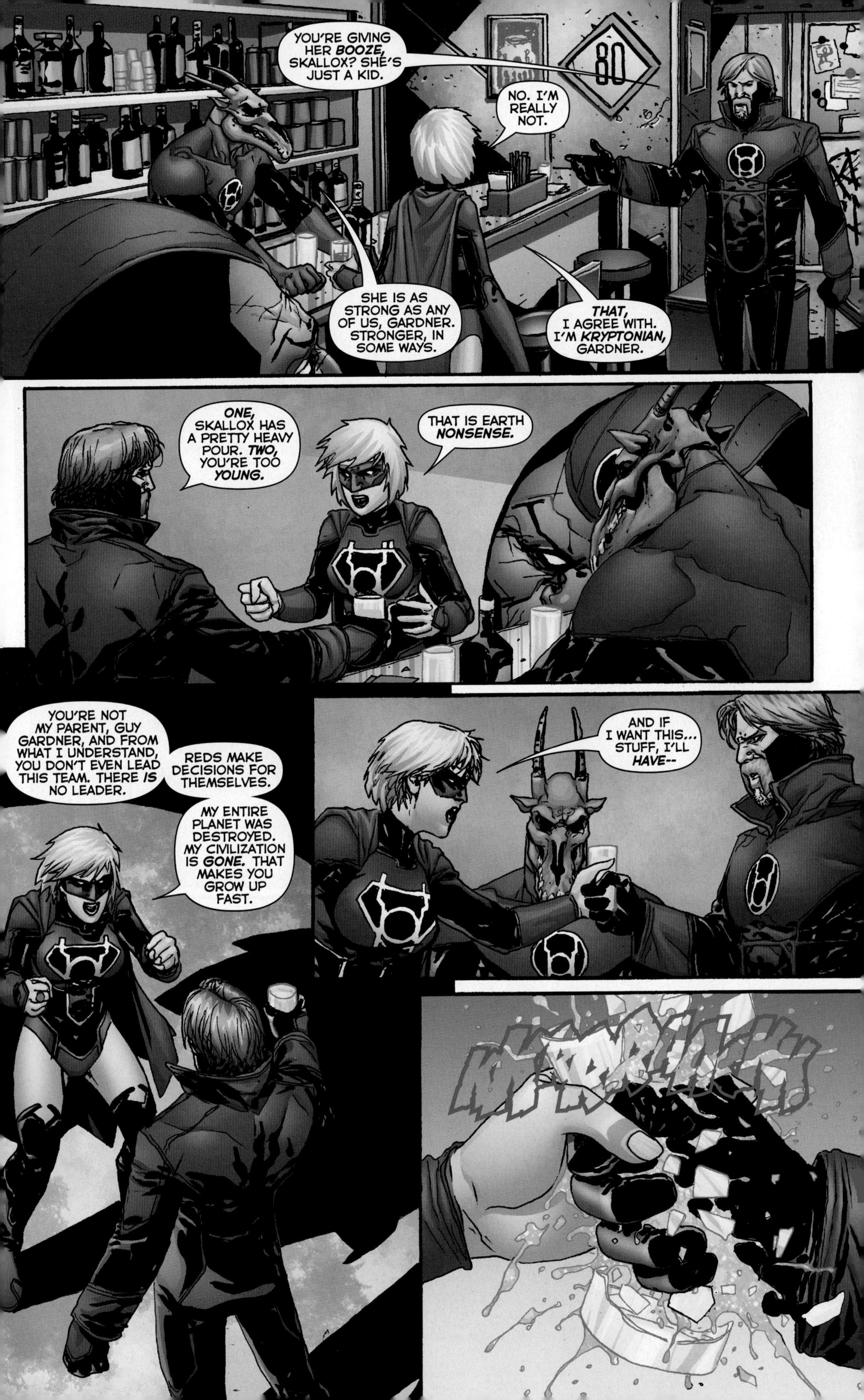
YOU'RE GIVING HER BOOZE, SKALLOX? SHE'S JUST A KID.
NO. I'M REALLY NOT.
SHE IS AS STRONG AS ANY OF US, GARDNER. STRONGER, IN SOME WAYS.
THAT, I AGREE WITH. I'M KRYPTONIAN, GARDNER.
ONE, SKALLOX HAS A PRETTY HEAVY POUR. TWO, YOU'RE TOO YOUNG.
THAT IS EARTH NONSENSE.
YOU'RE NOT MY PARENT, GUY GARDNER, AND FROM WHAT I UNDERSTAND, YOU DON'T EVEN LEAD THIS TEAM. THERE IS NO LEADER.
REDS MAKE DECISIONS FOR THEMSELVES.
MY ENTIRE PLANET WAS DESTROYED. MY CIVILIZATION IS GONE. THAT MAKES YOU GROW UP FAST.
AND IF I WANT THIS... STUFF, I'LL HAVE--

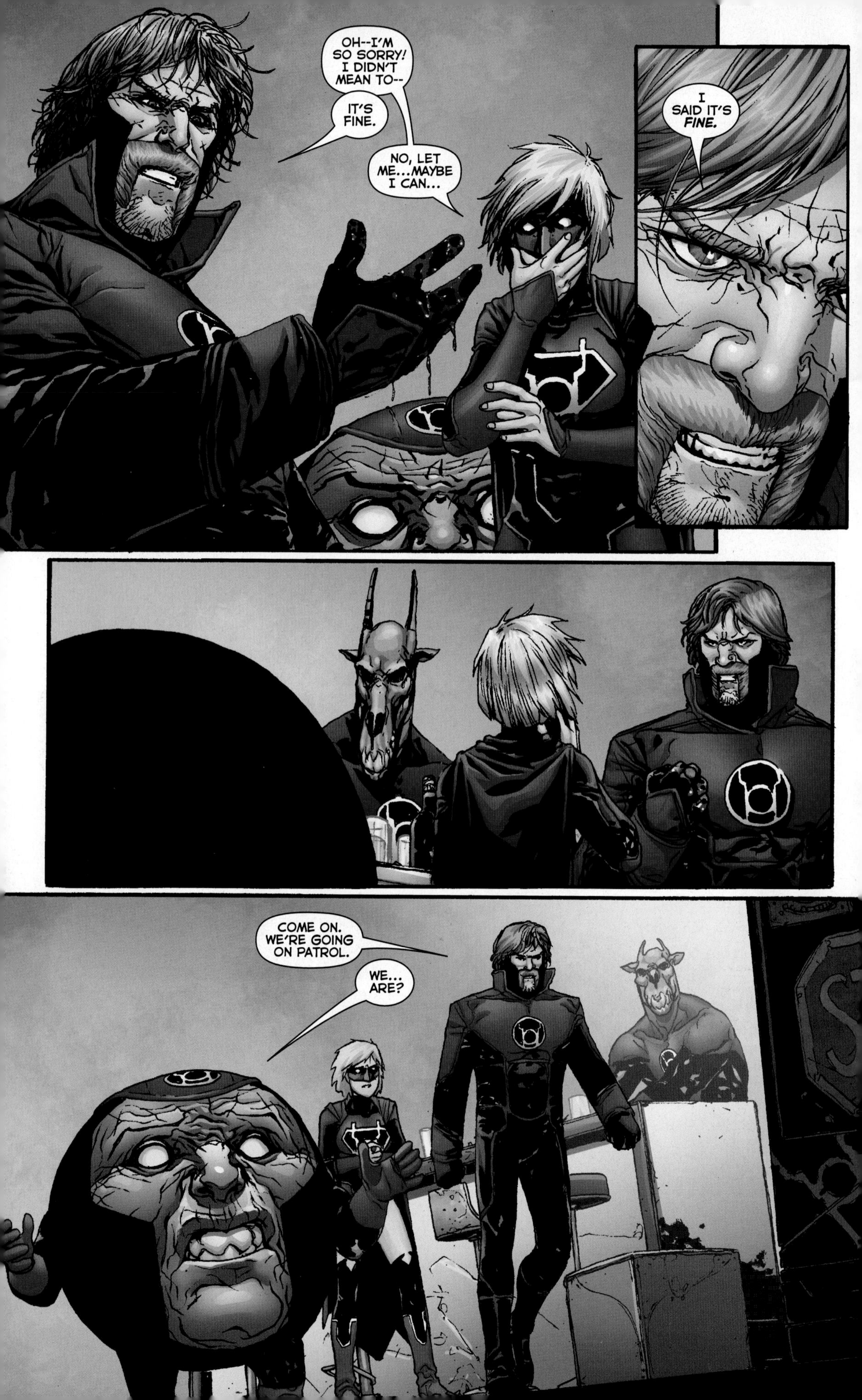
OH--I'M SO SORRY! I DIDN'T MEAN TO--
IT'S FINE.
NO, LET ME...MAYBE I CAN...
I SAID IT'S *FINE.*
COME ON. WE'RE GOING ON PATROL.
WE... ARE?

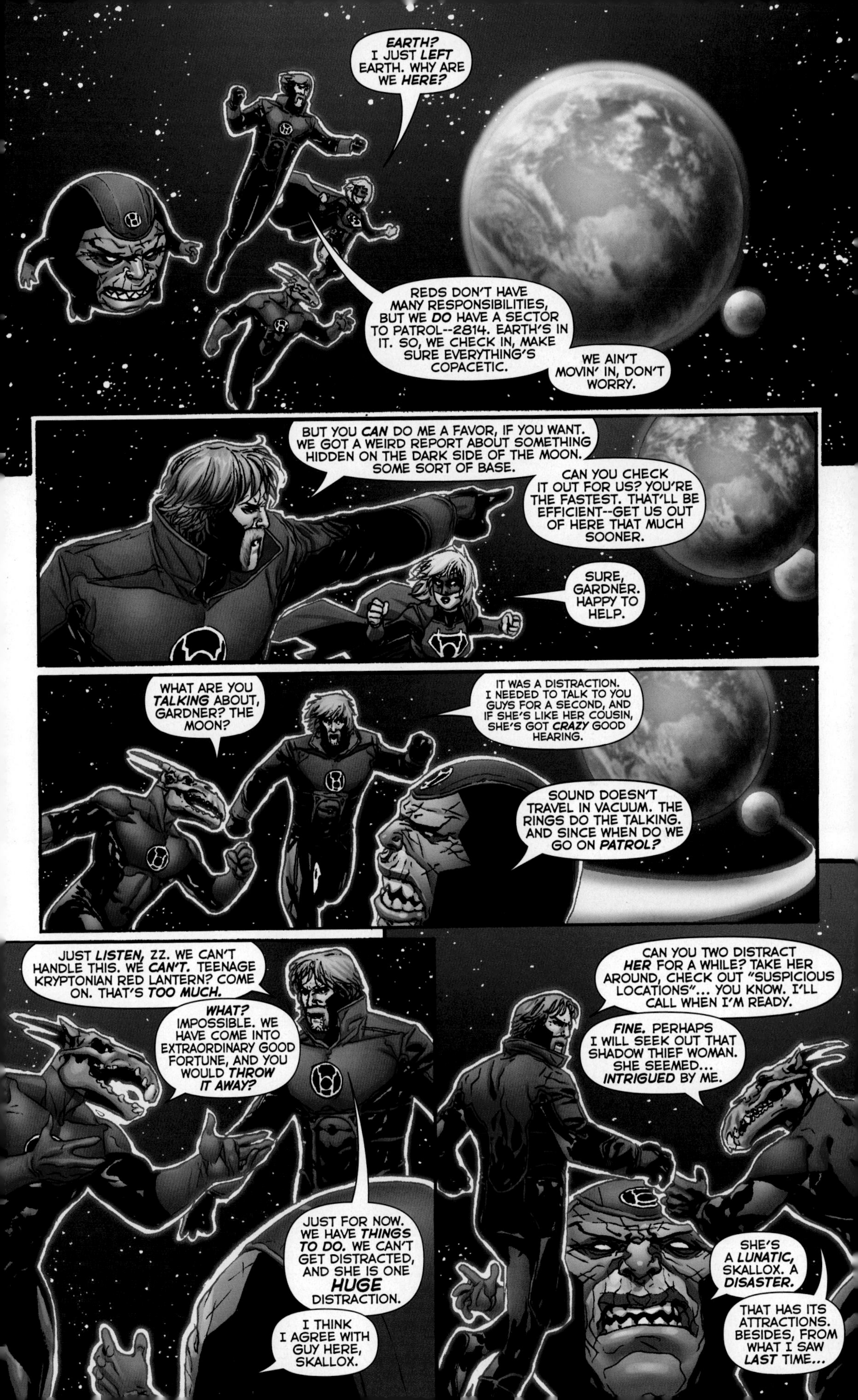
EARTH? I JUST LEFT EARTH. WHY ARE WE HERE?
REDS DON'T HAVE MANY RESPONSIBILITIES, BUT WE DO HAVE A SECTOR TO PATROL--2814. EARTH'S IN IT. SO, WE CHECK IN, MAKE SURE EVERYTHING'S COPACETIC.
WE AIN'T MOVIN' IN, DON'T WORRY.
BUT YOU CAN DO ME A FAVOR, IF YOU WANT. WE GOT A WEIRD REPORT ABOUT SOMETHING HIDDEN ON THE DARK SIDE OF THE MOON. SOME SORT OF BASE.
CAN YOU CHECK IT OUT FOR US? YOU'RE THE FASTEST. THAT'LL BE EFFICIENT--GET US OUT OF HERE THAT MUCH SOONER.
SURE, GARDNER. HAPPY TO HELP.
WHAT ARE YOU TALKING ABOUT, GARDNER? THE MOON?
IT WAS A DISTRACTION. I NEEDED TO TALK TO YOU GUYS FOR A SECOND, AND IF SHE'S LIKE HER COUSIN, SHE'S GOT CRAZY GOOD HEARING.
SOUND DOESN'T TRAVEL IN VACUUM. THE RINGS DO THE TALKING. AND SINCE WHEN DO WE GO ON PATROL?
JUST LISTEN, ZZ. WE CAN'T HANDLE THIS. WE CAN'T. TEENAGE KRYPTONIAN RED LANTERN? COME ON. THAT'S TOO MUCH.
WHAT? IMPOSSIBLE. WE HAVE COME INTO EXTRAORDINARY GOOD FORTUNE, AND YOU WOULD THROW IT AWAY?
JUST FOR NOW. WE HAVE THINGS TO DO. WE CAN'T GET DISTRACTED, AND SHE IS ONE HUGE DISTRACTION.
I THINK I AGREE WITH GUY HERE, SKALLOX.
CAN YOU TWO DISTRACT HER FOR A WHILE? TAKE HER AROUND, CHECK OUT "SUSPICIOUS LOCATIONS"... YOU KNOW. I'LL CALL WHEN I'M READY.
FINE. PERHAPS I WILL SEEK OUT THAT SHADOW THIEF WOMAN. SHE SEEMED... INTRIGUED BY ME.
SHE'S A LUNATIC, SKALLOX. A DISASTER.
THAT HAS ITS ATTRACTIONS. BESIDES, FROM WHAT I SAW LAST TIME...

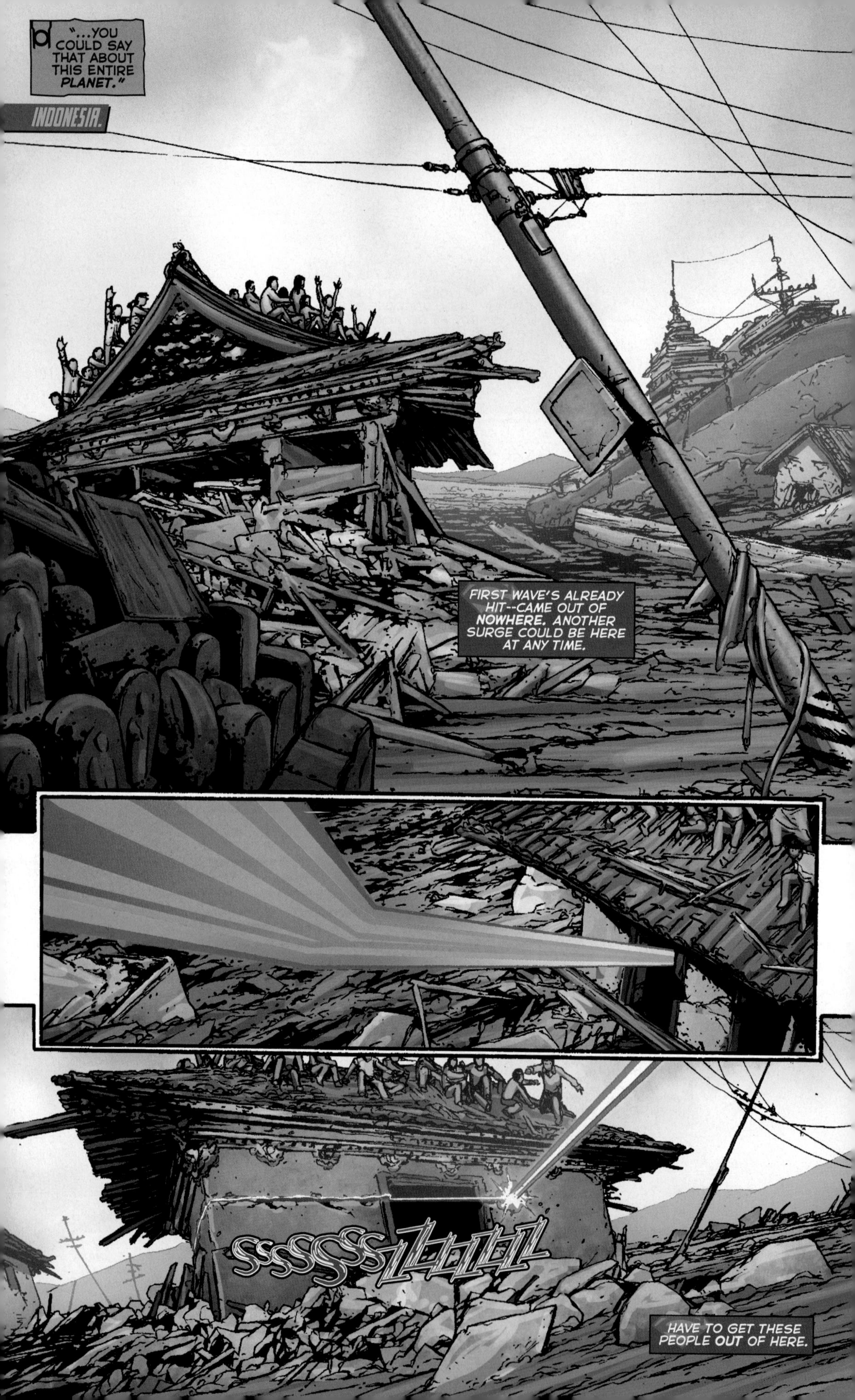
"...YOU COULD SAY THAT ABOUT THIS ENTIRE PLANET."
INDONESIA.
FIRST WAVE'S ALREADY HIT--CAME OUT OF NOWHERE. ANOTHER SURGE COULD BE HERE AT ANY TIME.
SSSSSSZZZZZZ
HAVE TO GET THESE PEOPLE OUT OF HERE.

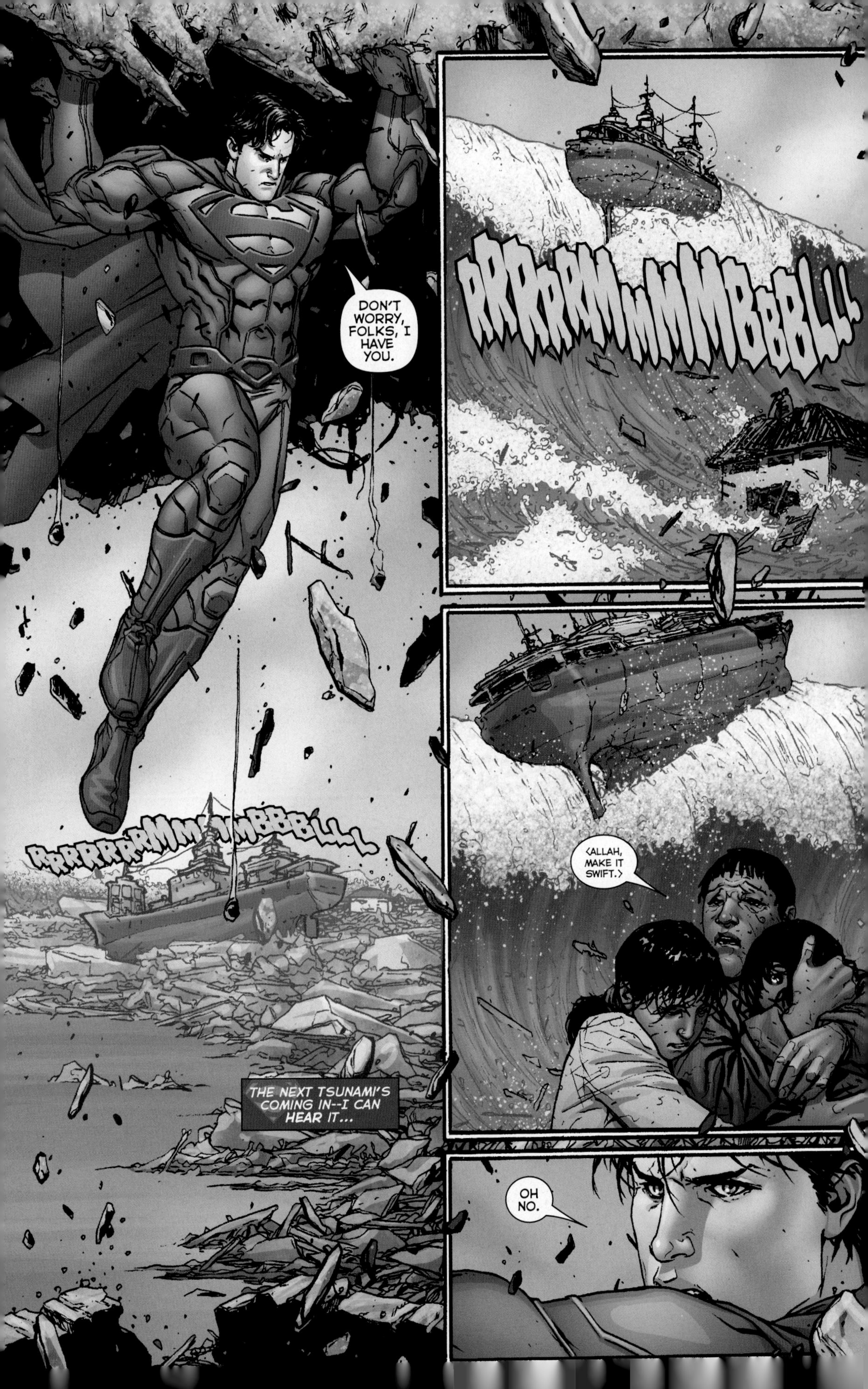
DON'T WORRY, FOLKS, I HAVE YOU.
RRRRRRMMMMMBBBLLL
THE NEXT TSUNAMI'S COMING IN--I CAN HEAR IT...
RRRRRRMMMMMMBBBLLL
<ALLAH, MAKE IT SWIFT.>
OH NO.

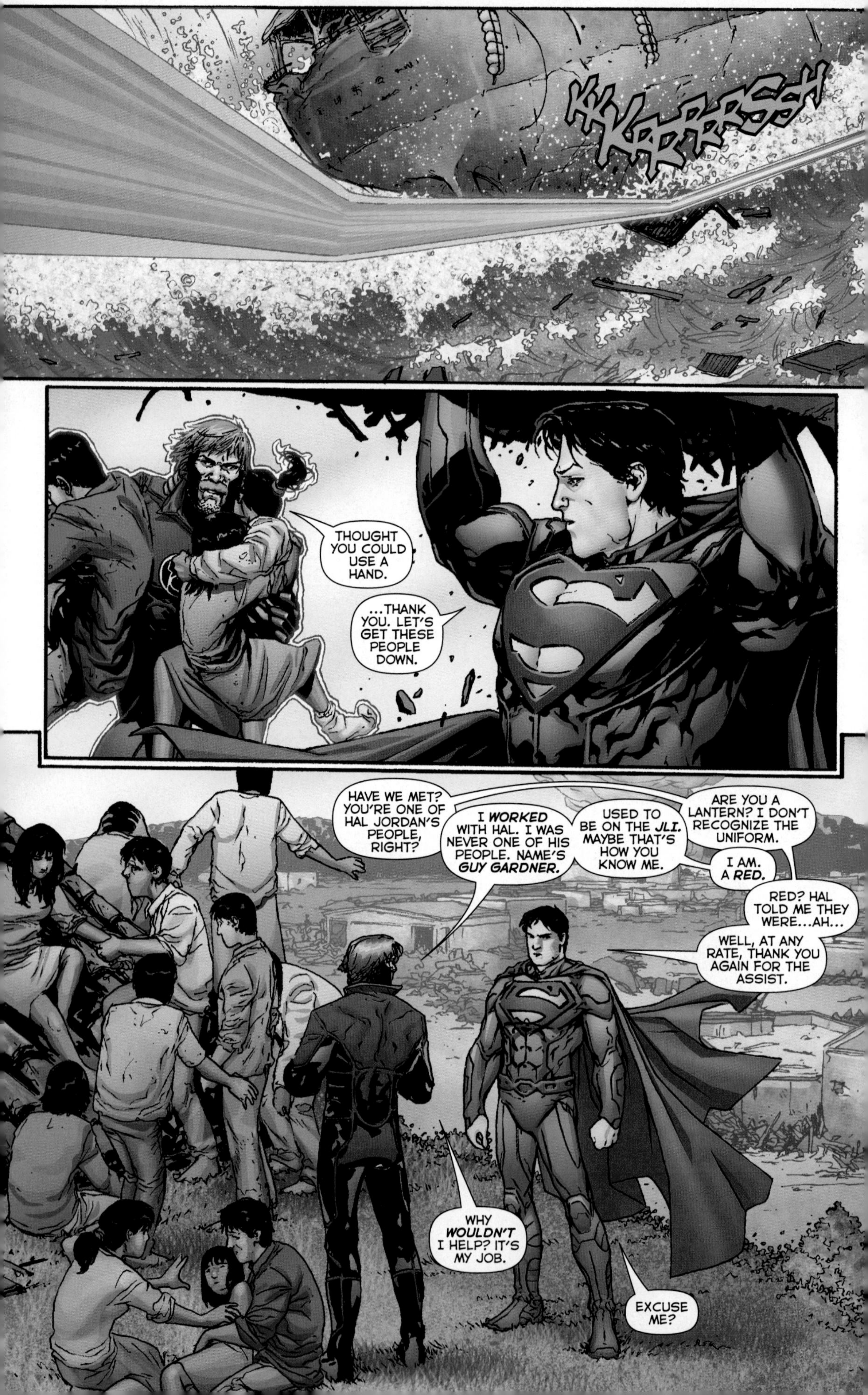
KKKARRSSH
THOUGHT YOU COULD USE A HAND.
...THANK YOU. LET'S GET THESE PEOPLE DOWN.
HAVE WE MET? YOU'RE ONE OF HAL JORDAN'S PEOPLE, RIGHT?
I WORKED WITH HAL. I WAS NEVER ONE OF HIS PEOPLE. NAME'S GUY GARDNER.
USED TO BE ON THE JLI. MAYBE THAT'S HOW YOU KNOW ME.
ARE YOU A LANTERN? I DON'T RECOGNIZE THE UNIFORM.
I AM. A RED.
RED? HAL TOLD ME THEY WERE...AH...
WELL, AT ANY RATE, THANK YOU AGAIN FOR THE ASSIST.
WHY WOULDN'T I HELP? IT'S MY JOB.
EXCUSE ME?

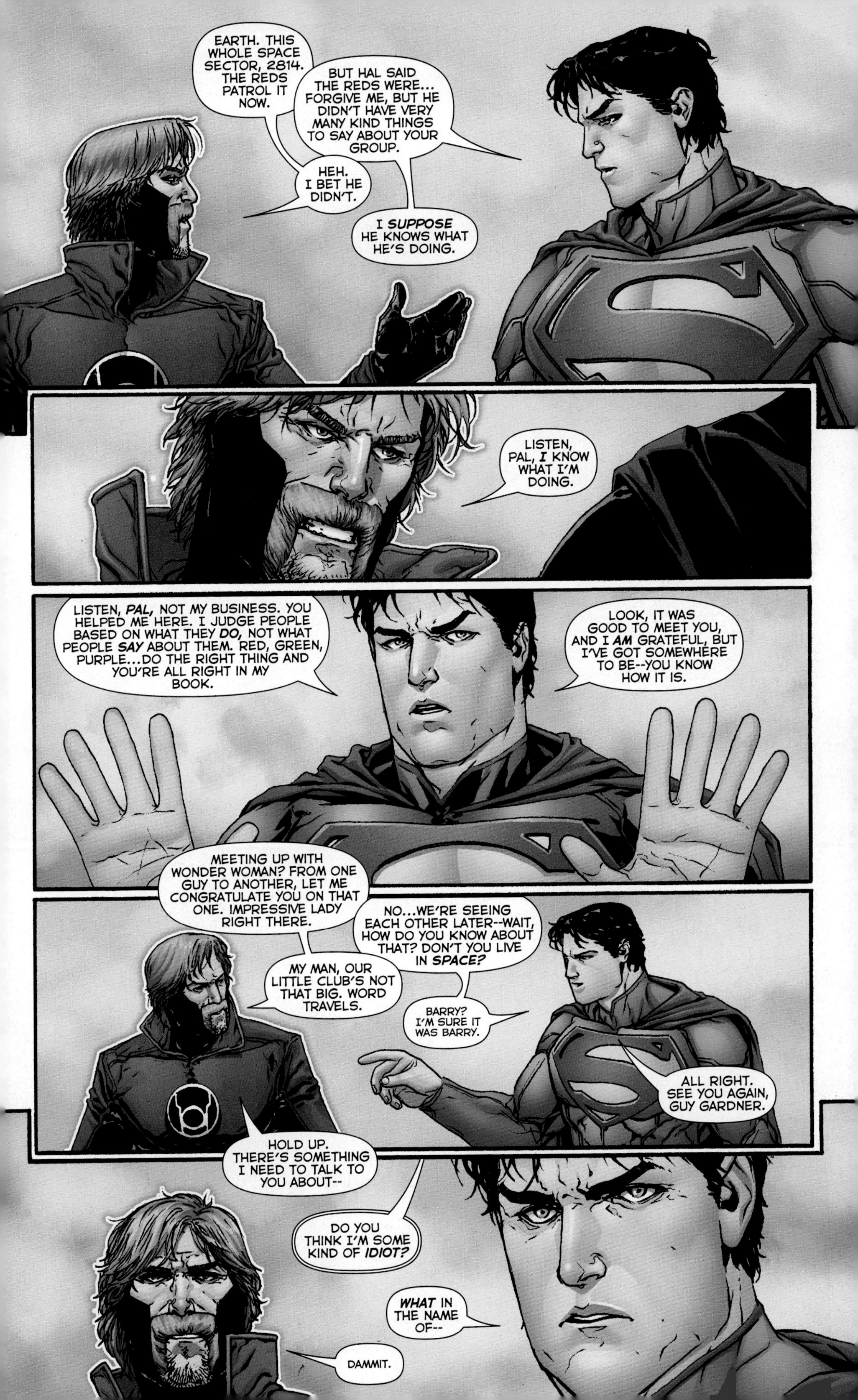
EARTH. THIS WHOLE SPACE SECTOR, 2814. THE REDS PATROL IT NOW.
BUT HAL SAID THE REDS WERE... FORGIVE ME, BUT HE DIDN'T HAVE VERY MANY KIND THINGS TO SAY ABOUT YOUR GROUP.
HEH. I BET HE DIDN'T.
I SUPPOSE HE KNOWS WHAT HE'S DOING.
LISTEN, PAL, I KNOW WHAT I'M DOING.
LISTEN, PAL, NOT MY BUSINESS. YOU HELPED ME HERE. I JUDGE PEOPLE BASED ON WHAT THEY DO, NOT WHAT PEOPLE SAY ABOUT THEM. RED, GREEN, PURPLE...DO THE RIGHT THING AND YOU'RE ALL RIGHT IN MY BOOK.
LOOK, IT WAS GOOD TO MEET YOU, AND I AM GRATEFUL, BUT I'VE GOT SOMEWHERE TO BE--YOU KNOW HOW IT IS.
MEETING UP WITH WONDER WOMAN? FROM ONE GUY TO ANOTHER, LET ME CONGRATULATE YOU ON THAT ONE. IMPRESSIVE LADY RIGHT THERE.
NO...WE'RE SEEING EACH OTHER LATER--WAIT, HOW DO YOU KNOW ABOUT THAT? DON'T YOU LIVE IN SPACE?
MY MAN, OUR LITTLE CLUB'S NOT THAT BIG. WORD TRAVELS.
BARRY? I'M SURE IT WAS BARRY.
ALL RIGHT. SEE YOU AGAIN, GUY GARDNER.
HOLD UP. THERE'S SOMETHING I NEED TO TALK TO YOU ABOUT--
DO YOU THINK I'M SOME KIND OF IDIOT?
WHAT IN THE NAME OF--
DAMMIT.

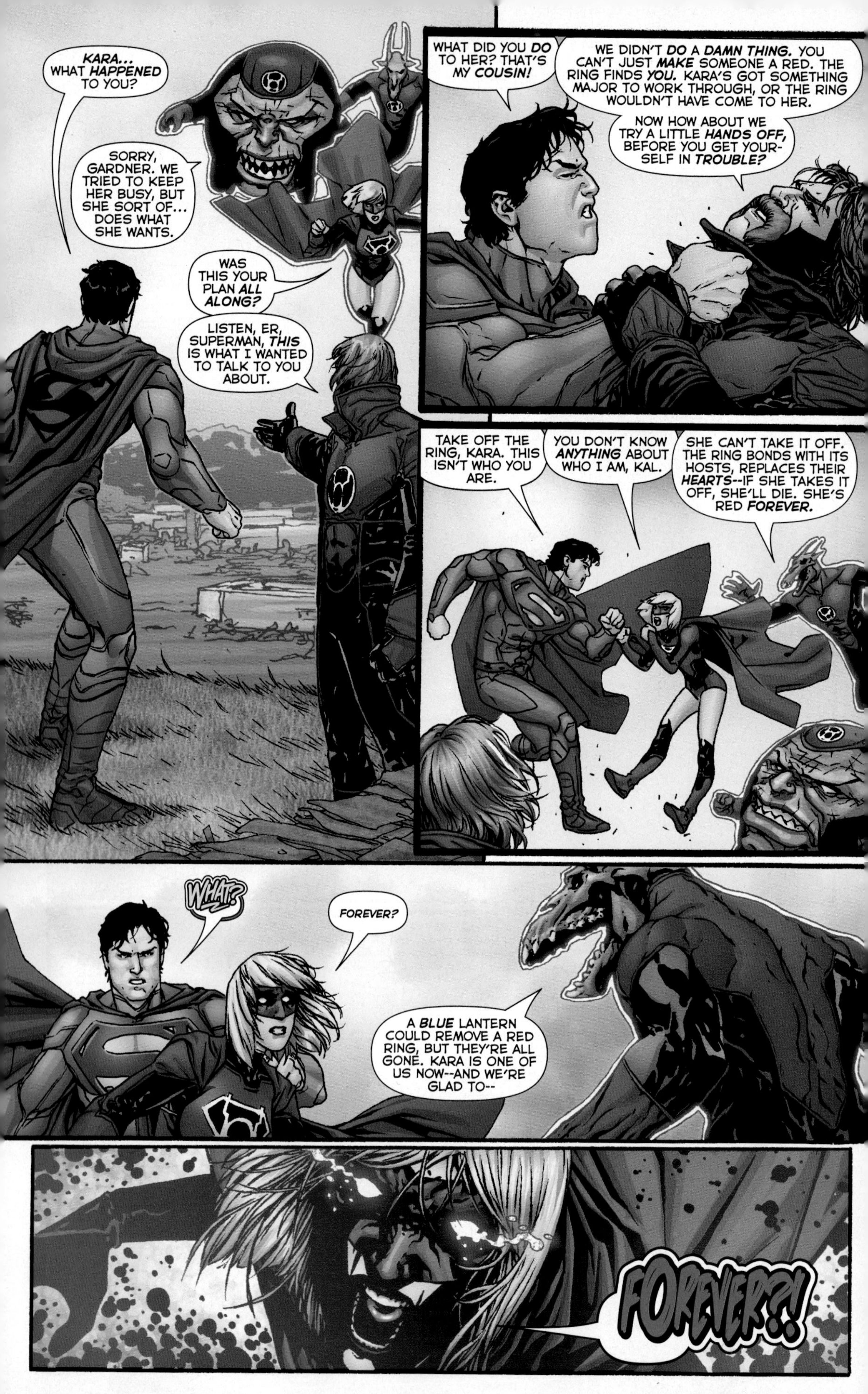

KARA... WHAT HAPPENED TO YOU?
SORRY, GARDNER. WE TRIED TO KEEP HER BUSY, BUT SHE SORT OF... DOES WHAT SHE WANTS.
WAS THIS YOUR PLAN ALL ALONG?
LISTEN, ER, SUPERMAN, THIS IS WHAT I WANTED TO TALK TO YOU ABOUT.
WHAT DID YOU DO TO HER? THAT'S MY COUSIN!
WE DIDN'T DO A DAMN THING. YOU CAN'T JUST MAKE SOMEONE A RED. THE RING FINDS YOU. KARA'S GOT SOMETHING MAJOR TO WORK THROUGH, OR THE RING WOULDN'T HAVE COME TO HER.
NOW HOW ABOUT WE TRY A LITTLE HANDS OFF, BEFORE YOU GET YOURSELF IN TROUBLE?
TAKE OFF THE RING, KARA. THIS ISN'T WHO YOU ARE.
YOU DON'T KNOW ANYTHING ABOUT WHO I AM, KAL.
SHE CAN'T TAKE IT OFF. THE RING BONDS WITH ITS HOSTS, REPLACES THEIR HEARTS--IF SHE TAKES IT OFF, SHE'LL DIE. SHE'S RED FOREVER.
WHAT?
FOREVER?
A BLUE LANTERN COULD REMOVE A RED RING, BUT THEY'RE ALL GONE. KARA IS ONE OF US NOW--AND WE'RE GLAD TO--
FOREVER?!

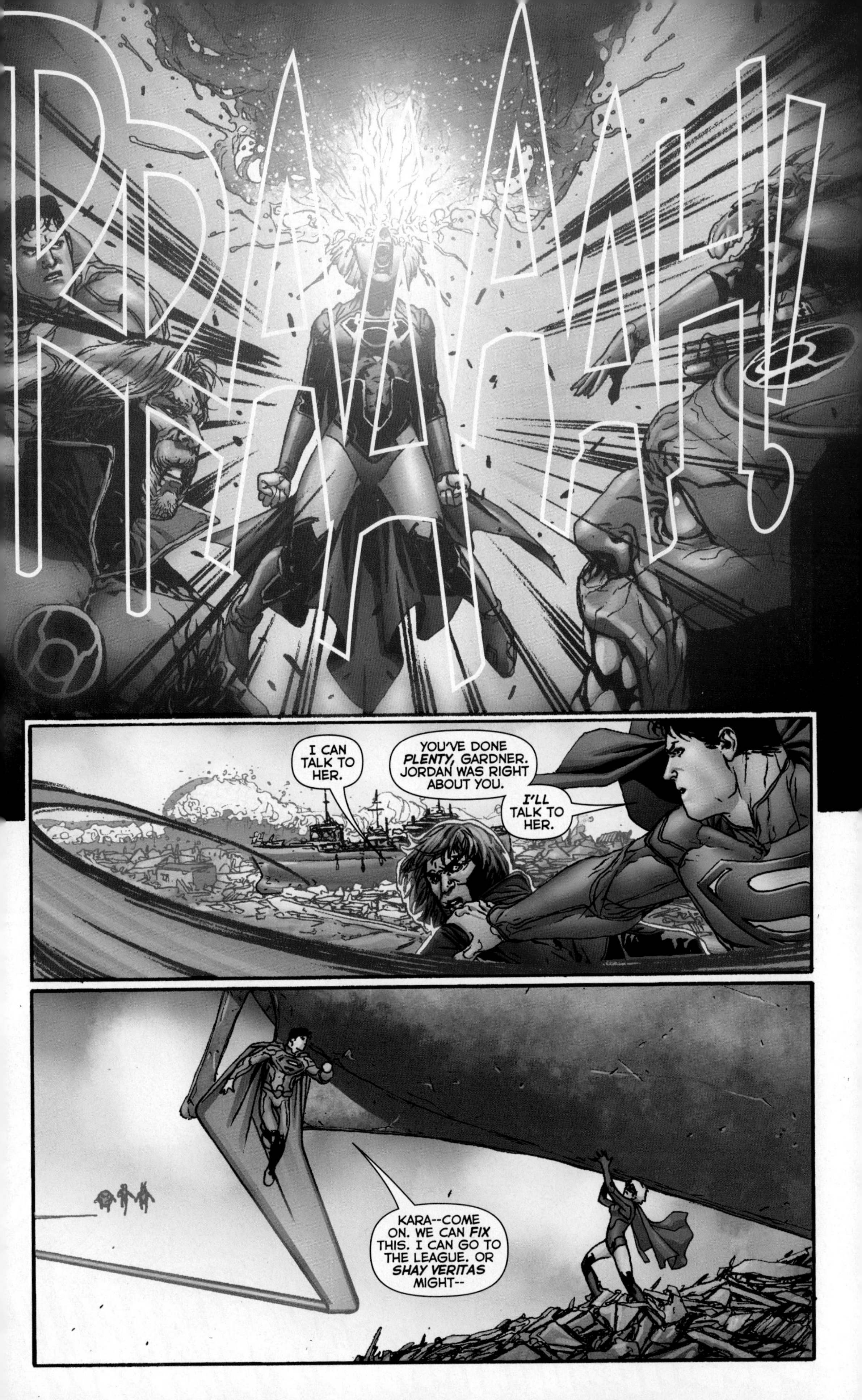
I CAN TALK TO HER.
YOU'VE DONE *PLENTY*, GARDNER. JORDAN WAS RIGHT ABOUT YOU.
I'LL TALK TO HER.
KARA--COME ON. WE CAN *FIX* THIS. I CAN GO TO THE LEAGUE. OR *SHAY VERITAS* MIGHT--

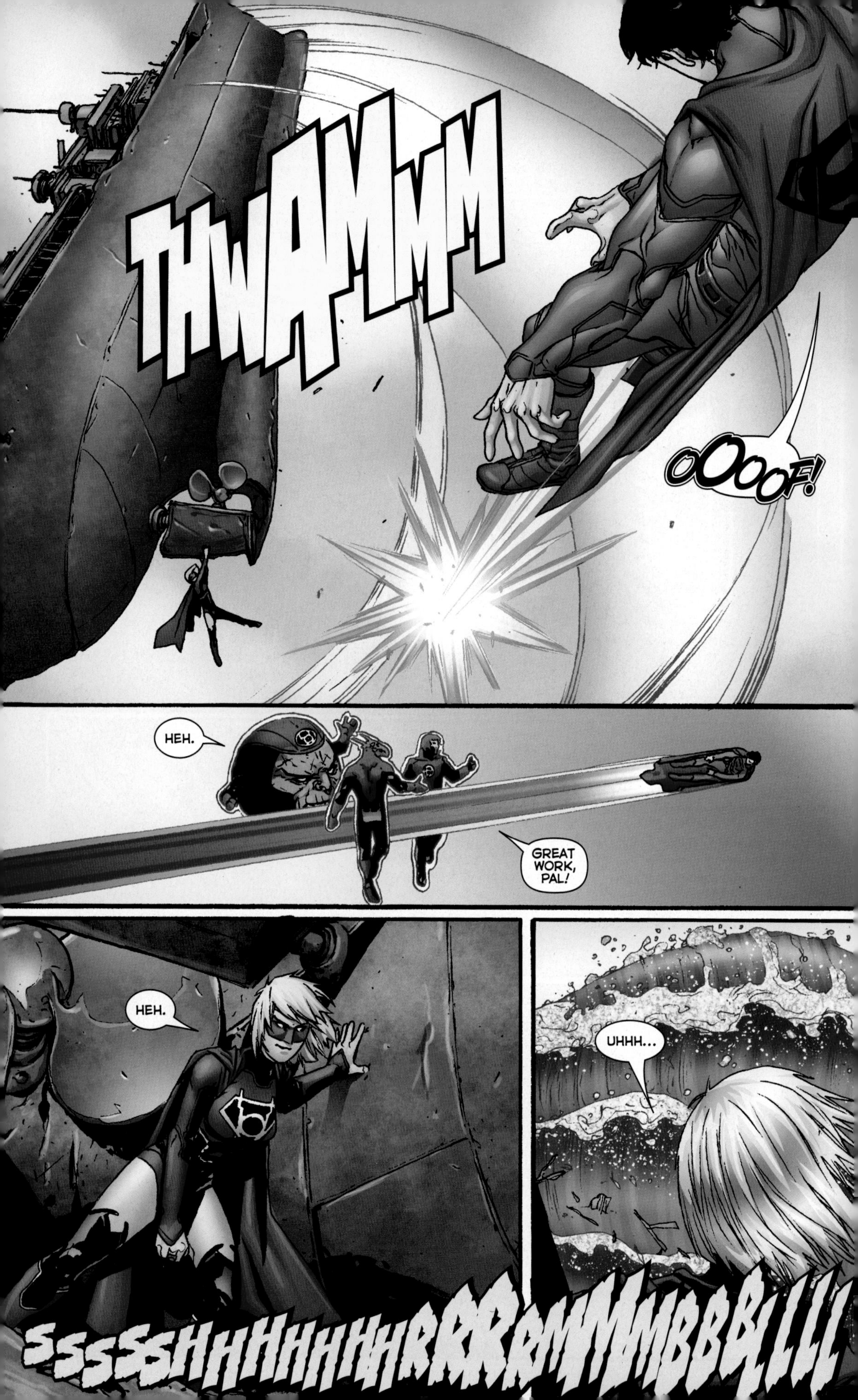
THWAMMMM
OOOOF!
HEH.
GREAT WORK, PAL!
HEH.
UHHH...
SSSSSHHHHHHHHRRRRMMMMBBBLLL

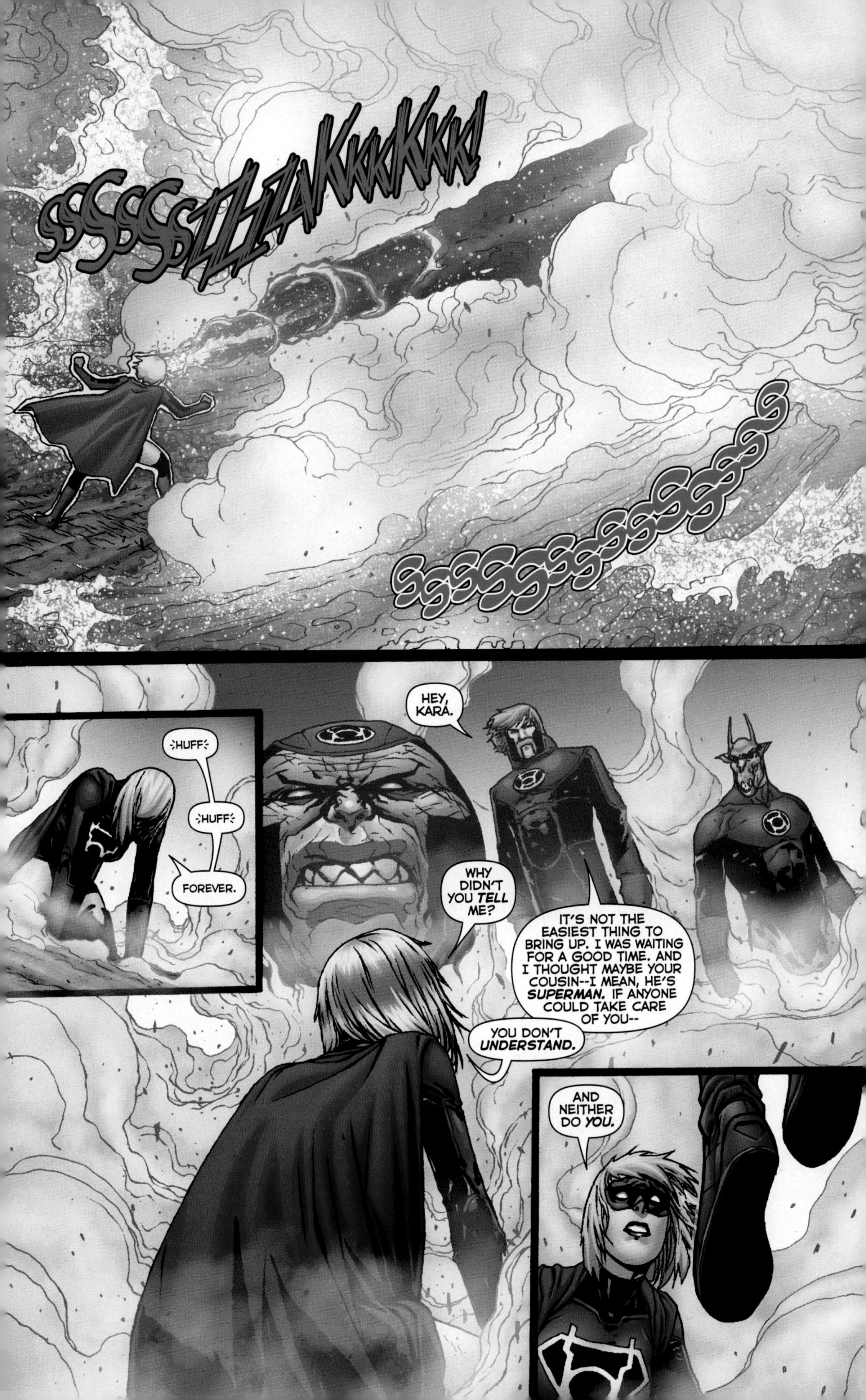
SSSSSSZZZZAKKKKKKK!
SSSSSSSSSSSSSSS
HUFF
HUFF
FOREVER.
HEY, KARA.
WHY DIDN'T YOU TELL ME?
IT'S NOT THE EASIEST THING TO BRING UP. I WAS WAITING FOR A GOOD TIME. AND I THOUGHT MAYBE YOUR COUSIN--I MEAN, HE'S SUPERMAN. IF ANYONE COULD TAKE CARE OF YOU--
YOU DON'T UNDERSTAND.
AND NEITHER DO YOU.

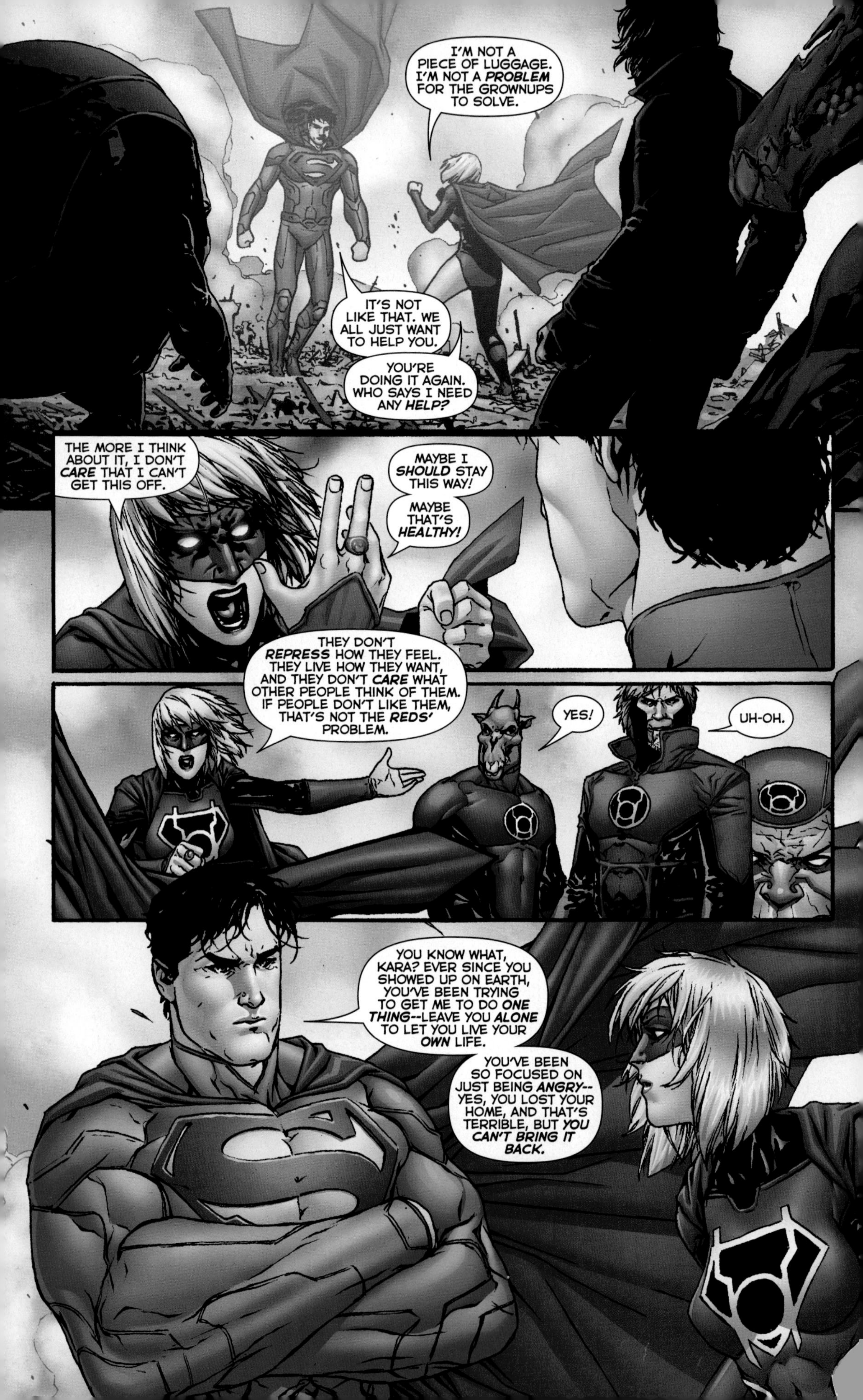
I'M NOT A PIECE OF LUGGAGE. I'M NOT A PROBLEM FOR THE GROWNUPS TO SOLVE.
IT'S NOT LIKE THAT. WE ALL JUST WANT TO HELP YOU.
YOU'RE DOING IT AGAIN. WHO SAYS I NEED ANY HELP?
THE MORE I THINK ABOUT IT, I DON'T CARE THAT I CAN'T GET THIS OFF.
MAYBE I SHOULD STAY THIS WAY!
MAYBE THAT'S HEALTHY!
THEY DON'T REPRESS HOW THEY FEEL. THEY LIVE HOW THEY WANT, AND THEY DON'T CARE WHAT OTHER PEOPLE THINK OF THEM. IF PEOPLE DON'T LIKE THEM, THAT'S NOT THE REDS' PROBLEM.
YES!
UH-OH.
YOU KNOW WHAT, KARA? EVER SINCE YOU SHOWED UP ON EARTH, YOU'VE BEEN TRYING TO GET ME TO DO ONE THING--LEAVE YOU ALONE TO LET YOU LIVE YOUR OWN LIFE.
YOU'VE BEEN SO FOCUSED ON JUST BEING ANGRY--YES, YOU LOST YOUR HOME, AND THAT'S TERRIBLE, BUT YOU CAN'T BRING IT BACK.

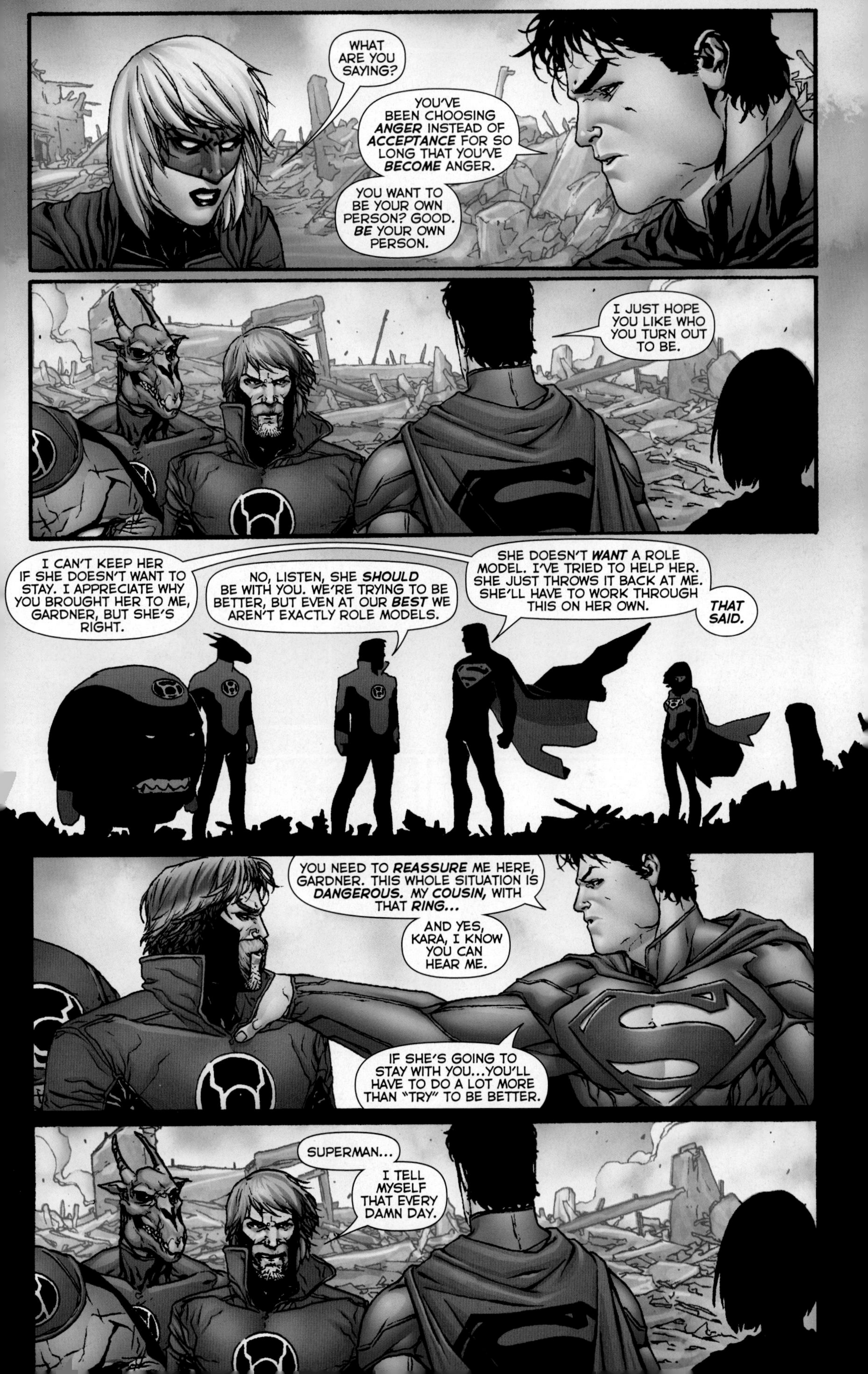
WHAT ARE YOU SAYING?
YOU'VE BEEN CHOOSING ANGER INSTEAD OF ACCEPTANCE FOR SO LONG THAT YOU'VE BECOME ANGER.
YOU WANT TO BE YOUR OWN PERSON? GOOD. BE YOUR OWN PERSON.
I JUST HOPE YOU LIKE WHO YOU TURN OUT TO BE.
I CAN'T KEEP HER IF SHE DOESN'T WANT TO STAY. I APPRECIATE WHY YOU BROUGHT HER TO ME, GARDNER, BUT SHE'S RIGHT.
NO, LISTEN, SHE SHOULD BE WITH YOU. WE'RE TRYING TO BE BETTER, BUT EVEN AT OUR BEST WE AREN'T EXACTLY ROLE MODELS.
SHE DOESN'T WANT A ROLE MODEL. I'VE TRIED TO HELP HER. SHE JUST THROWS IT BACK AT ME. SHE'LL HAVE TO WORK THROUGH THIS ON HER OWN.
THAT SAID.
YOU NEED TO REASSURE ME HERE, GARDNER. THIS WHOLE SITUATION IS DANGEROUS. MY COUSIN, WITH THAT RING...
AND YES, KARA, I KNOW YOU CAN HEAR ME.
IF SHE'S GOING TO STAY WITH YOU...YOU'LL HAVE TO DO A LOT MORE THAN "TRY" TO BE BETTER.
SUPERMAN...
I TELL MYSELF THAT EVERY DAMN DAY.

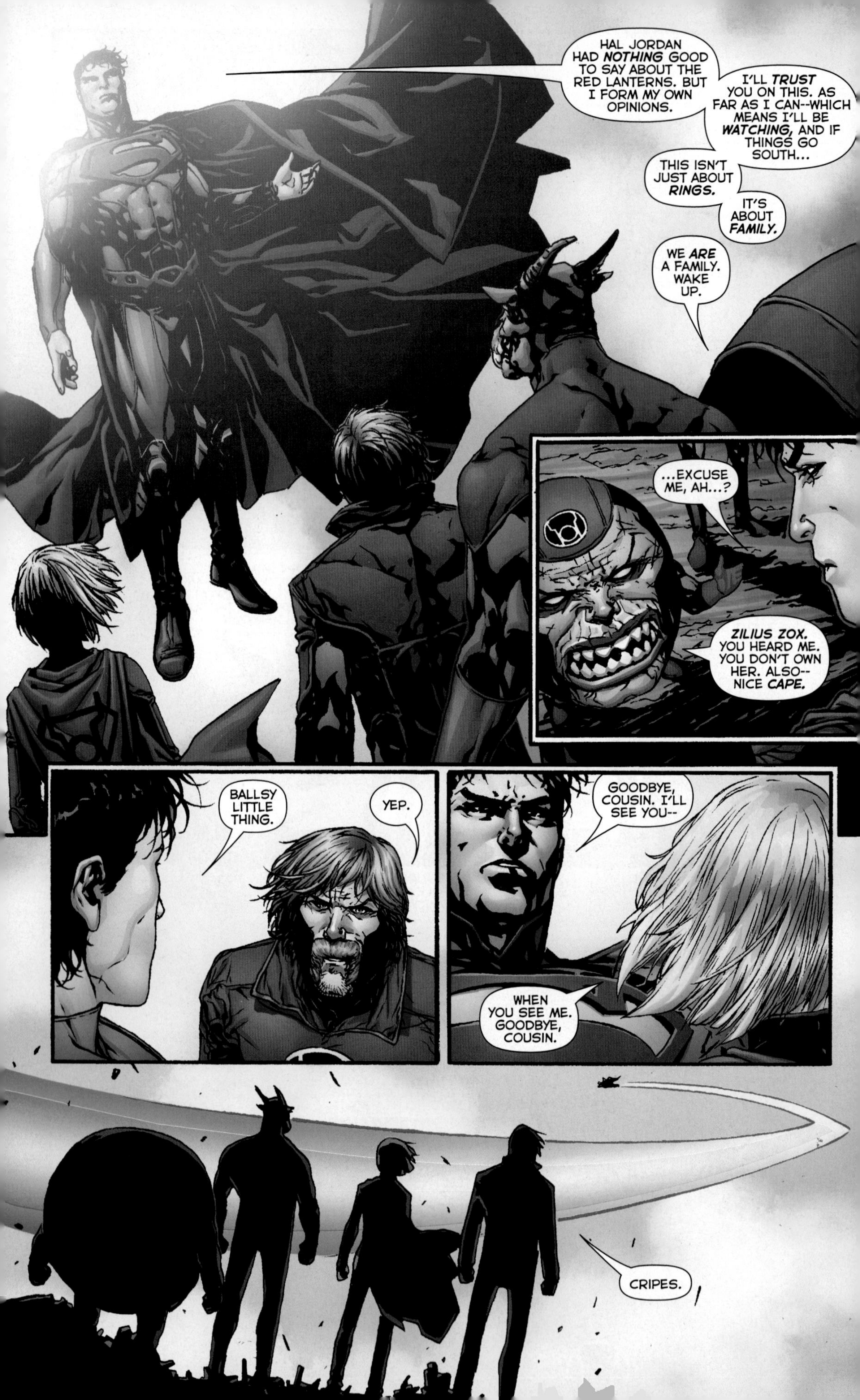
HAL JORDAN HAD *NOTHING* GOOD TO SAY ABOUT THE RED LANTERNS. BUT I FORM MY OWN OPINIONS.
I'LL *TRUST* YOU ON THIS. AS FAR AS I CAN--WHICH MEANS I'LL BE *WATCHING,* AND IF THINGS GO SOUTH...
THIS ISN'T JUST ABOUT *RINGS.*
IT'S ABOUT *FAMILY.*
WE *ARE* A FAMILY. WAKE UP.
...EXCUSE ME, AH...?
ZILIUS ZOX. YOU HEARD ME. YOU DON'T OWN HER. ALSO--NICE *CAPE.*
BALLSY LITTLE THING.
YEP.
GOODBYE, COUSIN. I'LL SEE YOU--
WHEN YOU SEE ME. GOODBYE, COUSIN.
CRIPES.

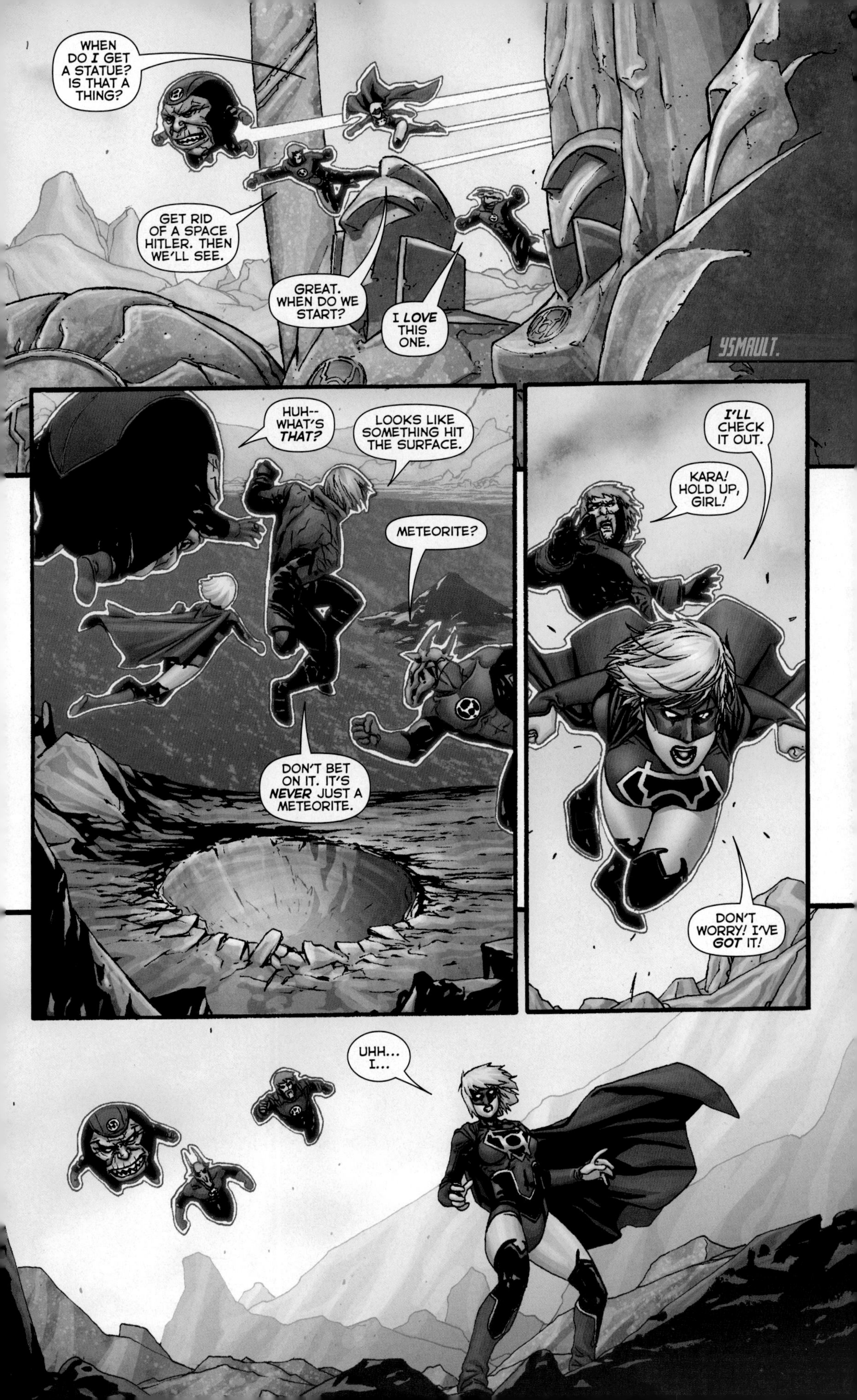
WHEN DO I GET A STATUE? IS THAT A THING?
GET RID OF A SPACE HITLER. THEN WE'LL SEE.
GREAT. WHEN DO WE START?
I LOVE THIS ONE.
YSMAULT.
HUH-- WHAT'S THAT?
LOOKS LIKE SOMETHING HIT THE SURFACE.
METEORITE?
DON'T BET ON IT. IT'S NEVER JUST A METEORITE.
I'LL CHECK IT OUT.
KARA! HOLD UP, GIRL!
DON'T WORRY! I'VE GOT IT!
UHH... I...

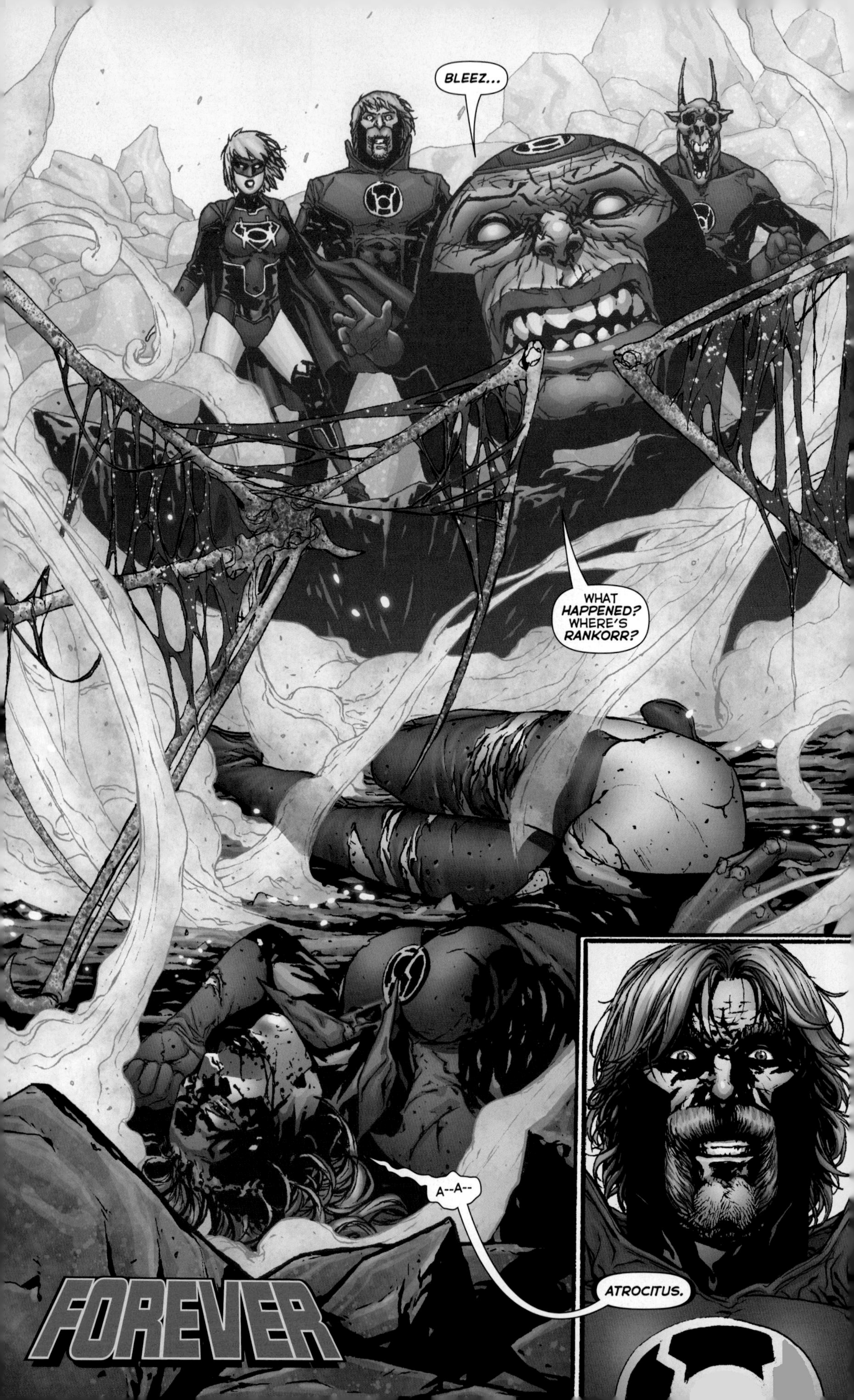
BLEEZ...
WHAT HAPPENED? WHERE'S RANKORR?
A--A--
ATROCITUS.
FOREVER

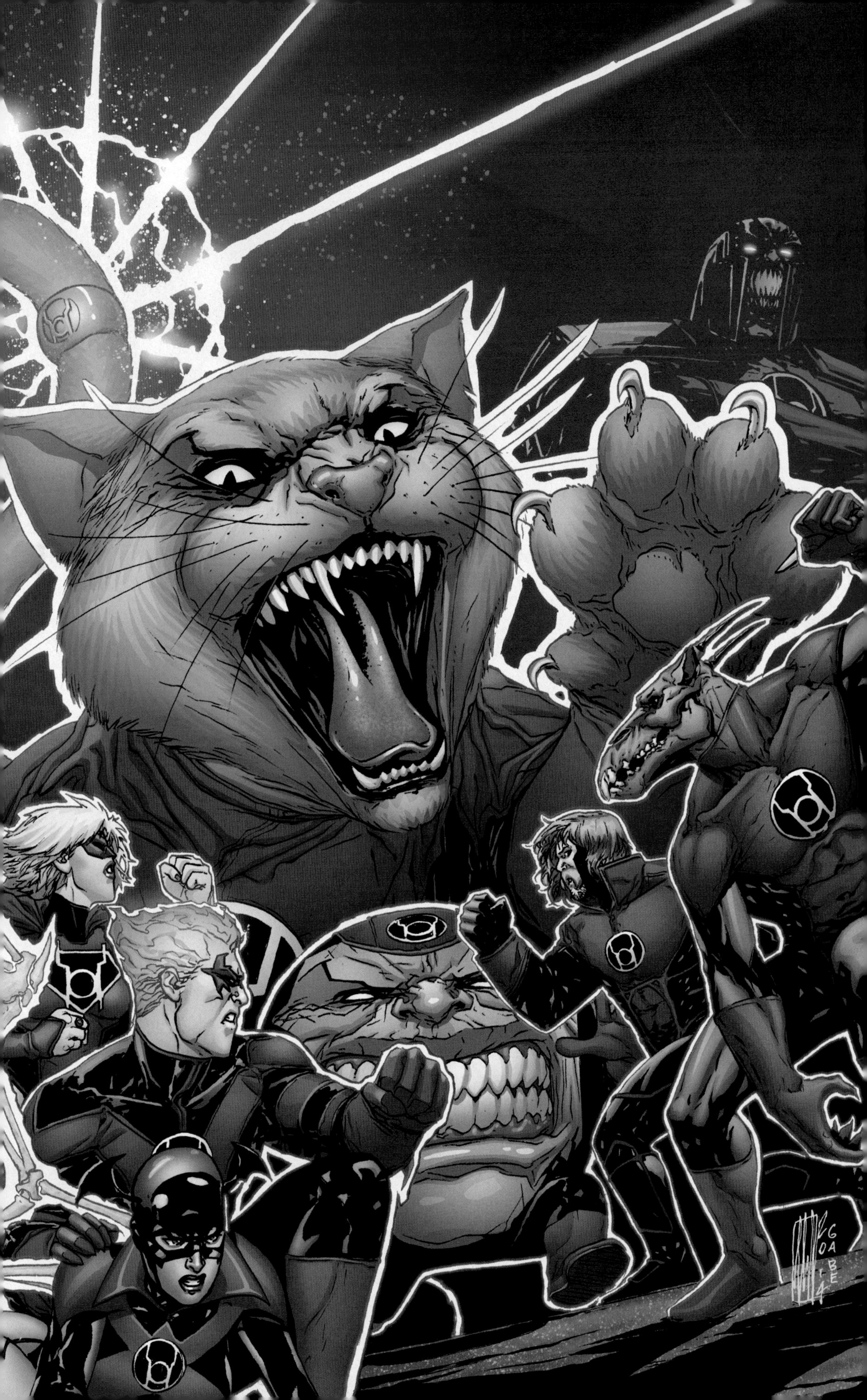

CHARLES SOULE writer **J. CALAFIORE ALESSANDRO VITTI** (97-100, 106-109) artists **GABE ELTAEB** colorist **DAVE SHARPE** letterer
cover art by **ALESSANDRO VITTI** with **GABE ELTAEB**

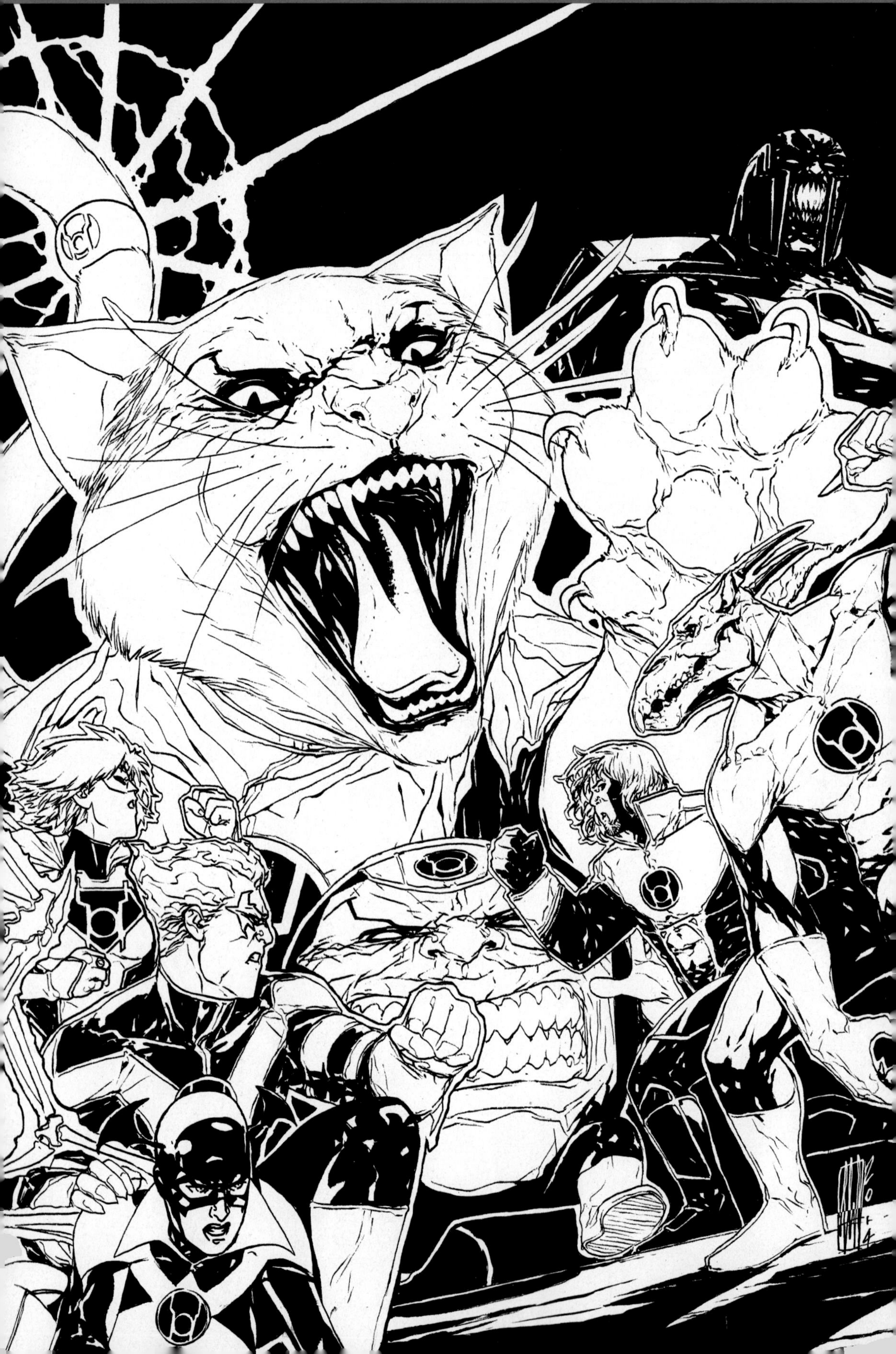

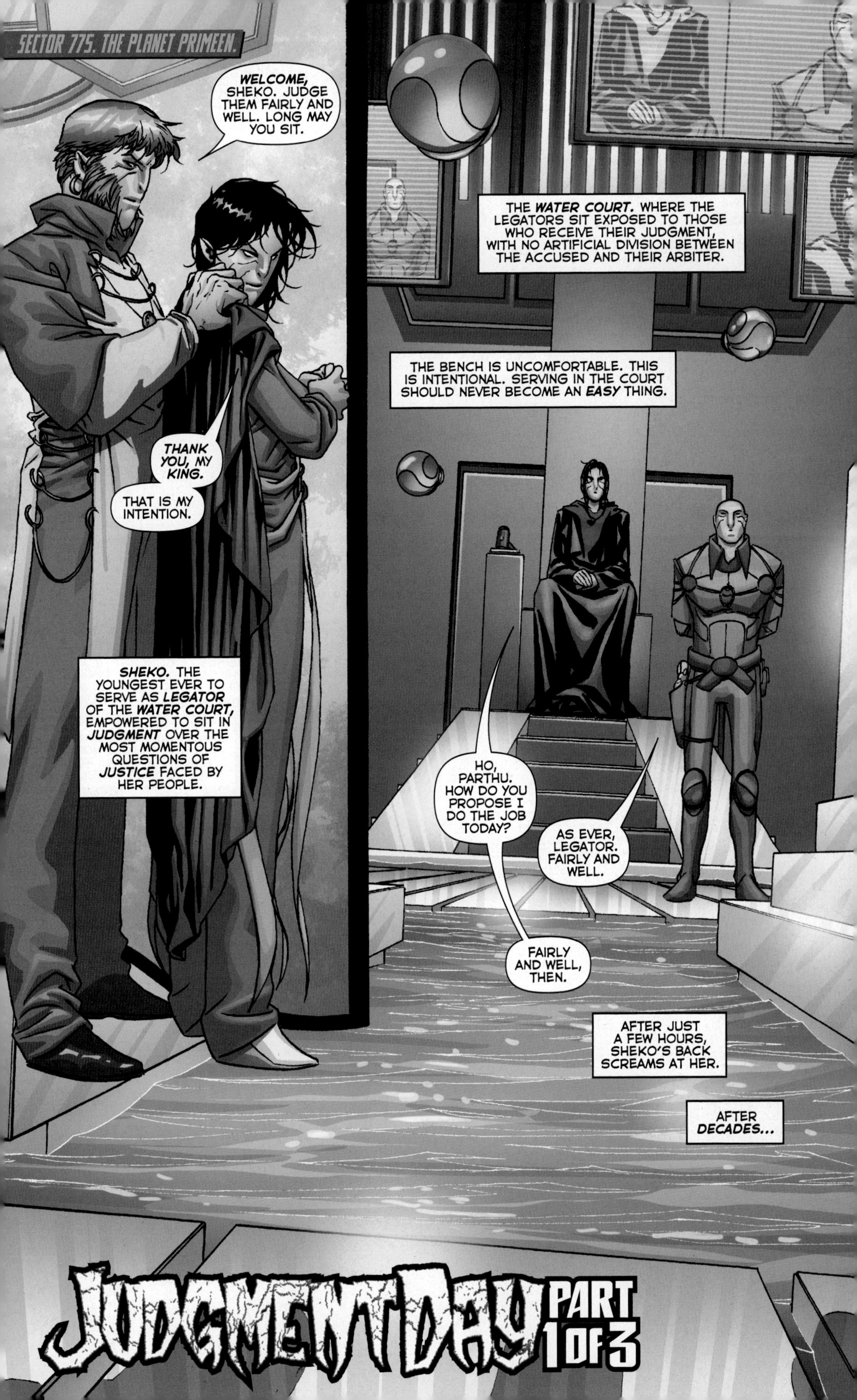
SECTOR 775. THE PLANET PRIMEEN.
WELCOME, SHEKO. JUDGE THEM FAIRLY AND WELL. LONG MAY YOU SIT.
THANK YOU, MY KING.
THAT IS MY INTENTION.
SHEKO. THE YOUNGEST EVER TO SERVE AS LEGATOR OF THE WATER COURT, EMPOWERED TO SIT IN JUDGMENT OVER THE MOST MOMENTOUS QUESTIONS OF JUSTICE FACED BY HER PEOPLE.
THE WATER COURT. WHERE THE LEGATORS SIT EXPOSED TO THOSE WHO RECEIVE THEIR JUDGMENT, WITH NO ARTIFICIAL DIVISION BETWEEN THE ACCUSED AND THEIR ARBITER.
THE BENCH IS UNCOMFORTABLE. THIS IS INTENTIONAL. SERVING IN THE COURT SHOULD NEVER BECOME AN EASY THING.
HO, PARTHU. HOW DO YOU PROPOSE I DO THE JOB TODAY?
AS EVER, LEGATOR. FAIRLY AND WELL.
FAIRLY AND WELL, THEN.
AFTER JUST A FEW HOURS, SHEKO'S BACK SCREAMS AT HER.
AFTER DECADES...
JUDGMENT DAY PART 1 OF 3

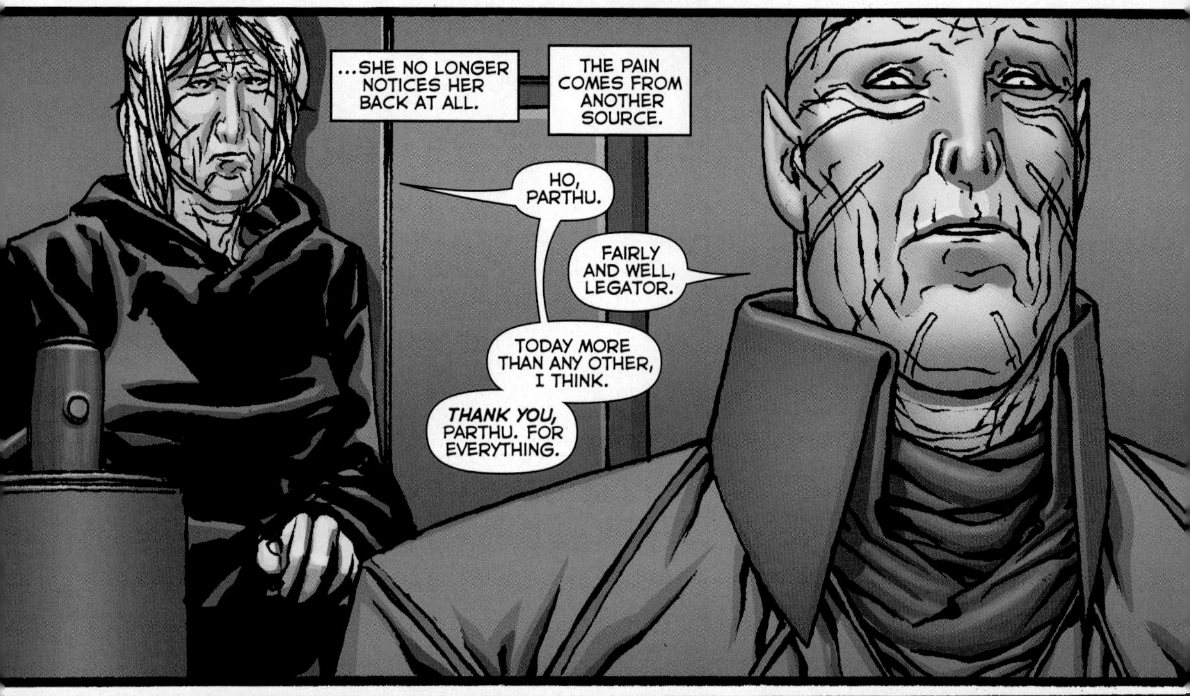
...SHE NO LONGER NOTICES HER BACK AT ALL.
THE PAIN COMES FROM ANOTHER SOURCE.
HO, PARTHU.
FAIRLY AND WELL, LEGATOR.
TODAY MORE THAN ANY OTHER, I THINK.
THANK YOU, PARTHU. FOR EVERYTHING.

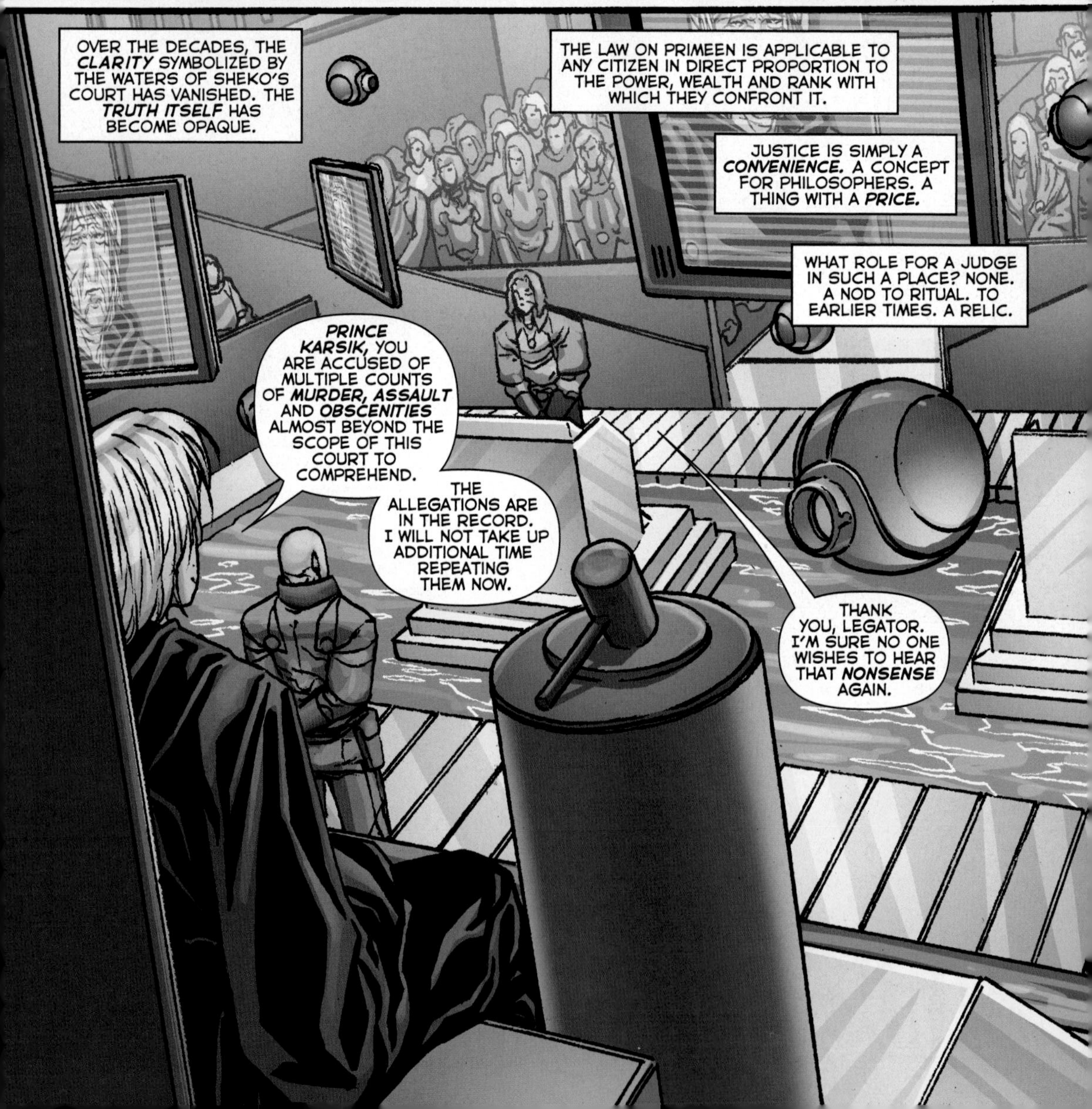
OVER THE DECADES, THE *CLARITY* SYMBOLIZED BY THE WATERS OF SHEKO'S COURT HAS VANISHED. THE *TRUTH ITSELF* HAS BECOME OPAQUE.
THE LAW ON PRIMEEN IS APPLICABLE TO ANY CITIZEN IN DIRECT PROPORTION TO THE POWER, WEALTH AND RANK WITH WHICH THEY CONFRONT IT.
JUSTICE IS SIMPLY A *CONVENIENCE.* A CONCEPT FOR PHILOSOPHERS. A THING WITH A *PRICE.*
WHAT ROLE FOR A JUDGE IN SUCH A PLACE? NONE. A NOD TO RITUAL. TO EARLIER TIMES. A RELIC.
PRINCE KARSIK, YOU ARE ACCUSED OF MULTIPLE COUNTS OF *MURDER, ASSAULT* AND *OBSCENITIES* ALMOST BEYOND THE SCOPE OF THIS COURT TO COMPREHEND.
THE ALLEGATIONS ARE IN THE RECORD. I WILL NOT TAKE UP ADDITIONAL TIME REPEATING THEM NOW.
THANK YOU, LEGATOR. I'M SURE NO ONE WISHES TO HEAR THAT *NONSENSE* AGAIN.

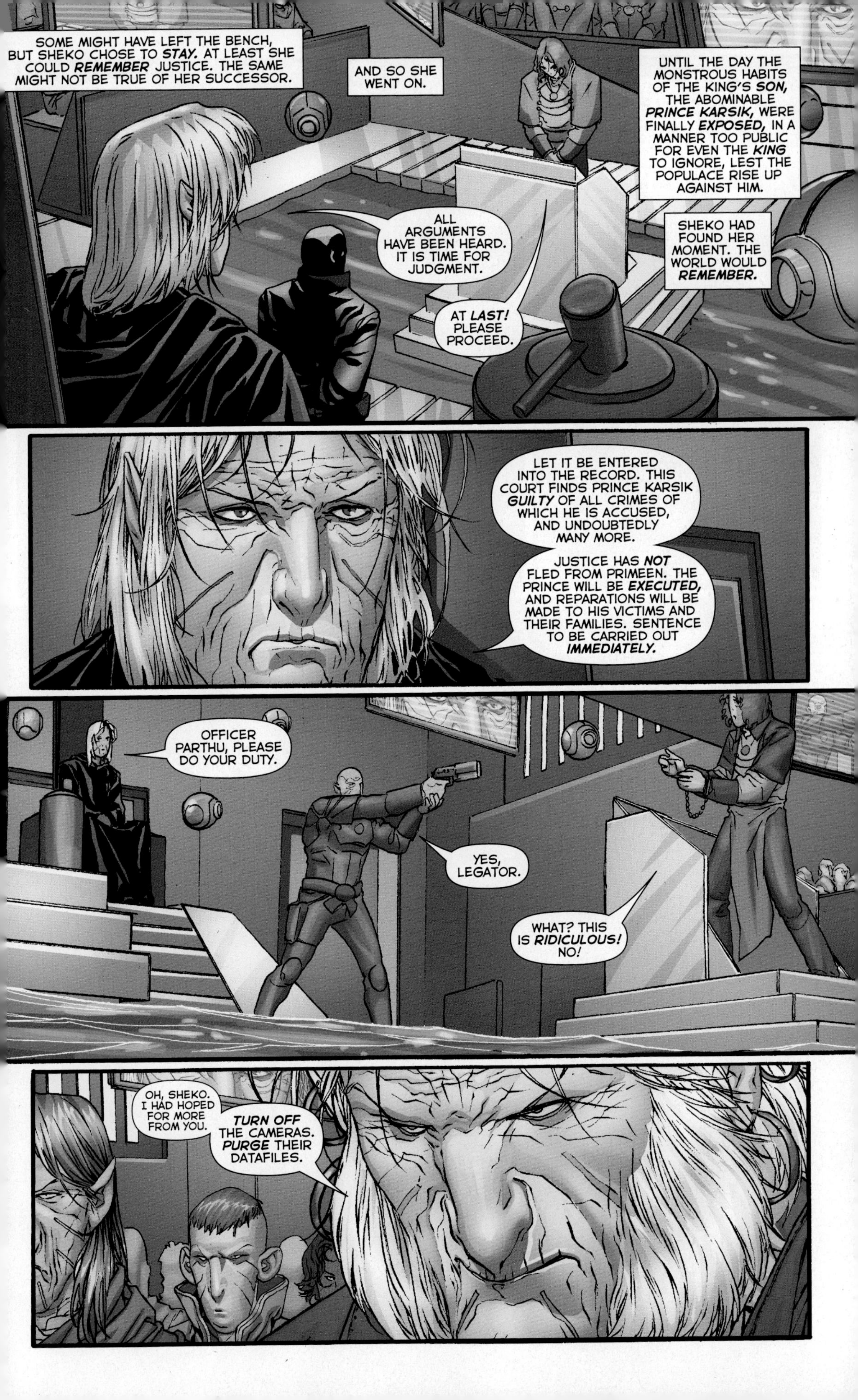
SOME MIGHT HAVE LEFT THE BENCH, BUT SHEKO CHOSE TO STAY. AT LEAST SHE COULD REMEMBER JUSTICE. THE SAME MIGHT NOT BE TRUE OF HER SUCCESSOR.
AND SO SHE WENT ON.
UNTIL THE DAY THE MONSTROUS HABITS OF THE KING'S SON, THE ABOMINABLE PRINCE KARSIK, WERE FINALLY EXPOSED, IN A MANNER TOO PUBLIC FOR EVEN THE KING TO IGNORE, LEST THE POPULACE RISE UP AGAINST HIM.
SHEKO HAD FOUND HER MOMENT. THE WORLD WOULD REMEMBER.
ALL ARGUMENTS HAVE BEEN HEARD. IT IS TIME FOR JUDGMENT.
AT LAST! PLEASE PROCEED.
LET IT BE ENTERED INTO THE RECORD. THIS COURT FINDS PRINCE KARSIK GUILTY OF ALL CRIMES OF WHICH HE IS ACCUSED, AND UNDOUBTEDLY MANY MORE.
JUSTICE HAS NOT FLED FROM PRIMEEN. THE PRINCE WILL BE EXECUTED, AND REPARATIONS WILL BE MADE TO HIS VICTIMS AND THEIR FAMILIES. SENTENCE TO BE CARRIED OUT IMMEDIATELY.
OFFICER PARTHU, PLEASE DO YOUR DUTY.
YES, LEGATOR.
WHAT? THIS IS RIDICULOUS! NO!
OH, SHEKO. I HAD HOPED FOR MORE FROM YOU.
TURN OFF THE CAMERAS. PURGE THEIR DATAFILES.

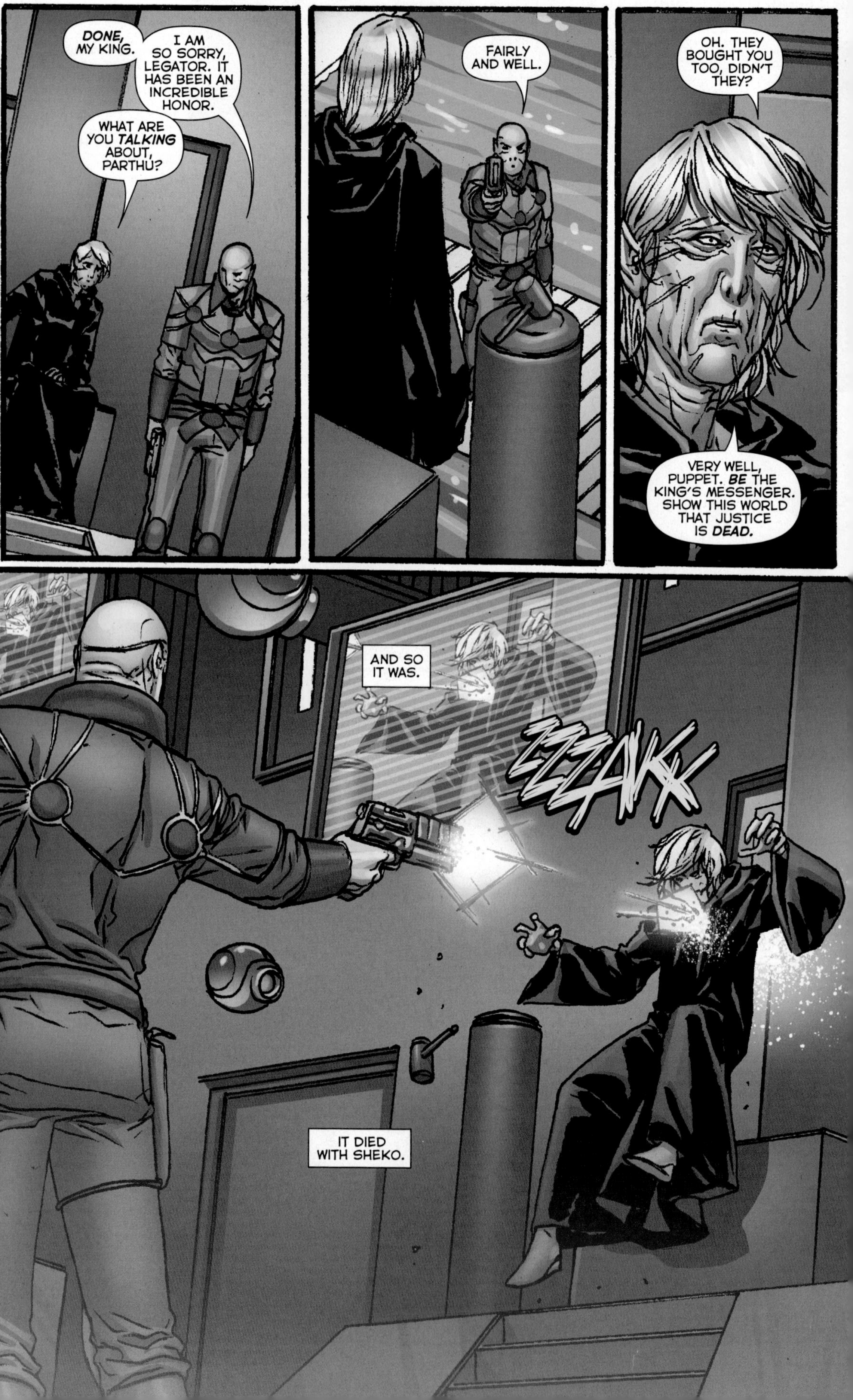
DONE, MY KING.
I AM SO SORRY, LEGATOR. IT HAS BEEN AN INCREDIBLE HONOR.
WHAT ARE YOU TALKING ABOUT, PARTHU?
FAIRLY AND WELL.
OH. THEY BOUGHT YOU TOO, DIDN'T THEY?
VERY WELL, PUPPET. BE THE KING'S MESSENGER. SHOW THIS WORLD THAT JUSTICE IS DEAD.
AND SO IT WAS.
ZZZAKK
IT DIED WITH SHEKO.

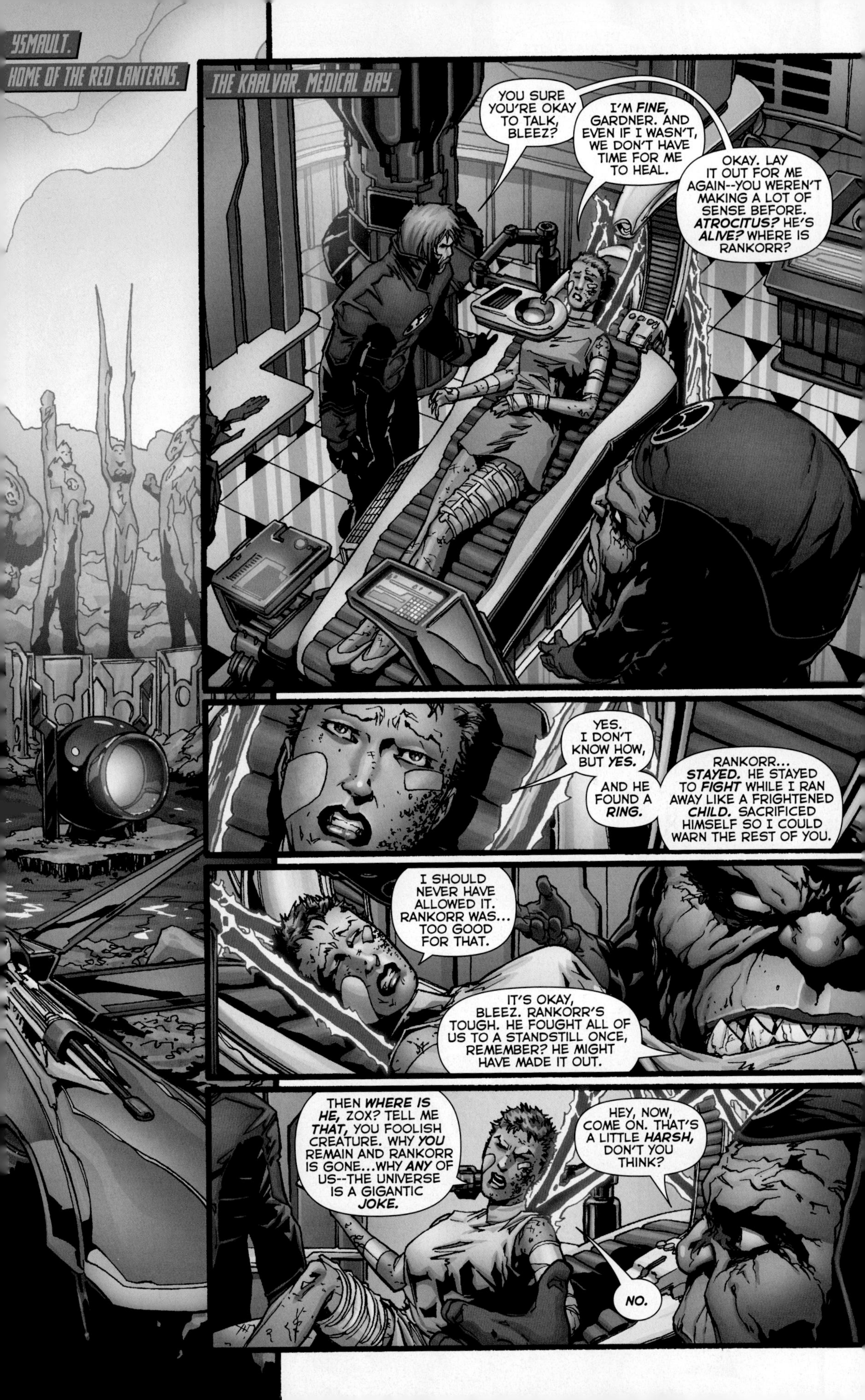
YSMAULT.
HOME OF THE RED LANTERNS.
THE KAALVAR. MEDICAL BAY.
YOU SURE YOU'RE OKAY TO TALK, BLEEZ?
I'M FINE, GARDNER. AND EVEN IF I WASN'T, WE DON'T HAVE TIME FOR ME TO HEAL.
OKAY. LAY IT OUT FOR ME AGAIN--YOU WEREN'T MAKING A LOT OF SENSE BEFORE. ATROCITUS? HE'S ALIVE? WHERE IS RANKORR?
YES. I DON'T KNOW HOW, BUT YES.
AND HE FOUND A RING.
RANKORR... STAYED. HE STAYED TO FIGHT WHILE I RAN AWAY LIKE A FRIGHTENED CHILD. SACRIFICED HIMSELF SO I COULD WARN THE REST OF YOU.
I SHOULD NEVER HAVE ALLOWED IT. RANKORR WAS... TOO GOOD FOR THAT.
IT'S OKAY, BLEEZ. RANKORR'S TOUGH. HE FOUGHT ALL OF US TO A STANDSTILL ONCE, REMEMBER? HE MIGHT HAVE MADE IT OUT.
THEN WHERE IS HE, ZOX? TELL ME THAT, YOU FOOLISH CREATURE. WHY YOU REMAIN AND RANKORR IS GONE...WHY ANY OF US--THE UNIVERSE IS A GIGANTIC JOKE.
HEY, NOW, COME ON. THAT'S A LITTLE HARSH, DON'T YOU THINK?
NO.

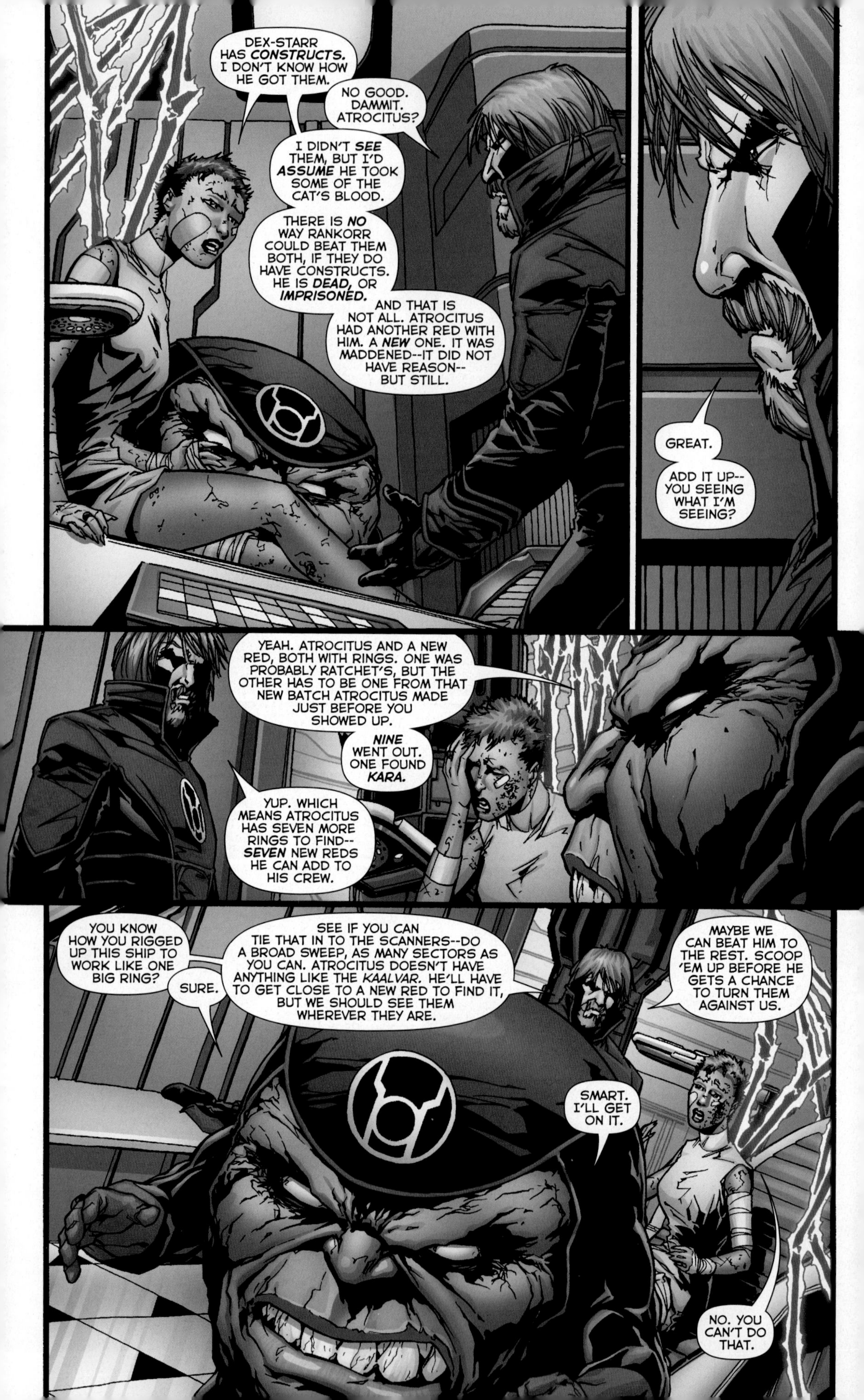

DEX-STARR HAS *CONSTRUCTS.* I DON'T KNOW HOW HE GOT THEM.
NO GOOD. DAMMIT. ATROCITUS?
I DIDN'T *SEE* THEM, BUT I'D *ASSUME* HE TOOK SOME OF THE CAT'S BLOOD.
THERE IS *NO* WAY RANKORR COULD BEAT THEM BOTH, IF THEY DO HAVE CONSTRUCTS. HE IS *DEAD,* OR *IMPRISONED.*
AND THAT IS NOT ALL. ATROCITUS HAD ANOTHER RED WITH HIM. A *NEW* ONE. IT WAS MADDENED--IT DID NOT HAVE REASON--BUT STILL.
GREAT.
ADD IT UP--YOU SEEING WHAT I'M SEEING?
YEAH. ATROCITUS AND A NEW RED, BOTH WITH RINGS. ONE WAS PROBABLY RATCHET'S, BUT THE OTHER HAS TO BE ONE FROM THAT NEW BATCH ATROCITUS MADE JUST BEFORE YOU SHOWED UP.
NINE WENT OUT. ONE FOUND *KARA.*
YUP. WHICH MEANS ATROCITUS HAS SEVEN MORE RINGS TO FIND--*SEVEN* NEW REDS HE CAN ADD TO HIS CREW.
YOU KNOW HOW YOU RIGGED UP THIS SHIP TO WORK LIKE ONE BIG RING?
SURE.
SEE IF YOU CAN TIE THAT IN TO THE SCANNERS--DO A BROAD SWEEP, AS MANY SECTORS AS YOU CAN. ATROCITUS DOESN'T HAVE ANYTHING LIKE THE *KAALVAR.* HE'LL HAVE TO GET CLOSE TO A NEW RED TO FIND IT, BUT WE SHOULD SEE THEM WHEREVER THEY ARE.
MAYBE WE CAN BEAT HIM TO THE REST. SCOOP 'EM UP BEFORE HE GETS A CHANCE TO TURN THEM AGAINST US.
SMART. I'LL GET ON IT.
NO. YOU CAN'T DO THAT.

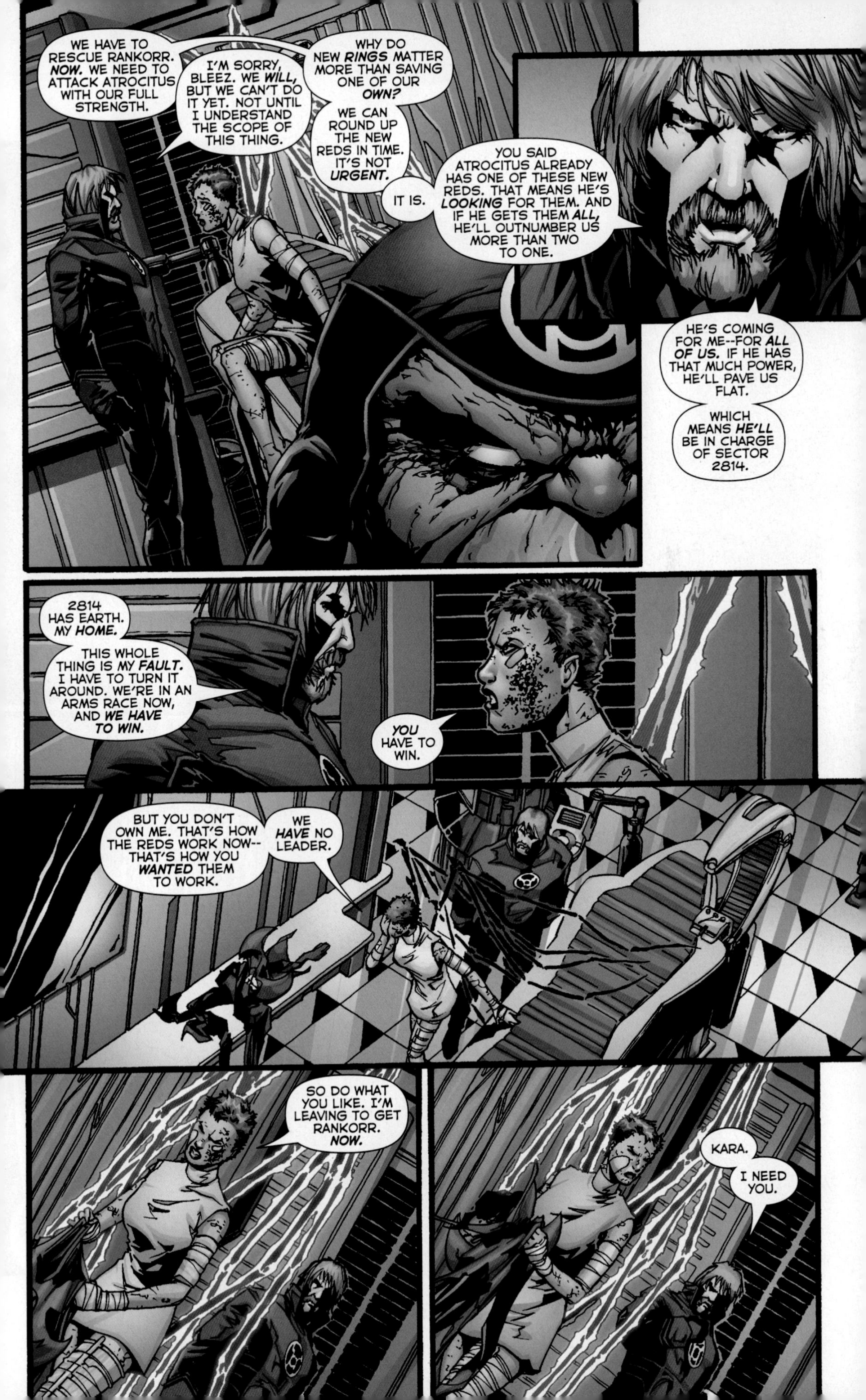
WE HAVE TO RESCUE RANKORR. NOW. WE NEED TO ATTACK ATROCITUS WITH OUR FULL STRENGTH.
I'M SORRY, BLEEZ. WE WILL, BUT WE CAN'T DO IT YET. NOT UNTIL I UNDERSTAND THE SCOPE OF THIS THING.
WHY DO NEW RINGS MATTER MORE THAN SAVING ONE OF OUR OWN?
WE CAN ROUND UP THE NEW REDS IN TIME. IT'S NOT URGENT.
IT IS.
YOU SAID ATROCITUS ALREADY HAS ONE OF THESE NEW REDS. THAT MEANS HE'S LOOKING FOR THEM. AND IF HE GETS THEM ALL, HE'LL OUTNUMBER US MORE THAN TWO TO ONE.
HE'S COMING FOR ME--FOR ALL OF US. IF HE HAS THAT MUCH POWER, HE'LL PAVE US FLAT.
WHICH MEANS HE'LL BE IN CHARGE OF SECTOR 2814.
2814 HAS EARTH. MY HOME.
THIS WHOLE THING IS MY FAULT. I HAVE TO TURN IT AROUND. WE'RE IN AN ARMS RACE NOW, AND WE HAVE TO WIN.
YOU HAVE TO WIN.
BUT YOU DON'T OWN ME. THAT'S HOW THE REDS WORK NOW--THAT'S HOW YOU WANTED THEM TO WORK.
WE HAVE NO LEADER.
SO DO WHAT YOU LIKE. I'M LEAVING TO GET RANKORR. NOW.
KARA.
I NEED YOU.

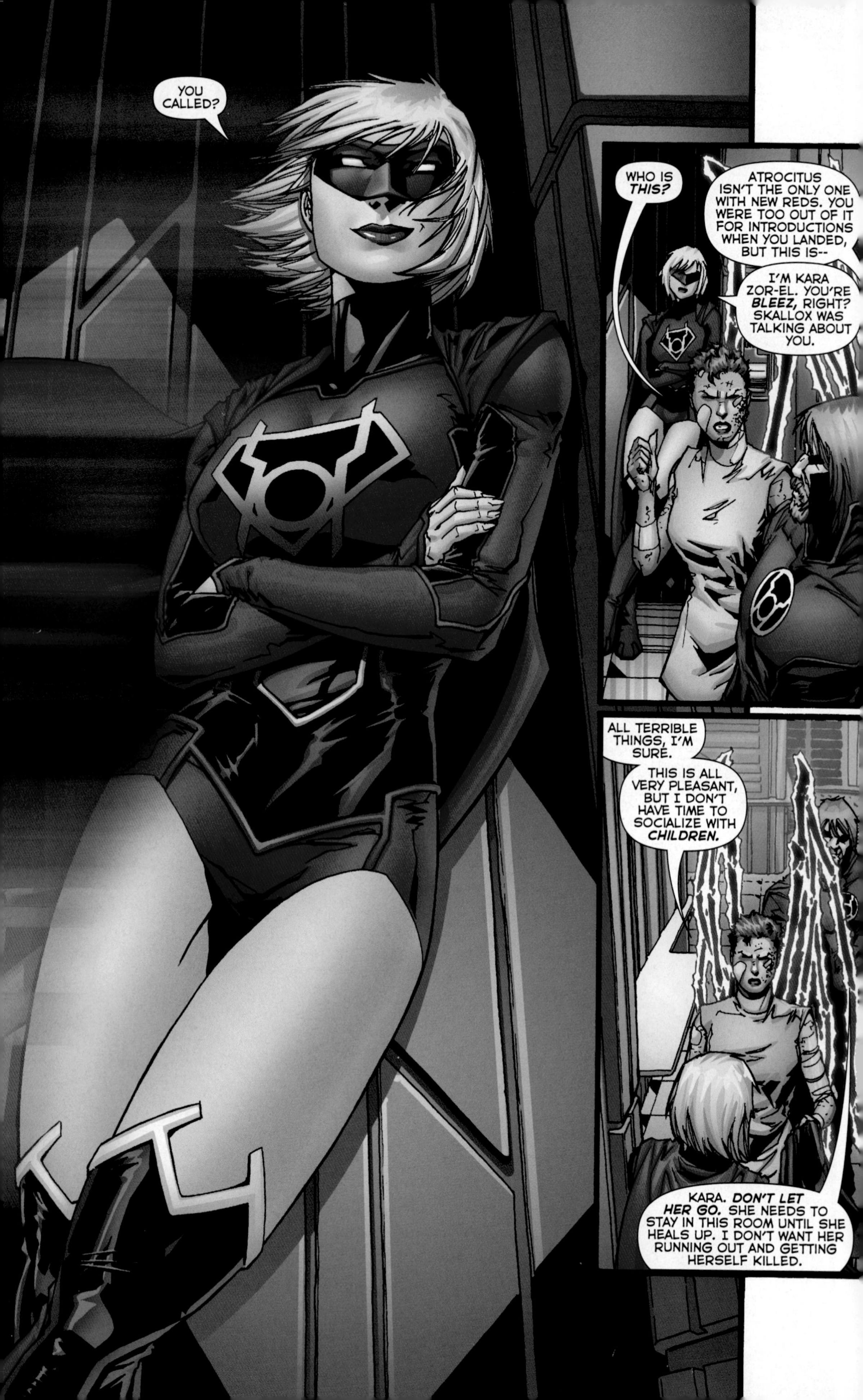
YOU CALLED?
WHO IS *THIS?*
ATROCITUS ISN'T THE ONLY ONE WITH NEW REDS. YOU WERE TOO OUT OF IT FOR INTRODUCTIONS WHEN YOU LANDED, BUT THIS IS--
I'M KARA ZOR-EL. YOU'RE *BLEEZ*, RIGHT? SKALLOX WAS TALKING ABOUT YOU.
ALL TERRIBLE THINGS, I'M SURE.
THIS IS ALL VERY PLEASANT, BUT I DON'T HAVE TIME TO SOCIALIZE WITH *CHILDREN.*
KARA. *DON'T LET HER GO.* SHE NEEDS TO STAY IN THIS ROOM UNTIL SHE HEALS UP. I DON'T WANT HER RUNNING OUT AND GETTING HERSELF KILLED.

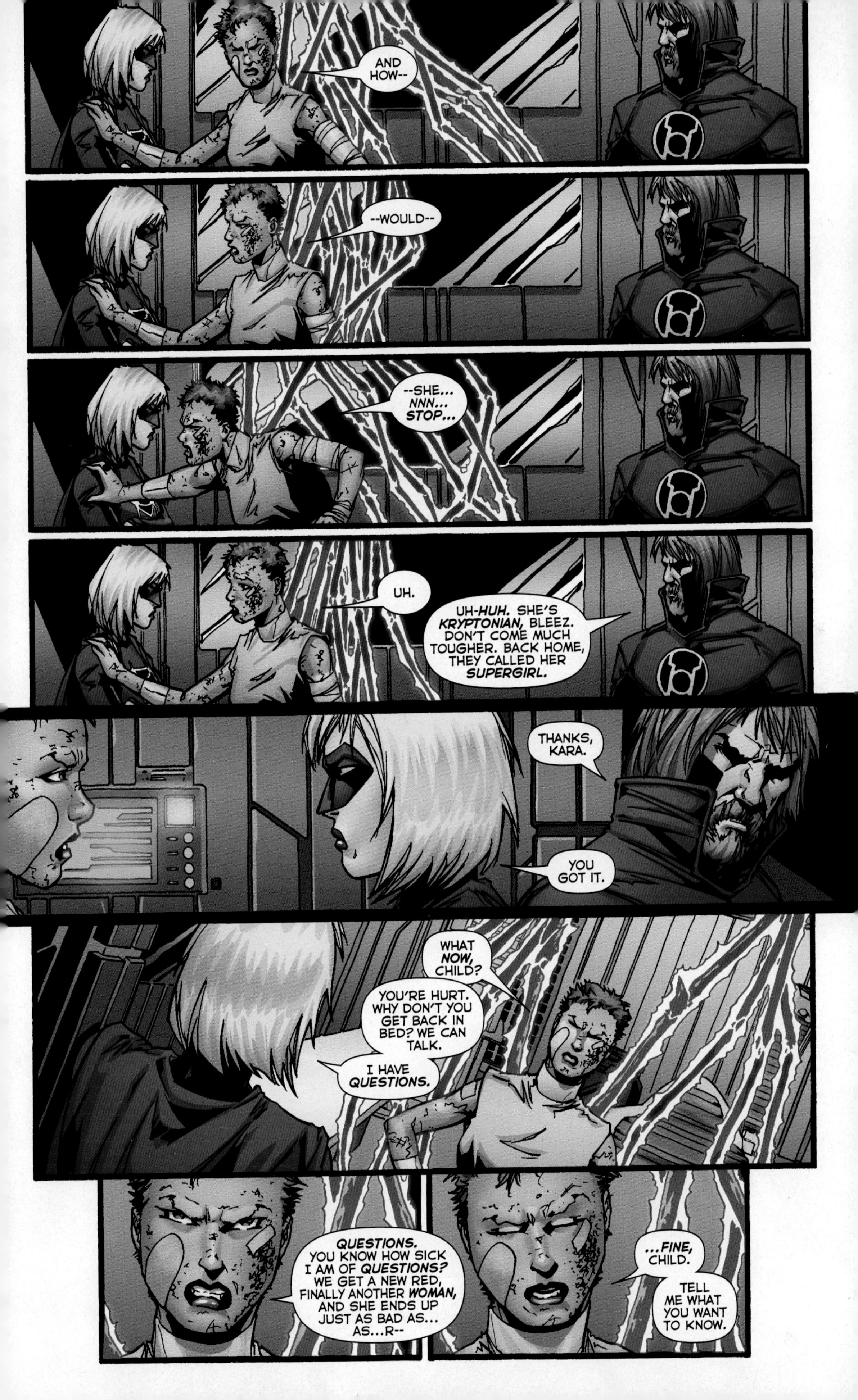
AND HOW--
--WOULD--
--SHE... NNN... STOP...
UH.
UH-HUH. SHE'S KRYPTONIAN, BLEEZ. DON'T COME MUCH TOUGHER. BACK HOME, THEY CALLED HER SUPERGIRL.
THANKS, KARA.
YOU GOT IT.
WHAT NOW, CHILD?
YOU'RE HURT. WHY DON'T YOU GET BACK IN BED? WE CAN TALK.
I HAVE QUESTIONS.
QUESTIONS. YOU KNOW HOW SICK I AM OF QUESTIONS? WE GET A NEW RED, FINALLY ANOTHER WOMAN, AND SHE ENDS UP JUST AS BAD AS... AS...R--
...FINE, CHILD.
TELL ME WHAT YOU WANT TO KNOW.

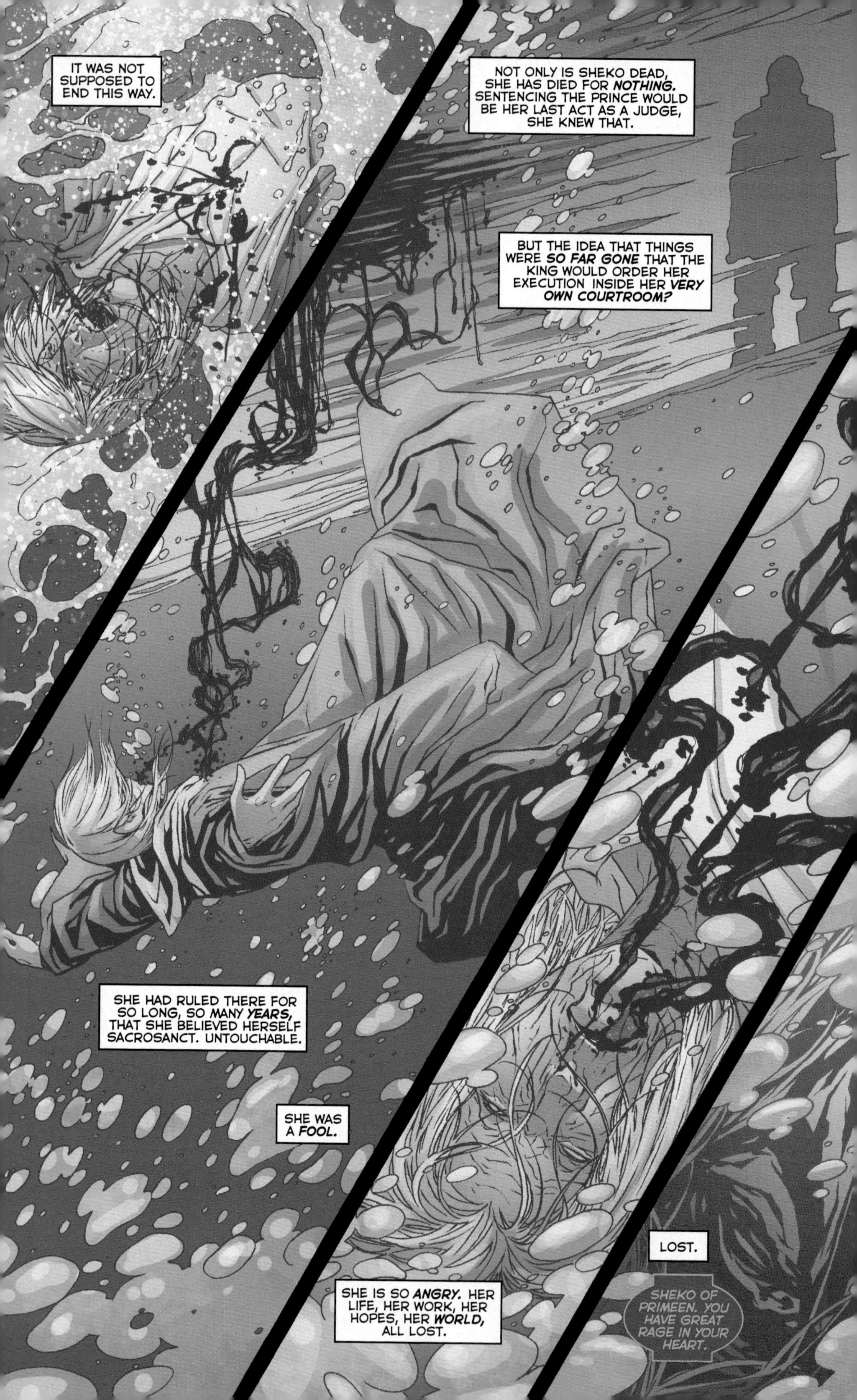
IT WAS NOT SUPPOSED TO END THIS WAY.
NOT ONLY IS SHEKO DEAD, SHE HAS DIED FOR *NOTHING.* SENTENCING THE PRINCE WOULD BE HER LAST ACT AS A JUDGE, SHE KNEW THAT.
BUT THE IDEA THAT THINGS WERE *SO FAR GONE* THAT THE KING WOULD ORDER HER EXECUTION INSIDE HER *VERY OWN COURTROOM?*
SHE HAD RULED THERE FOR SO LONG, SO MANY *YEARS,* THAT SHE BELIEVED HERSELF SACROSANCT. UNTOUCHABLE.
SHE WAS A *FOOL.*
SHE IS SO *ANGRY.* HER LIFE, HER WORK, HER HOPES, HER *WORLD,* ALL LOST.
LOST.
SHEKO OF PRIMEEN. YOU HAVE GREAT RAGE IN YOUR HEART.

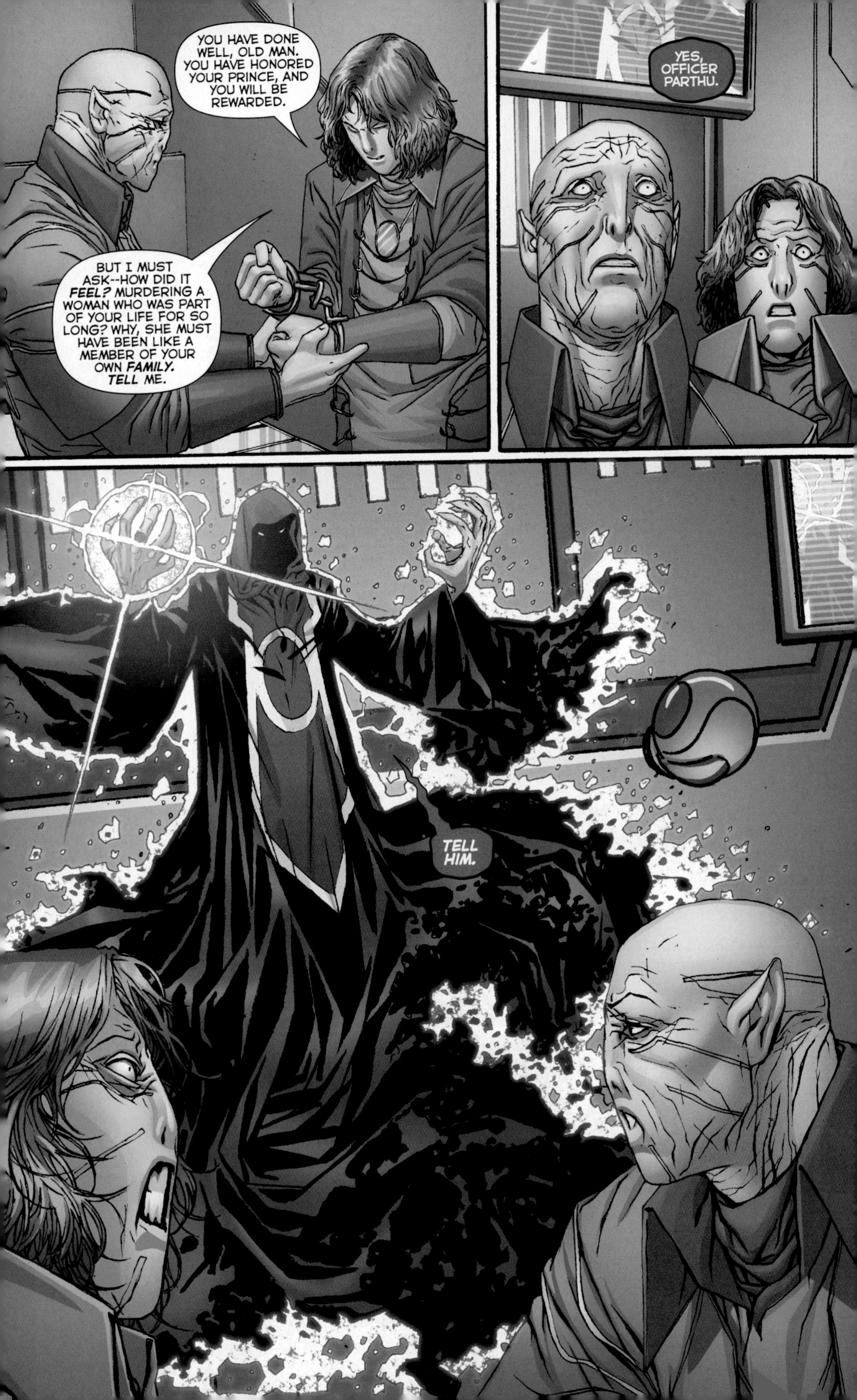
YOU HAVE DONE WELL, OLD MAN. YOU HAVE HONORED YOUR PRINCE, AND YOU WILL BE REWARDED.
BUT I MUST ASK--HOW DID IT FEEL? MURDERING A WOMAN WHO WAS PART OF YOUR LIFE FOR SO LONG? WHY, SHE MUST HAVE BEEN LIKE A MEMBER OF YOUR OWN FAMILY. TELL ME.
YES, OFFICER PARTHU.
TELL HIM.

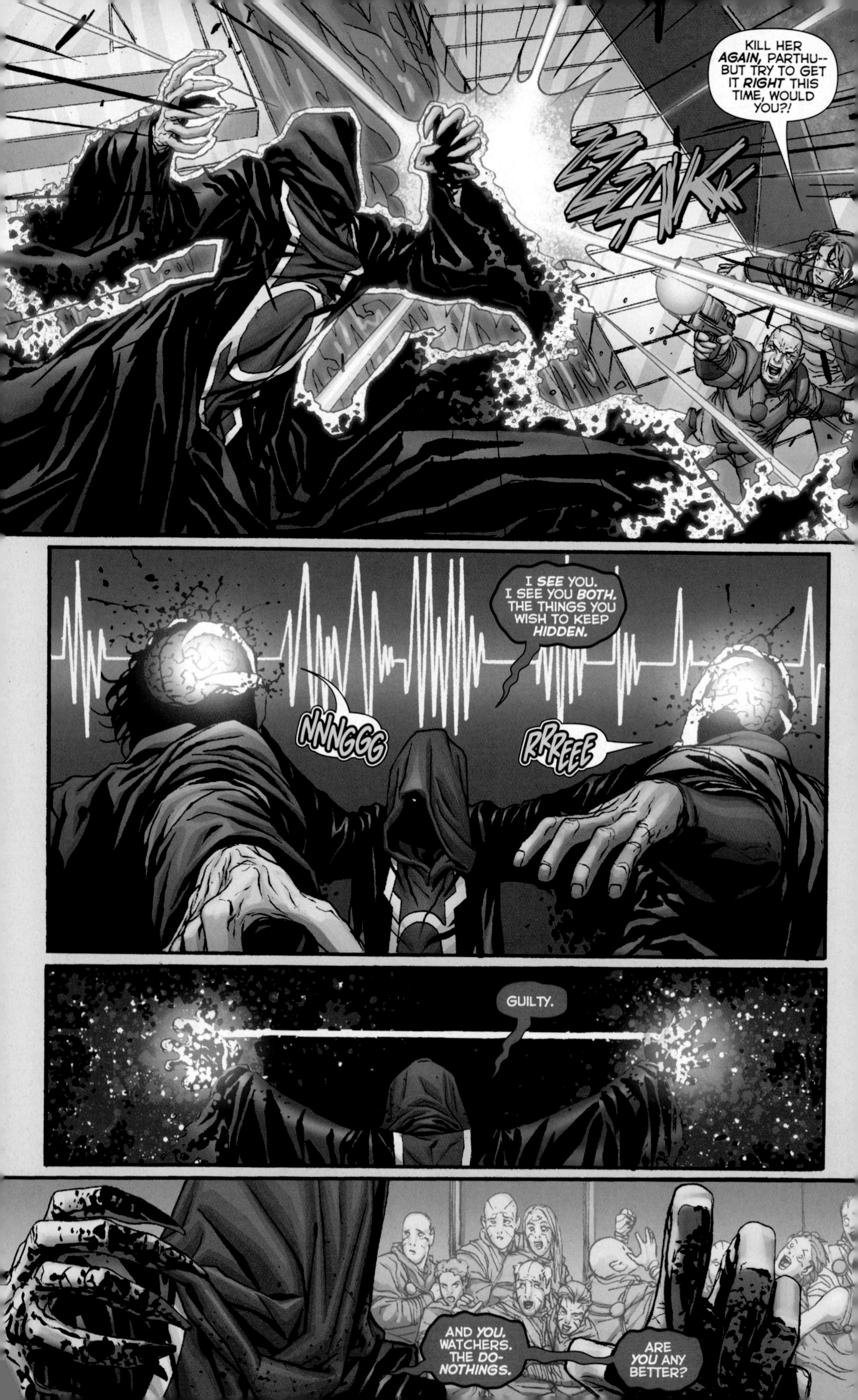
KILL HER AGAIN, PARTHU-- BUT TRY TO GET IT RIGHT THIS TIME, WOULD YOU?!
ZZZAKK
I SEE YOU. I SEE YOU BOTH. THE THINGS YOU WISH TO KEEP HIDDEN.
NNNGGG
RRREEE
GUILTY.
AND YOU. WATCHERS. THE DO-NOTHINGS.
ARE YOU ANY BETTER?

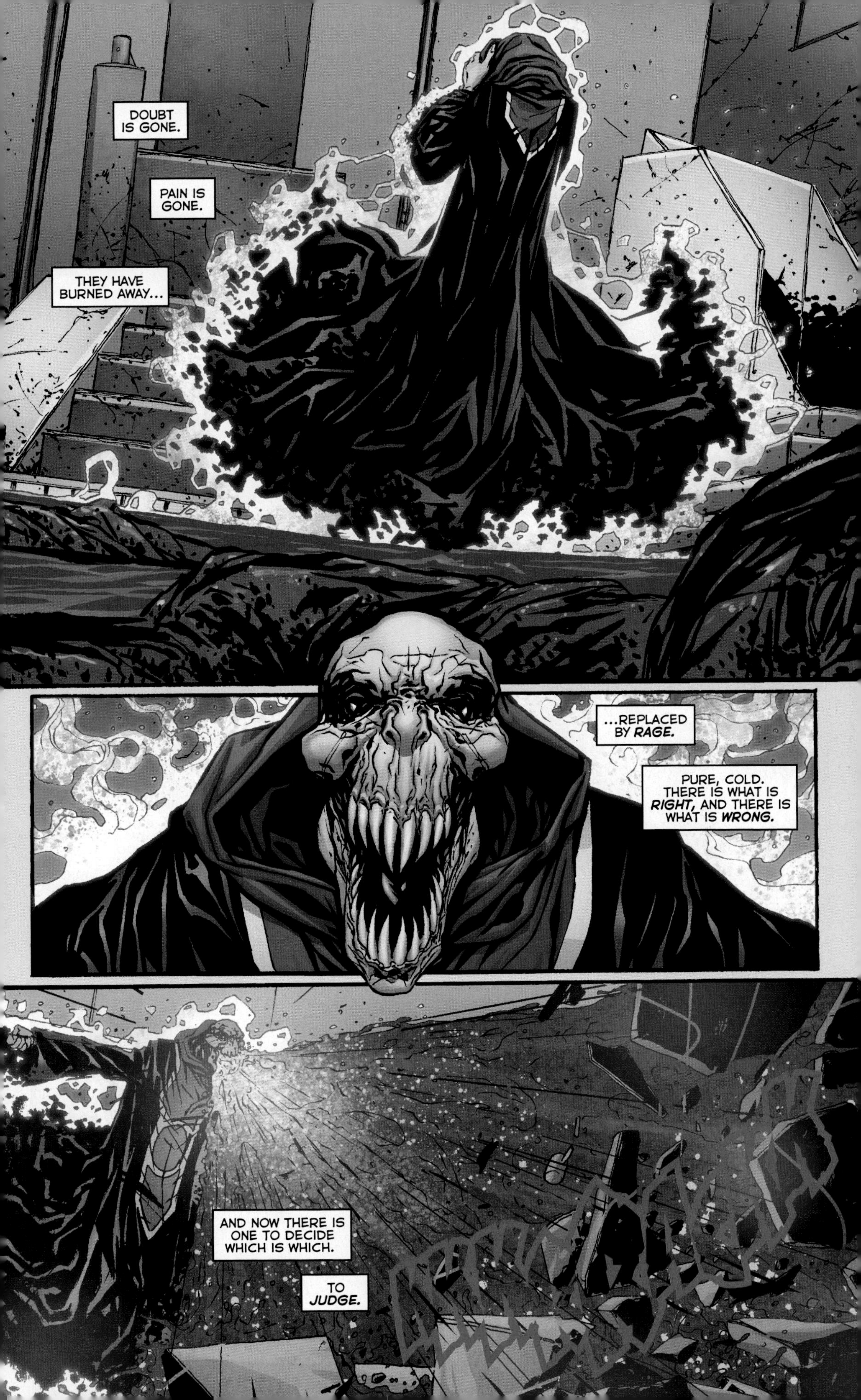
DOUBT IS GONE.
PAIN IS GONE.
THEY HAVE BURNED AWAY...
...REPLACED BY *RAGE.*
PURE, COLD. THERE IS WHAT IS *RIGHT,* AND THERE IS WHAT IS *WRONG.*
AND NOW THERE IS ONE TO DECIDE WHICH IS WHICH.
TO *JUDGE.*

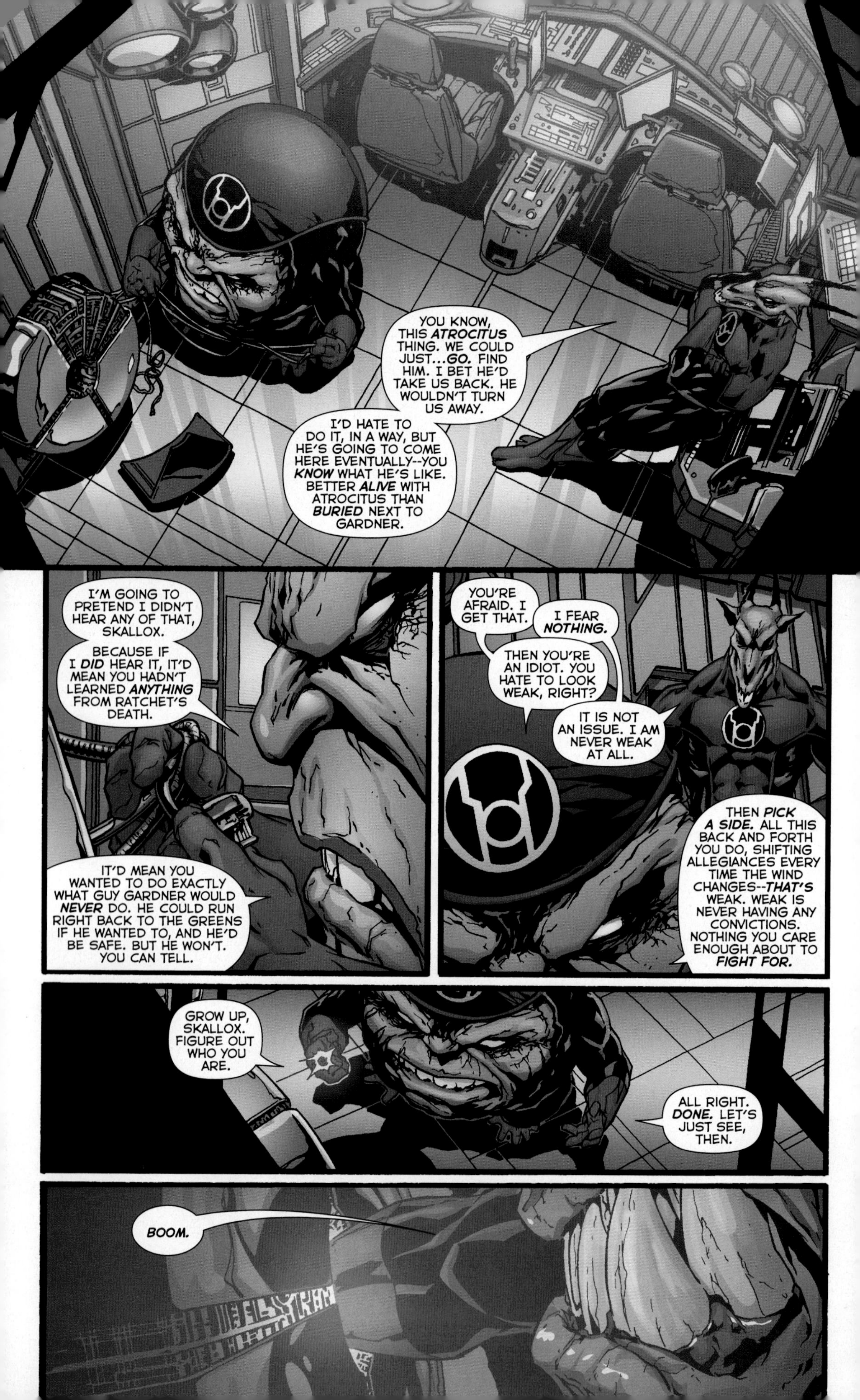
YOU KNOW, THIS ATROCITUS THING. WE COULD JUST...GO. FIND HIM. I BET HE'D TAKE US BACK. HE WOULDN'T TURN US AWAY.
I'D HATE TO DO IT, IN A WAY, BUT HE'S GOING TO COME HERE EVENTUALLY--YOU KNOW WHAT HE'S LIKE. BETTER ALIVE WITH ATROCITUS THAN BURIED NEXT TO GARDNER.
I'M GOING TO PRETEND I DIDN'T HEAR ANY OF THAT, SKALLOX.
BECAUSE IF I DID HEAR IT, IT'D MEAN YOU HADN'T LEARNED ANYTHING FROM RATCHET'S DEATH.
IT'D MEAN YOU WANTED TO DO EXACTLY WHAT GUY GARDNER WOULD NEVER DO. HE COULD RUN RIGHT BACK TO THE GREENS IF HE WANTED TO, AND HE'D BE SAFE. BUT HE WON'T. YOU CAN TELL.
YOU'RE AFRAID. I GET THAT.
I FEAR NOTHING.
THEN YOU'RE AN IDIOT. YOU HATE TO LOOK WEAK, RIGHT?
IT IS NOT AN ISSUE. I AM NEVER WEAK AT ALL.
THEN PICK A SIDE. ALL THIS BACK AND FORTH YOU DO, SHIFTING ALLEGIANCES EVERY TIME THE WIND CHANGES--THAT'S WEAK. WEAK IS NEVER HAVING ANY CONVICTIONS. NOTHING YOU CARE ENOUGH ABOUT TO FIGHT FOR.
GROW UP, SKALLOX. FIGURE OUT WHO YOU ARE.
ALL RIGHT. DONE. LET'S JUST SEE, THEN.
BOOM.

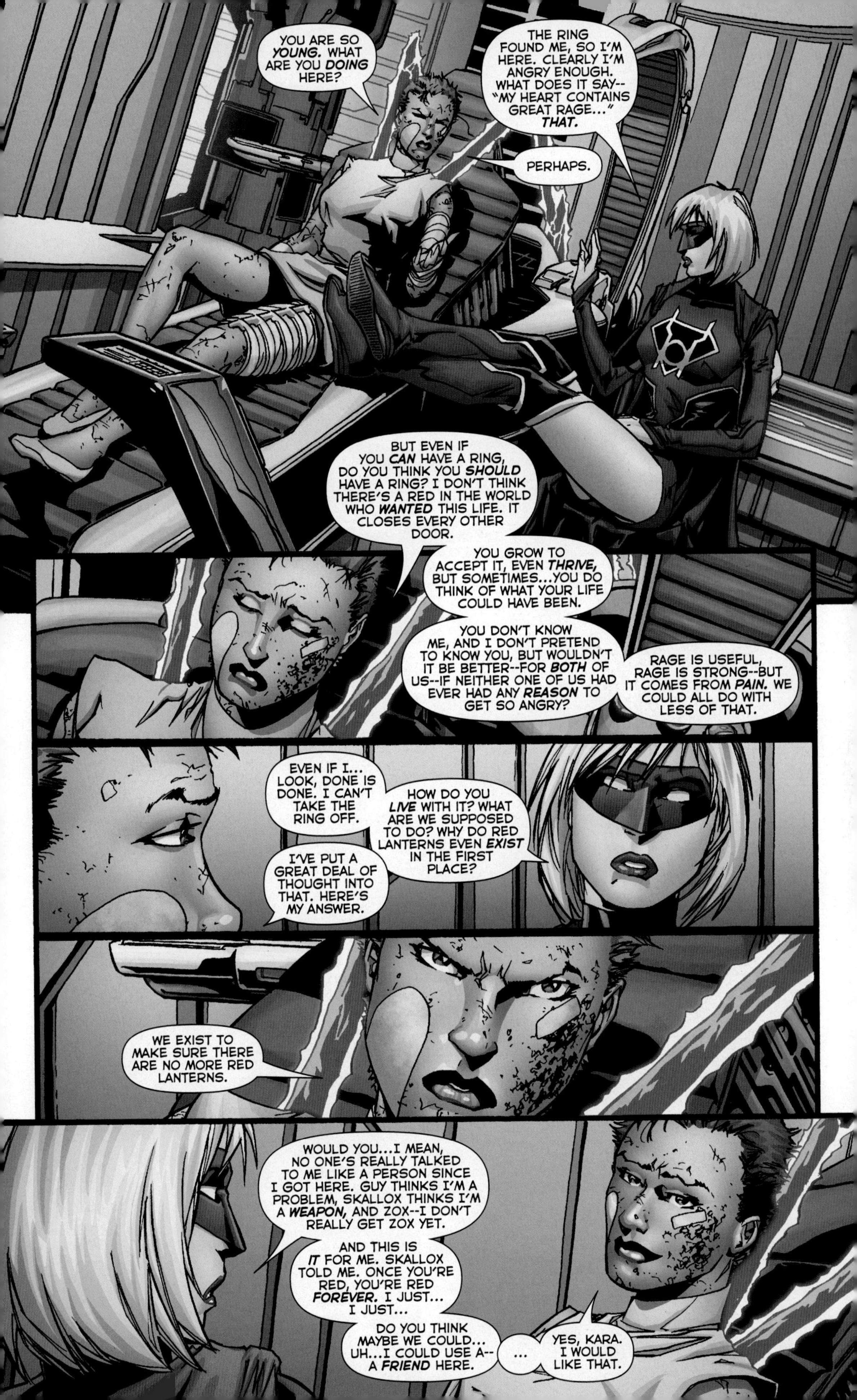

YOU ARE SO YOUNG. WHAT ARE YOU DOING HERE?
THE RING FOUND ME, SO I'M HERE. CLEARLY I'M ANGRY ENOUGH. WHAT DOES IT SAY--"MY HEART CONTAINS GREAT RAGE..." THAT.
PERHAPS.
BUT EVEN IF YOU CAN HAVE A RING, DO YOU THINK YOU SHOULD HAVE A RING? I DON'T THINK THERE'S A RED IN THE WORLD WHO WANTED THIS LIFE. IT CLOSES EVERY OTHER DOOR.
YOU GROW TO ACCEPT IT, EVEN THRIVE, BUT SOMETIMES...YOU DO THINK OF WHAT YOUR LIFE COULD HAVE BEEN.
YOU DON'T KNOW ME, AND I DON'T PRETEND TO KNOW YOU, BUT WOULDN'T IT BE BETTER--FOR BOTH OF US--IF NEITHER ONE OF US HAD EVER HAD ANY REASON TO GET SO ANGRY?
RAGE IS USEFUL, RAGE IS STRONG--BUT IT COMES FROM PAIN. WE COULD ALL DO WITH LESS OF THAT.
EVEN IF I... LOOK, DONE IS DONE. I CAN'T TAKE THE RING OFF.
HOW DO YOU LIVE WITH IT? WHAT ARE WE SUPPOSED TO DO? WHY DO RED LANTERNS EVEN EXIST IN THE FIRST PLACE?
I'VE PUT A GREAT DEAL OF THOUGHT INTO THAT. HERE'S MY ANSWER.
WE EXIST TO MAKE SURE THERE ARE NO MORE RED LANTERNS.
WOULD YOU...I MEAN, NO ONE'S REALLY TALKED TO ME LIKE A PERSON SINCE I GOT HERE. GUY THINKS I'M A PROBLEM, SKALLOX THINKS I'M A WEAPON, AND ZOX--I DON'T REALLY GET ZOX YET.
AND THIS IS IT FOR ME. SKALLOX TOLD ME. ONCE YOU'RE RED, YOU'RE RED FOREVER. I JUST... I JUST...
DO YOU THINK MAYBE WE COULD... UH...I COULD USE A-- A FRIEND HERE.
...
YES, KARA. I WOULD LIKE THAT.

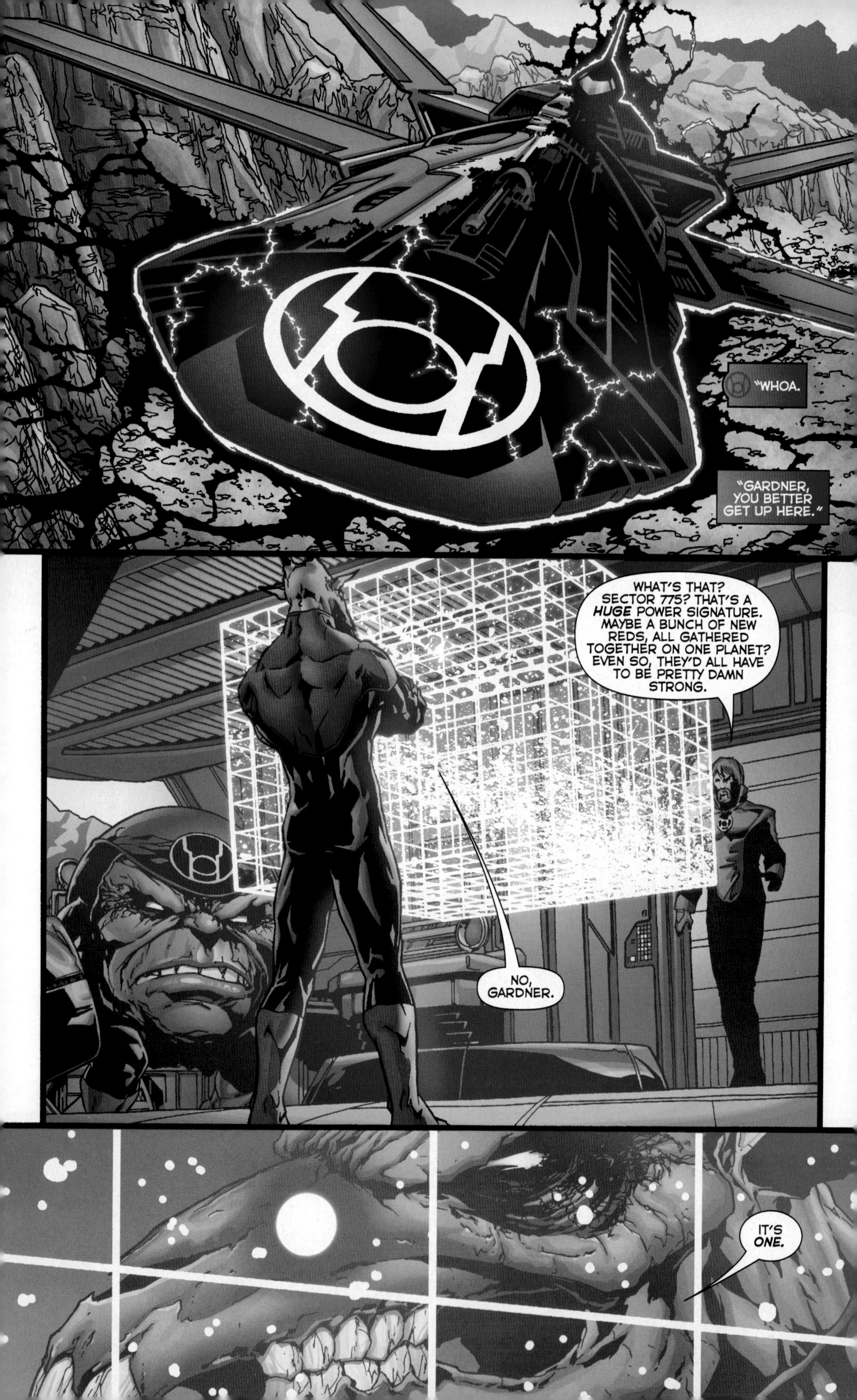

"WHOA.
"GARDNER, YOU BETTER GET UP HERE."
WHAT'S THAT? SECTOR 775? THAT'S A HUGE POWER SIGNATURE. MAYBE A BUNCH OF NEW REDS, ALL GATHERED TOGETHER ON ONE PLANET? EVEN SO, THEY'D ALL HAVE TO BE PRETTY DAMN STRONG.
NO, GARDNER.
IT'S ONE.

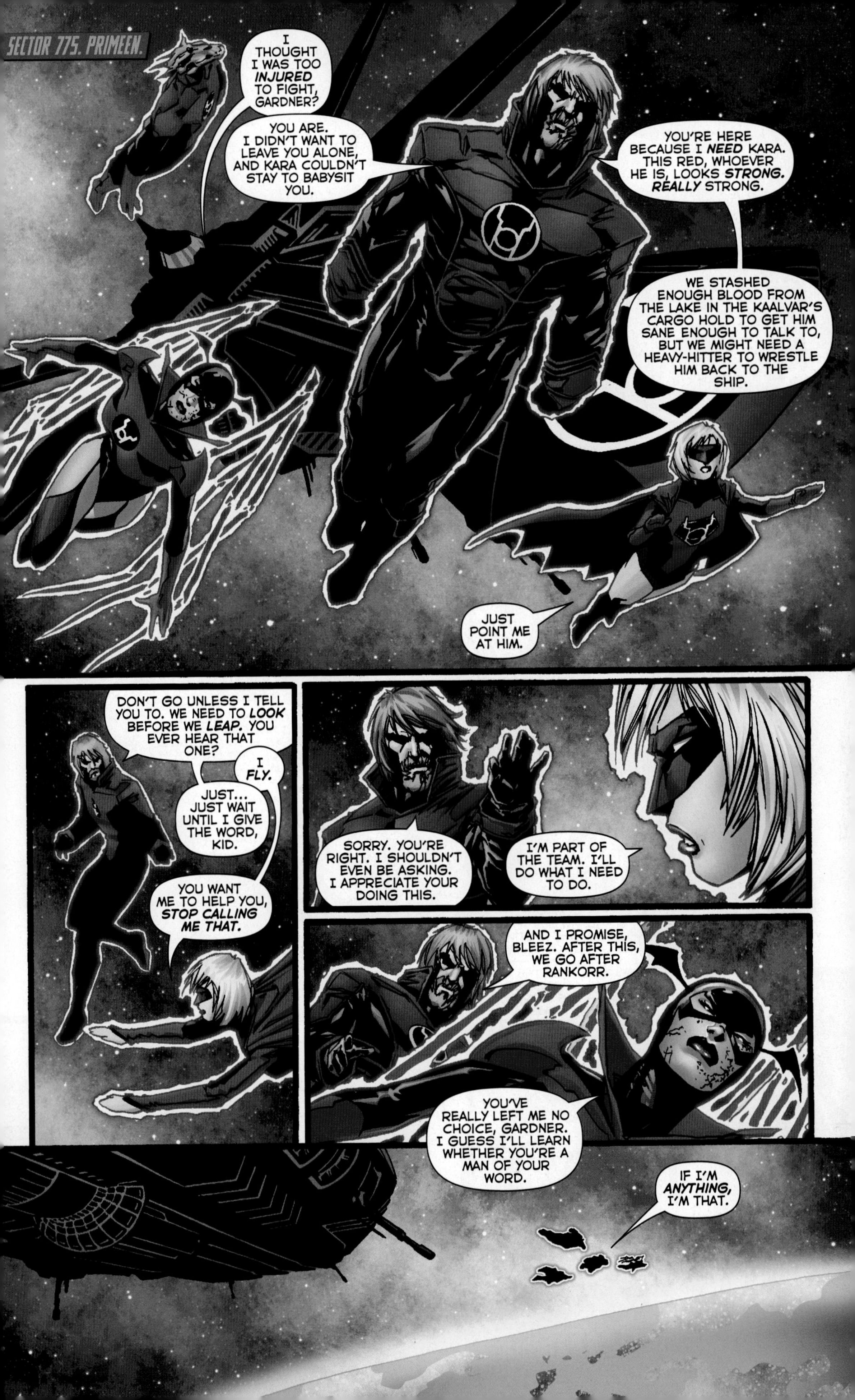
SECTOR 775. PRIMEEN.
I THOUGHT I WAS TOO INJURED TO FIGHT, GARDNER?
YOU ARE. I DIDN'T WANT TO LEAVE YOU ALONE, AND KARA COULDN'T STAY TO BABYSIT YOU.
YOU'RE HERE BECAUSE I NEED KARA. THIS RED, WHOEVER HE IS, LOOKS STRONG. REALLY STRONG.
WE STASHED ENOUGH BLOOD FROM THE LAKE IN THE KAALVAR'S CARGO HOLD TO GET HIM SANE ENOUGH TO TALK TO, BUT WE MIGHT NEED A HEAVY-HITTER TO WRESTLE HIM BACK TO THE SHIP.
JUST POINT ME AT HIM.
DON'T GO UNLESS I TELL YOU TO. WE NEED TO LOOK BEFORE WE LEAP. YOU EVER HEAR THAT ONE?
I FLY.
JUST... JUST WAIT UNTIL I GIVE THE WORD, KID.
YOU WANT ME TO HELP YOU, STOP CALLING ME THAT.
SORRY. YOU'RE RIGHT. I SHOULDN'T EVEN BE ASKING. I APPRECIATE YOUR DOING THIS.
I'M PART OF THE TEAM. I'LL DO WHAT I NEED TO DO.
AND I PROMISE, BLEEZ. AFTER THIS, WE GO AFTER RANKORR.
YOU'VE REALLY LEFT ME NO CHOICE, GARDNER. I GUESS I'LL LEARN WHETHER YOU'RE A MAN OF YOUR WORD.
IF I'M ANYTHING, I'M THAT.

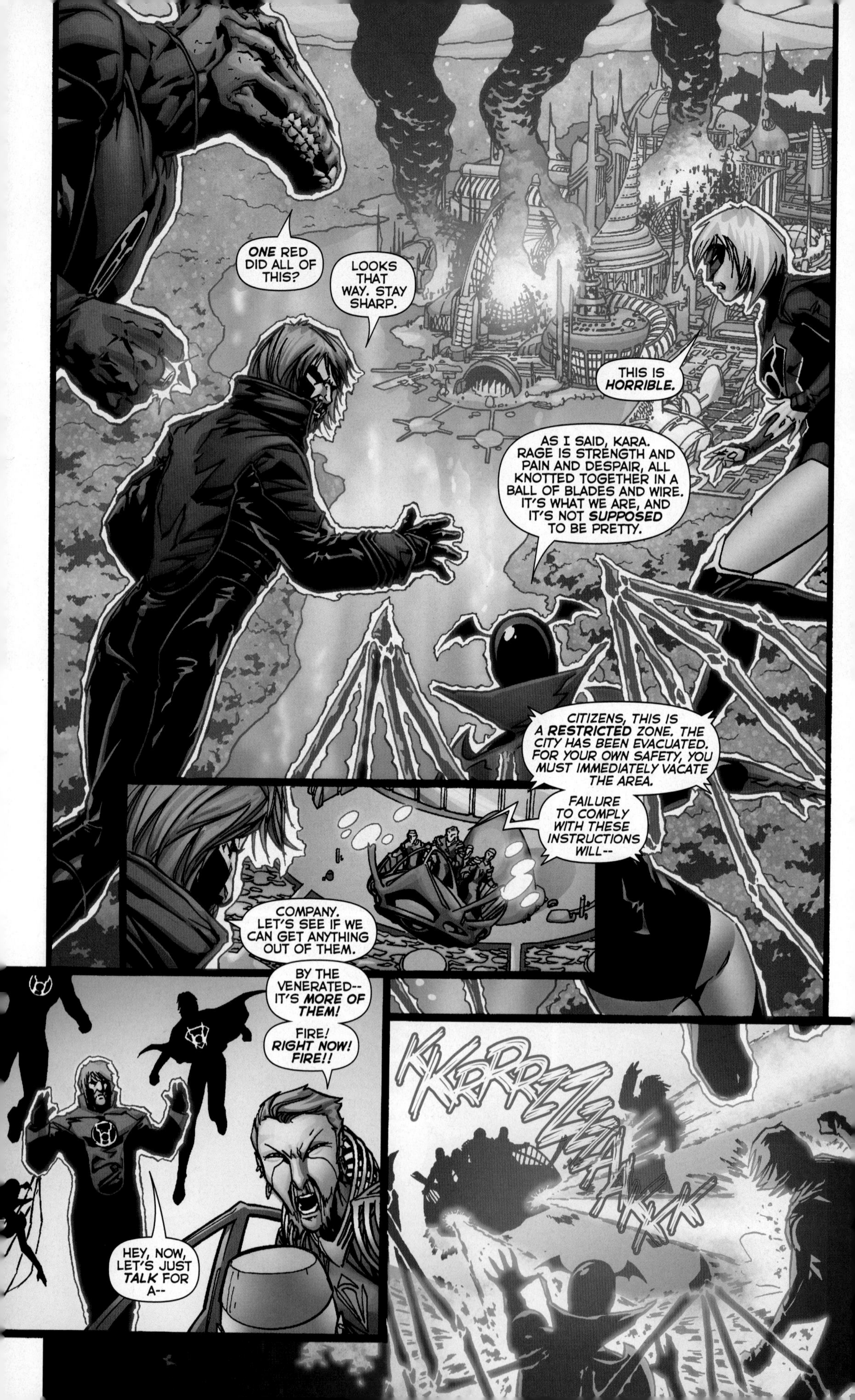
ONE RED DID ALL OF THIS?
LOOKS THAT WAY. STAY SHARP.
THIS IS HORRIBLE.
AS I SAID, KARA. RAGE IS STRENGTH AND PAIN AND DESPAIR, ALL KNOTTED TOGETHER IN A BALL OF BLADES AND WIRE. IT'S WHAT WE ARE, AND IT'S NOT SUPPOSED TO BE PRETTY.
CITIZENS, THIS IS A RESTRICTED ZONE. THE CITY HAS BEEN EVACUATED. FOR YOUR OWN SAFETY, YOU MUST IMMEDIATELY VACATE THE AREA.
FAILURE TO COMPLY WITH THESE INSTRUCTIONS WILL--
COMPANY. LET'S SEE IF WE CAN GET ANYTHING OUT OF THEM.
BY THE VENERATED-- IT'S MORE OF THEM!
FIRE! RIGHT NOW! FIRE!!
HEY, NOW, LET'S JUST TALK FOR A--

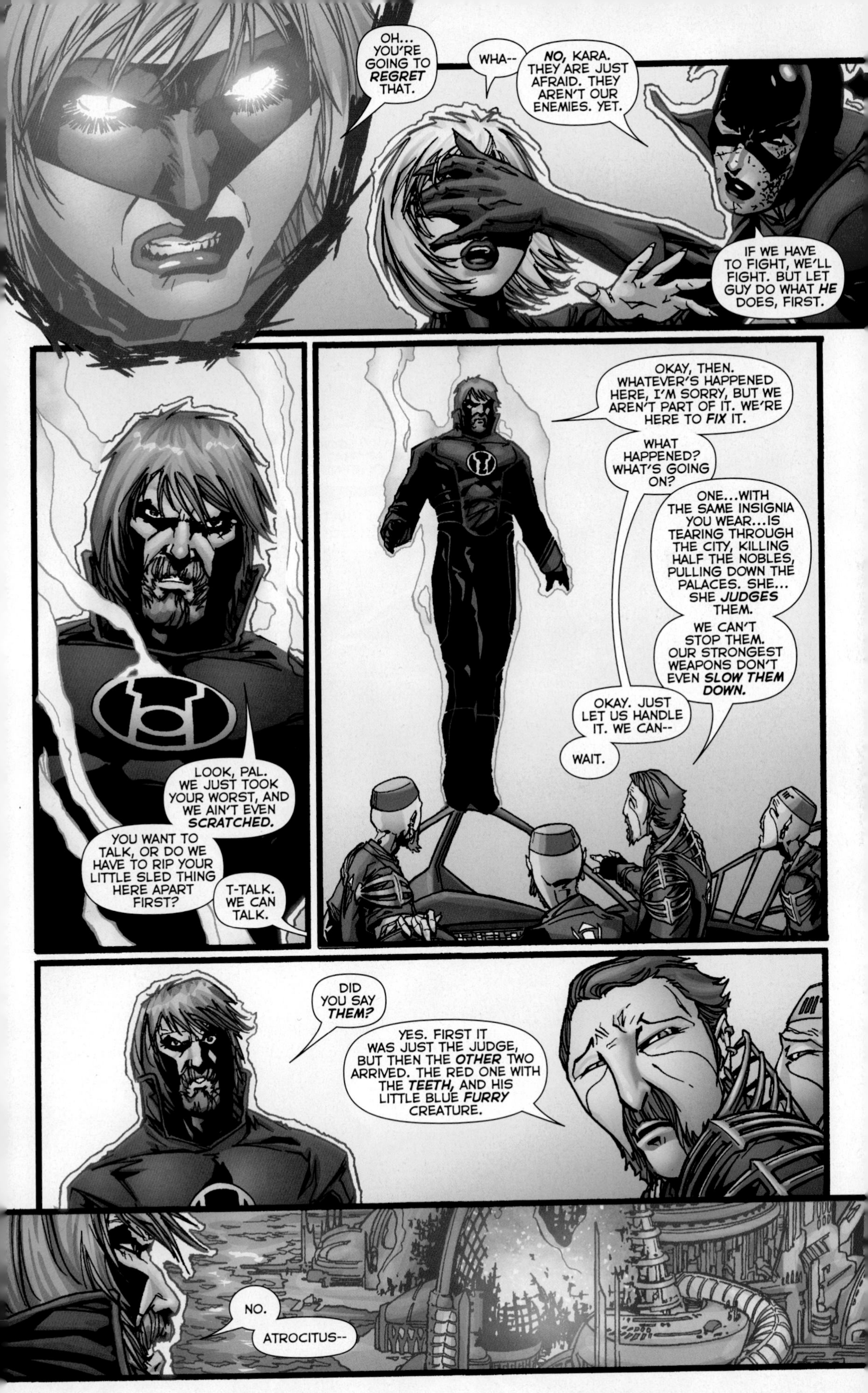
OH... YOU'RE GOING TO REGRET THAT.
WHA--
NO, KARA. THEY ARE JUST AFRAID. THEY AREN'T OUR ENEMIES. YET.
IF WE HAVE TO FIGHT, WE'LL FIGHT. BUT LET GUY DO WHAT HE DOES, FIRST.
LOOK, PAL. WE JUST TOOK YOUR WORST, AND WE AIN'T EVEN SCRATCHED.
YOU WANT TO TALK, OR DO WE HAVE TO RIP YOUR LITTLE SLED THING HERE APART FIRST?
T-TALK. WE CAN TALK.
OKAY, THEN. WHATEVER'S HAPPENED HERE, I'M SORRY, BUT WE AREN'T PART OF IT. WE'RE HERE TO FIX IT.
WHAT HAPPENED? WHAT'S GOING ON?
ONE...WITH THE SAME INSIGNIA YOU WEAR...IS TEARING THROUGH THE CITY, KILLING HALF THE NOBLES, PULLING DOWN THE PALACES. SHE... SHE JUDGES THEM.
WE CAN'T STOP THEM. OUR STRONGEST WEAPONS DON'T EVEN SLOW THEM DOWN.
OKAY. JUST LET US HANDLE IT. WE CAN--
WAIT.
DID YOU SAY THEM?
YES. FIRST IT WAS JUST THE JUDGE, BUT THEN THE OTHER TWO ARRIVED. THE RED ONE WITH THE TEETH, AND HIS LITTLE BLUE FURRY CREATURE.
NO.
ATROCITUS--

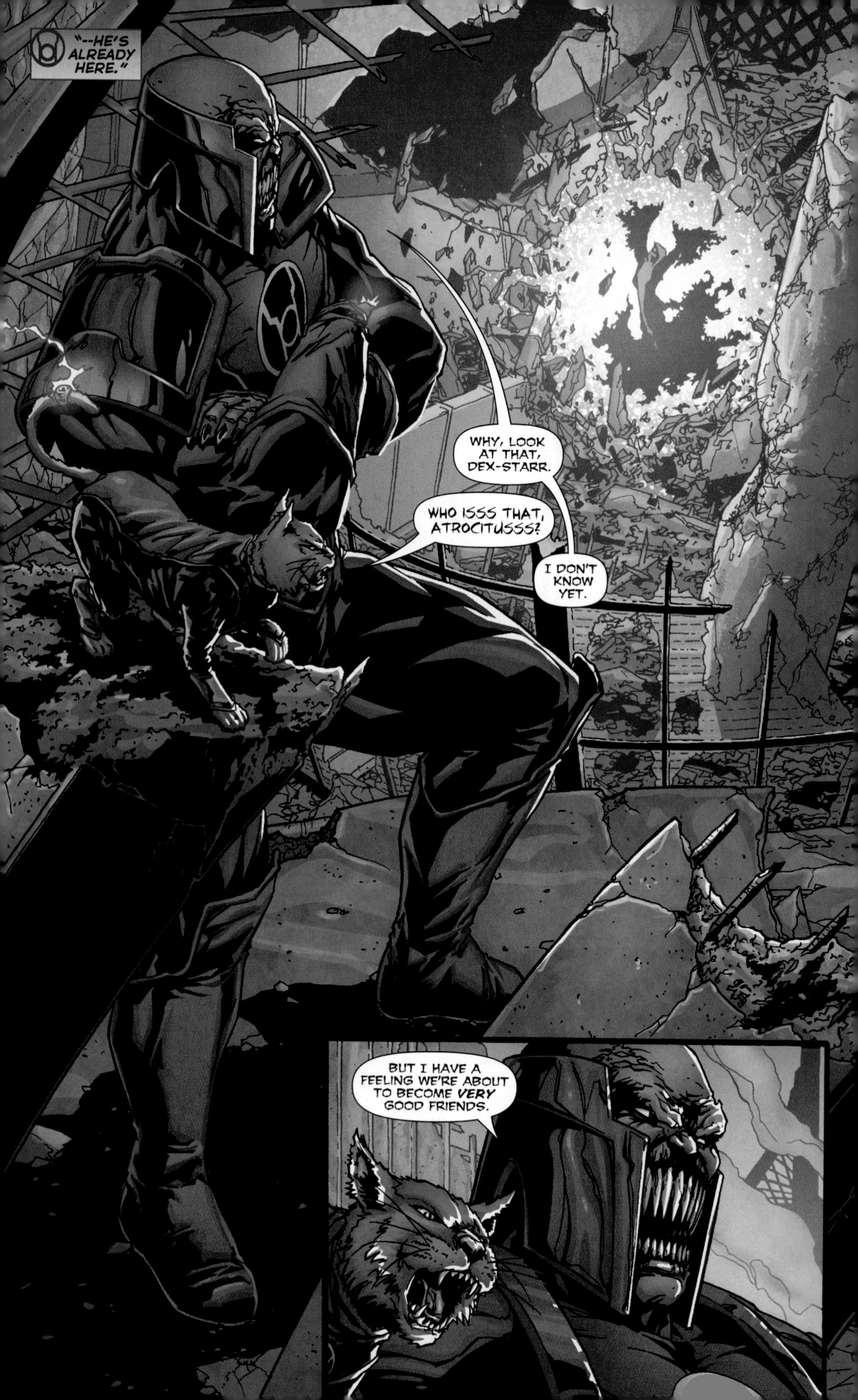
"--HE'S ALREADY HERE."
WHY, LOOK AT THAT, DEX-STARR.
WHO ISSS THAT, ATROCITUSSS?
I DON'T KNOW YET.
BUT I HAVE A FEELING WE'RE ABOUT TO BECOME *VERY* GOOD FRIENDS.

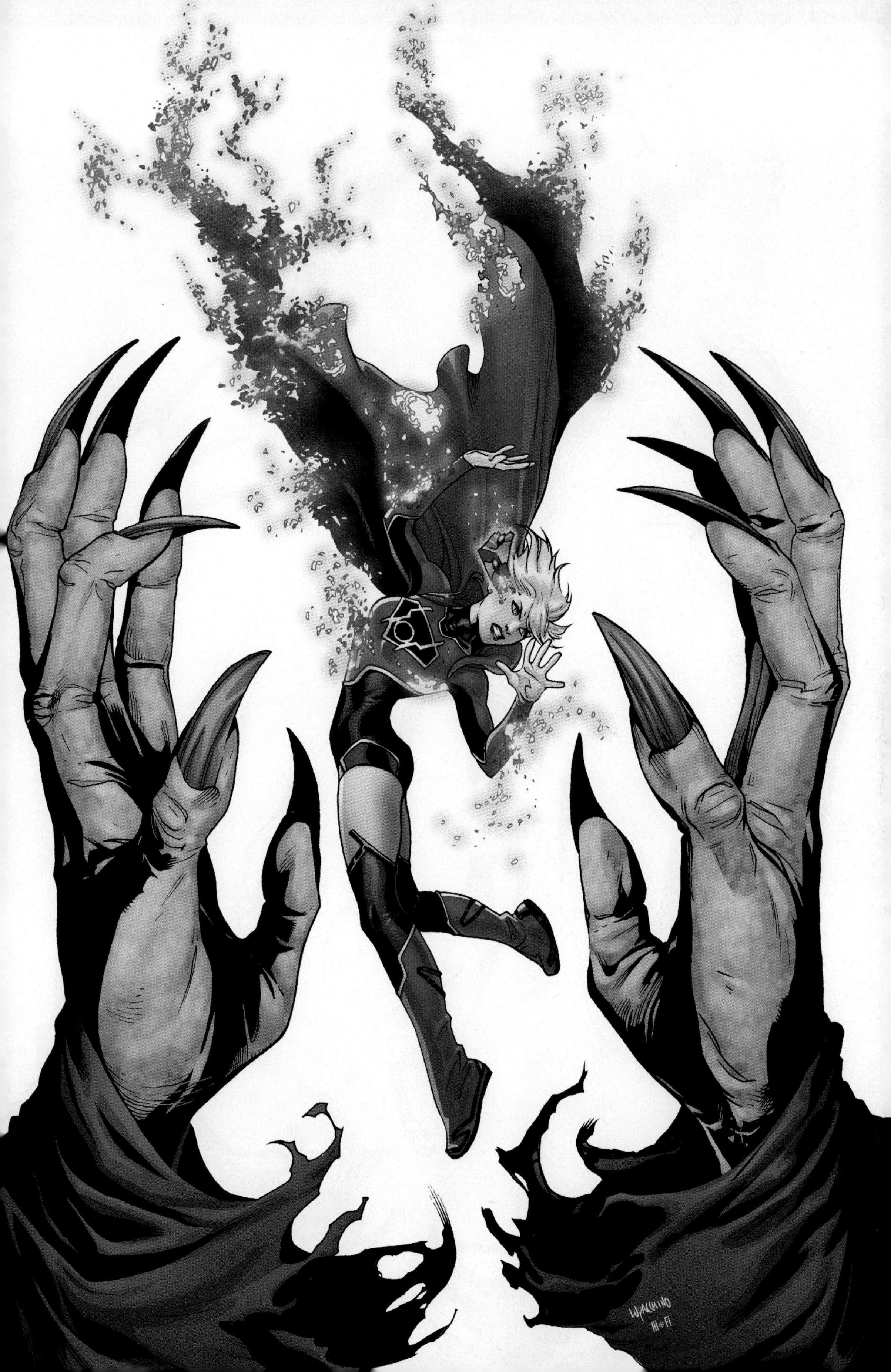

TONY BEDARD writer **EMANUELA LUPACCHINO RAY MCCARTHY** (pages 119-124, 126-131, 134-135)
GUILLERMO ORTEGO (page 137) **YILDIRAY CINAR** (pages 132-134) **CORY SMITH** (pages 125-138) artists
HI-FI (pages 119-131, 135-137) **YILDIRAY CINAR** (pages 132-134) colorists **ROB LEIGH** letterer cover art by **EMANUELA LUPACCHINO** and **HI-FI**

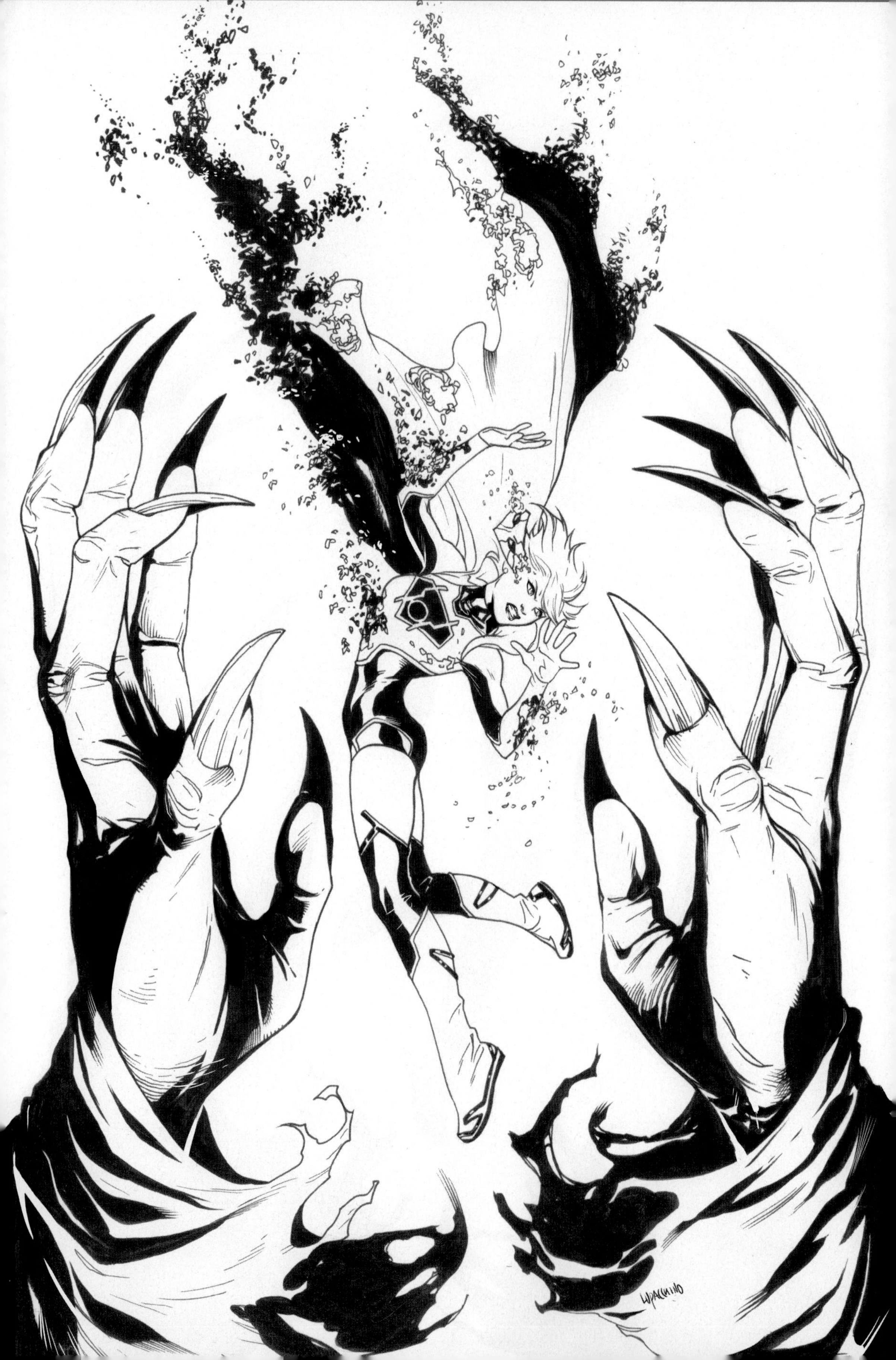
LUPACCHINO

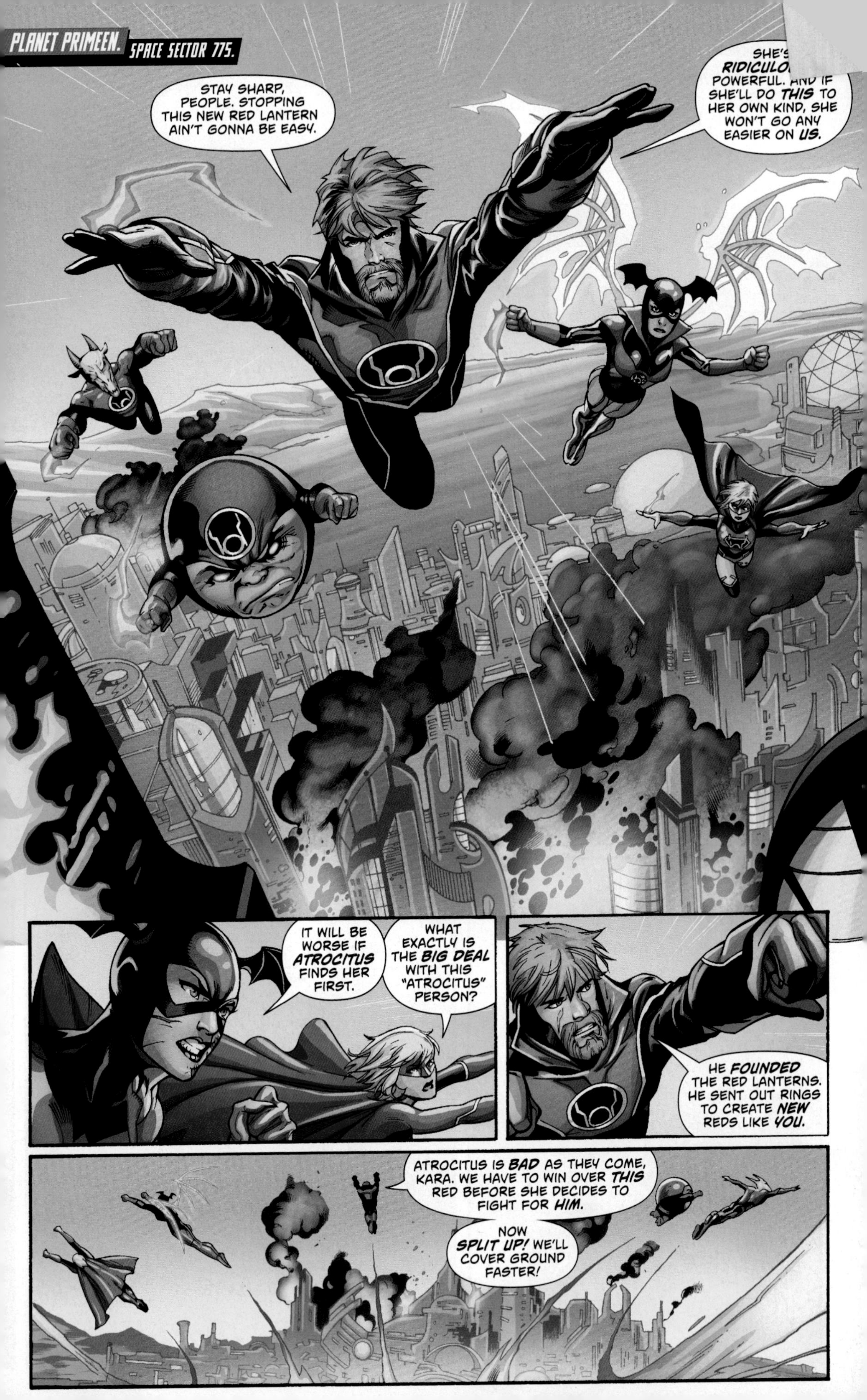
PLANET PRIMEEN. SPACE SECTOR 775.
STAY SHARP, PEOPLE. STOPPING THIS NEW RED LANTERN AIN'T GONNA BE EASY.
SHE'S RIDICULO POWERFUL. AND IF SHE'LL DO THIS TO HER OWN KIND, SHE WON'T GO ANY EASIER ON US.
IT WILL BE WORSE IF ATROCITUS FINDS HER FIRST.
WHAT EXACTLY IS THE BIG DEAL WITH THIS "ATROCITUS" PERSON?
HE FOUNDED THE RED LANTERNS. HE SENT OUT RINGS TO CREATE NEW REDS LIKE YOU.
ATROCITUS IS BAD AS THEY COME, KARA. WE HAVE TO WIN OVER THIS RED BEFORE SHE DECIDES TO FIGHT FOR HIM.
NOW SPLIT UP! WE'LL COVER GROUND FASTER!

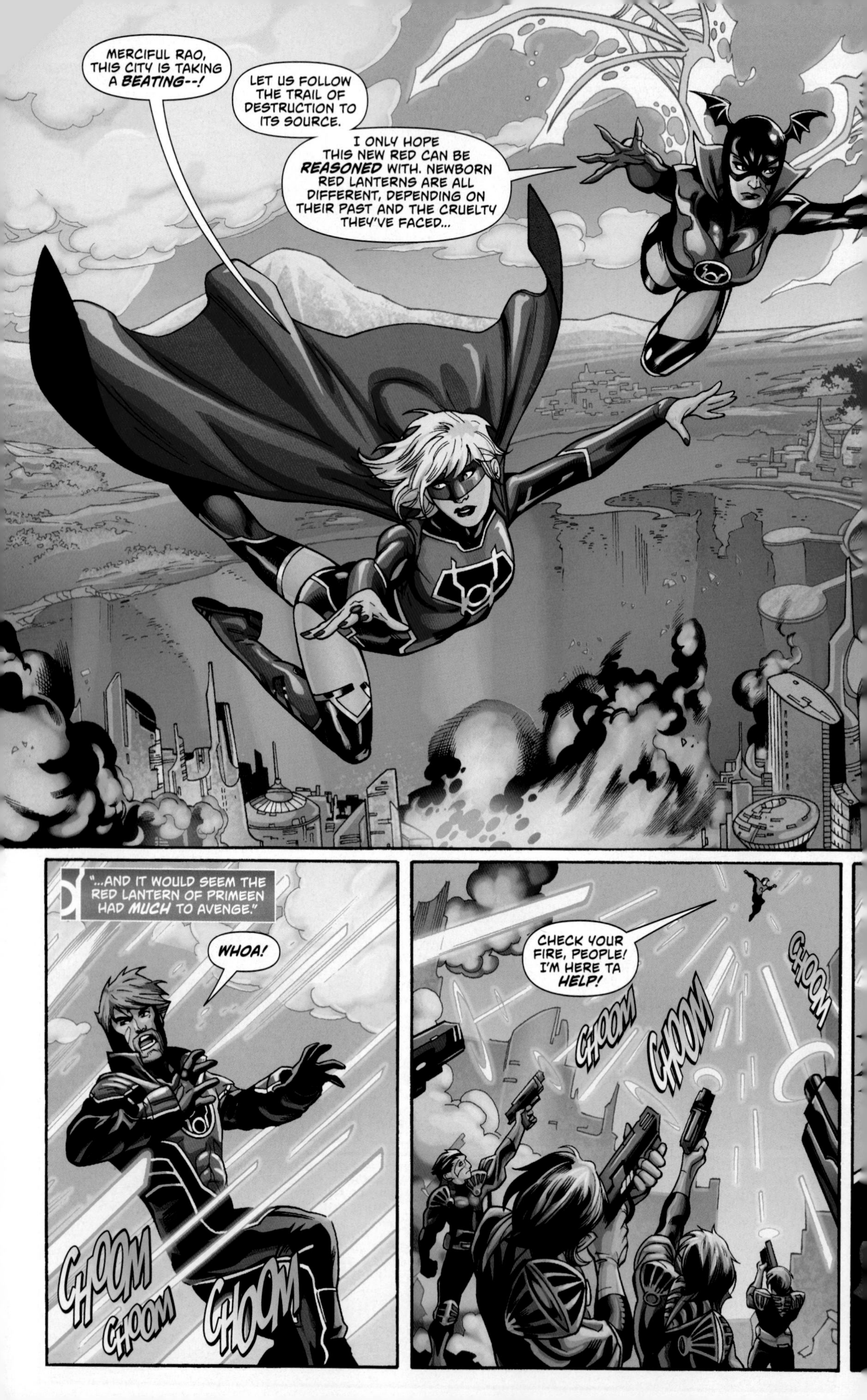
MERCIFUL RAO, THIS CITY IS TAKING A BEATING--!
LET US FOLLOW THE TRAIL OF DESTRUCTION TO ITS SOURCE.
I ONLY HOPE THIS NEW RED CAN BE REASONED WITH. NEWBORN RED LANTERNS ARE ALL DIFFERENT, DEPENDING ON THEIR PAST AND THE CRUELTY THEY'VE FACED...
"...AND IT WOULD SEEM THE RED LANTERN OF PRIMEEN HAD MUCH TO AVENGE."
WHOA!
CHOOM
CHOOM
CHOOM
CHECK YOUR FIRE, PEOPLE! I'M HERE TA HELP!
CHOOM
CHOOM
CHOOM

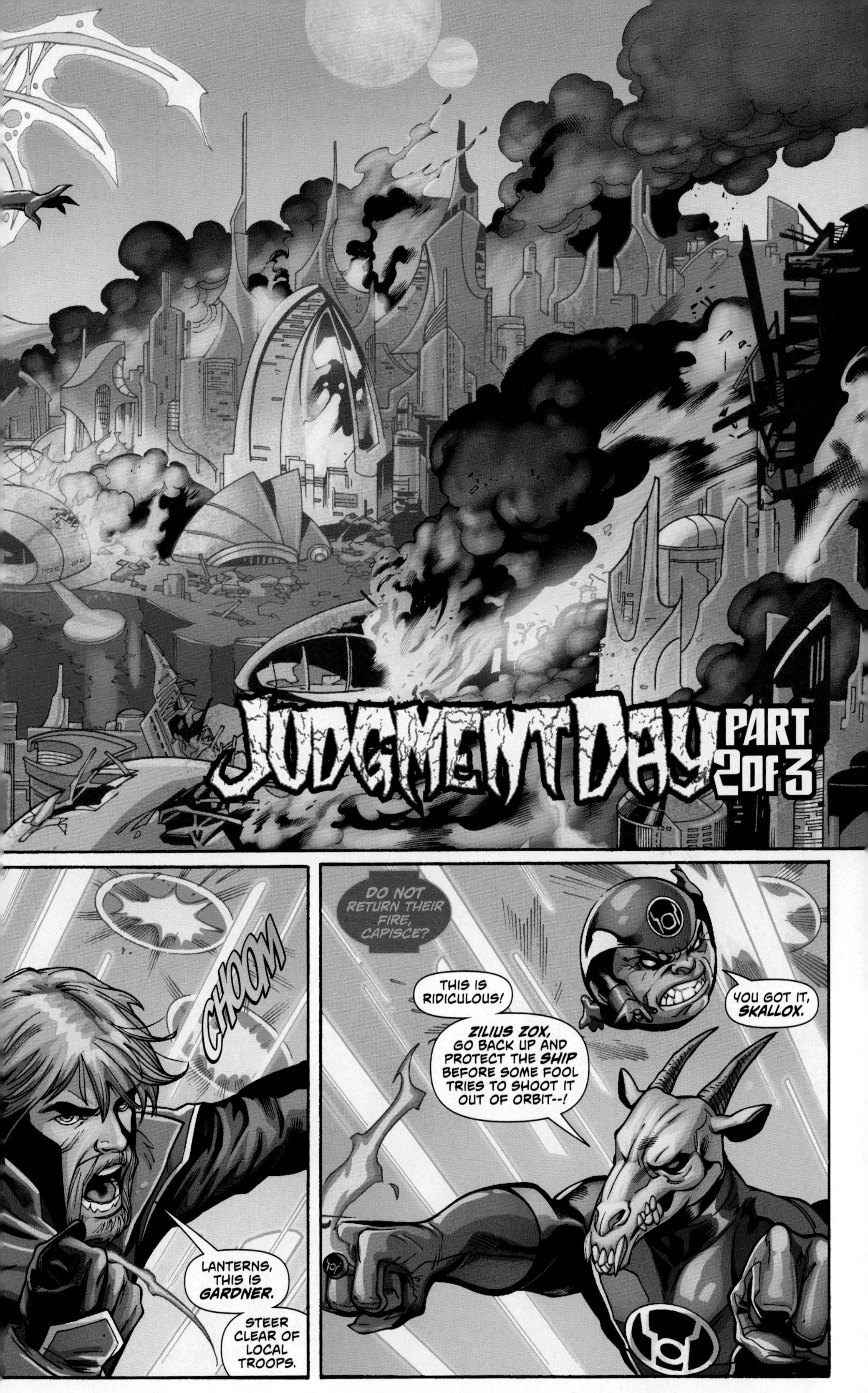
JUDGMENT DAY PART 2 OF 3
CHOOM
LANTERNS, THIS IS GARDNER.
STEER CLEAR OF LOCAL TROOPS.
DO NOT RETURN THEIR FIRE, CAPISCE?
THIS IS RIDICULOUS!
ZILIUS ZOX, GO BACK UP AND PROTECT THE SHIP BEFORE SOME FOOL TRIES TO SHOOT IT OUT OF ORBIT--!
YOU GOT IT, SKALLOX.

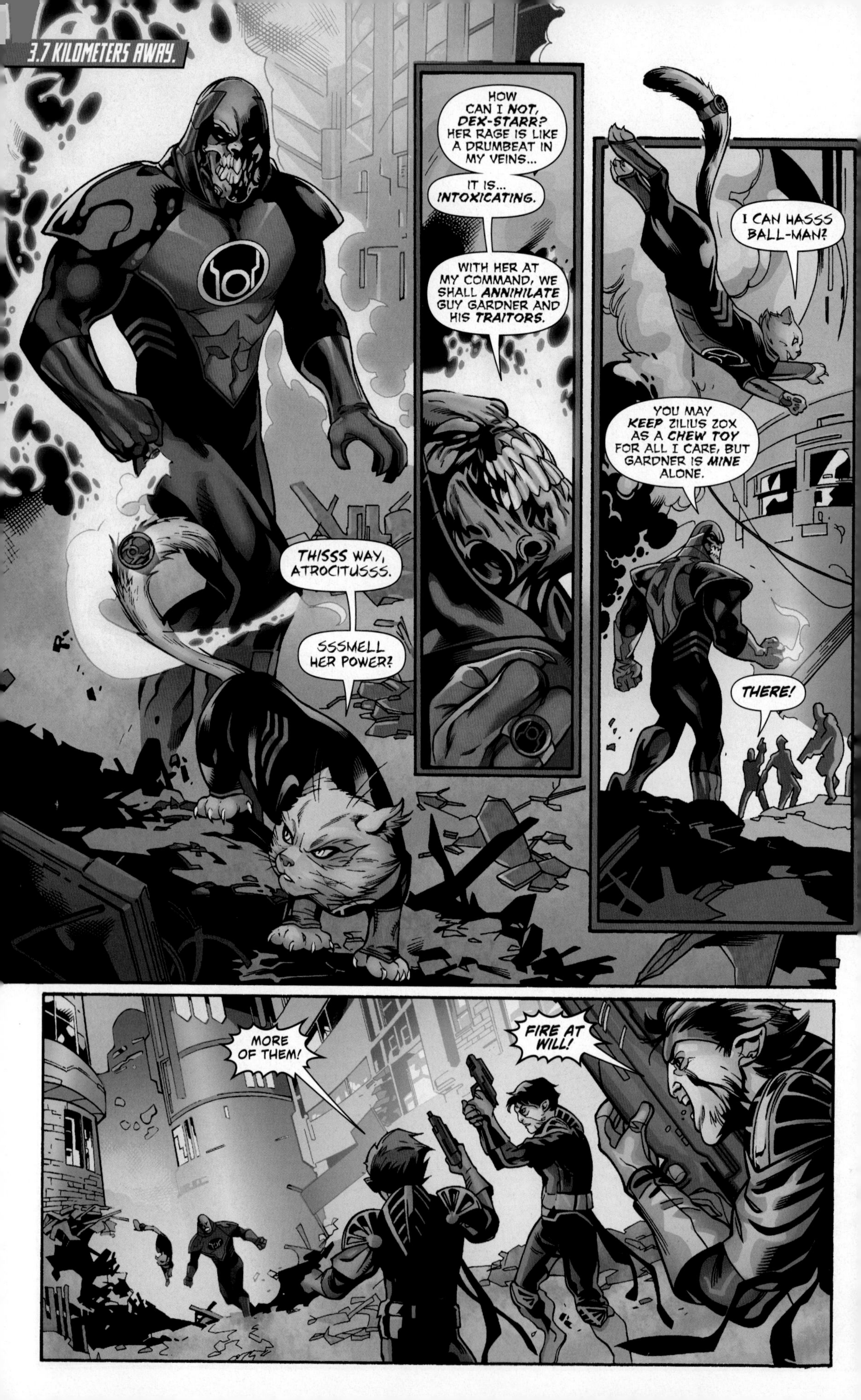
3.7 KILOMETERS AWAY.
THISSS WAY, ATROCITUSSS.
SSSMELL HER POWER?
HOW CAN I NOT, DEX-STARR? HER RAGE IS LIKE A DRUMBEAT IN MY VEINS...
IT IS... INTOXICATING.
WITH HER AT MY COMMAND, WE SHALL ANNIHILATE GUY GARDNER AND HIS TRAITORS.
I CAN HASSS BALL-MAN?
YOU MAY KEEP ZILIUS ZOX AS A CHEW TOY FOR ALL I CARE, BUT GARDNER IS MINE ALONE.
THERE!
MORE OF THEM!
FIRE AT WILL!

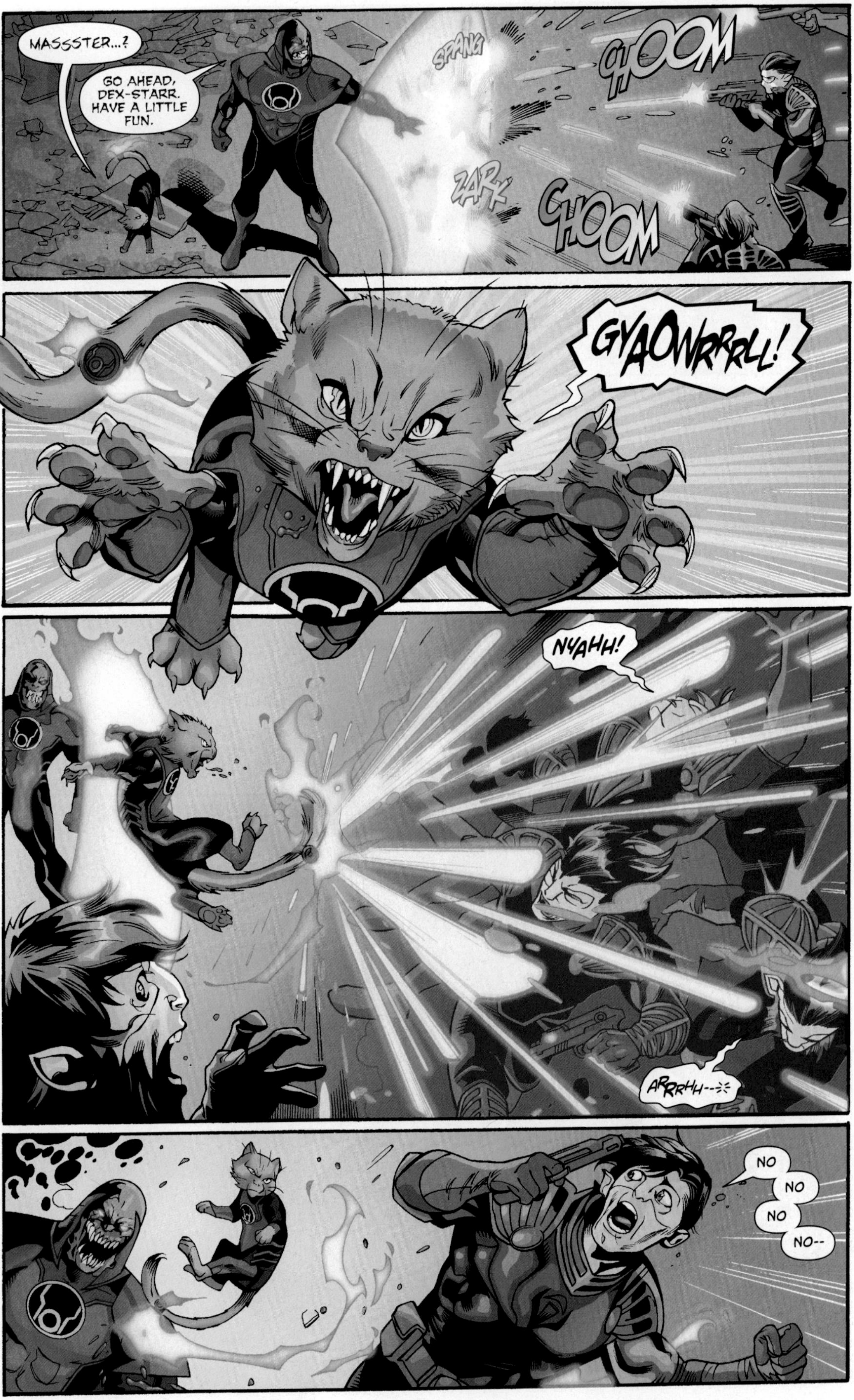
MASSSTER...?
GO AHEAD, DEX-STARR. HAVE A LITTLE FUN.
SPANG
CHOOM
ZARK
CHOOM
GYAOWRRRLL!
NYAHH!
ARRRHH--
NO
NO
NO
NO--

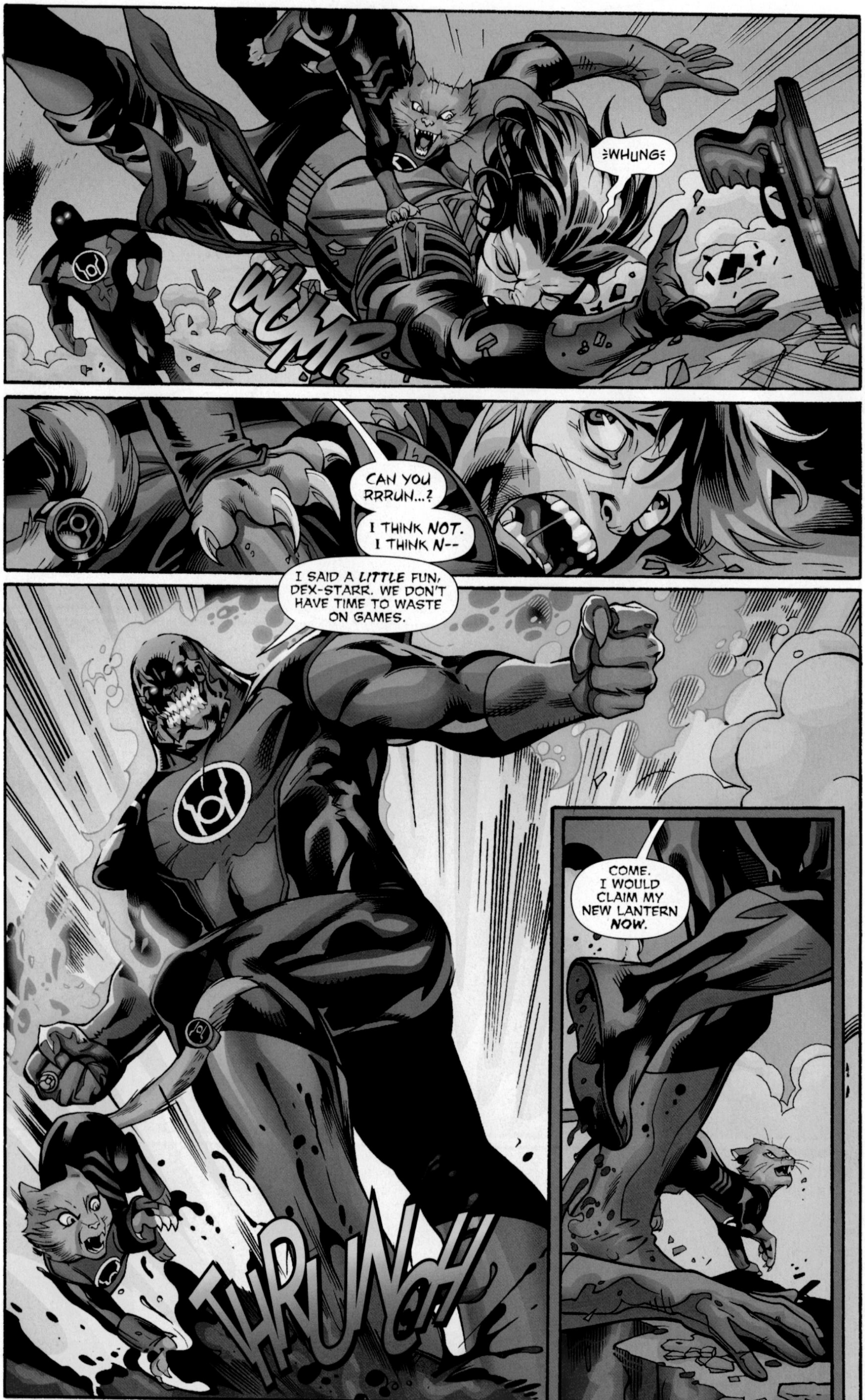
WHUNG
WUMP
CAN YOU RRRUN...?
I THINK NOT. I THINK N--
I SAID A LITTLE FUN, DEX-STARR. WE DON'T HAVE TIME TO WASTE ON GAMES.
COME. I WOULD CLAIM MY NEW LANTERN NOW.
THRUNCH

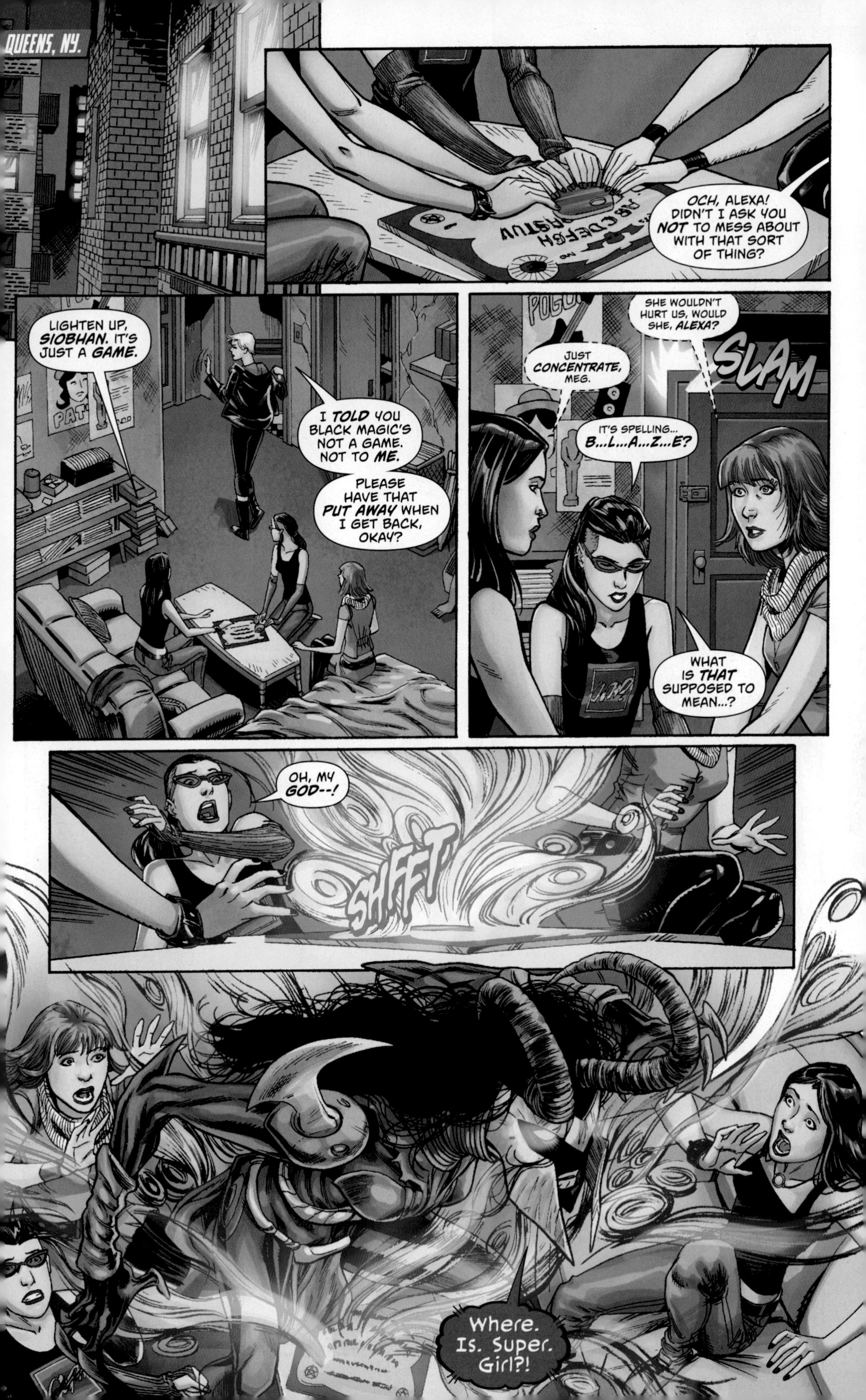
QUEENS, NY.
OCH, ALEXA! DIDN'T I ASK YOU NOT TO MESS ABOUT WITH THAT SORT OF THING?
LIGHTEN UP, SIOBHAN. IT'S JUST A GAME.
I TOLD YOU BLACK MAGIC'S NOT A GAME. NOT TO ME.
PLEASE HAVE THAT PUT AWAY WHEN I GET BACK, OKAY?
SHE WOULDN'T HURT US, WOULD SHE, ALEXA?
SLAM
JUST CONCENTRATE, MEG.
IT'S SPELLING... B...L...A...Z...E?
WHAT IS THAT SUPPOSED TO MEAN...?
OH, MY GOD--!
SHFFT
Where. Is. Super. Girl?!

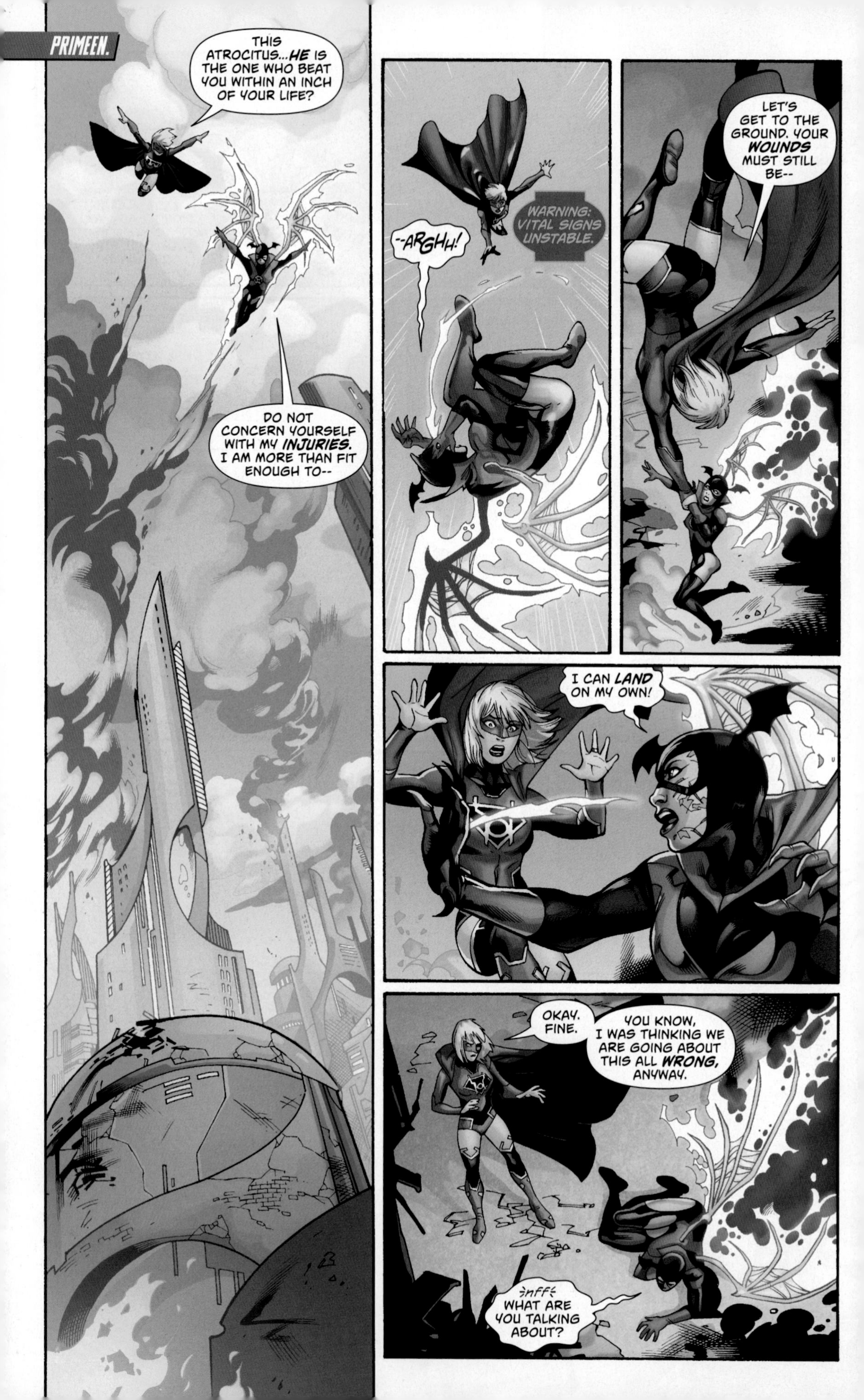
PRIMEEN.
THIS ATROCITUS...HE IS THE ONE WHO BEAT YOU WITHIN AN INCH OF YOUR LIFE?
DO NOT CONCERN YOURSELF WITH MY INJURIES. I AM MORE THAN FIT ENOUGH TO--
--ARGHH!
WARNING: VITAL SIGNS UNSTABLE.
LET'S GET TO THE GROUND. YOUR WOUNDS MUST STILL BE--
I CAN LAND ON MY OWN!
OKAY. FINE.
YOU KNOW, I WAS THINKING WE ARE GOING ABOUT THIS ALL WRONG, ANYWAY.
SNFF WHAT ARE YOU TALKING ABOUT?

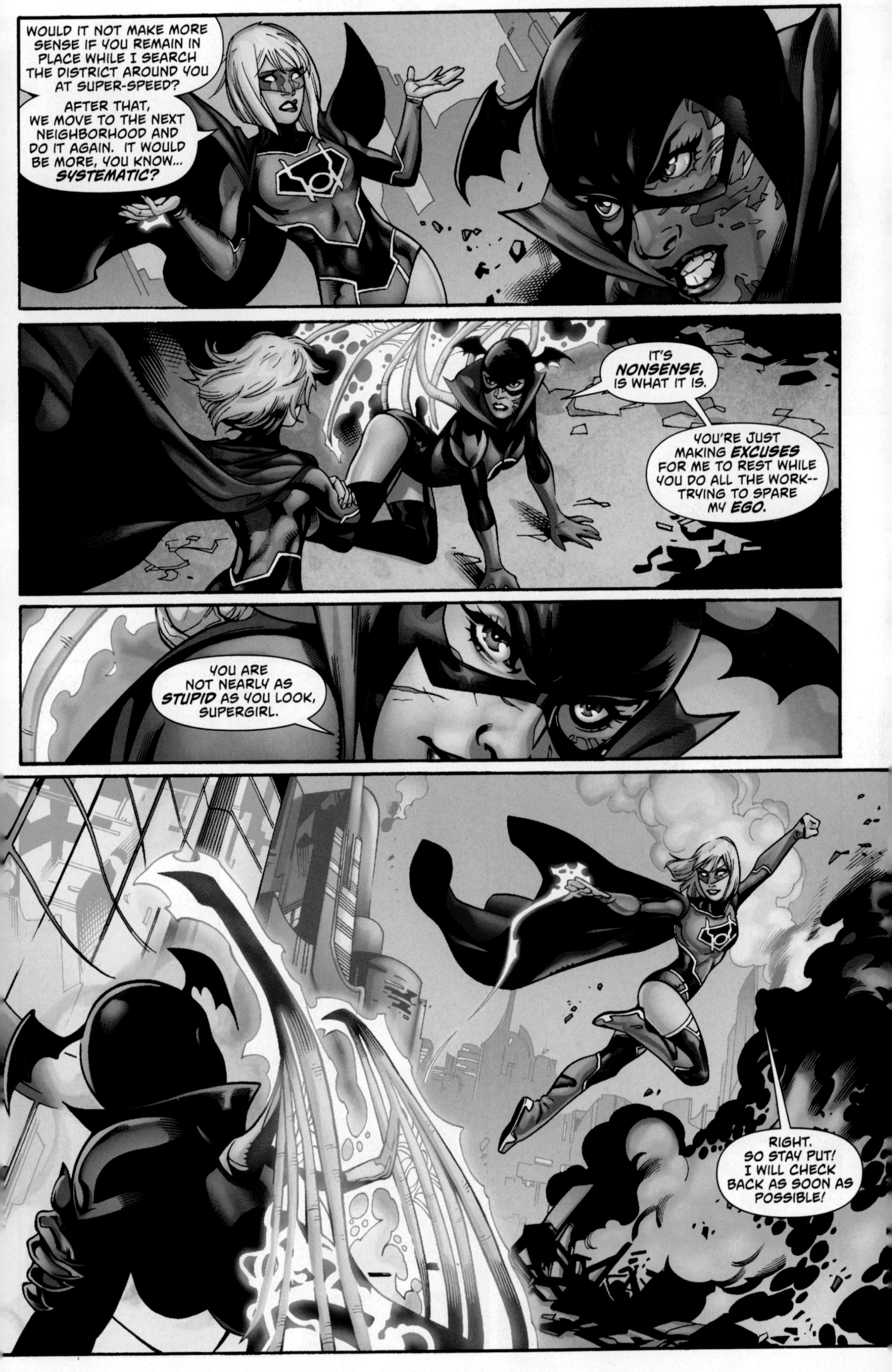
WOULD IT NOT MAKE MORE SENSE IF YOU REMAIN IN PLACE WHILE I SEARCH THE DISTRICT AROUND YOU AT SUPER-SPEED?
AFTER THAT, WE MOVE TO THE NEXT NEIGHBORHOOD AND DO IT AGAIN. IT WOULD BE MORE, YOU KNOW... SYSTEMATIC?
IT'S NONSENSE, IS WHAT IT IS.
YOU'RE JUST MAKING EXCUSES FOR ME TO REST WHILE YOU DO ALL THE WORK-- TRYING TO SPARE MY EGO.
YOU ARE NOT NEARLY AS STUPID AS YOU LOOK, SUPERGIRL.
RIGHT. SO STAY PUT! I WILL CHECK BACK AS SOON AS POSSIBLE!

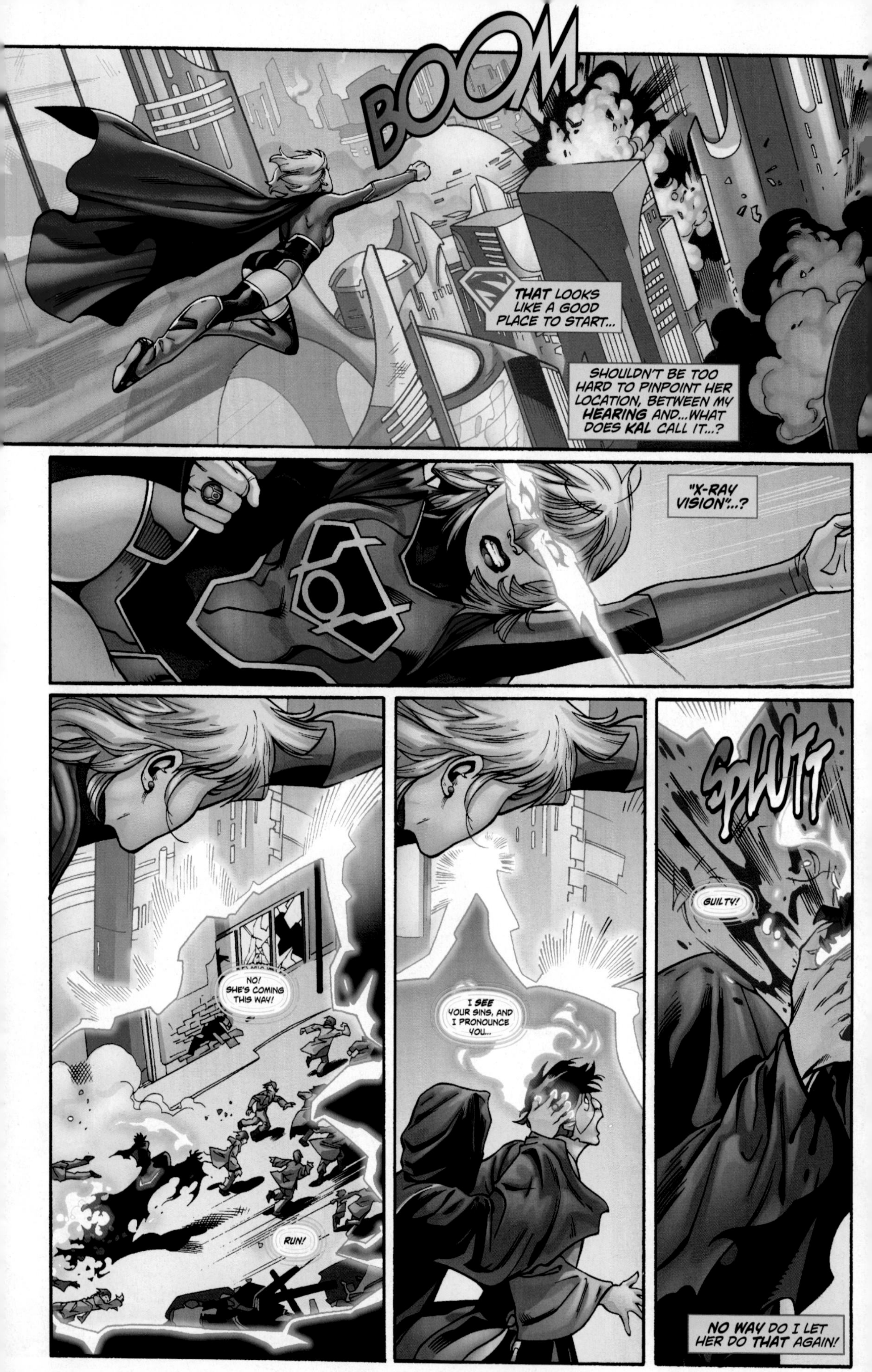
BOOM
THAT LOOKS LIKE A GOOD PLACE TO START...
SHOULDN'T BE TOO HARD TO PINPOINT HER LOCATION, BETWEEN MY HEARING AND...WHAT DOES KAL CALL IT...?
"X-RAY VISION"...?
NO! SHE'S COMING THIS WAY!
RUN!
I SEE YOUR SINS, AND I PRONOUNCE YOU...
SPLUTT
GUILTY!
NO WAY DO I LET HER DO THAT AGAIN!

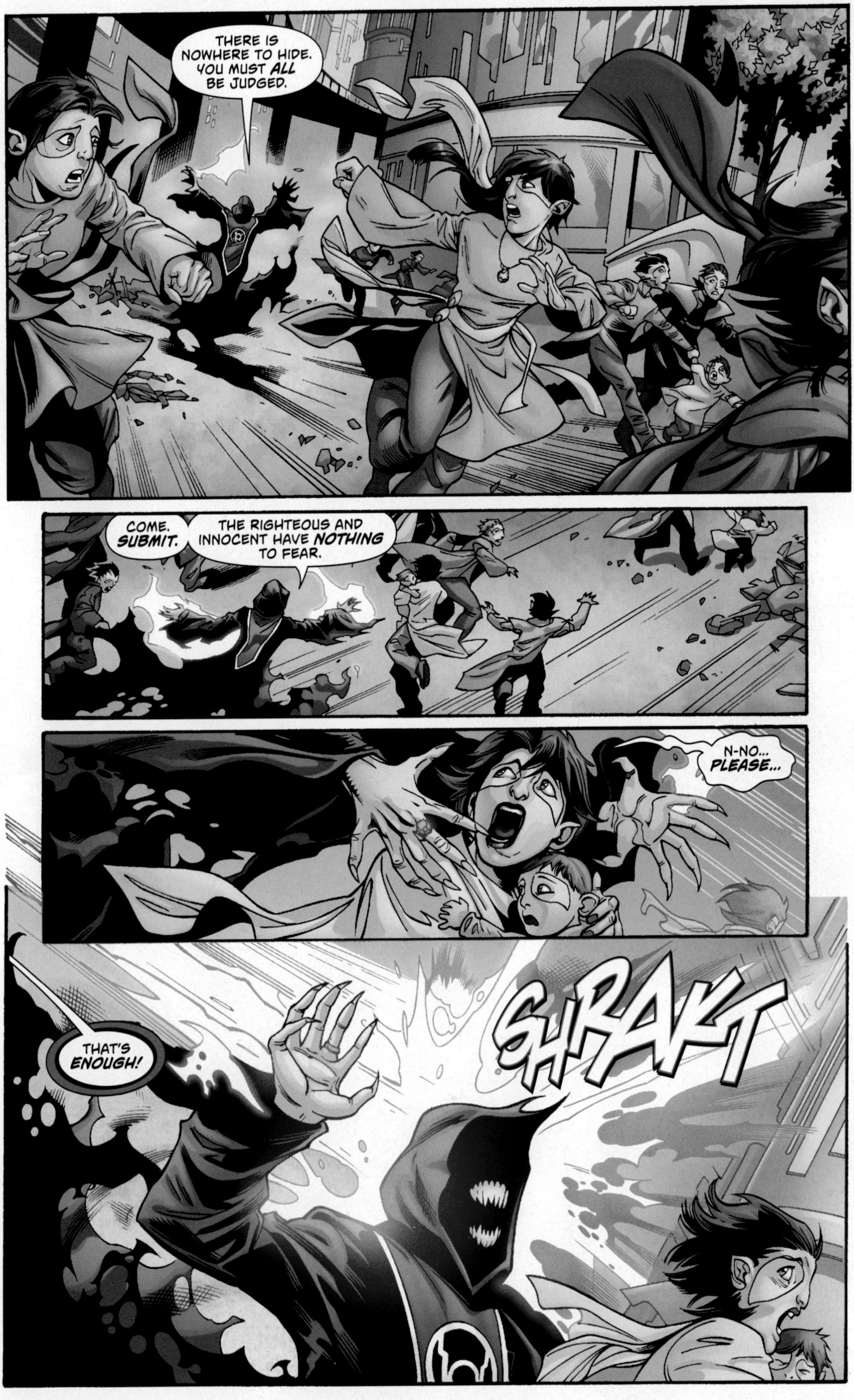
THERE IS NOWHERE TO HIDE. YOU MUST ALL BE JUDGED.
COME. SUBMIT.
THE RIGHTEOUS AND INNOCENT HAVE NOTHING TO FEAR.
N-NO... PLEASE...
THAT'S ENOUGH!
SHRAKT

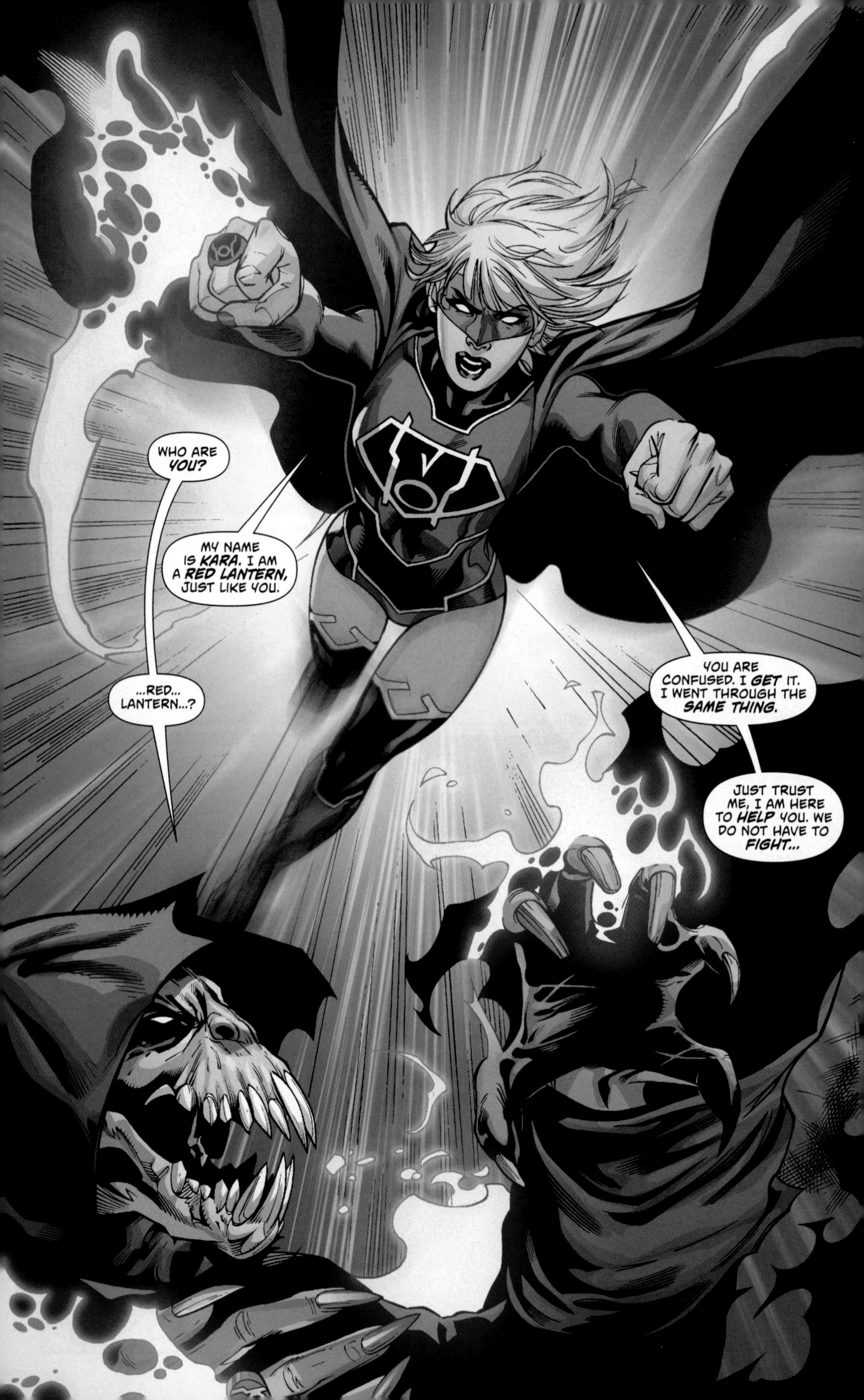
WHO ARE YOU?
MY NAME IS KARA. I AM A RED LANTERN, JUST LIKE YOU.
...RED... LANTERN...?
YOU ARE CONFUSED. I GET IT. I WENT THROUGH THE SAME THING.
JUST TRUST ME, I AM HERE TO HELP YOU. WE DO NOT HAVE TO FIGHT...

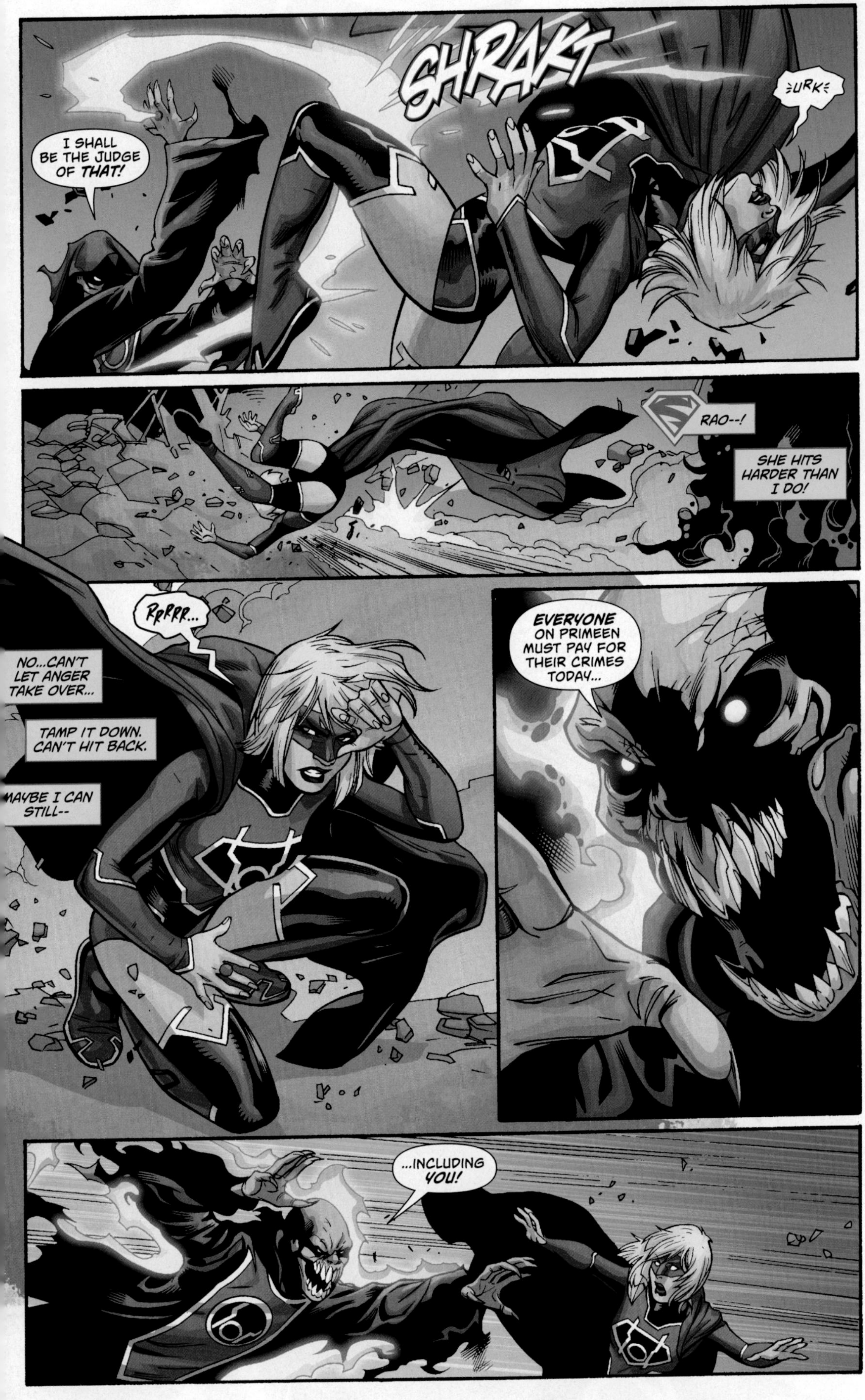
SHRAKT
I SHALL BE THE JUDGE OF THAT!
URK
RAO--!
SHE HITS HARDER THAN I DO!
RRRRR...
NO...CAN'T LET ANGER TAKE OVER...
TAMP IT DOWN. CAN'T HIT BACK.
MAYBE I CAN STILL--
EVERYONE ON PRIMEEN MUST PAY FOR THEIR CRIMES TODAY...
...INCLUDING YOU!

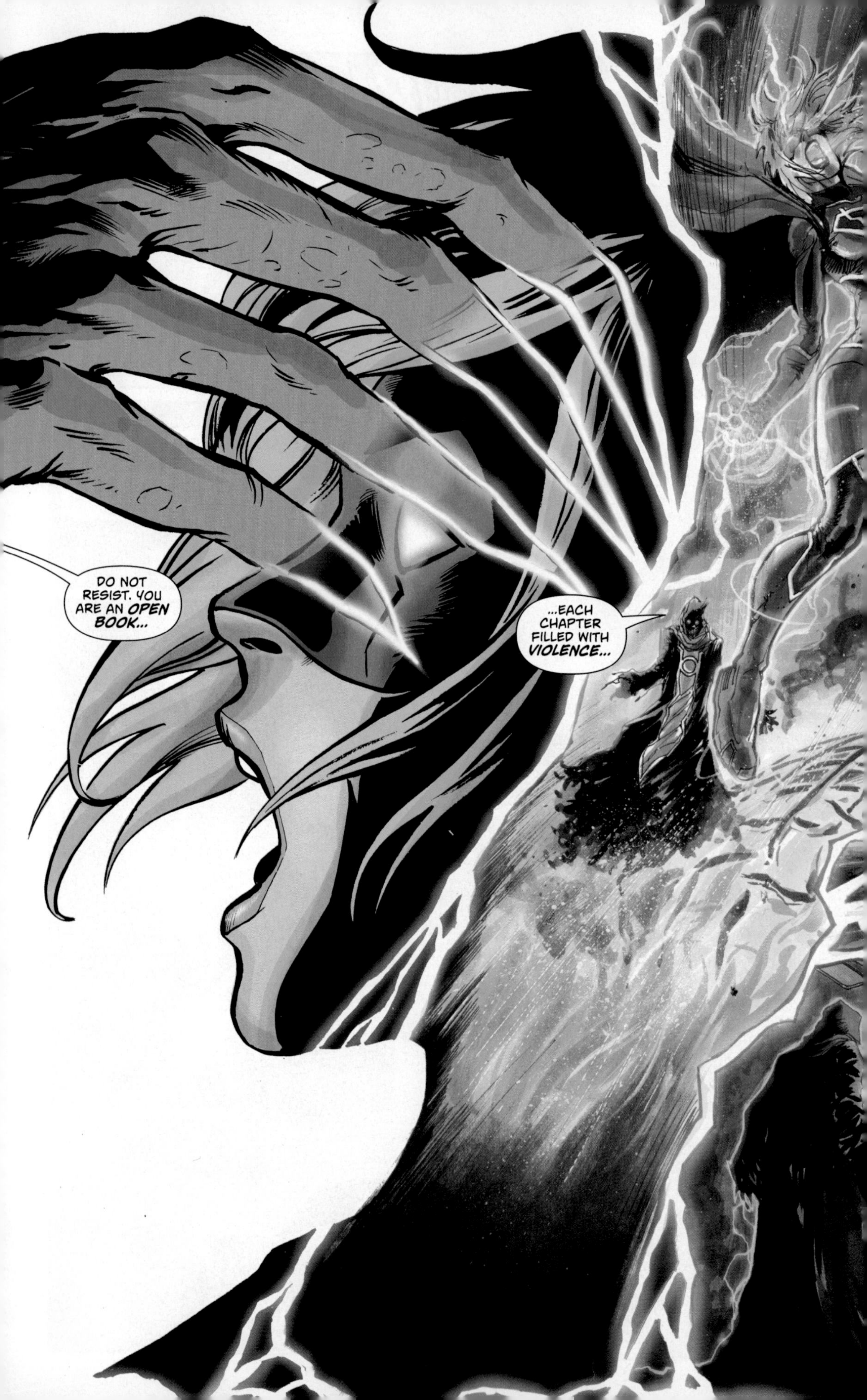
DO NOT RESIST. YOU ARE AN OPEN BOOK...
...EACH CHAPTER FILLED WITH VIOLENCE...

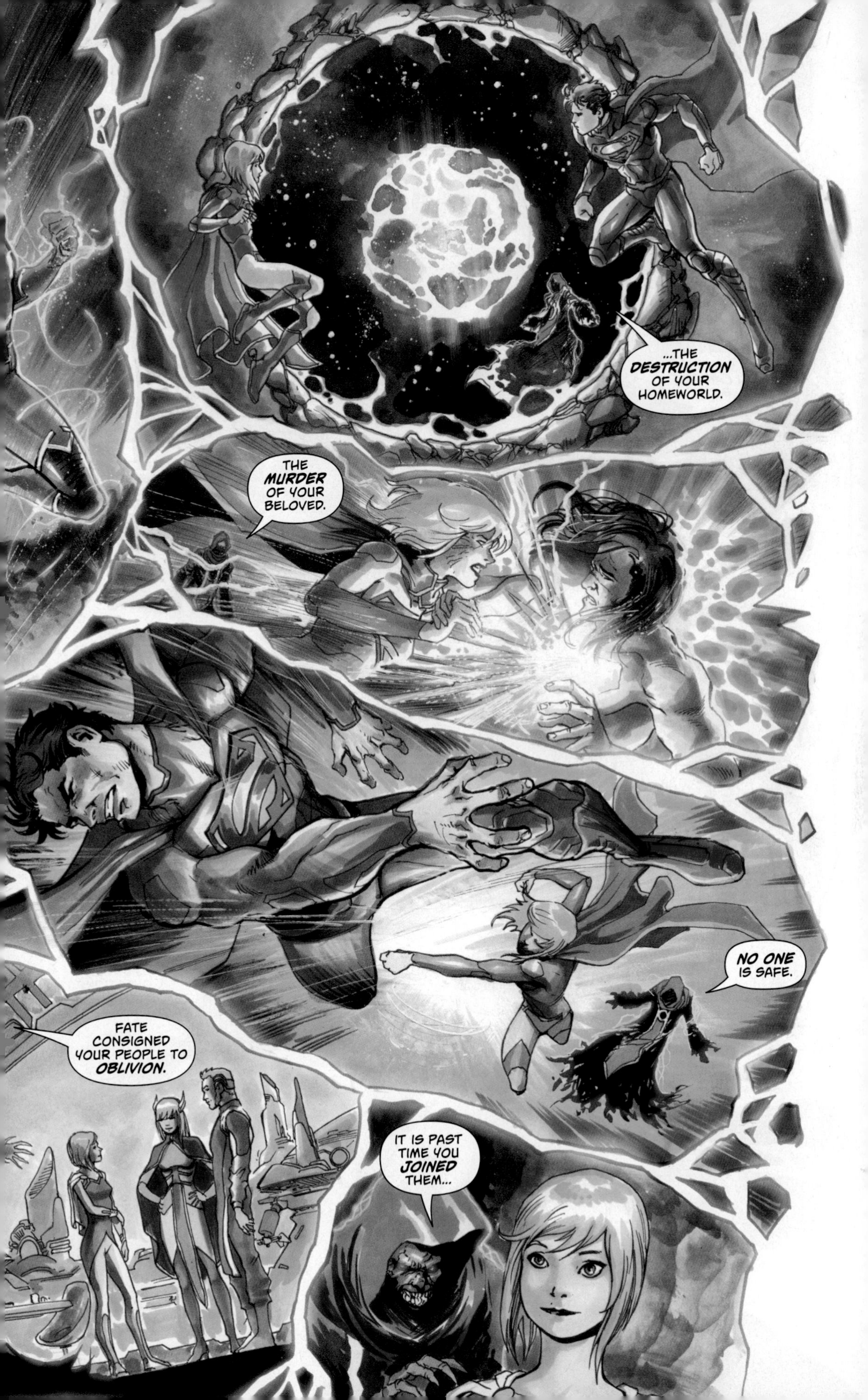
...THE DESTRUCTION OF YOUR HOMEWORLD.
THE MURDER OF YOUR BELOVED.
NO ONE IS SAFE.
FATE CONSIGNED YOUR PEOPLE TO OBLIVION.
IT IS PAST TIME YOU JOINED THEM...

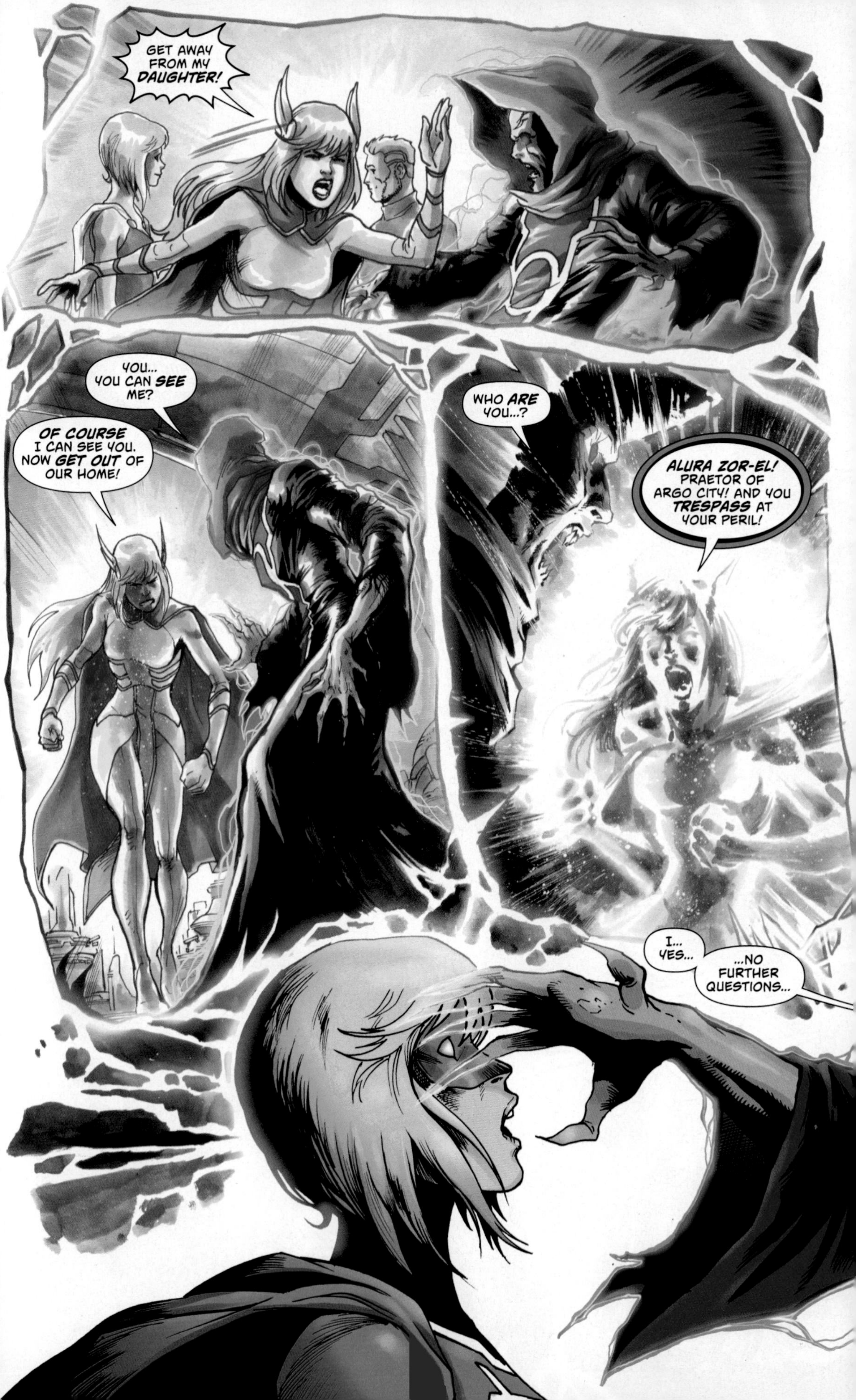

GET AWAY FROM MY DAUGHTER!
YOU... YOU CAN SEE ME?
OF COURSE I CAN SEE YOU. NOW GET OUT OF OUR HOME!
WHO ARE YOU...?
ALURA ZOR-EL! PRAETOR OF ARGO CITY! AND YOU TRESPASS AT YOUR PERIL!
I... YES...
...NO FURTHER QUESTIONS...

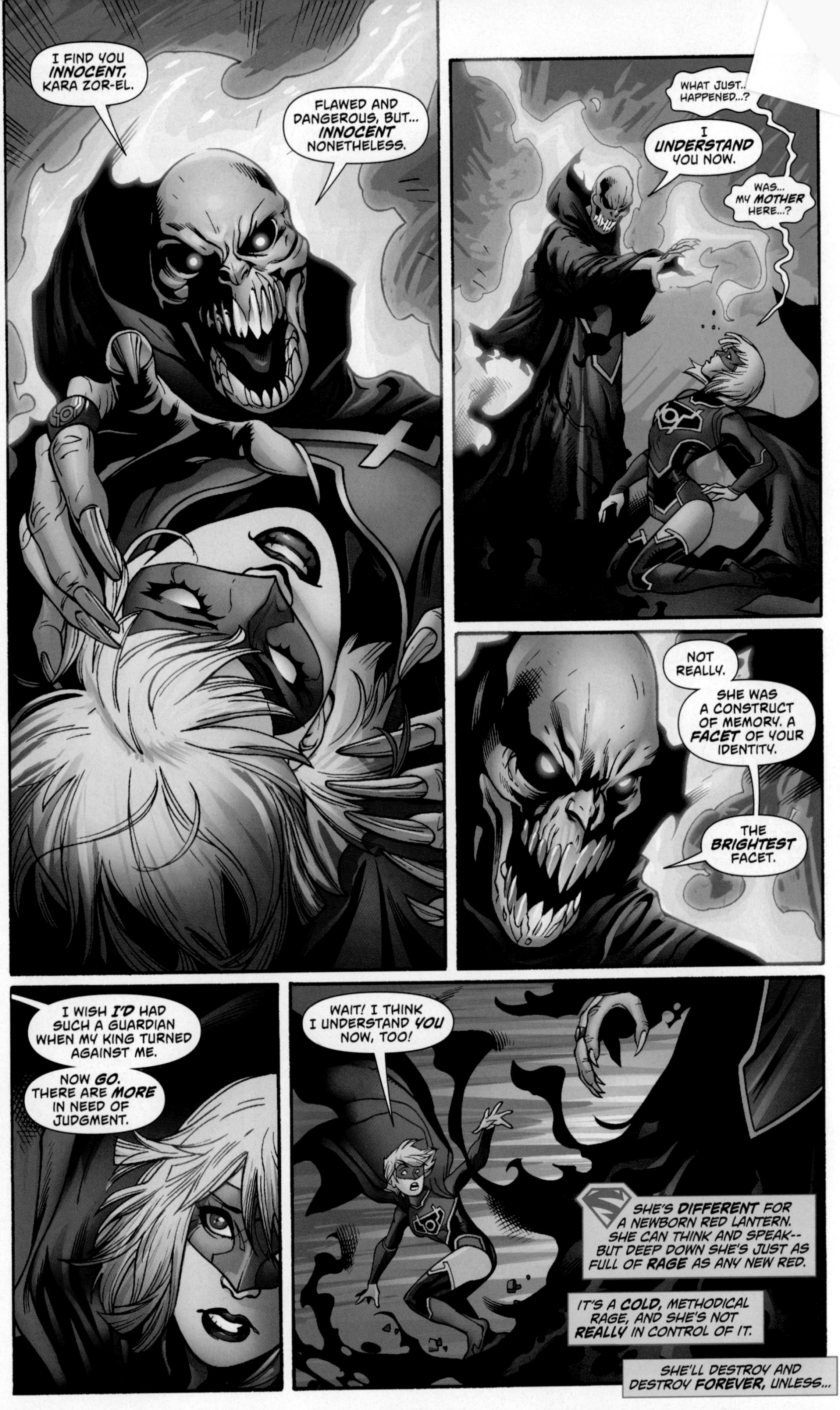
I FIND YOU INNOCENT, KARA ZOR-EL.
FLAWED AND DANGEROUS, BUT... INNOCENT NONETHELESS.
WHAT JUST... HAPPENED...?
I UNDERSTAND YOU NOW.
WAS... MY MOTHER HERE...?
NOT REALLY.
SHE WAS A CONSTRUCT OF MEMORY. A FACET OF YOUR IDENTITY.
THE BRIGHTEST FACET.
I WISH I'D HAD SUCH A GUARDIAN WHEN MY KING TURNED AGAINST ME.
NOW GO. THERE ARE MORE IN NEED OF JUDGMENT.
WAIT! I THINK I UNDERSTAND YOU NOW, TOO!
SHE'S DIFFERENT FOR A NEWBORN RED LANTERN. SHE CAN THINK AND SPEAK-- BUT DEEP DOWN SHE'S JUST AS FULL OF RAGE AS ANY NEW RED.
IT'S A COLD, METHODICAL RAGE, AND SHE'S NOT REALLY IN CONTROL OF IT.
SHE'LL DESTROY AND DESTROY FOREVER, UNLESS...

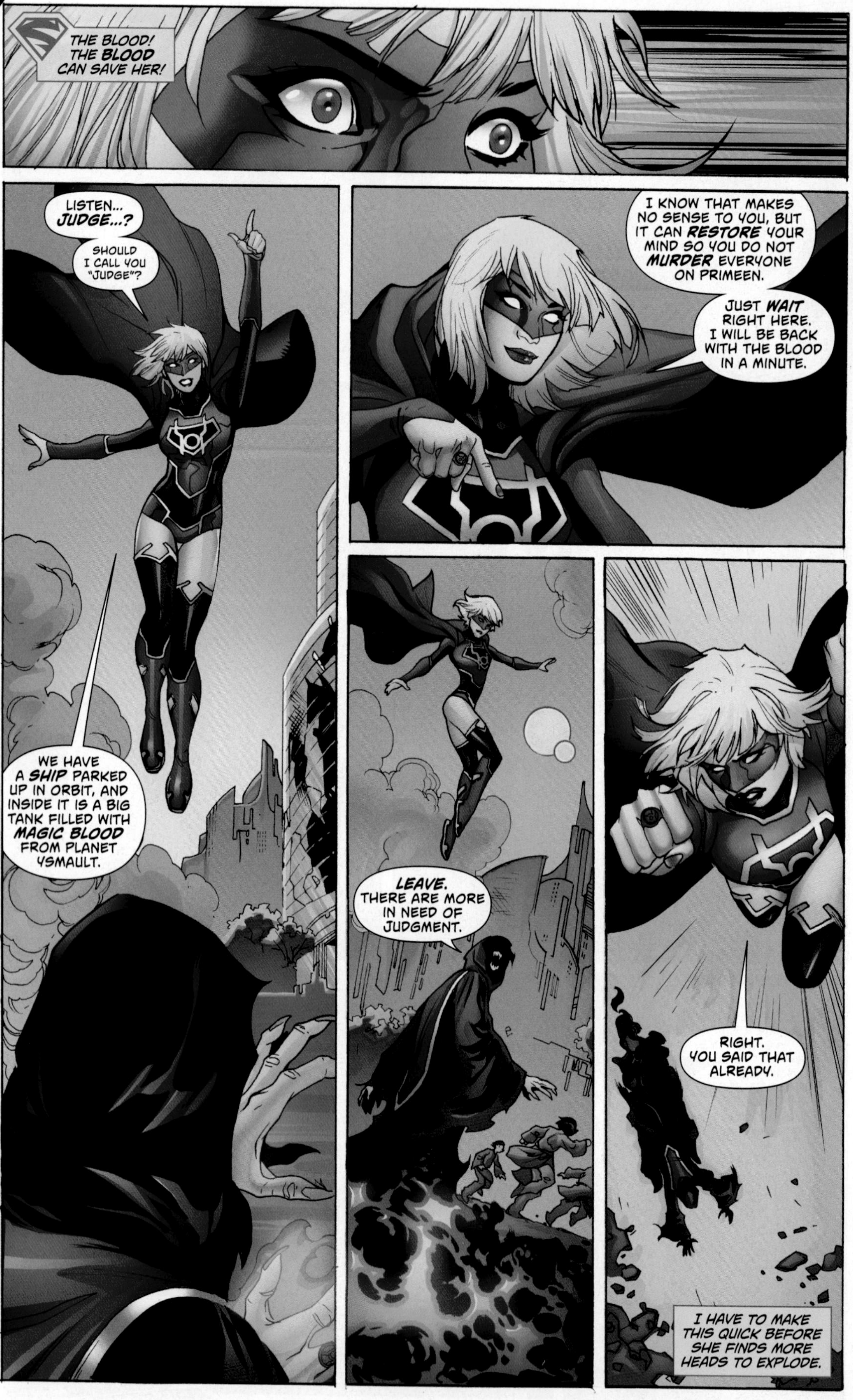
THE BLOOD! THE BLOOD CAN SAVE HER!
LISTEN... JUDGE...?
SHOULD I CALL YOU "JUDGE"?
WE HAVE A SHIP PARKED UP IN ORBIT, AND INSIDE IT IS A BIG TANK FILLED WITH MAGIC BLOOD FROM PLANET YSMAULT.
I KNOW THAT MAKES NO SENSE TO YOU, BUT IT CAN RESTORE YOUR MIND SO YOU DO NOT MURDER EVERYONE ON PRIMEEN.
JUST WAIT RIGHT HERE. I WILL BE BACK WITH THE BLOOD IN A MINUTE.
LEAVE. THERE ARE MORE IN NEED OF JUDGMENT.
RIGHT. YOU SAID THAT ALREADY.
I HAVE TO MAKE THIS QUICK BEFORE SHE FINDS MORE HEADS TO EXPLODE.

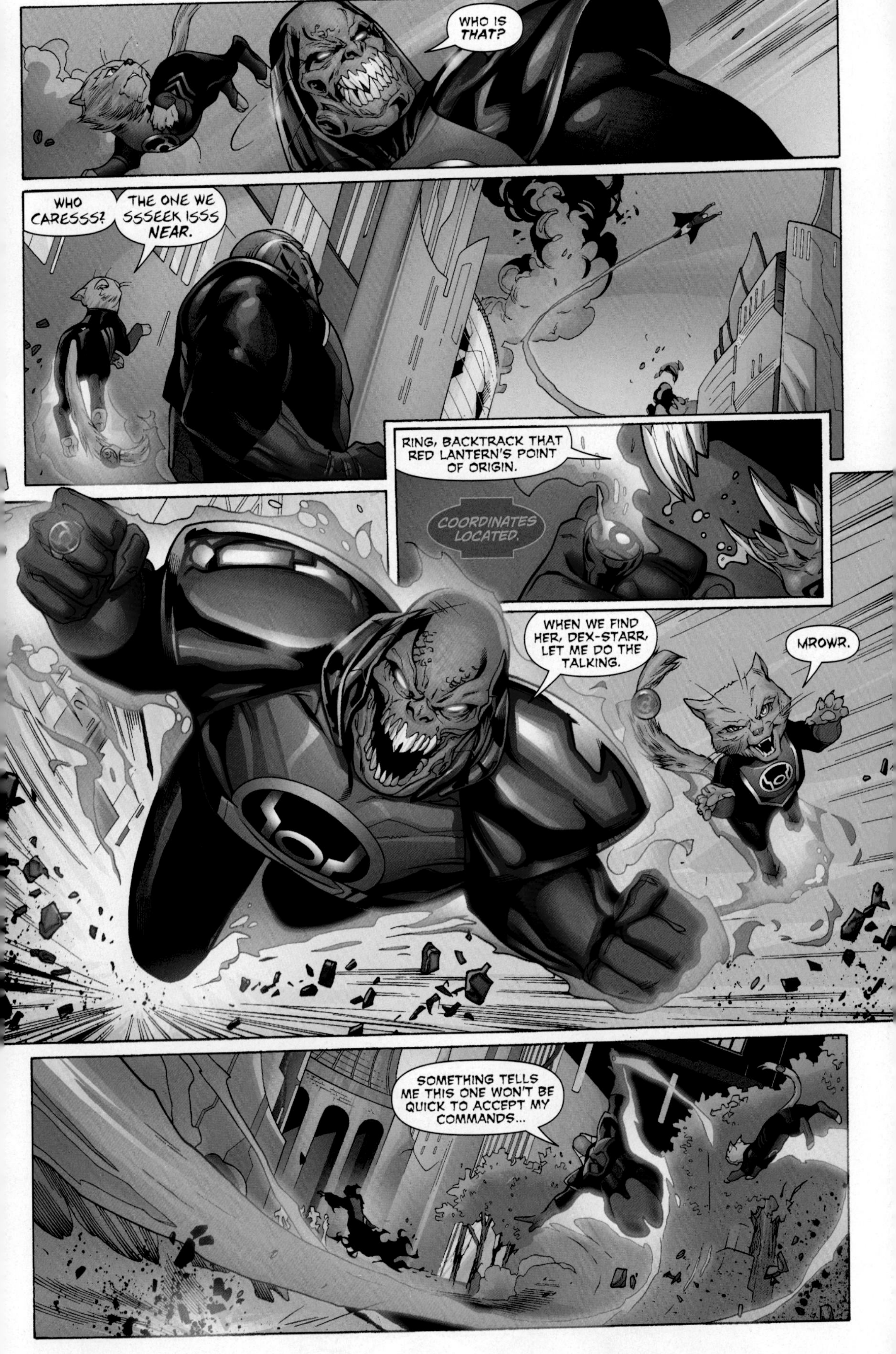
WHO IS THAT?
WHO CARESSS?
THE ONE WE SSSEEK ISSS NEAR.
RING, BACKTRACK THAT RED LANTERN'S POINT OF ORIGIN.
COORDINATES LOCATED.
WHEN WE FIND HER, DEX-STARR, LET ME DO THE TALKING.
MROWR.
SOMETHING TELLS ME THIS ONE WON'T BE QUICK TO ACCEPT MY COMMANDS...

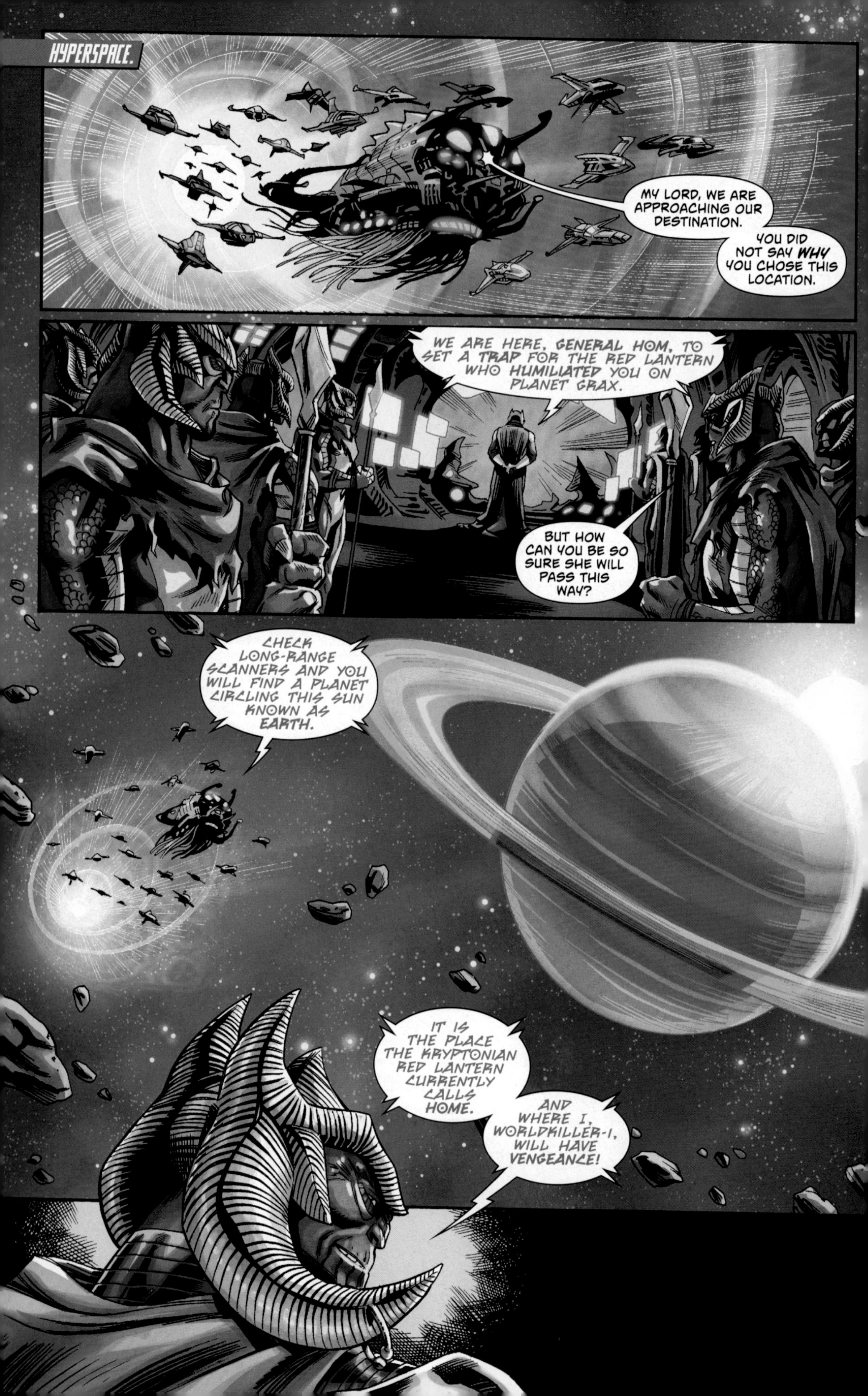
HYPERSPACE.
MY LORD, WE ARE APPROACHING OUR DESTINATION.
YOU DID NOT SAY WHY YOU CHOSE THIS LOCATION.
WE ARE HERE, GENERAL HOM, TO SET A TRAP FOR THE RED LANTERN WHO HUMILIATED YOU ON PLANET GRAX.
BUT HOW CAN YOU BE SO SURE SHE WILL PASS THIS WAY?
CHECK LONG-RANGE SCANNERS AND YOU WILL FIND A PLANET CIRCLING THIS SUN KNOWN AS EARTH.
IT IS THE PLACE THE KRYPTONIAN RED LANTERN CURRENTLY CALLS HOME.
AND WHERE I, WORLDKILLER-1, WILL HAVE VENGEANCE!

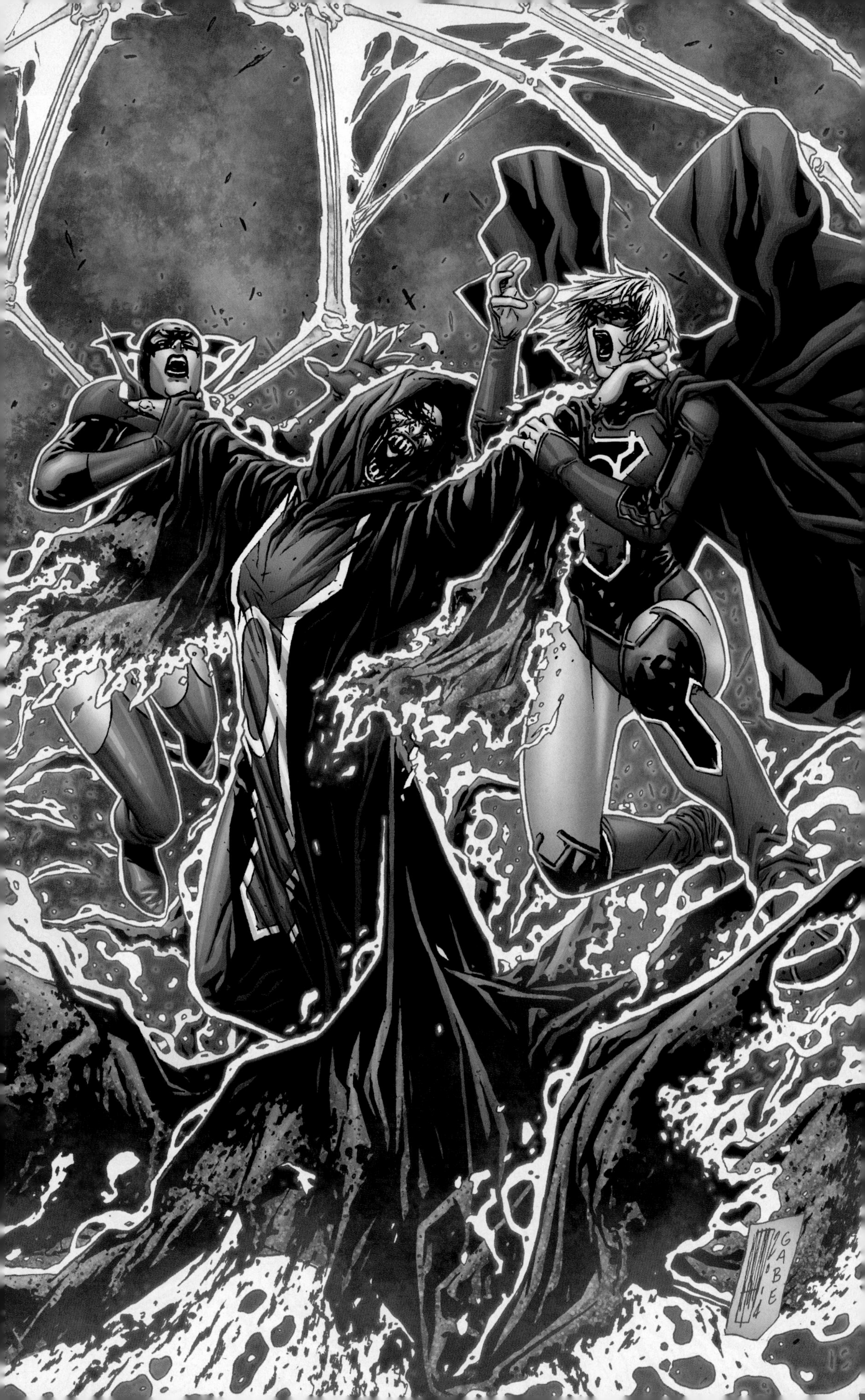
GABE

CHARLES SOULE writer ALESSANDRO VITTI J. CALAFIORE (146, 147, 150, 160) artists GABE ELTAEB colorist DAVE SHARPE letterer
cover art by ALESSANDRO VITTI with GABE ELTAEB

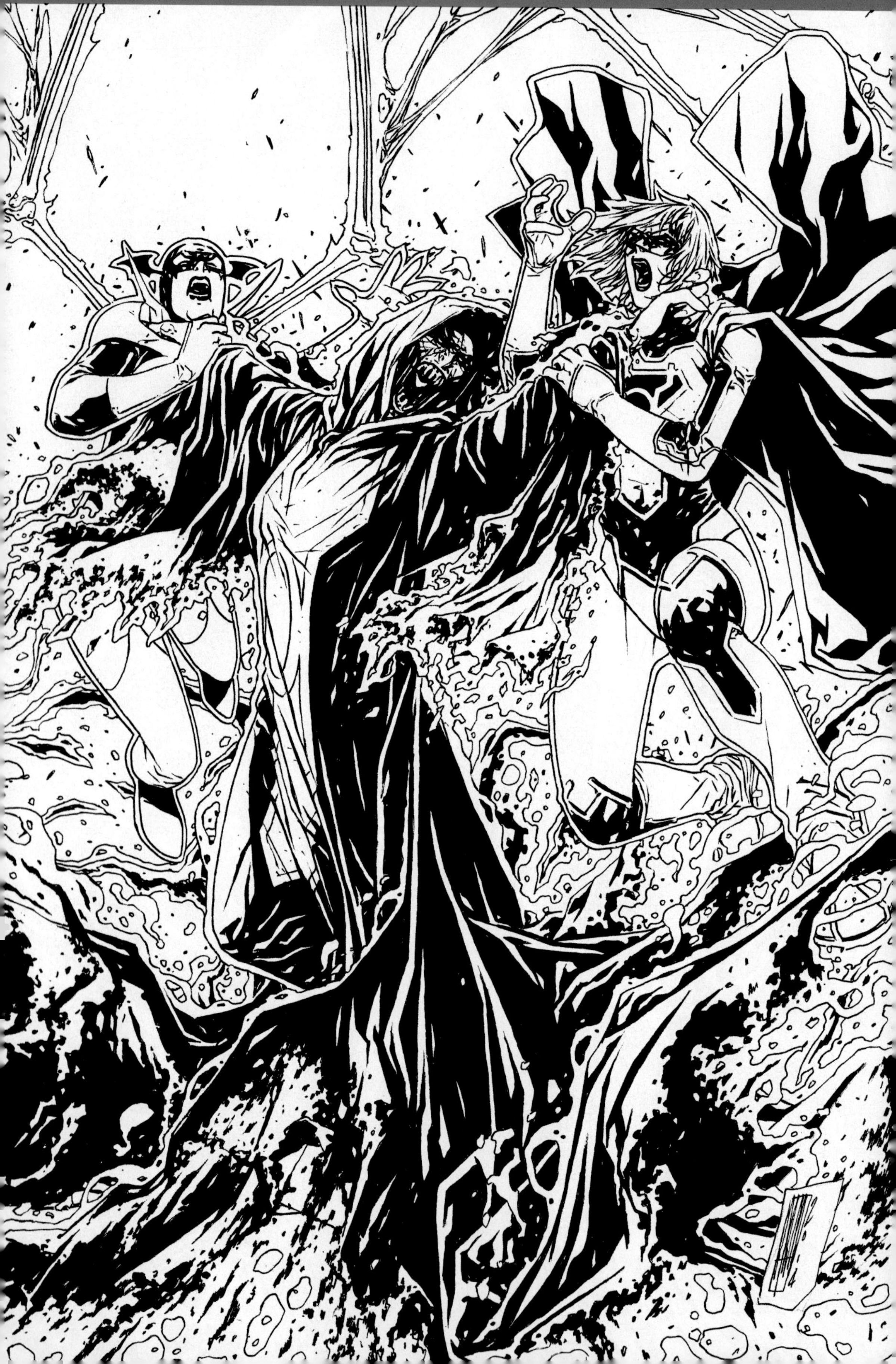

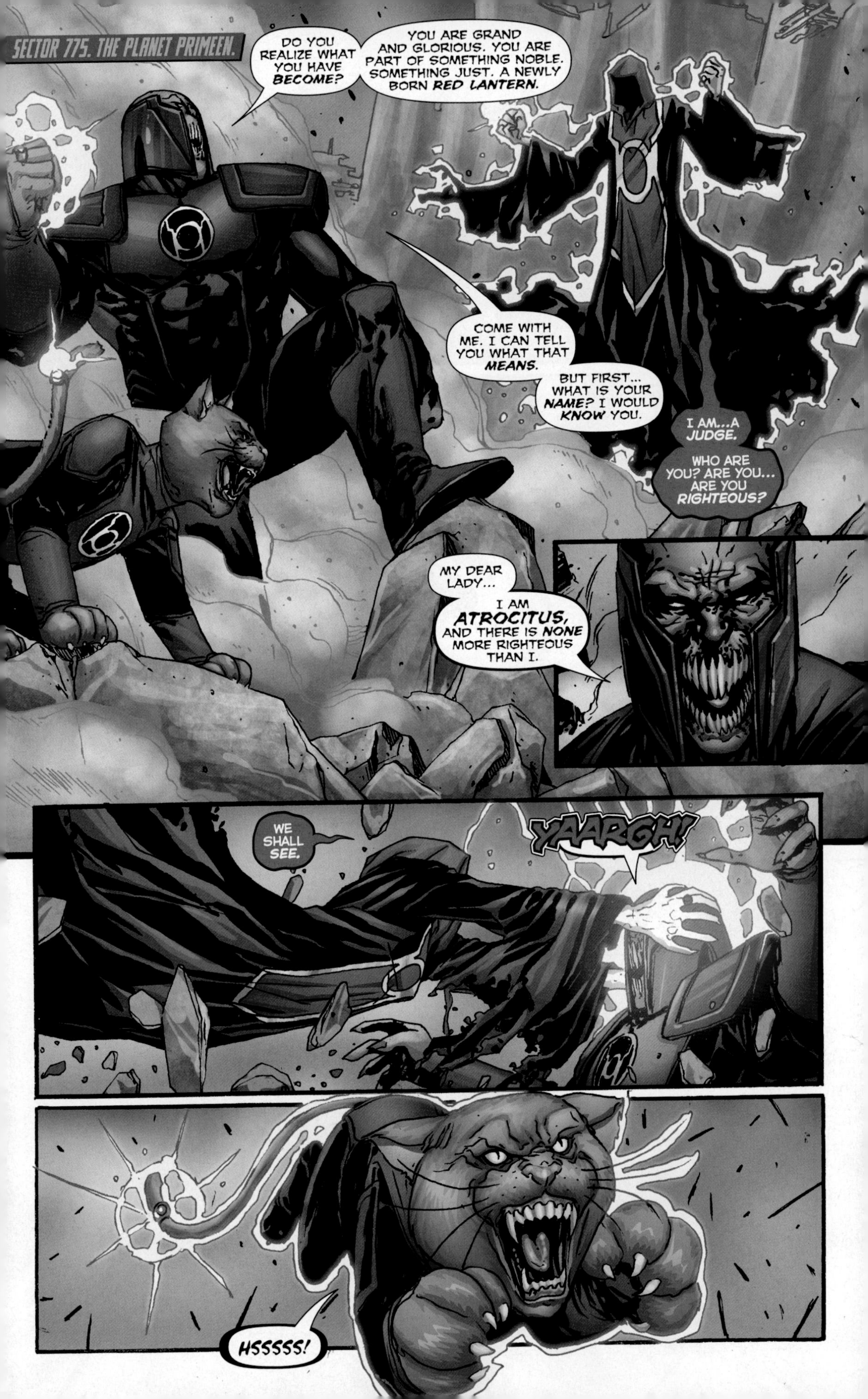
SECTOR 775. THE PLANET PRIMEEN.
DO YOU REALIZE WHAT YOU HAVE BECOME?
YOU ARE GRAND AND GLORIOUS. YOU ARE PART OF SOMETHING NOBLE. SOMETHING JUST. A NEWLY BORN RED LANTERN.
COME WITH ME. I CAN TELL YOU WHAT THAT MEANS.
BUT FIRST... WHAT IS YOUR NAME? I WOULD KNOW YOU.
I AM...A JUDGE.
WHO ARE YOU? ARE YOU... ARE YOU RIGHTEOUS?
MY DEAR LADY...
I AM ATROCITUS, AND THERE IS NONE MORE RIGHTEOUS THAN I.
WE SHALL SEE.
YAARGH!
HSSSSS!

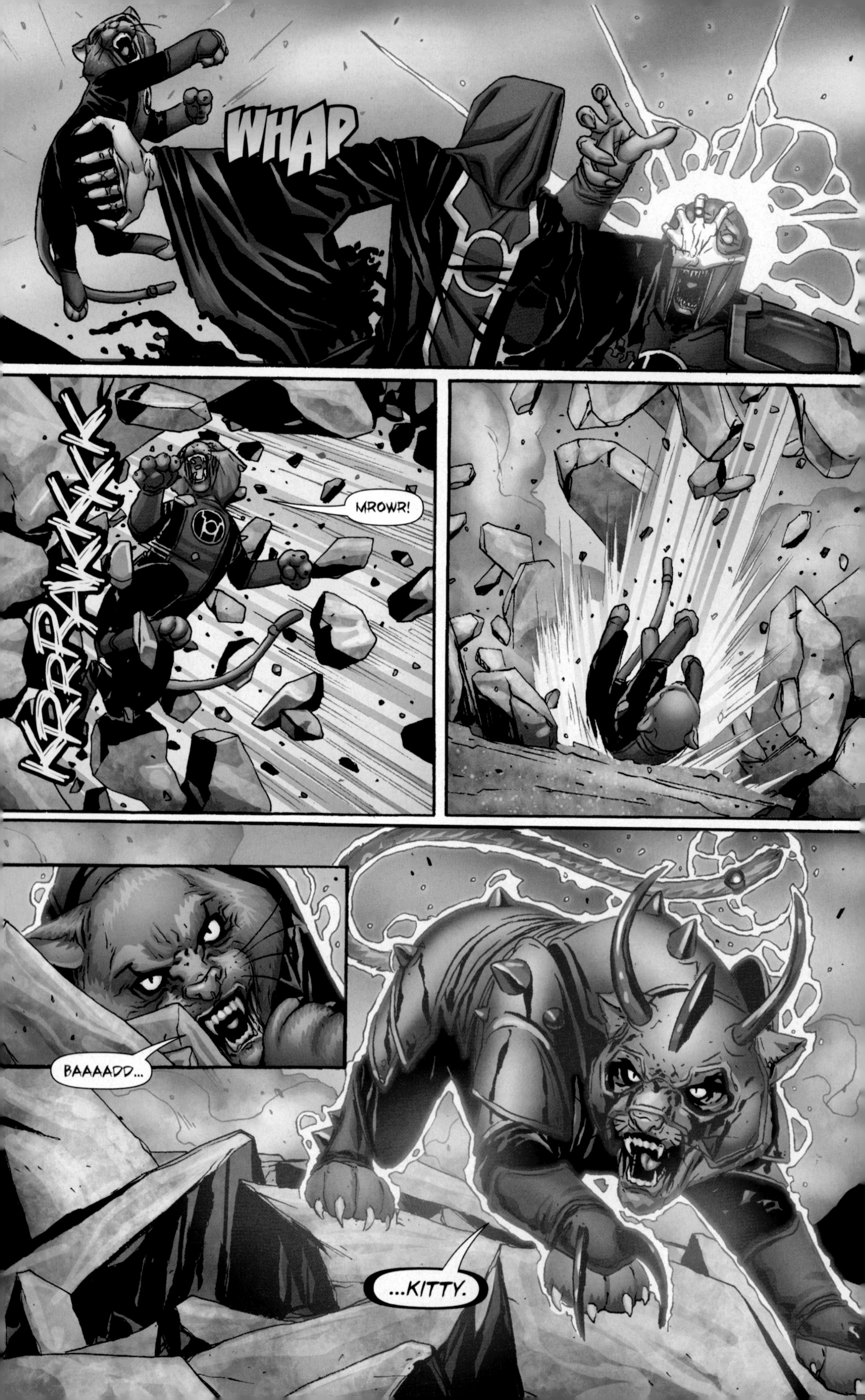
WHAP
KRRRAKKKK
MROWR!
BAAAADD...
...KITTY.

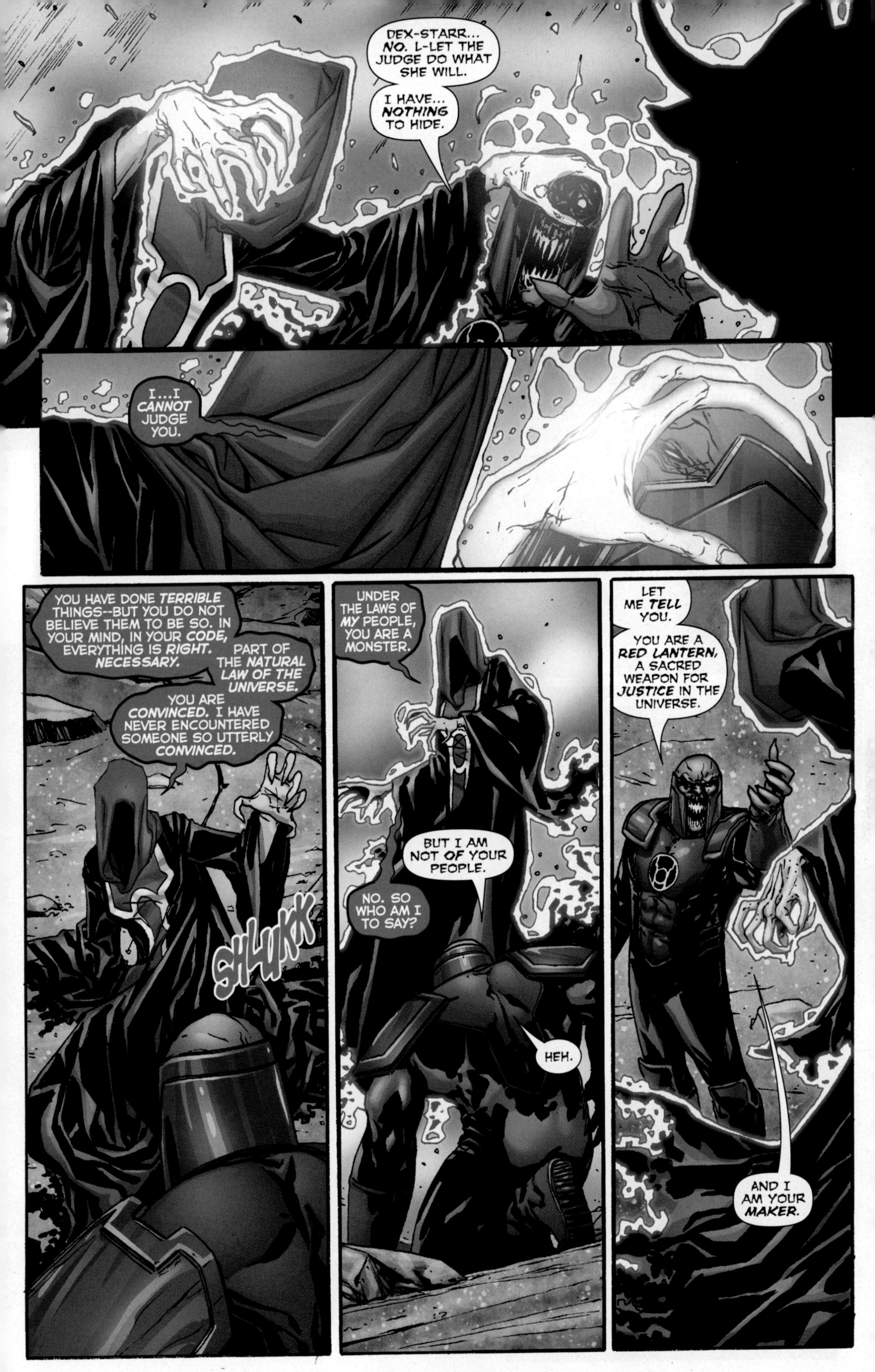
DEX-STARR... NO. L-LET THE JUDGE DO WHAT SHE WILL.
I HAVE... NOTHING TO HIDE.
I...I CANNOT JUDGE YOU.
YOU HAVE DONE TERRIBLE THINGS--BUT YOU DO NOT BELIEVE THEM TO BE SO. IN YOUR MIND, IN YOUR CODE, EVERYTHING IS RIGHT. NECESSARY.
PART OF THE NATURAL LAW OF THE UNIVERSE.
YOU ARE CONVINCED. I HAVE NEVER ENCOUNTERED SOMEONE SO UTTERLY CONVINCED.
SHLUKK
UNDER THE LAWS OF MY PEOPLE, YOU ARE A MONSTER.
BUT I AM NOT OF YOUR PEOPLE.
NO. SO WHO AM I TO SAY?
HEH.
LET ME TELL YOU.
YOU ARE A RED LANTERN, A SACRED WEAPON FOR JUSTICE IN THE UNIVERSE.
AND I AM YOUR MAKER.

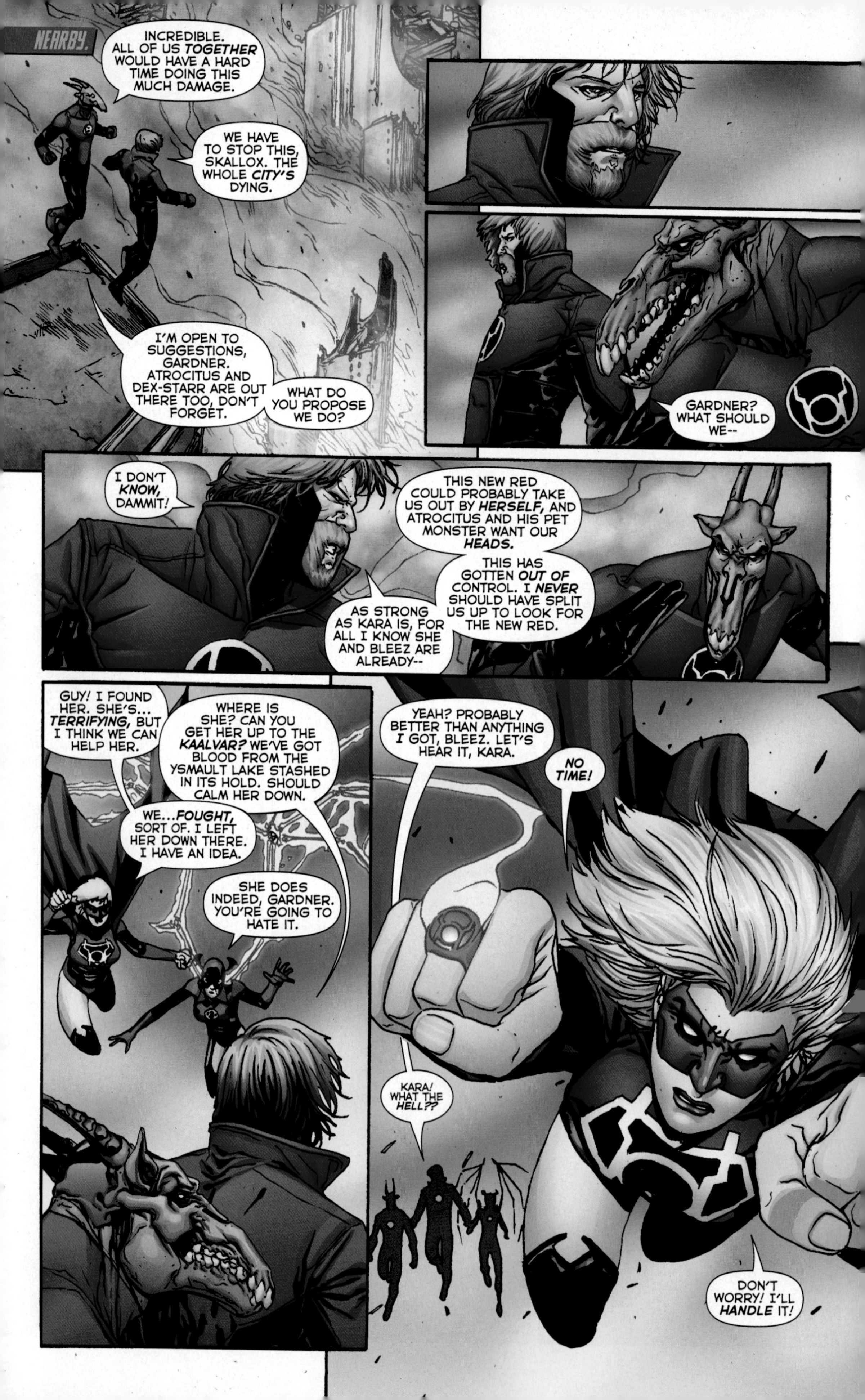
NEARBY.
INCREDIBLE. ALL OF US TOGETHER WOULD HAVE A HARD TIME DOING THIS MUCH DAMAGE.
WE HAVE TO STOP THIS, SKALLOX. THE WHOLE CITY'S DYING.
I'M OPEN TO SUGGESTIONS, GARDNER. ATROCITUS AND DEX-STARR ARE OUT THERE TOO, DON'T FORGET.
WHAT DO YOU PROPOSE WE DO?
GARDNER? WHAT SHOULD WE--
I DON'T KNOW, DAMMIT!
THIS NEW RED COULD PROBABLY TAKE US OUT BY HERSELF, AND ATROCITUS AND HIS PET MONSTER WANT OUR HEADS.
THIS HAS GOTTEN OUT OF CONTROL. I NEVER SHOULD HAVE SPLIT US UP TO LOOK FOR THE NEW RED.
AS STRONG AS KARA IS, FOR ALL I KNOW SHE AND BLEEZ ARE ALREADY--
GUY! I FOUND HER. SHE'S... TERRIFYING, BUT I THINK WE CAN HELP HER.
WHERE IS SHE? CAN YOU GET HER UP TO THE KAALVAR? WE'VE GOT BLOOD FROM THE YSMAULT LAKE STASHED IN ITS HOLD. SHOULD CALM HER DOWN.
WE...FOUGHT, SORT OF. I LEFT HER DOWN THERE. I HAVE AN IDEA.
SHE DOES INDEED, GARDNER. YOU'RE GOING TO HATE IT.
YEAH? PROBABLY BETTER THAN ANYTHING I GOT, BLEEZ. LET'S HEAR IT, KARA.
NO TIME!
KARA! WHAT THE HELL??
DON'T WORRY! I'LL HANDLE IT!

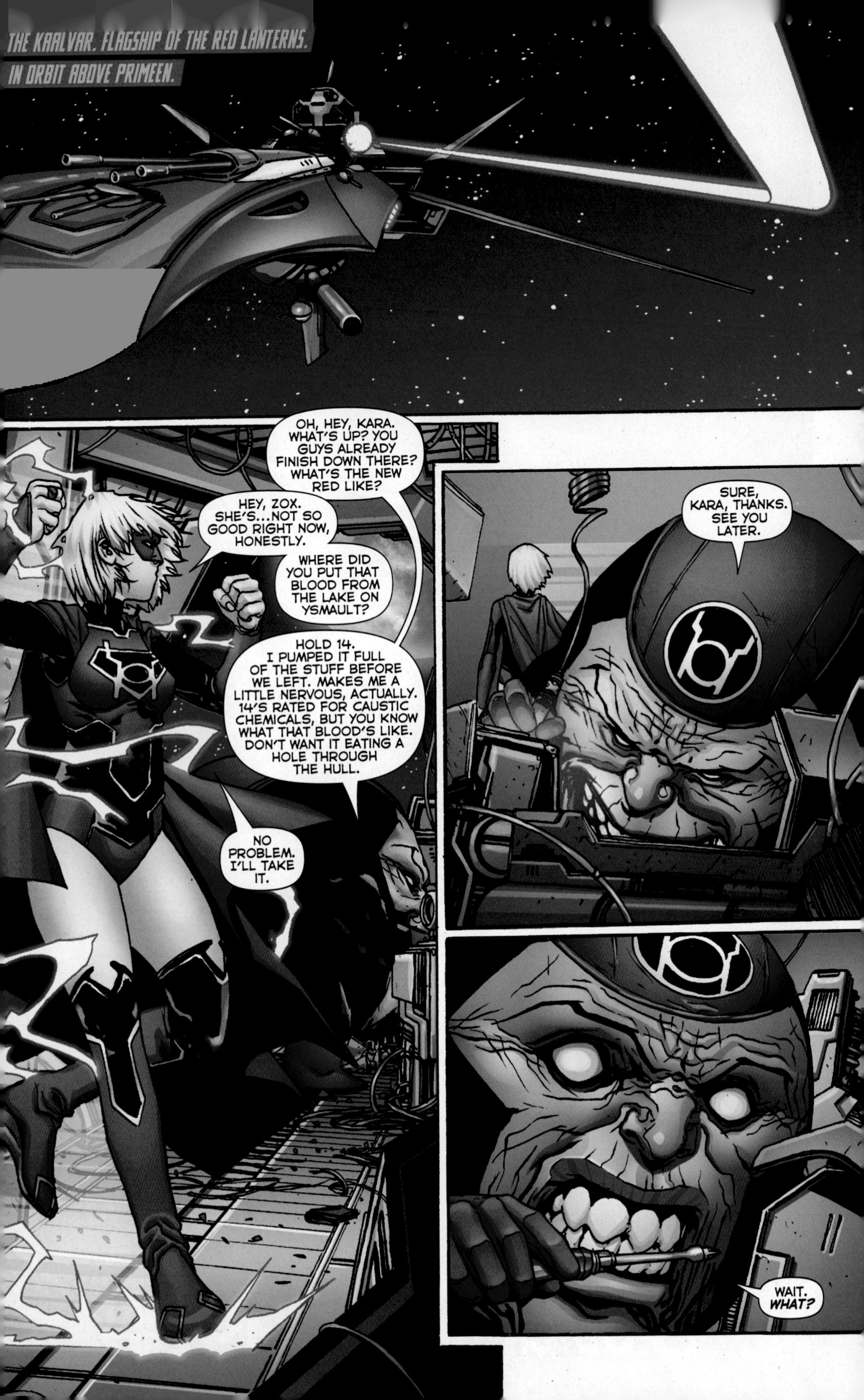
THE KAALVAR. FLAGSHIP OF THE RED LANTERNS.
IN ORBIT ABOVE PRIMEEN.
OH, HEY, KARA. WHAT'S UP? YOU GUYS ALREADY FINISH DOWN THERE? WHAT'S THE NEW RED LIKE?
HEY, ZOX. SHE'S...NOT SO GOOD RIGHT NOW, HONESTLY.
WHERE DID YOU PUT THAT BLOOD FROM THE LAKE ON YSMAULT?
HOLD 14. I PUMPED IT FULL OF THE STUFF BEFORE WE LEFT. MAKES ME A LITTLE NERVOUS, ACTUALLY. 14'S RATED FOR CAUSTIC CHEMICALS, BUT YOU KNOW WHAT THAT BLOOD'S LIKE. DON'T WANT IT EATING A HOLE THROUGH THE HULL.
NO PROBLEM. I'LL TAKE IT.
SURE, KARA, THANKS. SEE YOU LATER.
WAIT. WHAT?

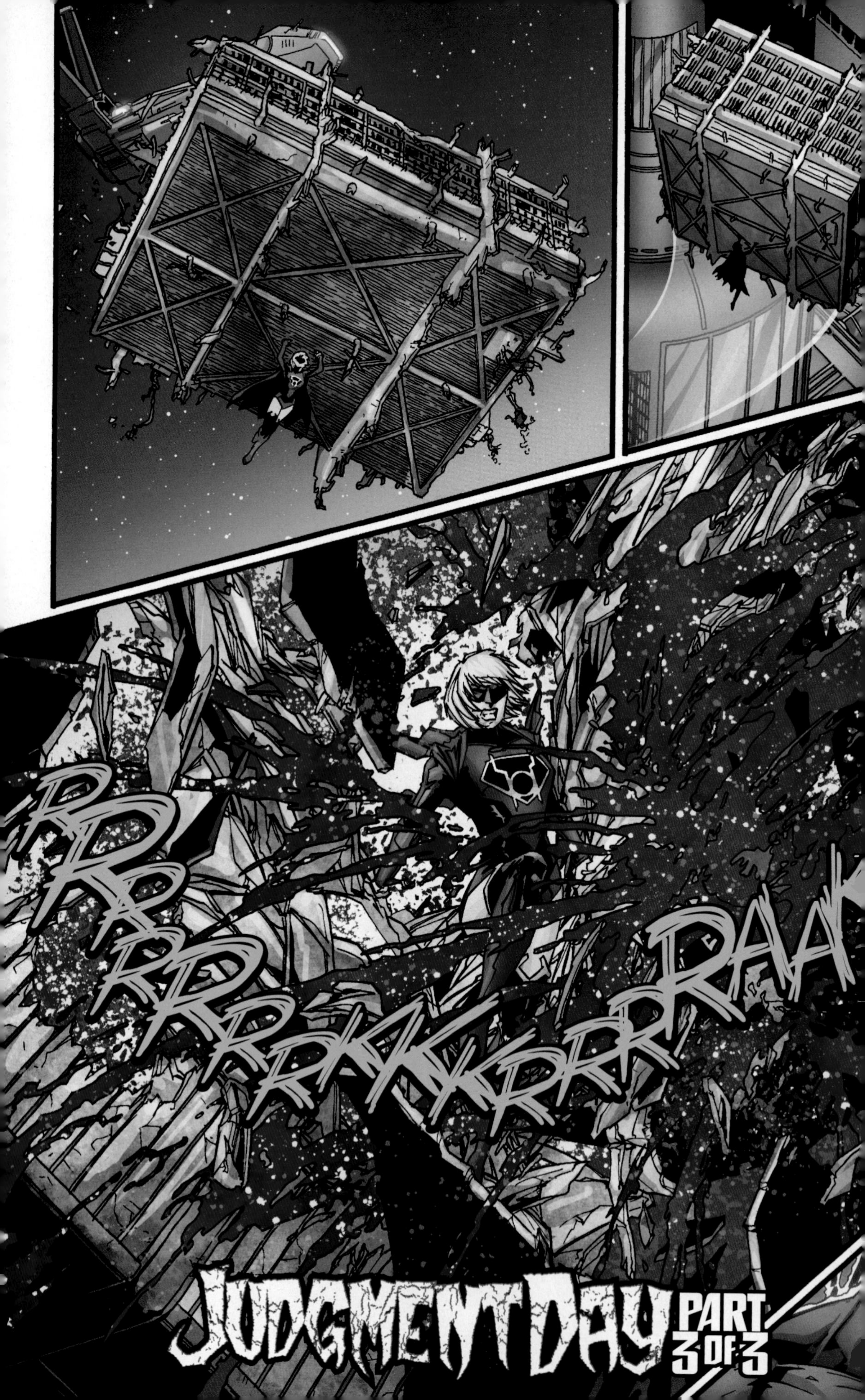
JUDGMENT DAY PART 3 OF 3

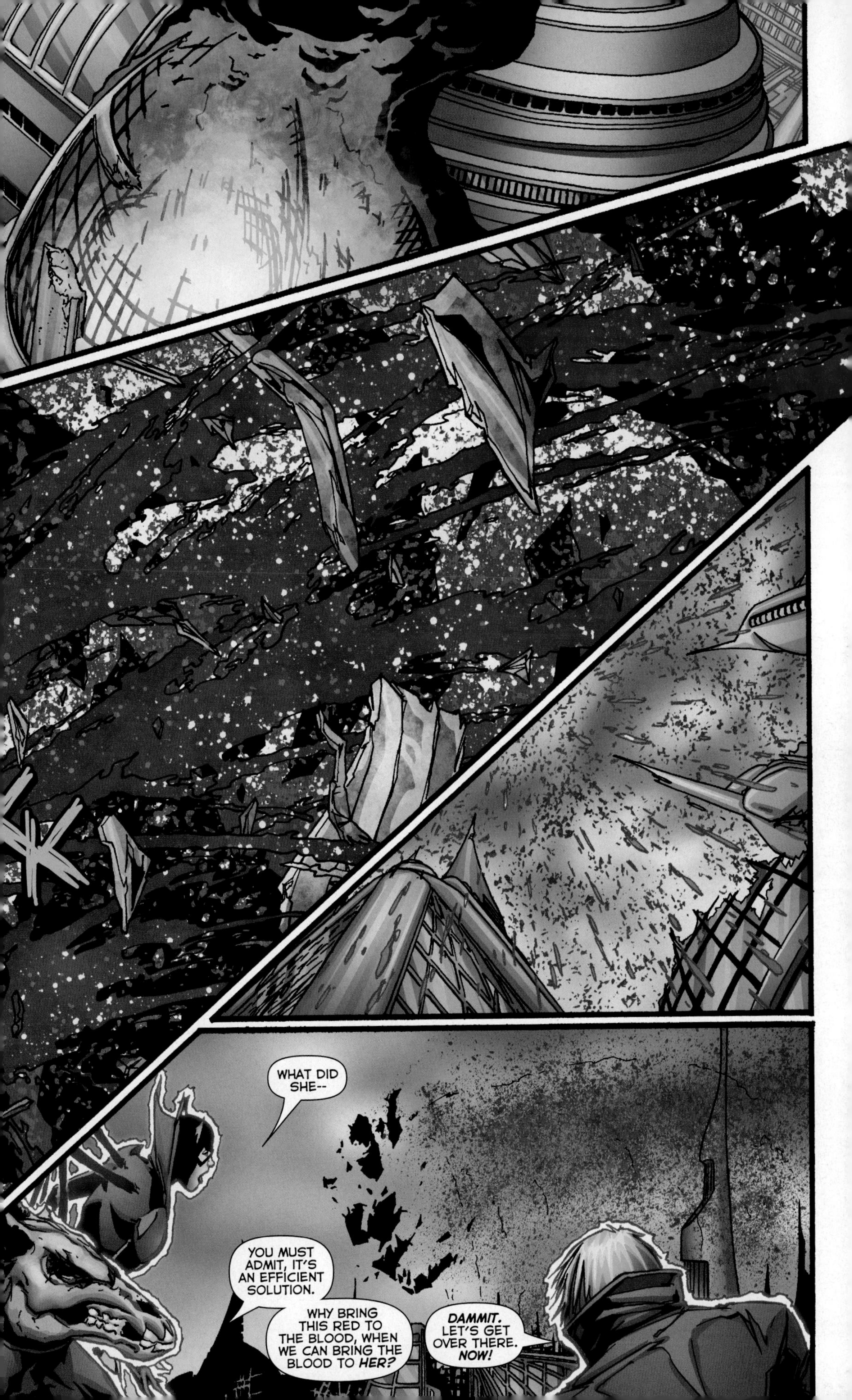
WHAT DID SHE--
YOU MUST ADMIT, IT'S AN EFFICIENT SOLUTION.
WHY BRING THIS RED TO THE BLOOD, WHEN WE CAN BRING THE BLOOD TO *HER?*
DAMMIT. LET'S GET OVER THERE. *NOW!*

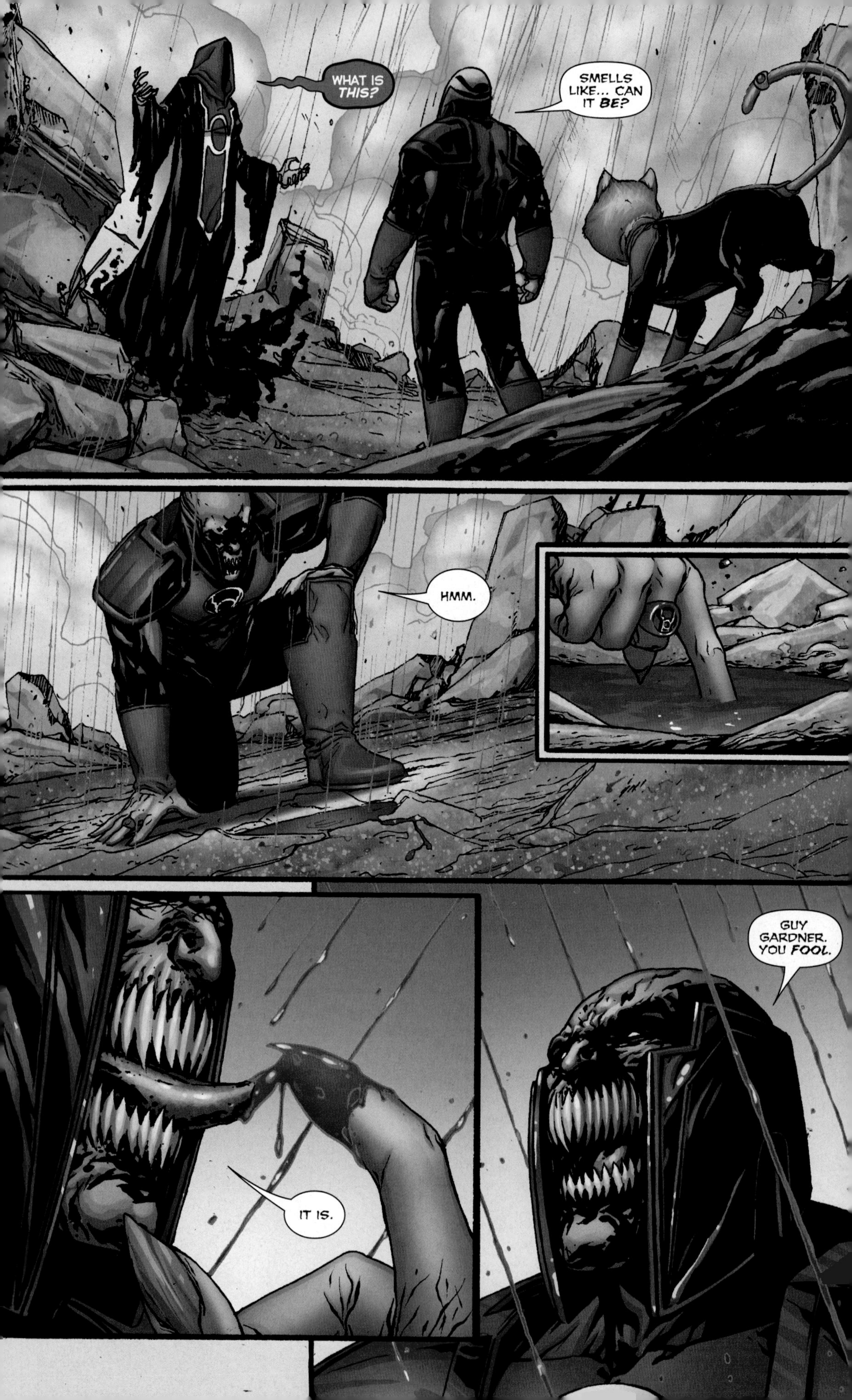
WHAT IS THIS?
SMELLS LIKE... CAN IT BE?
HMM.
IT IS.
GUY GARDNER. YOU FOOL.

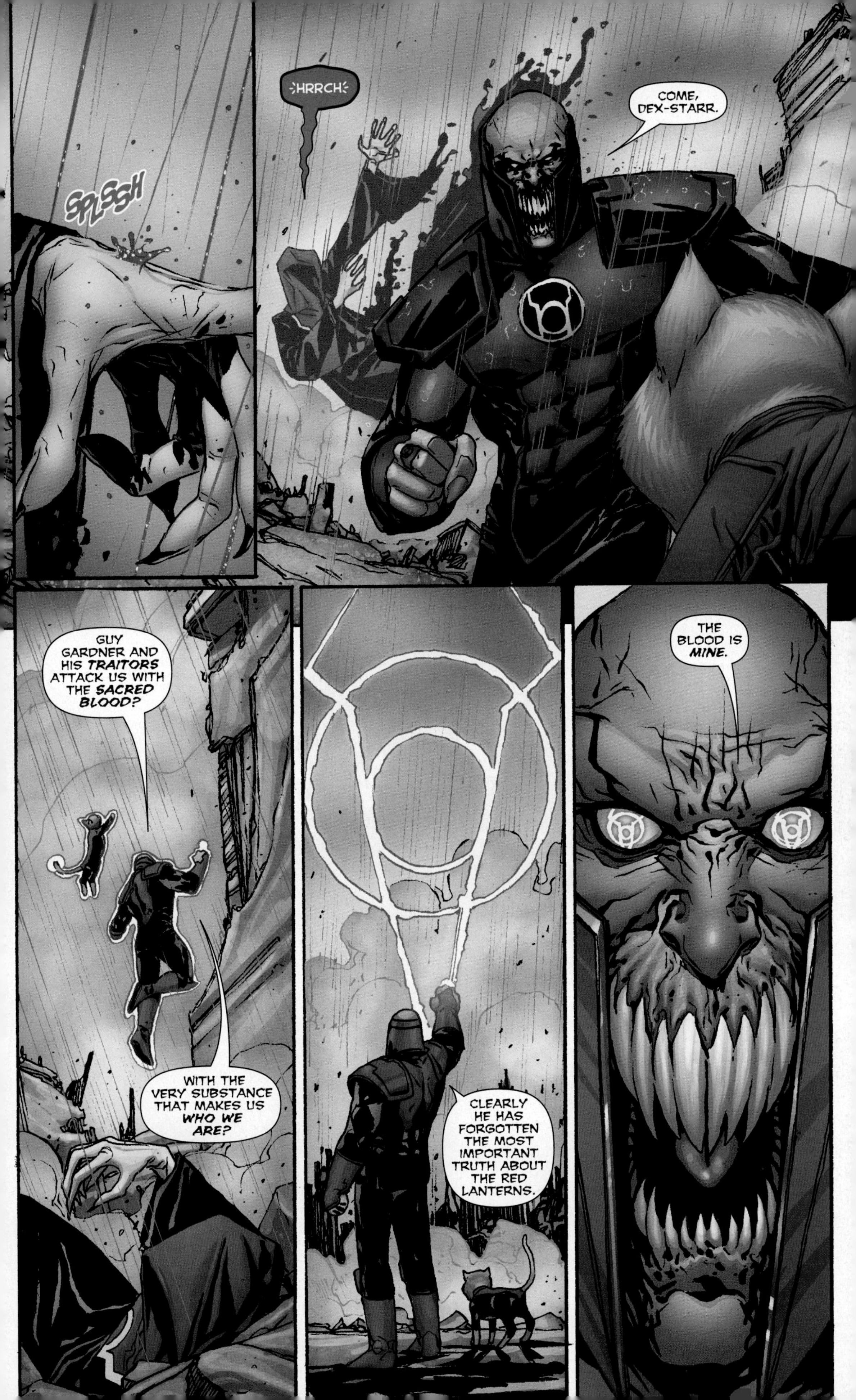

SPLSSH
HRRCH
COME, DEX-STARR.
GUY GARDNER AND HIS *TRAITORS* ATTACK US WITH THE *SACRED BLOOD?*
WITH THE VERY SUBSTANCE THAT MAKES US *WHO WE ARE?*
CLEARLY HE HAS FORGOTTEN THE MOST IMPORTANT TRUTH ABOUT THE RED LANTERNS.
THE BLOOD IS *MINE.*

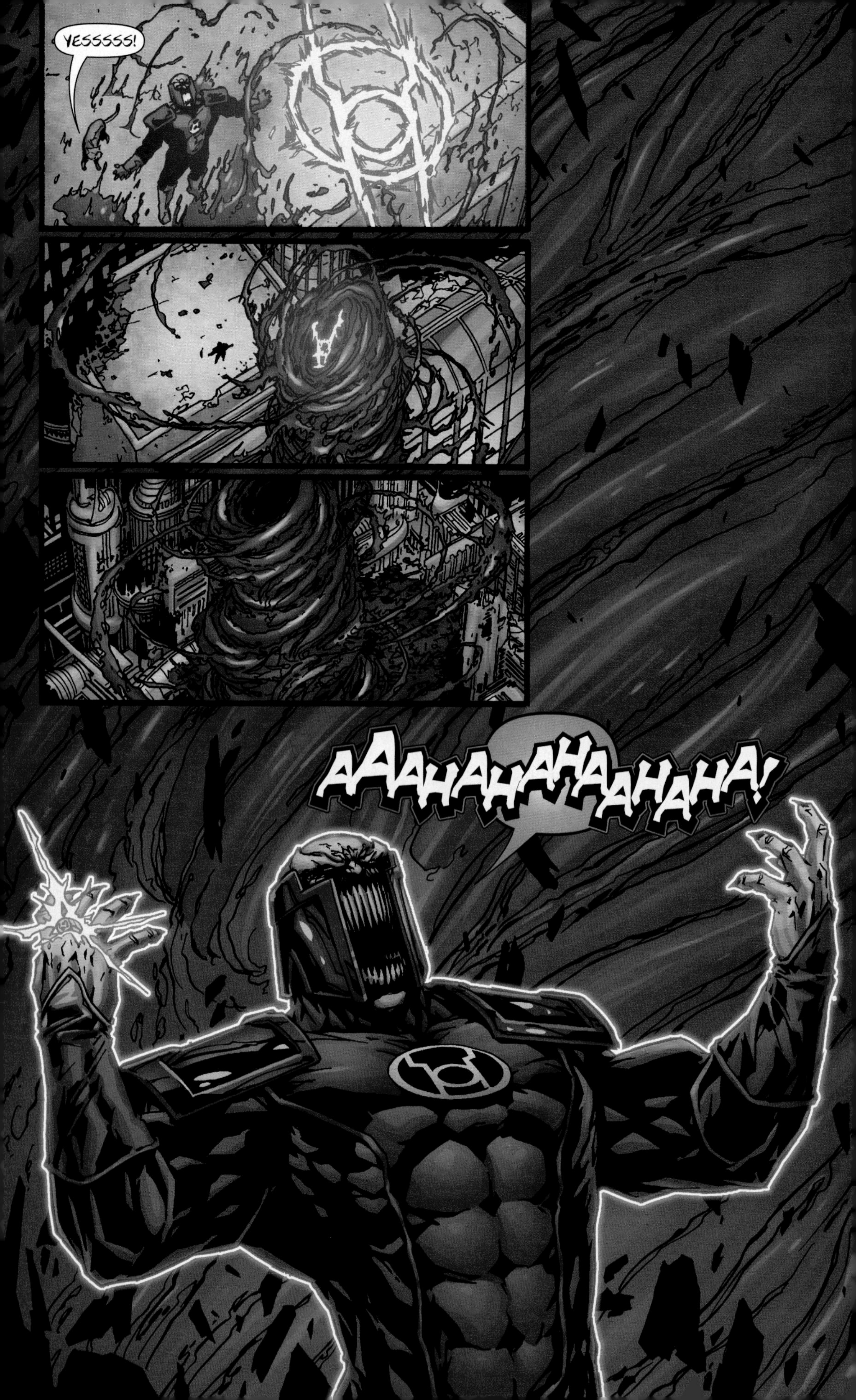
YESSSSS!
AAAHAHAHAAHAHA!

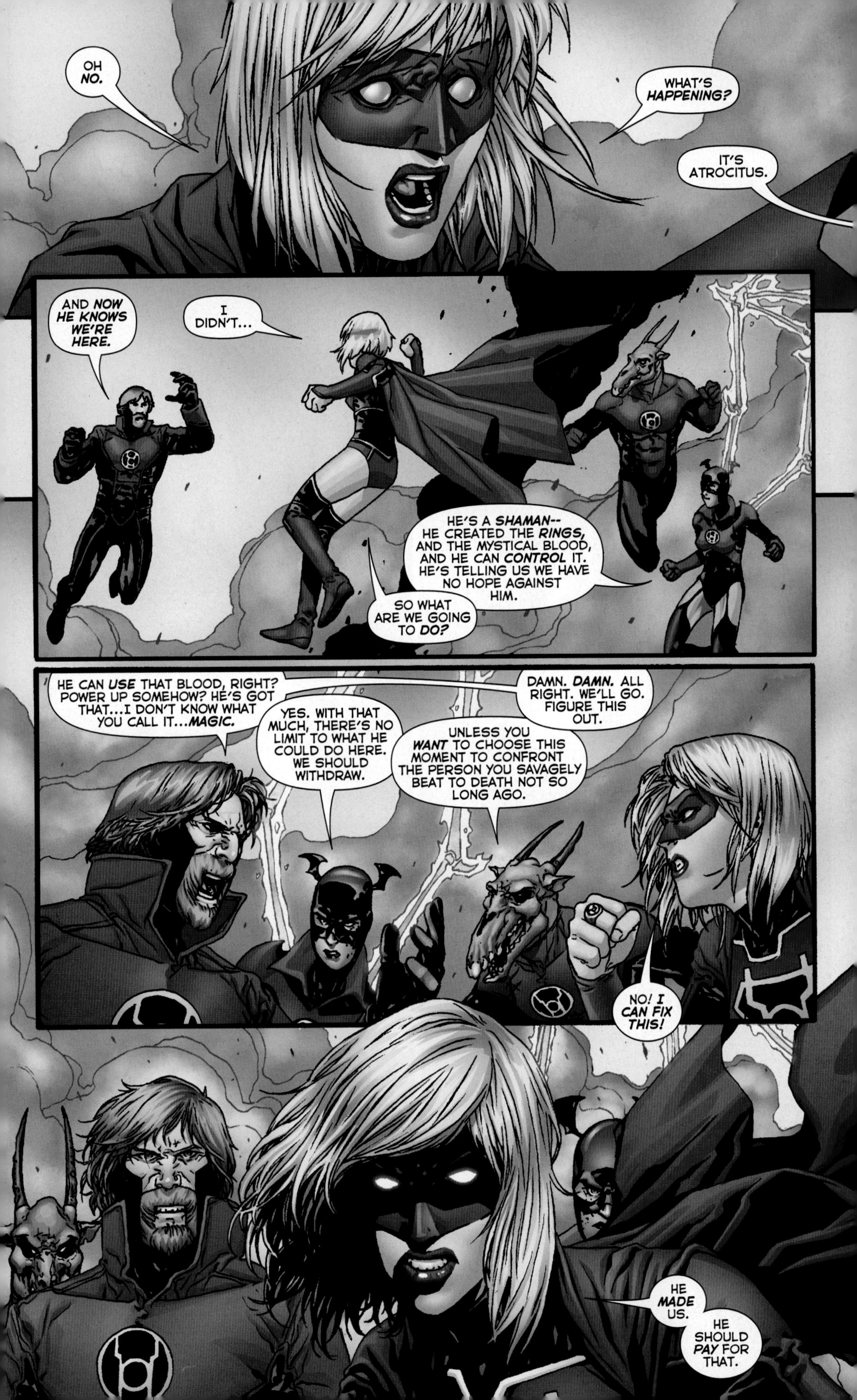
OH NO.
WHAT'S HAPPENING?
IT'S ATROCITUS.
AND NOW HE KNOWS WE'RE HERE.
I DIDN'T...
HE'S A SHAMAN-- HE CREATED THE RINGS, AND THE MYSTICAL BLOOD, AND HE CAN CONTROL IT. HE'S TELLING US WE HAVE NO HOPE AGAINST HIM.
SO WHAT ARE WE GOING TO DO?
HE CAN USE THAT BLOOD, RIGHT? POWER UP SOMEHOW? HE'S GOT THAT...I DON'T KNOW WHAT YOU CALL IT...MAGIC.
YES. WITH THAT MUCH, THERE'S NO LIMIT TO WHAT HE COULD DO HERE. WE SHOULD WITHDRAW.
DAMN. DAMN. ALL RIGHT. WE'LL GO. FIGURE THIS OUT.
UNLESS YOU WANT TO CHOOSE THIS MOMENT TO CONFRONT THE PERSON YOU SAVAGELY BEAT TO DEATH NOT SO LONG AGO.
NO! I CAN FIX THIS!
HE MADE US.
HE SHOULD PAY FOR THAT.

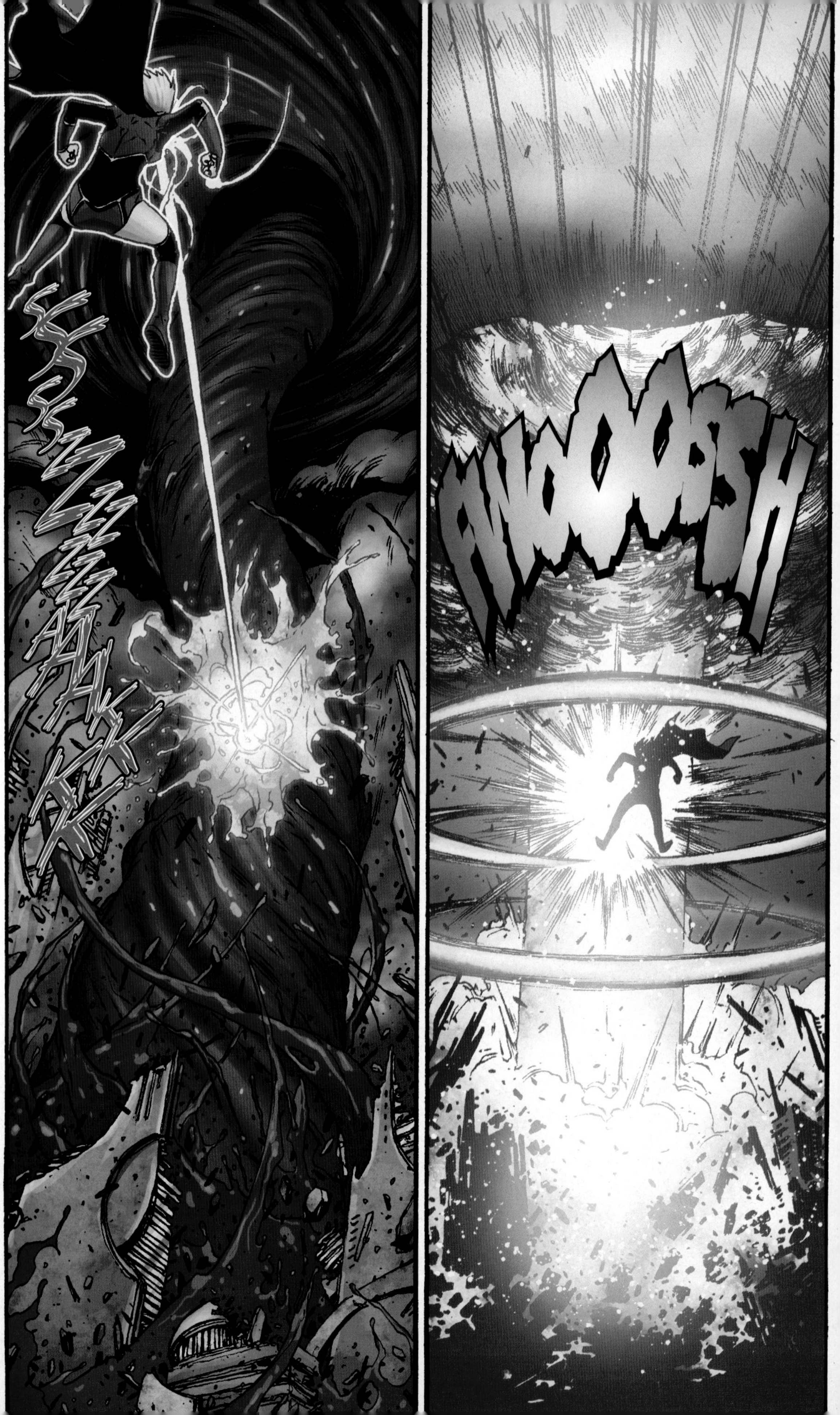
SSSSZZZZZZZAAAKKKK
WHOOOSH

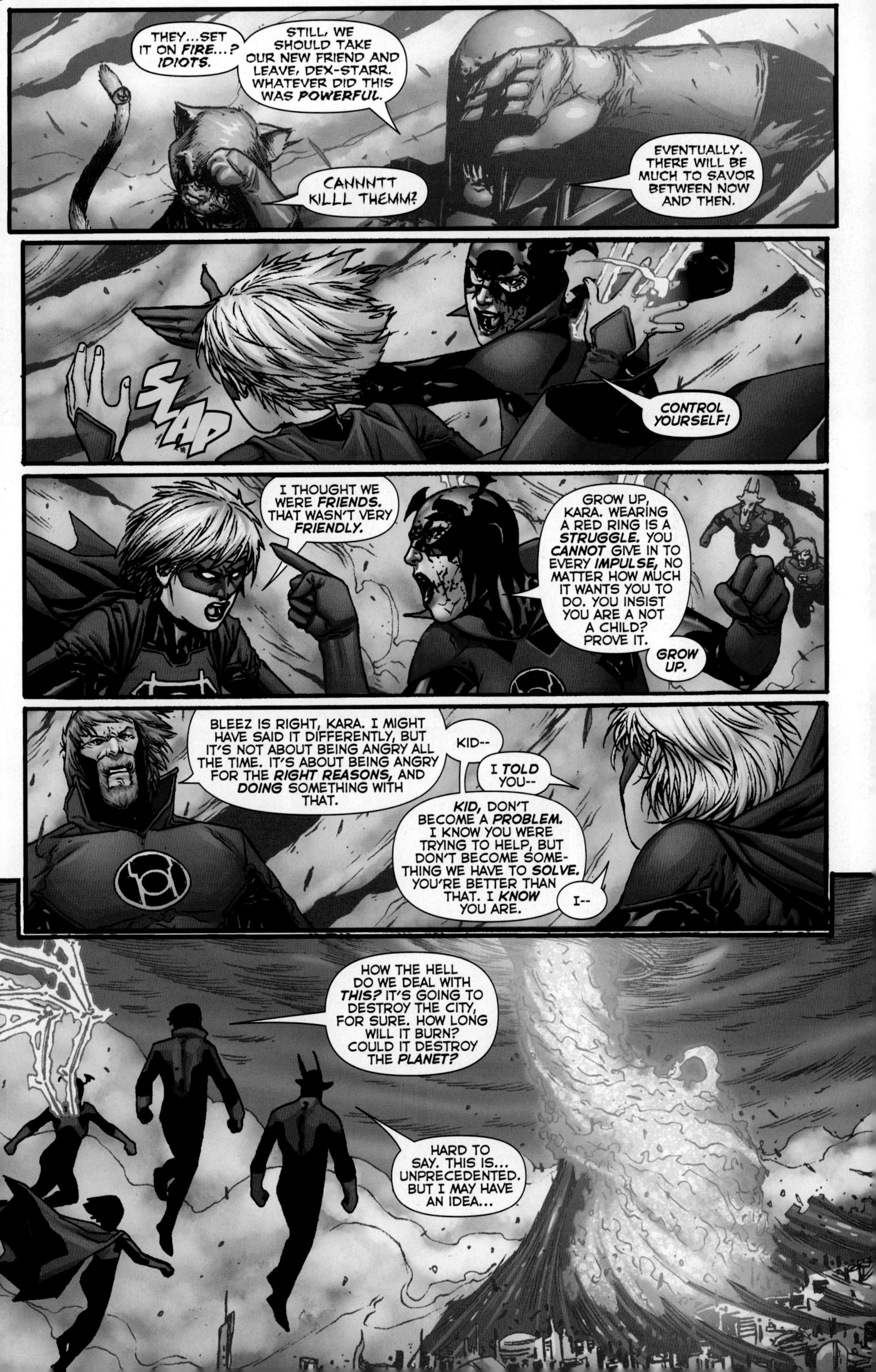
THEY...SET IT ON FIRE...? IDIOTS.
STILL, WE SHOULD TAKE OUR NEW FRIEND AND LEAVE, DEX-STARR. WHATEVER DID THIS WAS POWERFUL.
CANNNTT KILLL THEMM?
EVENTUALLY. THERE WILL BE MUCH TO SAVOR BETWEEN NOW AND THEN.
SLAP
CONTROL YOURSELF!
I THOUGHT WE WERE FRIENDS. THAT WASN'T VERY FRIENDLY.
GROW UP, KARA. WEARING A RED RING IS A STRUGGLE. YOU CANNOT GIVE IN TO EVERY IMPULSE, NO MATTER HOW MUCH IT WANTS YOU TO DO. YOU INSIST YOU ARE A NOT A CHILD? PROVE IT.
GROW UP.
BLEEZ IS RIGHT, KARA. I MIGHT HAVE SAID IT DIFFERENTLY, BUT IT'S NOT ABOUT BEING ANGRY ALL THE TIME. IT'S ABOUT BEING ANGRY FOR THE RIGHT REASONS, AND DOING SOMETHING WITH THAT.
KID--
I TOLD YOU--
KID, DON'T BECOME A PROBLEM. I KNOW YOU WERE TRYING TO HELP, BUT DON'T BECOME SOMETHING WE HAVE TO SOLVE. YOU'RE BETTER THAN THAT. I KNOW YOU ARE.
I--
HOW THE HELL DO WE DEAL WITH THIS? IT'S GOING TO DESTROY THE CITY, FOR SURE. HOW LONG WILL IT BURN? COULD IT DESTROY THE PLANET?
HARD TO SAY. THIS IS... UNPRECEDENTED. BUT I MAY HAVE AN IDEA...

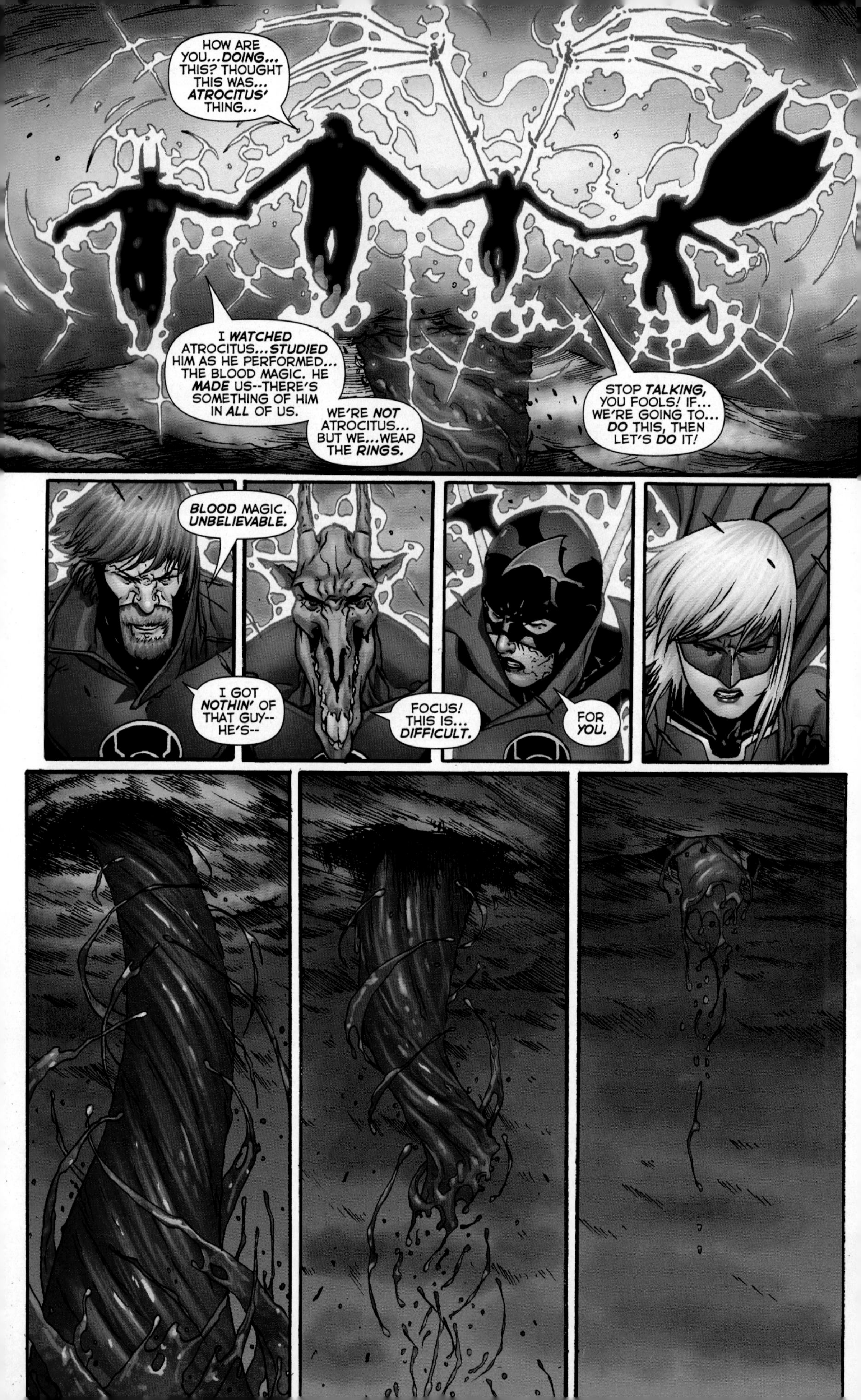
HOW ARE YOU...DOING... THIS? THOUGHT THIS WAS... ATROCITUS' THING...
I WATCHED ATROCITUS...STUDIED HIM AS HE PERFORMED... THE BLOOD MAGIC. HE MADE US--THERE'S SOMETHING OF HIM IN ALL OF US.
WE'RE NOT ATROCITUS... BUT WE...WEAR THE RINGS.
STOP TALKING, YOU FOOLS! IF... WE'RE GOING TO... DO THIS, THEN LET'S DO IT!
BLOOD MAGIC. UNBELIEVABLE.
I GOT NOTHIN' OF THAT GUY-- HE'S--
FOCUS! THIS IS... DIFFICULT.
FOR YOU.

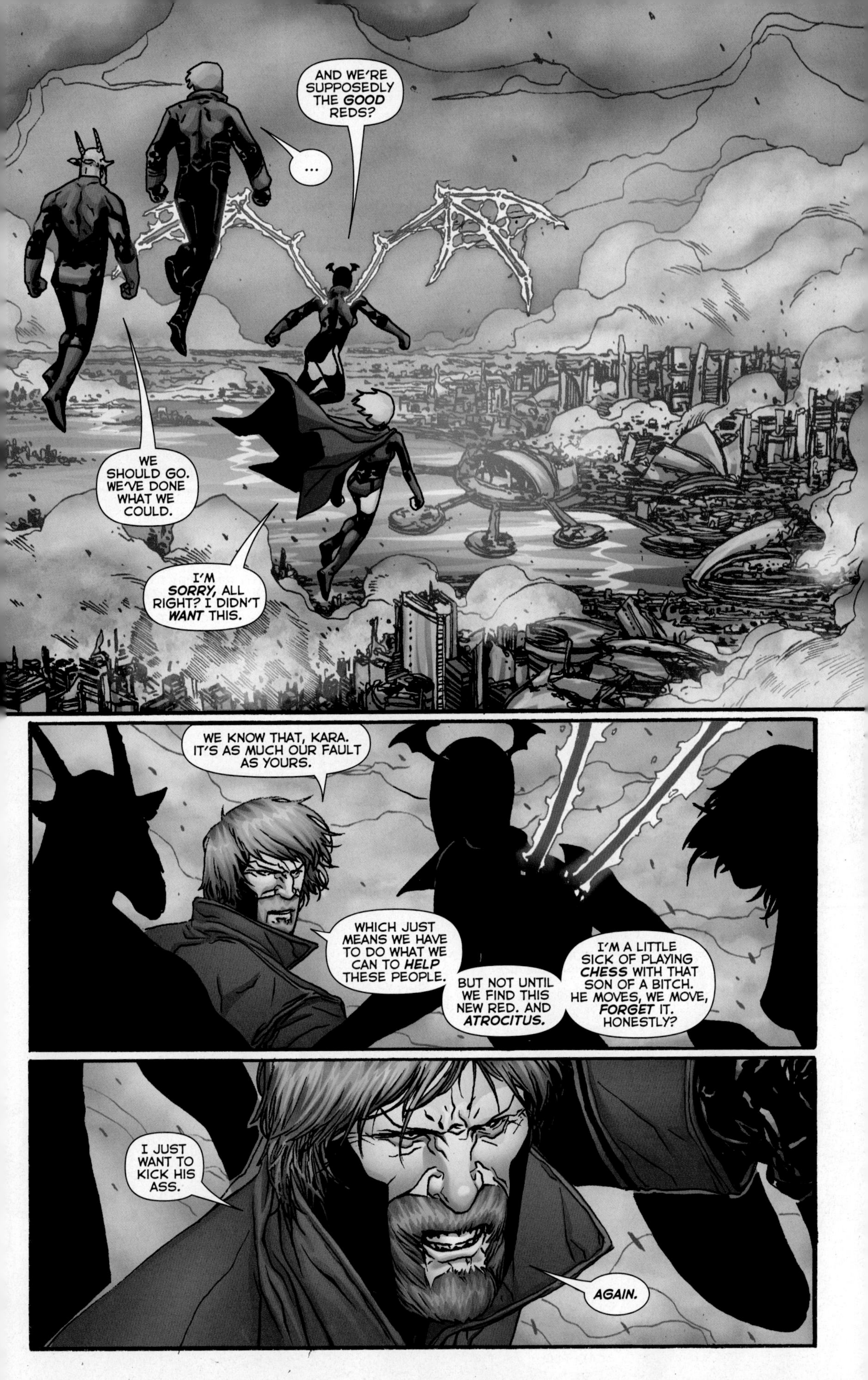
AND WE'RE SUPPOSEDLY THE GOOD REDS?
...
WE SHOULD GO. WE'VE DONE WHAT WE COULD.
I'M SORRY, ALL RIGHT? I DIDN'T WANT THIS.
WE KNOW THAT, KARA. IT'S AS MUCH OUR FAULT AS YOURS.
WHICH JUST MEANS WE HAVE TO DO WHAT WE CAN TO HELP THESE PEOPLE.
BUT NOT UNTIL WE FIND THIS NEW RED. AND ATROCITUS.
I'M A LITTLE SICK OF PLAYING CHESS WITH THAT SON OF A BITCH. HE MOVES, WE MOVE, FORGET IT. HONESTLY?
I JUST WANT TO KICK HIS ASS.
AGAIN.

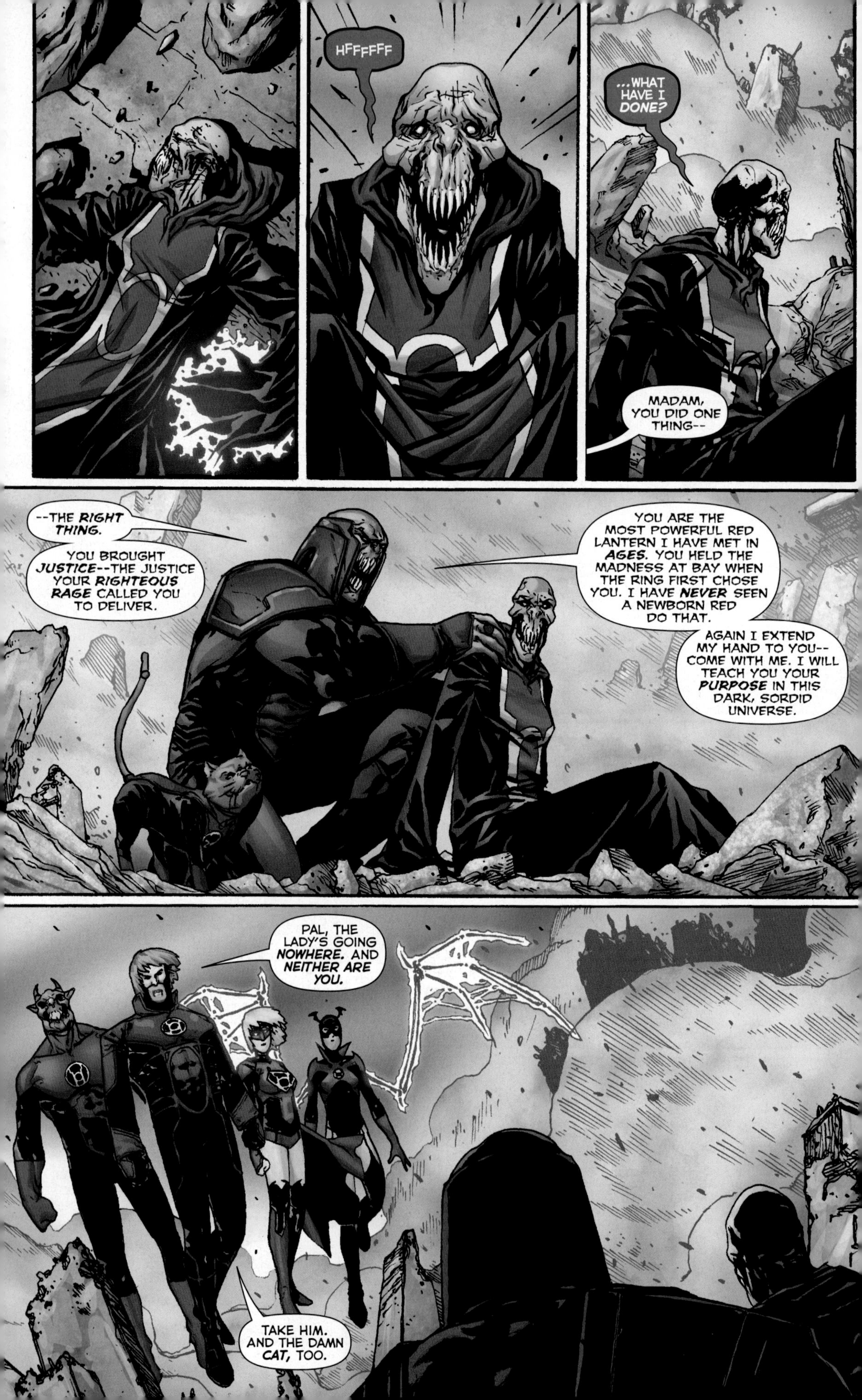
HFFFFFF
...WHAT HAVE I DONE?
MADAM, YOU DID ONE THING--
--THE RIGHT THING.
YOU BROUGHT JUSTICE--THE JUSTICE YOUR RIGHTEOUS RAGE CALLED YOU TO DELIVER.
YOU ARE THE MOST POWERFUL RED LANTERN I HAVE MET IN AGES. YOU HELD THE MADNESS AT BAY WHEN THE RING FIRST CHOSE YOU. I HAVE NEVER SEEN A NEWBORN RED DO THAT.
AGAIN I EXTEND MY HAND TO YOU-- COME WITH ME. I WILL TEACH YOU YOUR PURPOSE IN THIS DARK, SORDID UNIVERSE.
PAL, THE LADY'S GOING NOWHERE. AND NEITHER ARE YOU.
TAKE HIM. AND THE DAMN CAT, TOO.

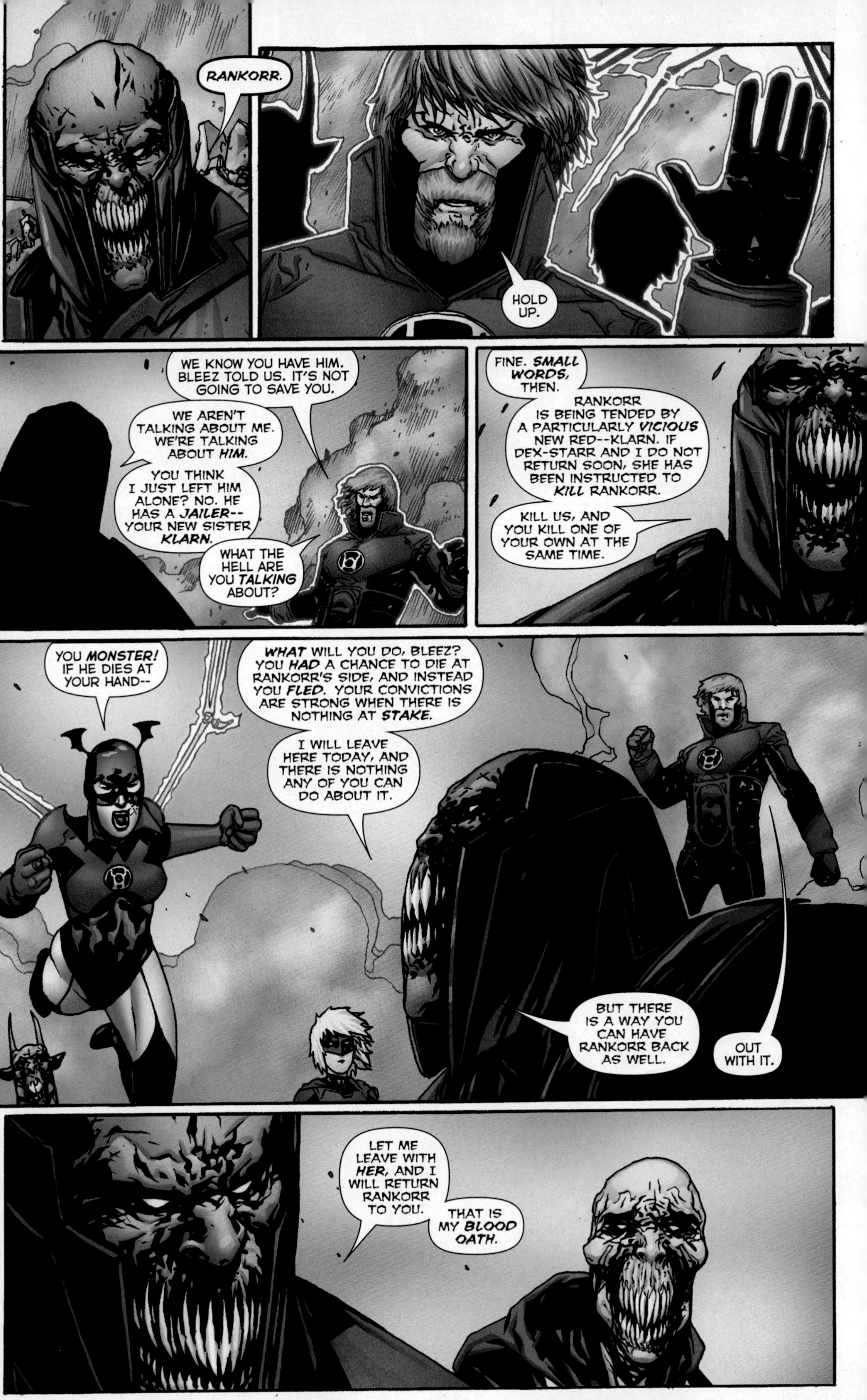
RANKORR.
HOLD UP.
WE KNOW YOU HAVE HIM. BLEEZ TOLD US. IT'S NOT GOING TO SAVE YOU.
WE AREN'T TALKING ABOUT ME. WE'RE TALKING ABOUT HIM.
YOU THINK I JUST LEFT HIM ALONE? NO. HE HAS A JAILER-- YOUR NEW SISTER KLARN.
WHAT THE HELL ARE YOU TALKING ABOUT?
FINE. SMALL WORDS, THEN.
RANKORR IS BEING TENDED BY A PARTICULARLY VICIOUS NEW RED--KLARN. IF DEX-STARR AND I DO NOT RETURN SOON, SHE HAS BEEN INSTRUCTED TO KILL RANKORR.
KILL US, AND YOU KILL ONE OF YOUR OWN AT THE SAME TIME.
YOU MONSTER! IF HE DIES AT YOUR HAND--
WHAT WILL YOU DO, BLEEZ? YOU HAD A CHANCE TO DIE AT RANKORR'S SIDE, AND INSTEAD YOU FLED. YOUR CONVICTIONS ARE STRONG WHEN THERE IS NOTHING AT STAKE.
I WILL LEAVE HERE TODAY, AND THERE IS NOTHING ANY OF YOU CAN DO ABOUT IT.
BUT THERE IS A WAY YOU CAN HAVE RANKORR BACK AS WELL.
OUT WITH IT.
LET ME LEAVE WITH HER, AND I WILL RETURN RANKORR TO YOU.
THAT IS MY BLOOD OATH.

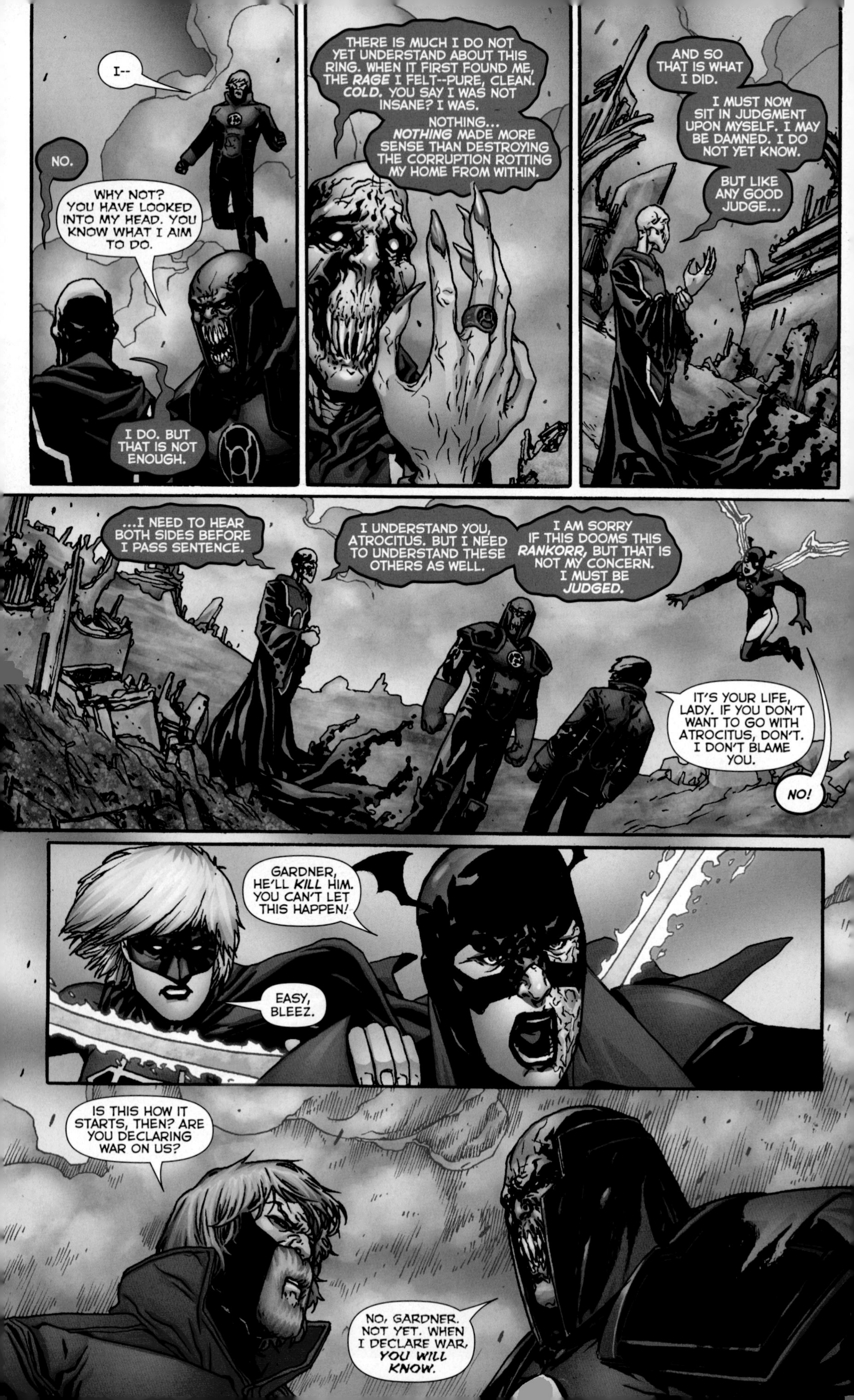
I--
NO.
WHY NOT? YOU HAVE LOOKED INTO MY HEAD. YOU KNOW WHAT I AIM TO DO.
I DO. BUT THAT IS NOT ENOUGH.
THERE IS MUCH I DO NOT YET UNDERSTAND ABOUT THIS RING. WHEN IT FIRST FOUND ME, THE RAGE I FELT--PURE, CLEAN. COLD. YOU SAY I WAS NOT INSANE? I WAS.
NOTHING... NOTHING MADE MORE SENSE THAN DESTROYING THE CORRUPTION ROTTING MY HOME FROM WITHIN.
AND SO THAT IS WHAT I DID.
I MUST NOW SIT IN JUDGMENT UPON MYSELF. I MAY BE DAMNED. I DO NOT YET KNOW.
BUT LIKE ANY GOOD JUDGE...
...I NEED TO HEAR BOTH SIDES BEFORE I PASS SENTENCE.
I UNDERSTAND YOU, ATROCITUS. BUT I NEED TO UNDERSTAND THESE OTHERS AS WELL.
I AM SORRY IF THIS DOOMS THIS RANKORR, BUT THAT IS NOT MY CONCERN. I MUST BE JUDGED.
IT'S YOUR LIFE, LADY. IF YOU DON'T WANT TO GO WITH ATROCITUS, DON'T. I DON'T BLAME YOU.
NO!
GARDNER, HE'LL KILL HIM. YOU CAN'T LET THIS HAPPEN!
EASY, BLEEZ.
IS THIS HOW IT STARTS, THEN? ARE YOU DECLARING WAR ON US?
NO, GARDNER. NOT YET. WHEN I DECLARE WAR, YOU WILL KNOW.

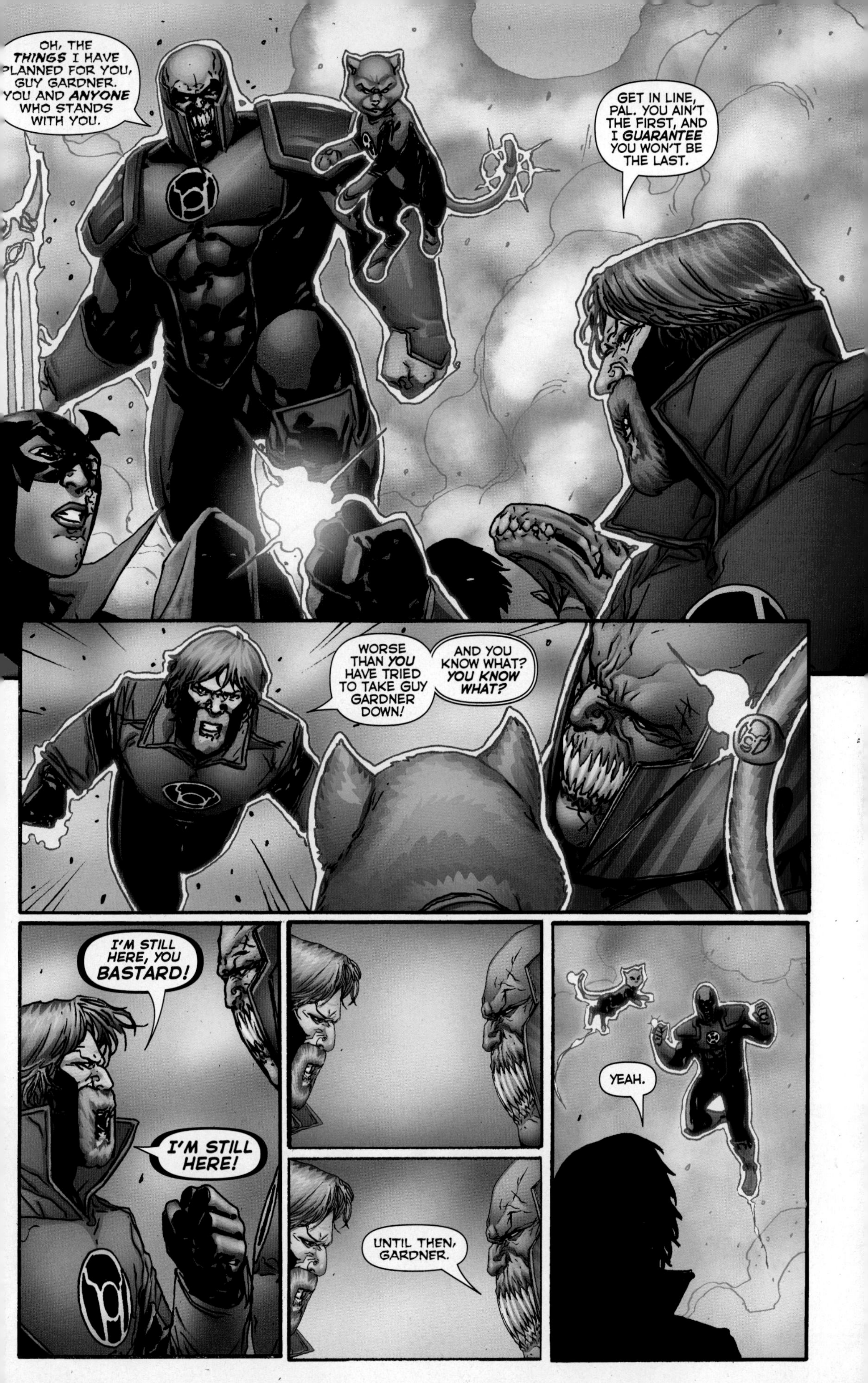
OH, THE THINGS I HAVE PLANNED FOR YOU, GUY GARDNER. YOU AND ANYONE WHO STANDS WITH YOU.
GET IN LINE, PAL. YOU AIN'T THE FIRST, AND I GUARANTEE YOU WON'T BE THE LAST.
WORSE THAN YOU HAVE TRIED TO TAKE GUY GARDNER DOWN!
AND YOU KNOW WHAT? YOU KNOW WHAT?
I'M STILL HERE, YOU BASTARD!
I'M STILL HERE!
UNTIL THEN, GARDNER.
YEAH.

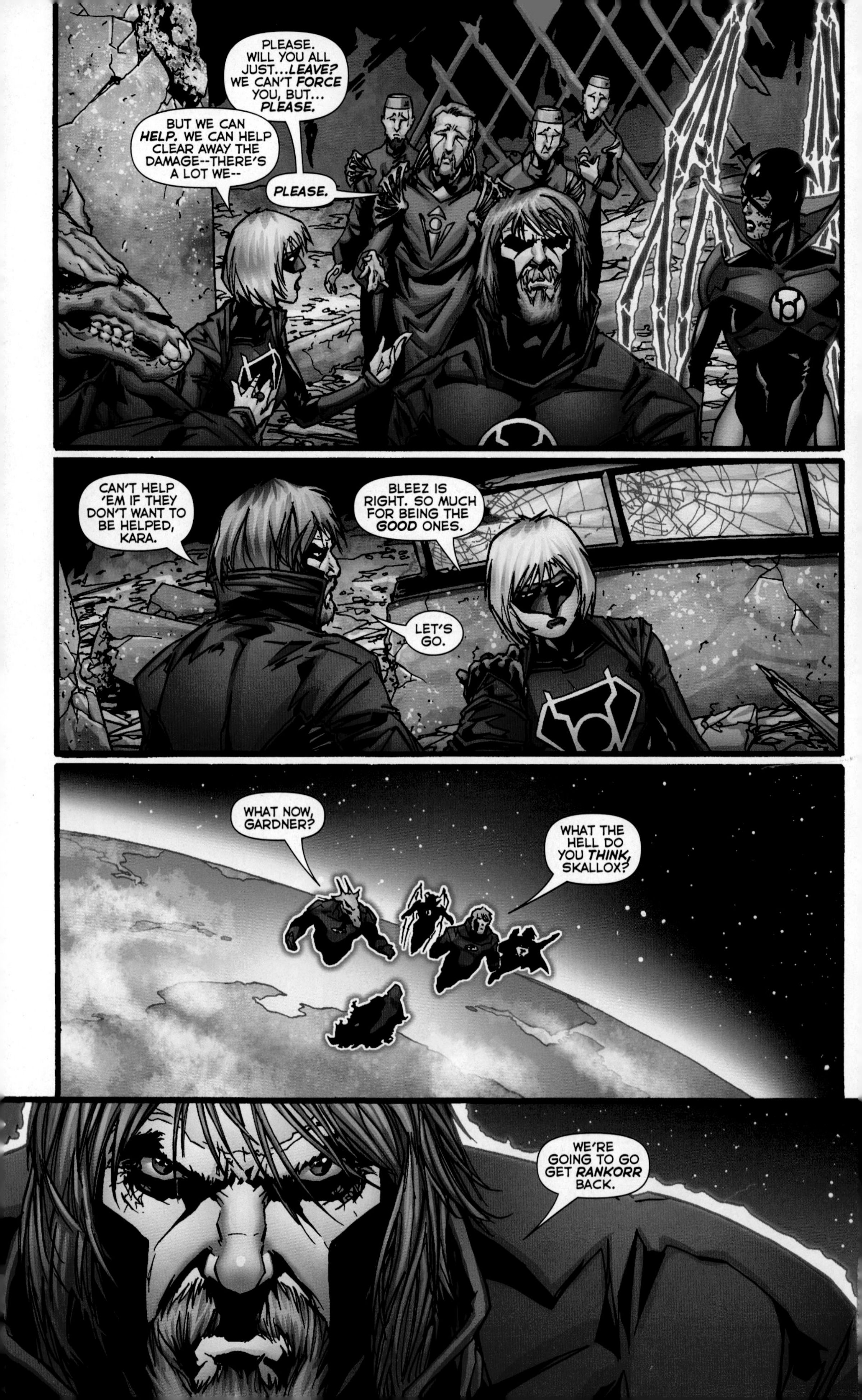
PLEASE. WILL YOU ALL JUST...LEAVE? WE CAN'T FORCE YOU, BUT... PLEASE.
BUT WE CAN HELP. WE CAN HELP CLEAR AWAY THE DAMAGE--THERE'S A LOT WE--
PLEASE.
CAN'T HELP 'EM IF THEY DON'T WANT TO BE HELPED, KARA.
BLEEZ IS RIGHT. SO MUCH FOR BEING THE GOOD ONES.
LET'S GO.
WHAT NOW, GARDNER?
WHAT THE HELL DO YOU THINK, SKALLOX?
WE'RE GOING TO GO GET RANKORR BACK.

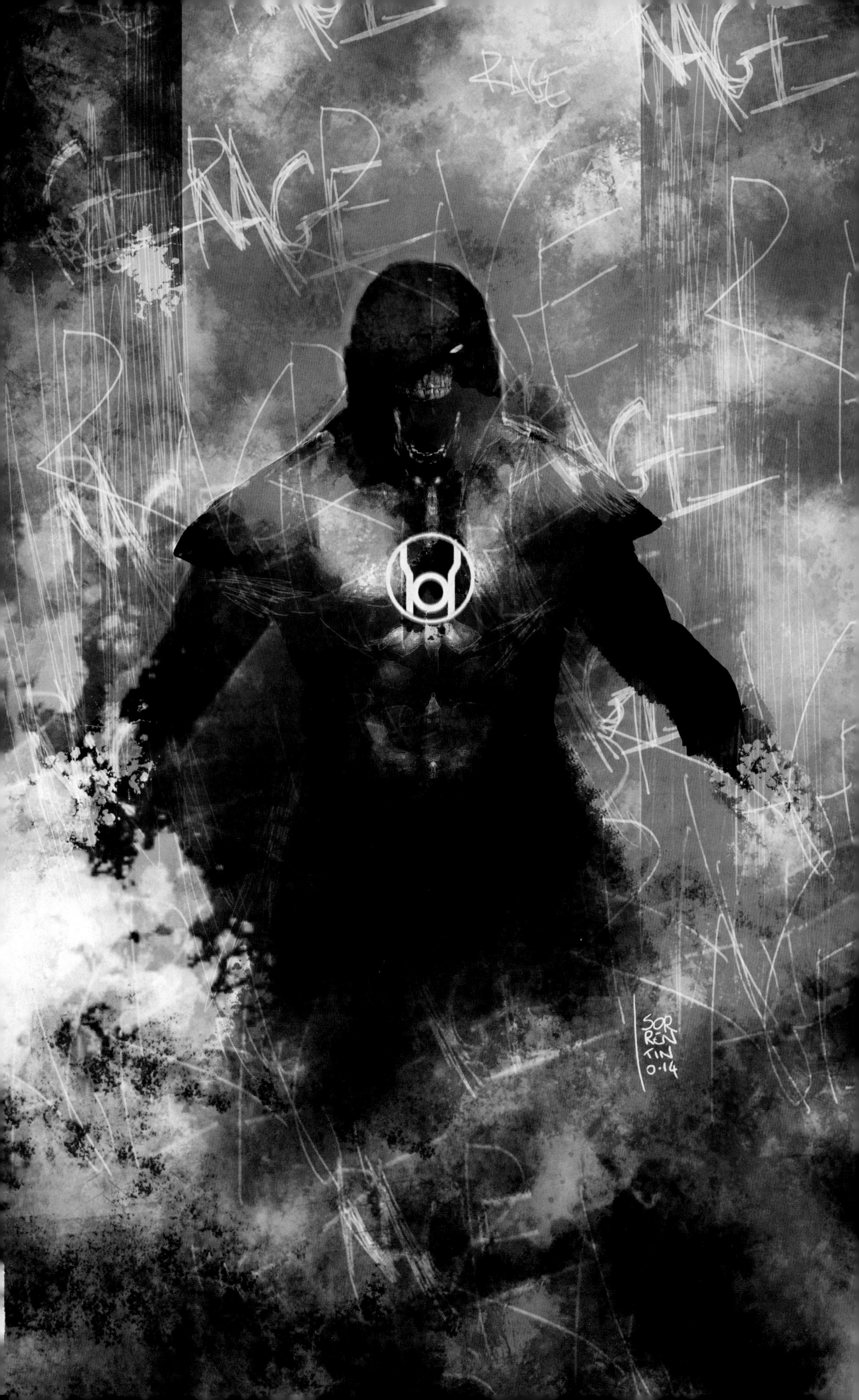
RAGE
SOR
REN
TIN
O·14

CHARLES SOULE writer **J. CALAFIORE** artist **GABE ELTAEB** colorist **TAYLOR ESPOSITO** letterer
cover art by **ANDREA SORRENTINO**

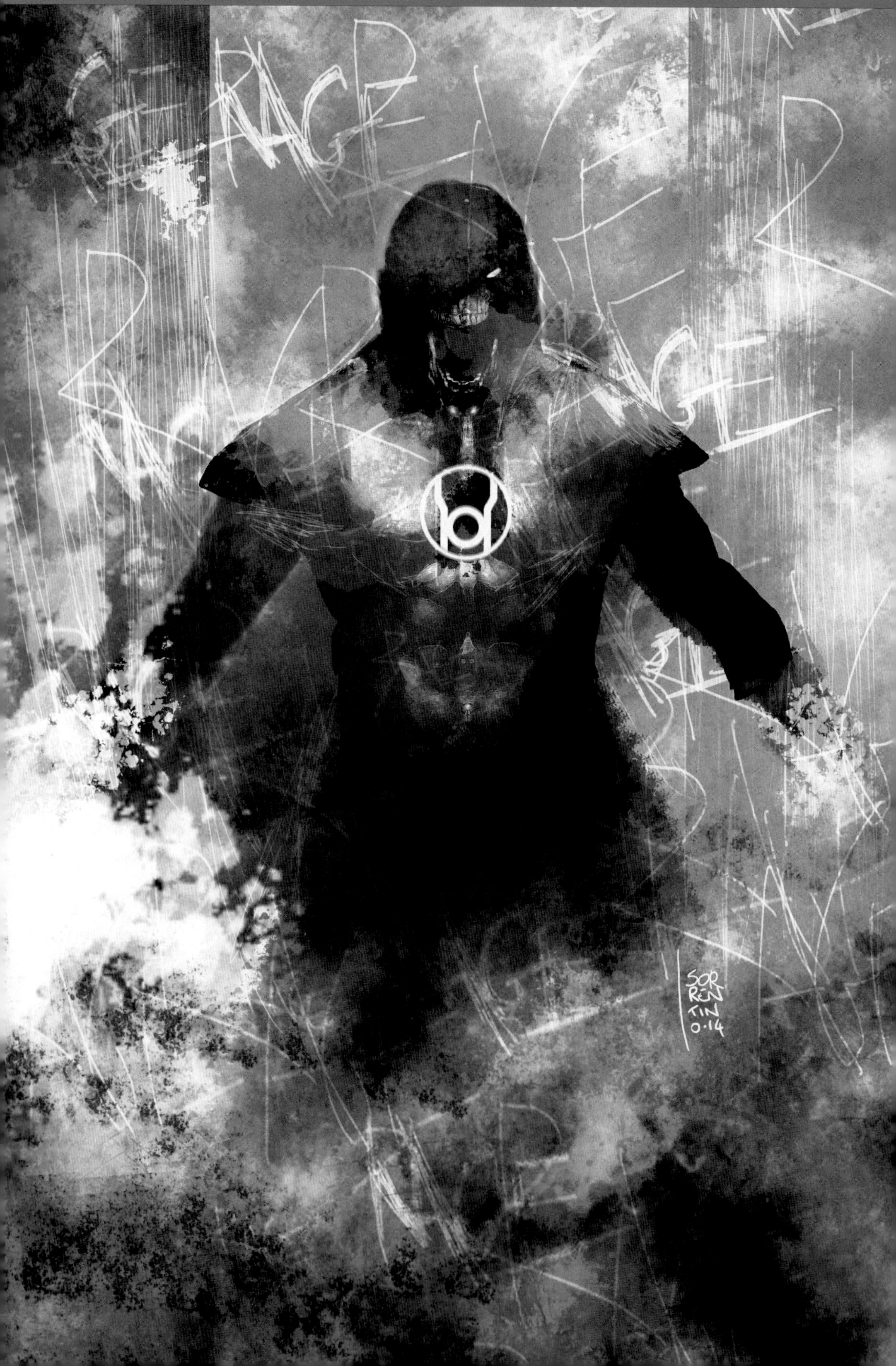
RAGE

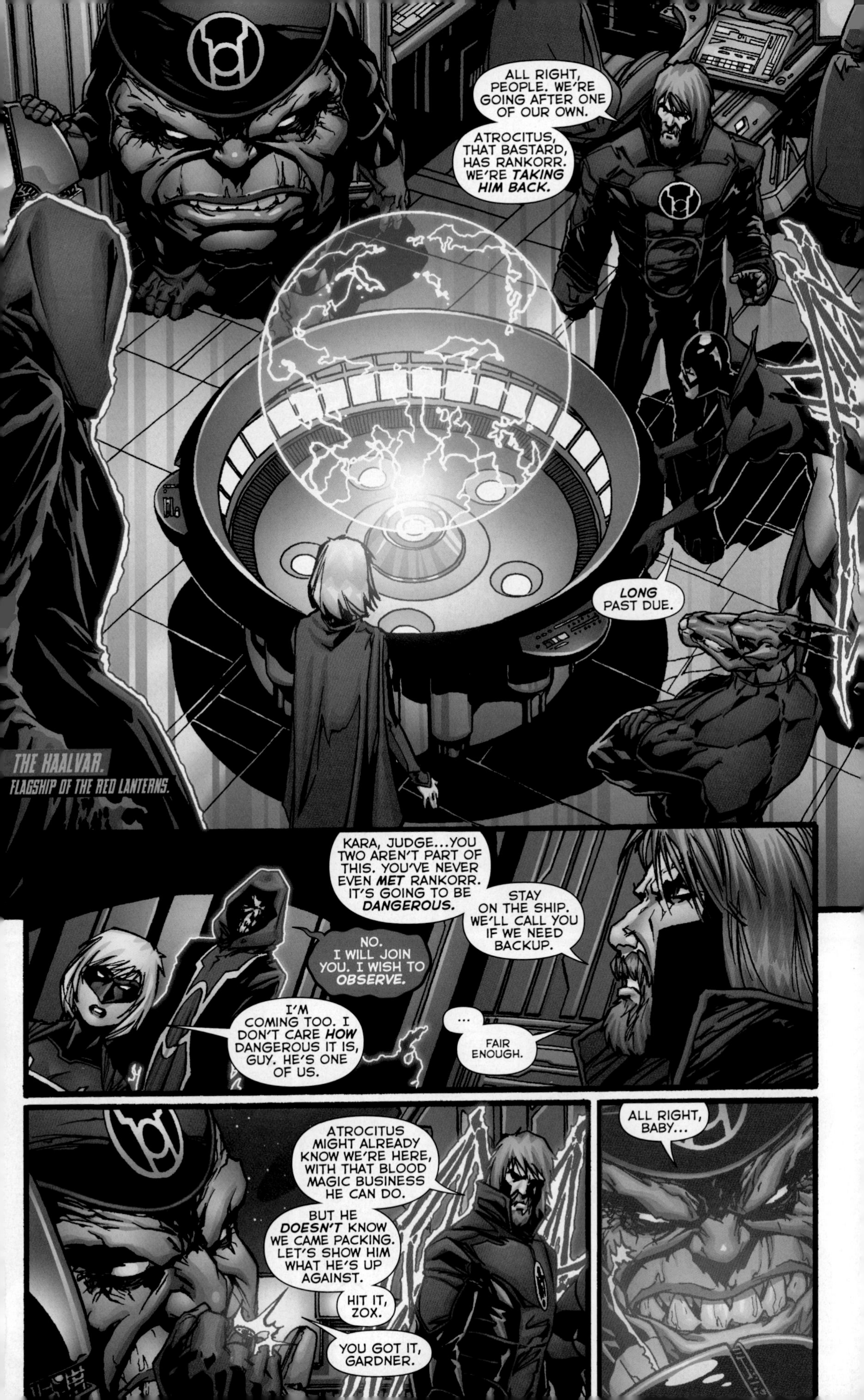
ALL RIGHT, PEOPLE. WE'RE GOING AFTER ONE OF OUR OWN.
ATROCITUS, THAT BASTARD, HAS RANKORR. WE'RE TAKING HIM BACK.
LONG PAST DUE.
THE HAALVAR.
FLAGSHIP OF THE RED LANTERNS.
KARA, JUDGE...YOU TWO AREN'T PART OF THIS. YOU'VE NEVER EVEN MET RANKORR. IT'S GOING TO BE DANGEROUS.
STAY ON THE SHIP. WE'LL CALL YOU IF WE NEED BACKUP.
NO. I WILL JOIN YOU. I WISH TO OBSERVE.
I'M COMING TOO. I DON'T CARE HOW DANGEROUS IT IS, GUY. HE'S ONE OF US.
...
FAIR ENOUGH.
ATROCITUS MIGHT ALREADY KNOW WE'RE HERE, WITH THAT BLOOD MAGIC BUSINESS HE CAN DO.
BUT HE DOESN'T KNOW WE CAME PACKING. LET'S SHOW HIM WHAT HE'S UP AGAINST.
HIT IT, ZOX.
YOU GOT IT, GARDNER.
ALL RIGHT, BABY...

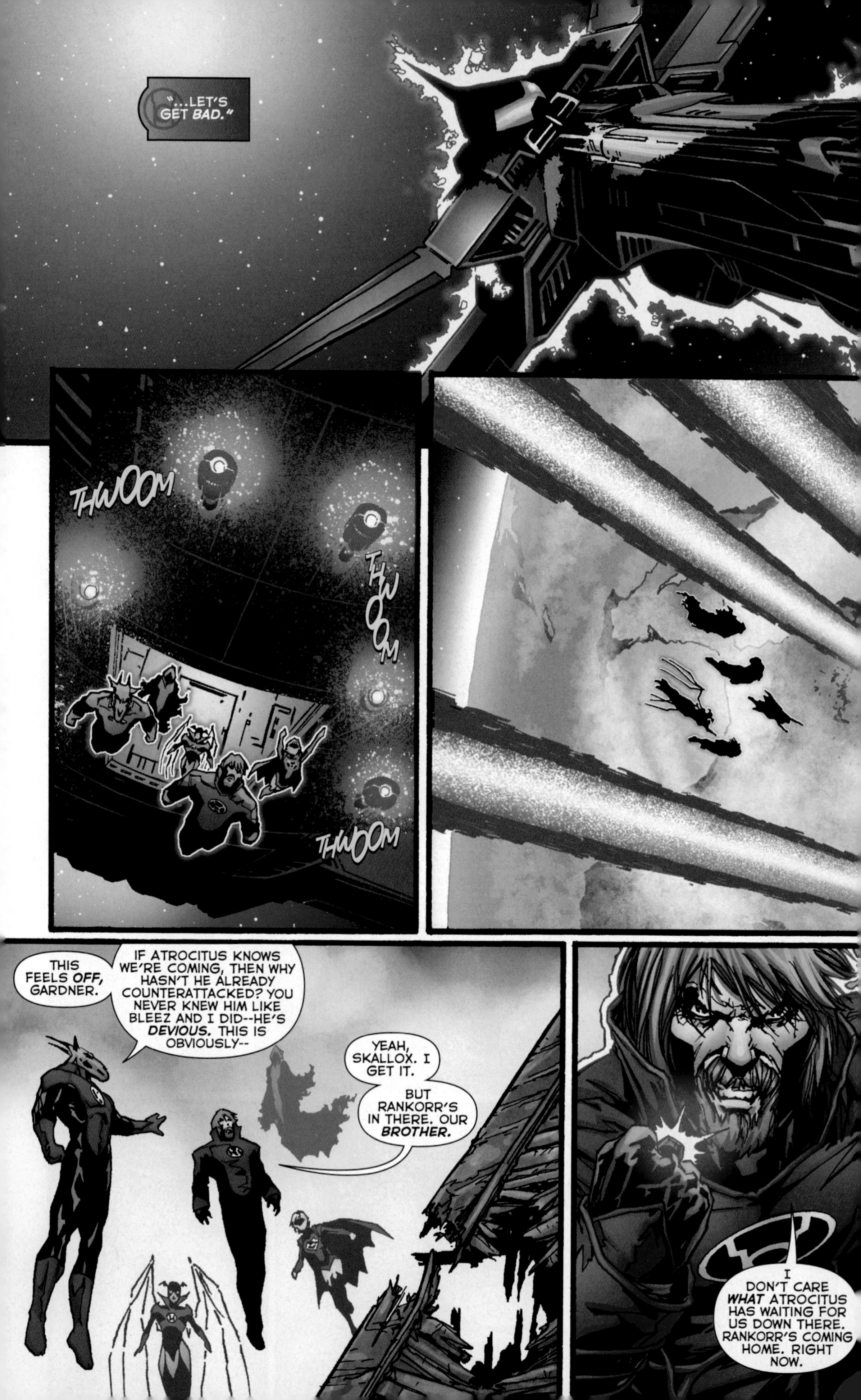
"...LET'S GET BAD."
THWOOM
THWOOM
THWOOM
THIS FEELS OFF, GARDNER.
IF ATROCITUS KNOWS WE'RE COMING, THEN WHY HASN'T HE ALREADY COUNTERATTACKED? YOU NEVER KNEW HIM LIKE BLEEZ AND I DID--HE'S DEVIOUS. THIS IS OBVIOUSLY--
YEAH, SKALLOX. I GET IT.
BUT RANKORR'S IN THERE. OUR BROTHER.
I DON'T CARE WHAT ATROCITUS HAS WAITING FOR US DOWN THERE. RANKORR'S COMING HOME. RIGHT NOW.

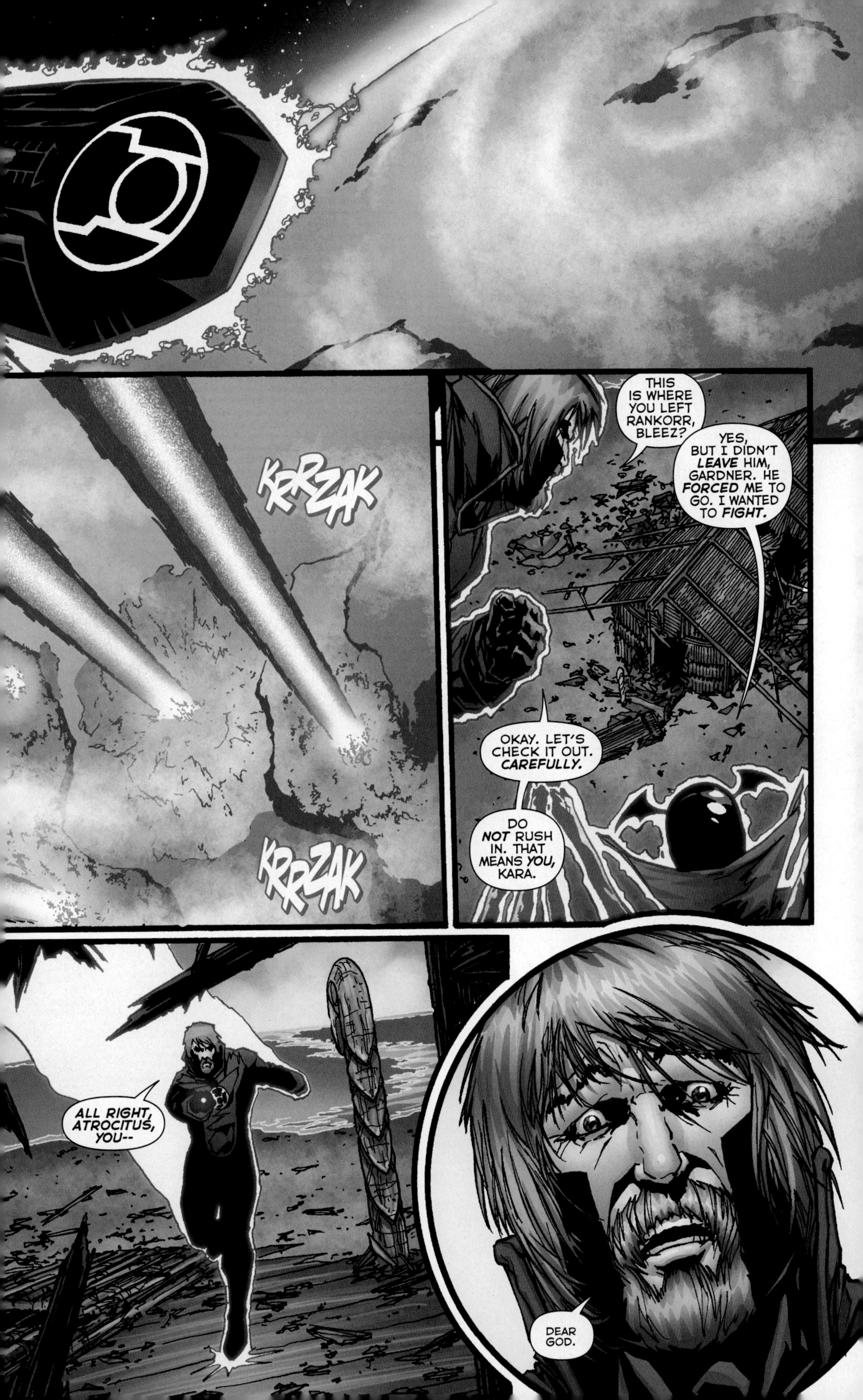

KRRZAK
KRRZAK
THIS IS WHERE YOU LEFT RANKORR, BLEEZ?
YES, BUT I DIDN'T LEAVE HIM, GARDNER. HE FORCED ME TO GO. I WANTED TO FIGHT.
OKAY. LET'S CHECK IT OUT. CAREFULLY.
DO NOT RUSH IN. THAT MEANS YOU, KARA.
ALL RIGHT, ATROCITUS, YOU--
DEAR GOD.

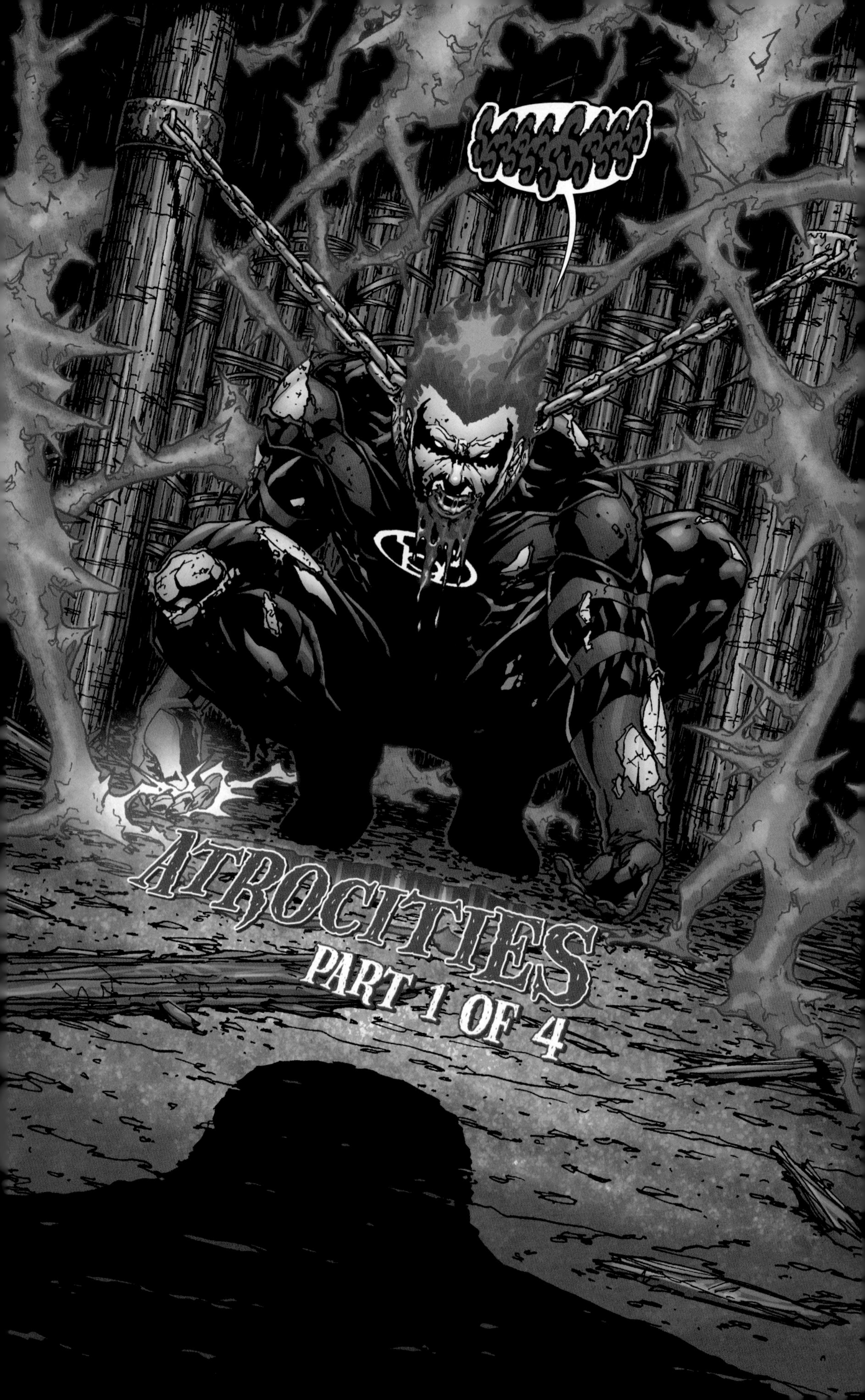
SSSSSSSSSSS
ATROCITIES
PART 1 OF 4

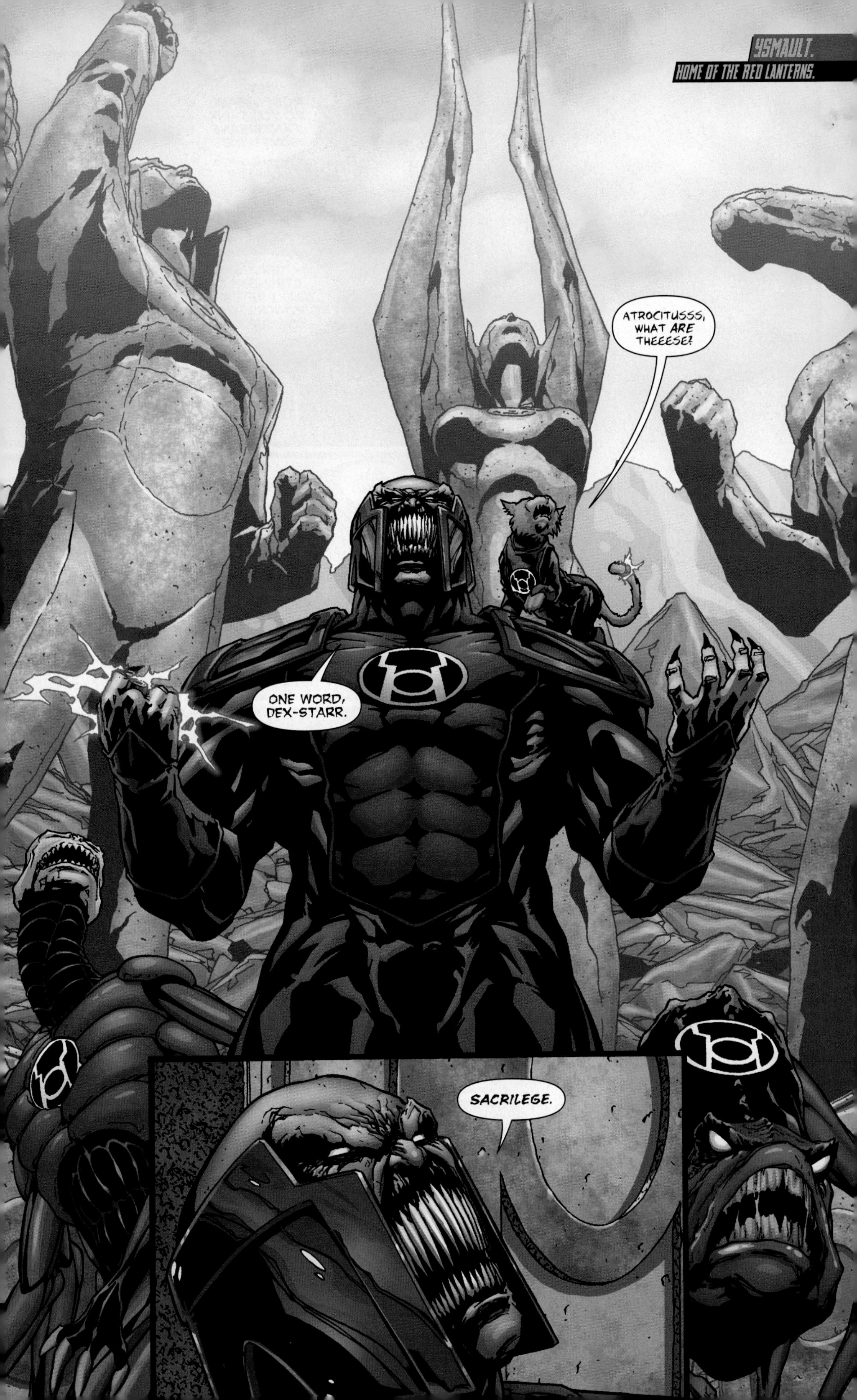
YSMAULT.
HOME OF THE RED LANTERNS.
ATROCITUSSS, WHAT ARE THEEESE?
ONE WORD, DEX-STARR.
SACRILEGE.

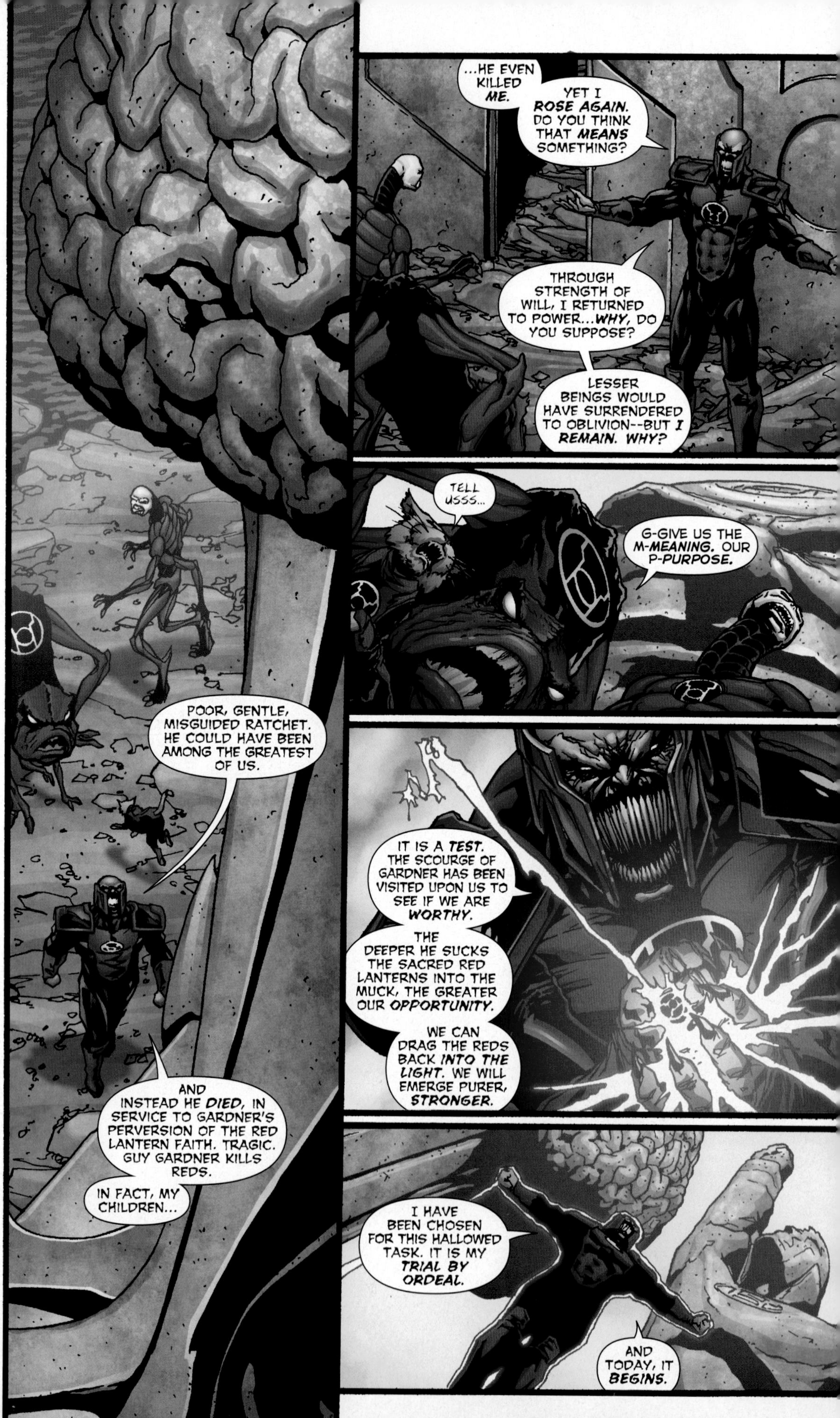
...HE EVEN KILLED ME.
YET I ROSE AGAIN. DO YOU THINK THAT MEANS SOMETHING?
THROUGH STRENGTH OF WILL, I RETURNED TO POWER...WHY, DO YOU SUPPOSE?
LESSER BEINGS WOULD HAVE SURRENDERED TO OBLIVION--BUT I REMAIN. WHY?
TELL USSS...
G-GIVE US THE M-MEANING. OUR P-PURPOSE.
POOR, GENTLE, MISGUIDED RATCHET. HE COULD HAVE BEEN AMONG THE GREATEST OF US.
AND INSTEAD HE DIED, IN SERVICE TO GARDNER'S PERVERSION OF THE RED LANTERN FAITH. TRAGIC. GUY GARDNER KILLS REDS.
IN FACT, MY CHILDREN...
IT IS A TEST. THE SCOURGE OF GARDNER HAS BEEN VISITED UPON US TO SEE IF WE ARE WORTHY.
THE DEEPER HE SUCKS THE SACRED RED LANTERNS INTO THE MUCK, THE GREATER OUR OPPORTUNITY.
WE CAN DRAG THE REDS BACK INTO THE LIGHT. WE WILL EMERGE PURER, STRONGER.
I HAVE BEEN CHOSEN FOR THIS HALLOWED TASK. IT IS MY TRIAL BY ORDEAL.
AND TODAY, IT BEGINS.

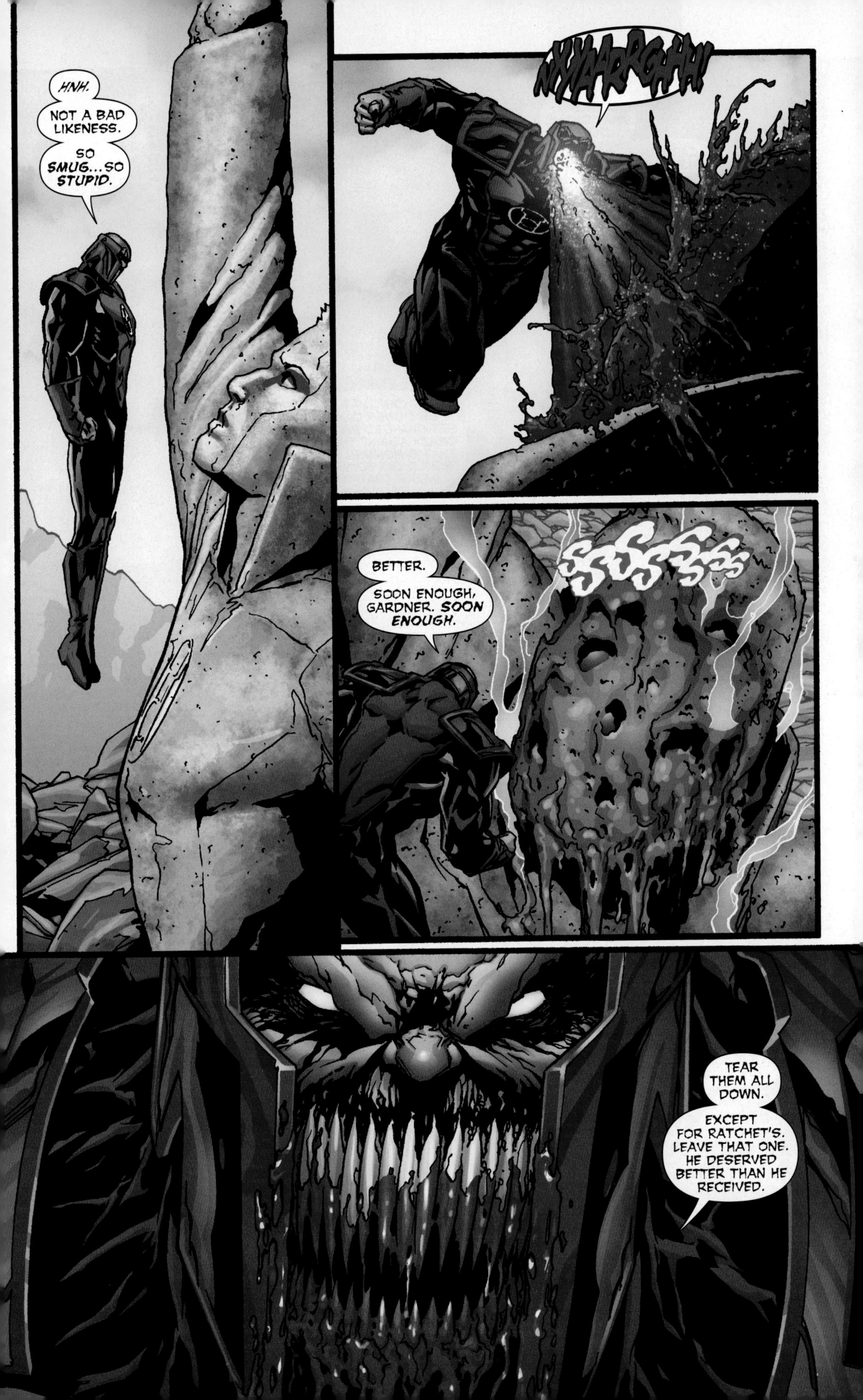
HNH.
NOT A BAD LIKENESS.
SO SMUG...SO STUPID.
NYYAARRGHHH!
BETTER.
SOON ENOUGH, GARDNER. SOON ENOUGH.
TEAR THEM ALL DOWN.
EXCEPT FOR RATCHET'S. LEAVE THAT ONE. HE DESERVED BETTER THAN HE RECEIVED.

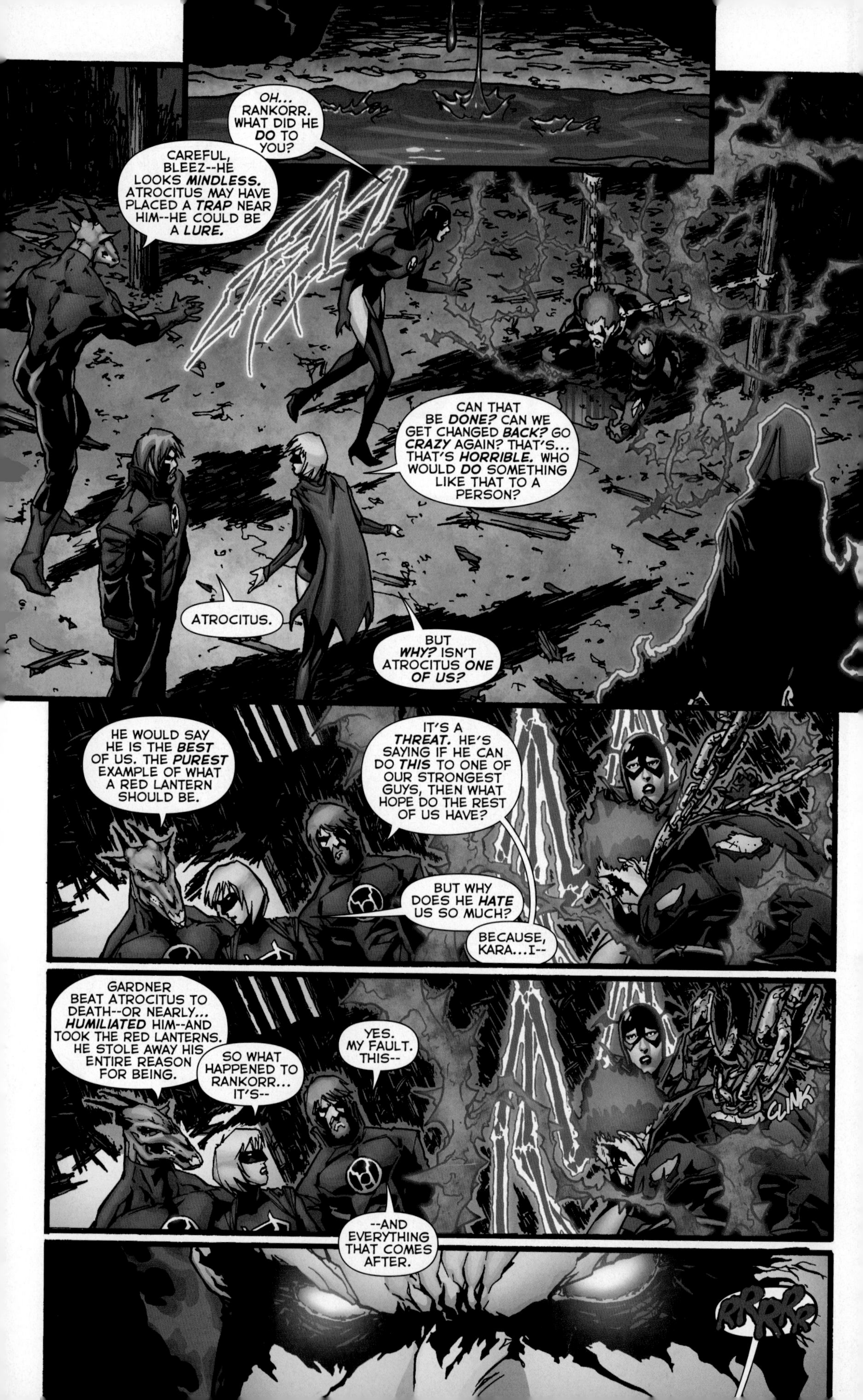
OH... RANKORR. WHAT DID HE DO TO YOU?
CAREFUL, BLEEZ--HE LOOKS MINDLESS. ATROCITUS MAY HAVE PLACED A TRAP NEAR HIM--HE COULD BE A LURE.
CAN THAT BE DONE? CAN WE GET CHANGED BACK? GO CRAZY AGAIN? THAT'S... THAT'S HORRIBLE. WHO WOULD DO SOMETHING LIKE THAT TO A PERSON?
ATROCITUS.
BUT WHY? ISN'T ATROCITUS ONE OF US?
HE WOULD SAY HE IS THE BEST OF US. THE PUREST EXAMPLE OF WHAT A RED LANTERN SHOULD BE.
IT'S A THREAT. HE'S SAYING IF HE CAN DO THIS TO ONE OF OUR STRONGEST GUYS, THEN WHAT HOPE DO THE REST OF US HAVE?
BUT WHY DOES HE HATE US SO MUCH?
BECAUSE, KARA...I--
GARDNER BEAT ATROCITUS TO DEATH--OR NEARLY... HUMILIATED HIM--AND TOOK THE RED LANTERNS. HE STOLE AWAY HIS ENTIRE REASON FOR BEING.
SO WHAT HAPPENED TO RANKORR... IT'S--
YES. MY FAULT. THIS--
CLINK
--AND EVERYTHING THAT COMES AFTER.
RRRRR

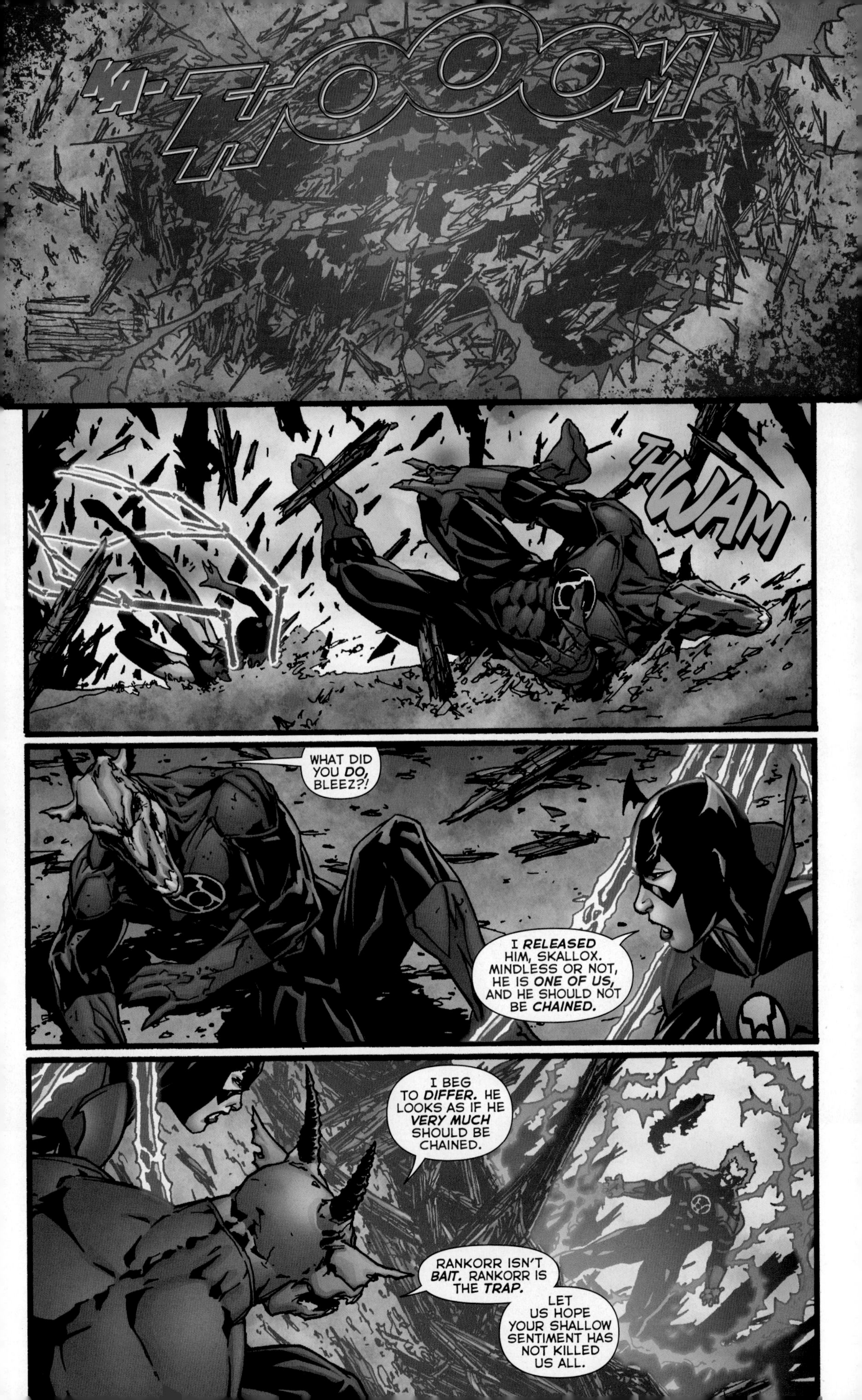
KA-TOOOOM
THWAM
WHAT DID YOU DO, BLEEZ?!
I RELEASED HIM, SKALLOX. MINDLESS OR NOT, HE IS ONE OF US, AND HE SHOULD NOT BE CHAINED.
I BEG TO DIFFER. HE LOOKS AS IF HE VERY MUCH SHOULD BE CHAINED.
RANKORR ISN'T BAIT. RANKORR IS THE TRAP.
LET US HOPE YOUR SHALLOW SENTIMENT HAS NOT KILLED US ALL.

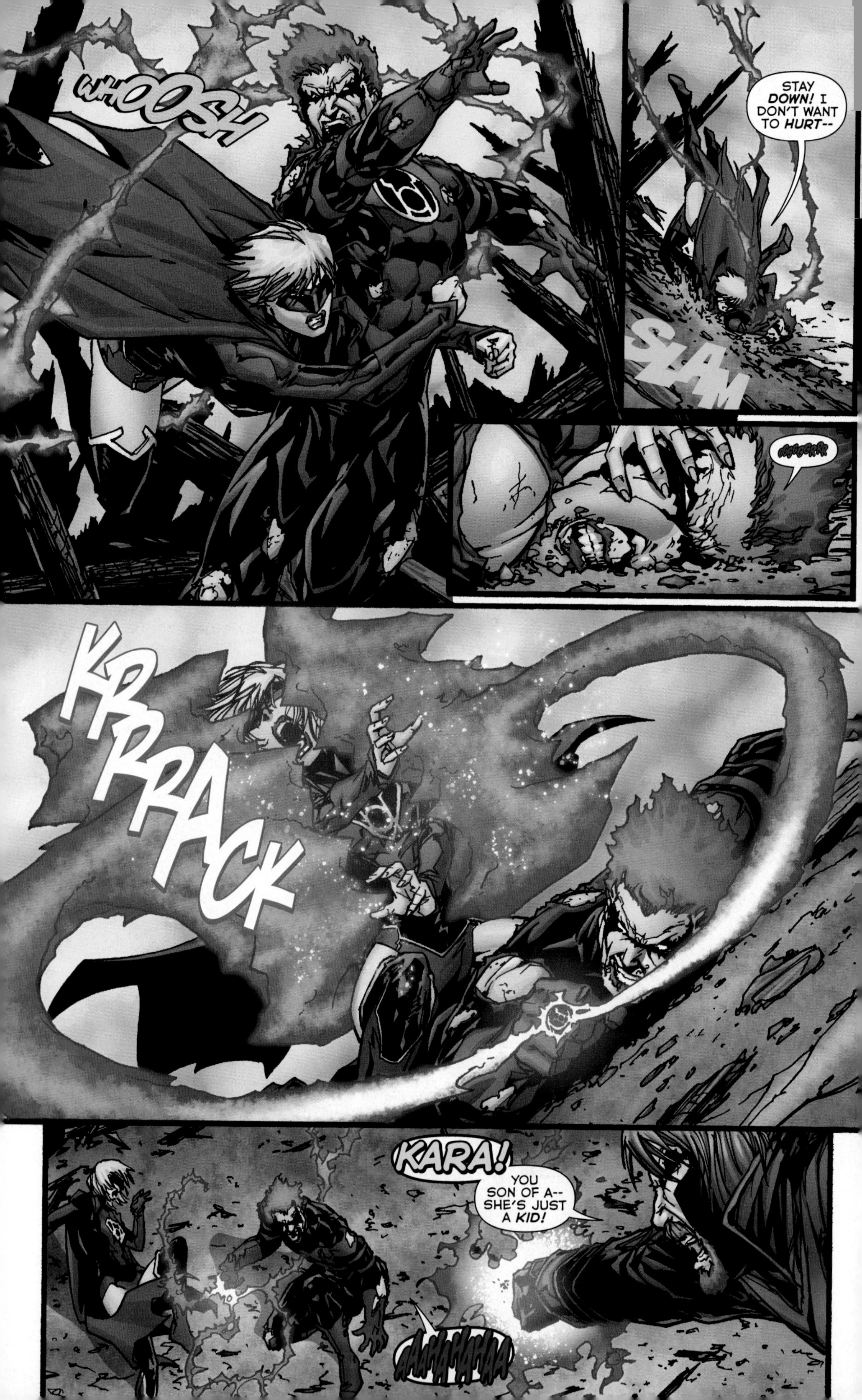
WHOOSH
STAY DOWN! I DON'T WANT TO HURT--
SLAM
KRRRACK
KARA!
YOU SON OF A-- SHE'S JUST A KID!

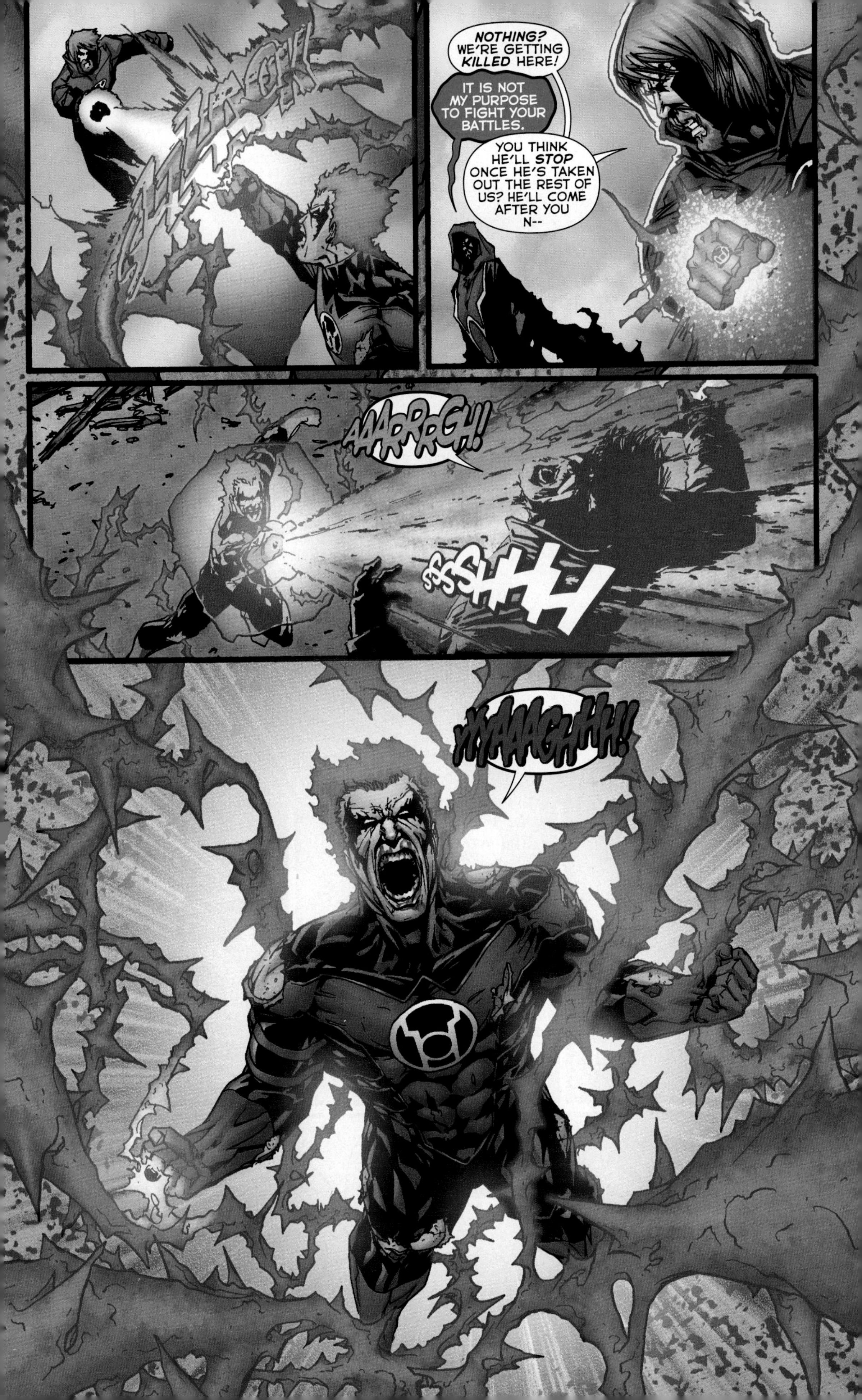
NOTHING? WE'RE GETTING KILLED HERE!
IT IS NOT MY PURPOSE TO FIGHT YOUR BATTLES.
YOU THINK HE'LL STOP ONCE HE'S TAKEN OUT THE REST OF US? HE'LL COME AFTER YOU N--
AAARRRGH!
SSSHHH
YYYAAAGHHHH!

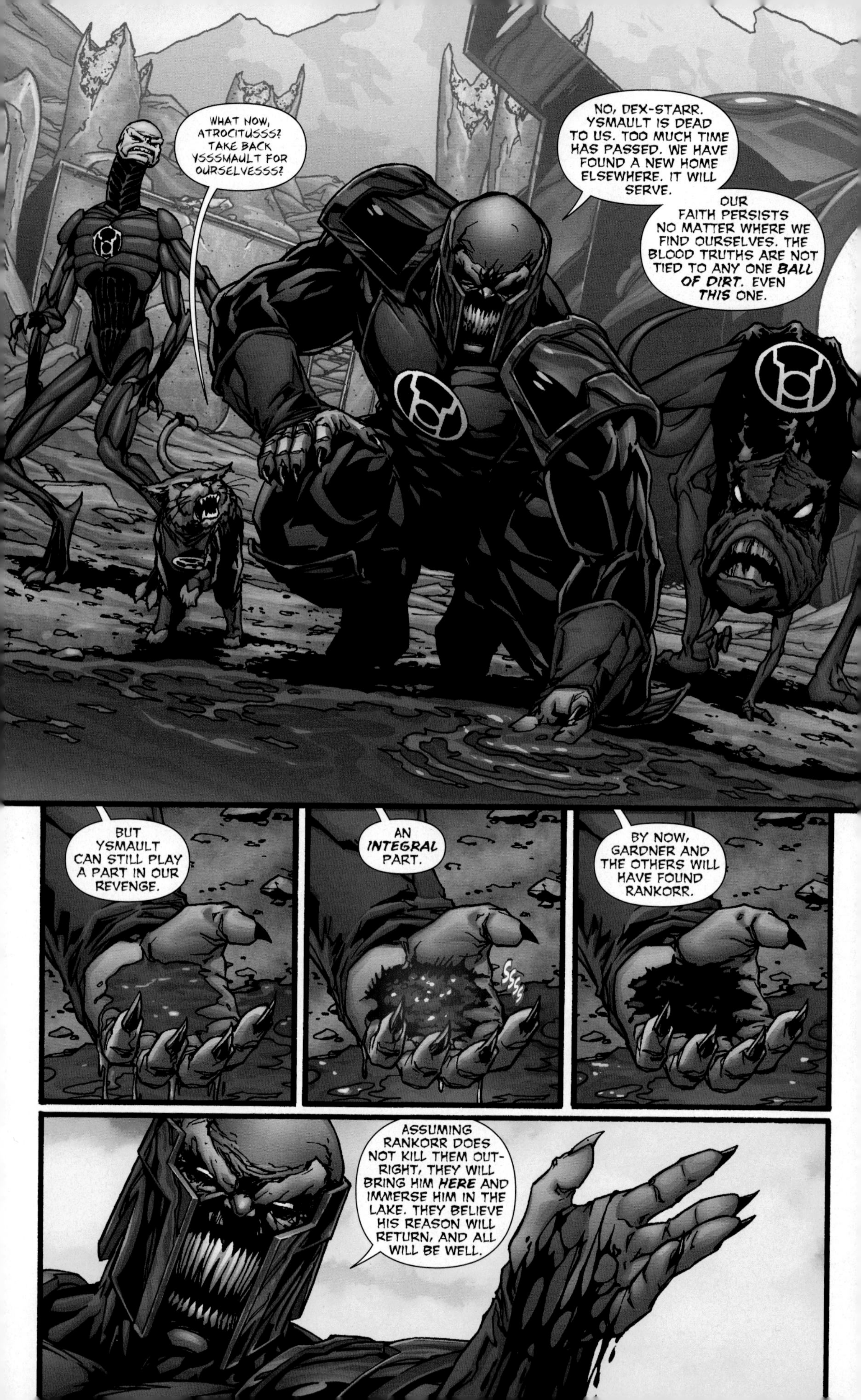
WHAT NOW, ATROCITUSSS? TAKE BACK YSSSMAULT FOR OURSELVESSS?
NO, DEX-STARR. YSMAULT IS DEAD TO US. TOO MUCH TIME HAS PASSED. WE HAVE FOUND A NEW HOME ELSEWHERE. IT WILL SERVE.
OUR FAITH PERSISTS NO MATTER WHERE WE FIND OURSELVES. THE BLOOD TRUTHS ARE NOT TIED TO ANY ONE BALL OF DIRT. EVEN THIS ONE.
BUT YSMAULT CAN STILL PLAY A PART IN OUR REVENGE.
AN INTEGRAL PART.
SSSS
BY NOW, GARDNER AND THE OTHERS WILL HAVE FOUND RANKORR.
ASSUMING RANKORR DOES NOT KILL THEM OUT-RIGHT, THEY WILL BRING HIM HERE AND IMMERSE HIM IN THE LAKE. THEY BELIEVE HIS REASON WILL RETURN, AND ALL WILL BE WELL.

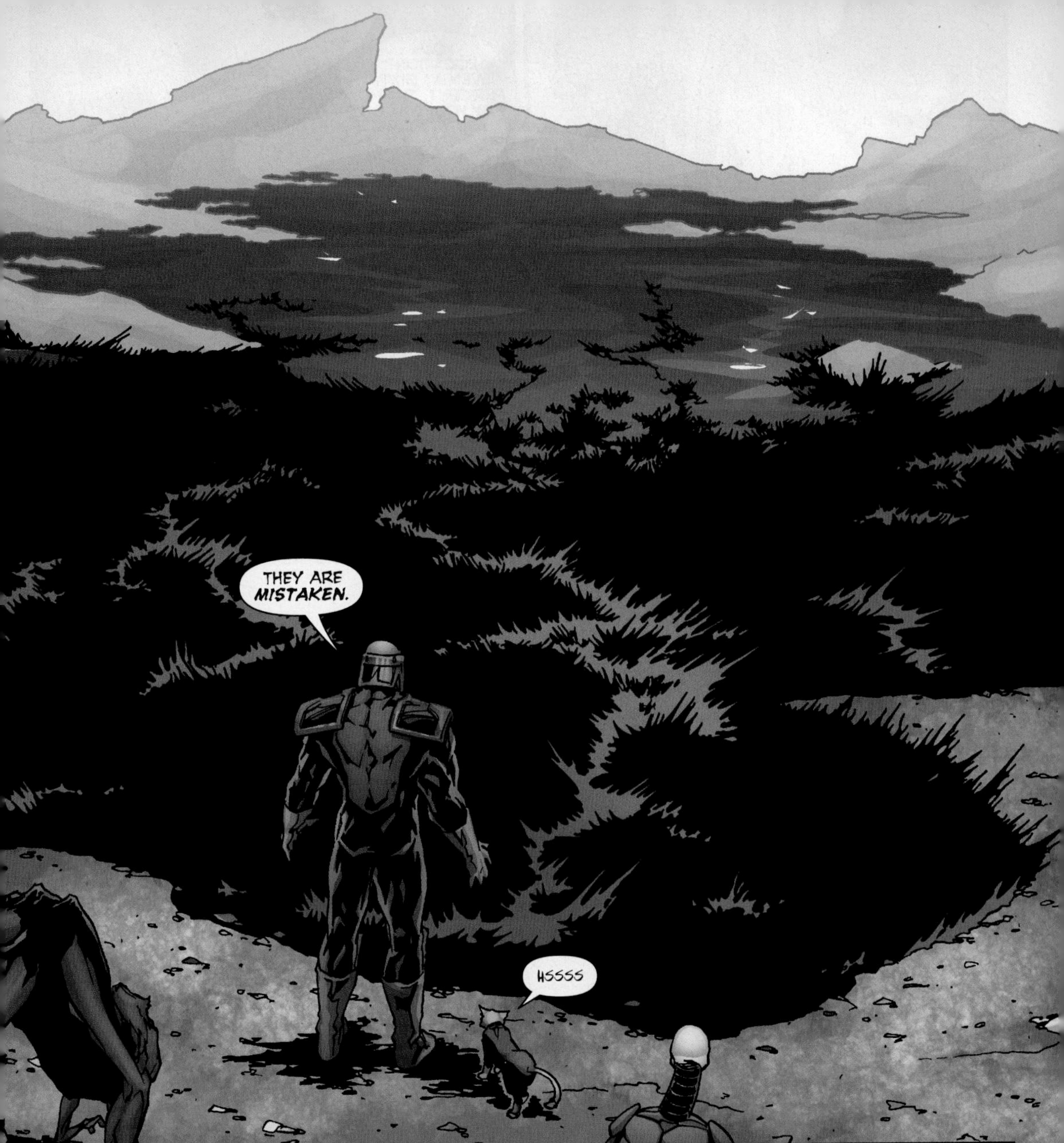
THEY ARE MISTAKEN.
HSSSS

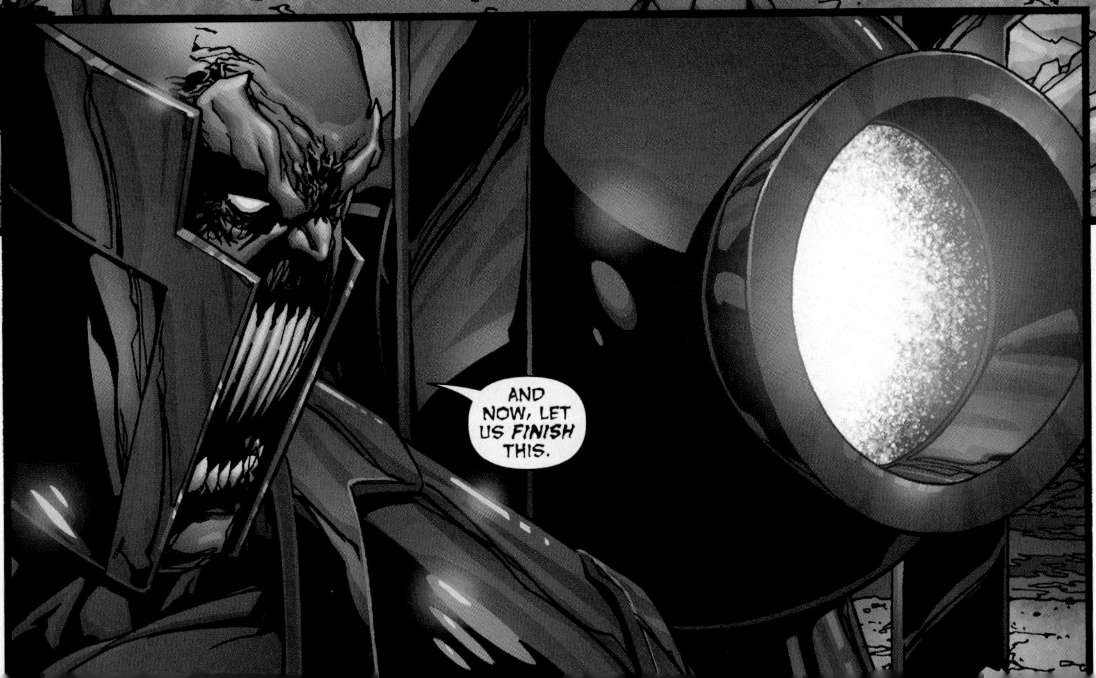
AND NOW, LET US FINISH THIS.

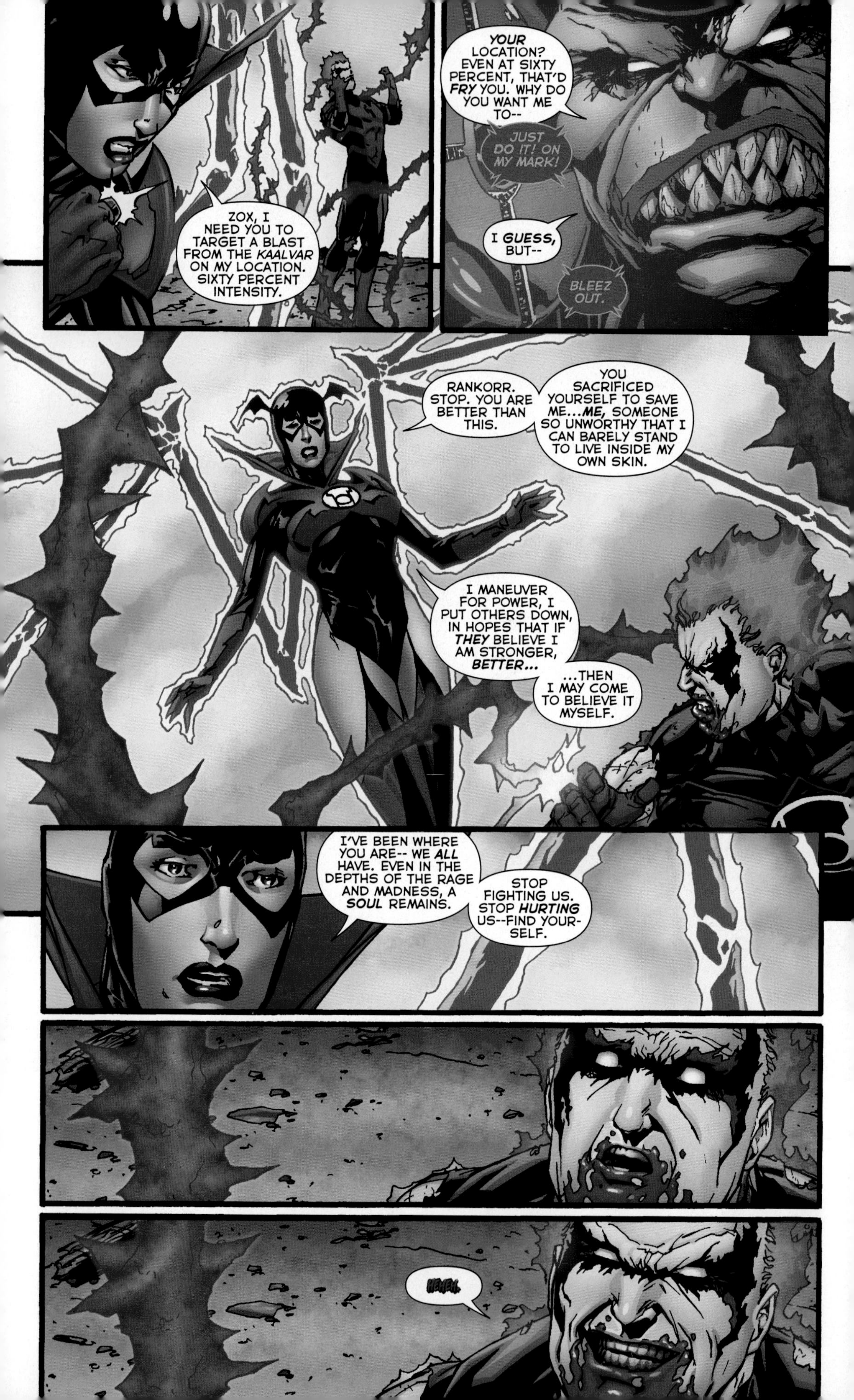
ZOX, I NEED YOU TO TARGET A BLAST FROM THE KAALVAR ON MY LOCATION. SIXTY PERCENT INTENSITY.
YOUR LOCATION? EVEN AT SIXTY PERCENT, THAT'D FRY YOU. WHY DO YOU WANT ME TO--
JUST DO IT! ON MY MARK!
I GUESS, BUT--
BLEEZ OUT.
RANKORR. STOP. YOU ARE BETTER THAN THIS.
YOU SACRIFICED YOURSELF TO SAVE ME...ME, SOMEONE SO UNWORTHY THAT I CAN BARELY STAND TO LIVE INSIDE MY OWN SKIN.
I MANEUVER FOR POWER, I PUT OTHERS DOWN, IN HOPES THAT IF THEY BELIEVE I AM STRONGER, BETTER...
...THEN I MAY COME TO BELIEVE IT MYSELF.
I'VE BEEN WHERE YOU ARE-- WE ALL HAVE. EVEN IN THE DEPTHS OF THE RAGE AND MADNESS, A SOUL REMAINS.
STOP FIGHTING US. STOP HURTING US--FIND YOURSELF.
HEHEH.

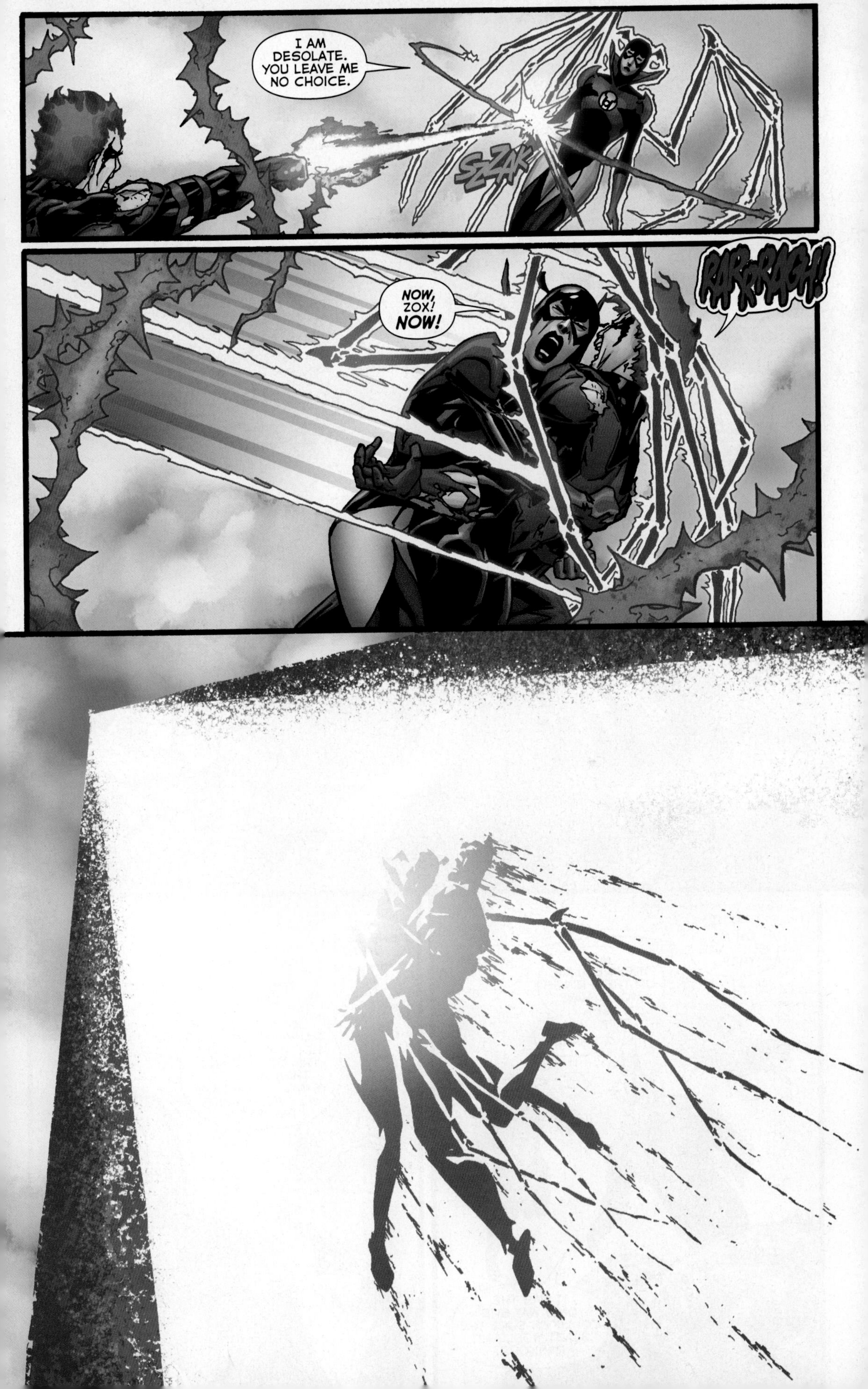
I AM DESOLATE. YOU LEAVE ME NO CHOICE.
SZZAK
NOW, ZOX! NOW!
RAR-R-RAGH!

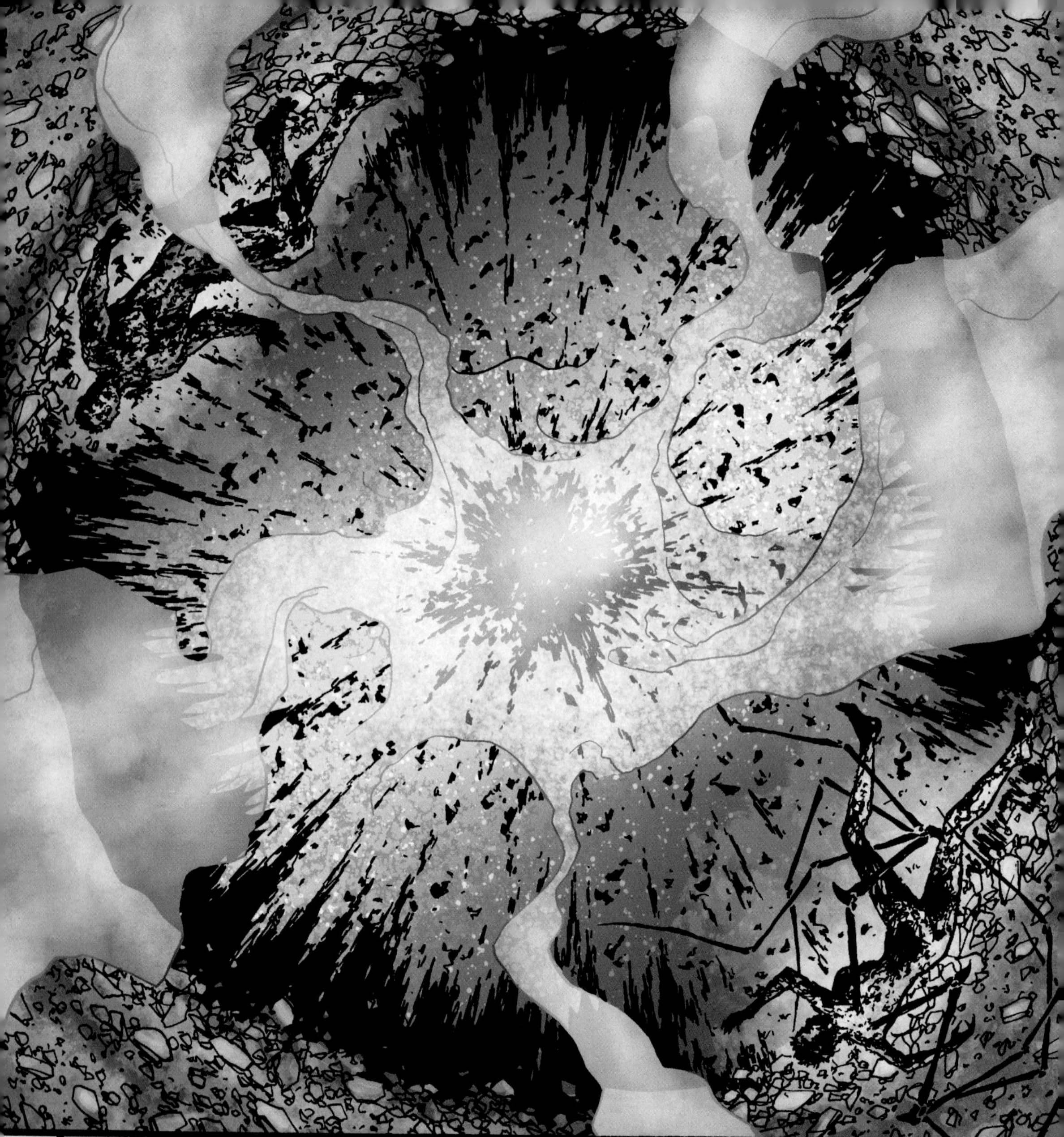

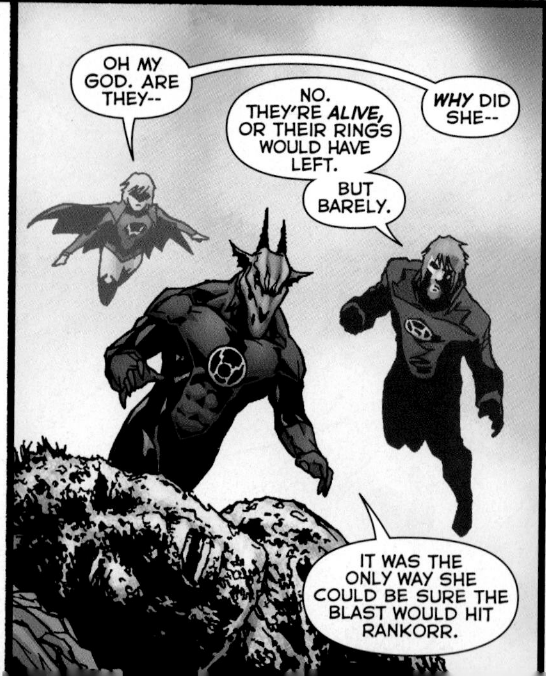
OH MY GOD. ARE THEY--
NO. THEY'RE *ALIVE*, OR THEIR RINGS WOULD HAVE LEFT.
WHY DID SHE--
BUT BARELY.
IT WAS THE ONLY WAY SHE COULD BE SURE THE BLAST WOULD HIT RANKORR.

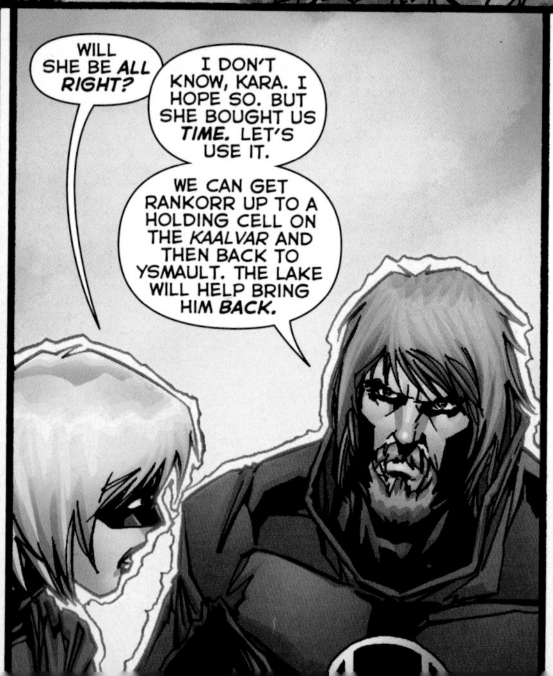
WILL SHE BE *ALL RIGHT?*
I DON'T KNOW, KARA. I HOPE SO. BUT SHE BOUGHT US *TIME.* LET'S USE IT.
WE CAN GET RANKORR UP TO A HOLDING CELL ON THE *KAALVAR* AND THEN BACK TO YSMAULT. THE LAKE WILL HELP BRING HIM *BACK.*

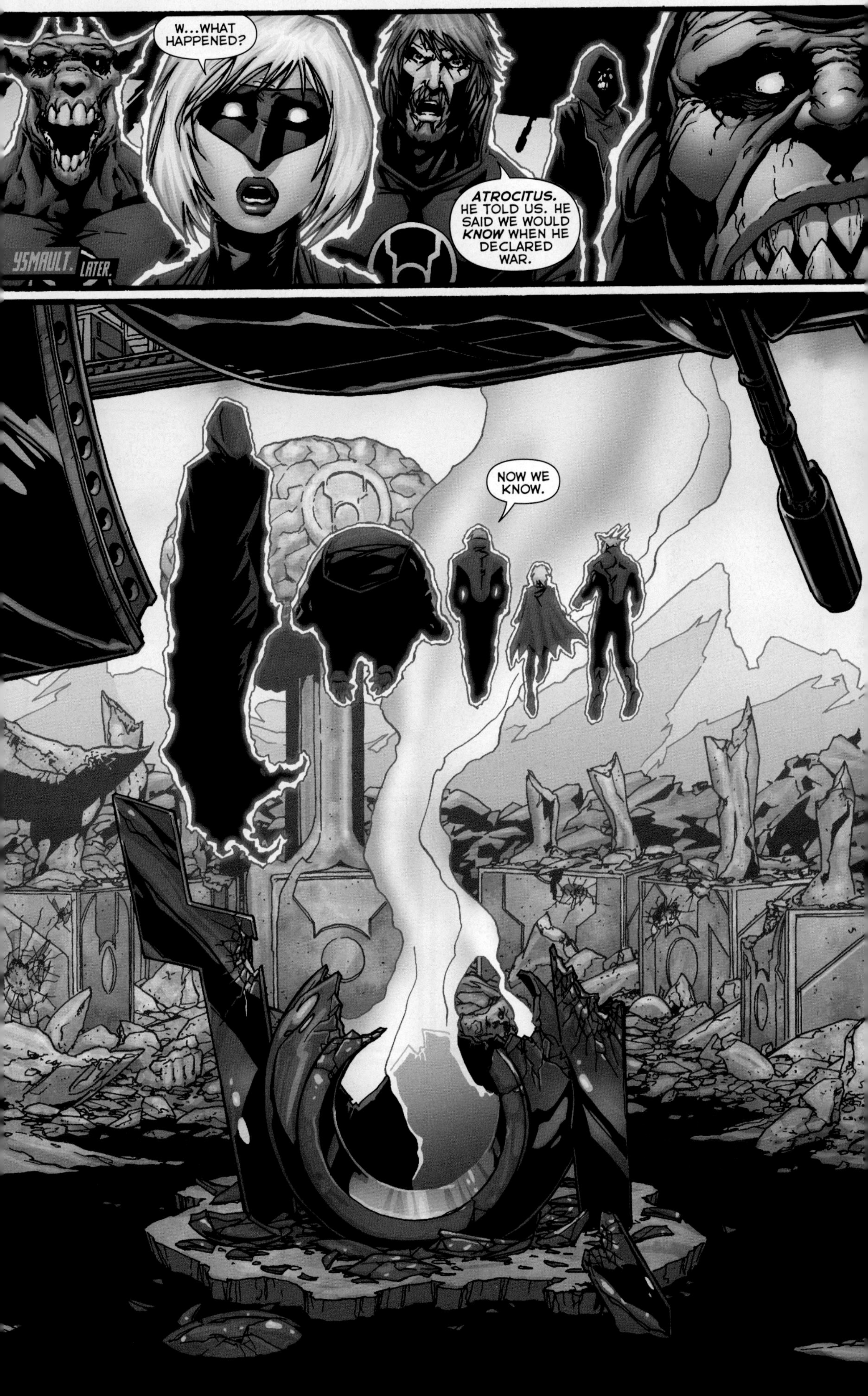
YSMAULT. LATER.
W...WHAT HAPPENED?
ATROCITUS. HE TOLD US. HE SAID WE WOULD KNOW WHEN HE DECLARED WAR.
NOW WE KNOW.

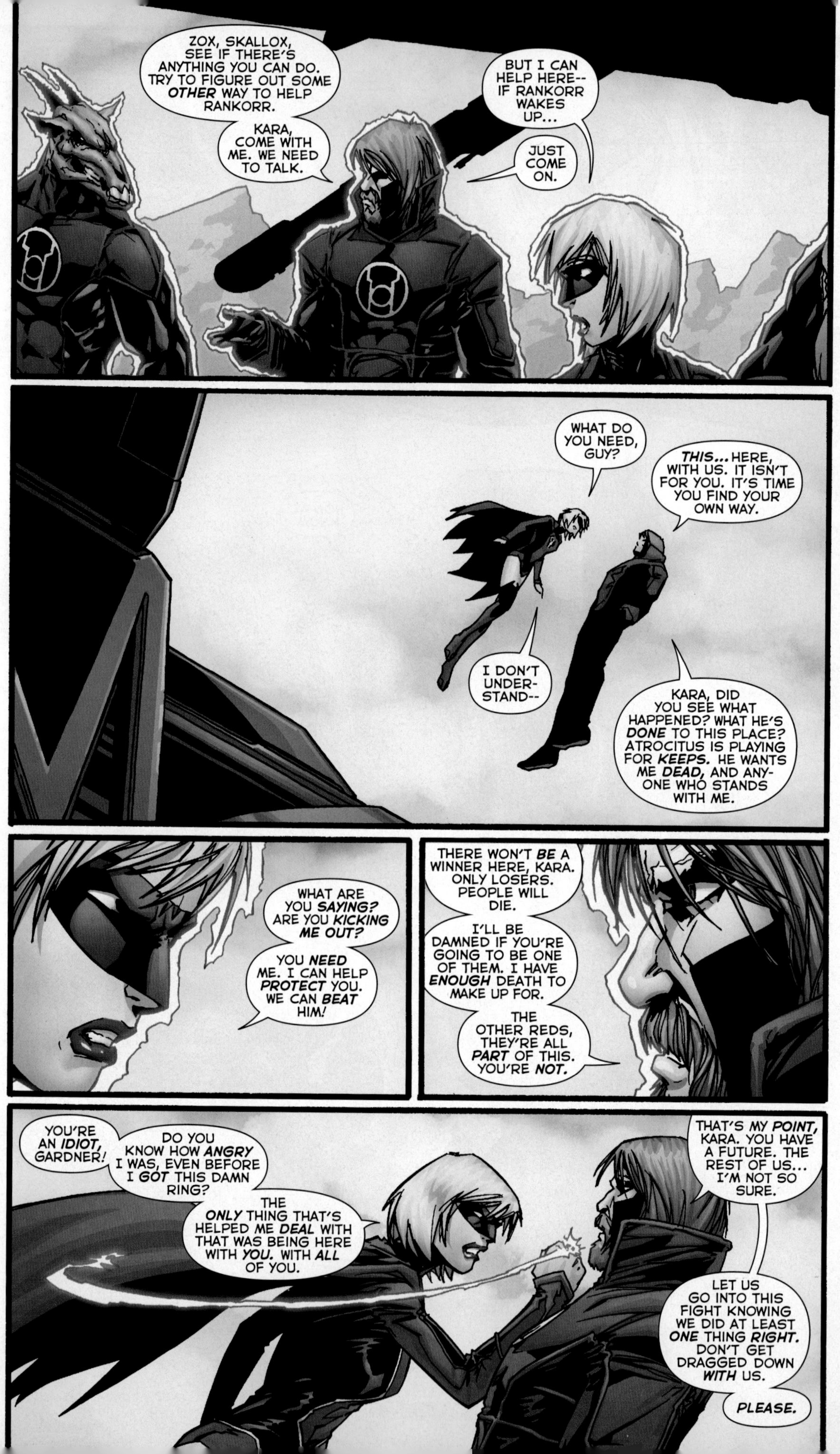
ZOX, SKALLOX, SEE IF THERE'S ANYTHING YOU CAN DO. TRY TO FIGURE OUT SOME OTHER WAY TO HELP RANKORR.
KARA, COME WITH ME. WE NEED TO TALK.
BUT I CAN HELP HERE-- IF RANKORR WAKES UP...
JUST COME ON.
WHAT DO YOU NEED, GUY?
THIS... HERE, WITH US. IT ISN'T FOR YOU. IT'S TIME YOU FIND YOUR OWN WAY.
I DON'T UNDER-STAND--
KARA, DID YOU SEE WHAT HAPPENED? WHAT HE'S DONE TO THIS PLACE? ATROCITUS IS PLAYING FOR KEEPS. HE WANTS ME DEAD, AND ANY-ONE WHO STANDS WITH ME.
WHAT ARE YOU SAYING? ARE YOU KICKING ME OUT?
YOU NEED ME. I CAN HELP PROTECT YOU. WE CAN BEAT HIM!
THERE WON'T BE A WINNER HERE, KARA. ONLY LOSERS. PEOPLE WILL DIE.
I'LL BE DAMNED IF YOU'RE GOING TO BE ONE OF THEM. I HAVE ENOUGH DEATH TO MAKE UP FOR.
THE OTHER REDS, THEY'RE ALL PART OF THIS. YOU'RE NOT.
YOU'RE AN IDIOT, GARDNER!
DO YOU KNOW HOW ANGRY I WAS, EVEN BEFORE I GOT THIS DAMN RING?
THE ONLY THING THAT'S HELPED ME DEAL WITH THAT WAS BEING HERE WITH YOU. WITH ALL OF YOU.
THAT'S MY POINT, KARA. YOU HAVE A FUTURE. THE REST OF US... I'M NOT SO SURE.
LET US GO INTO THIS FIGHT KNOWING WE DID AT LEAST ONE THING RIGHT. DON'T GET DRAGGED DOWN WITH US.
PLEASE.

BUT EVEN IF I *DO* GO...THE RING...I CAN'T TAKE IT *OFF*. I'M A RED *FOREVER.*

WITHOUT YOU AND THE *OTHERS*, HOW WILL I--WHAT AM I SUPPOSED TO *DO*?

YOU'LL FIND YOUR WAY. YOU'RE *STRONG*, KARA. YOU DIDN'T CHOOSE THIS LIFE, BUT I'VE SEEN ENOUGH IN OUR TIME TOGETHER TO KNOW THAT YOU CAN MAKE SOMETHING OF IT.

YOU'RE BETTER THAN ALL OF US.

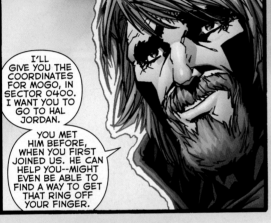

I'LL GIVE YOU THE COORDINATES FOR MOGO, IN SECTOR 0400. I WANT YOU TO GO TO HAL JORDAN.

YOU MET HIM BEFORE, WHEN YOU FIRST JOINED US. HE CAN HELP YOU--MIGHT EVEN BE ABLE TO FIND A WAY TO GET THAT RING OFF YOUR FINGER.

WHO SAYS I WANT THAT?

OH, KID.

DON'T CALL ME THAT.

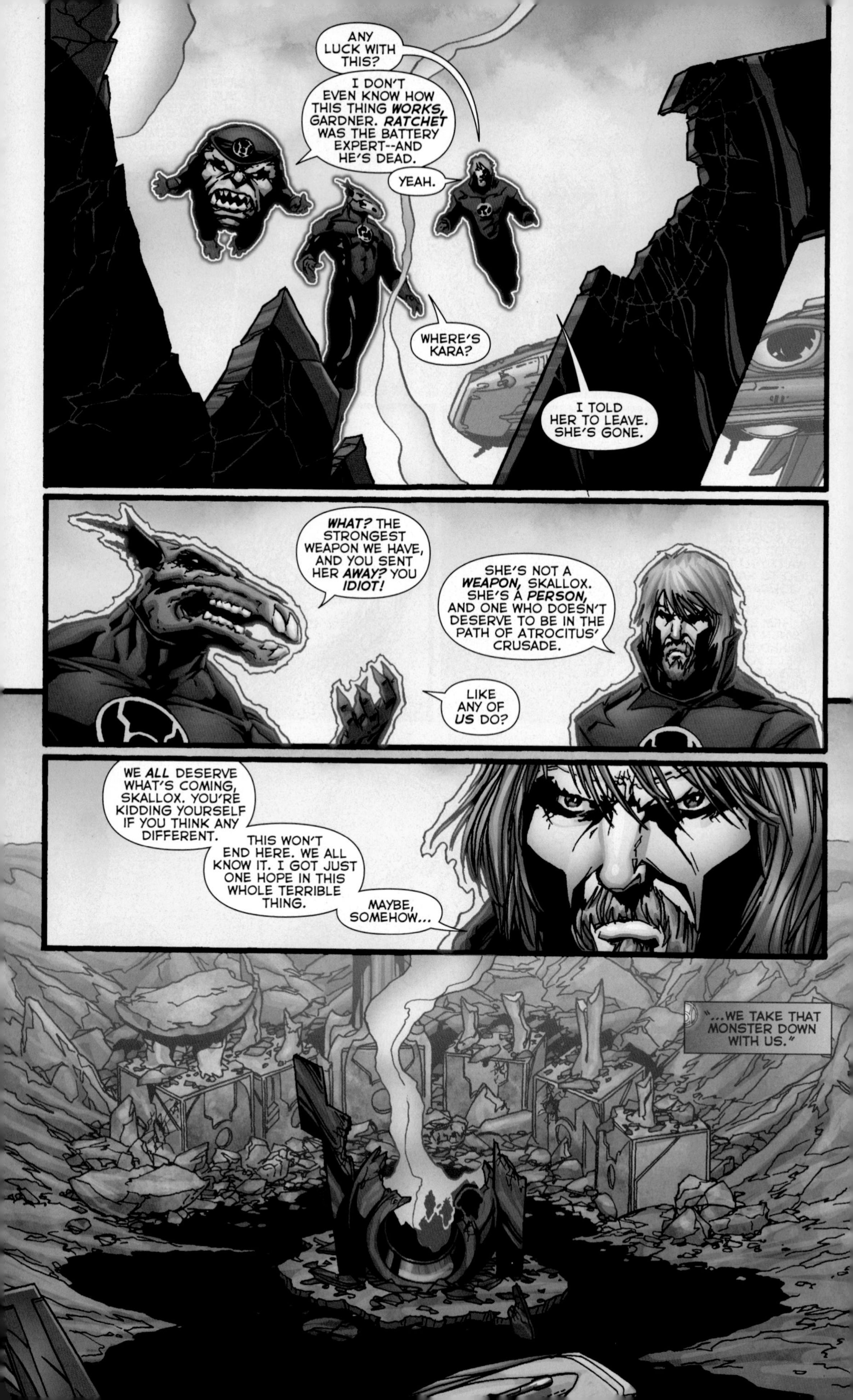
ANY LUCK WITH THIS?
I DON'T EVEN KNOW HOW THIS THING *WORKS,* GARDNER. *RATCHET* WAS THE BATTERY EXPERT--AND HE'S DEAD.
YEAH.
WHERE'S KARA?
I TOLD HER TO LEAVE. SHE'S GONE.
WHAT? THE STRONGEST WEAPON WE HAVE, AND YOU SENT HER *AWAY?* YOU *IDIOT!*
SHE'S NOT A *WEAPON,* SKALLOX. SHE'S A *PERSON,* AND ONE WHO DOESN'T DESERVE TO BE IN THE PATH OF ATROCITUS' CRUSADE.
LIKE ANY OF *US* DO?
WE *ALL* DESERVE WHAT'S COMING, SKALLOX. YOU'RE KIDDING YOURSELF IF YOU THINK ANY DIFFERENT.
THIS WON'T END HERE. WE ALL KNOW IT. I GOT JUST ONE HOPE IN THIS WHOLE TERRIBLE THING.
MAYBE, SOMEHOW...
"...WE TAKE THAT MONSTER DOWN WITH US."

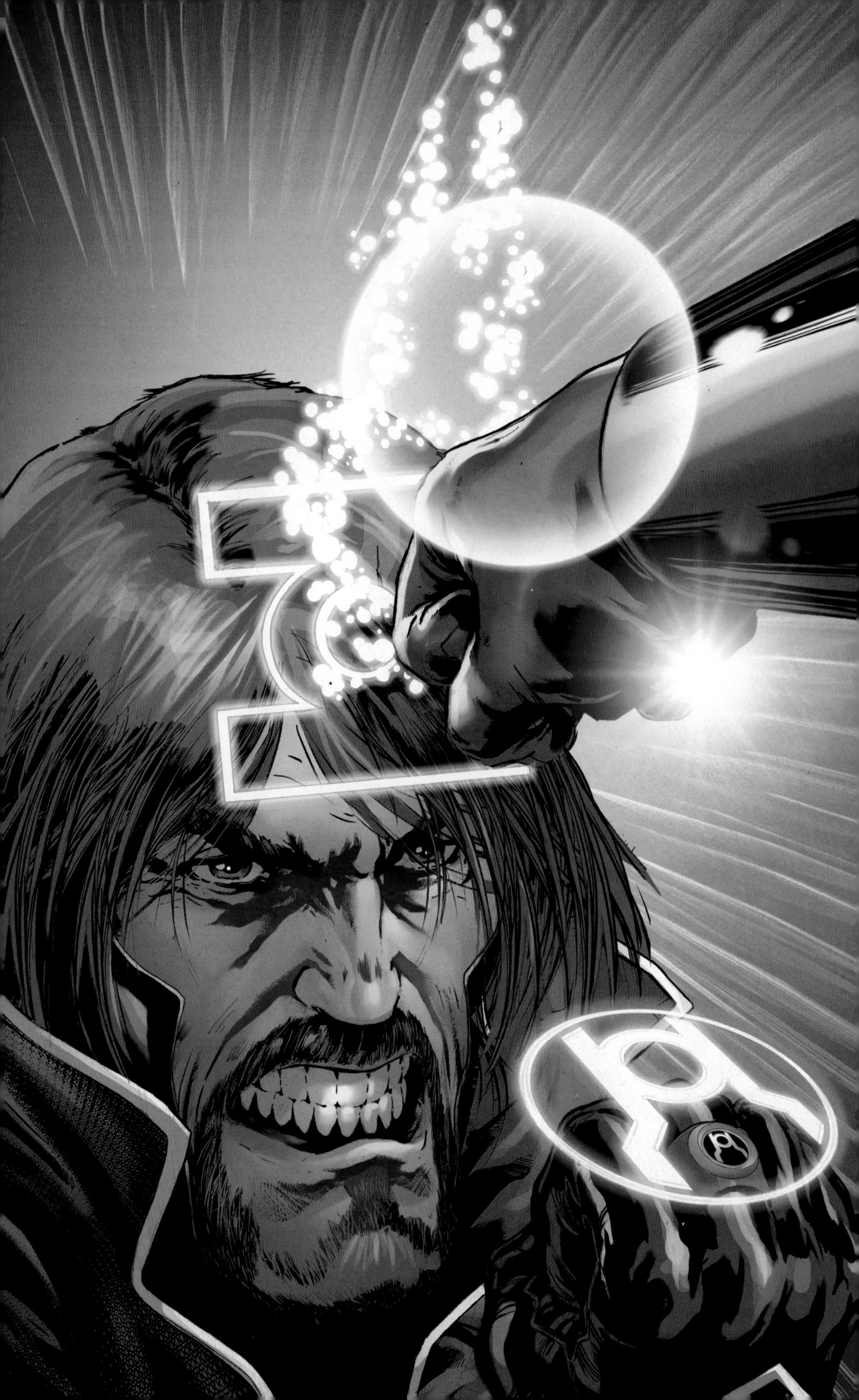

CHARLES SOULE writer **ALESSANDRO VITTI** artist **GABE ELTAEB** colorist **DAVE SHARPE** letterers
cover art by **MIGUEL SEPULVEDA** with **RAIN BEREDO**

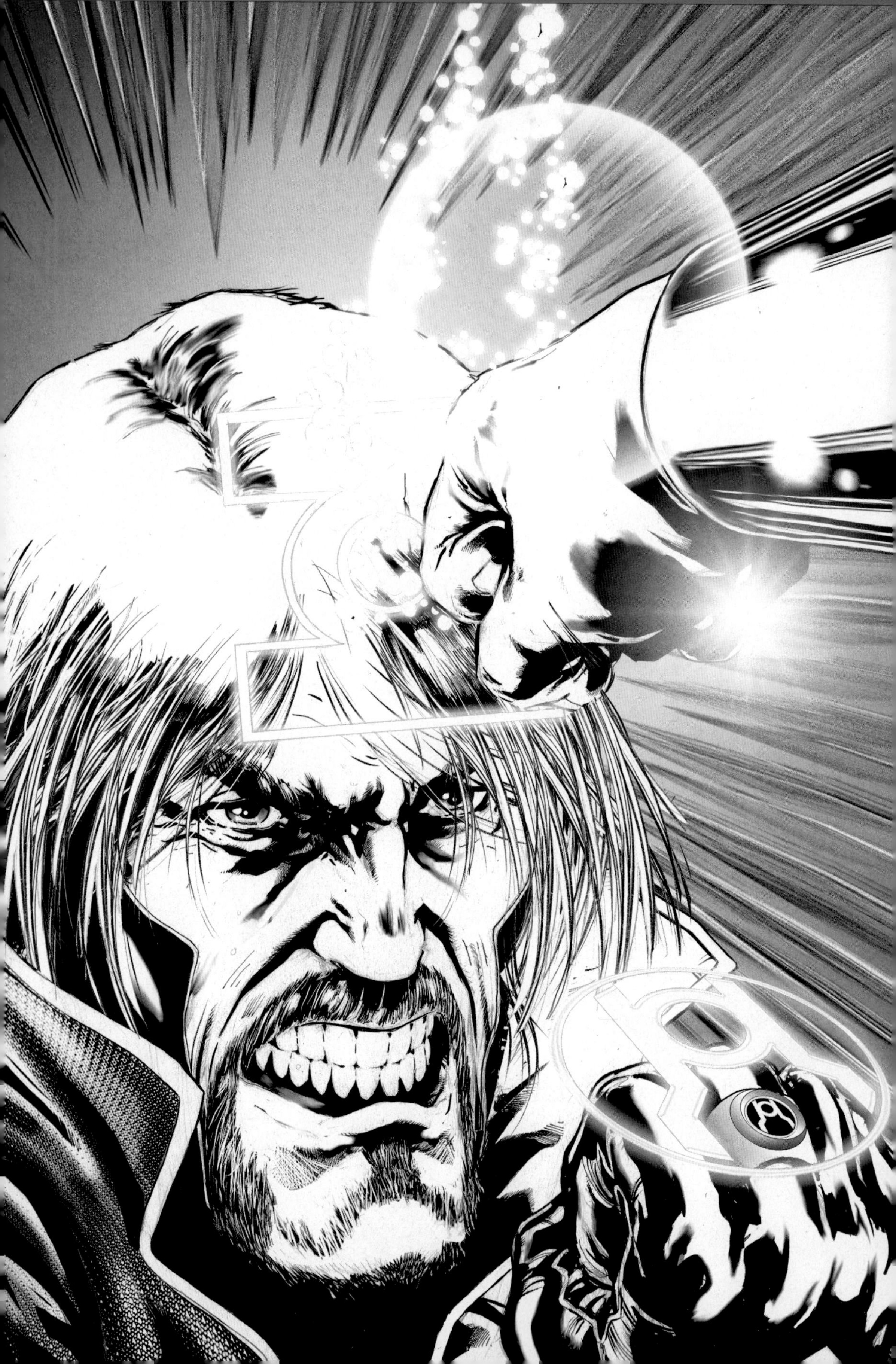

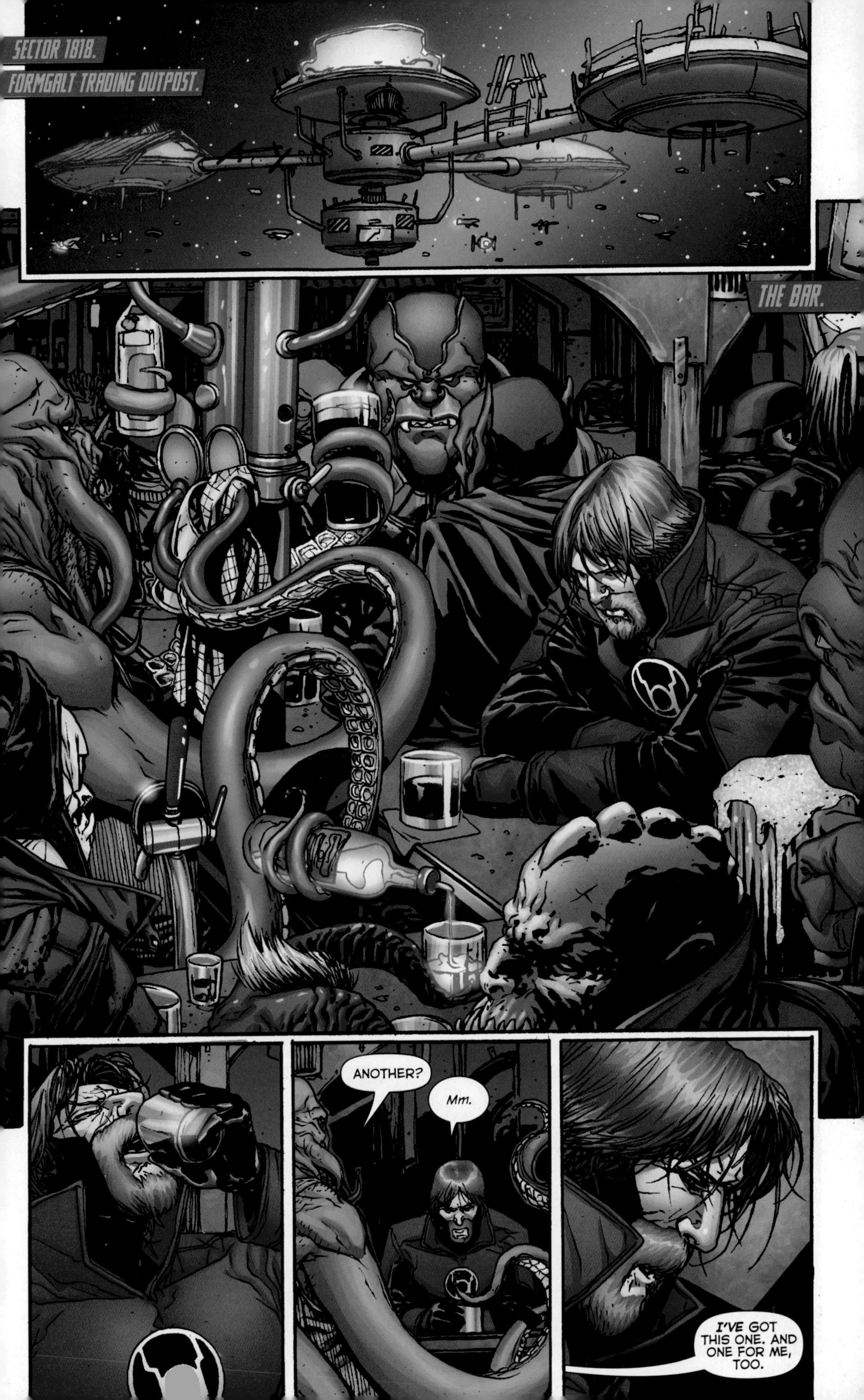
SECTOR 1818.
FORMGALT TRADING OUTPOST.
THE BAR.
ANOTHER?
Mm.
I'VE GOT THIS ONE. AND ONE FOR ME, TOO.

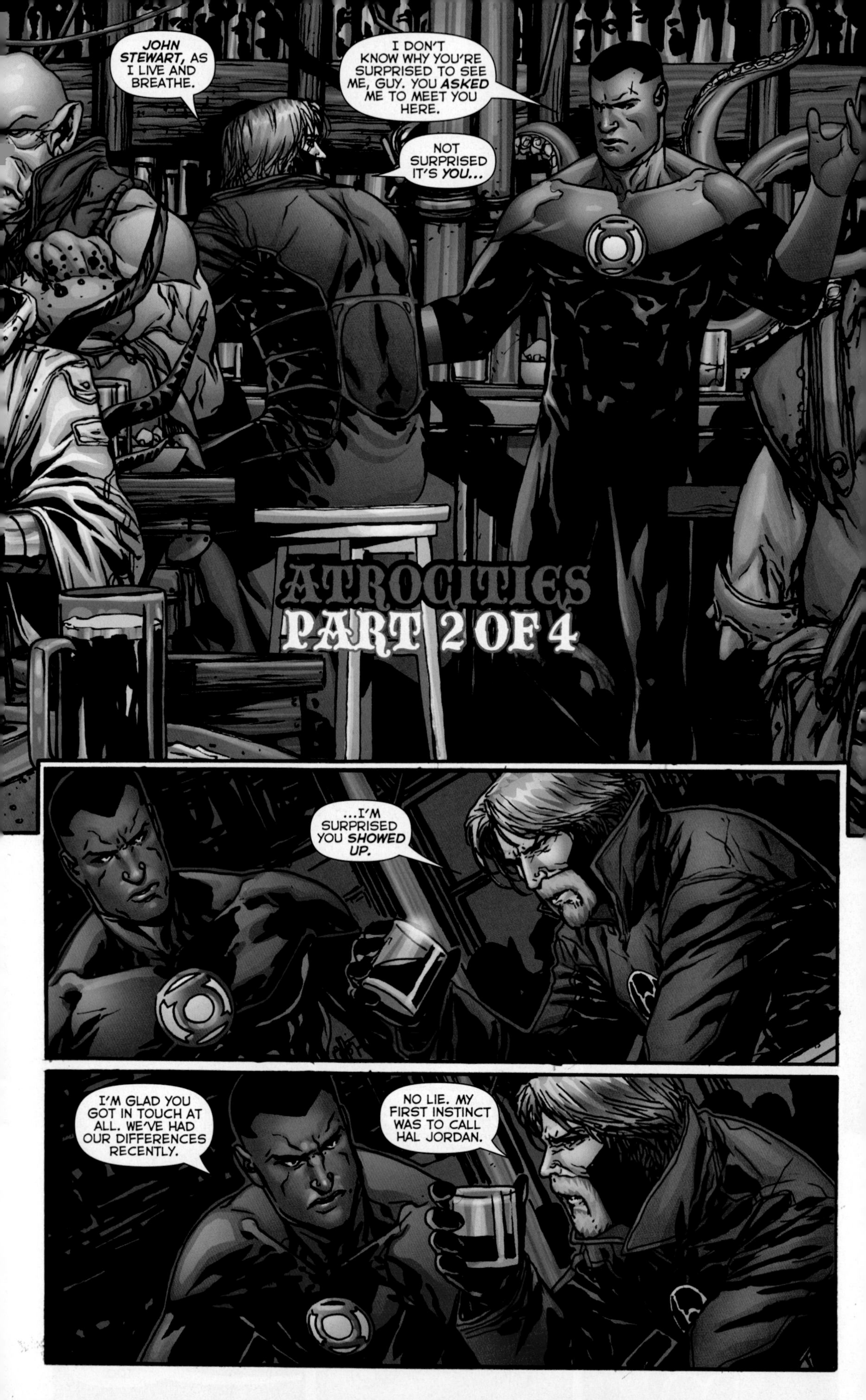
JOHN STEWART, AS I LIVE AND BREATHE.
I DON'T KNOW WHY YOU'RE SURPRISED TO SEE ME, GUY. YOU ASKED ME TO MEET YOU HERE.
NOT SURPRISED IT'S YOU...
ATROCITIES
PART 2 OF 4
...I'M SURPRISED YOU SHOWED UP.
I'M GLAD YOU GOT IN TOUCH AT ALL. WE'VE HAD OUR DIFFERENCES RECENTLY.
NO LIE. MY FIRST INSTINCT WAS TO CALL HAL JORDAN.

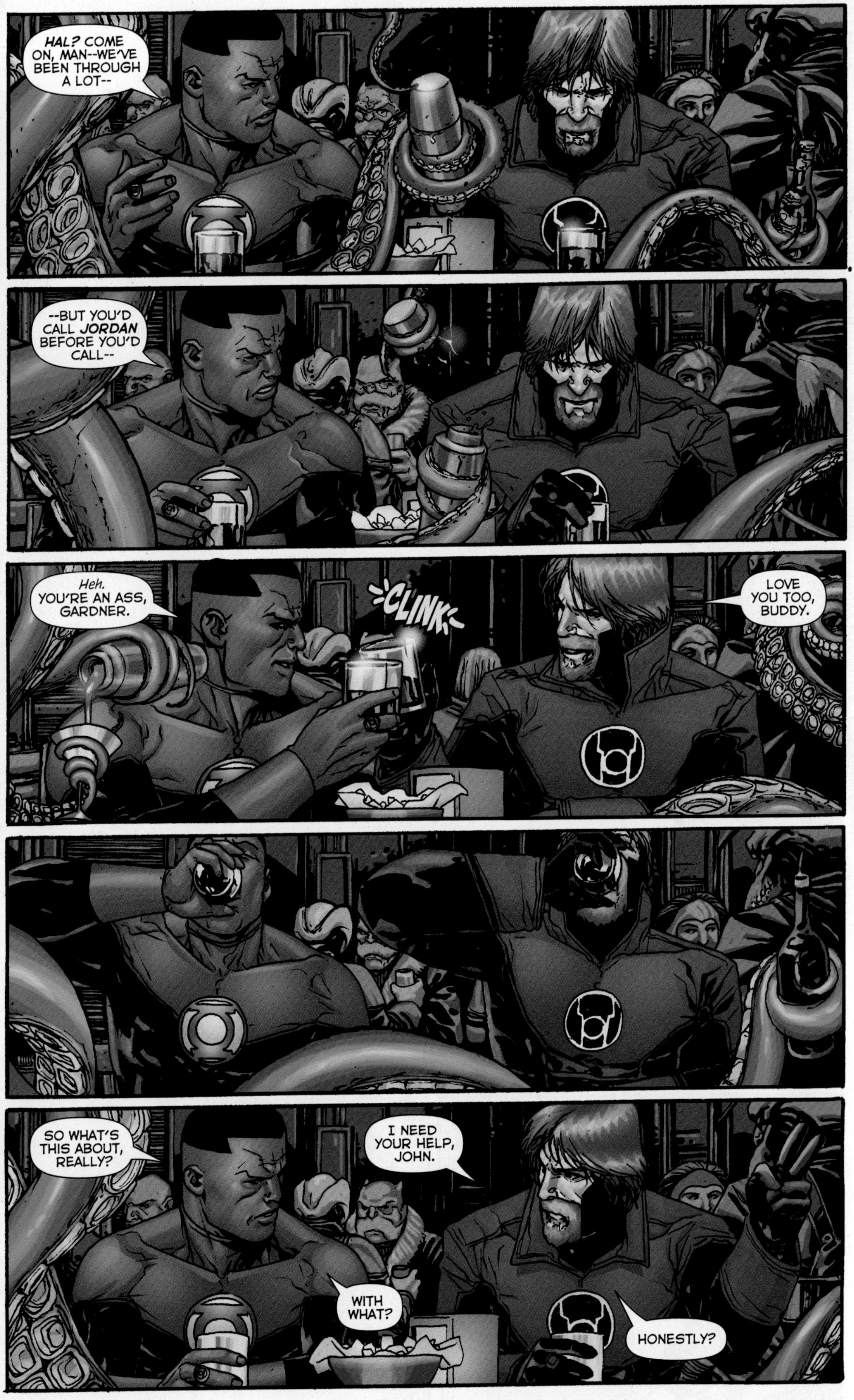
HAL? COME ON, MAN--WE'VE BEEN THROUGH A LOT--
--BUT YOU'D CALL JORDAN BEFORE YOU'D CALL--
Heh. YOU'RE AN ASS, GARDNER.
CLINK
LOVE YOU TOO, BUDDY.
SO WHAT'S THIS ABOUT, REALLY?
I NEED YOUR HELP, JOHN.
WITH WHAT?
HONESTLY?

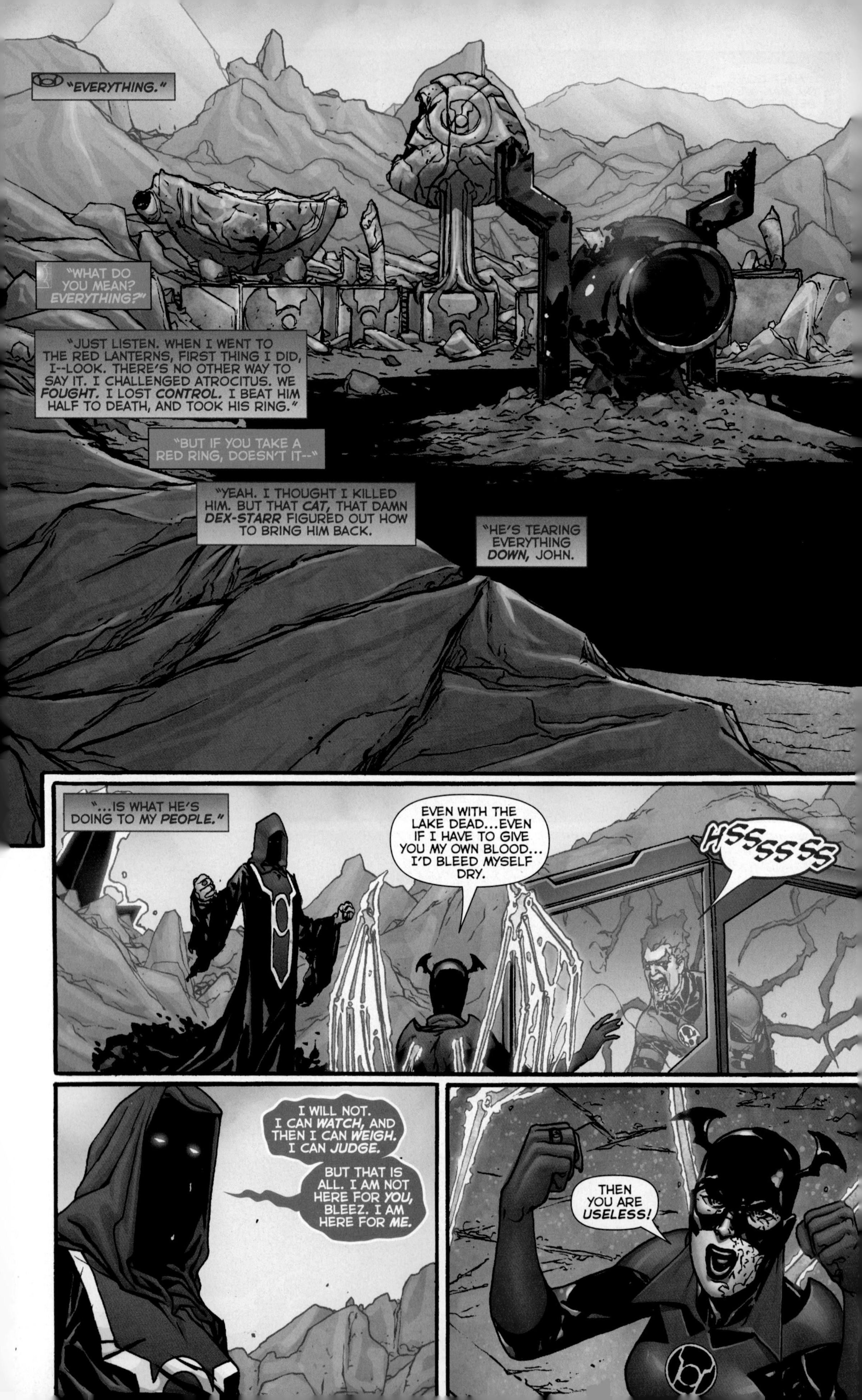

"EVERYTHING."
"WHAT DO YOU MEAN? EVERYTHING?"
"JUST LISTEN. WHEN I WENT TO THE RED LANTERNS, FIRST THING I DID, I--LOOK. THERE'S NO OTHER WAY TO SAY IT. I CHALLENGED ATROCITUS. WE FOUGHT. I LOST CONTROL. I BEAT HIM HALF TO DEATH, AND TOOK HIS RING."
"BUT IF YOU TAKE A RED RING, DOESN'T IT--"
"YEAH. I THOUGHT I KILLED HIM. BUT THAT CAT, THAT DAMN DEX-STARR FIGURED OUT HOW TO BRING HIM BACK.
"HE'S TEARING EVERYTHING DOWN, JOHN.
"...IS WHAT HE'S DOING TO MY PEOPLE."
EVEN WITH THE LAKE DEAD...EVEN IF I HAVE TO GIVE YOU MY OWN BLOOD... I'D BLEED MYSELF DRY.
HSSSSSS
I WILL NOT. I CAN WATCH, AND THEN I CAN WEIGH. I CAN JUDGE.
BUT THAT IS ALL. I AM NOT HERE FOR YOU, BLEEZ. I AM HERE FOR ME.
THEN YOU ARE USELESS!

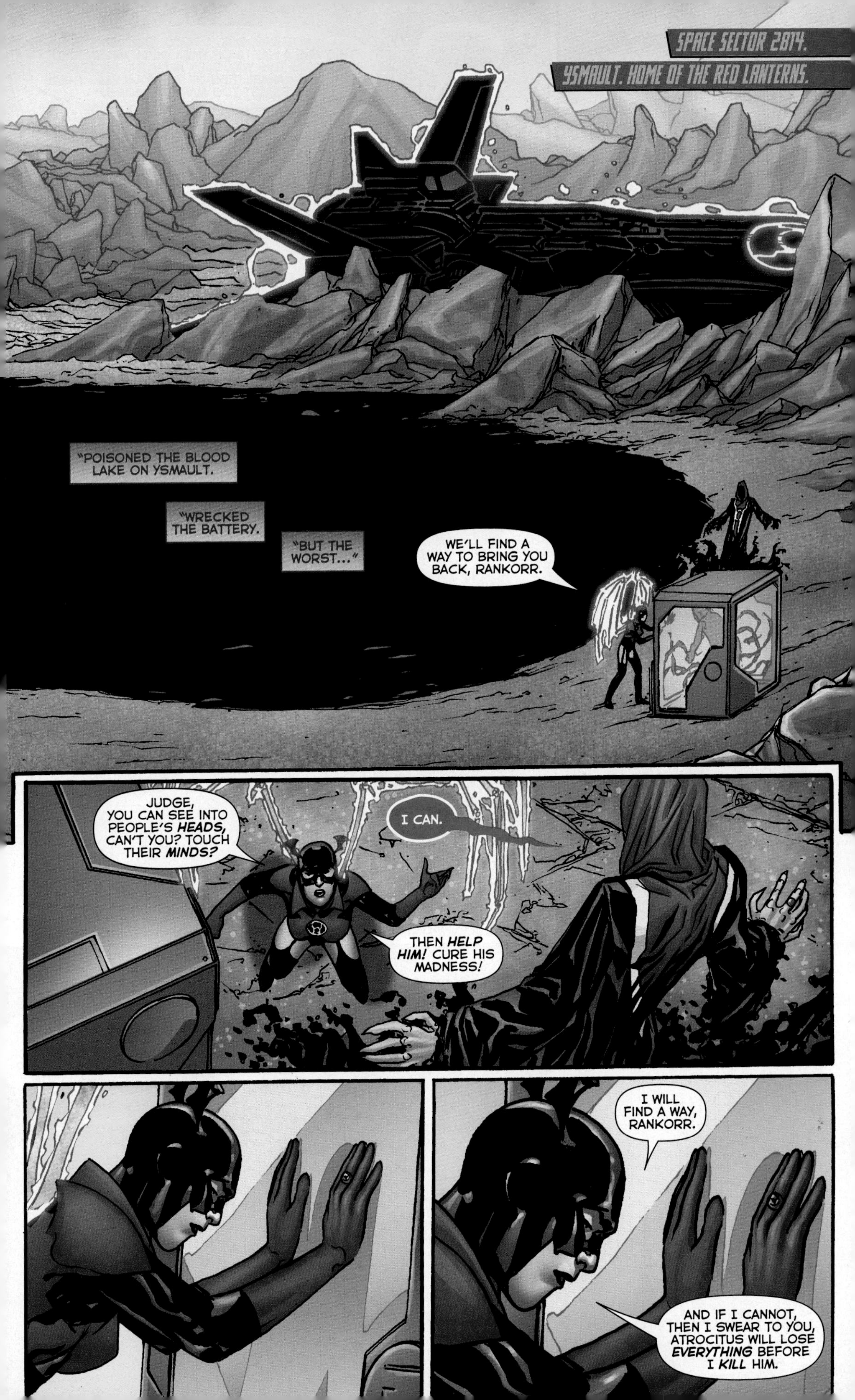
SPACE SECTOR 2814.
YSMAULT. HOME OF THE RED LANTERNS.
"POISONED THE BLOOD LAKE ON YSMAULT.
"WRECKED THE BATTERY.
"BUT THE WORST..."
WE'LL FIND A WAY TO BRING YOU BACK, RANKORR.
JUDGE, YOU CAN SEE INTO PEOPLE'S HEADS, CAN'T YOU? TOUCH THEIR MINDS?
I CAN.
THEN HELP HIM! CURE HIS MADNESS!
I WILL FIND A WAY, RANKORR.
AND IF I CANNOT, THEN I SWEAR TO YOU, ATROCITUS WILL LOSE EVERYTHING BEFORE I KILL HIM.

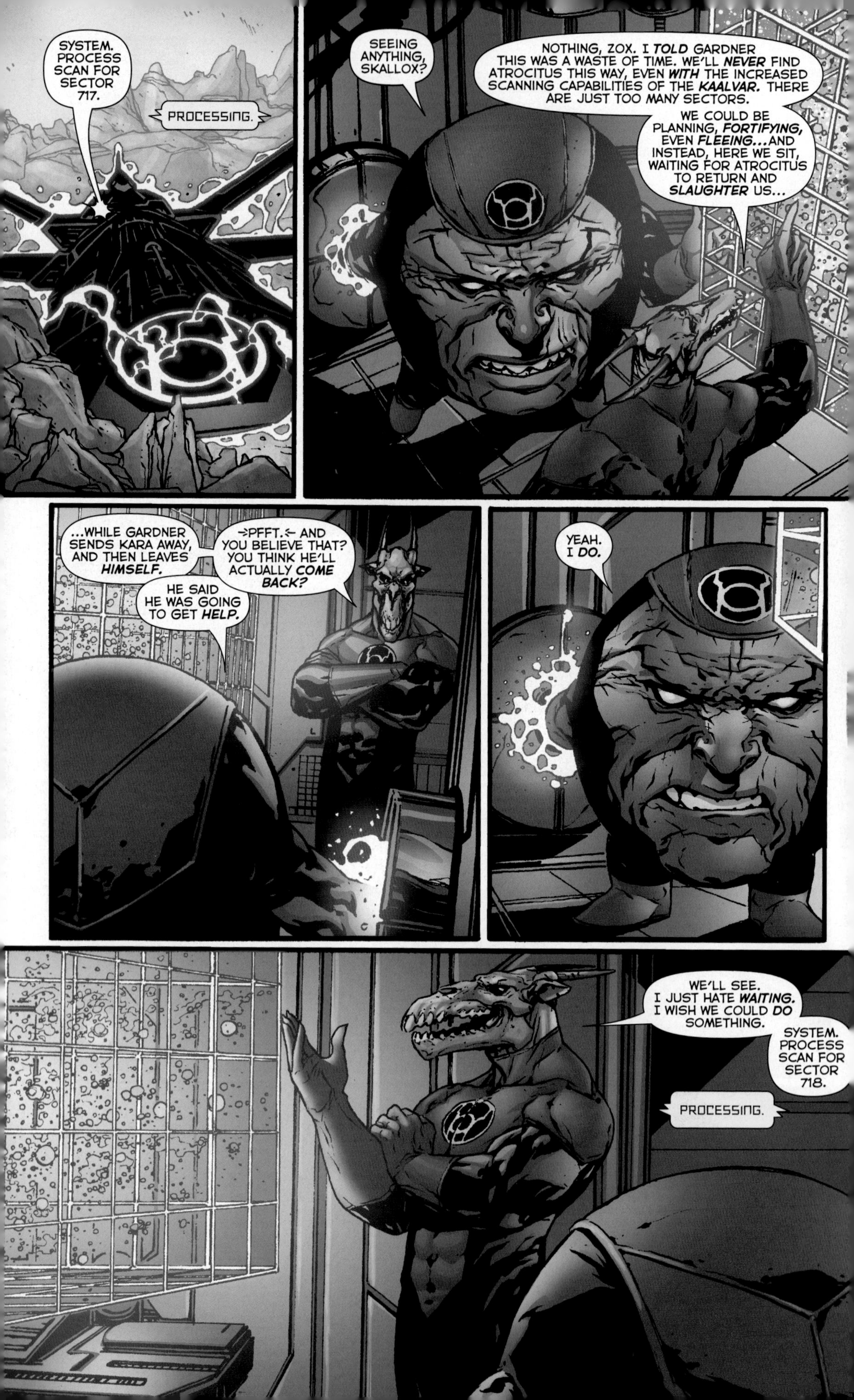
SYSTEM. PROCESS SCAN FOR SECTOR 717.
PROCESSING.
SEEING ANYTHING, SKALLOX?
NOTHING, ZOX. I TOLD GARDNER THIS WAS A WASTE OF TIME. WE'LL NEVER FIND ATROCITUS THIS WAY, EVEN WITH THE INCREASED SCANNING CAPABILITIES OF THE KAALVAR. THERE ARE JUST TOO MANY SECTORS.
WE COULD BE PLANNING, FORTIFYING, EVEN FLEEING...AND INSTEAD, HERE WE SIT, WAITING FOR ATROCITUS TO RETURN AND SLAUGHTER US...
...WHILE GARDNER SENDS KARA AWAY, AND THEN LEAVES HIMSELF.
HE SAID HE WAS GOING TO GET HELP.
PFFT. AND YOU BELIEVE THAT? YOU THINK HE'LL ACTUALLY COME BACK?
YEAH. I DO.
WE'LL SEE. I JUST HATE WAITING. I WISH WE COULD DO SOMETHING.
SYSTEM. PROCESS SCAN FOR SECTOR 718.
PROCESSING.

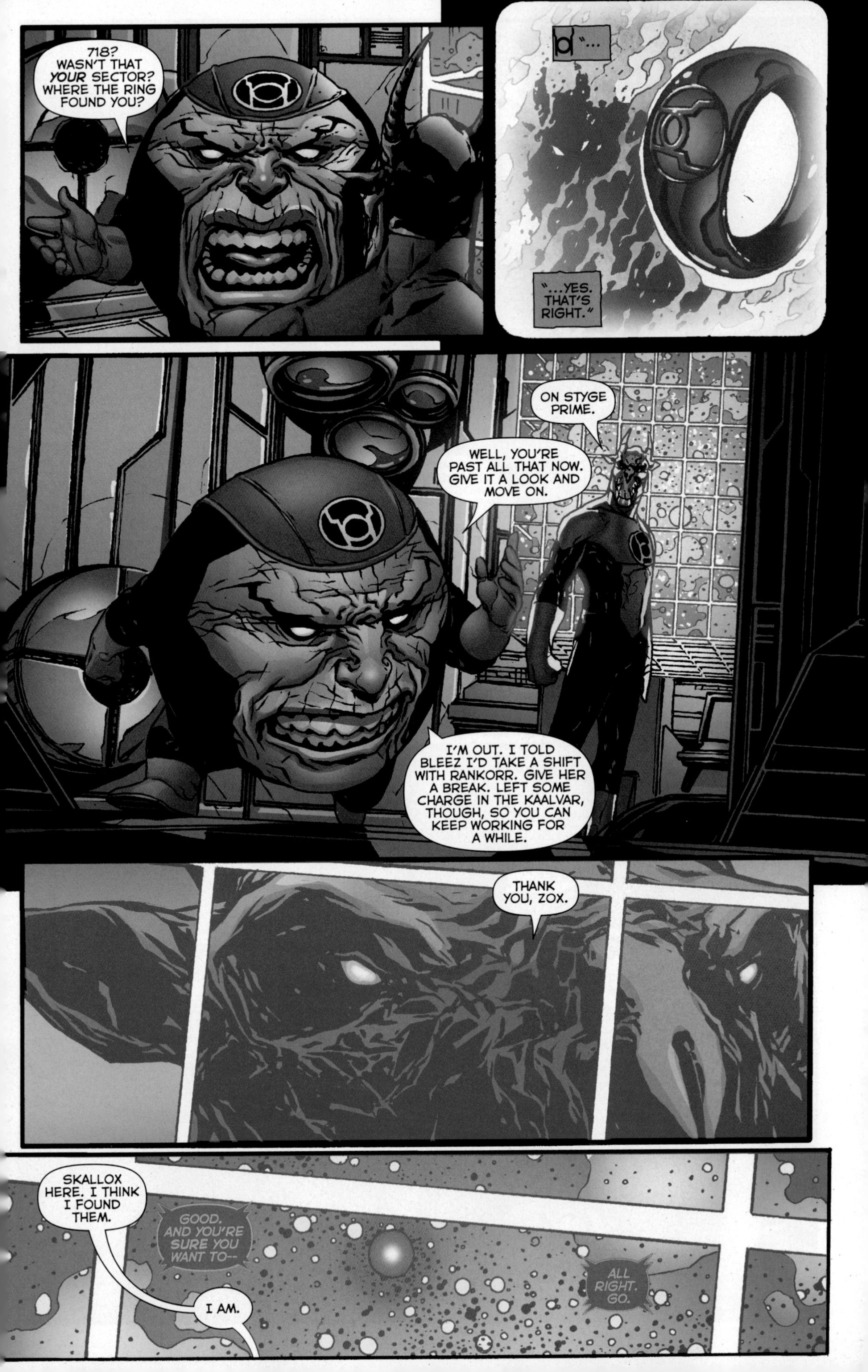
718? WASN'T THAT YOUR SECTOR? WHERE THE RING FOUND YOU?
"...
"...YES. THAT'S RIGHT."
ON STYGE PRIME.
WELL, YOU'RE PAST ALL THAT NOW. GIVE IT A LOOK AND MOVE ON.
I'M OUT. I TOLD BLEEZ I'D TAKE A SHIFT WITH RANKORR. GIVE HER A BREAK. LEFT SOME CHARGE IN THE KAALVAR, THOUGH, SO YOU CAN KEEP WORKING FOR A WHILE.
THANK YOU, ZOX.
SKALLOX HERE. I THINK I FOUND THEM.
GOOD. AND YOU'RE SURE YOU WANT TO--
I AM.
ALL RIGHT. GO.

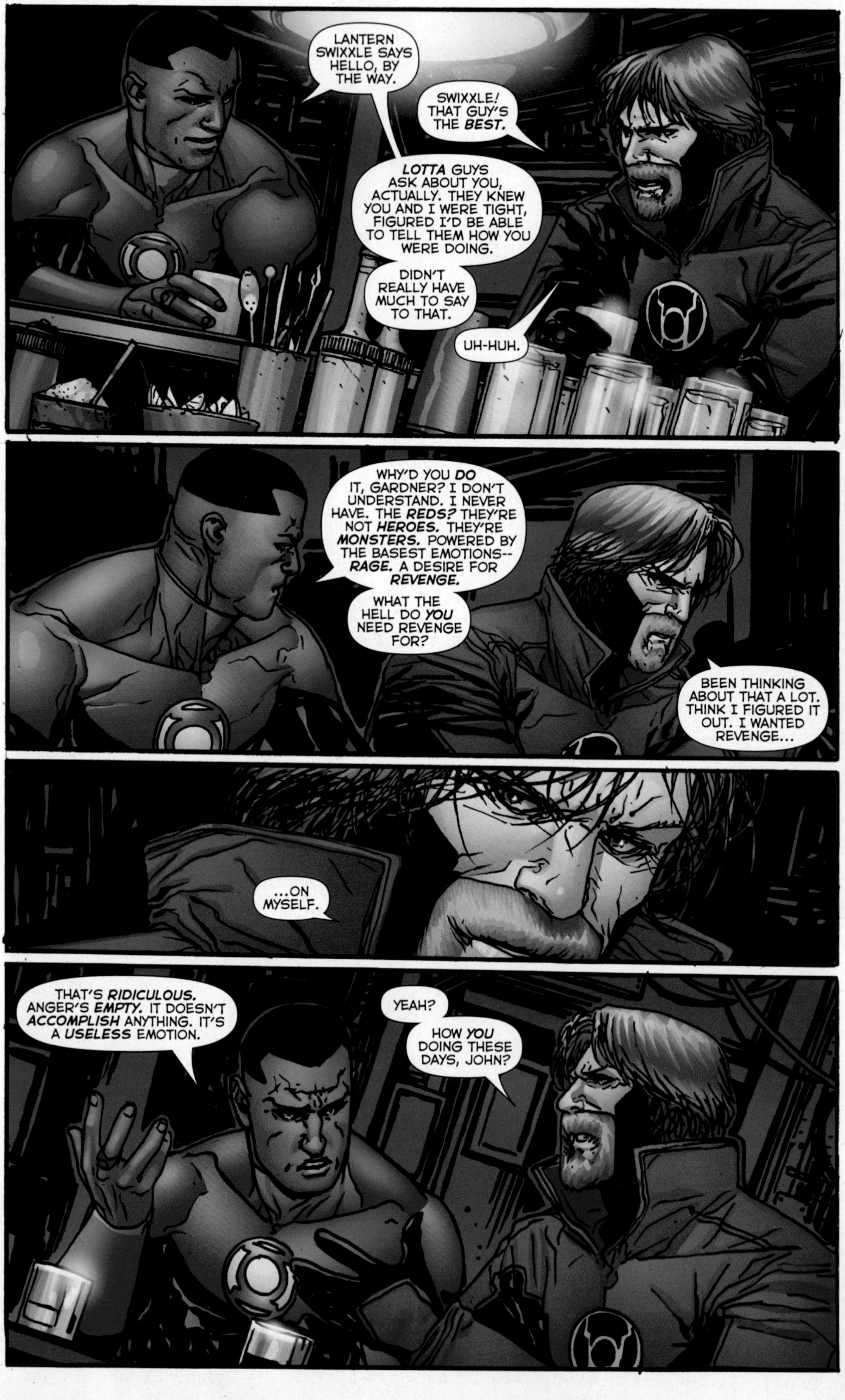
LANTERN SWIXXLE SAYS HELLO, BY THE WAY.
SWIXXLE! THAT GUY'S THE BEST.
LOTTA GUYS ASK ABOUT YOU, ACTUALLY. THEY KNEW YOU AND I WERE TIGHT, FIGURED I'D BE ABLE TO TELL THEM HOW YOU WERE DOING.
DIDN'T REALLY HAVE MUCH TO SAY TO THAT.
UH-HUH.
WHY'D YOU DO IT, GARDNER? I DON'T UNDERSTAND. I NEVER HAVE. THE REDS? THEY'RE NOT HEROES. THEY'RE MONSTERS. POWERED BY THE BASEST EMOTIONS--RAGE. A DESIRE FOR REVENGE.
WHAT THE HELL DO YOU NEED REVENGE FOR?
BEEN THINKING ABOUT THAT A LOT. THINK I FIGURED IT OUT. I WANTED REVENGE...
...ON MYSELF.
THAT'S RIDICULOUS. ANGER'S EMPTY. IT DOESN'T ACCOMPLISH ANYTHING. IT'S A USELESS EMOTION.
YEAH?
HOW YOU DOING THESE DAYS, JOHN?

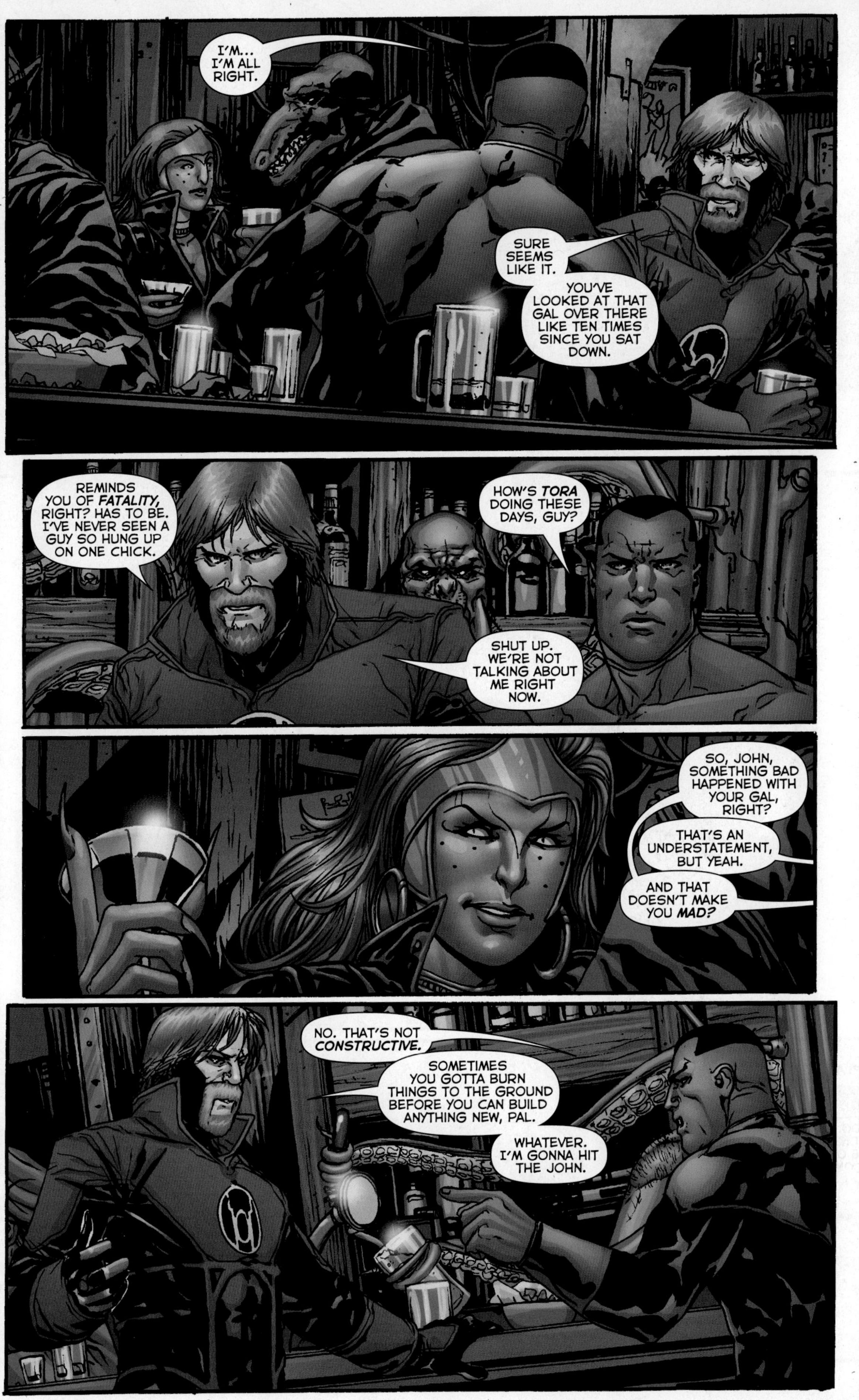
I'M... I'M ALL RIGHT.
SURE SEEMS LIKE IT.
YOU'VE LOOKED AT THAT GAL OVER THERE LIKE TEN TIMES SINCE YOU SAT DOWN.
REMINDS YOU OF FATALITY, RIGHT? HAS TO BE. I'VE NEVER SEEN A GUY SO HUNG UP ON ONE CHICK.
HOW'S TORA DOING THESE DAYS, GUY?
SHUT UP. WE'RE NOT TALKING ABOUT ME RIGHT NOW.
SO, JOHN, SOMETHING BAD HAPPENED WITH YOUR GAL, RIGHT?
THAT'S AN UNDERSTATEMENT, BUT YEAH.
AND THAT DOESN'T MAKE YOU MAD?
NO. THAT'S NOT CONSTRUCTIVE.
SOMETIMES YOU GOTTA BURN THINGS TO THE GROUND BEFORE YOU CAN BUILD ANYTHING NEW, PAL.
WHATEVER. I'M GONNA HIT THE JOHN.

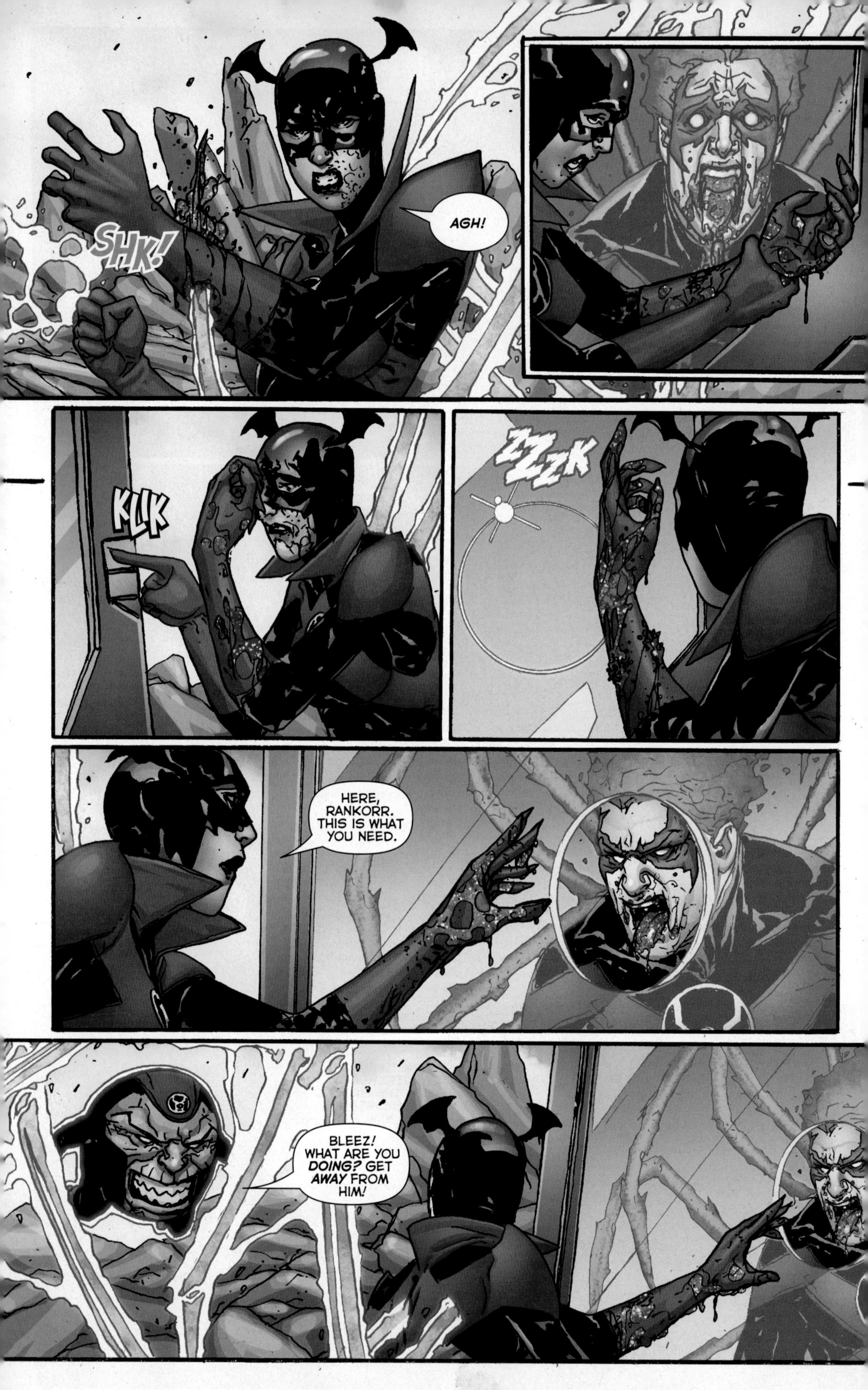
SHK!
AGH!
KLIK
ZZZK
HERE, RANKORR. THIS IS WHAT YOU NEED.
BLEEZ! WHAT ARE YOU DOING? GET AWAY FROM HIM!

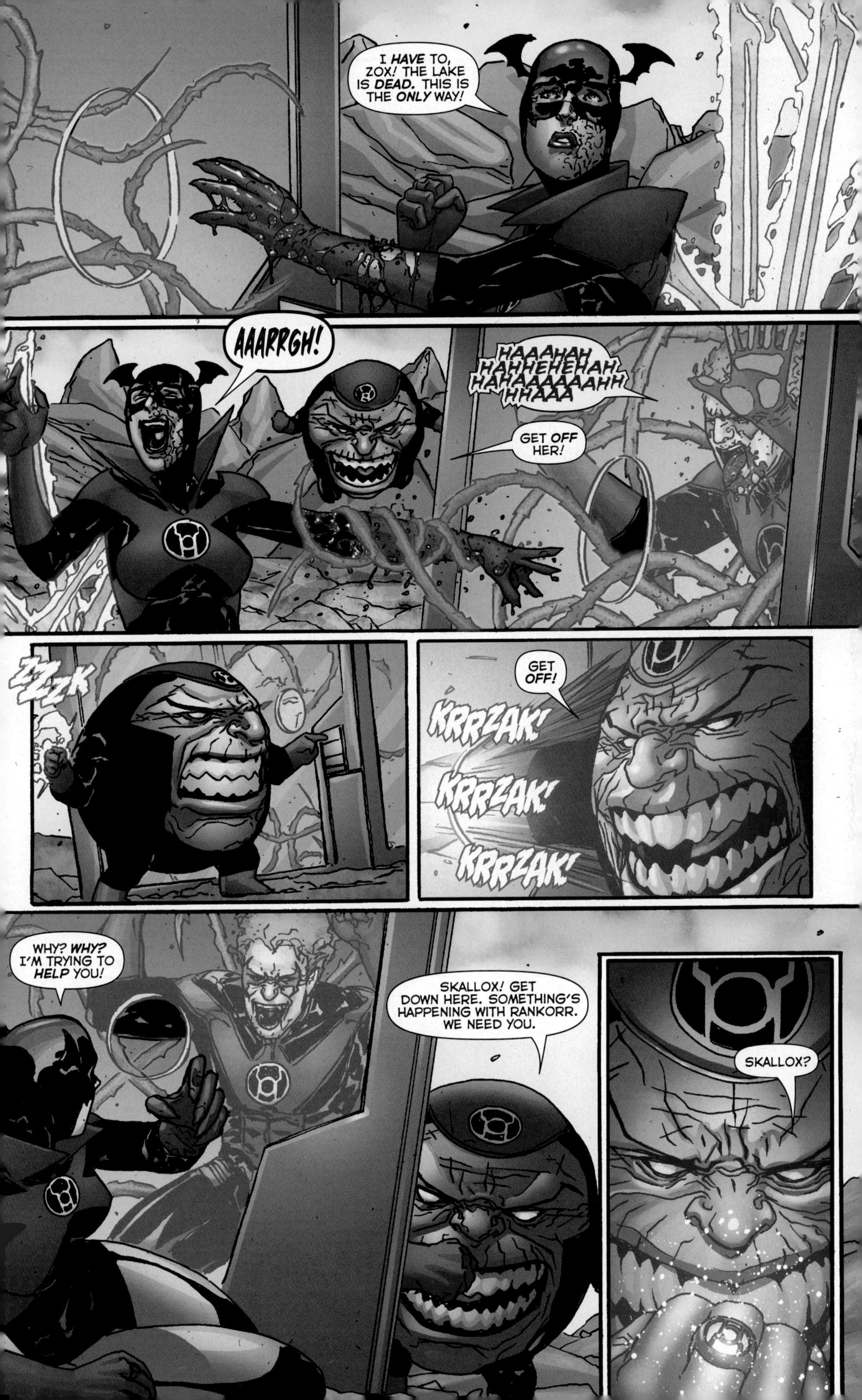

I HAVE TO, ZOX! THE LAKE IS DEAD. THIS IS THE ONLY WAY!
AAARRGH!
HAAAHAH HAHHEHEHAH HAHAAAAAAAHH HHAAA
GET OFF HER!
ZZZK
GET OFF!
KRRZAK!
KRRZAK!
KRRZAK!
WHY? WHY? I'M TRYING TO HELP YOU!
SKALLOX! GET DOWN HERE. SOMETHING'S HAPPENING WITH RANKORR. WE NEED YOU.
SKALLOX?

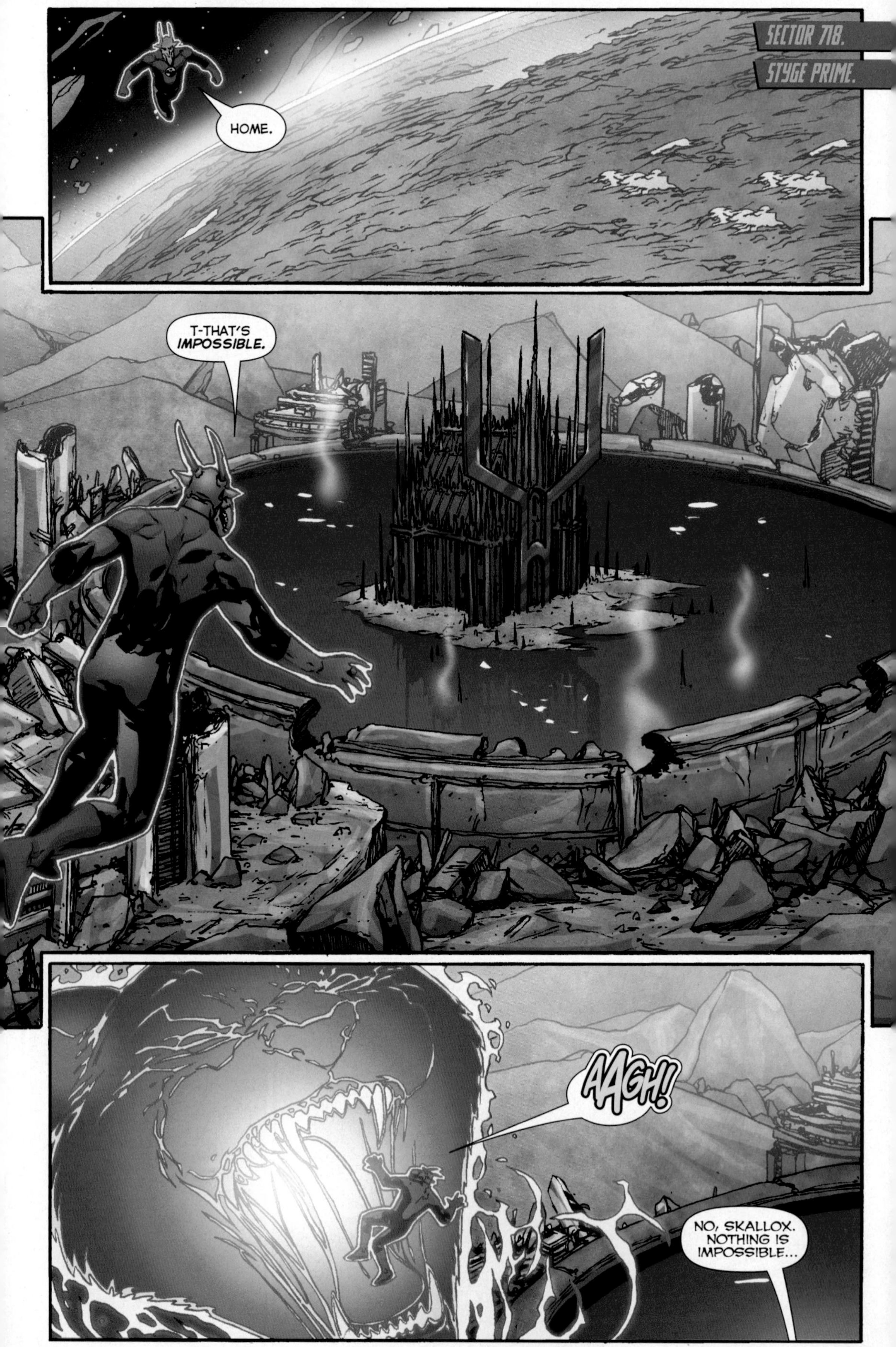
SECTOR 718.
STYGE PRIME.
HOME.
T-THAT'S IMPOSSIBLE.
AAGH!
NO, SKALLOX. NOTHING IS IMPOSSIBLE...

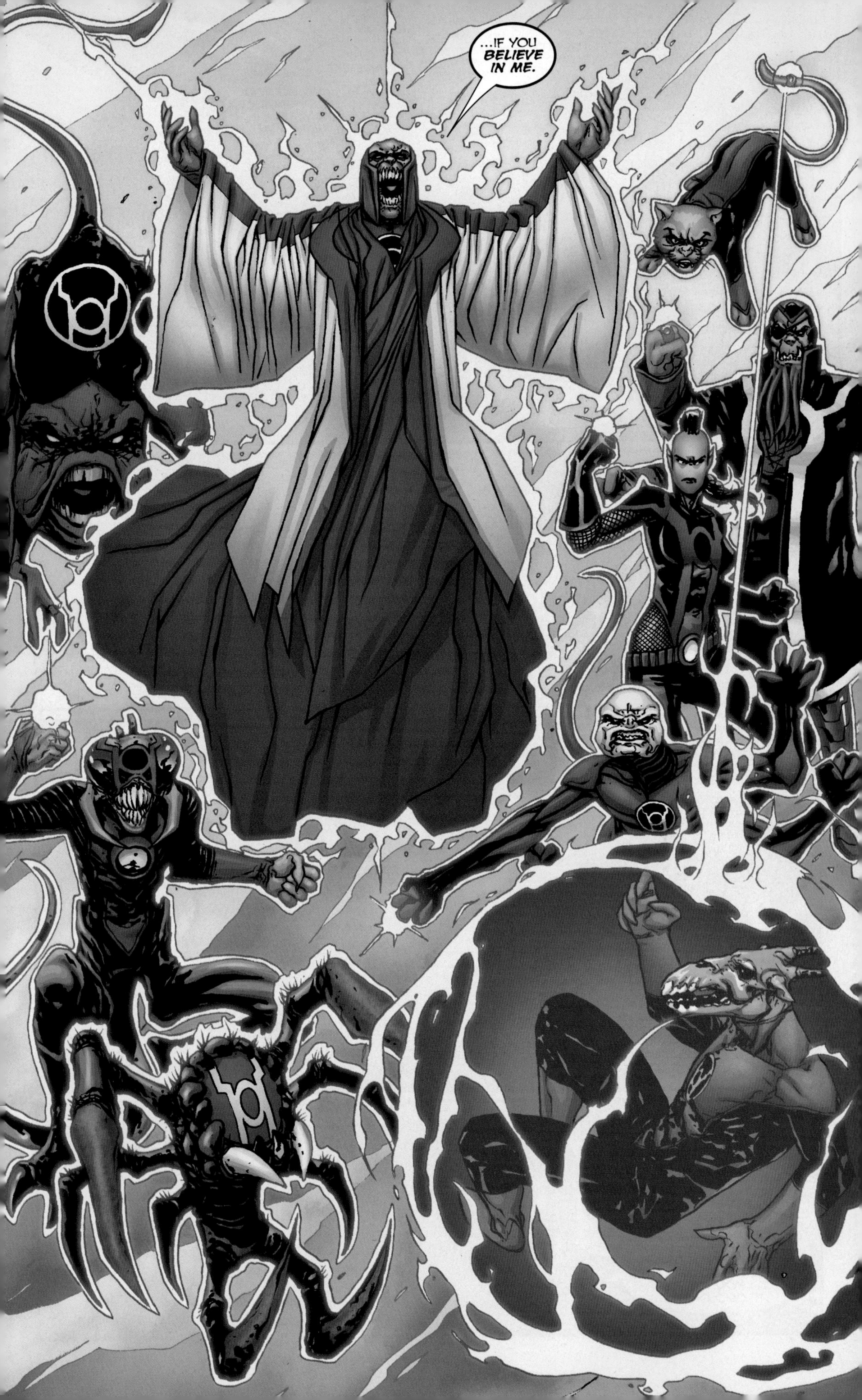
...IF YOU BELIEVE IN ME.

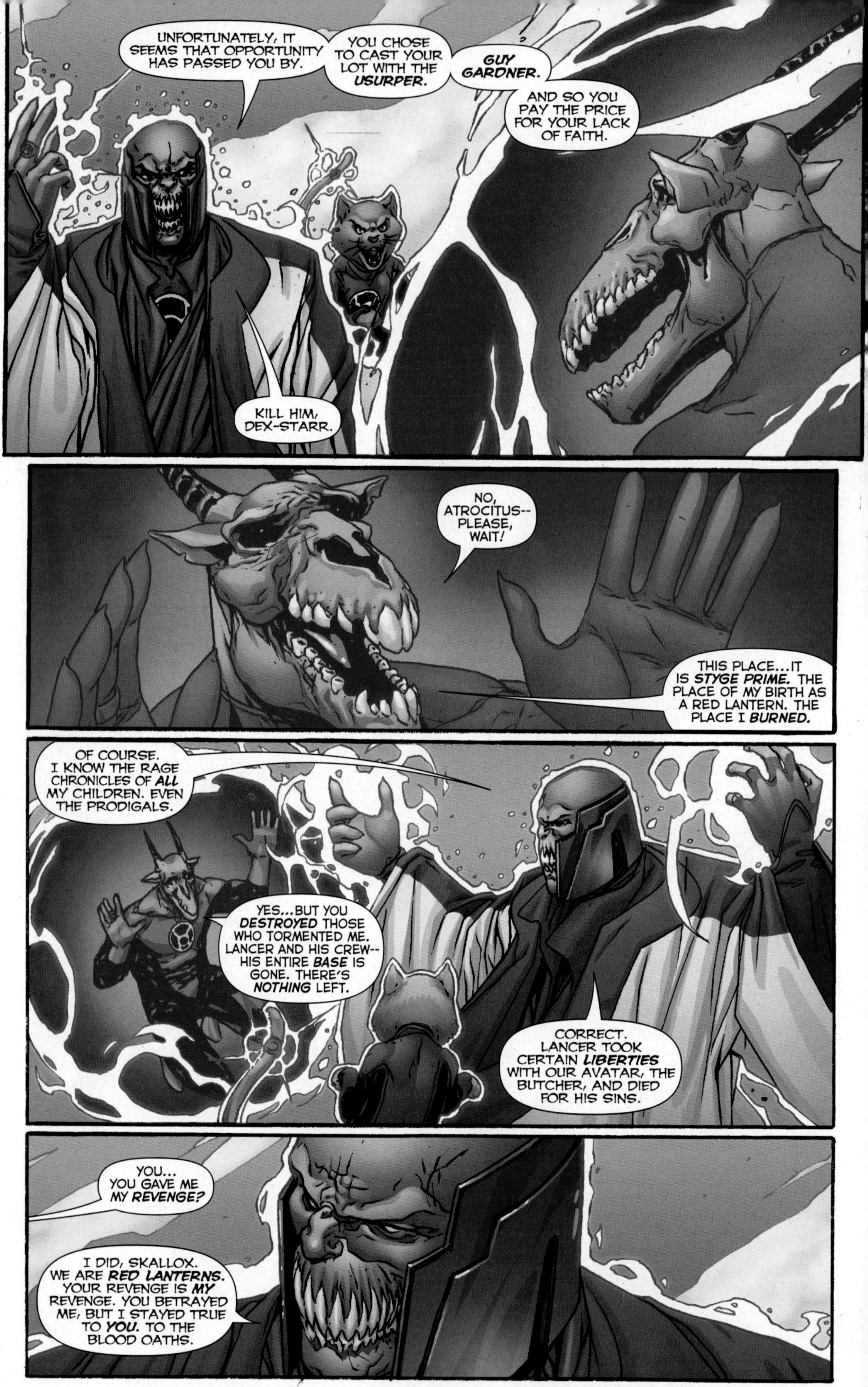

UNFORTUNATELY, IT SEEMS THAT OPPORTUNITY HAS PASSED YOU BY.
YOU CHOSE TO CAST YOUR LOT WITH THE USURPER.
GUY GARDNER.
AND SO YOU PAY THE PRICE FOR YOUR LACK OF FAITH.
KILL HIM, DEX-STARR.
NO, ATROCITUS-- PLEASE, WAIT!
THIS PLACE...IT IS STYGE PRIME. THE PLACE OF MY BIRTH AS A RED LANTERN. THE PLACE I BURNED.
OF COURSE. I KNOW THE RAGE CHRONICLES OF ALL MY CHILDREN. EVEN THE PRODIGALS.
YES...BUT YOU DESTROYED THOSE WHO TORMENTED ME. LANCER AND HIS CREW-- HIS ENTIRE BASE IS GONE. THERE'S NOTHING LEFT.
CORRECT. LANCER TOOK CERTAIN LIBERTIES WITH OUR AVATAR, THE BUTCHER, AND DIED FOR HIS SINS.
YOU... YOU GAVE ME MY REVENGE?
I DID, SKALLOX. WE ARE RED LANTERNS. YOUR REVENGE IS MY REVENGE. YOU BETRAYED ME, BUT I STAYED TRUE TO YOU. TO THE BLOOD OATHS.

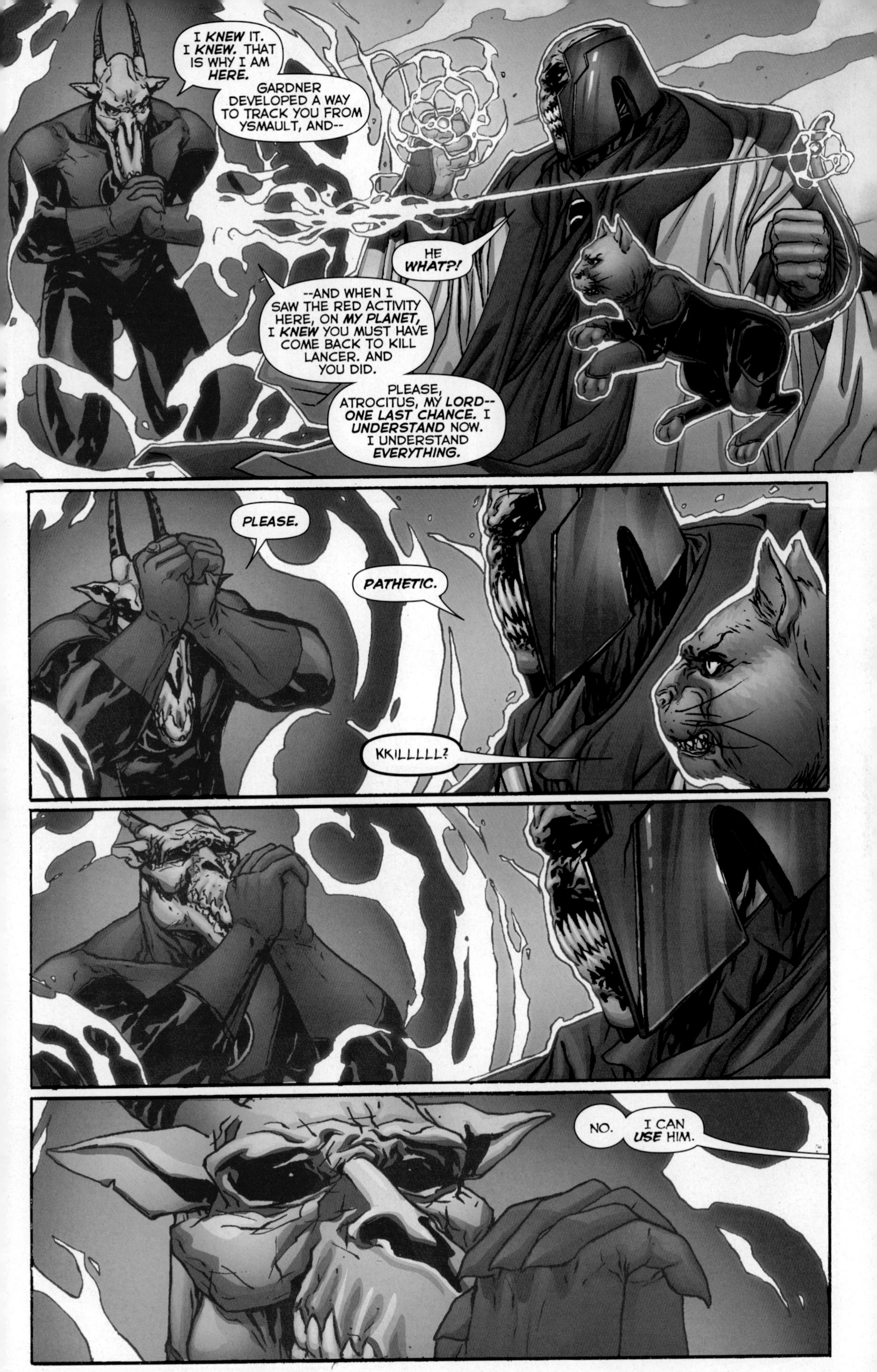
I KNEW IT. I KNEW. THAT IS WHY I AM HERE.
GARDNER DEVELOPED A WAY TO TRACK YOU FROM YSMAULT, AND--
HE WHAT?!
--AND WHEN I SAW THE RED ACTIVITY HERE, ON MY PLANET, I KNEW YOU MUST HAVE COME BACK TO KILL LANCER. AND YOU DID.
PLEASE, ATROCITUS, MY LORD-- ONE LAST CHANCE. I UNDERSTAND NOW. I UNDERSTAND EVERYTHING.
PLEASE.
PATHETIC.
KKILLLLL?
NO. I CAN USE HIM.

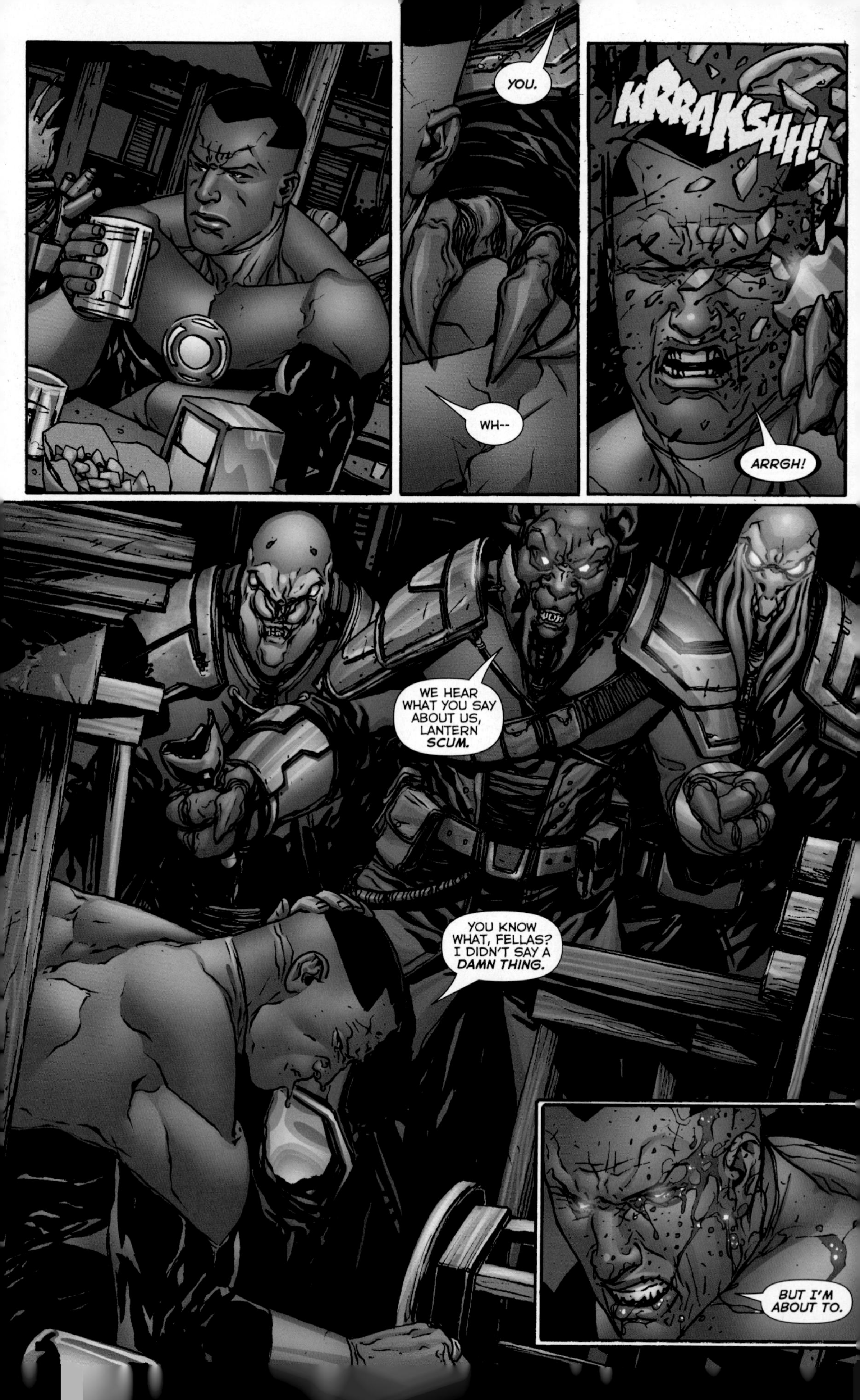
YOU.
WH--
KRRAKSHH!
ARRGH!
WE HEAR WHAT YOU SAY ABOUT US, LANTERN SCUM.
YOU KNOW WHAT, FELLAS? I DIDN'T SAY A DAMN THING.
BUT I'M ABOUT TO.

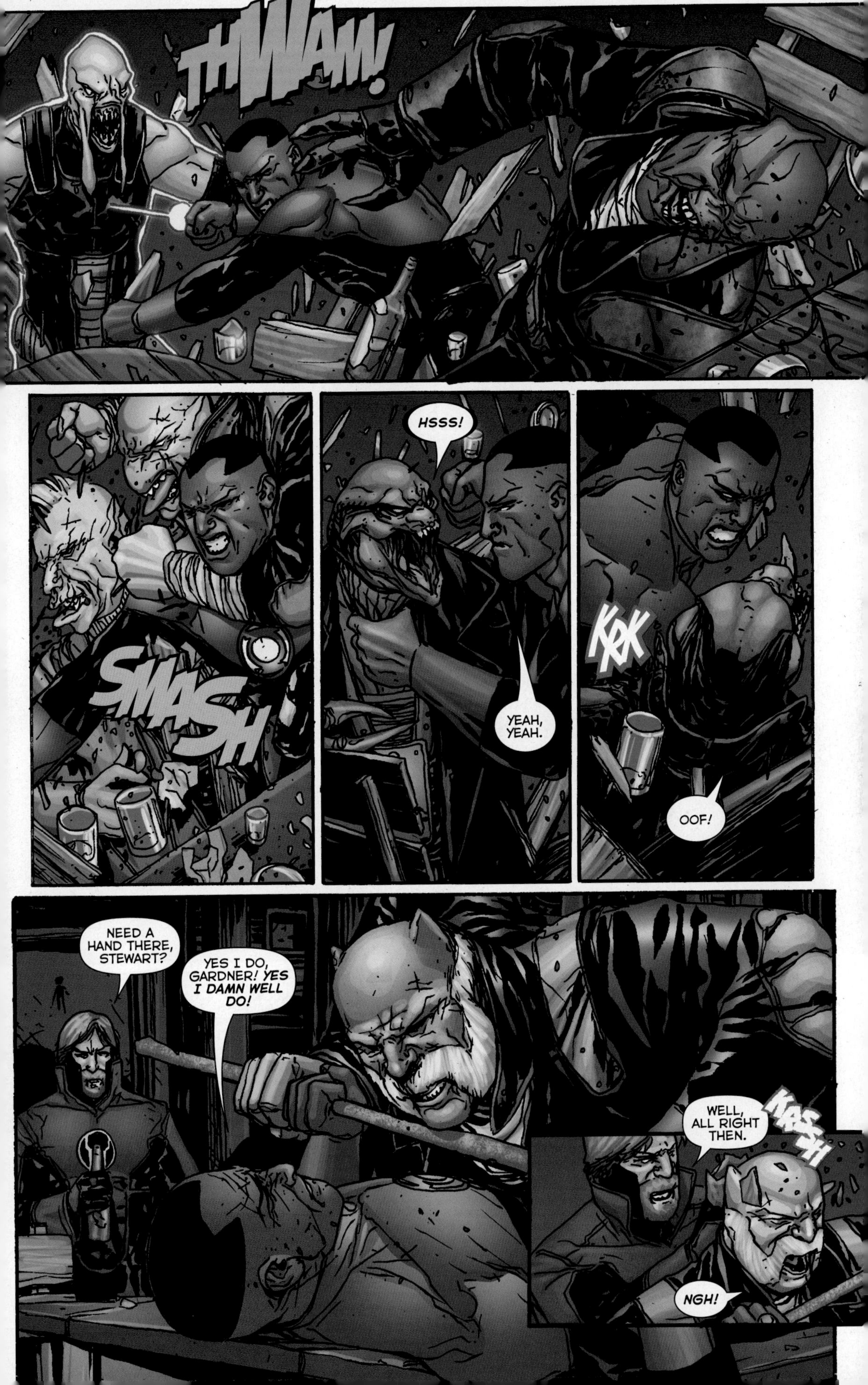
THWAM!
SMASH
HSSS!
YEAH, YEAH.
KRK
OOF!
NEED A HAND THERE, STEWART?
YES I DO, GARDNER! YES I DAMN WELL DO!
WELL, ALL RIGHT THEN.
KASSH
NGH!

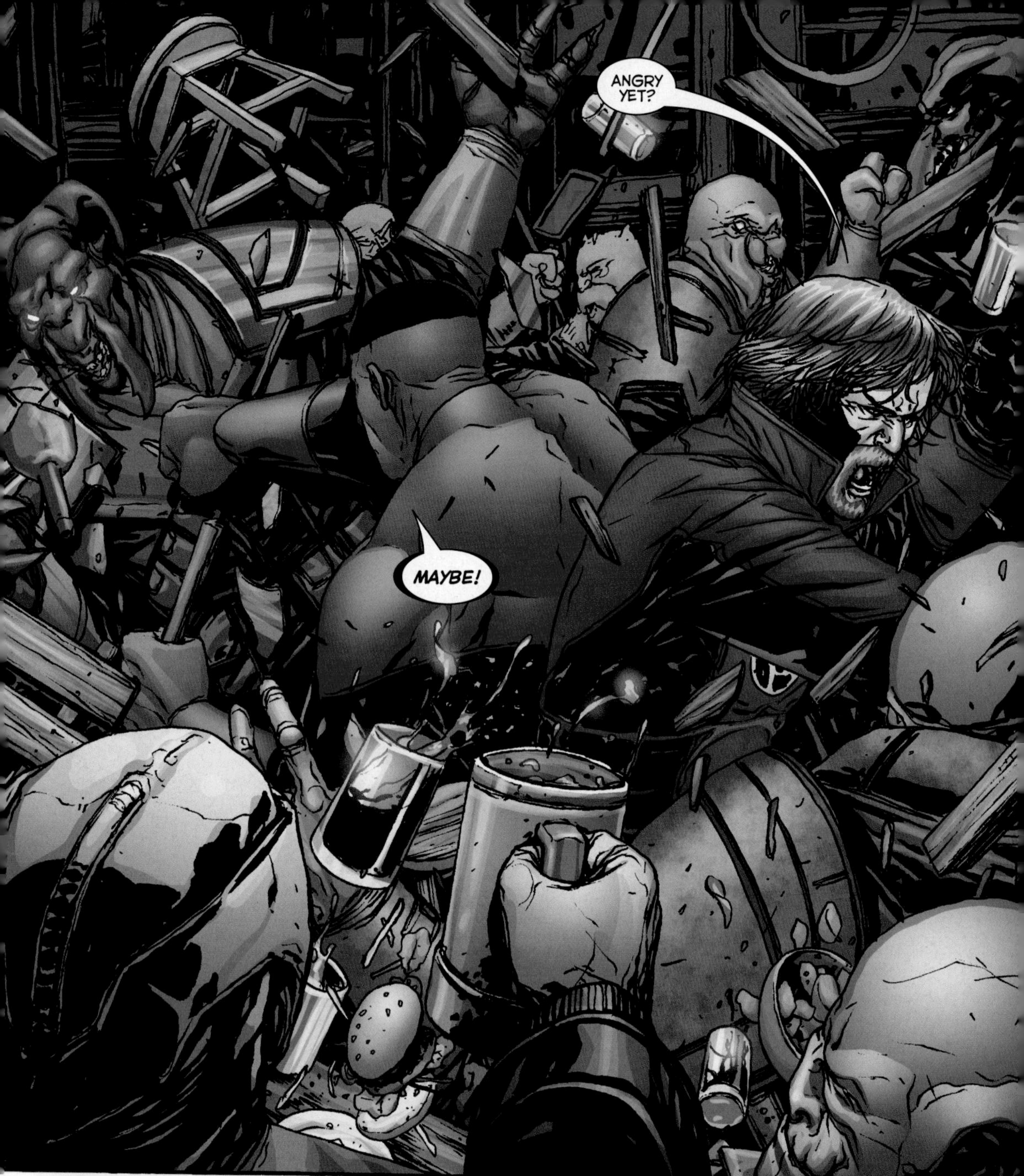
ANGRY YET?
MAYBE!

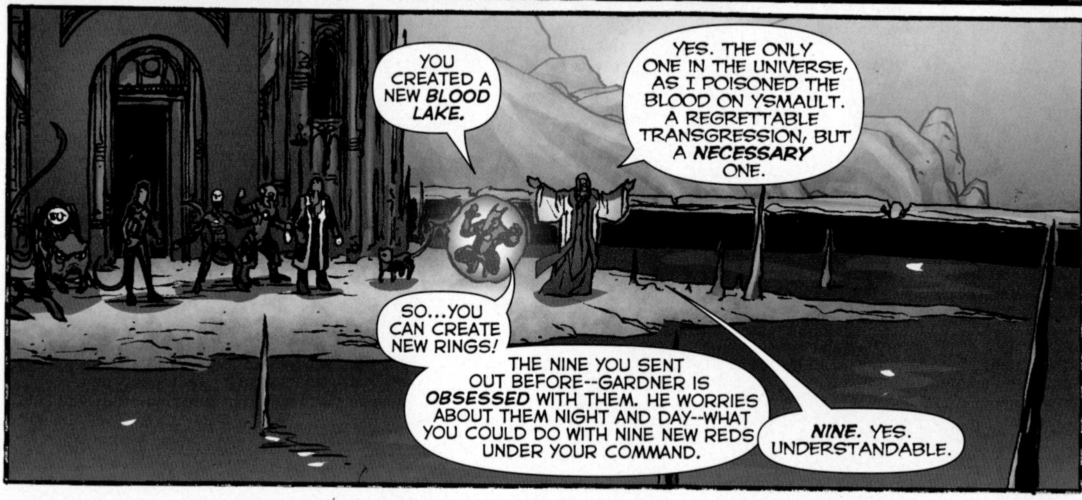
YOU CREATED A NEW *BLOOD LAKE.*
YES. THE ONLY ONE IN THE UNIVERSE, AS I POISONED THE BLOOD ON YSMAULT. A REGRETTABLE TRANSGRESSION, BUT A ***NECESSARY*** ONE.
SO...YOU CAN CREATE NEW RINGS!
THE NINE YOU SENT OUT BEFORE--GARDNER IS ***OBSESSED*** WITH THEM. HE WORRIES ABOUT THEM NIGHT AND DAY--WHAT YOU COULD DO WITH NINE NEW REDS UNDER YOUR COMMAND.
NINE. YES. UNDERSTANDABLE.

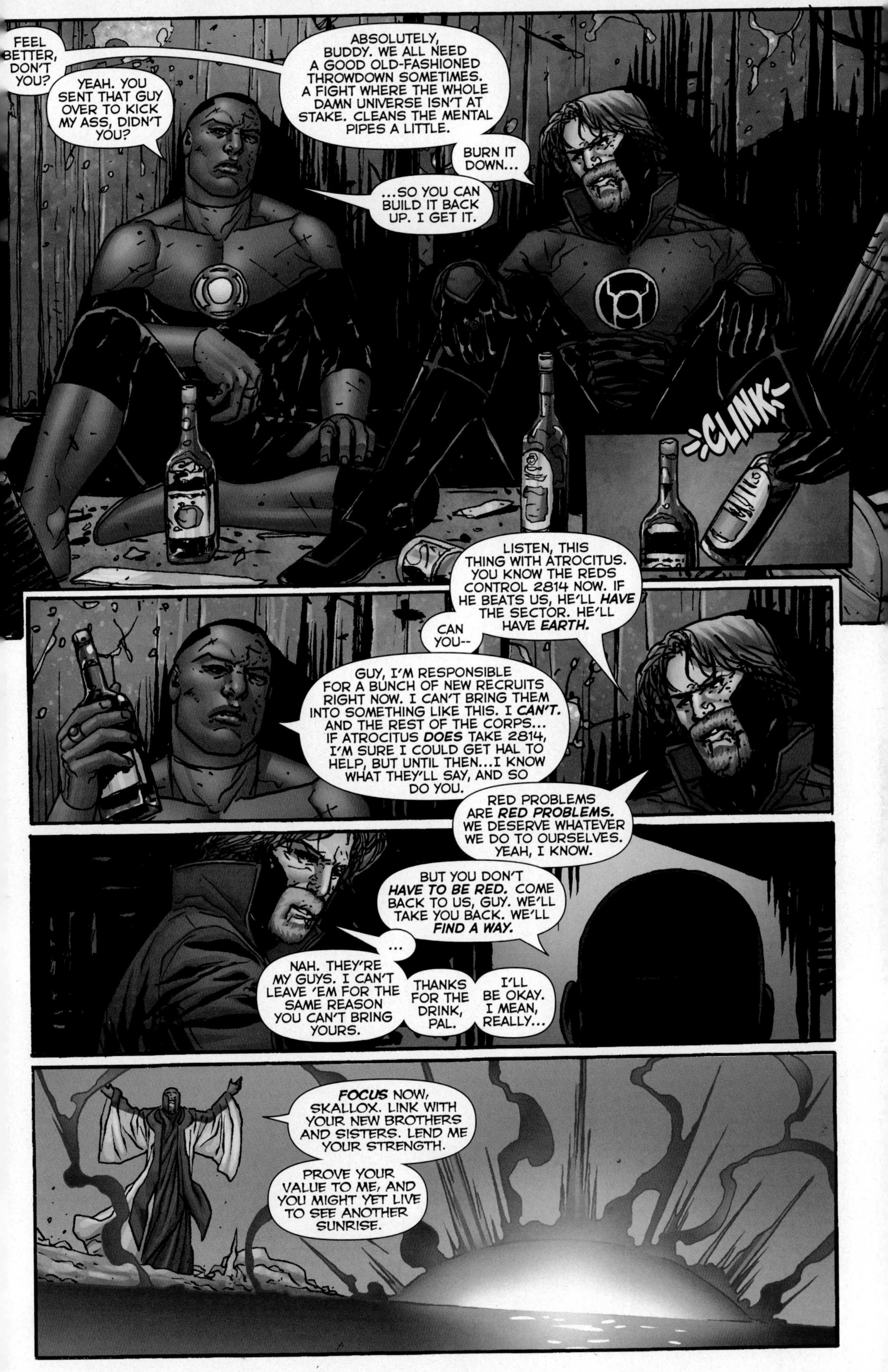
FEEL BETTER, DON'T YOU?
YEAH. YOU SENT THAT GUY OVER TO KICK MY ASS, DIDN'T YOU?
ABSOLUTELY, BUDDY. WE ALL NEED A GOOD OLD-FASHIONED THROWDOWN SOMETIMES. A FIGHT WHERE THE WHOLE DAMN UNIVERSE ISN'T AT STAKE. CLEANS THE MENTAL PIPES A LITTLE.
BURN IT DOWN...
...SO YOU CAN BUILD IT BACK UP. I GET IT.
CLINK
LISTEN, THIS THING WITH ATROCITUS. YOU KNOW THE REDS CONTROL 2814 NOW. IF HE BEATS US, HE'LL *HAVE* THE SECTOR. HE'LL HAVE *EARTH.*
CAN YOU--
GUY, I'M RESPONSIBLE FOR A BUNCH OF NEW RECRUITS RIGHT NOW. I CAN'T BRING THEM INTO SOMETHING LIKE THIS. I *CAN'T.* AND THE REST OF THE CORPS... IF ATROCITUS *DOES* TAKE 2814, I'M SURE I COULD GET HAL TO HELP, BUT UNTIL THEN...I KNOW WHAT THEY'LL SAY, AND SO DO YOU.
RED PROBLEMS ARE *RED PROBLEMS.* WE DESERVE WHATEVER WE DO TO OURSELVES. YEAH, I KNOW.
BUT YOU DON'T *HAVE TO BE RED.* COME BACK TO US, GUY. WE'LL TAKE YOU BACK. WE'LL *FIND A WAY.*
...
NAH. THEY'RE MY GUYS. I CAN'T LEAVE 'EM FOR THE SAME REASON YOU CAN'T BRING YOURS.
THANKS FOR THE DRINK, PAL.
I'LL BE OKAY. I MEAN, REALLY...
FOCUS NOW, SKALLOX. LINK WITH YOUR NEW BROTHERS AND SISTERS. LEND ME YOUR STRENGTH.
PROVE YOUR VALUE TO ME, AND YOU MIGHT YET LIVE TO SEE ANOTHER SUNRISE.

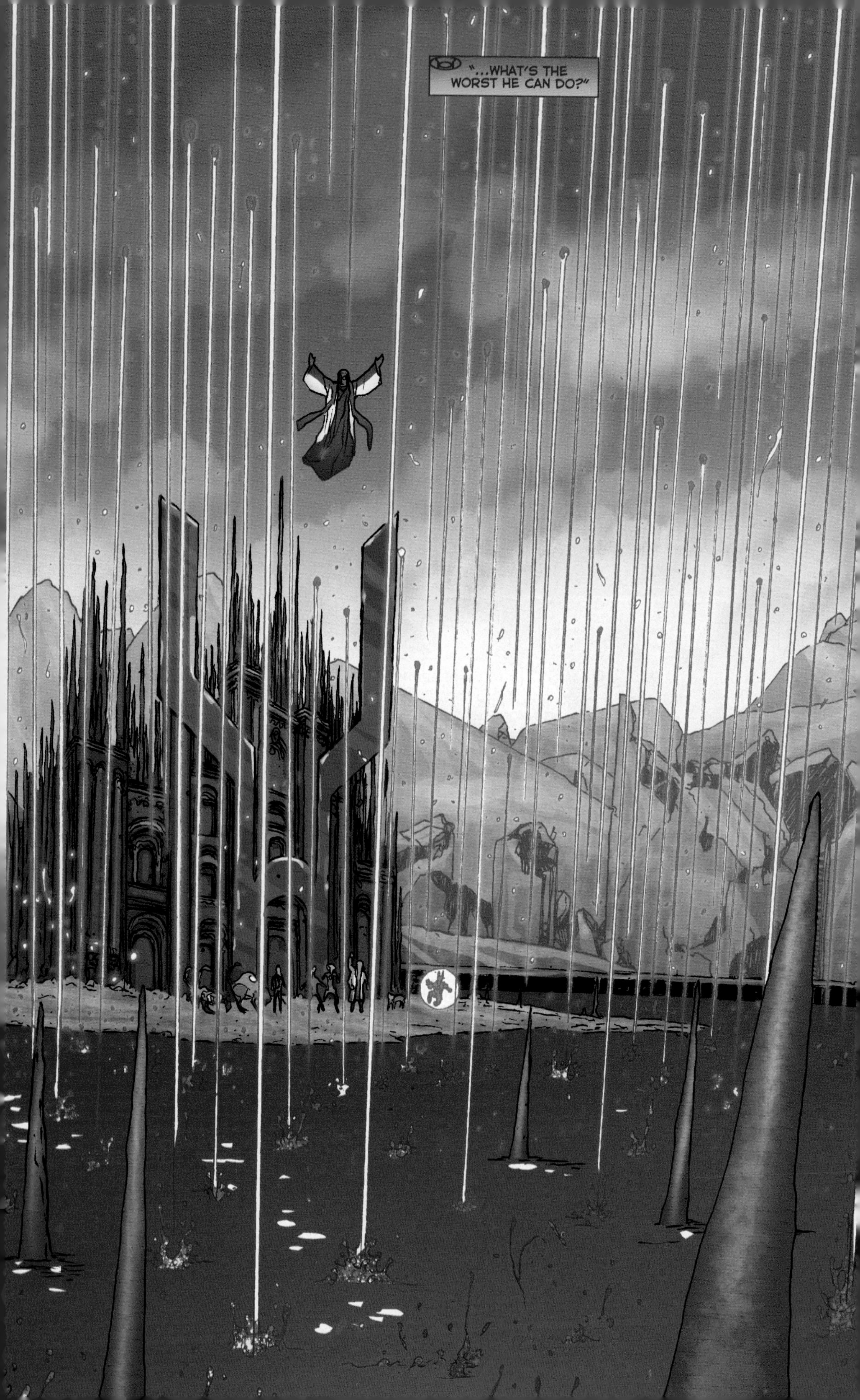
"...WHAT'S THE WORST HE CAN DO?"

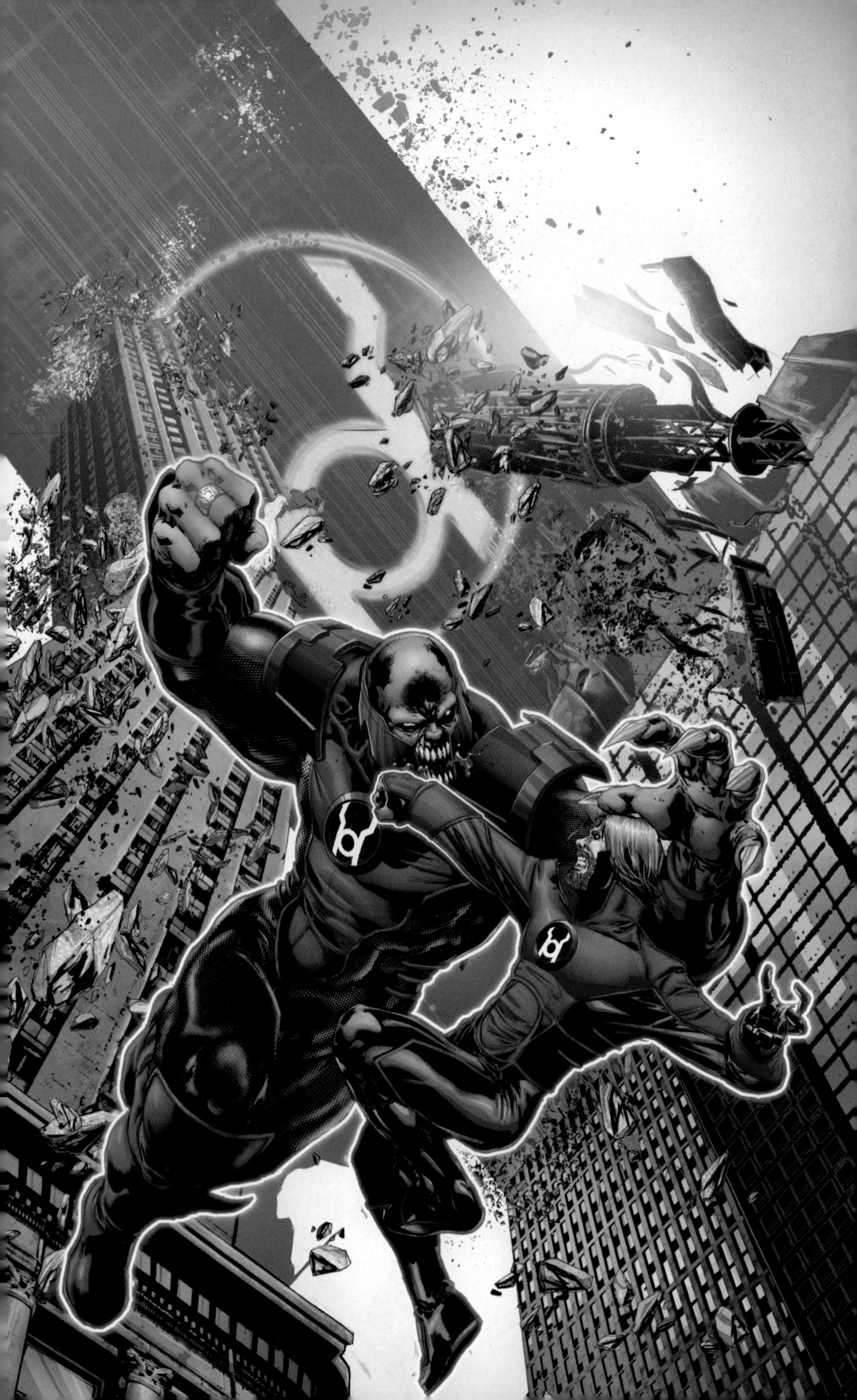

CHARLES SOULE writer **MIGUEL SEPULVEDA** artist **CHRIS SOTOMAYOR** colorist **DEZI SIENTY TAYLOR ESPOSITO** letterers
cover art by **MIGUEL SEPULVEDA** with **GABE ELTAEB**

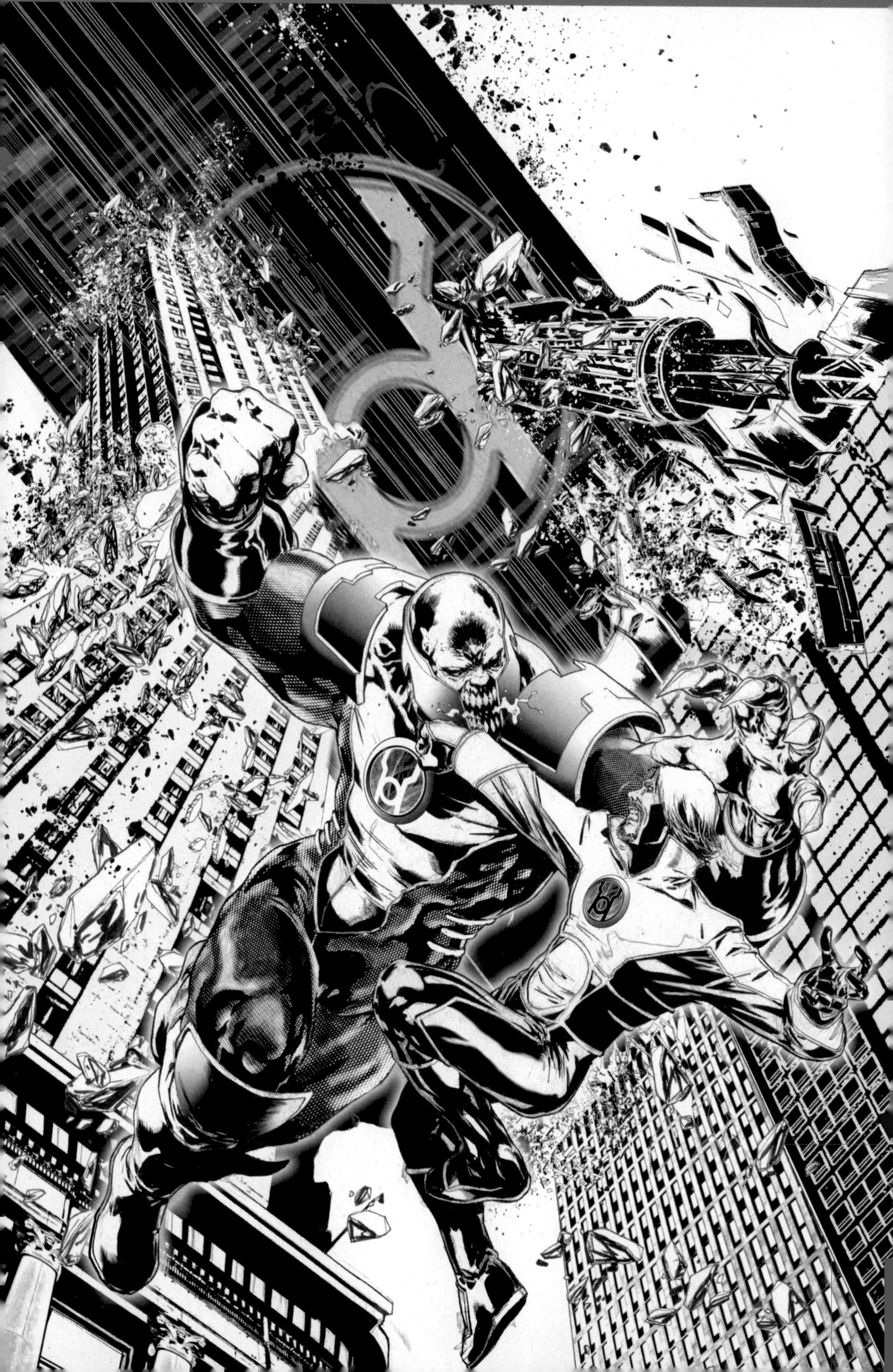

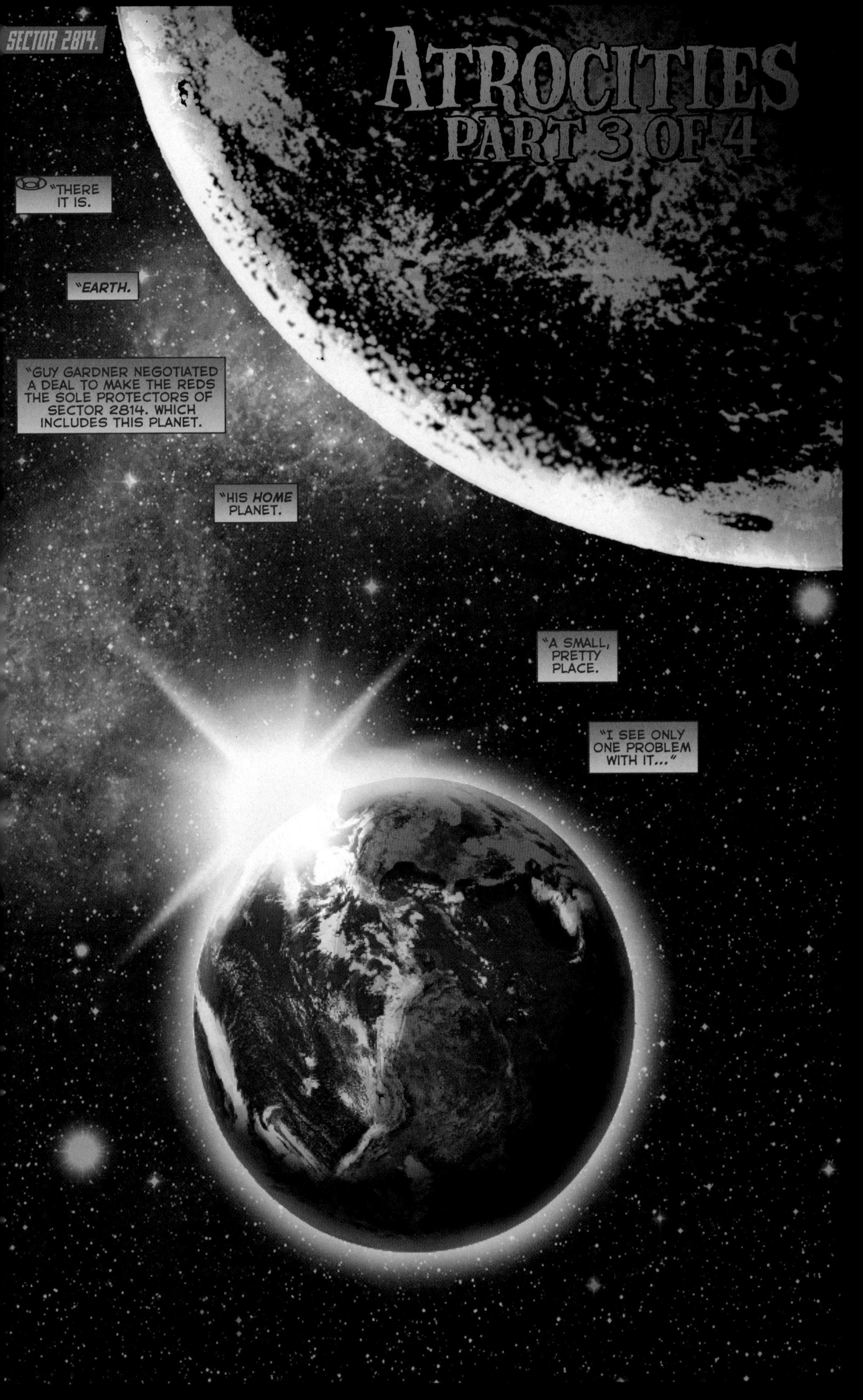
SECTOR 2814.
ATROCITIES
PART 3 OF 4
"THERE IT IS.
"EARTH.
"GUY GARDNER NEGOTIATED A DEAL TO MAKE THE REDS THE SOLE PROTECTORS OF SECTOR 2814. WHICH INCLUDES THIS PLANET.
"HIS HOME PLANET.
"A SMALL, PRETTY PLACE.
"I SEE ONLY ONE PROBLEM WITH IT..."

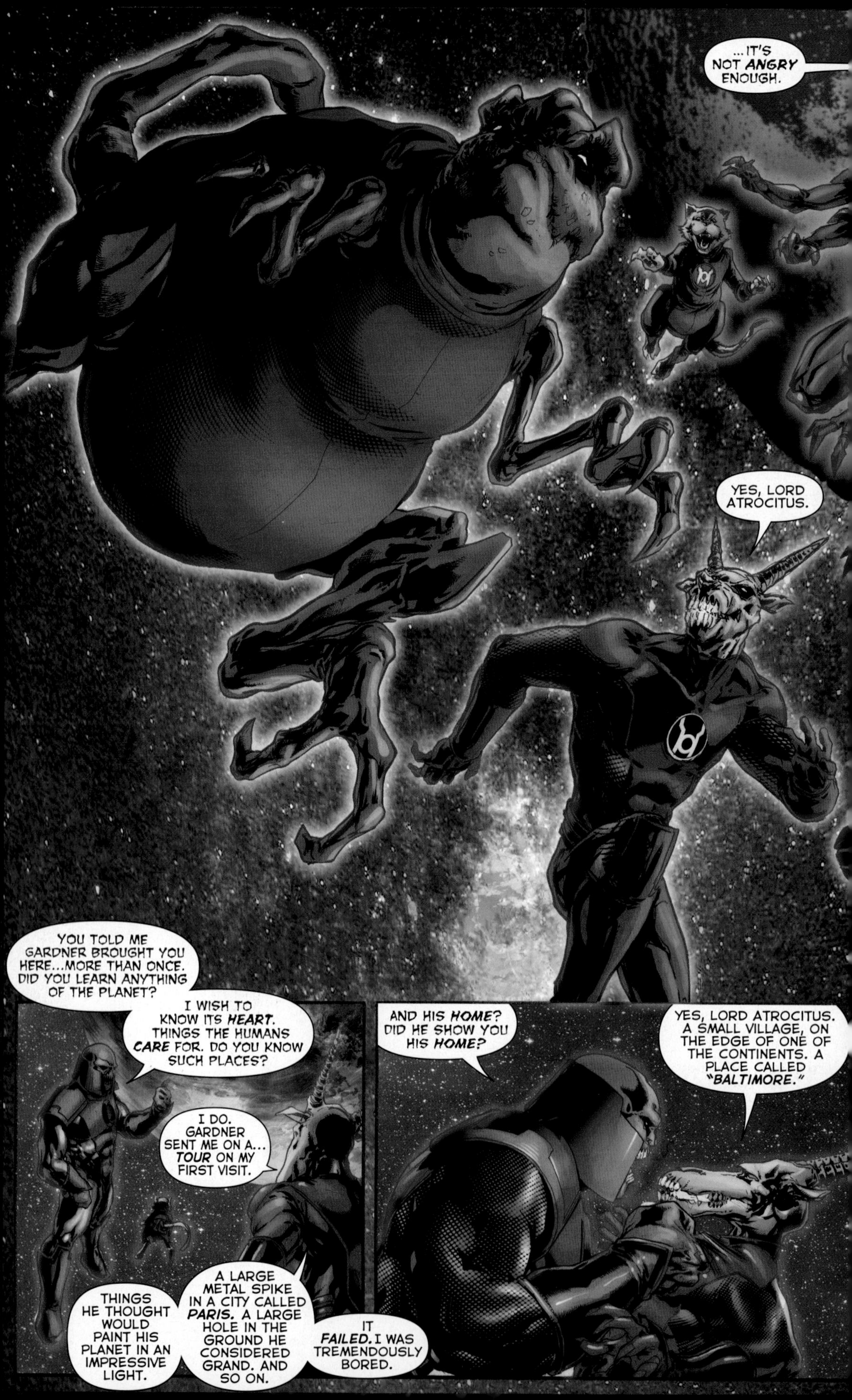
...IT'S NOT ANGRY ENOUGH.
YES, LORD ATROCITUS.
YOU TOLD ME GARDNER BROUGHT YOU HERE...MORE THAN ONCE. DID YOU LEARN ANYTHING OF THE PLANET?
I WISH TO KNOW ITS HEART. THINGS THE HUMANS CARE FOR. DO YOU KNOW SUCH PLACES?
I DO. GARDNER SENT ME ON A... TOUR ON MY FIRST VISIT.
THINGS HE THOUGHT WOULD PAINT HIS PLANET IN AN IMPRESSIVE LIGHT.
A LARGE METAL SPIKE IN A CITY CALLED PARIS. A LARGE HOLE IN THE GROUND HE CONSIDERED GRAND. AND SO ON.
IT FAILED. I WAS TREMENDOUSLY BORED.
AND HIS HOME? DID HE SHOW YOU HIS HOME?
YES, LORD ATROCITUS. A SMALL VILLAGE, ON THE EDGE OF ONE OF THE CONTINENTS. A PLACE CALLED "BALTIMORE."

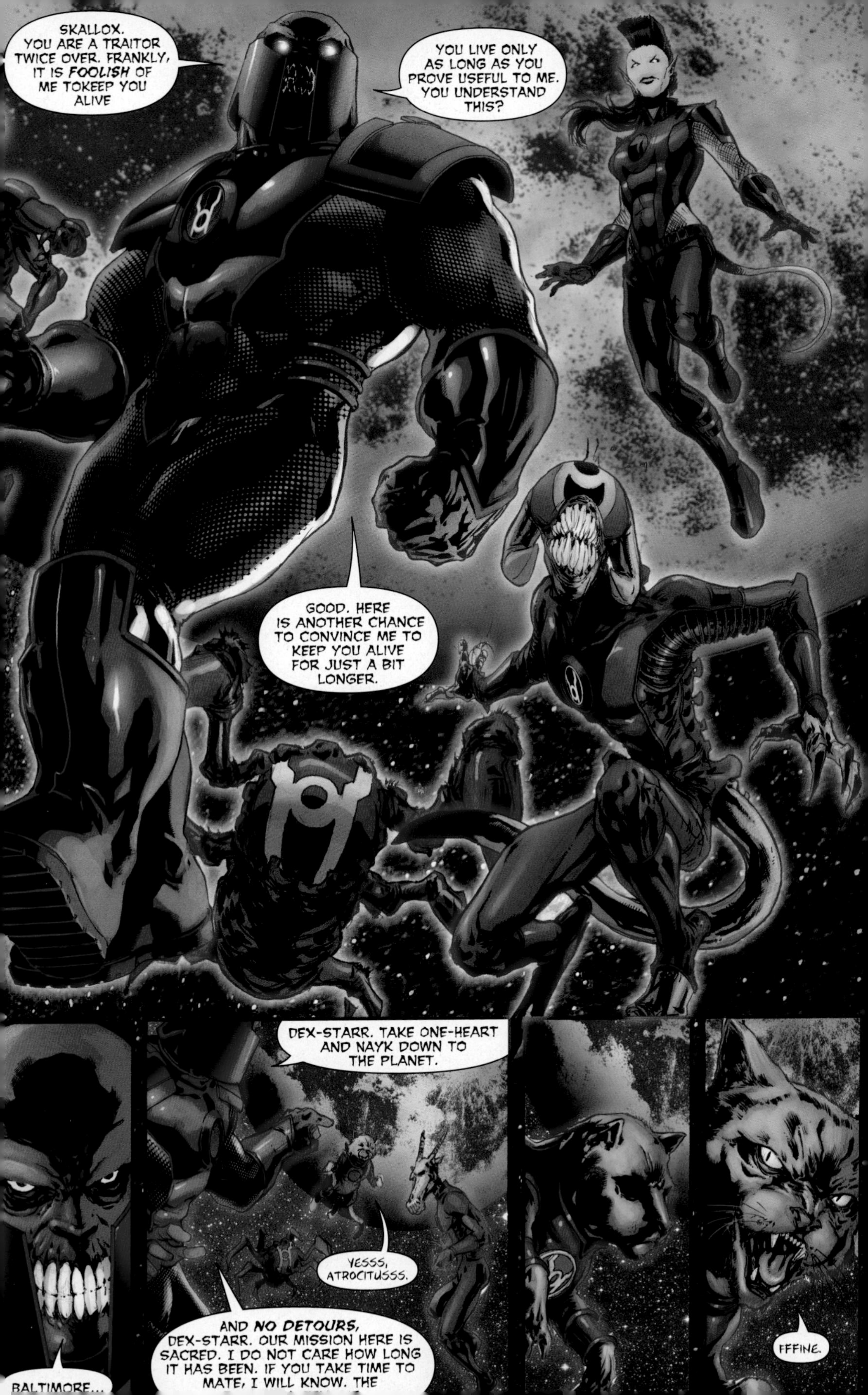
SKALLOX. YOU ARE A TRAITOR TWICE OVER. FRANKLY, IT IS *FOOLISH* OF ME TOKEEP YOU ALIVE
YOU LIVE ONLY AS LONG AS YOU PROVE USEFUL TO ME. YOU UNDERSTAND THIS?
GOOD. HERE IS ANOTHER CHANCE TO CONVINCE ME TO KEEP YOU ALIVE FOR JUST A BIT LONGER.
BALTIMORE...
DEX-STARR. TAKE ONE-HEART AND NAYK DOWN TO THE PLANET.
YESSS, ATROCITUSSS.
AND *NO DETOURS,* DEX-STARR. OUR MISSION HERE IS SACRED. I DO NOT CARE HOW LONG IT HAS BEEN. IF YOU TAKE TIME TO MATE, I WILL KNOW. THE
FFFINE.

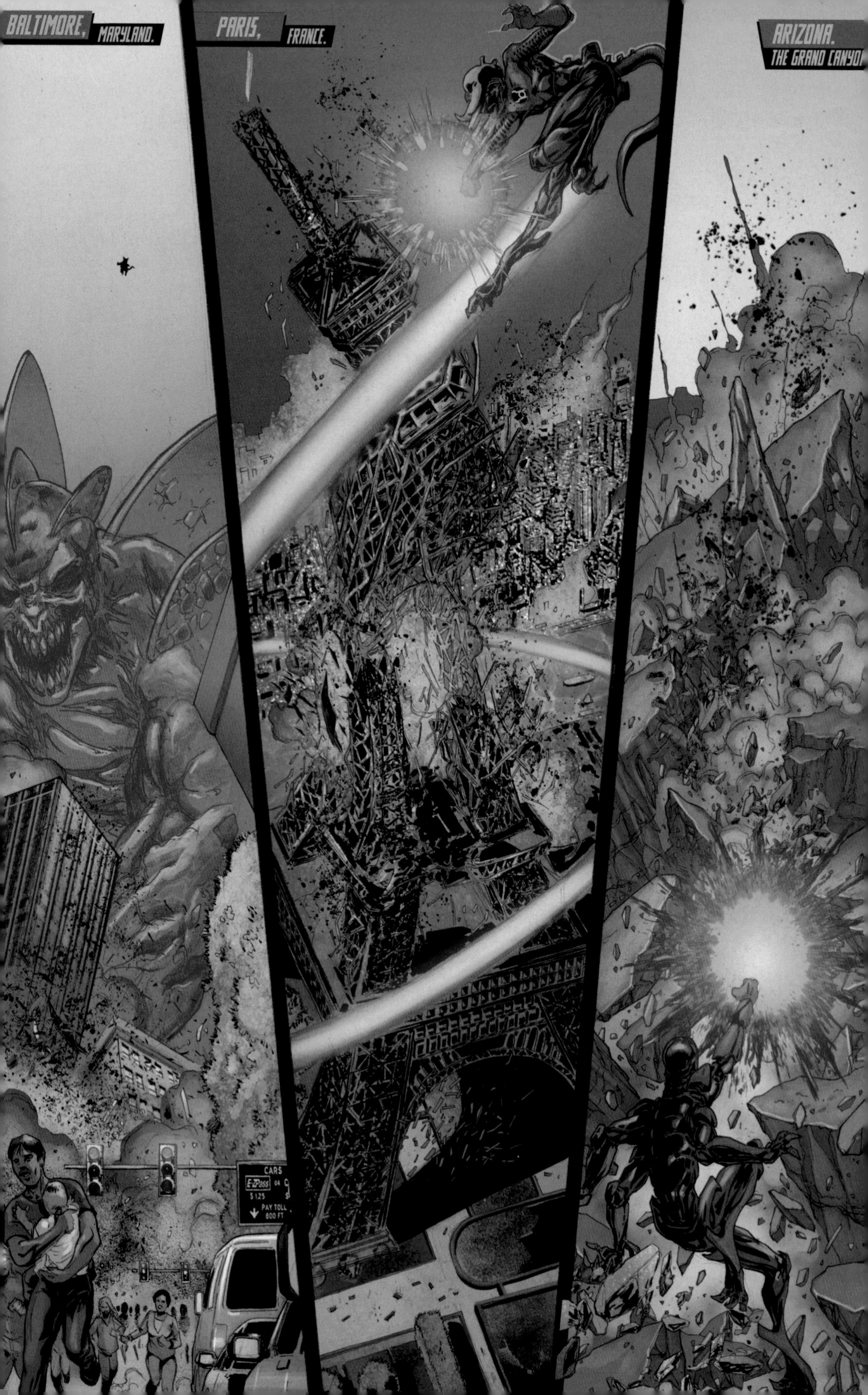
BALTIMORE, MARYLAND.
PARIS, FRANCE.
ARIZONA. THE GRAND CANYO
CARS
E-ZPass
$ 1.25
PAY TOLL
800 FT

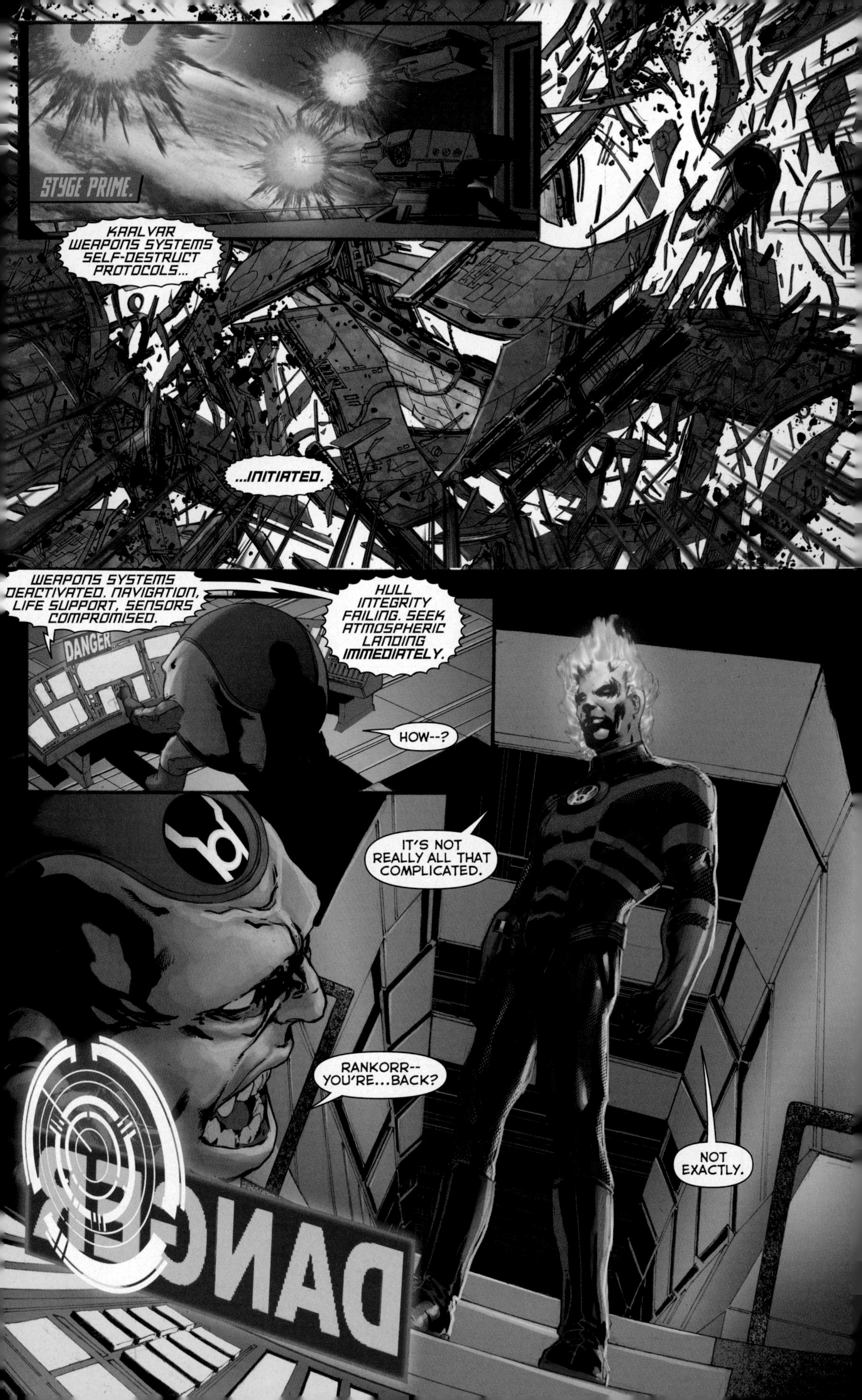
STYGE PRIME.
KAALVAR WEAPONS SYSTEMS SELF-DESTRUCT PROTOCOLS...
...INITIATED.
WEAPONS SYSTEMS DEACTIVATED. NAVIGATION, LIFE SUPPORT, SENSORS COMPROMISED.
HULL INTEGRITY FAILING. SEEK ATMOSPHERIC LANDING IMMEDIATELY.
DANGER
HOW--?
IT'S NOT REALLY ALL THAT COMPLICATED.
RANKORR-- YOU'RE...BACK?
NOT EXACTLY.

OF ALL OF 'EM, I NEVER THOUGHT IT'D BE *YOU.* ALL THIS TIME, PRETENDING TO BE NUTS. YOU *TURNED* ON US.
NOT EXACTLY.
EH. WHO CARES? I'M RED.
YOU'RE DEAD!
SHKK
NOT EXACTLY.
NNNNNGH

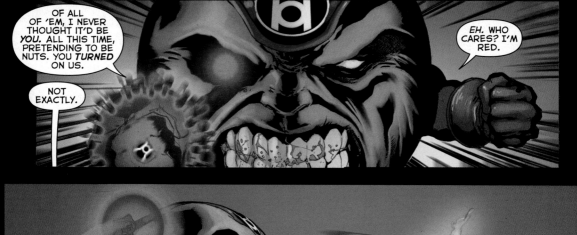

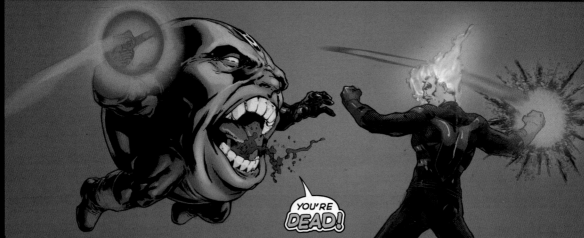

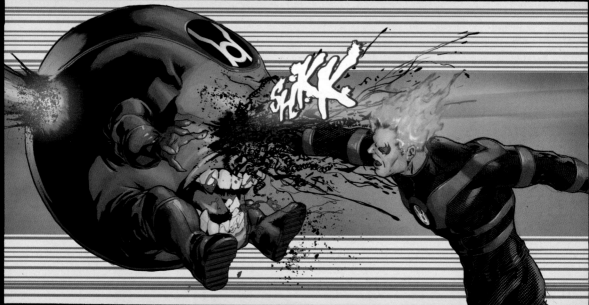

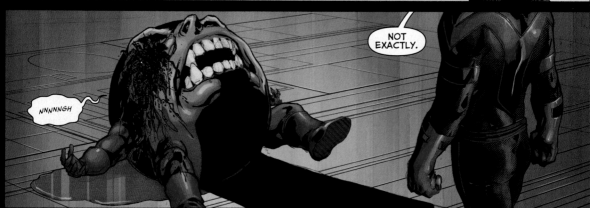

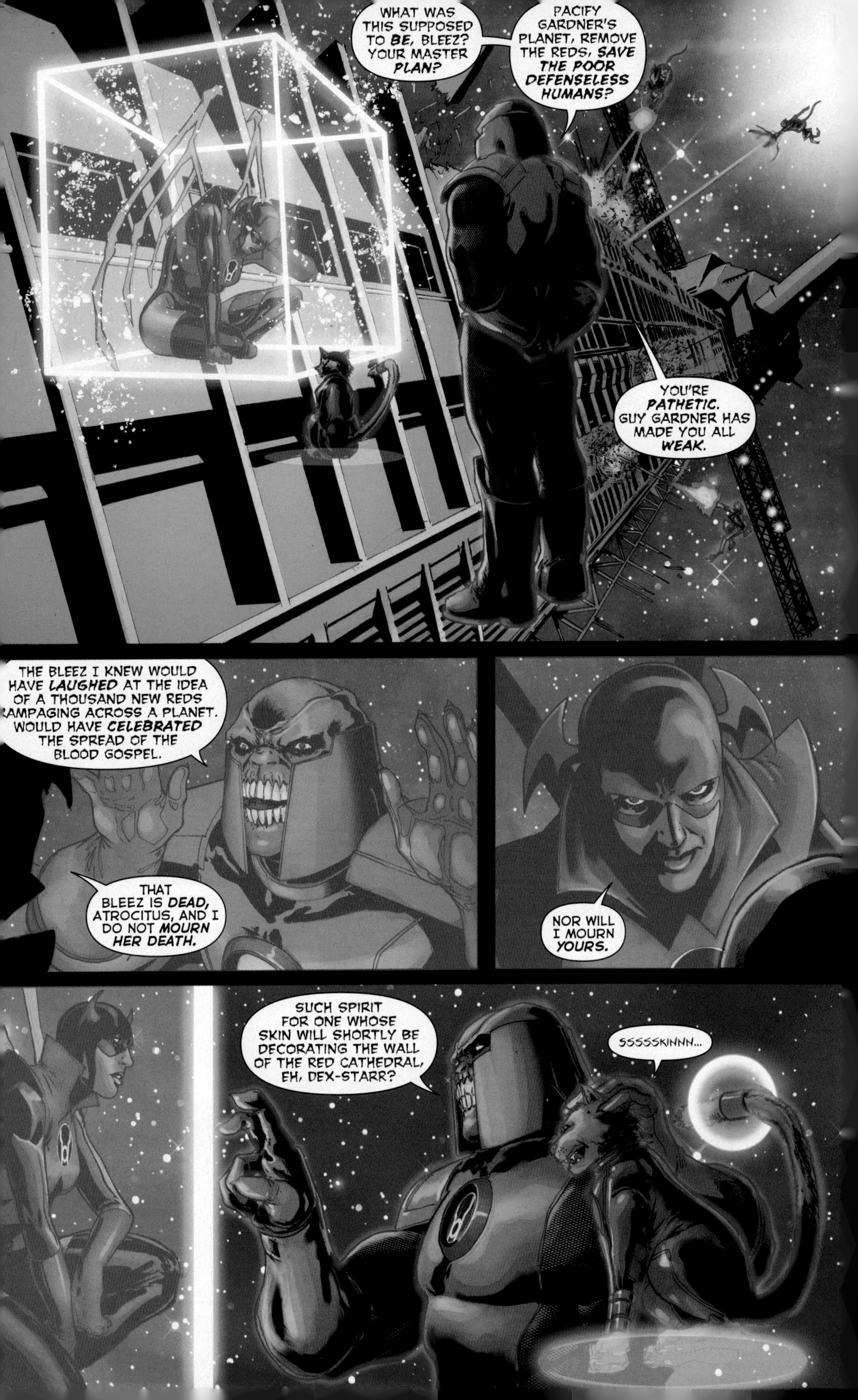

WHAT WAS THIS SUPPOSED TO *BE*, BLEEZ? YOUR MASTER *PLAN?*
PACIFY GARDNER'S PLANET, REMOVE THE REDS, ***SAVE THE POOR DEFENSELESS HUMANS?***
YOU'RE ***PATHETIC.*** GUY GARDNER HAS MADE YOU ALL ***WEAK.***
THE BLEEZ I KNEW WOULD HAVE ***LAUGHED*** AT THE IDEA OF A THOUSAND NEW REDS RAMPAGING ACROSS A PLANET. WOULD HAVE ***CELEBRATED*** THE SPREAD OF THE BLOOD GOSPEL.
THAT BLEEZ IS ***DEAD,*** ATROCITUS, AND I DO NOT ***MOURN HER DEATH.***
NOR WILL I MOURN ***YOURS.***
SUCH SPIRIT FOR ONE WHOSE SKIN WILL SHORTLY BE DECORATING THE WALL OF THE RED CATHEDRAL, EH, DEX-STARR?
SSSSSKINNN...

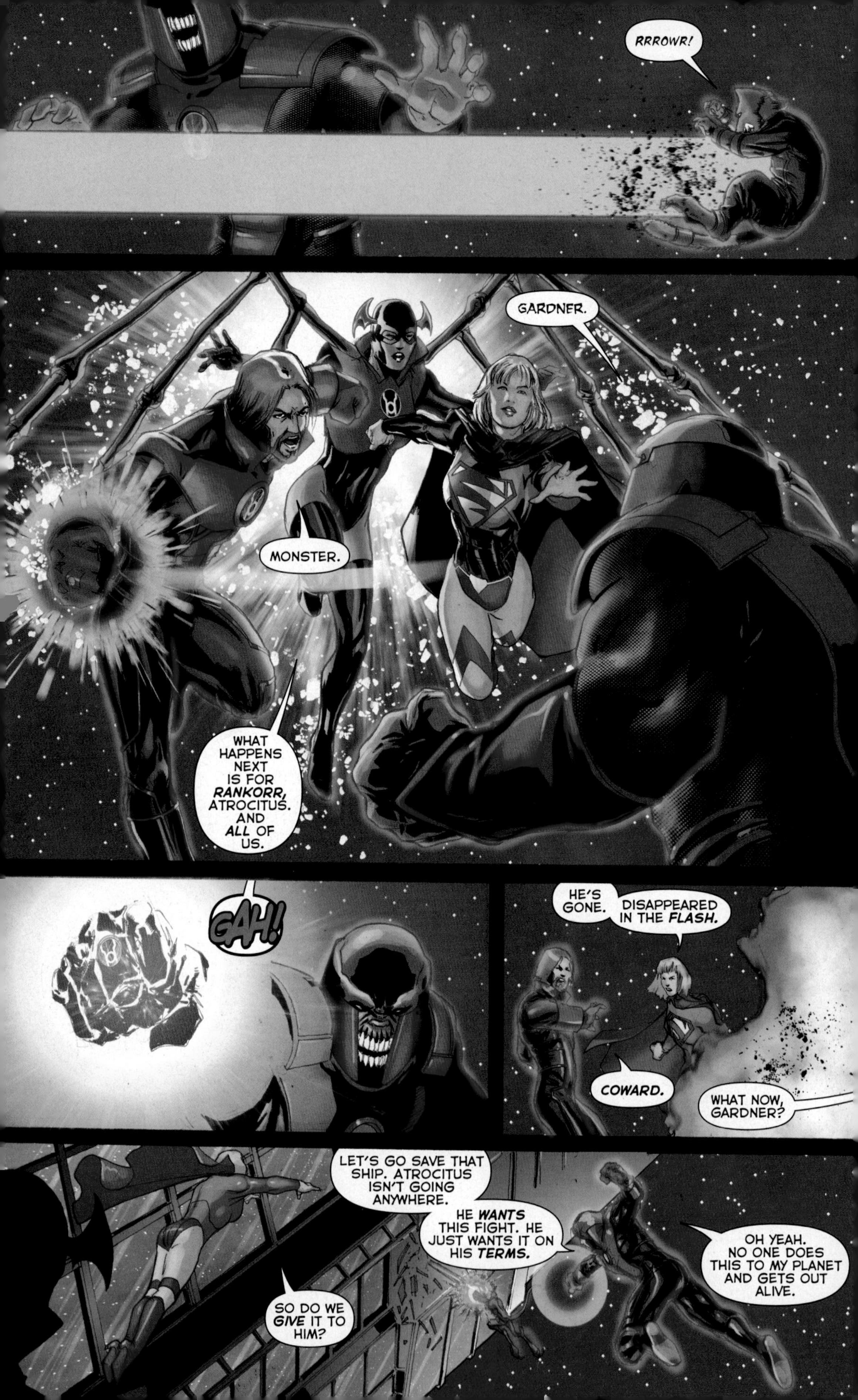
RRROWR!
GARDNER.
MONSTER.
WHAT HAPPENS NEXT IS FOR RANKORR, ATROCITUS. AND ALL OF US.
GAH!
HE'S GONE.
DISAPPEARED IN THE FLASH.
COWARD.
WHAT NOW, GARDNER?
LET'S GO SAVE THAT SHIP. ATROCITUS ISN'T GOING ANYWHERE.
HE WANTS THIS FIGHT. HE JUST WANTS IT ON HIS TERMS.
SO DO WE GIVE IT TO HIM?
OH YEAH. NO ONE DOES THIS TO MY PLANET AND GETS OUT ALIVE.

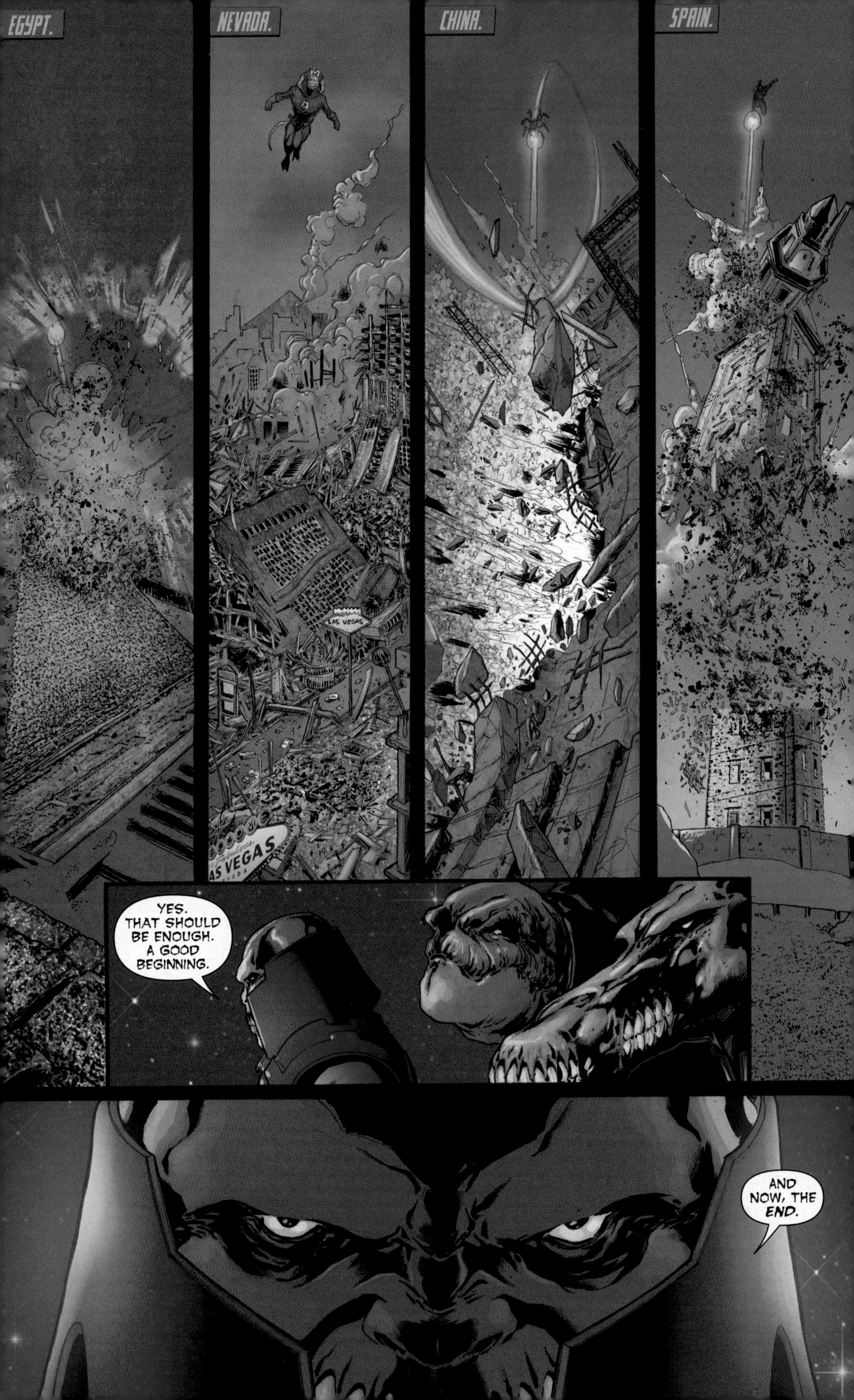
EGYPT.
NEVADA.
CHINA.
SPAIN.
LAS VEGAS
WELCOME TO Fabulous LAS VEGAS NEVADA
YES. THAT SHOULD BE ENOUGH. A GOOD BEGINNING.
AND NOW, THE END.

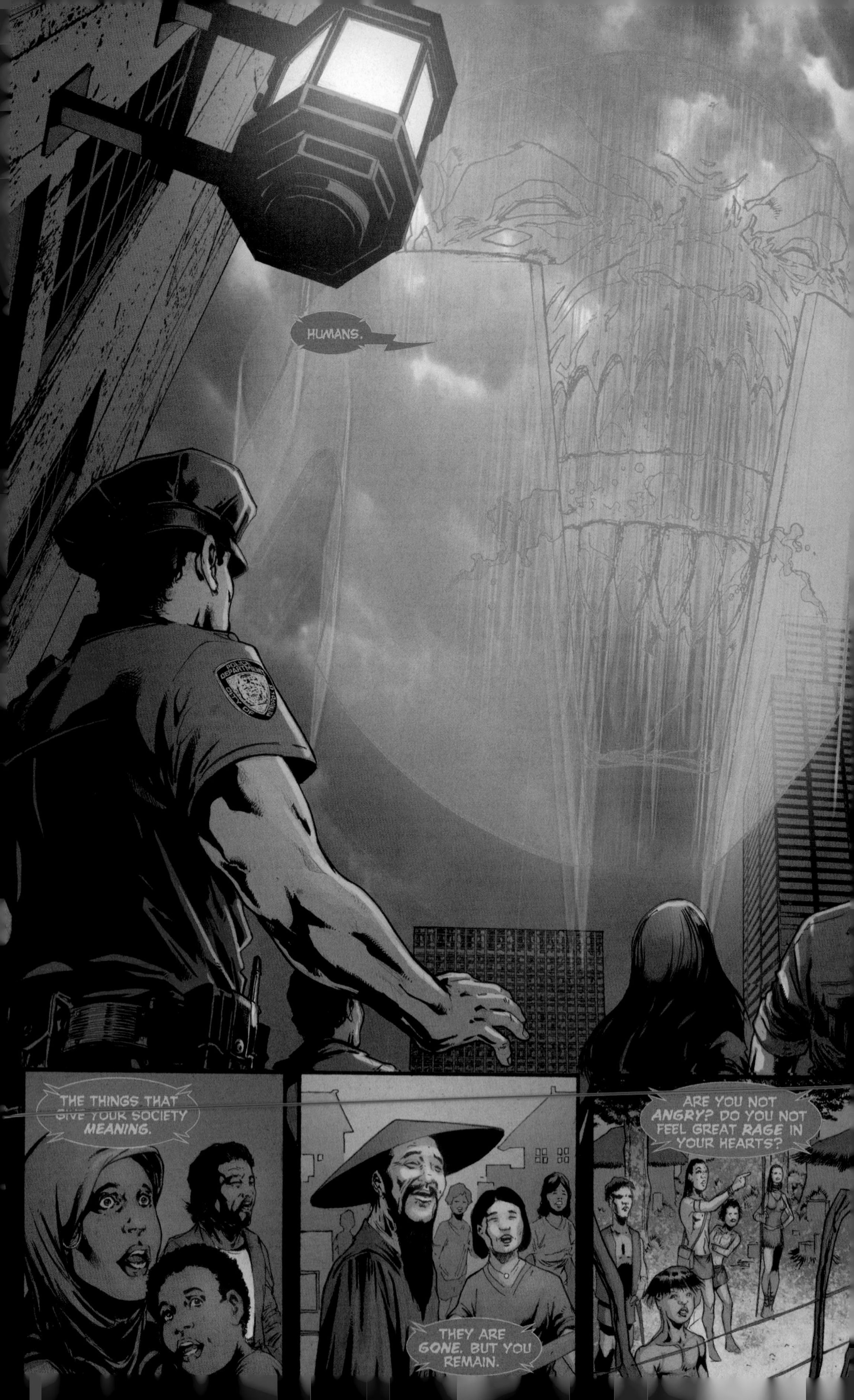
HUMANS.
THE THINGS THAT GIVE YOUR SOCIETY MEANING.
THEY ARE GONE, BUT YOU REMAIN.
ARE YOU NOT ANGRY? DO YOU NOT FEEL GREAT RAGE IN YOUR HEARTS?

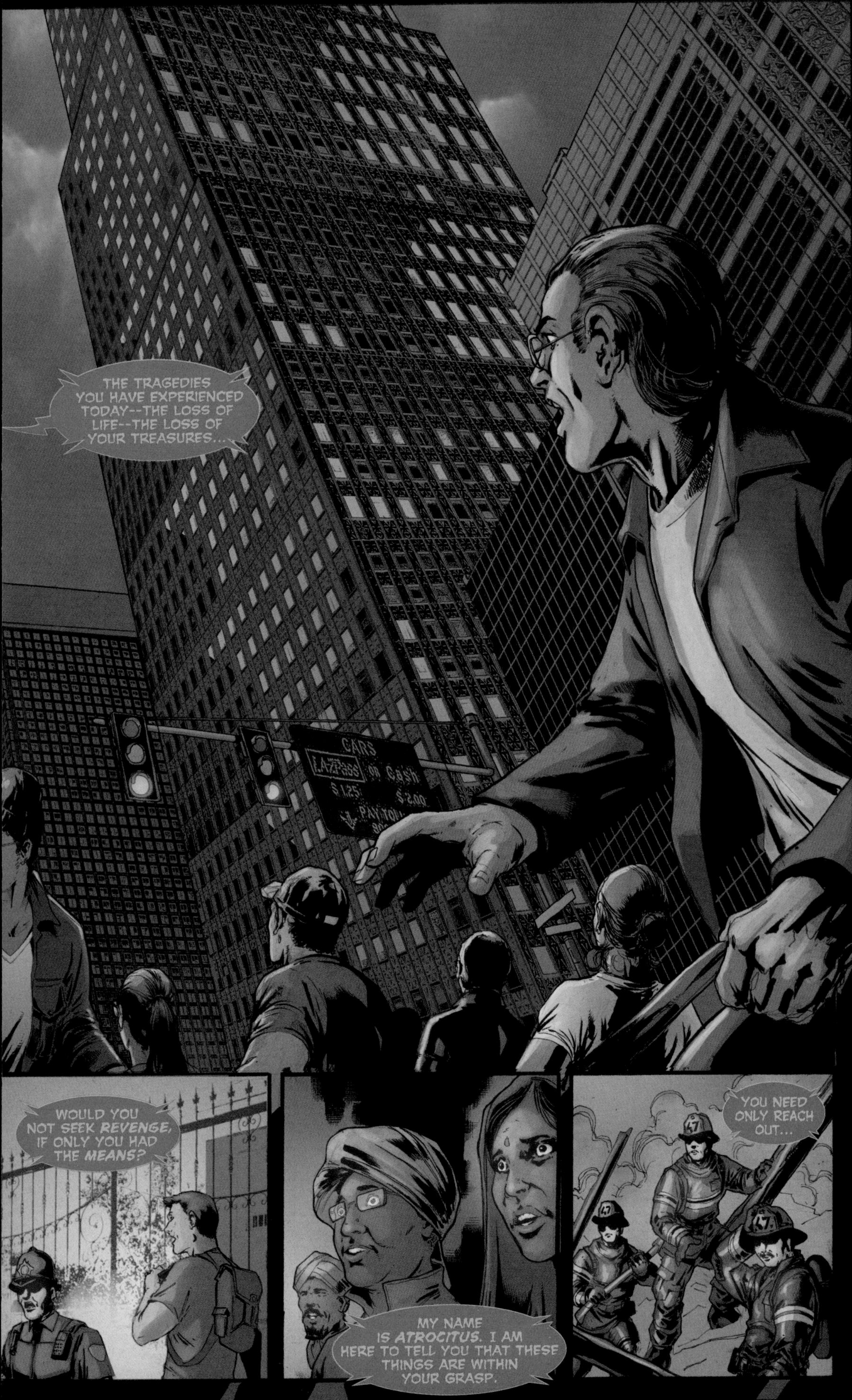
THE TRAGEDIES YOU HAVE EXPERIENCED TODAY--THE LOSS OF LIFE--THE LOSS OF YOUR TREASURES...
CARS
WOULD YOU NOT SEEK *REVENGE,* IF ONLY YOU HAD THE *MEANS?*
MY NAME IS *ATROCITUS.* I AM HERE TO TELL YOU THAT THESE THINGS ARE WITHIN YOUR GRASP.
YOU NEED ONLY REACH OUT...

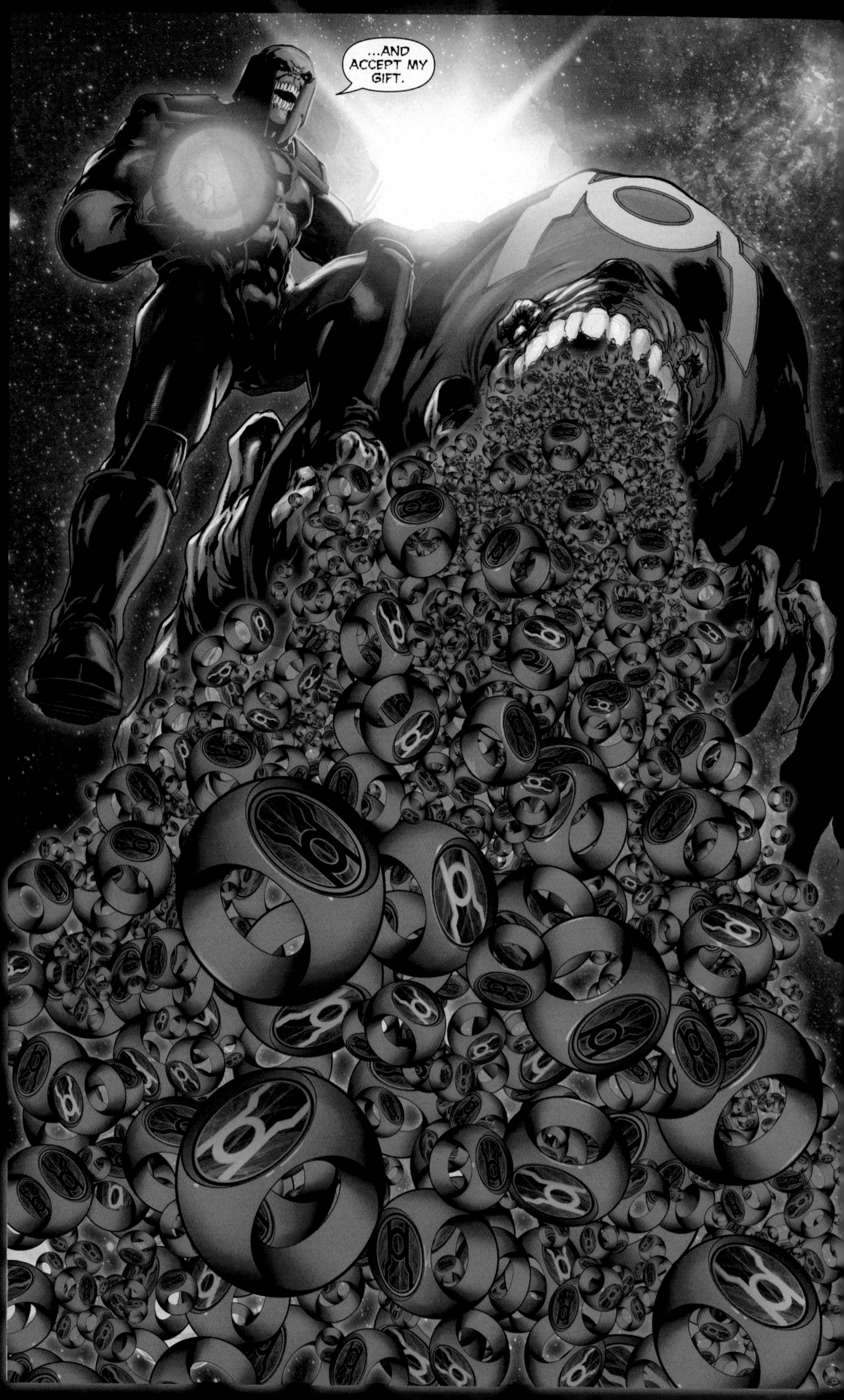
...AND ACCEPT MY GIFT.

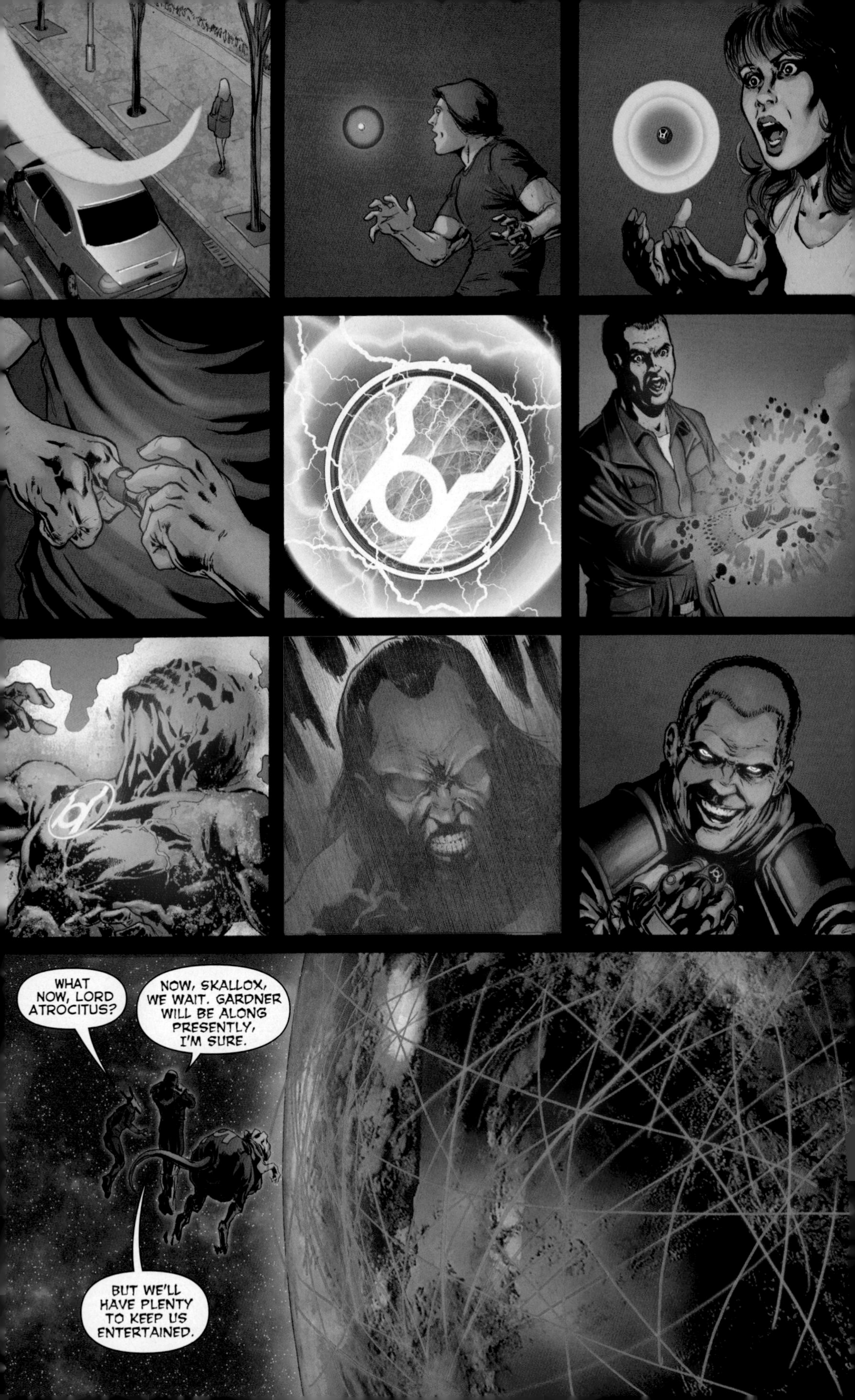
WHAT NOW, LORD ATROCITUS?
NOW, SKALLOX, WE WAIT. GARDNER WILL BE ALONG PRESENTLY, I'M SURE.
BUT WE'LL HAVE PLENTY TO KEEP US ENTERTAINED.

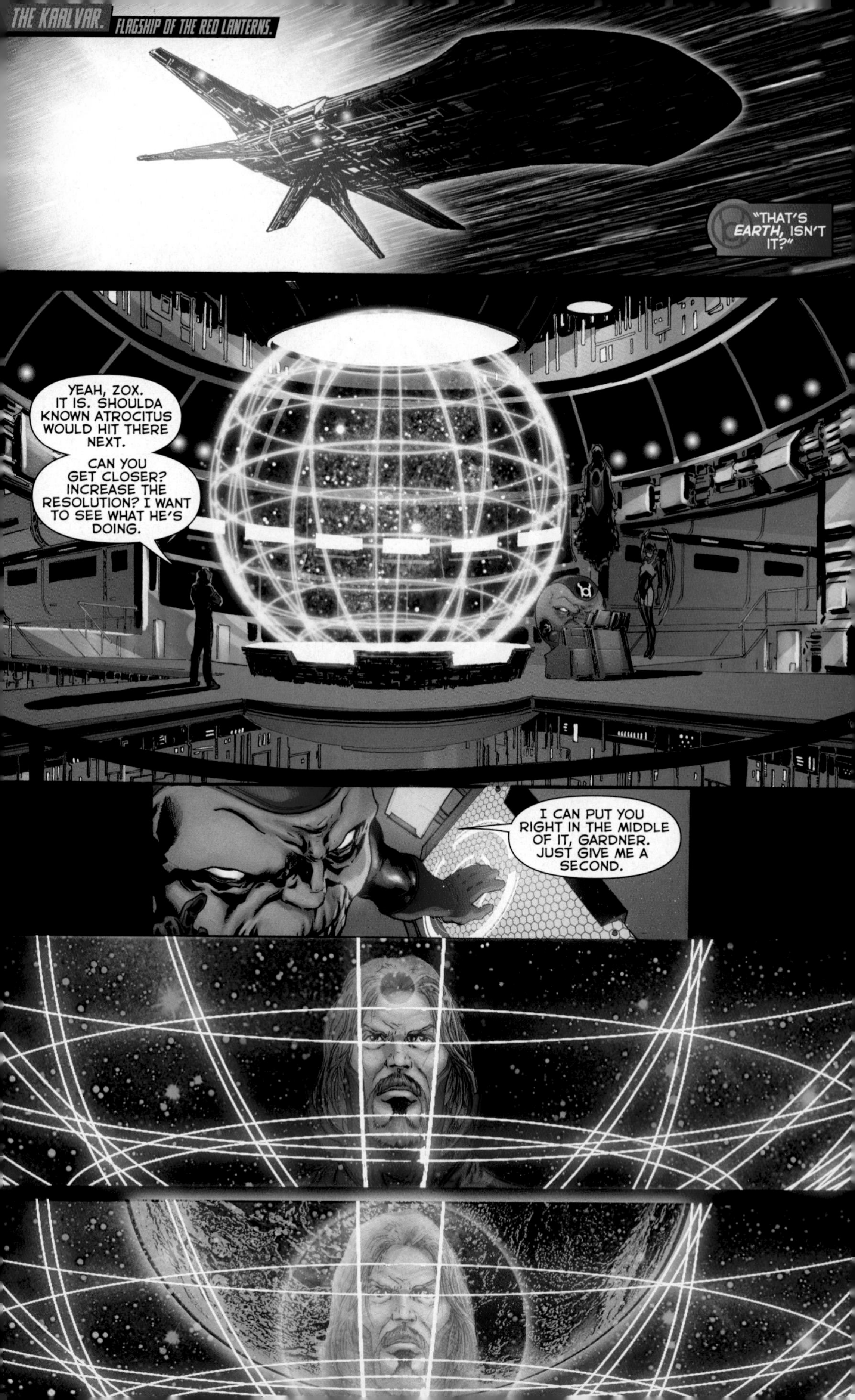
THE KAALVAR. FLAGSHIP OF THE RED LANTERNS.
"THAT'S EARTH, ISN'T IT?"
YEAH, ZOX. IT IS. SHOULDA KNOWN ATROCITUS WOULD HIT THERE NEXT.
CAN YOU GET CLOSER? INCREASE THE RESOLUTION? I WANT TO SEE WHAT HE'S DOING.
I CAN PUT YOU RIGHT IN THE MIDDLE OF IT, GARDNER. JUST GIVE ME A SECOND.

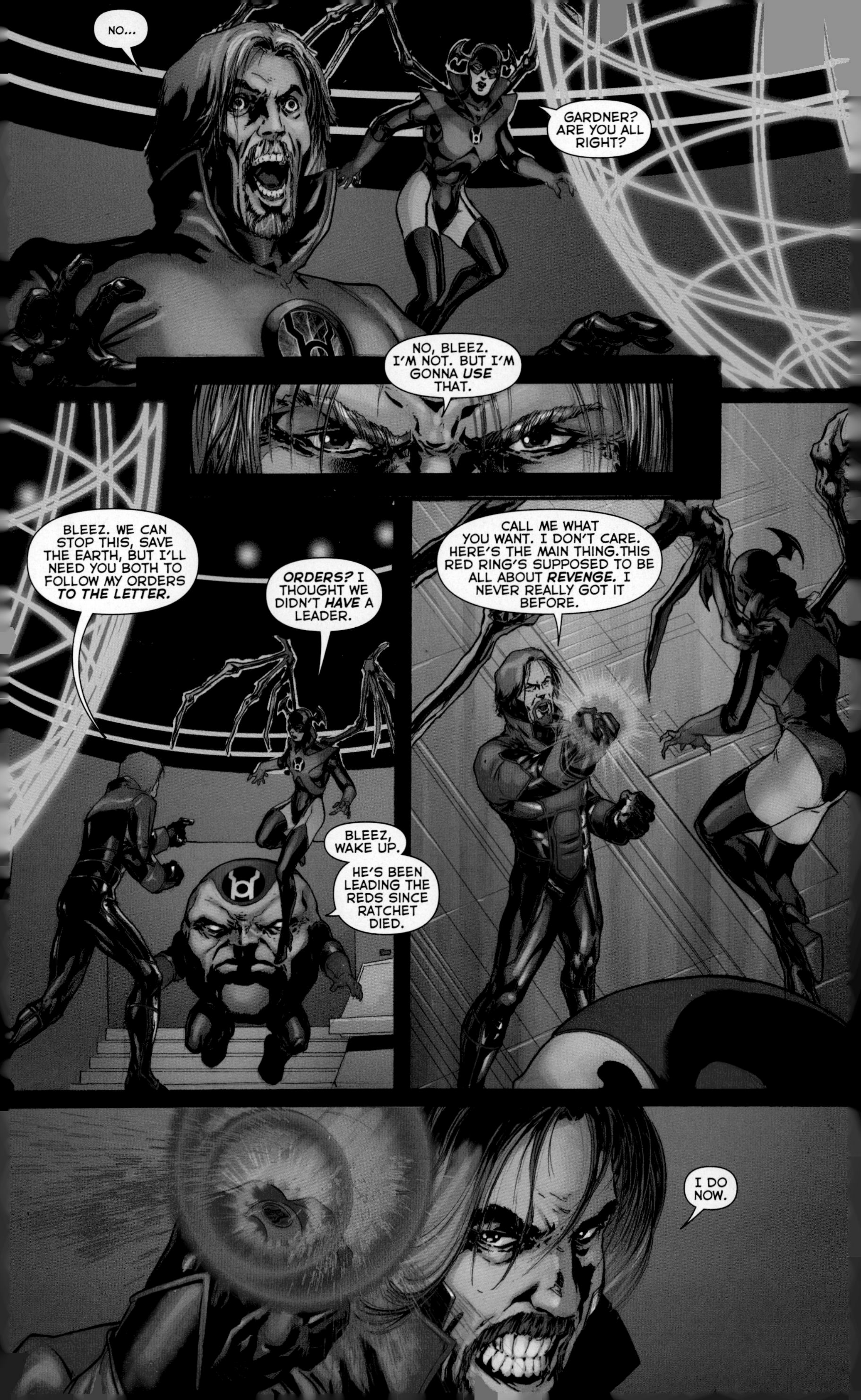
NO...
GARDNER? ARE YOU ALL RIGHT?
NO, BLEEZ. I'M NOT. BUT I'M GONNA USE THAT.
BLEEZ. WE CAN STOP THIS, SAVE THE EARTH, BUT I'LL NEED YOU BOTH TO FOLLOW MY ORDERS TO THE LETTER.
ORDERS? I THOUGHT WE DIDN'T HAVE A LEADER.
BLEEZ, WAKE UP.
HE'S BEEN LEADING THE REDS SINCE RATCHET DIED.
CALL ME WHAT YOU WANT. I DON'T CARE. HERE'S THE MAIN THING.THIS RED RING'S SUPPOSED TO BE ALL ABOUT REVENGE. I NEVER REALLY GOT IT BEFORE.
I DO NOW.

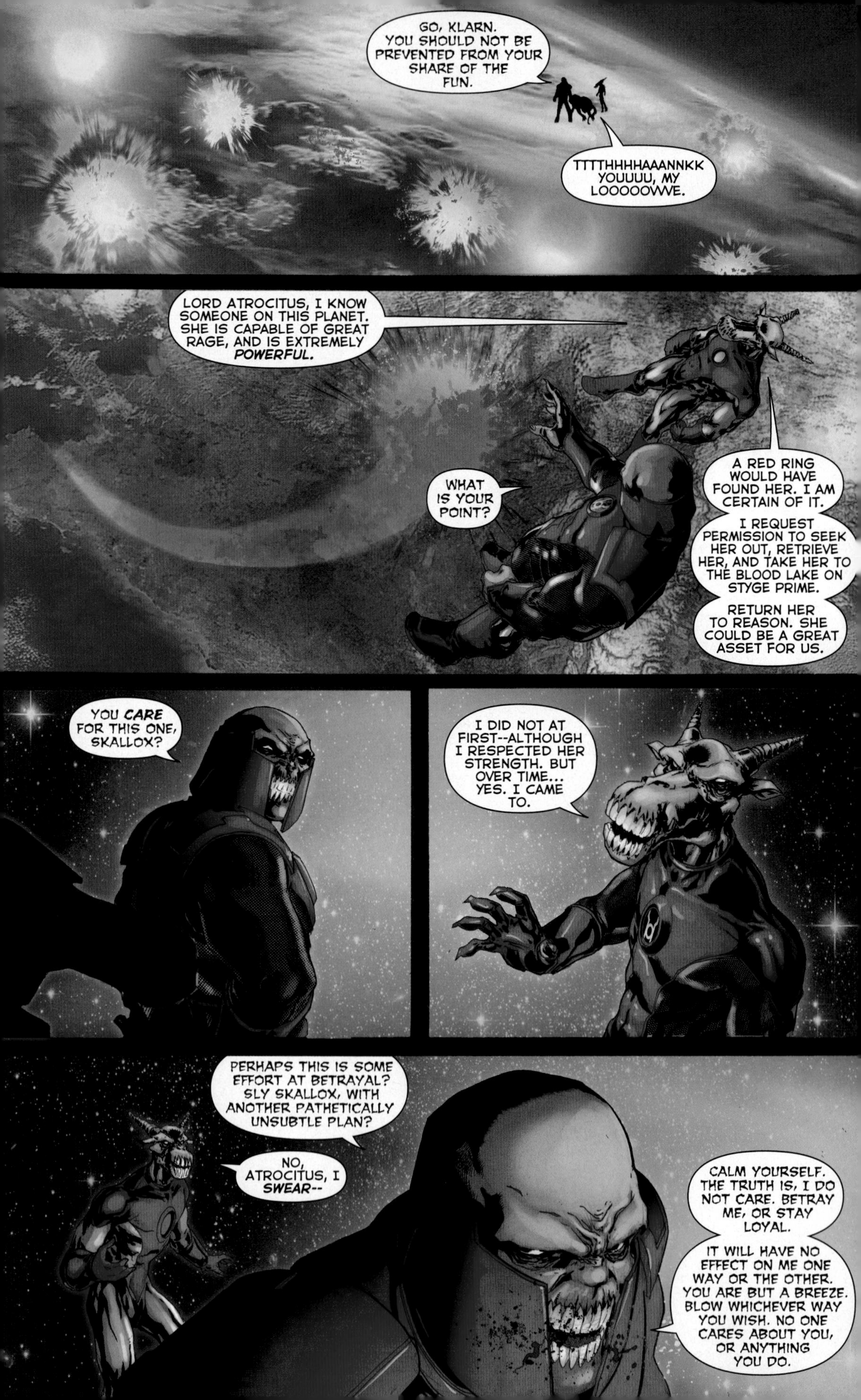
GO, KLARN. YOU SHOULD NOT BE PREVENTED FROM YOUR SHARE OF THE FUN.
TTTTHHHHAAANNKK YOUUUU, MY LOOOOOWVE.
LORD ATROCITUS, I KNOW SOMEONE ON THIS PLANET. SHE IS CAPABLE OF GREAT RAGE, AND IS EXTREMELY POWERFUL.
WHAT IS YOUR POINT?
A RED RING WOULD HAVE FOUND HER. I AM CERTAIN OF IT.
I REQUEST PERMISSION TO SEEK HER OUT, RETRIEVE HER, AND TAKE HER TO THE BLOOD LAKE ON STYGE PRIME.
RETURN HER TO REASON. SHE COULD BE A GREAT ASSET FOR US.
YOU CARE FOR THIS ONE, SKALLOX?
I DID NOT AT FIRST--ALTHOUGH I RESPECTED HER STRENGTH. BUT OVER TIME... YES. I CAME TO.
PERHAPS THIS IS SOME EFFORT AT BETRAYAL? SLY SKALLOX, WITH ANOTHER PATHETICALLY UNSUBTLE PLAN?
NO, ATROCITUS, I SWEAR--
CALM YOURSELF. THE TRUTH IS, I DO NOT CARE. BETRAY ME, OR STAY LOYAL.
IT WILL HAVE NO EFFECT ON ME ONE WAY OR THE OTHER. YOU ARE BUT A BREEZE. BLOW WHICHEVER WAY YOU WISH. NO ONE CARES ABOUT YOU, OR ANYTHING YOU DO.

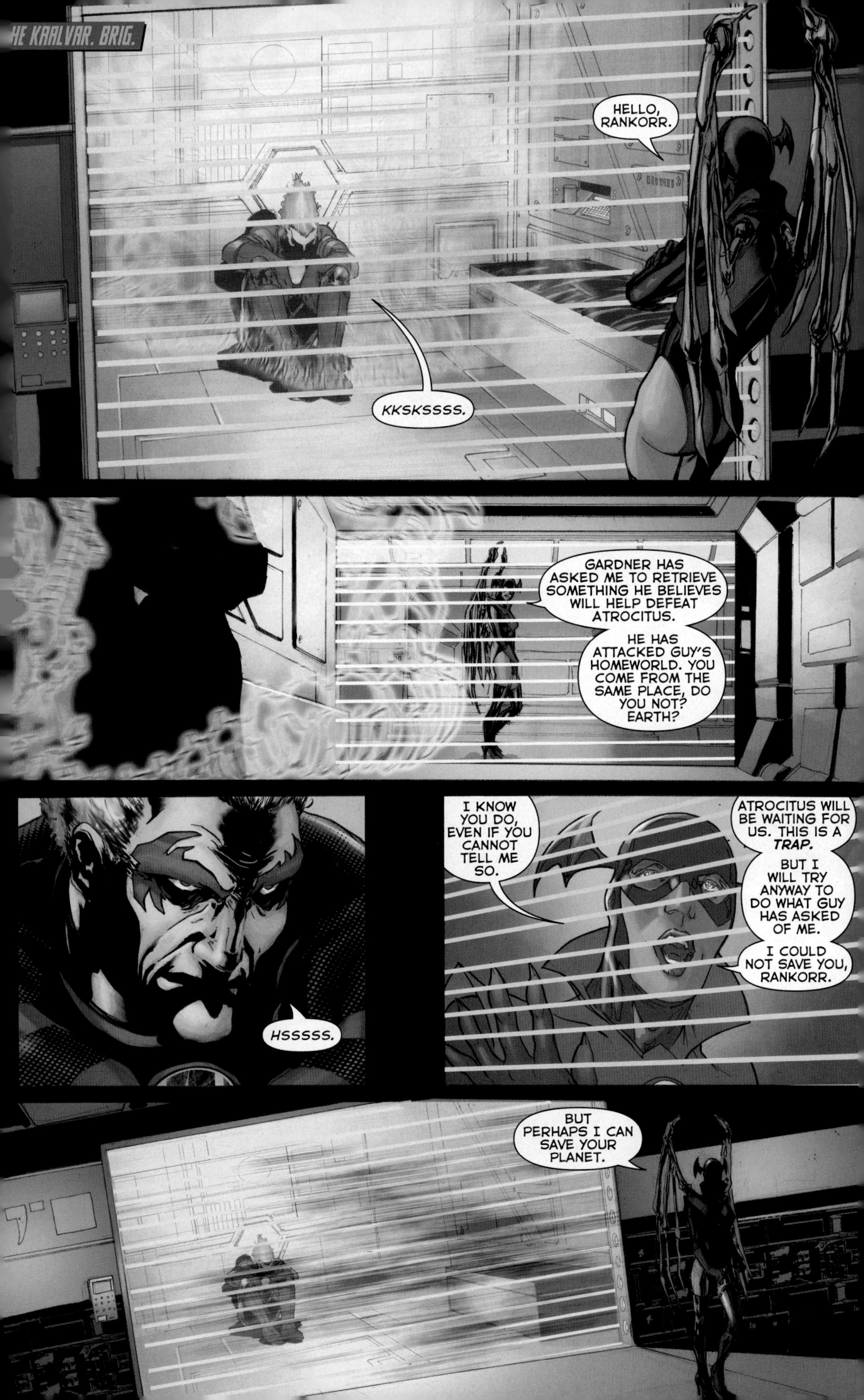
HE KAALVAR. BRIG.
HELLO, RANKORR.
KKSKSSSS.
GARDNER HAS ASKED ME TO RETRIEVE SOMETHING HE BELIEVES WILL HELP DEFEAT ATROCITUS.
HE HAS ATTACKED GUY'S HOMEWORLD. YOU COME FROM THE SAME PLACE, DO YOU NOT? EARTH?
HSSSSS.
I KNOW YOU DO, EVEN IF YOU CANNOT TELL ME SO.
ATROCITUS WILL BE WAITING FOR US. THIS IS A *TRAP.*
BUT I WILL TRY ANYWAY TO DO WHAT GUY HAS ASKED OF ME.
I COULD NOT SAVE YOU, RANKORR.
BUT PERHAPS I CAN SAVE YOUR PLANET.

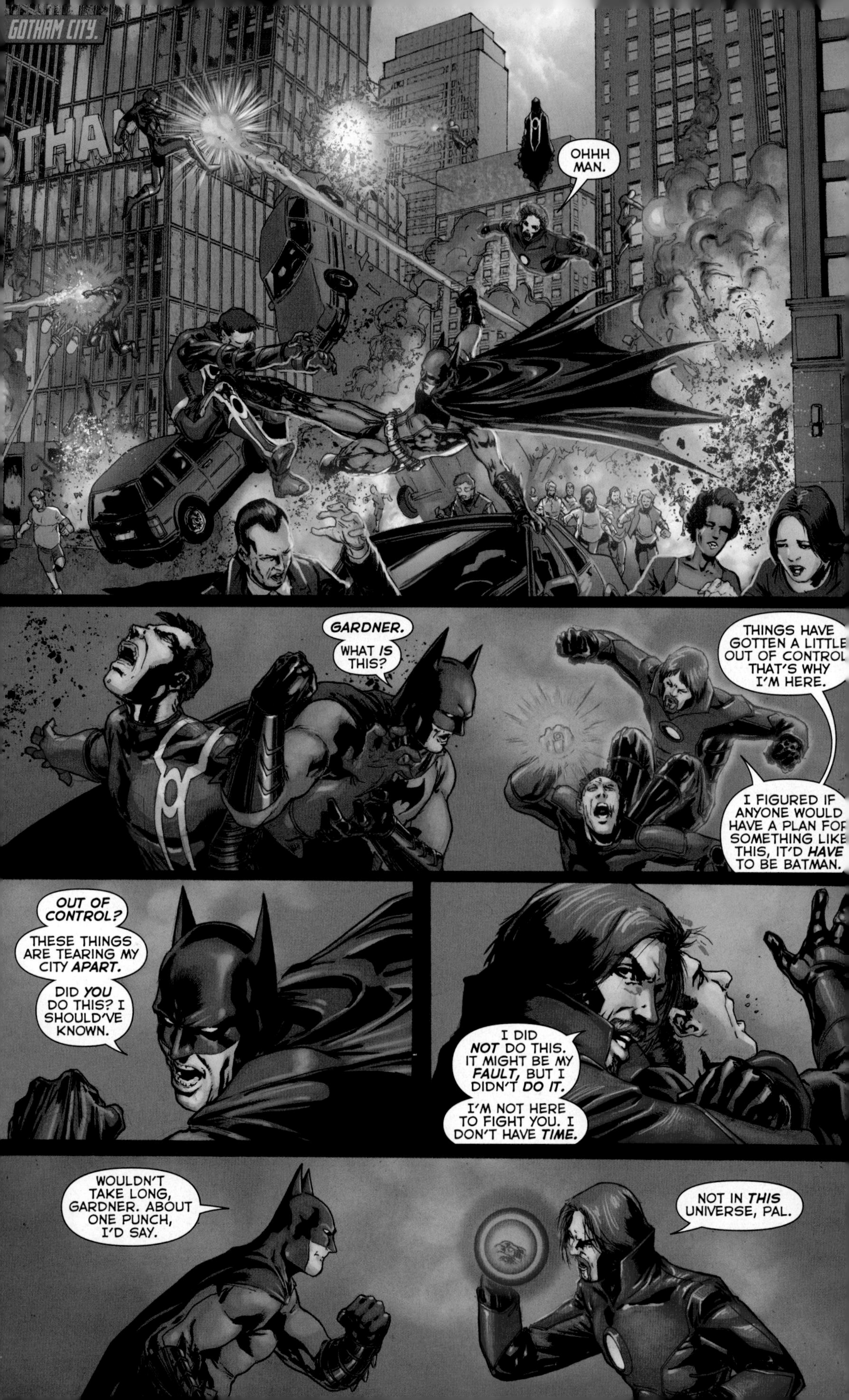
GOTHAM CITY.
OHHH MAN.
GARDNER. WHAT IS THIS?
THINGS HAVE GOTTEN A LITTLE OUT OF CONTROL THAT'S WHY I'M HERE.
I FIGURED IF ANYONE WOULD HAVE A PLAN FOR SOMETHING LIKE THIS, IT'D HAVE TO BE BATMAN.
OUT OF CONTROL?
THESE THINGS ARE TEARING MY CITY APART.
DID YOU DO THIS? I SHOULD'VE KNOWN.
I DID NOT DO THIS. IT MIGHT BE MY FAULT, BUT I DIDN'T DO IT.
I'M NOT HERE TO FIGHT YOU. I DON'T HAVE TIME.
WOULDN'T TAKE LONG, GARDNER. ABOUT ONE PUNCH, I'D SAY.
NOT IN THIS UNIVERSE, PAL.

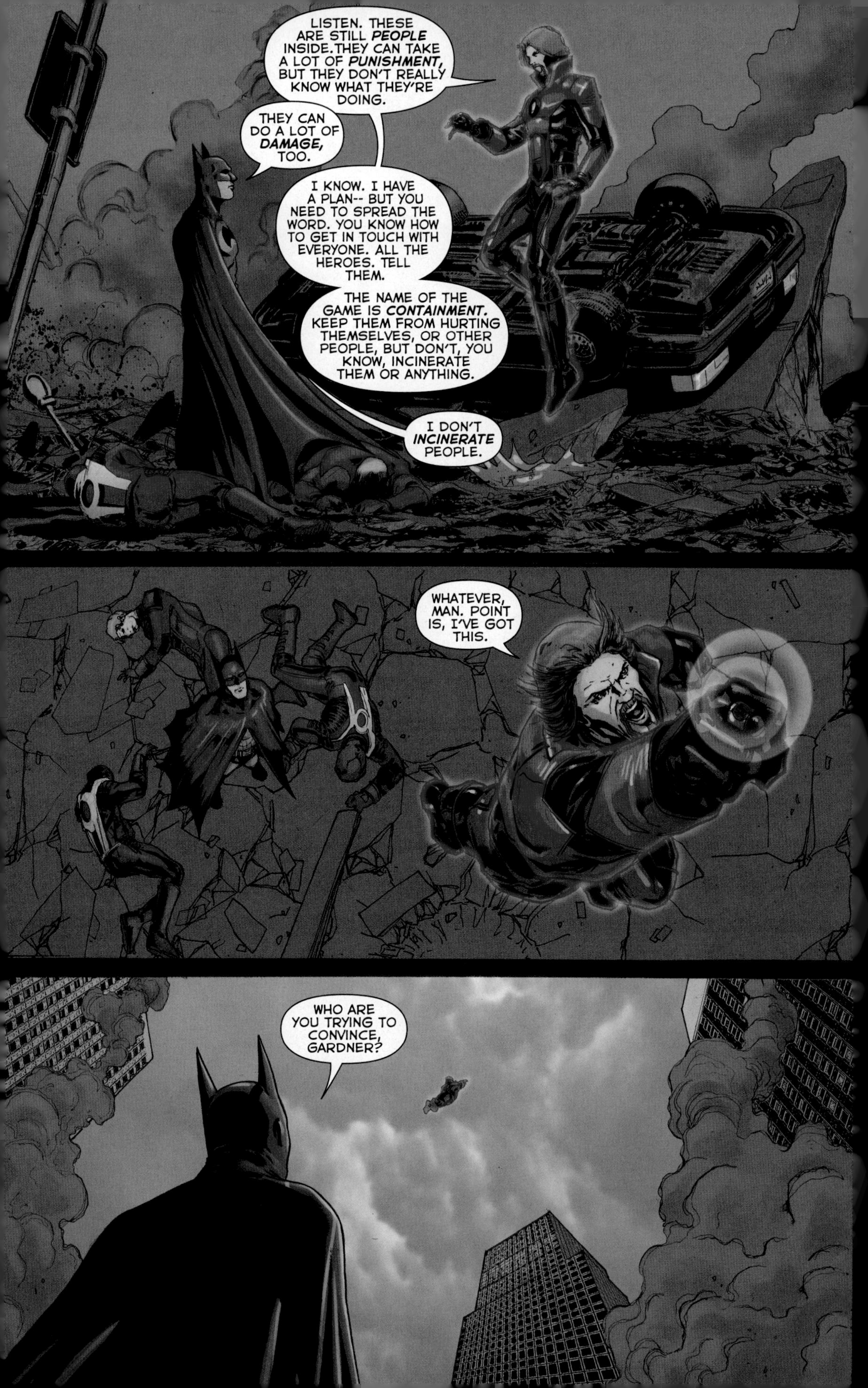
LISTEN. THESE ARE STILL PEOPLE INSIDE. THEY CAN TAKE A LOT OF PUNISHMENT, BUT THEY DON'T REALLY KNOW WHAT THEY'RE DOING.
THEY CAN DO A LOT OF DAMAGE, TOO.
I KNOW. I HAVE A PLAN-- BUT YOU NEED TO SPREAD THE WORD. YOU KNOW HOW TO GET IN TOUCH WITH EVERYONE. ALL THE HEROES. TELL THEM.
THE NAME OF THE GAME IS CONTAINMENT. KEEP THEM FROM HURTING THEMSELVES, OR OTHER PEOPLE, BUT DON'T, YOU KNOW, INCINERATE THEM OR ANYTHING.
I DON'T INCINERATE PEOPLE.
WHATEVER, MAN. POINT IS, I'VE GOT THIS.
WHO ARE YOU TRYING TO CONVINCE, GARDNER?

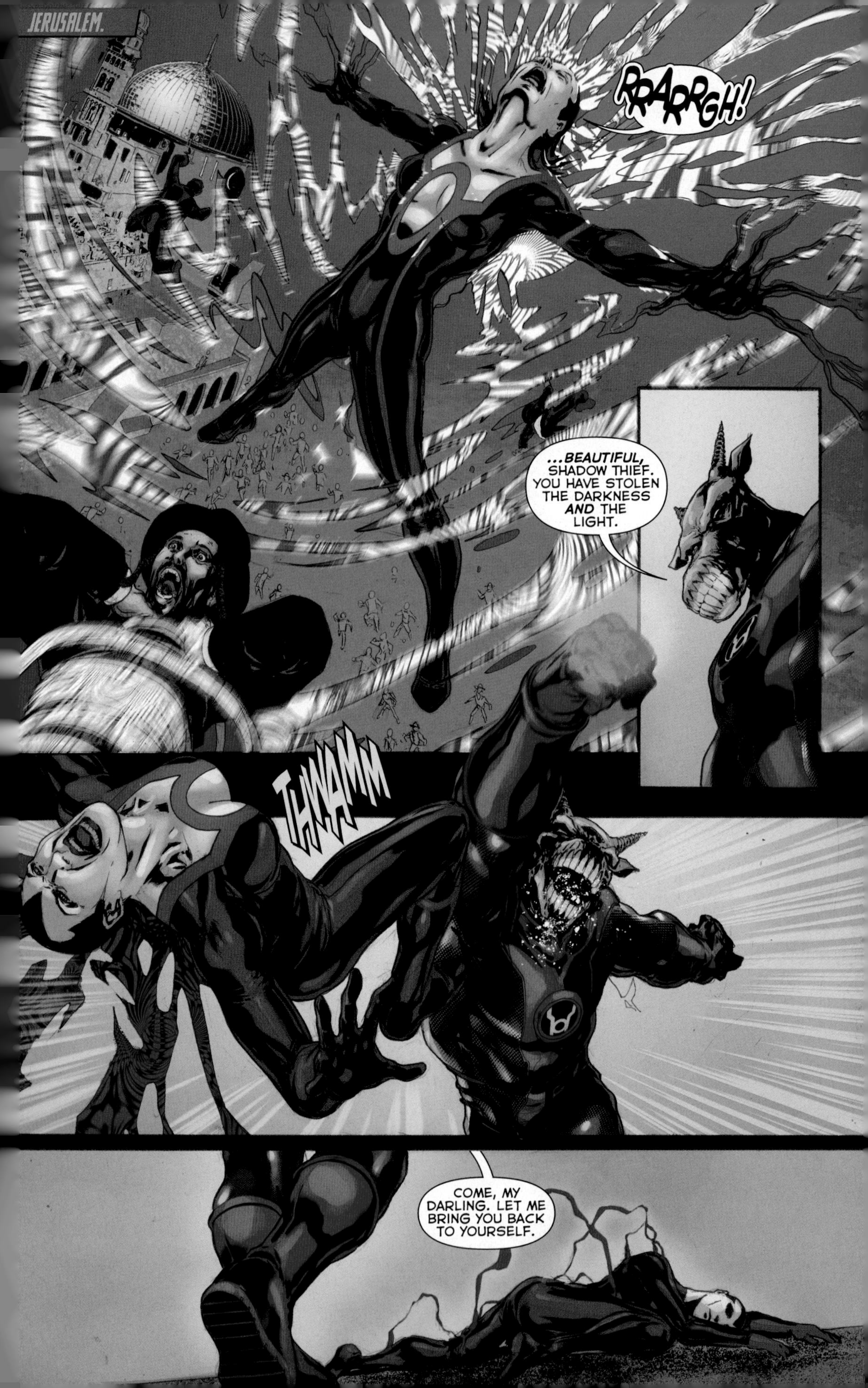
JERUSALEM.
RRARRGH!
...BEAUTIFUL, SHADOW THIEF. YOU HAVE STOLEN THE DARKNESS AND THE LIGHT.
THWAMM
COME, MY DARLING. LET ME BRING YOU BACK TO YOURSELF.

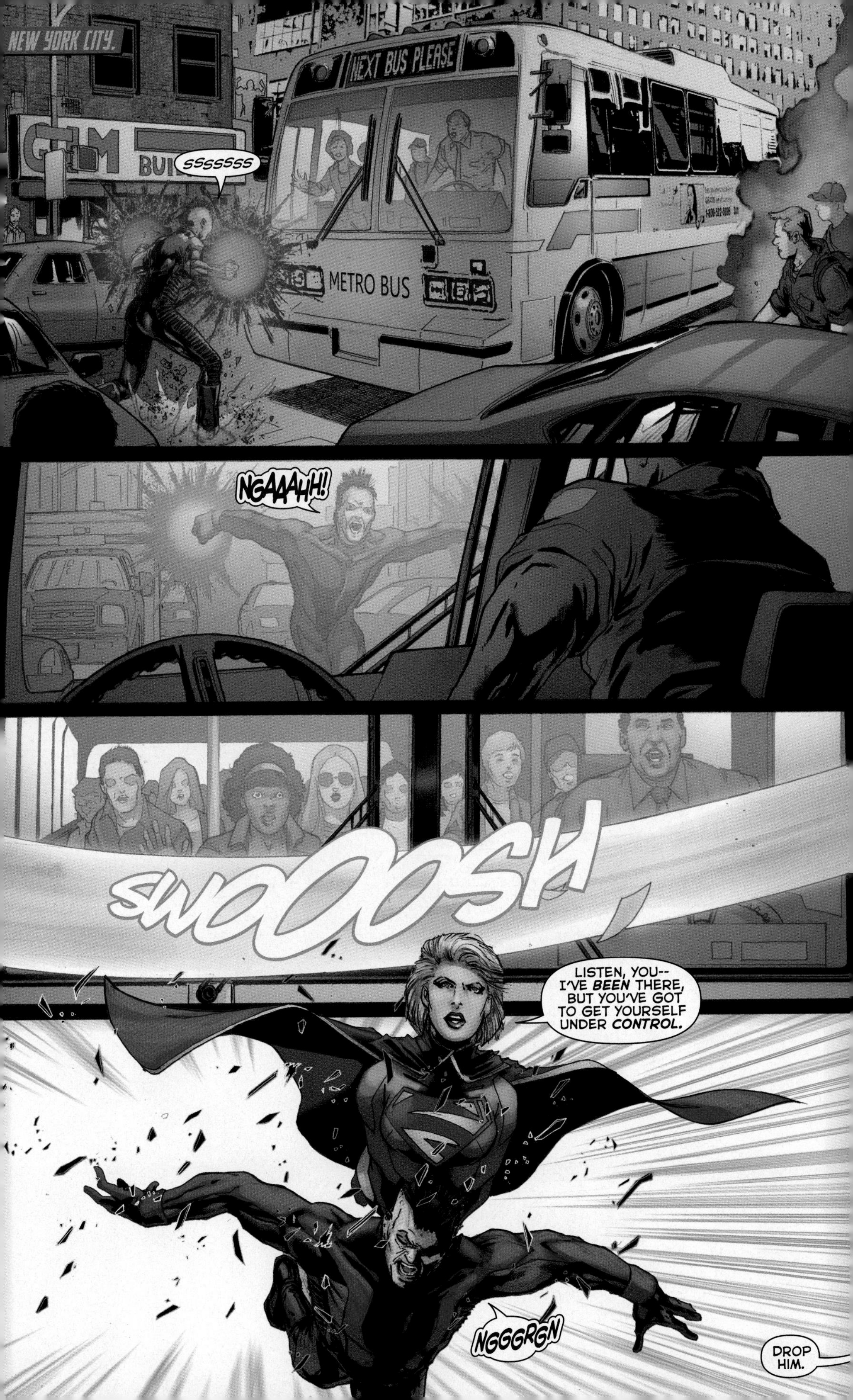
NEW YORK CITY.
NEXT BUS PLEASE
METRO BUS
SSSSSSS
NGAAAHH!
SWOOOSH
LISTEN, YOU-- I'VE BEEN THERE, BUT YOU'VE GOT TO GET YOURSELF UNDER CONTROL.
NGGGRGN
DROP HIM.

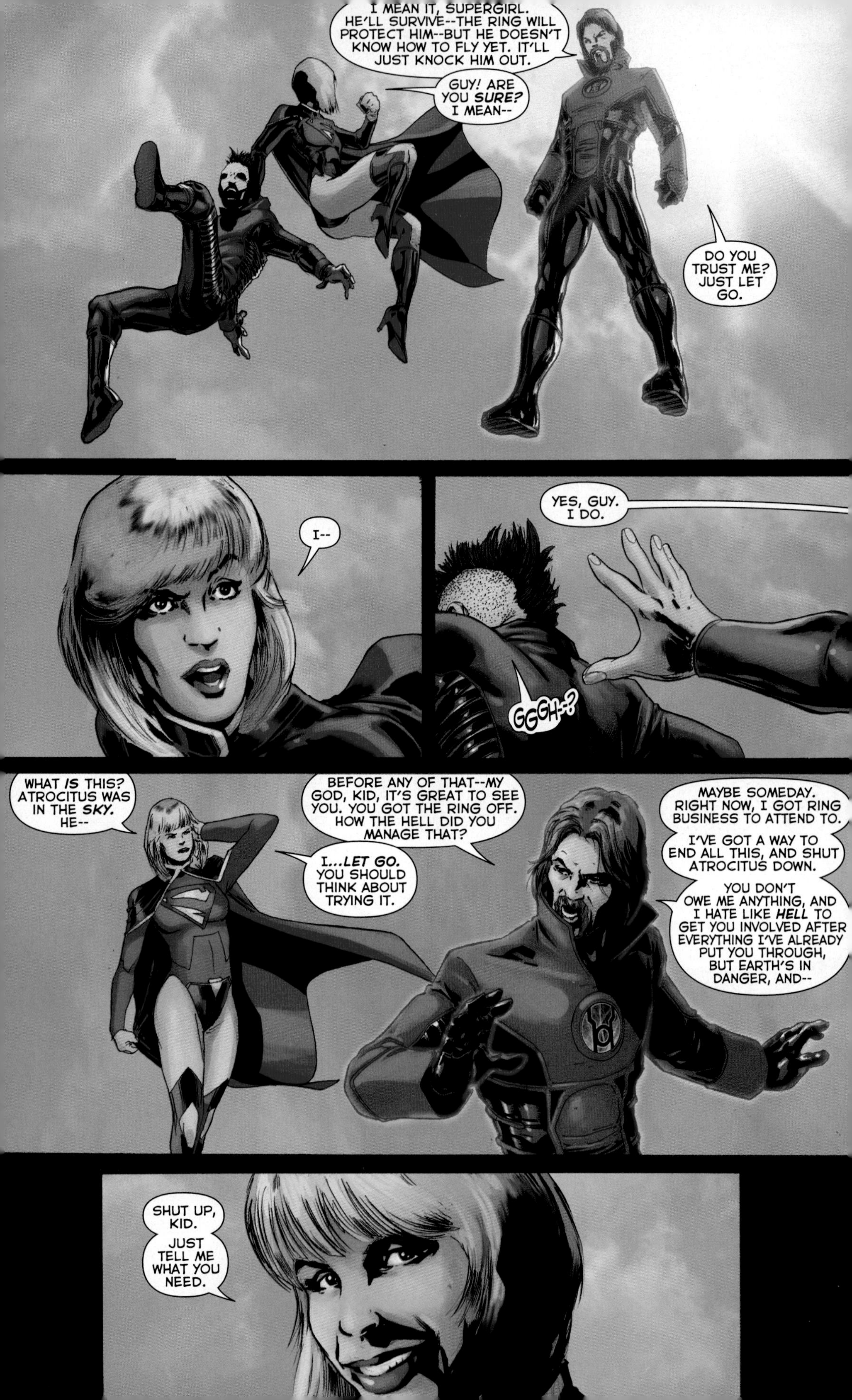
I MEAN IT, SUPERGIRL. HE'LL SURVIVE--THE RING WILL PROTECT HIM--BUT HE DOESN'T KNOW HOW TO FLY YET. IT'LL JUST KNOCK HIM OUT.
GUY! ARE YOU *SURE?* I MEAN--
DO YOU TRUST ME? JUST LET GO.
I--
YES, GUY. I DO.
GGGH--?
WHAT *IS* THIS? ATROCITUS WAS IN THE *SKY.* HE--
BEFORE ANY OF THAT--MY GOD, KID, IT'S GREAT TO SEE YOU. YOU GOT THE RING OFF. HOW THE HELL DID YOU MANAGE THAT?
I...*LET GO.* YOU SHOULD THINK ABOUT TRYING IT.
MAYBE SOMEDAY. RIGHT NOW, I GOT RING BUSINESS TO ATTEND TO.
I'VE GOT A WAY TO END ALL THIS, AND SHUT ATROCITUS DOWN.
YOU DON'T OWE ME ANYTHING, AND I HATE LIKE *HELL* TO GET YOU INVOLVED AFTER EVERYTHING I'VE ALREADY PUT YOU THROUGH, BUT EARTH'S IN DANGER, AND--
SHUT UP, KID.
JUST TELL ME WHAT YOU NEED.

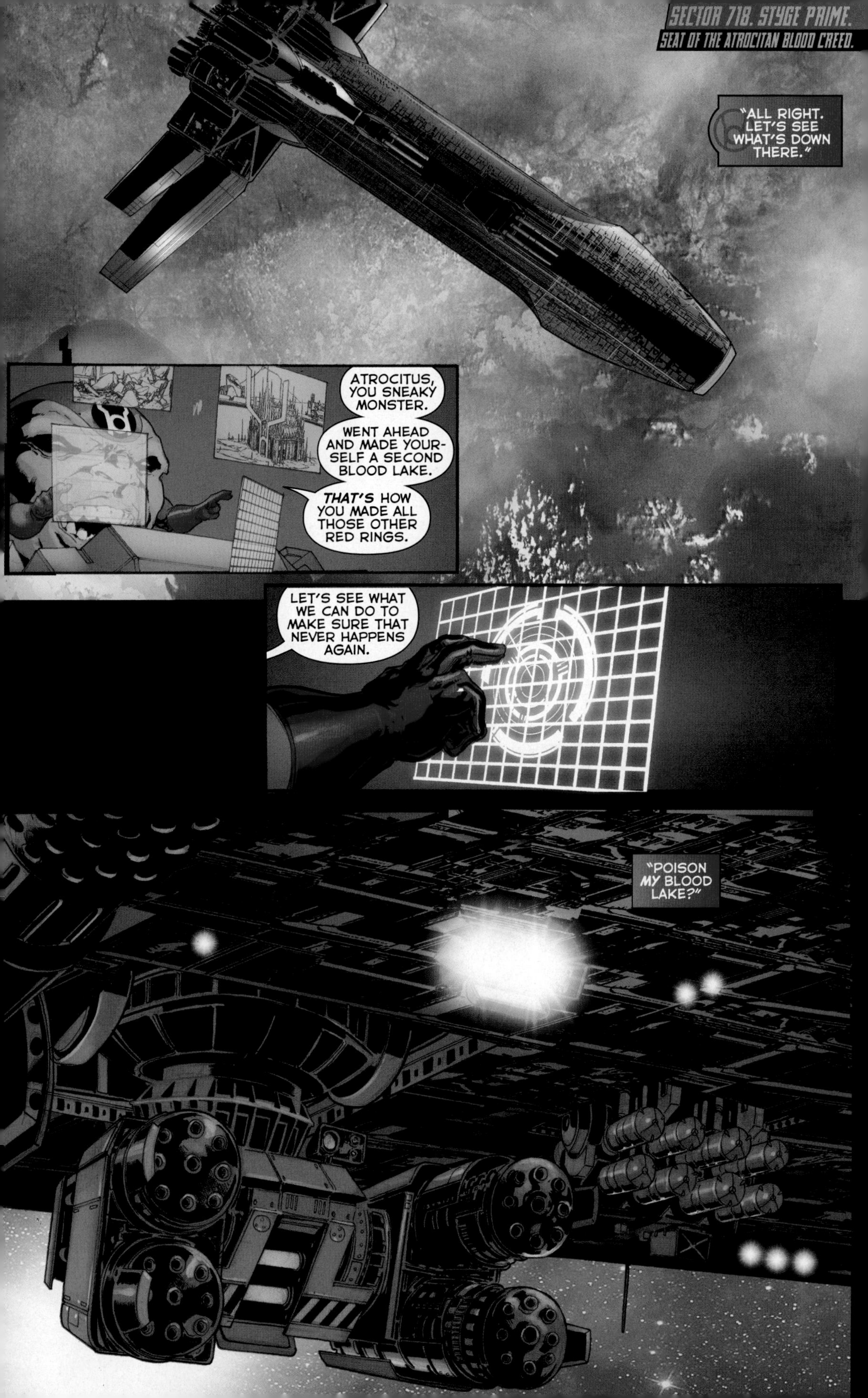
SECTOR 718. STYGE PRIME.
SEAT OF THE ATROCITAN BLOOD CREED.
"ALL RIGHT. LET'S SEE WHAT'S DOWN THERE."
ATROCITUS, YOU SNEAKY MONSTER.
WENT AHEAD AND MADE YOURSELF A SECOND BLOOD LAKE.
THAT'S HOW YOU MADE ALL THOSE OTHER RED RINGS.
LET'S SEE WHAT WE CAN DO TO MAKE SURE THAT NEVER HAPPENS AGAIN.
"POISON *MY* BLOOD LAKE?"

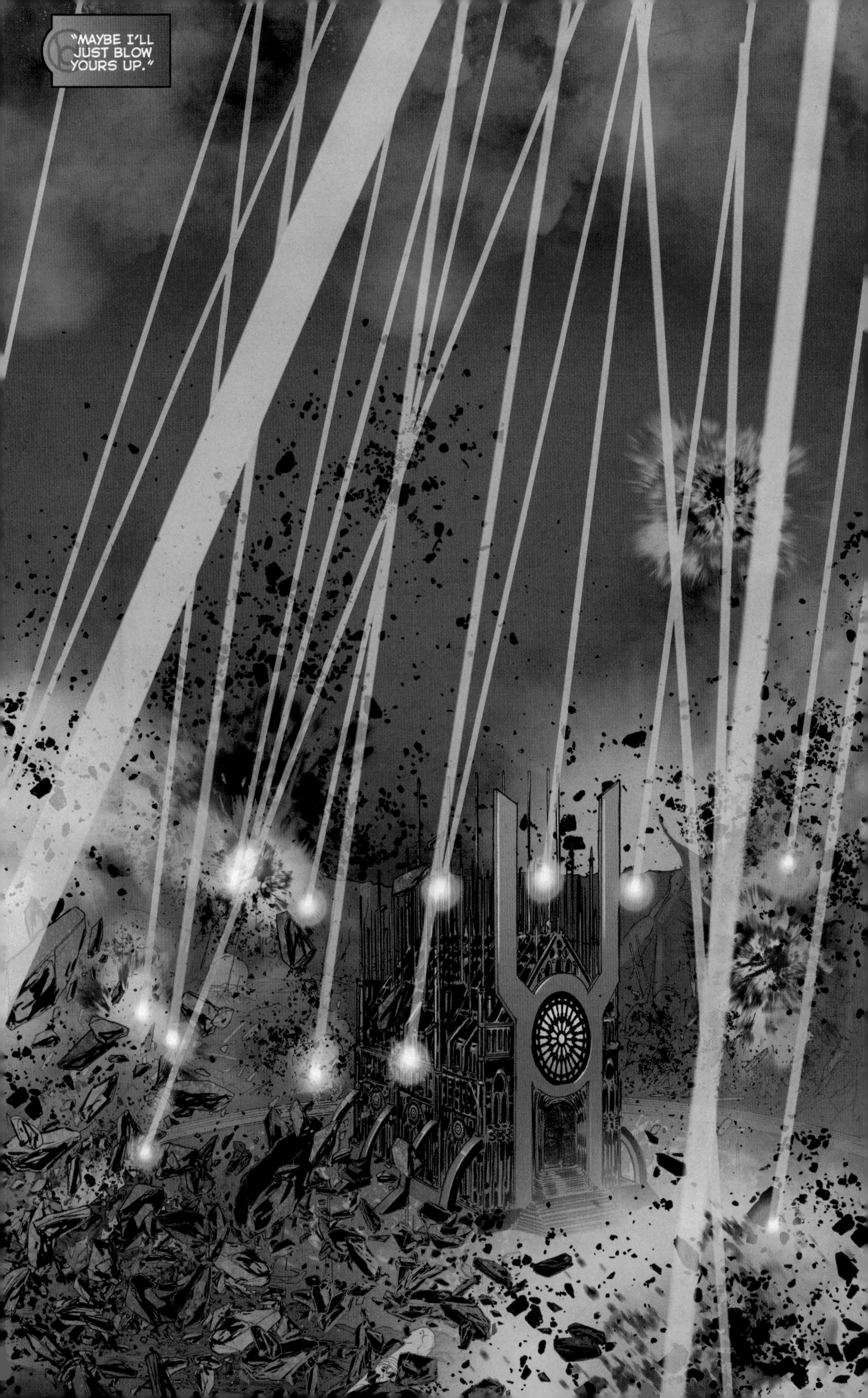
"MAYBE I'LL JUST BLOW YOURS UP."

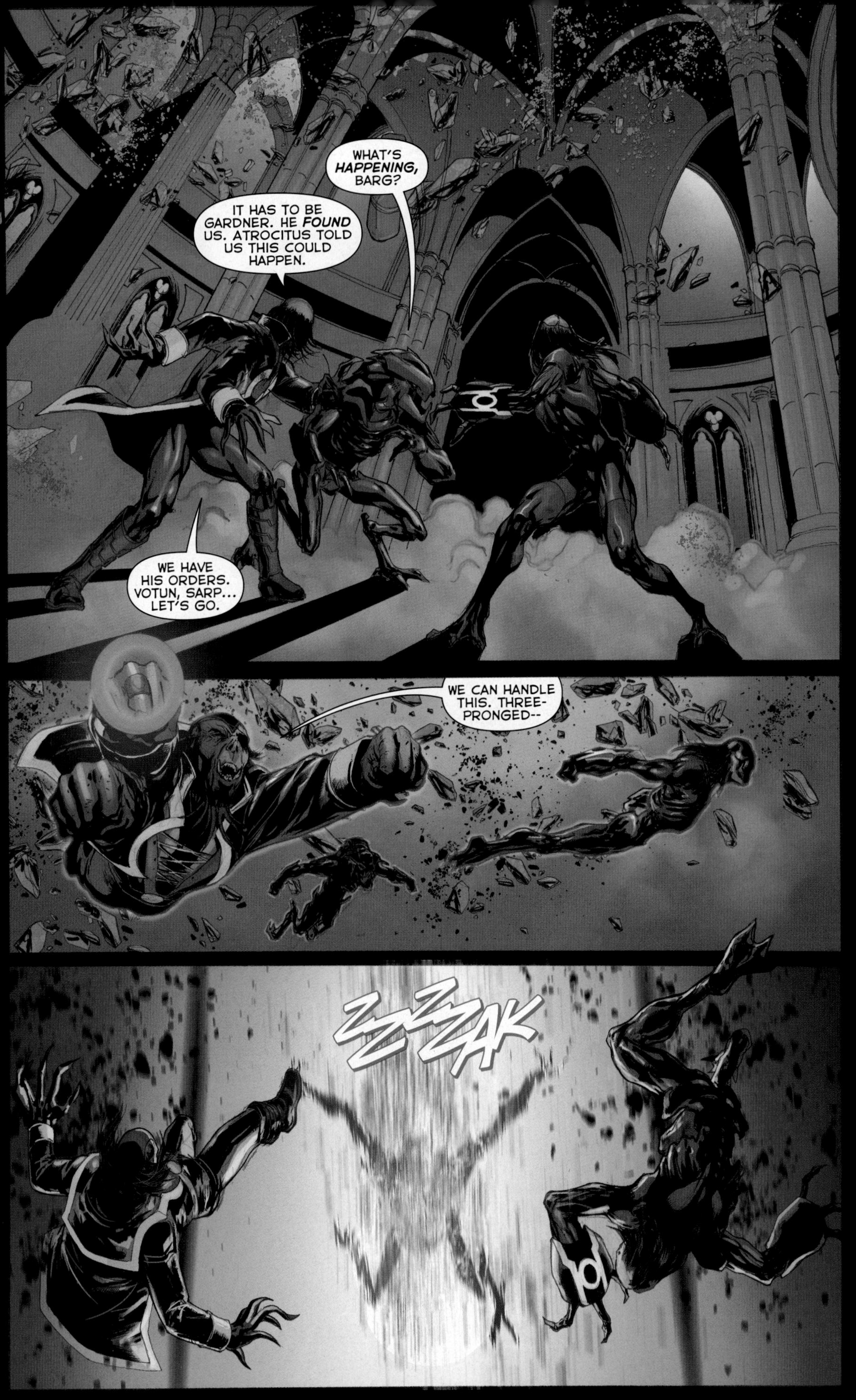
WHAT'S *HAPPENING,* BARG?
IT HAS TO BE GARDNER. HE *FOUND* US. ATROCITUS TOLD US THIS COULD HAPPEN.
WE HAVE HIS ORDERS. VOTUN, SARP... LET'S GO.
WE CAN HANDLE THIS. THREE-PRONGED--
ZZZZZAK

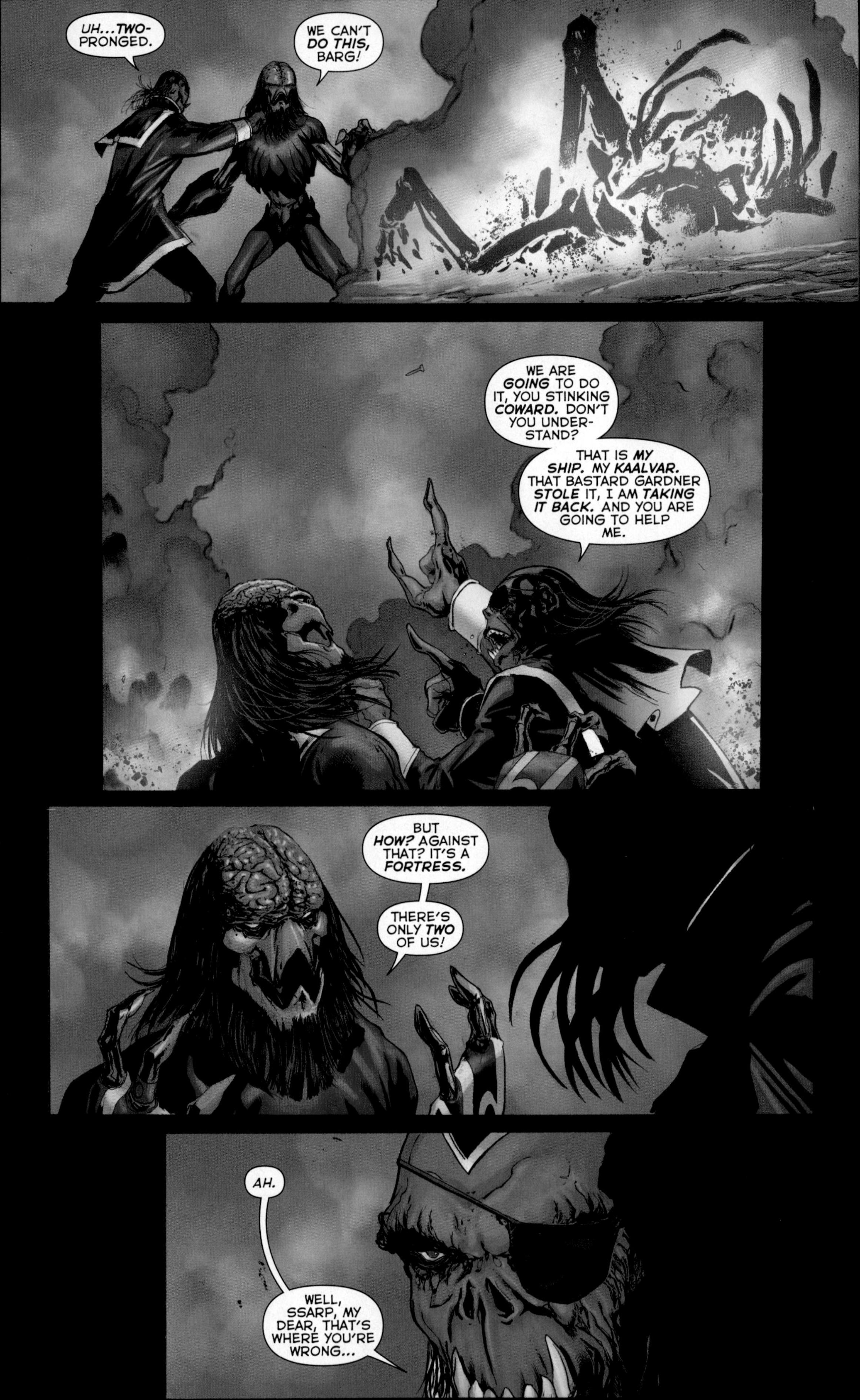
UH...TWO-PRONGED.
WE CAN'T DO THIS, BARG!
WE ARE GOING TO DO IT, YOU STINKING COWARD. DON'T YOU UNDER-STAND?
THAT IS MY SHIP. MY KAALVAR. THAT BASTARD GARDNER STOLE IT, I AM TAKING IT BACK. AND YOU ARE GOING TO HELP ME.
BUT HOW? AGAINST THAT? IT'S A FORTRESS.
THERE'S ONLY TWO OF US!
AH.
WELL, SSARP, MY DEAR, THAT'S WHERE YOU'RE WRONG...

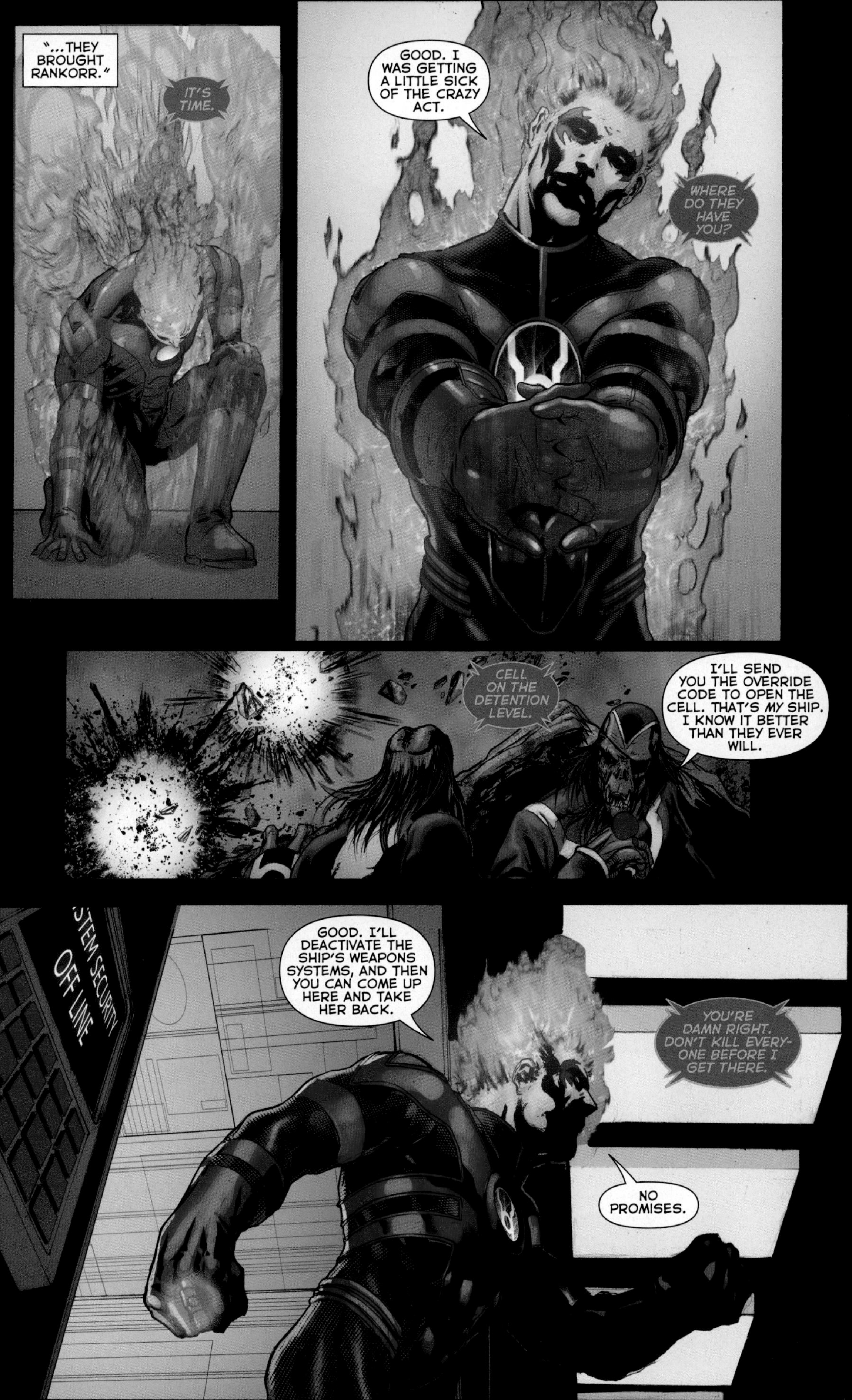
"...THEY BROUGHT RANKORR."
IT'S TIME.
GOOD. I WAS GETTING A LITTLE SICK OF THE CRAZY ACT.
WHERE DO THEY HAVE YOU?
CELL ON THE DETENTION LEVEL.
I'LL SEND YOU THE OVERRIDE CODE TO OPEN THE CELL. THAT'S MY SHIP. I KNOW IT BETTER THAN THEY EVER WILL.
STEM SECURITY OFF LINE
GOOD. I'LL DEACTIVATE THE SHIP'S WEAPONS SYSTEMS, AND THEN YOU CAN COME UP HERE AND TAKE HER BACK.
YOU'RE DAMN RIGHT. DON'T KILL EVERY-ONE BEFORE I GET THERE.
NO PROMISES.

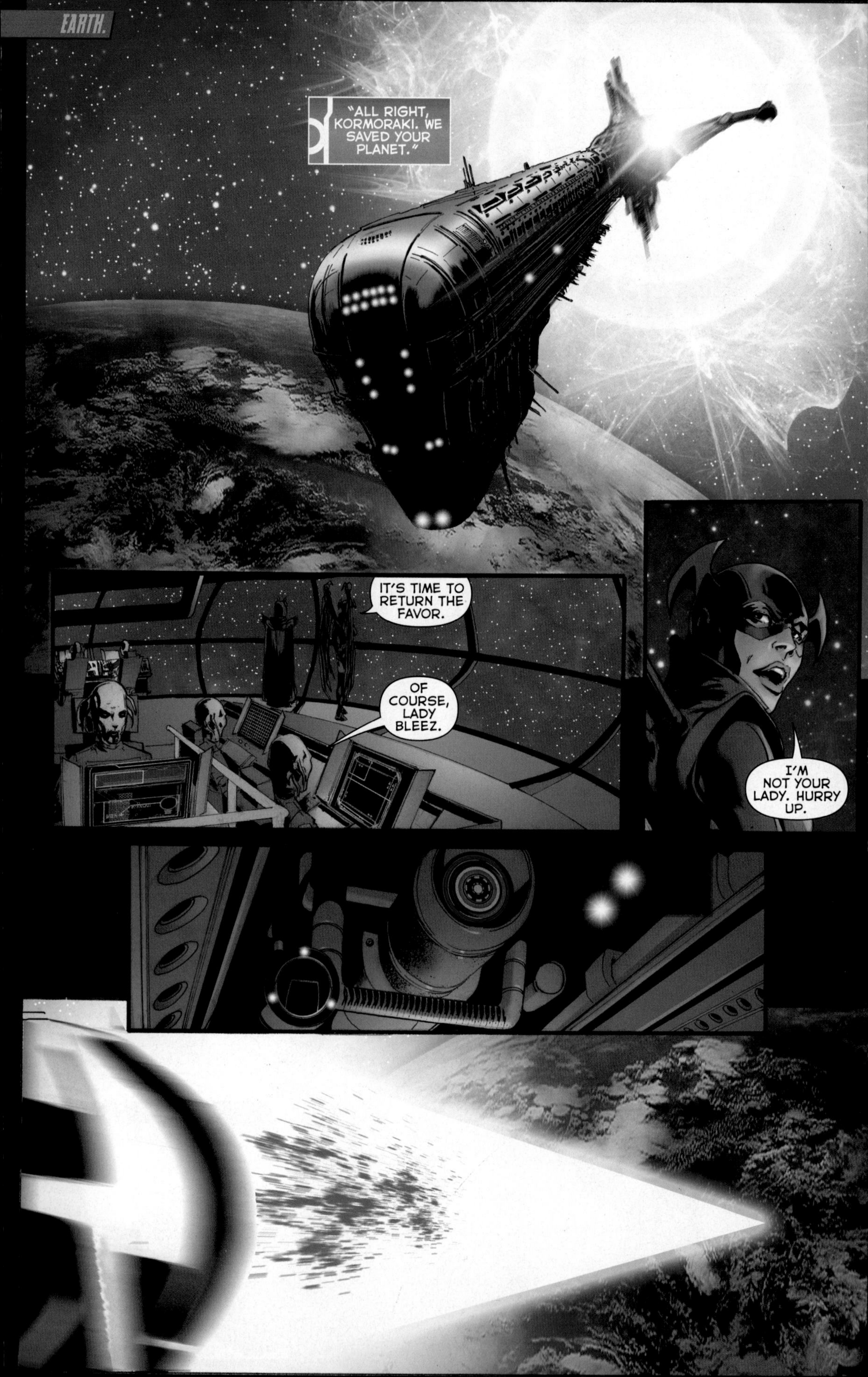
EARTH.
"ALL RIGHT, KORMORAKI. WE SAVED YOUR PLANET."
IT'S TIME TO RETURN THE FAVOR.
OF COURSE, LADY BLEEZ.
I'M NOT YOUR LADY. HURRY UP.

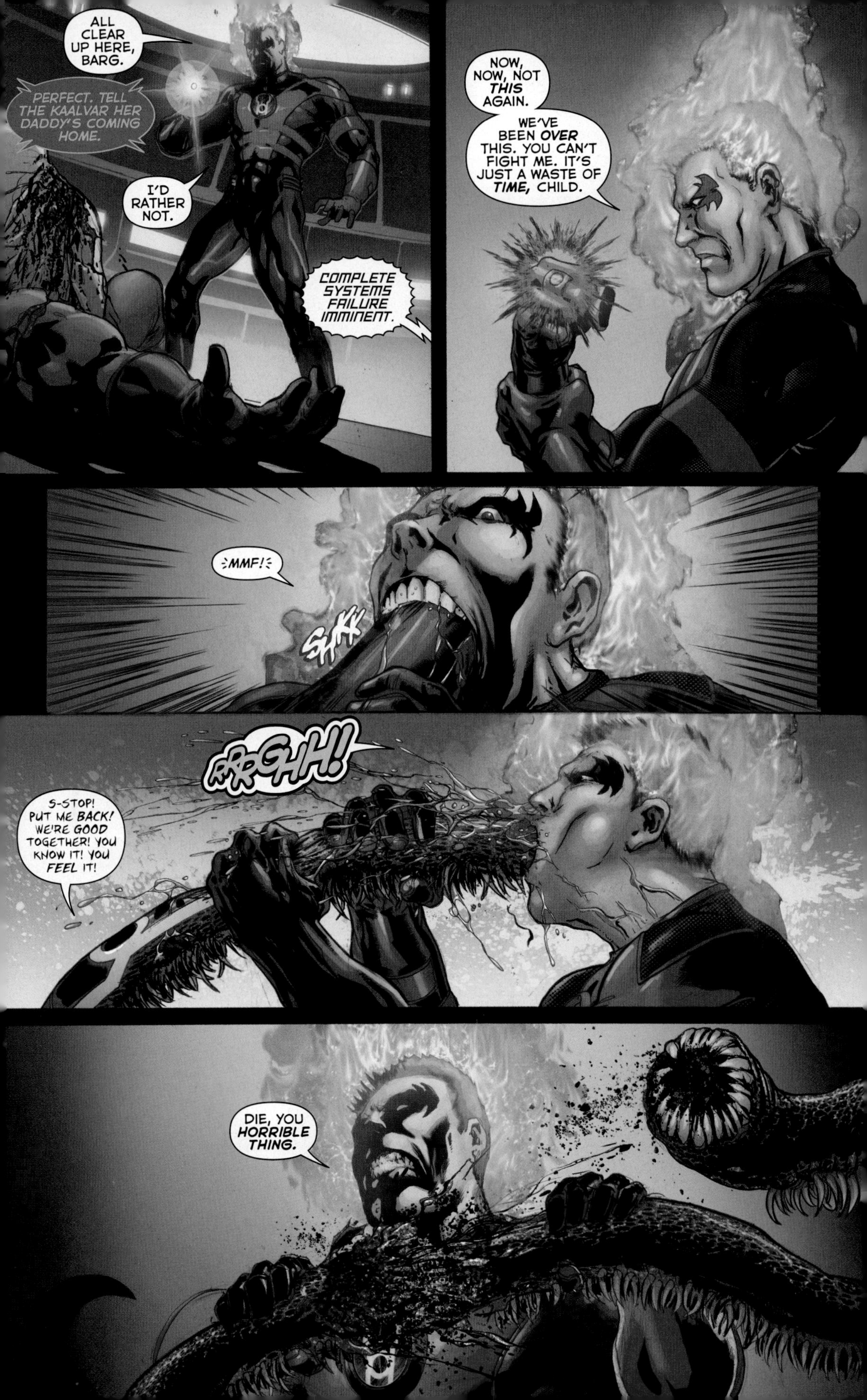
ALL CLEAR UP HERE, BARG.
PERFECT. TELL THE KAALVAR HER DADDY'S COMING HOME.
I'D RATHER NOT.
COMPLETE SYSTEMS FAILURE IMMINENT.
NOW, NOW, NOT THIS AGAIN.
WE'VE BEEN OVER THIS. YOU CAN'T FIGHT ME. IT'S JUST A WASTE OF TIME, CHILD.
MMF!
SHKK
RRRGHH!
S-STOP! PUT ME BACK! WE'RE GOOD TOGETHER! YOU KNOW IT! YOU FEEL IT!
DIE, YOU HORRIBLE THING.

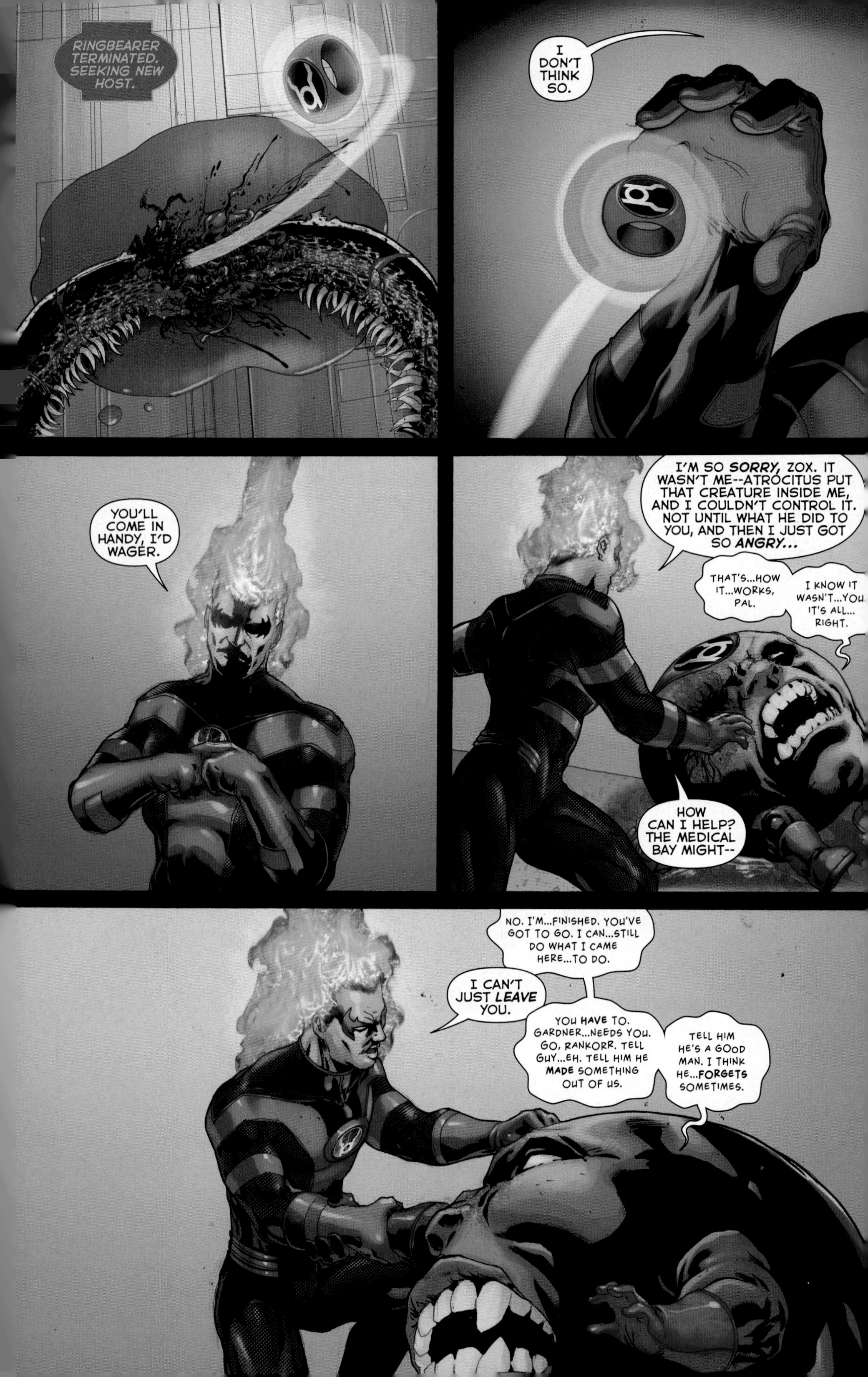
RINGBEARER TERMINATED. SEEKING NEW HOST.
I DON'T THINK SO.
YOU'LL COME IN HANDY, I'D WAGER.
I'M SO SORRY, ZOX. IT WASN'T ME--ATROCITUS PUT THAT CREATURE INSIDE ME, AND I COULDN'T CONTROL IT. NOT UNTIL WHAT HE DID TO YOU, AND THEN I JUST GOT SO ANGRY...
THAT'S...HOW IT...WORKS, PAL.
I KNOW IT WASN'T...YOU IT'S ALL... RIGHT.
HOW CAN I HELP? THE MEDICAL BAY MIGHT--
NO. I'M...FINISHED. YOU'VE GOT TO GO. I CAN...STILL DO WHAT I CAME HERE...TO DO.
I CAN'T JUST LEAVE YOU.
YOU HAVE TO. GARDNER...NEEDS YOU. GO, RANKORR. TELL GUY...EH. TELL HIM HE MADE SOMETHING OUT OF US.
TELL HIM HE'S A GOOD MAN. I THINK HE...FORGETS SOMETIMES.

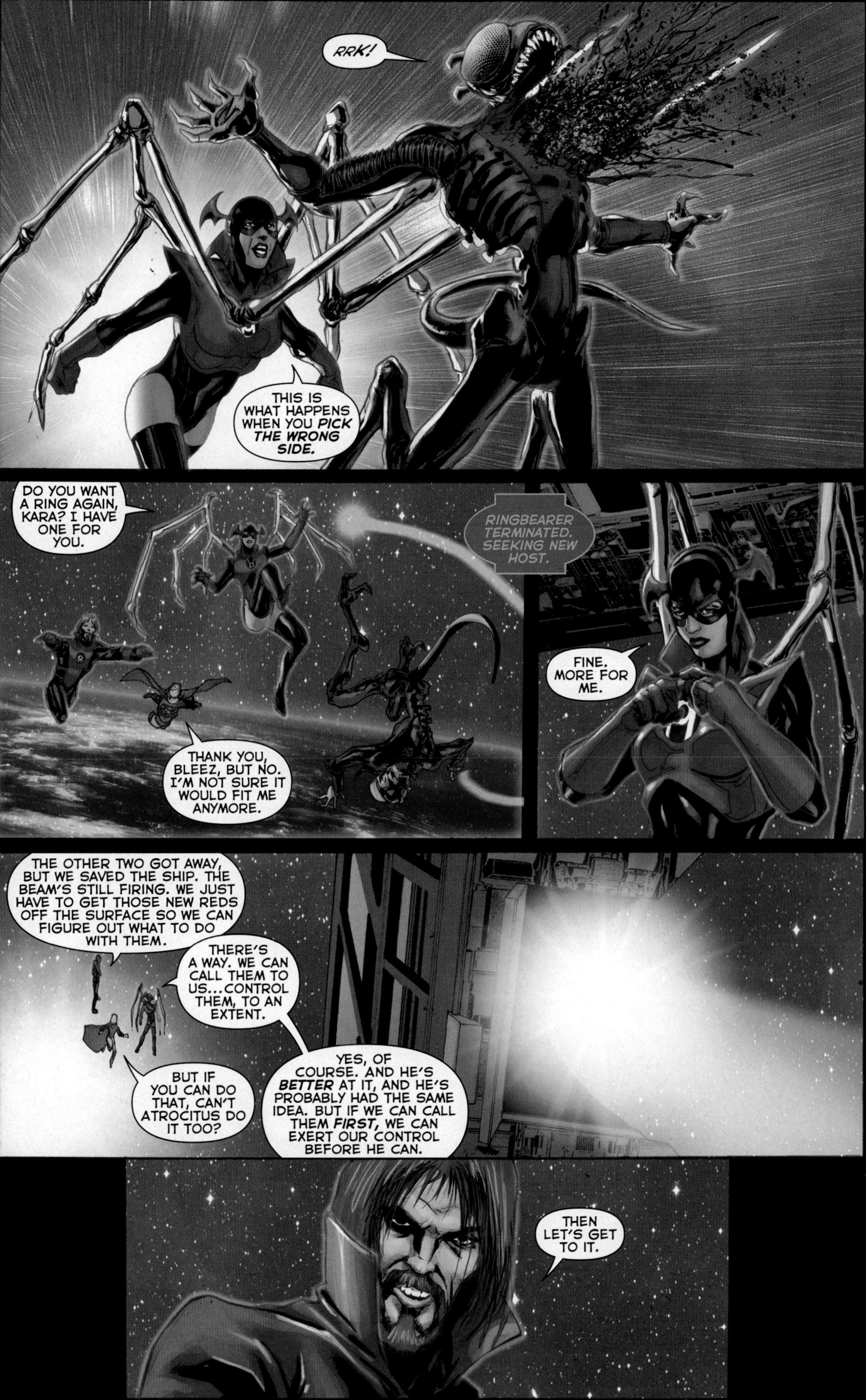
RRK!
THIS IS WHAT HAPPENS WHEN YOU PICK THE WRONG SIDE.
DO YOU WANT A RING AGAIN, KARA? I HAVE ONE FOR YOU.
THANK YOU, BLEEZ, BUT NO. I'M NOT SURE IT WOULD FIT ME ANYMORE.
RINGBEARER TERMINATED. SEEKING NEW HOST.
FINE. MORE FOR ME.
THE OTHER TWO GOT AWAY, BUT WE SAVED THE SHIP. THE BEAM'S STILL FIRING. WE JUST HAVE TO GET THOSE NEW REDS OFF THE SURFACE SO WE CAN FIGURE OUT WHAT TO DO WITH THEM.
THERE'S A WAY. WE CAN CALL THEM TO US...CONTROL THEM, TO AN EXTENT.
BUT IF YOU CAN DO THAT, CAN'T ATROCITUS DO IT TOO?
YES, OF COURSE. AND HE'S BETTER AT IT, AND HE'S PROBABLY HAD THE SAME IDEA. BUT IF WE CAN CALL THEM FIRST, WE CAN EXERT OUR CONTROL BEFORE HE CAN.
THEN LET'S GET TO IT.

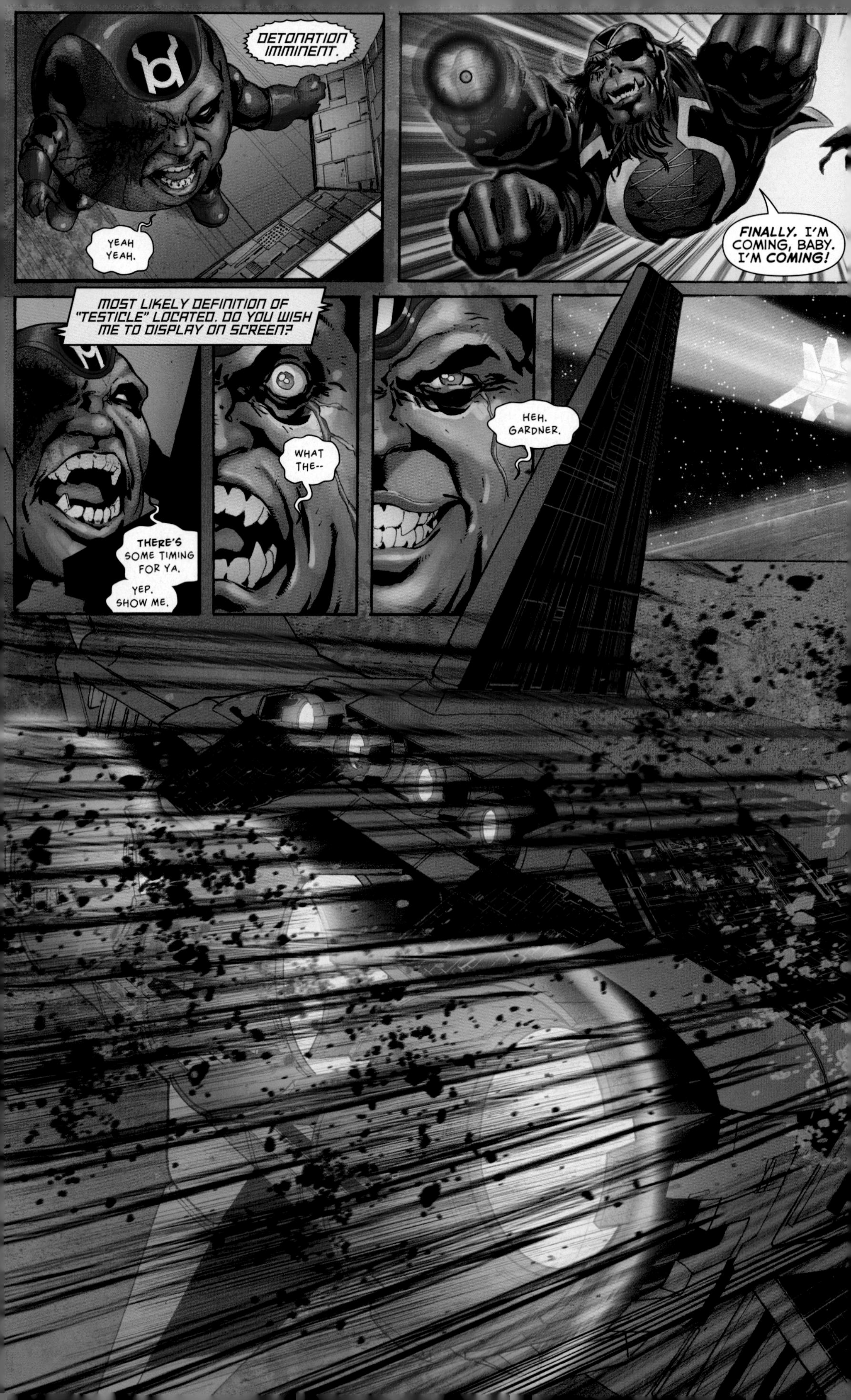
DETONATION IMMINENT.
YEAH YEAH.
FINALLY. I'M COMING, BABY. I'M COMING!
MOST LIKELY DEFINITION OF "TESTICLE" LOCATED. DO YOU WISH ME TO DISPLAY ON SCREEN?
THERE'S SOME TIMING FOR YA.
YEP. SHOW ME.
WHAT THE--
HEH. GARDNER.

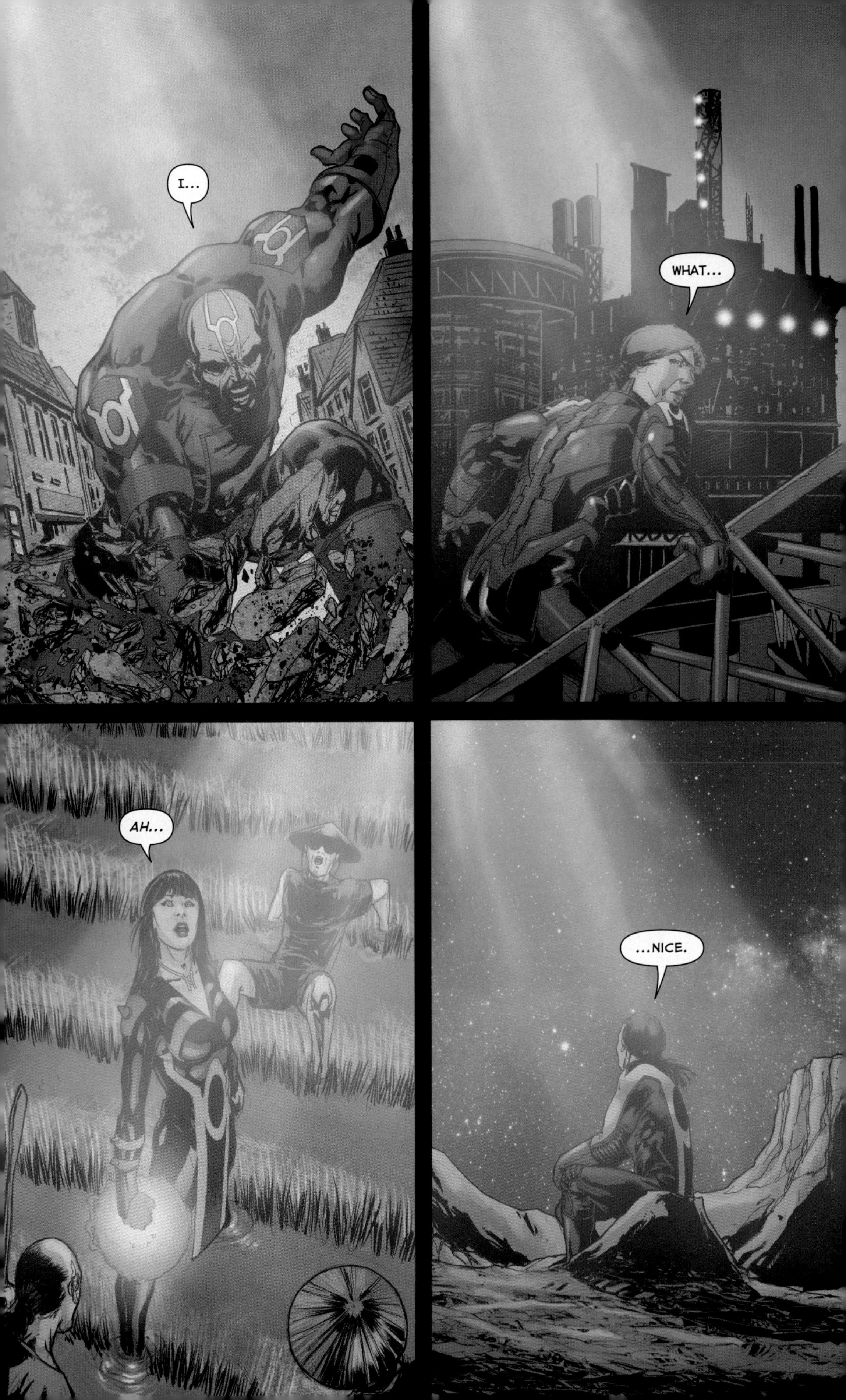
I...
WHAT...
AH...
...NICE.

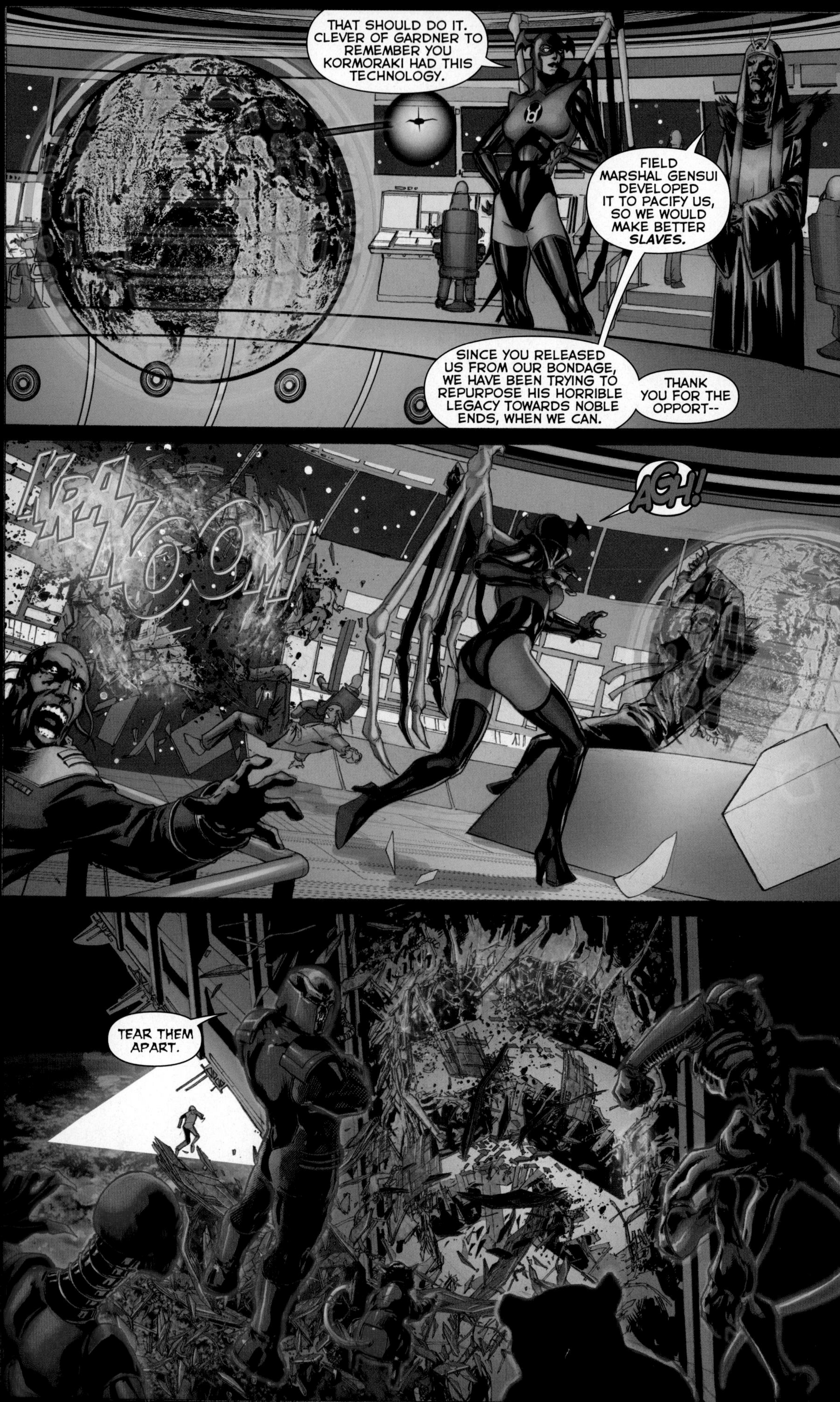
THAT SHOULD DO IT. CLEVER OF GARDNER TO REMEMBER YOU KORMORAKI HAD THIS TECHNOLOGY.
FIELD MARSHAL GENSUI DEVELOPED IT TO PACIFY US, SO WE WOULD MAKE BETTER SLAVES.
SINCE YOU RELEASED US FROM OUR BONDAGE, WE HAVE BEEN TRYING TO REPURPOSE HIS HORRIBLE LEGACY TOWARDS NOBLE ENDS, WHEN WE CAN.
THANK YOU FOR THE OPPORT--
KRA-KOOOM
AGH!
TEAR THEM APART.

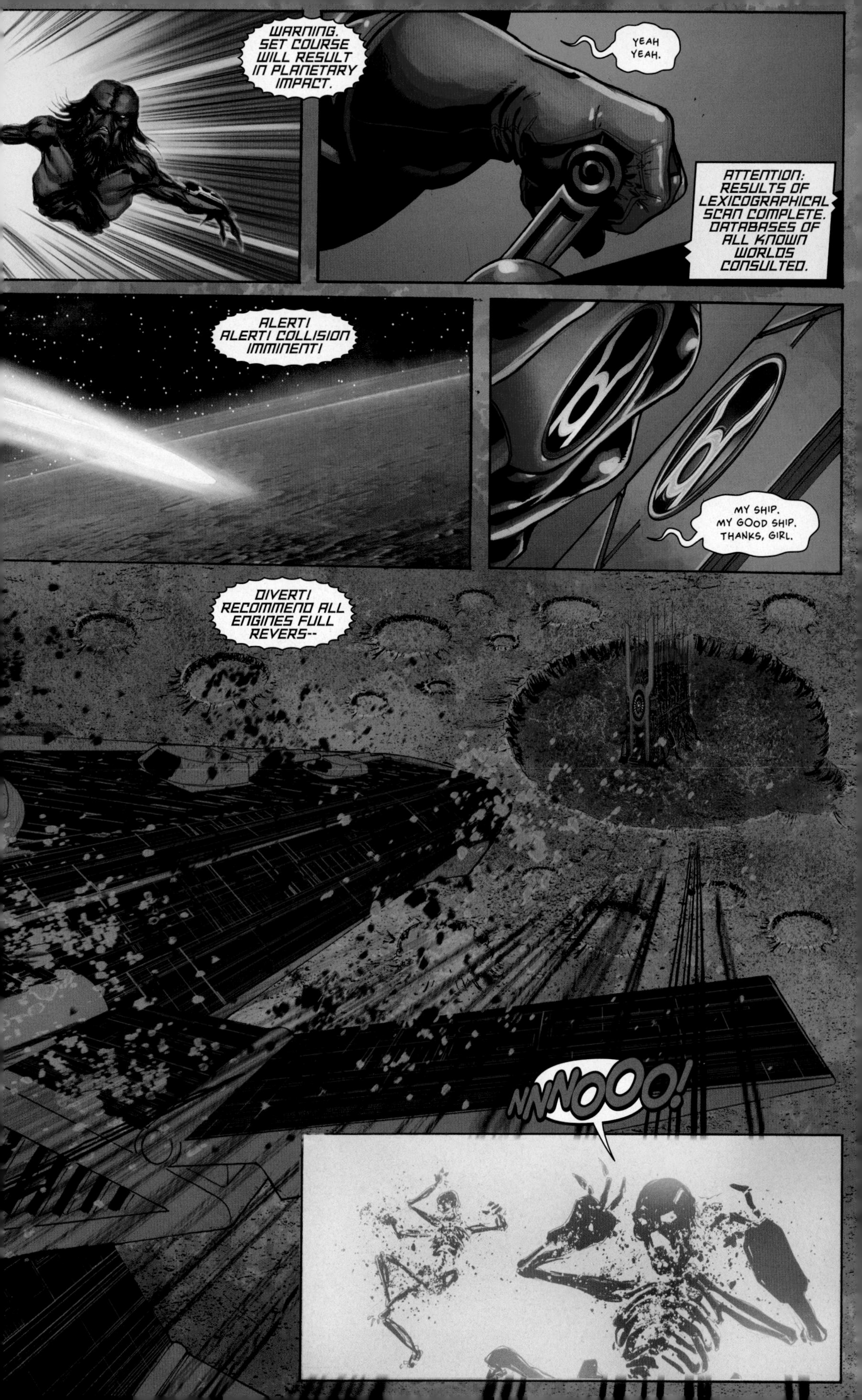
WARNING. SET COURSE WILL RESULT IN PLANETARY IMPACT.
YEAH YEAH.
ATTENTION: RESULTS OF LEXICOGRAPHICAL SCAN COMPLETE. DATABASES OF ALL KNOWN WORLDS CONSULTED.
ALERT! ALERT! COLLISION IMMINENT!
MY SHIP. MY GOOD SHIP. THANKS, GIRL.
DIVERT! RECOMMEND ALL ENGINES FULL REVERS--
NNNOOO!

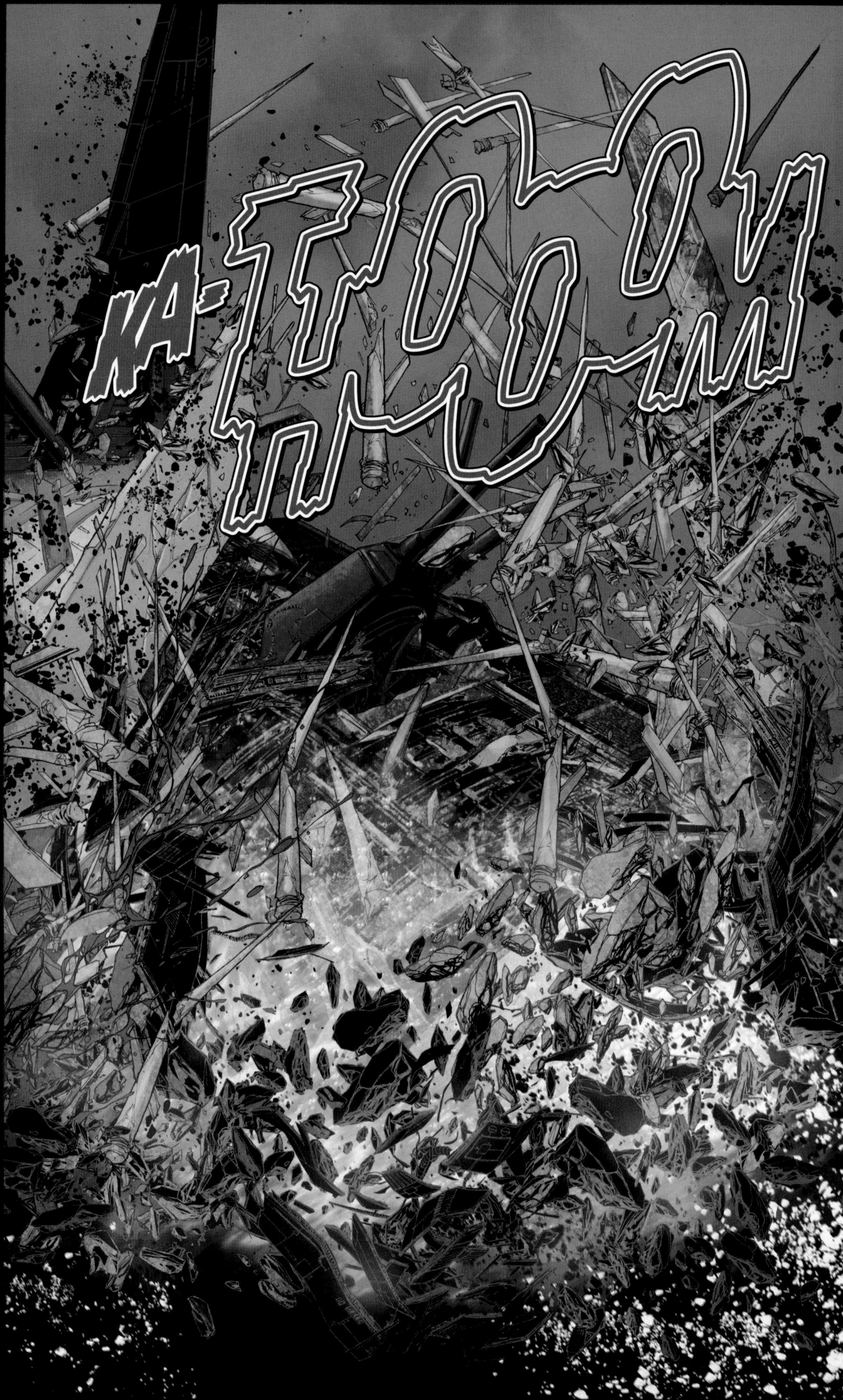
KA-THOOOM

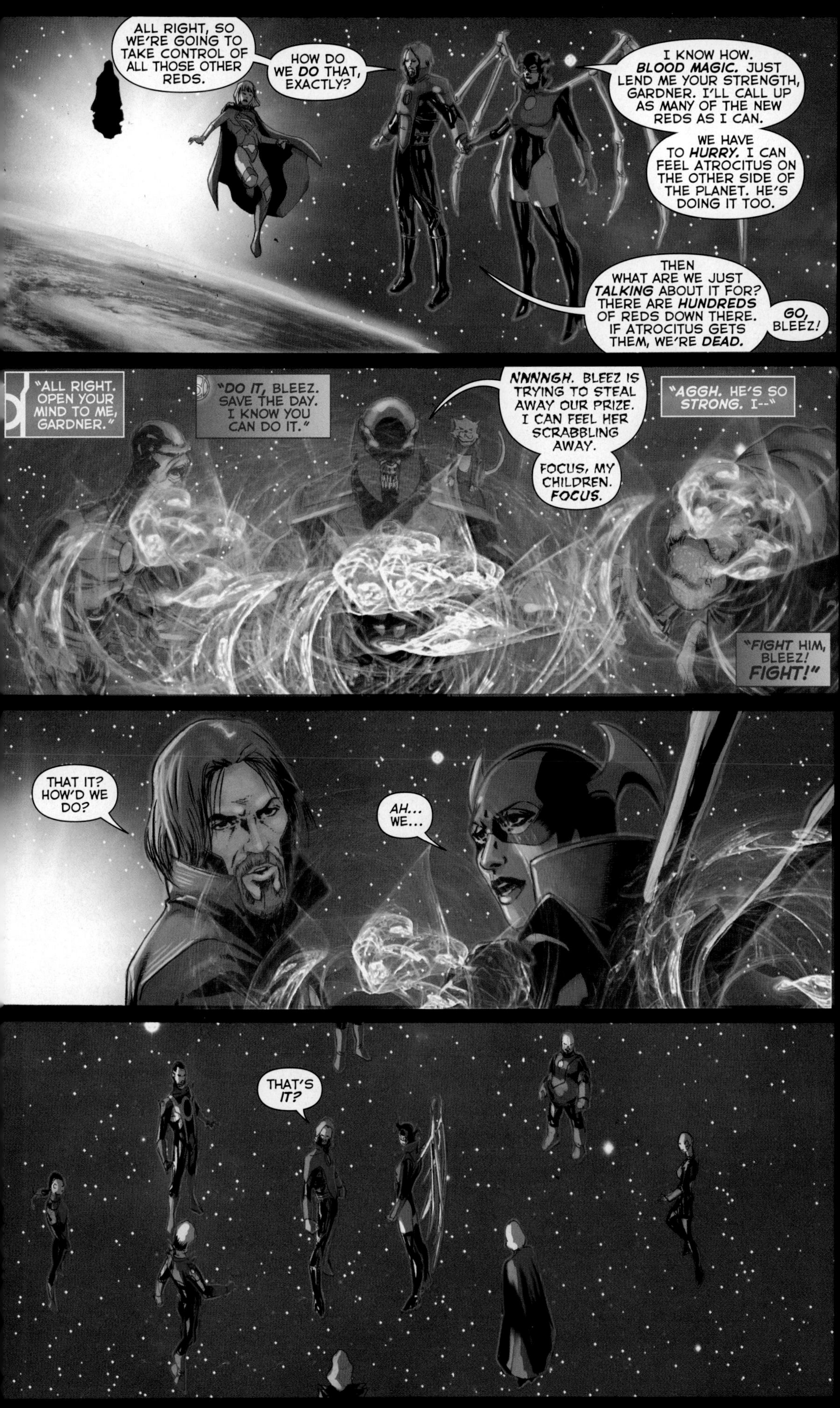
ALL RIGHT, SO WE'RE GOING TO TAKE CONTROL OF ALL THOSE OTHER REDS.
HOW DO WE DO THAT, EXACTLY?
I KNOW HOW. BLOOD MAGIC. JUST LEND ME YOUR STRENGTH, GARDNER. I'LL CALL UP AS MANY OF THE NEW REDS AS I CAN.
WE HAVE TO HURRY. I CAN FEEL ATROCITUS ON THE OTHER SIDE OF THE PLANET. HE'S DOING IT TOO.
THEN WHAT ARE WE JUST TALKING ABOUT IT FOR? THERE ARE HUNDREDS OF REDS DOWN THERE. IF ATROCITUS GETS THEM, WE'RE DEAD.
GO, BLEEZ!
"ALL RIGHT. OPEN YOUR MIND TO ME, GARDNER."
"DO IT, BLEEZ. SAVE THE DAY. I KNOW YOU CAN DO IT."
NNNNGH. BLEEZ IS TRYING TO STEAL AWAY OUR PRIZE. I CAN FEEL HER SCRABBLING AWAY.
FOCUS, MY CHILDREN. FOCUS.
"AGGH. HE'S SO STRONG. I--"
"FIGHT HIM, BLEEZ! FIGHT!"
THAT IT? HOW'D WE DO?
AH... WE...
THAT'S IT?

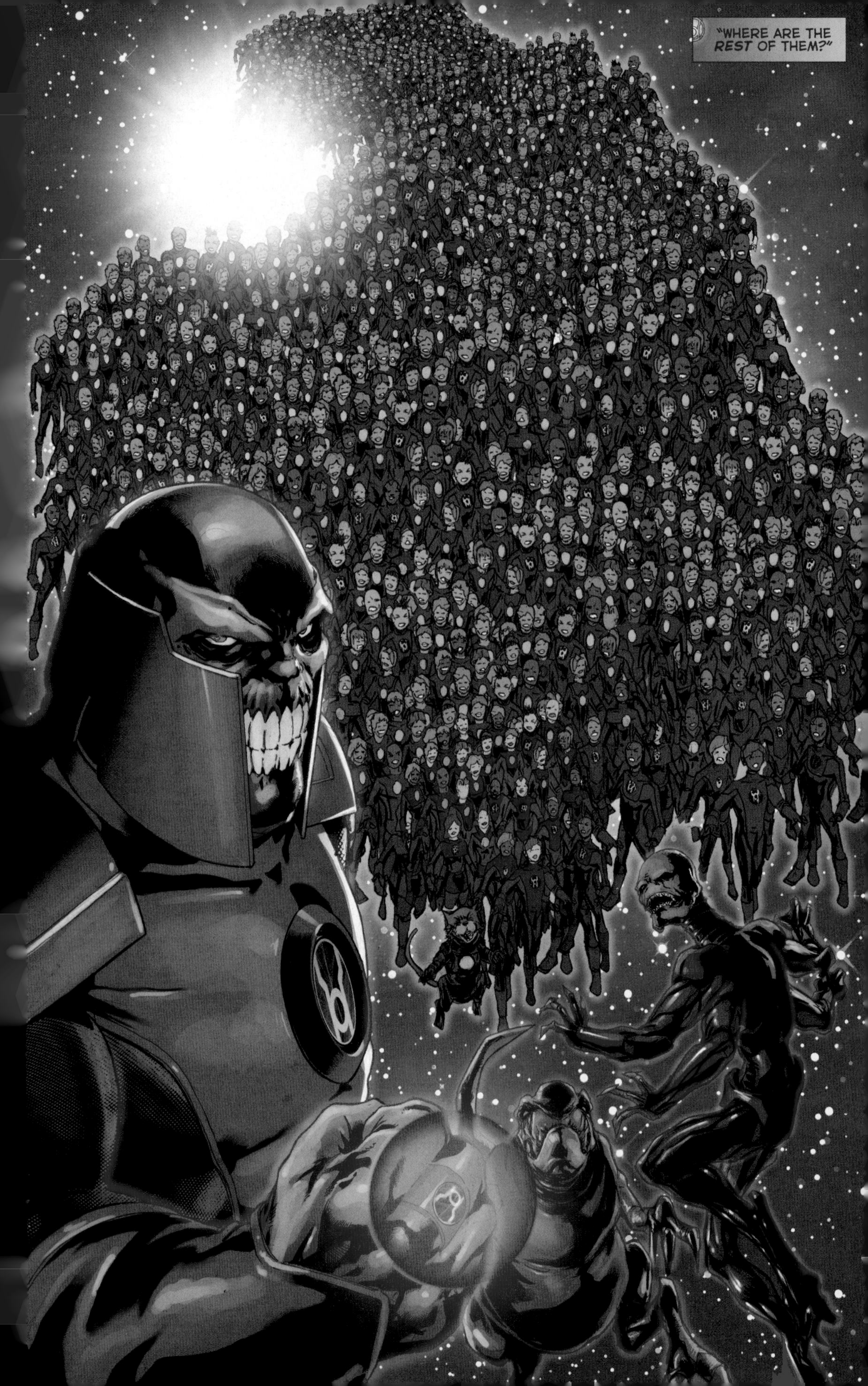
"WHERE ARE THE REST OF THEM?"

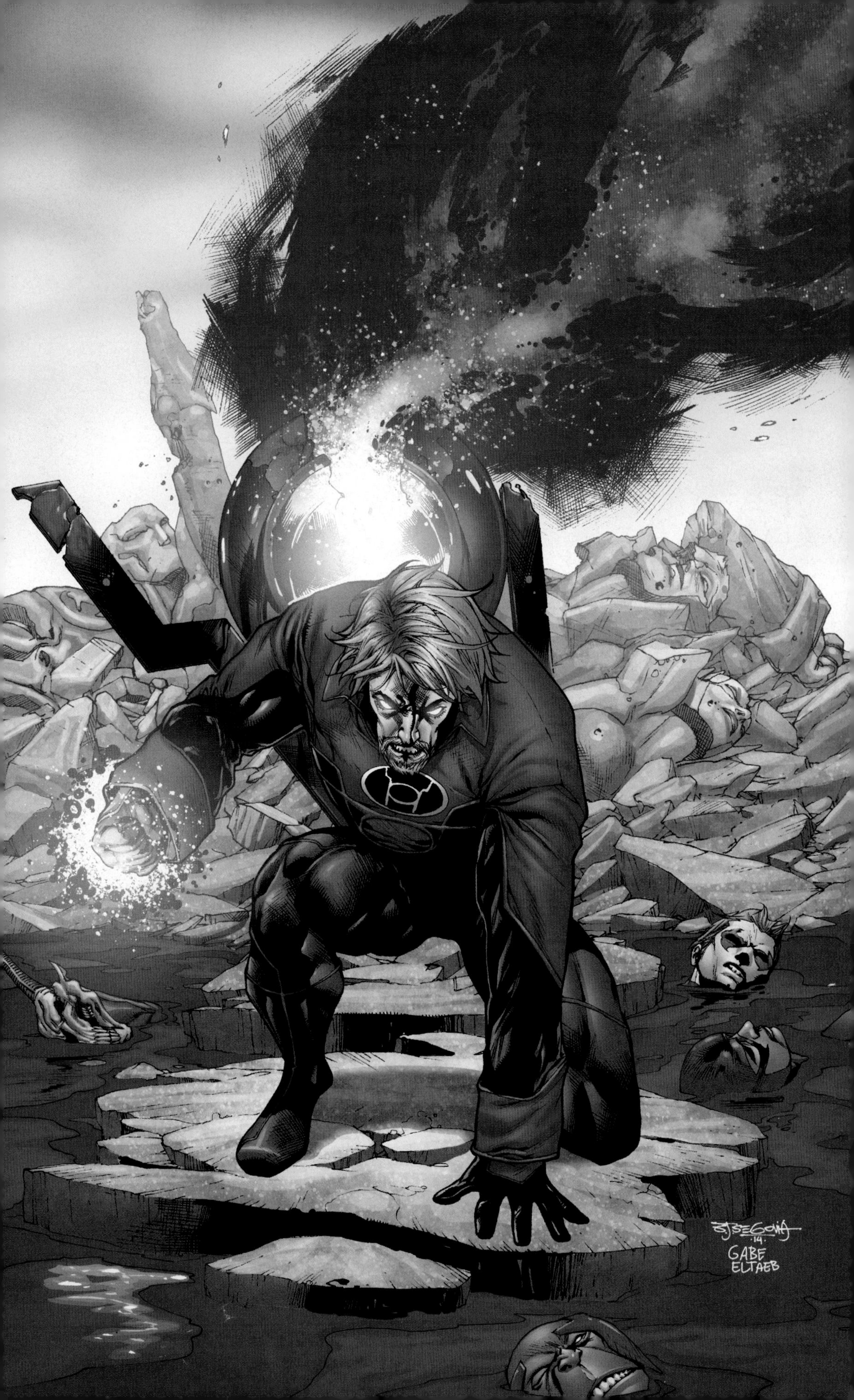
GABE
ELTAEB

CHARLES SOULE writer ALESSANDRO VITTI J. CALAFIORE artists GABE ELTAEB colorist DAVE SHARPE letterer
cover art by STEPHEN SEGOVIA with GABE ELTAEB

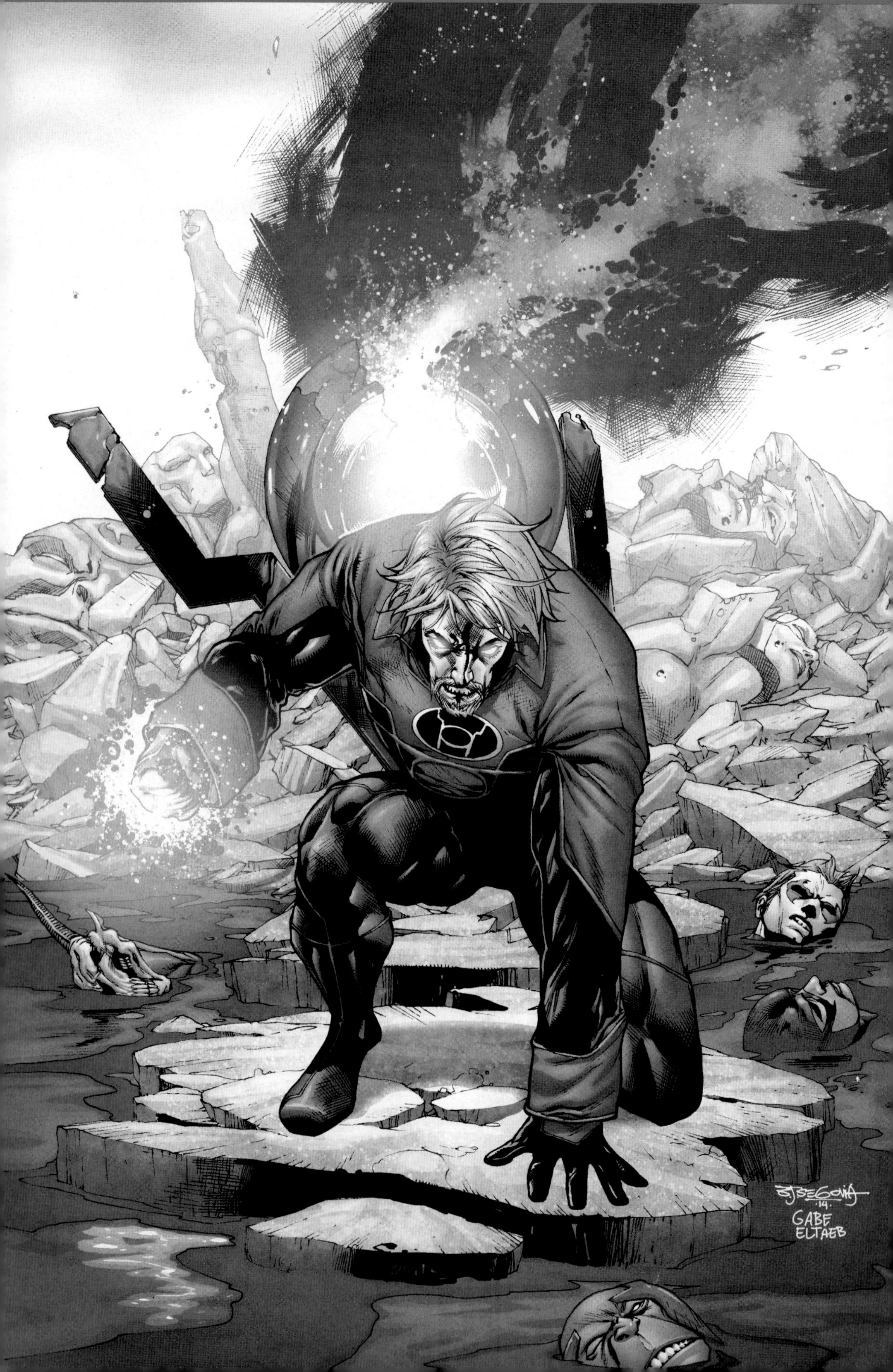
GABE
ELTAEB

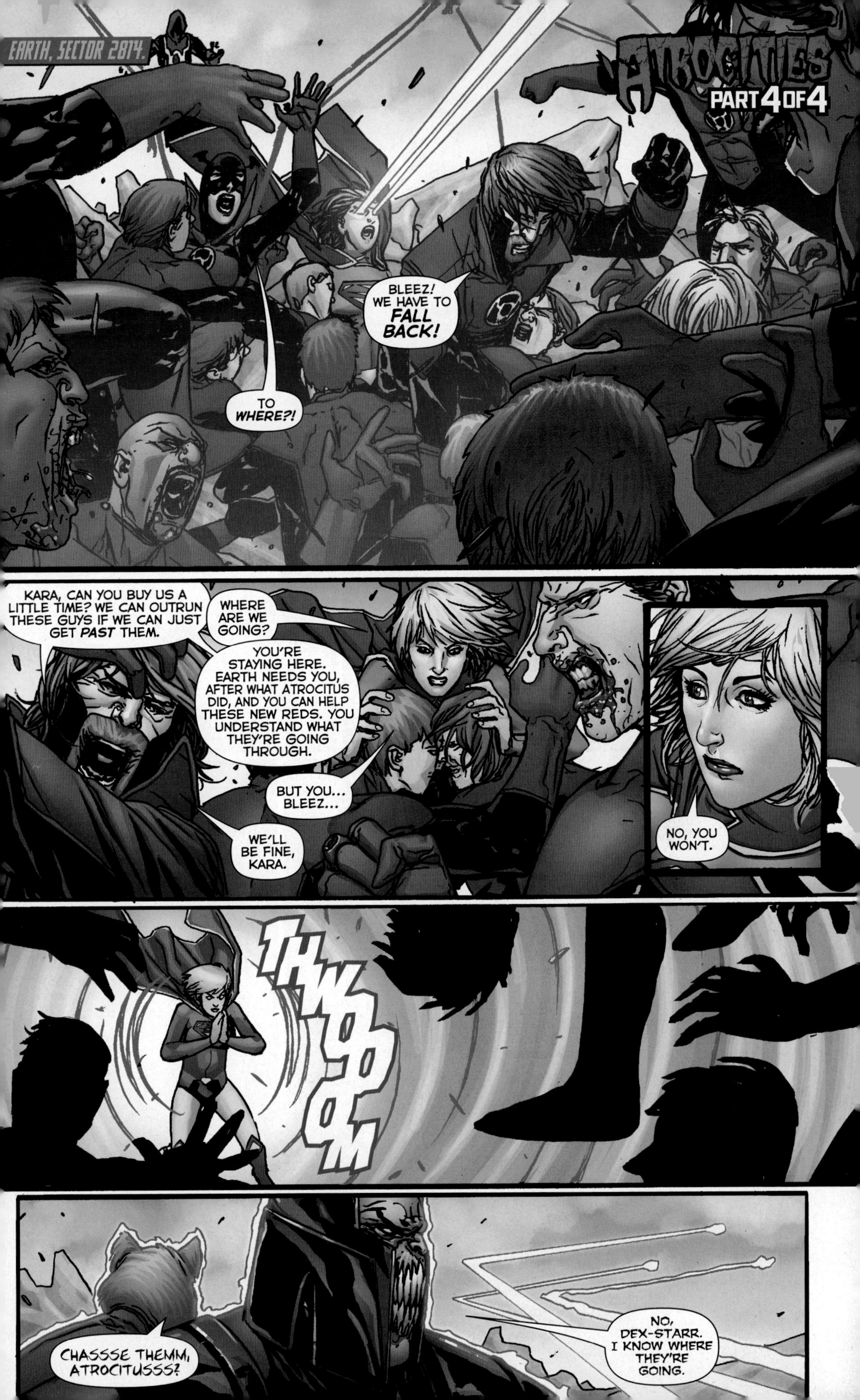
EARTH, SECTOR 2814.
ATROCITIES
PART 4 OF 4
BLEEZ! WE HAVE TO FALL BACK!
TO WHERE?!
KARA, CAN YOU BUY US A LITTLE TIME? WE CAN OUTRUN THESE GUYS IF WE CAN JUST GET PAST THEM.
WHERE ARE WE GOING?
YOU'RE STAYING HERE. EARTH NEEDS YOU, AFTER WHAT ATROCITUS DID, AND YOU CAN HELP THESE NEW REDS. YOU UNDERSTAND WHAT THEY'RE GOING THROUGH.
BUT YOU... BLEEZ...
WE'LL BE FINE, KARA.
NO, YOU WON'T.
THWOOOM
CHASSSE THEMM, ATROCITUSSS?
NO, DEX-STARR. I KNOW WHERE THEY'RE GOING.

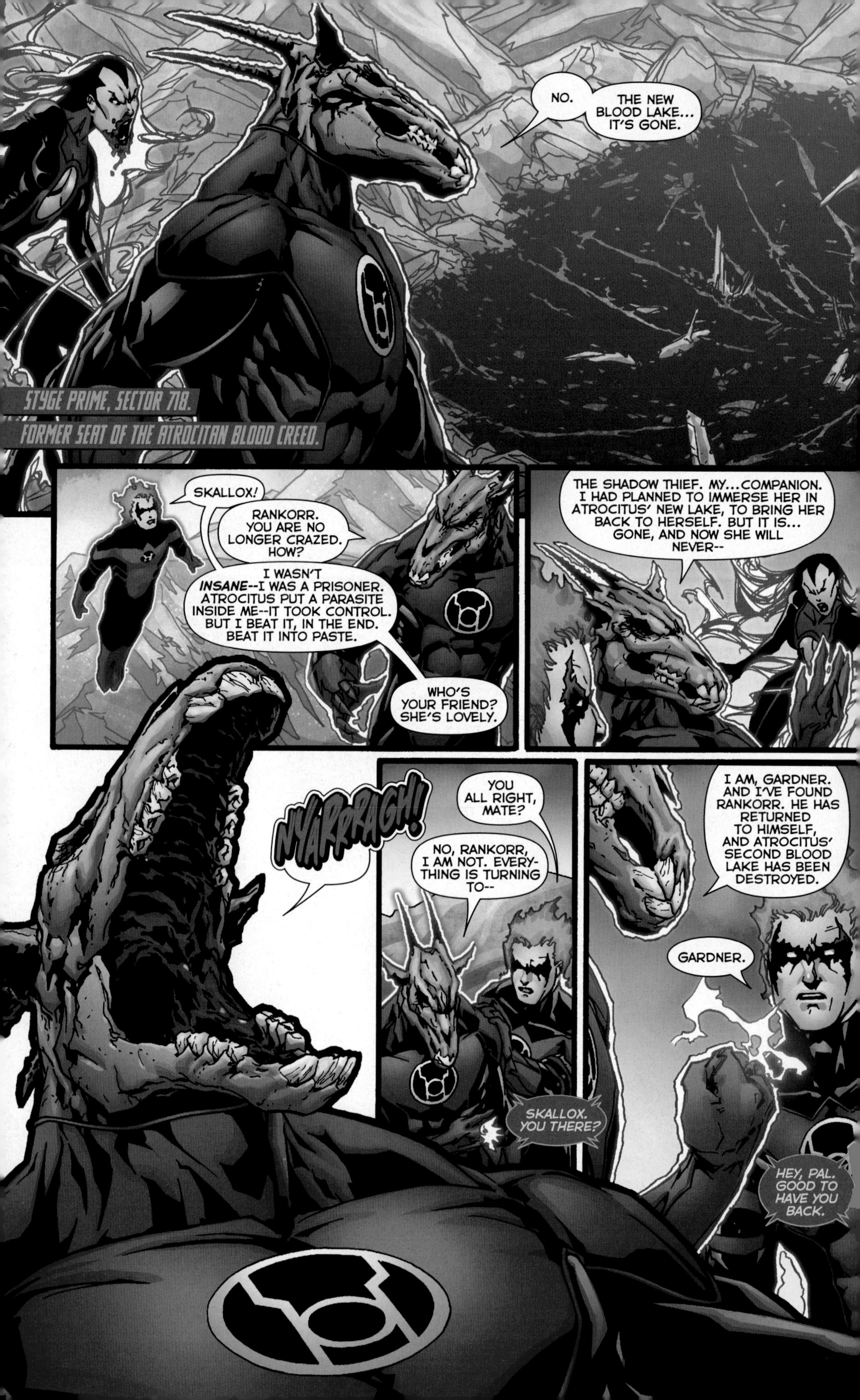
NO.
THE NEW BLOOD LAKE... IT'S GONE.
STYGE PRIME, SECTOR 718.
FORMER SEAT OF THE ATROCITAN BLOOD CREED.
SKALLOX!
RANKORR. YOU ARE NO LONGER CRAZED. HOW?
I WASN'T *INSANE*--I WAS A PRISONER. ATROCITUS PUT A PARASITE INSIDE ME--IT TOOK CONTROL. BUT I BEAT IT, IN THE END. BEAT IT INTO PASTE.
WHO'S YOUR FRIEND? SHE'S LOVELY.
THE SHADOW THIEF. MY...COMPANION. I HAD PLANNED TO IMMERSE HER IN ATROCITUS' NEW LAKE, TO BRING HER BACK TO HERSELF. BUT IT IS... GONE, AND NOW SHE WILL NEVER--
NYARRRAGH!
YOU ALL RIGHT, MATE?
NO, RANKORR, I AM NOT. EVERY-THING IS TURNING TO--
SKALLOX. YOU THERE?
I AM, GARDNER. AND I'VE FOUND RANKORR. HE HAS RETURNED TO HIMSELF, AND ATROCITUS' SECOND BLOOD LAKE HAS BEEN DESTROYED.
GARDNER.
HEY, PAL. GOOD TO HAVE YOU BACK.

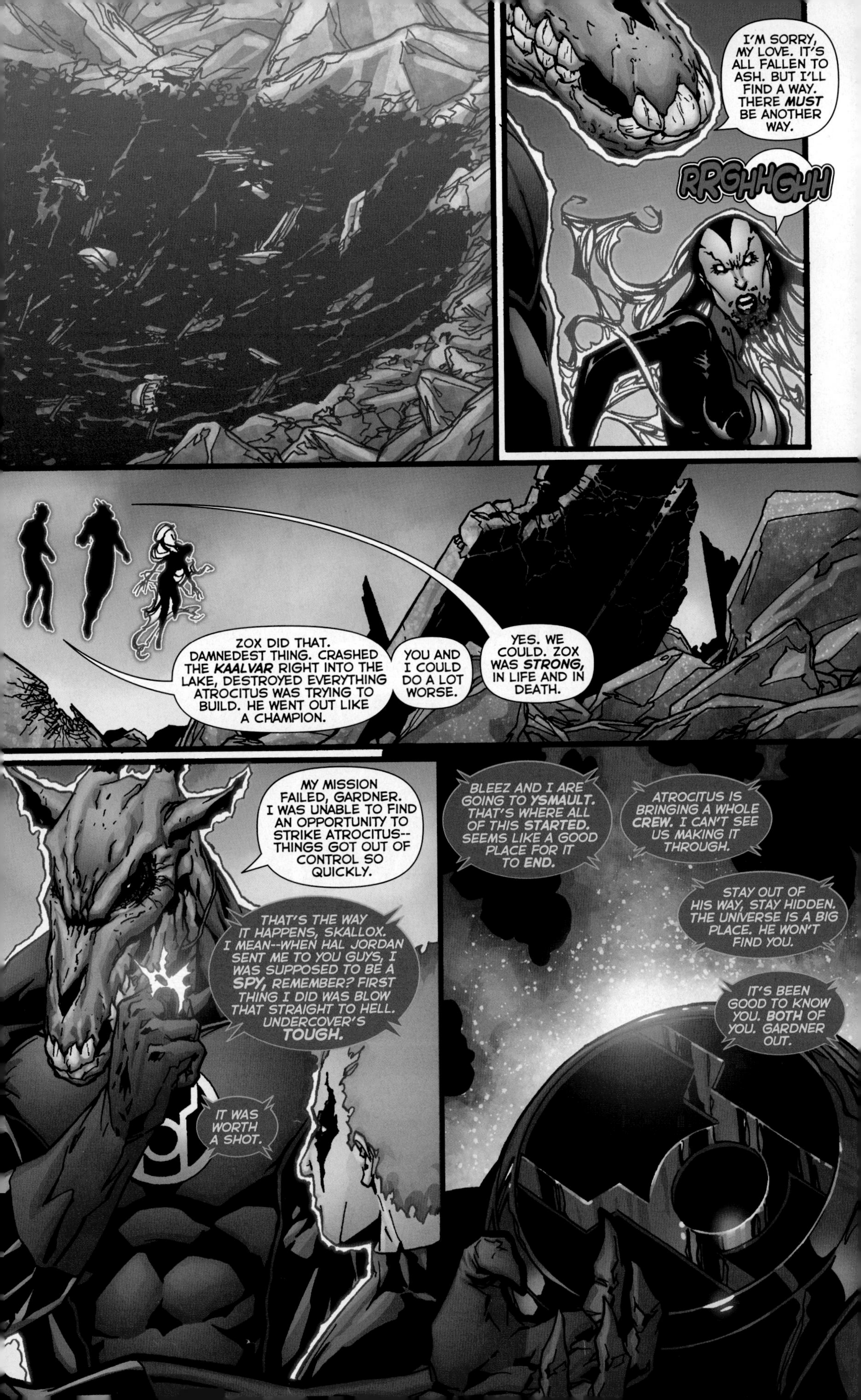
I'M SORRY, MY LOVE. IT'S ALL FALLEN TO ASH. BUT I'LL FIND A WAY. THERE MUST BE ANOTHER WAY.
RRGHHGHH
ZOX DID THAT. DAMNEDEST THING. CRASHED THE KAALVAR RIGHT INTO THE LAKE, DESTROYED EVERYTHING ATROCITUS WAS TRYING TO BUILD. HE WENT OUT LIKE A CHAMPION.
YOU AND I COULD DO A LOT WORSE.
YES. WE COULD. ZOX WAS STRONG, IN LIFE AND IN DEATH.
MY MISSION FAILED, GARDNER. I WAS UNABLE TO FIND AN OPPORTUNITY TO STRIKE ATROCITUS-- THINGS GOT OUT OF CONTROL SO QUICKLY.
THAT'S THE WAY IT HAPPENS, SKALLOX. I MEAN--WHEN HAL JORDAN SENT ME TO YOU GUYS, I WAS SUPPOSED TO BE A SPY, REMEMBER? FIRST THING I DID WAS BLOW THAT STRAIGHT TO HELL. UNDERCOVER'S TOUGH.
IT WAS WORTH A SHOT.
BLEEZ AND I ARE GOING TO YSMAULT. THAT'S WHERE ALL OF THIS STARTED. SEEMS LIKE A GOOD PLACE FOR IT TO END.
ATROCITUS IS BRINGING A WHOLE CREW. I CAN'T SEE US MAKING IT THROUGH.
STAY OUT OF HIS WAY, STAY HIDDEN. THE UNIVERSE IS A BIG PLACE. HE WON'T FIND YOU.
IT'S BEEN GOOD TO KNOW YOU. BOTH OF YOU. GARDNER OUT.

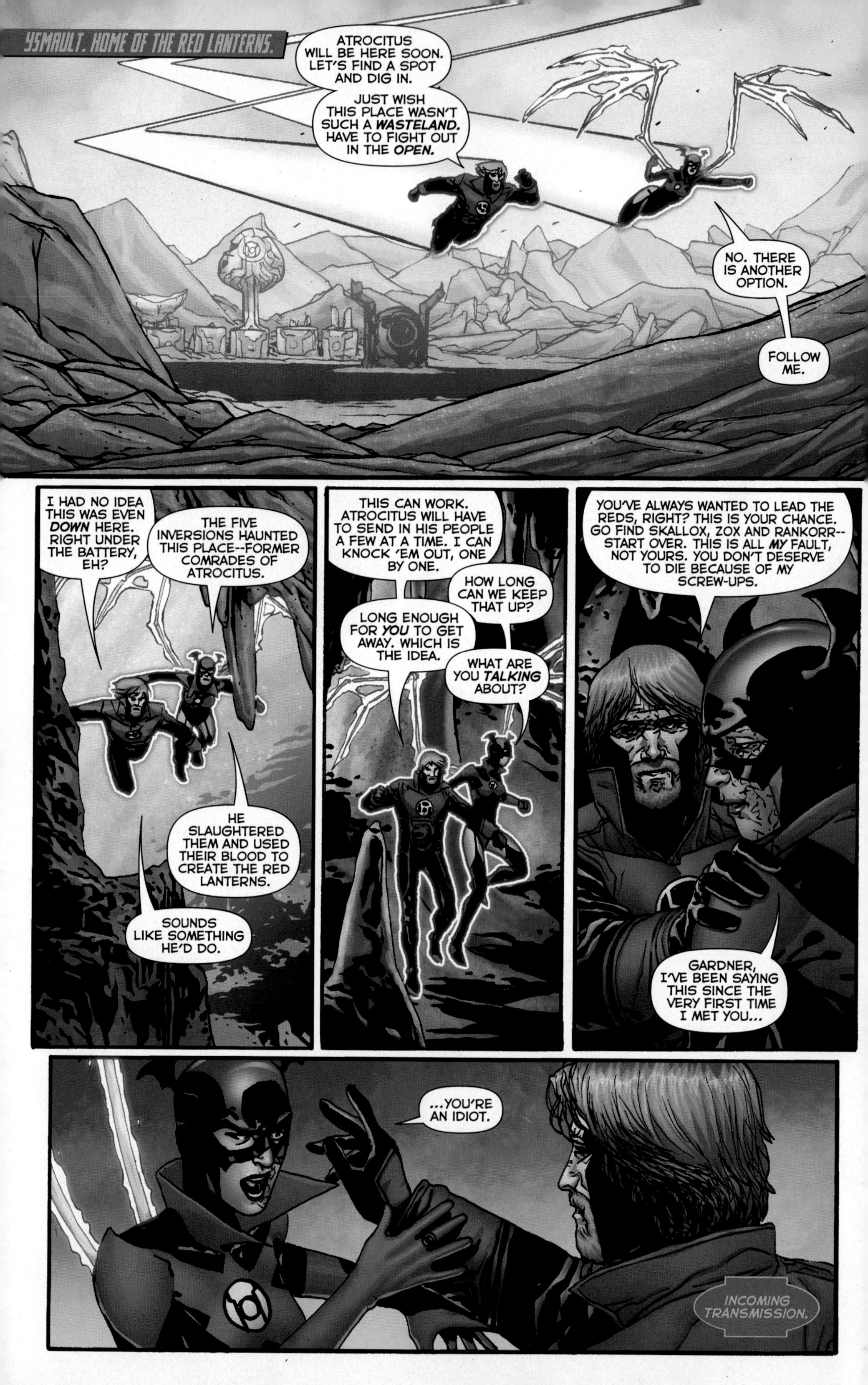
YSMAULT. HOME OF THE RED LANTERNS.
ATROCITUS WILL BE HERE SOON. LET'S FIND A SPOT AND DIG IN.
JUST WISH THIS PLACE WASN'T SUCH A *WASTELAND.* HAVE TO FIGHT OUT IN THE *OPEN.*
NO. THERE IS ANOTHER OPTION.
FOLLOW ME.
I HAD NO IDEA THIS WAS EVEN *DOWN* HERE. RIGHT UNDER THE BATTERY, EH?
THE FIVE INVERSIONS HAUNTED THIS PLACE--FORMER COMRADES OF ATROCITUS.
HE SLAUGHTERED THEM AND USED THEIR BLOOD TO CREATE THE RED LANTERNS.
SOUNDS LIKE SOMETHING HE'D DO.
THIS CAN WORK. ATROCITUS WILL HAVE TO SEND IN HIS PEOPLE A FEW AT A TIME. I CAN KNOCK 'EM OUT, ONE BY ONE.
HOW LONG CAN WE KEEP THAT UP?
LONG ENOUGH FOR *YOU* TO GET AWAY. WHICH IS THE IDEA.
WHAT ARE YOU *TALKING* ABOUT?
YOU'VE ALWAYS WANTED TO LEAD THE REDS, RIGHT? THIS IS YOUR CHANCE. GO FIND SKALLOX, ZOX AND RANKORR--START OVER. THIS IS ALL *MY* FAULT, NOT YOURS. YOU DON'T DESERVE TO DIE BECAUSE OF MY SCREW-UPS.
GARDNER, I'VE BEEN SAYING THIS SINCE THE VERY FIRST TIME I MET YOU...
...YOU'RE AN IDIOT.
INCOMING TRANSMISSION.

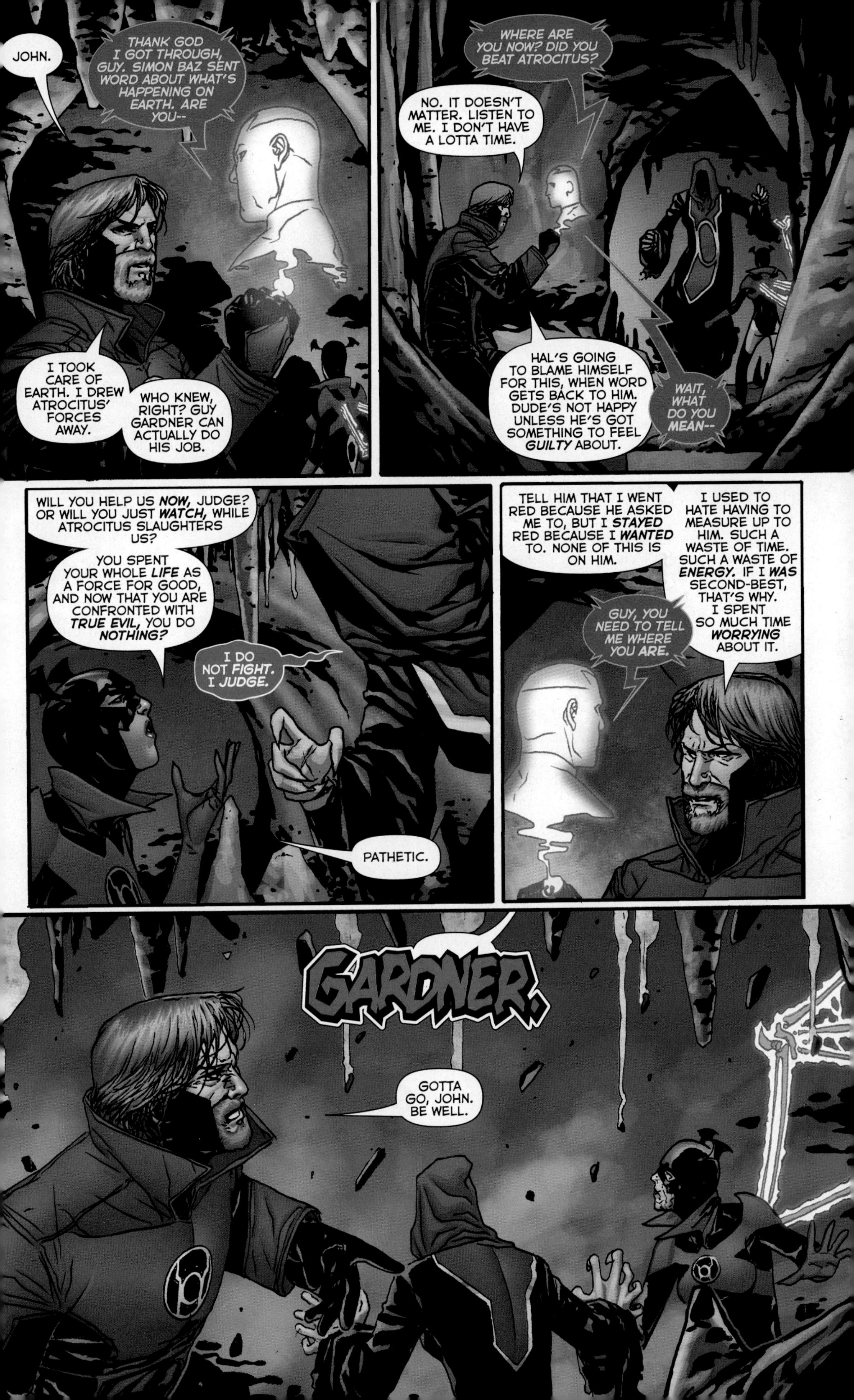
JOHN.
THANK GOD I GOT THROUGH, GUY. SIMON BAZ SENT WORD ABOUT WHAT'S HAPPENING ON EARTH. ARE YOU--
I TOOK CARE OF EARTH. I DREW ATROCITUS' FORCES AWAY.
WHO KNEW, RIGHT? GUY GARDNER CAN ACTUALLY DO HIS JOB.
WHERE ARE YOU NOW? DID YOU BEAT ATROCITUS?
NO. IT DOESN'T MATTER. LISTEN TO ME. I DON'T HAVE A LOTTA TIME.
HAL'S GOING TO BLAME HIMSELF FOR THIS, WHEN WORD GETS BACK TO HIM. DUDE'S NOT HAPPY UNLESS HE'S GOT SOMETHING TO FEEL GUILTY ABOUT.
WAIT, WHAT DO YOU MEAN--
WILL YOU HELP US NOW, JUDGE? OR WILL YOU JUST WATCH, WHILE ATROCITUS SLAUGHTERS US?
YOU SPENT YOUR WHOLE LIFE AS A FORCE FOR GOOD, AND NOW THAT YOU ARE CONFRONTED WITH TRUE EVIL, YOU DO NOTHING?
I DO NOT FIGHT. I JUDGE.
PATHETIC.
TELL HIM THAT I WENT RED BECAUSE HE ASKED ME TO, BUT I STAYED RED BECAUSE I WANTED TO. NONE OF THIS IS ON HIM.
I USED TO HATE HAVING TO MEASURE UP TO HIM. SUCH A WASTE OF TIME. SUCH A WASTE OF ENERGY. IF I WAS SECOND-BEST, THAT'S WHY. I SPENT SO MUCH TIME WORRYING ABOUT IT.
GUY, YOU NEED TO TELL ME WHERE YOU ARE.
GARDNER.
GOTTA GO, JOHN. BE WELL.

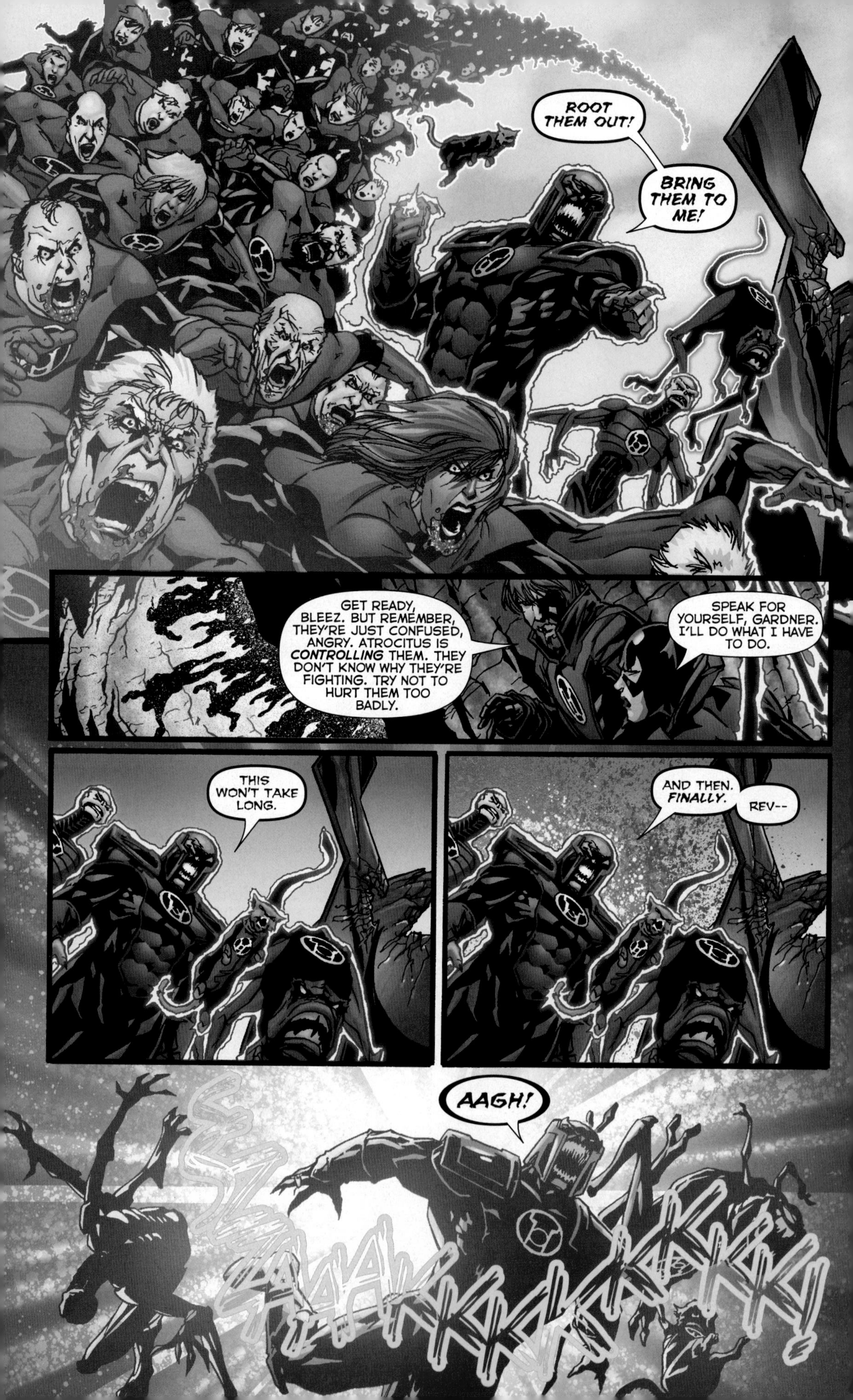
ROOT THEM OUT!
BRING THEM TO ME!
GET READY, BLEEZ. BUT REMEMBER, THEY'RE JUST CONFUSED, ANGRY. ATROCITUS IS **CONTROLLING** THEM. THEY DON'T KNOW WHY THEY'RE FIGHTING. TRY NOT TO HURT THEM TOO BADLY.
SPEAK FOR YOURSELF, GARDNER. I'LL DO WHAT I HAVE TO DO.
THIS WON'T TAKE LONG.
AND THEN. ***FINALLY.***
REV--
AAGH!
SZZAAAAKKKKKKKKK!

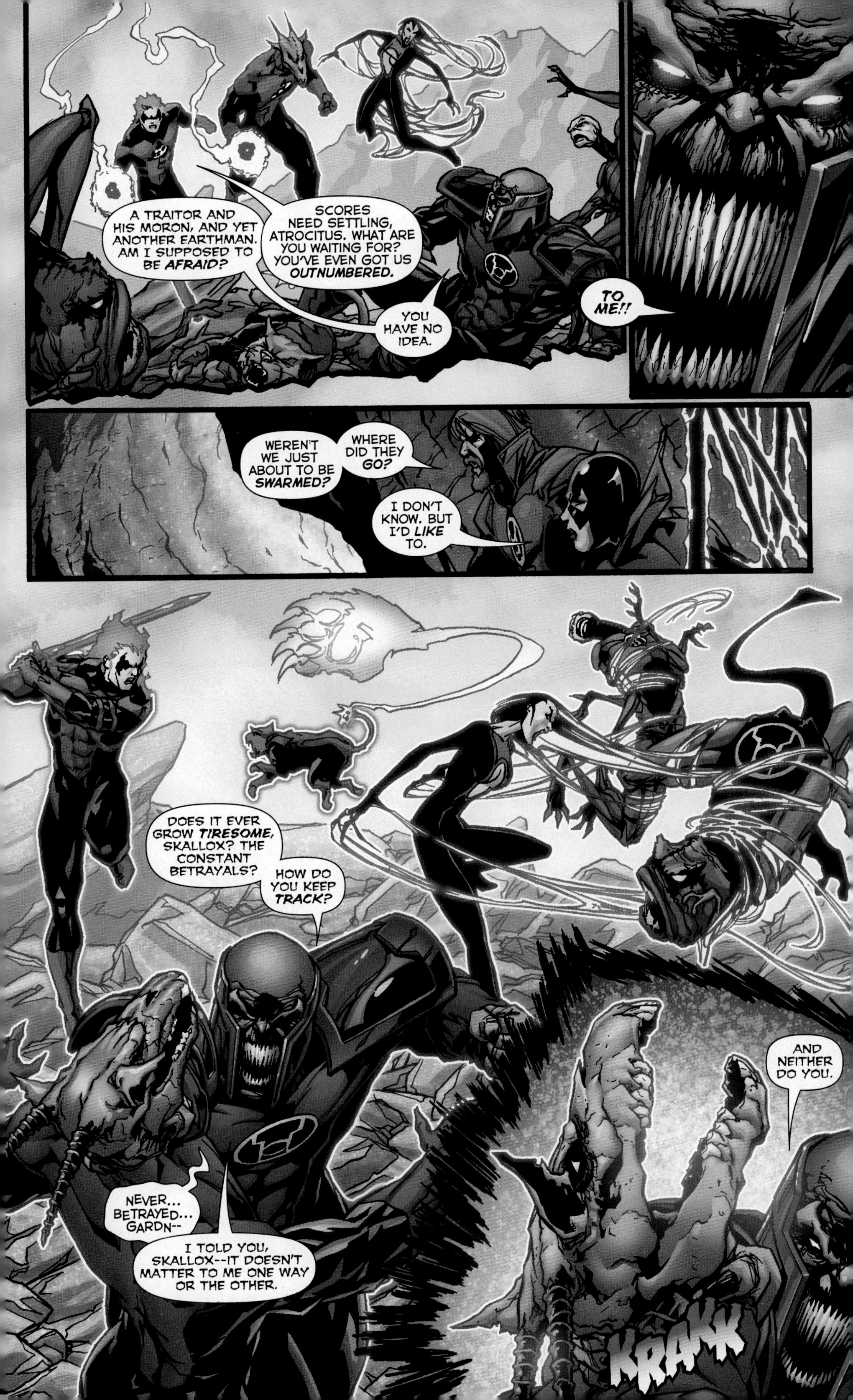
A TRAITOR AND HIS MORON, AND YET ANOTHER EARTHMAN. AM I SUPPOSED TO BE AFRAID?
SCORES NEED SETTLING, ATROCITUS. WHAT ARE YOU WAITING FOR? YOU'VE EVEN GOT US OUTNUMBERED.
YOU HAVE NO IDEA.
TO ME!!
WEREN'T WE JUST ABOUT TO BE SWARMED?
WHERE DID THEY GO?
I DON'T KNOW. BUT I'D LIKE TO.
DOES IT EVER GROW TIRESOME, SKALLOX? THE CONSTANT BETRAYALS?
HOW DO YOU KEEP TRACK?
AND NEITHER DO YOU.
NEVER... BETRAYED... GARDN--
I TOLD YOU, SKALLOX--IT DOESN'T MATTER TO ME ONE WAY OR THE OTHER.
KRAKK

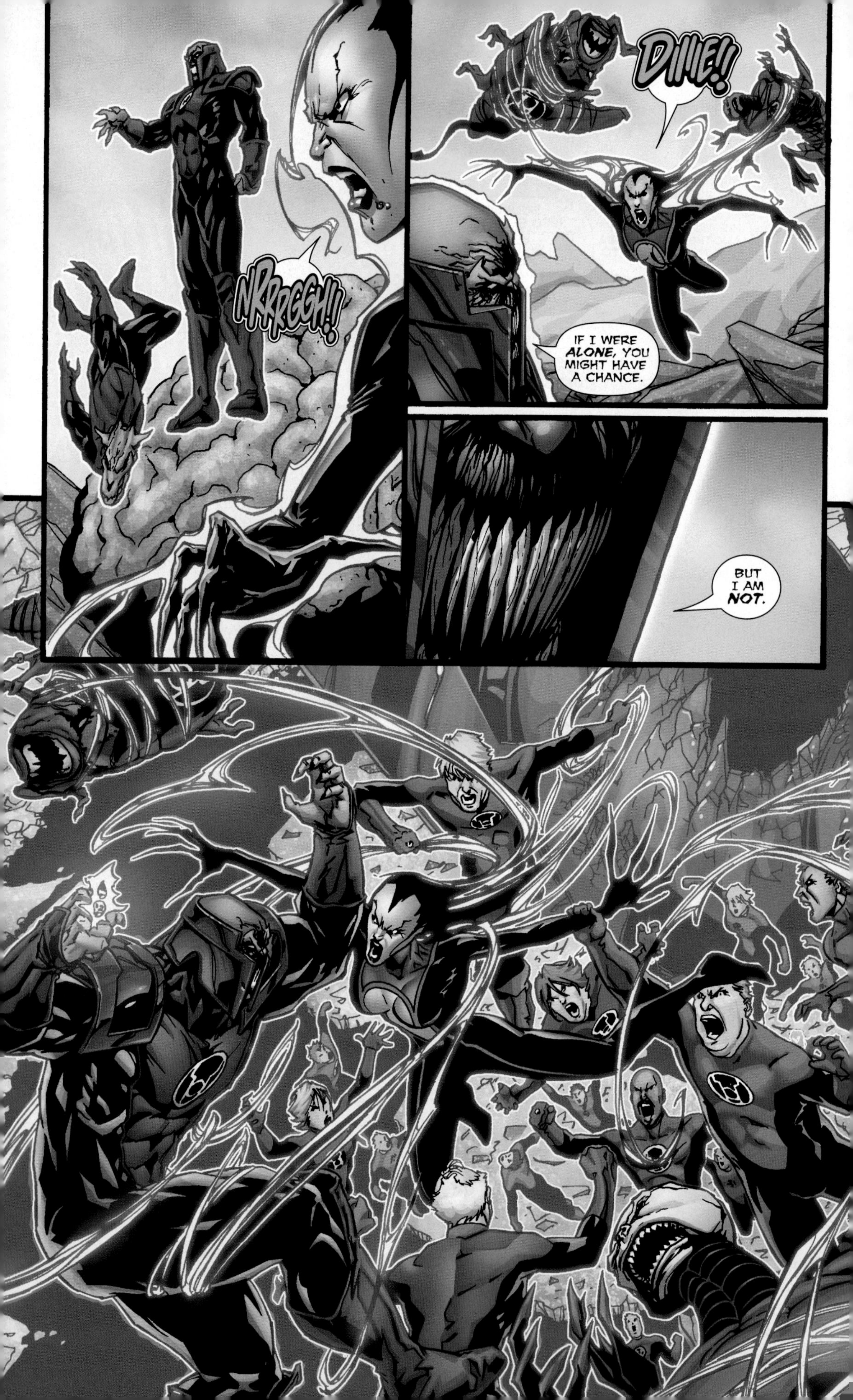
NRRRGGH!!
DIIIE!!
IF I WERE ALONE, YOU MIGHT HAVE A CHANCE.
BUT I AM NOT.

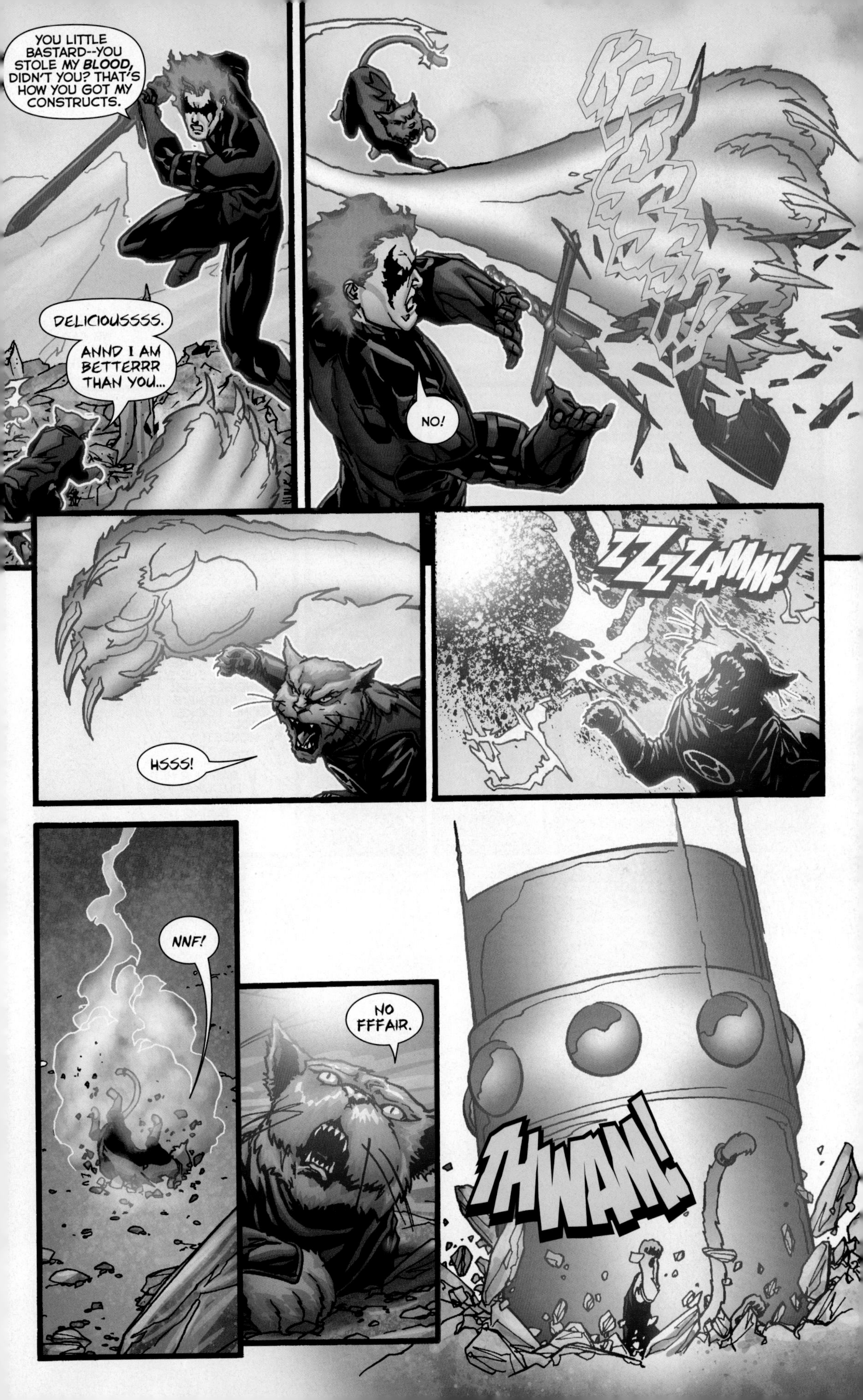
YOU LITTLE BASTARD--YOU STOLE MY BLOOD, DIDN'T YOU? THAT'S HOW YOU GOT MY CONSTRUCTS.
DELICIOUSSSS.
ANND I AM BETTERRR THAN YOU...
KRRSSSH
NO!
HSSS!
ZZZZAMM!
NNF!
NO FFFAIR.
THWAM!

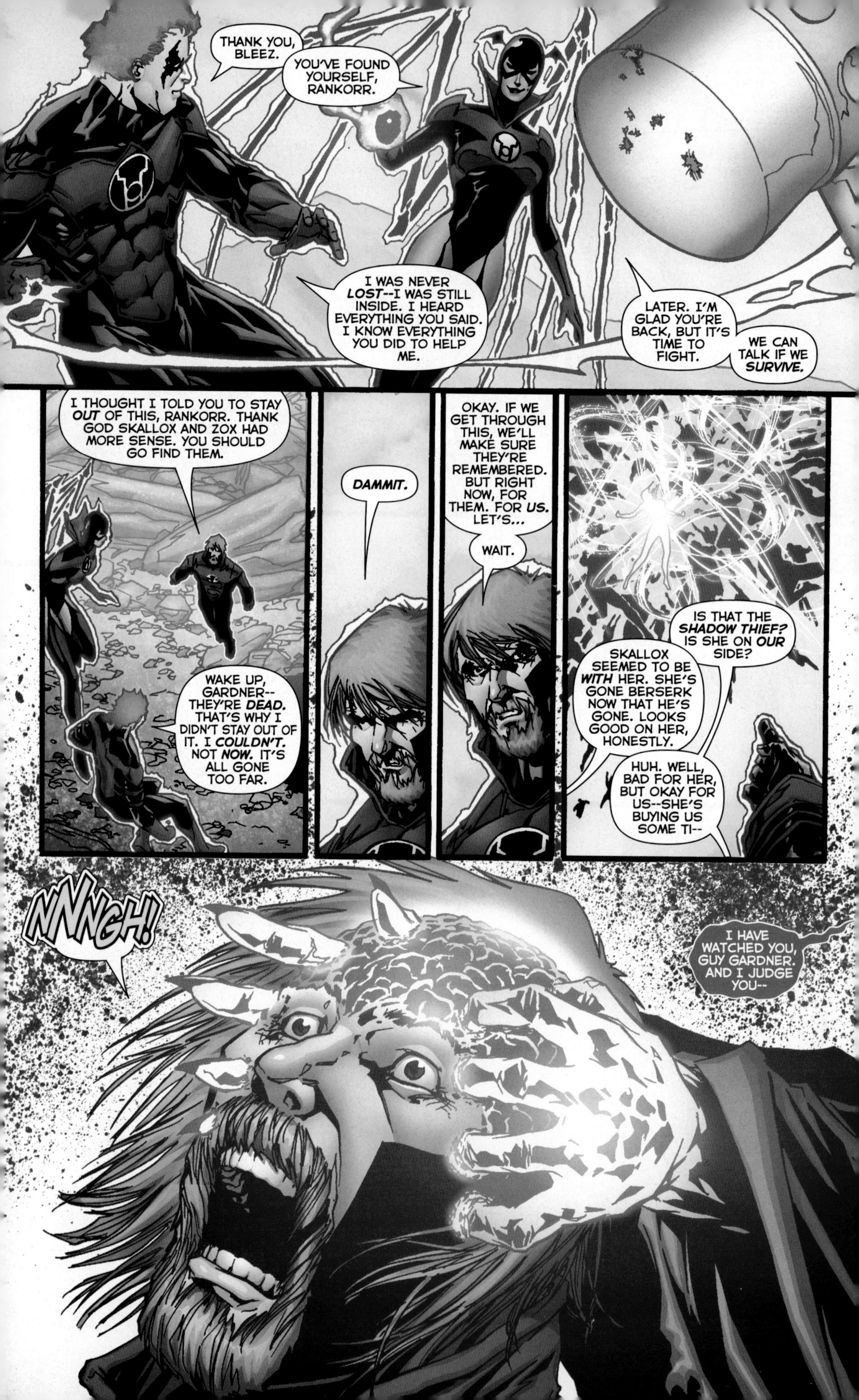
THANK YOU, BLEEZ.
YOU'VE FOUND YOURSELF, RANKORR.
I WAS NEVER LOST--I WAS STILL INSIDE. I HEARD EVERYTHING YOU SAID. I KNOW EVERYTHING YOU DID TO HELP ME.
LATER. I'M GLAD YOU'RE BACK, BUT IT'S TIME TO FIGHT.
WE CAN TALK IF WE SURVIVE.
I THOUGHT I TOLD YOU TO STAY OUT OF THIS, RANKORR. THANK GOD SKALLOX AND ZOX HAD MORE SENSE. YOU SHOULD GO FIND THEM.
WAKE UP, GARDNER--THEY'RE DEAD. THAT'S WHY I DIDN'T STAY OUT OF IT. I COULDN'T. NOT NOW. IT'S ALL GONE TOO FAR.
DAMMIT.
OKAY. IF WE GET THROUGH THIS, WE'LL MAKE SURE THEY'RE REMEMBERED. BUT RIGHT NOW, FOR THEM. FOR US. LET'S...
WAIT.
IS THAT THE SHADOW THIEF? IS SHE ON OUR SIDE?
SKALLOX SEEMED TO BE WITH HER. SHE'S GONE BERSERK NOW THAT HE'S GONE. LOOKS GOOD ON HER, HONESTLY.
HUH. WELL, BAD FOR HER, BUT OKAY FOR US--SHE'S BUYING US SOME TI--
NNNGH!
I HAVE WATCHED YOU, GUY GARDNER. AND I JUDGE YOU--

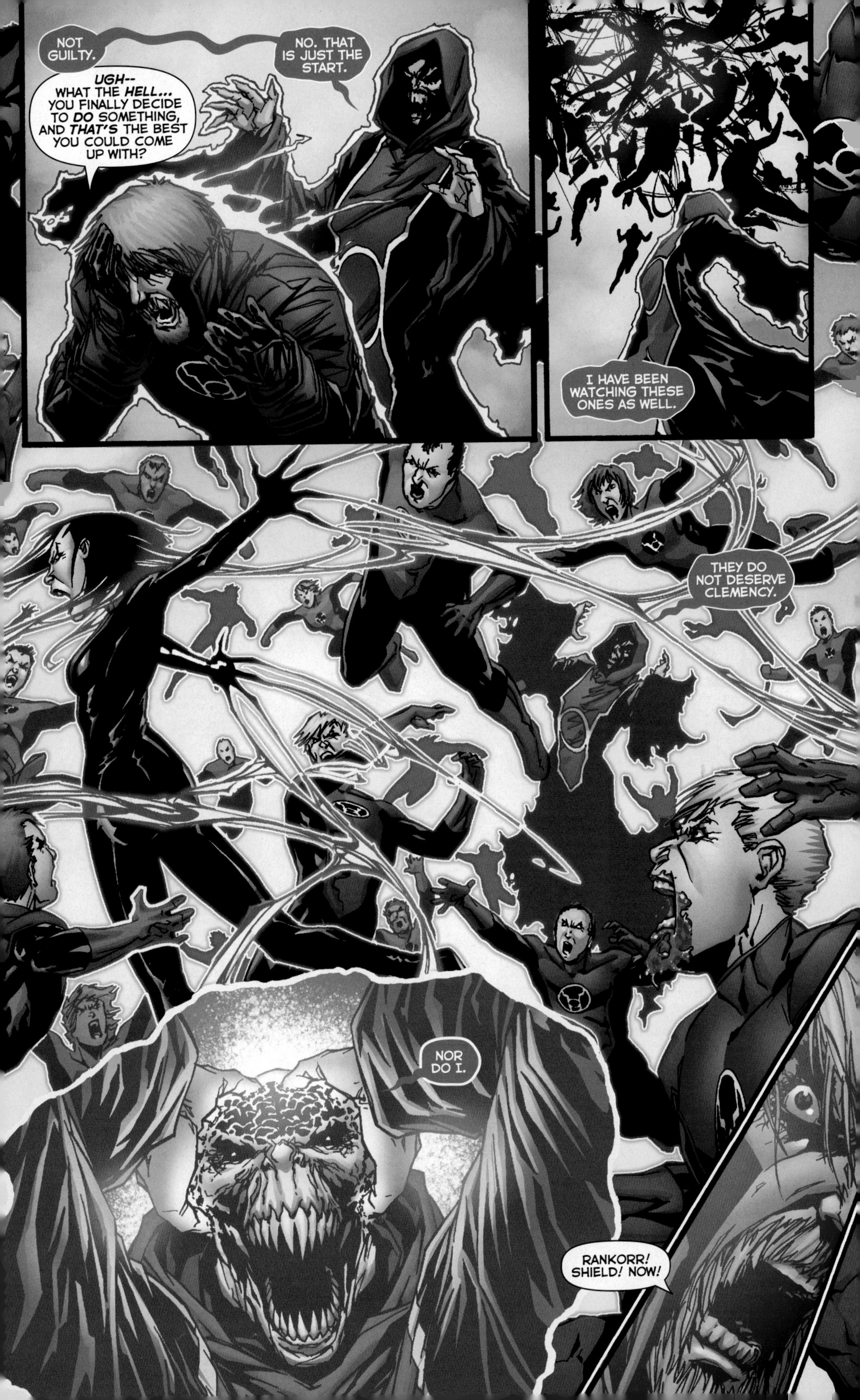
NOT GUILTY.
NO. THAT IS JUST THE START.
UGH-- WHAT THE HELL... YOU FINALLY DECIDE TO DO SOMETHING, AND THAT'S THE BEST YOU COULD COME UP WITH?
I HAVE BEEN WATCHING THESE ONES AS WELL.
THEY DO NOT DESERVE CLEMENCY.
NOR DO I.
RANKORR! SHIELD! NOW!

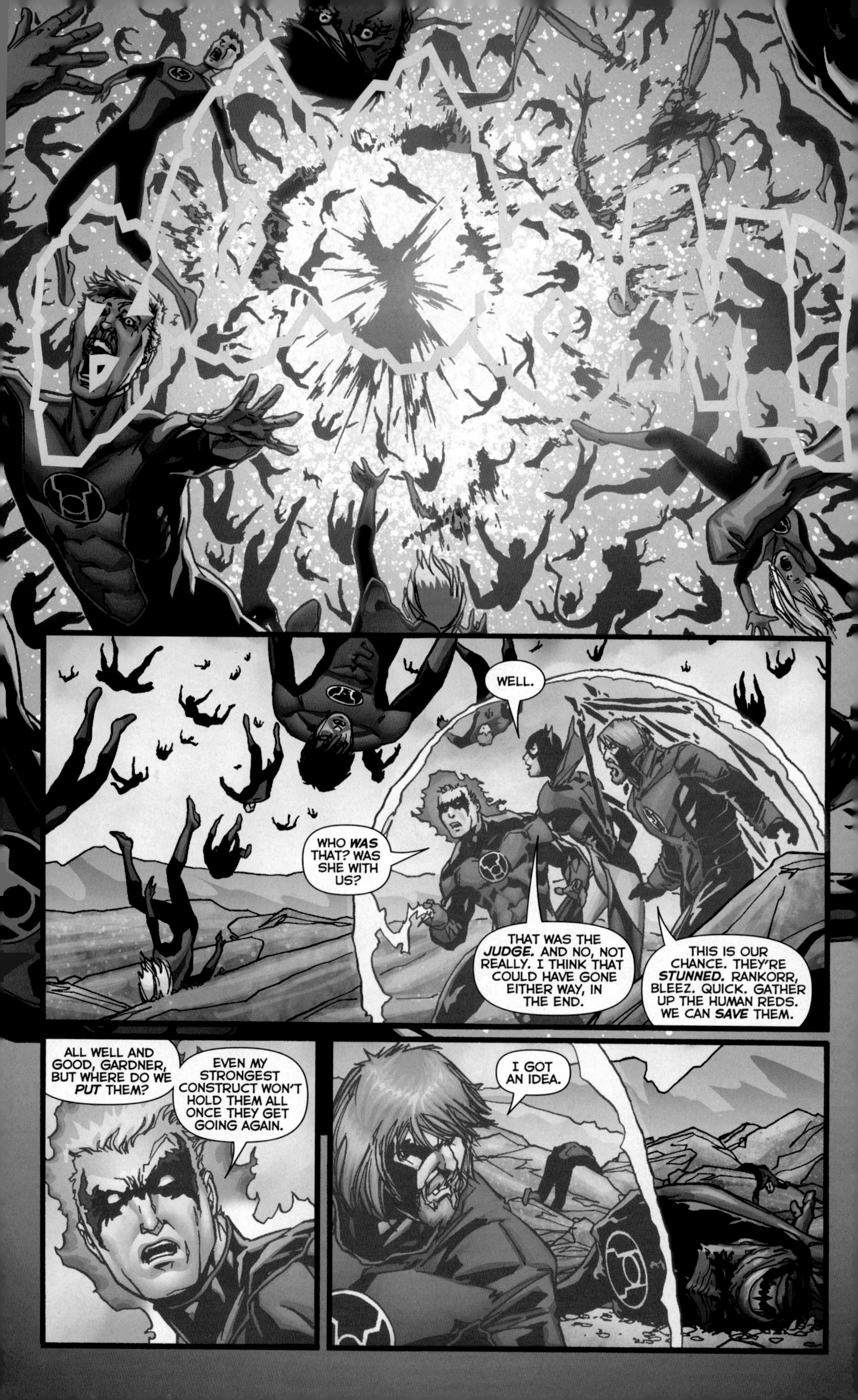
WELL.
WHO *WAS* THAT? WAS SHE WITH US?
THAT WAS THE *JUDGE.* AND NO, NOT REALLY. I THINK THAT COULD HAVE GONE EITHER WAY, IN THE END.
THIS IS OUR CHANCE. THEY'RE *STUNNED.* RANKORR, BLEEZ. QUICK. GATHER UP THE HUMAN REDS. WE CAN *SAVE* THEM.
ALL WELL AND GOOD, GARDNER, BUT WHERE DO WE *PUT* THEM?
EVEN MY STRONGEST CONSTRUCT WON'T HOLD THEM ALL ONCE THEY GET GOING AGAIN.
I GOT AN IDEA.

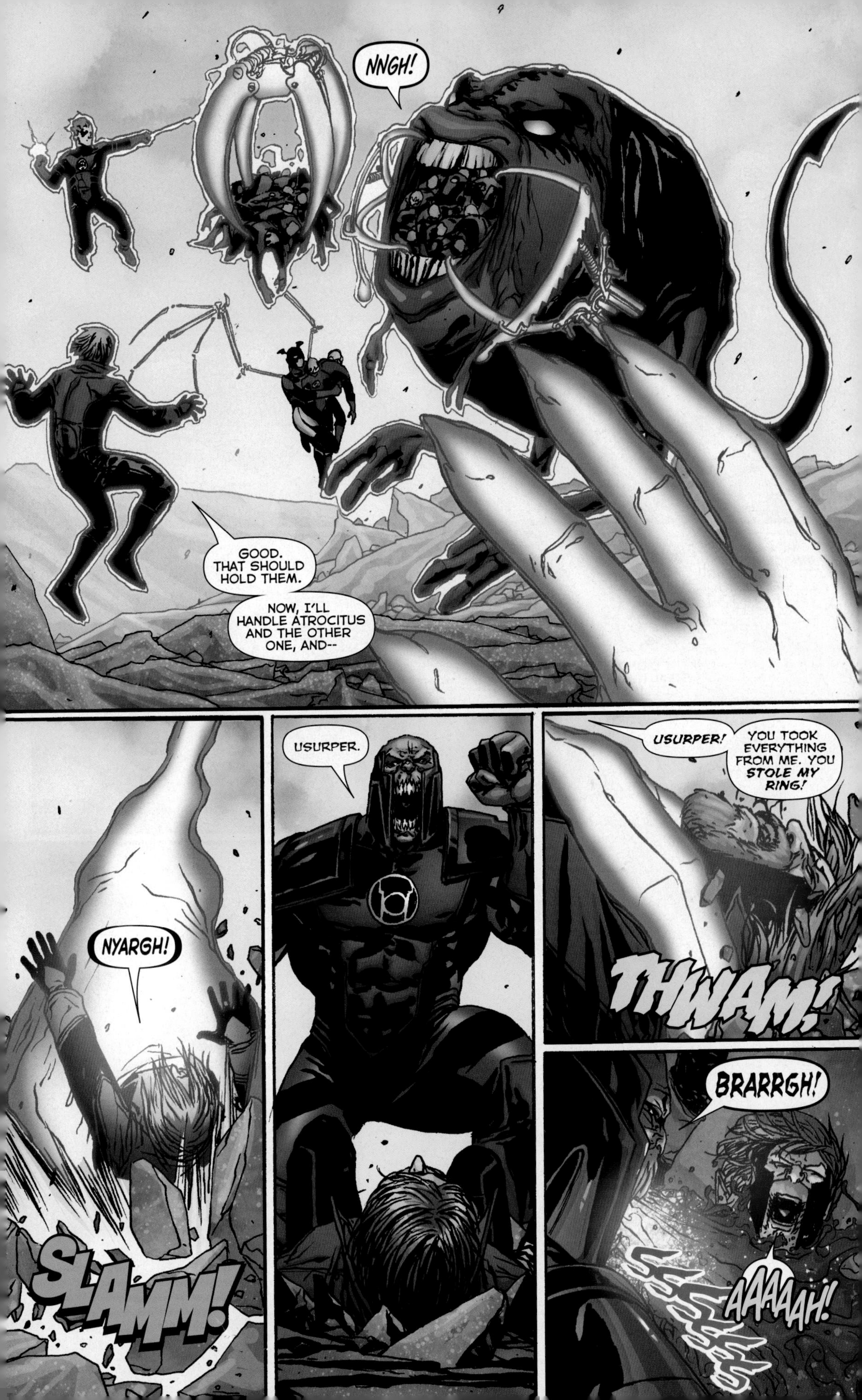
NNGH!
GOOD. THAT SHOULD HOLD THEM.
NOW, I'LL HANDLE ATROCITUS AND THE OTHER ONE, AND--
NYARGH!
SLAMM!
USURPER.
USURPER!
YOU TOOK EVERYTHING FROM ME. YOU STOLE MY RING!
THWAM!
BRARRGH!
AAAAAH!

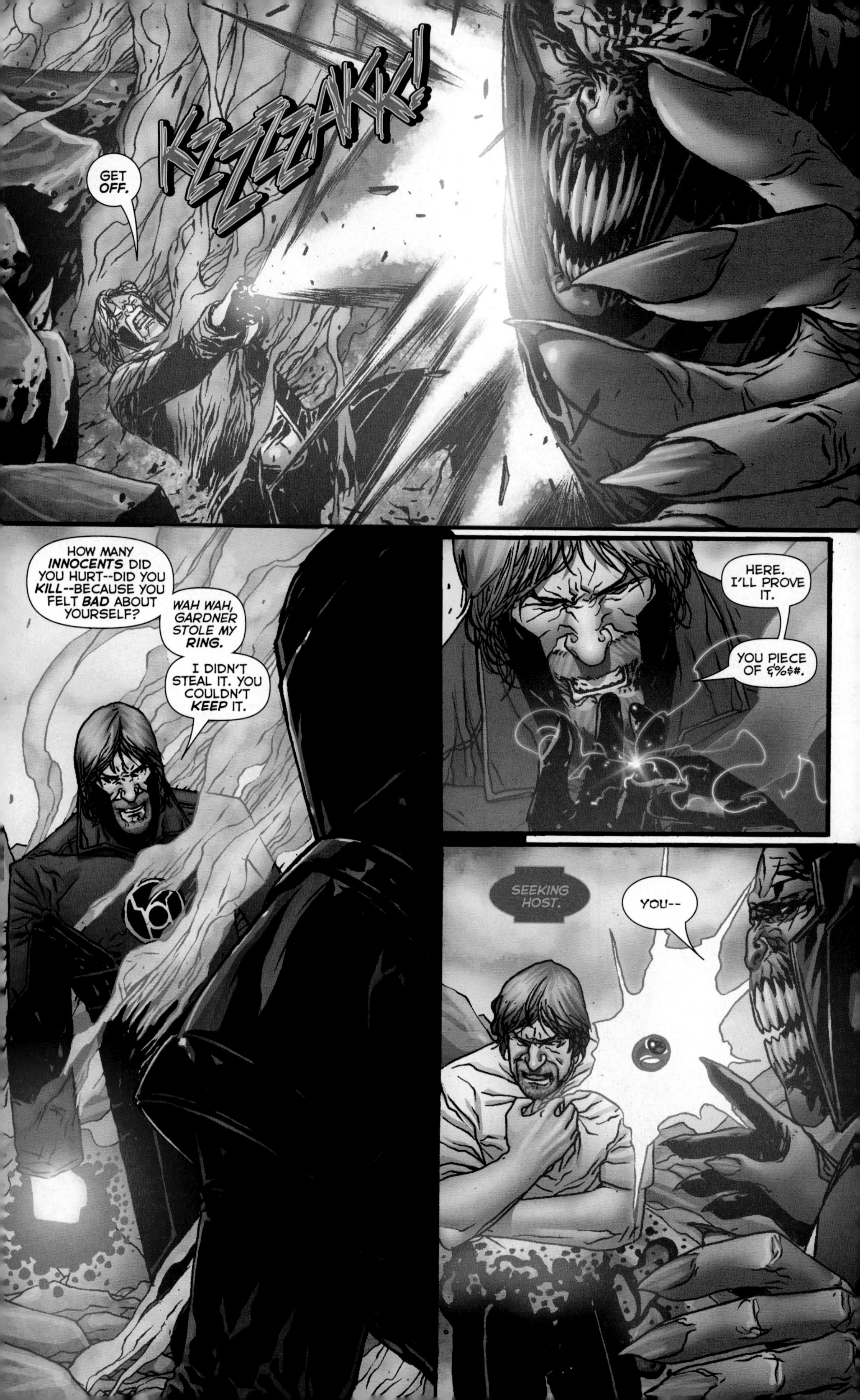
KZZZZAKK!
GET OFF.
HOW MANY INNOCENTS DID YOU HURT--DID YOU KILL--BECAUSE YOU FELT BAD ABOUT YOURSELF?
WAH WAH, GARDNER STOLE MY RING.
I DIDN'T STEAL IT. YOU COULDN'T KEEP IT.
HERE. I'LL PROVE IT.
YOU PIECE OF &%$#.
SEEKING HOST.
YOU--

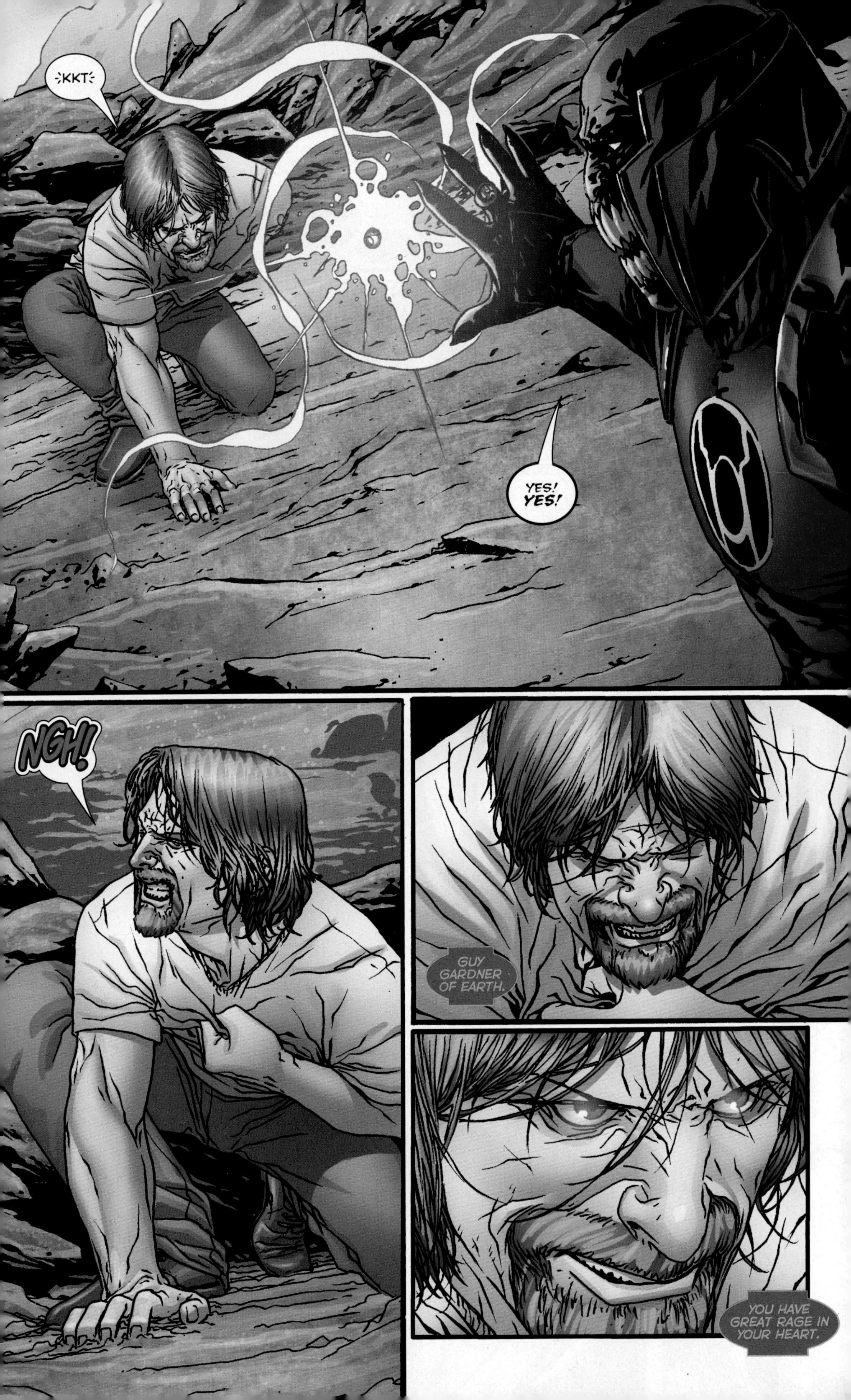
KKT
YES! YES!
NGH!
GUY GARDNER OF EARTH.
YOU HAVE GREAT RAGE IN YOUR HEART.

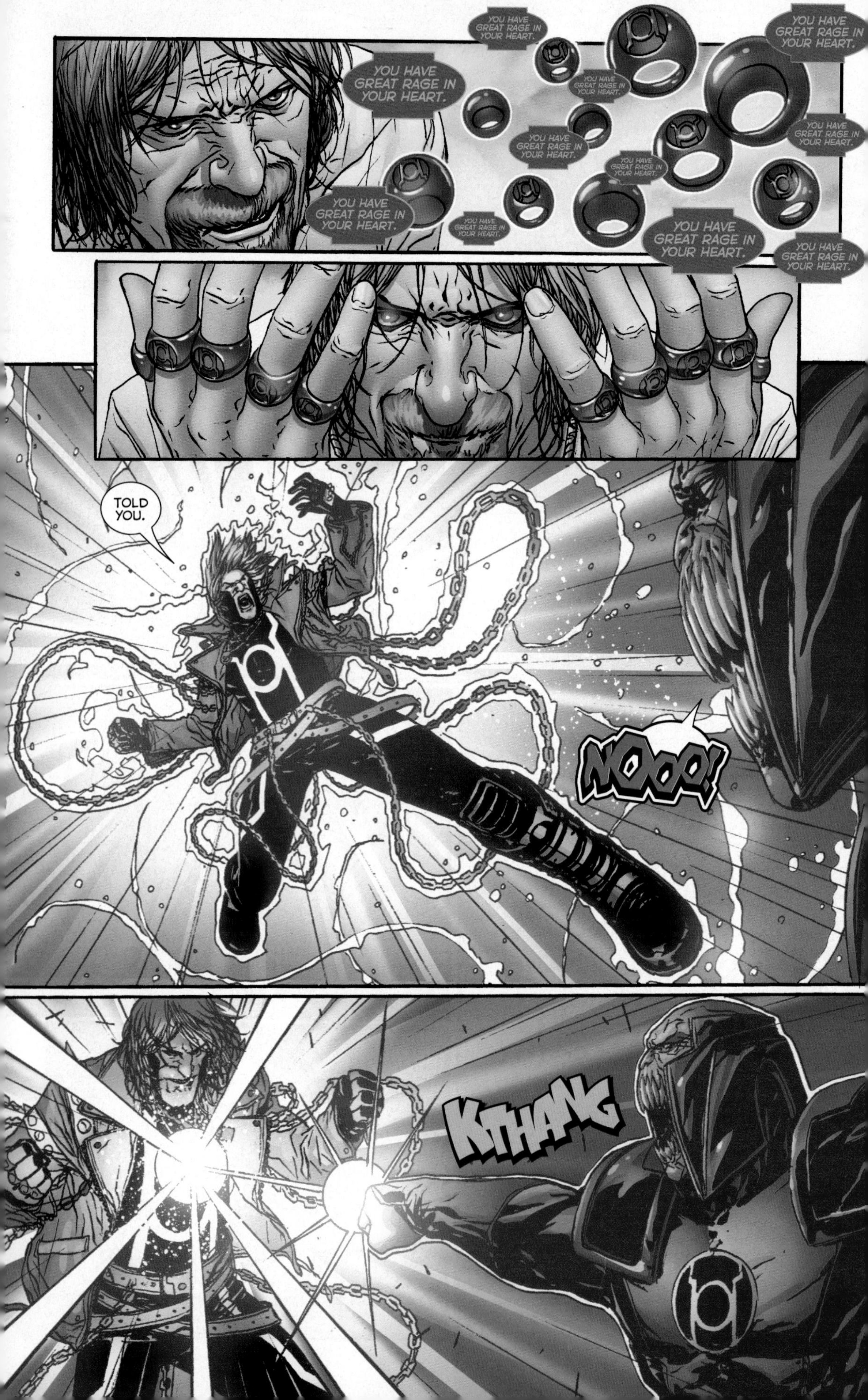
YOU HAVE GREAT RAGE IN YOUR HEART.
YOU HAVE GREAT RAGE IN YOUR HEART.
YOU HAVE GREAT RAGE IN YOUR HEART.
YOU HAVE GREAT RAGE IN YOUR HEART.
YOU HAVE GREAT RAGE IN YOUR HEART.
YOU HAVE GREAT RAGE IN YOUR HEART.
YOU HAVE GREAT RAGE IN YOUR HEART.
YOU HAVE GREAT RAGE IN YOUR HEART.
YOU HAVE GREAT RAGE IN YOUR HEART.
YOU HAVE GREAT RAGE IN YOUR HEART.
YOU HAVE GREAT RAGE IN YOUR HEART.
TOLD YOU.
NOOO!
KTHANG

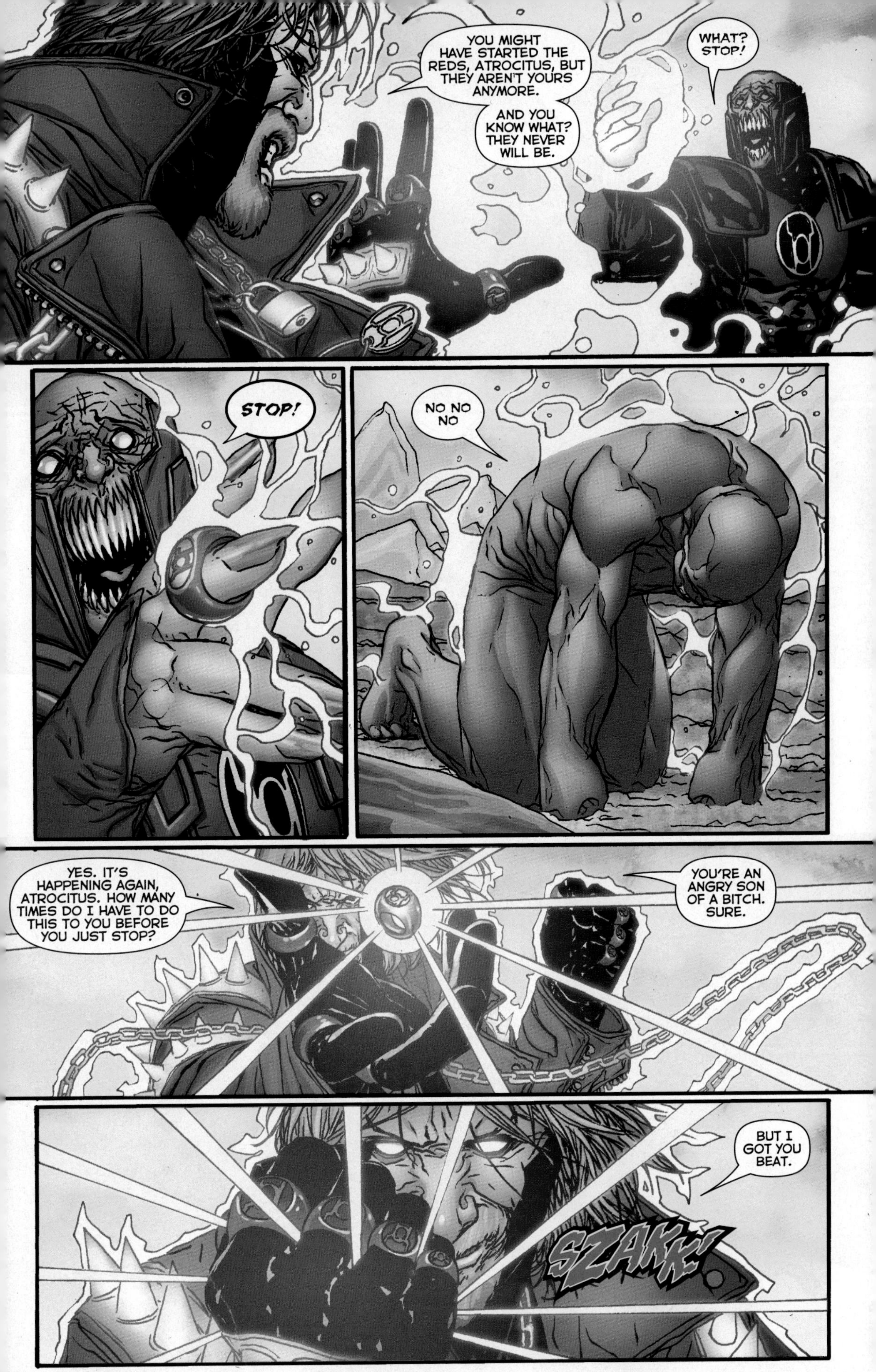
YOU MIGHT HAVE STARTED THE REDS, ATROCITUS, BUT THEY AREN'T YOURS ANYMORE.
AND YOU KNOW WHAT? THEY NEVER WILL BE.
WHAT? STOP!
STOP!
NO NO NO
YES. IT'S HAPPENING AGAIN, ATROCITUS. HOW MANY TIMES DO I HAVE TO DO THIS TO YOU BEFORE YOU JUST STOP?
YOU'RE AN ANGRY SON OF A BITCH. SURE.
BUT I GOT YOU BEAT.
SZAKK!

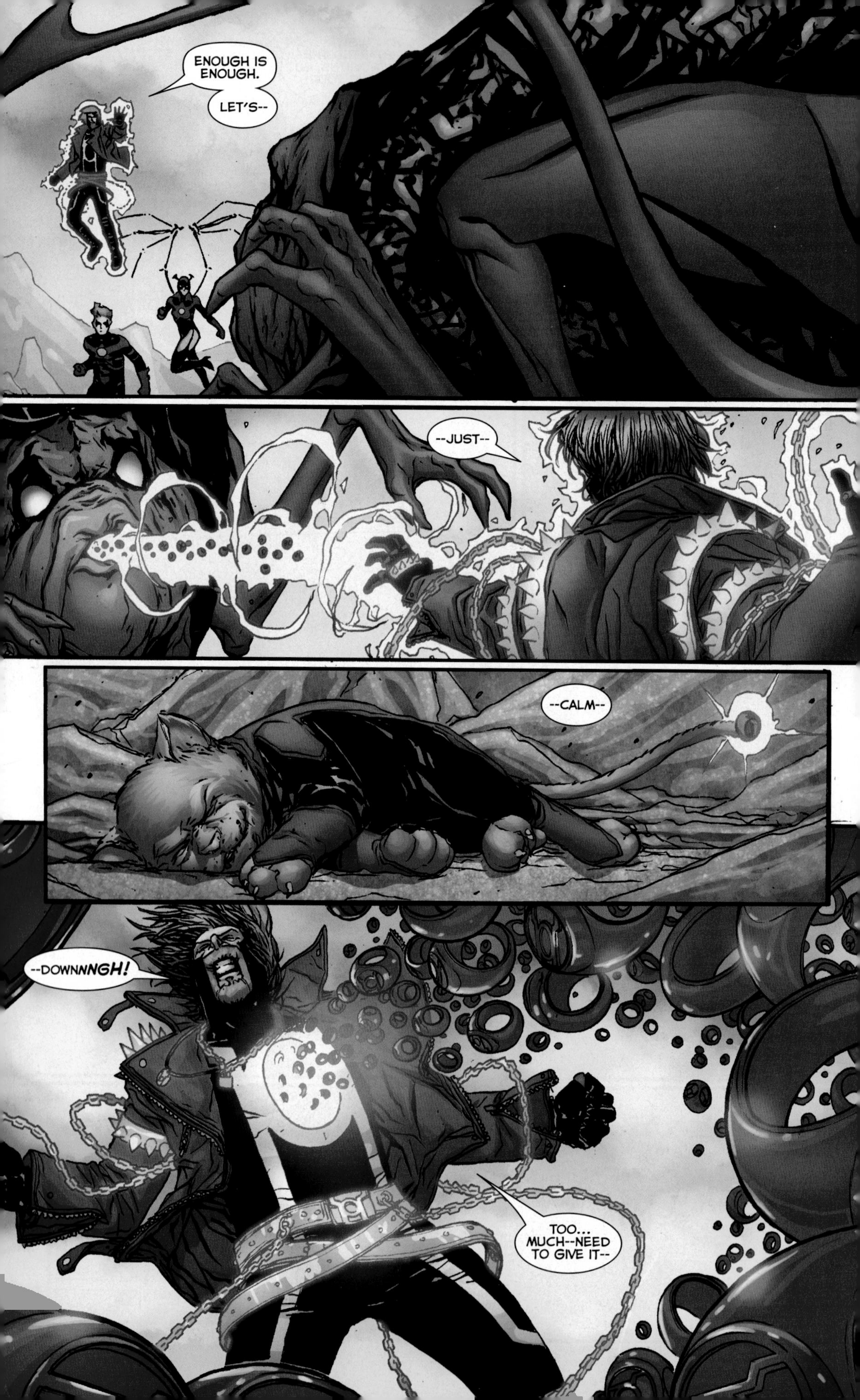
ENOUGH IS ENOUGH.
LET'S--
--JUST--
--CALM--
--DOWNNNGH!
TOO... MUCH--NEED TO GIVE IT--

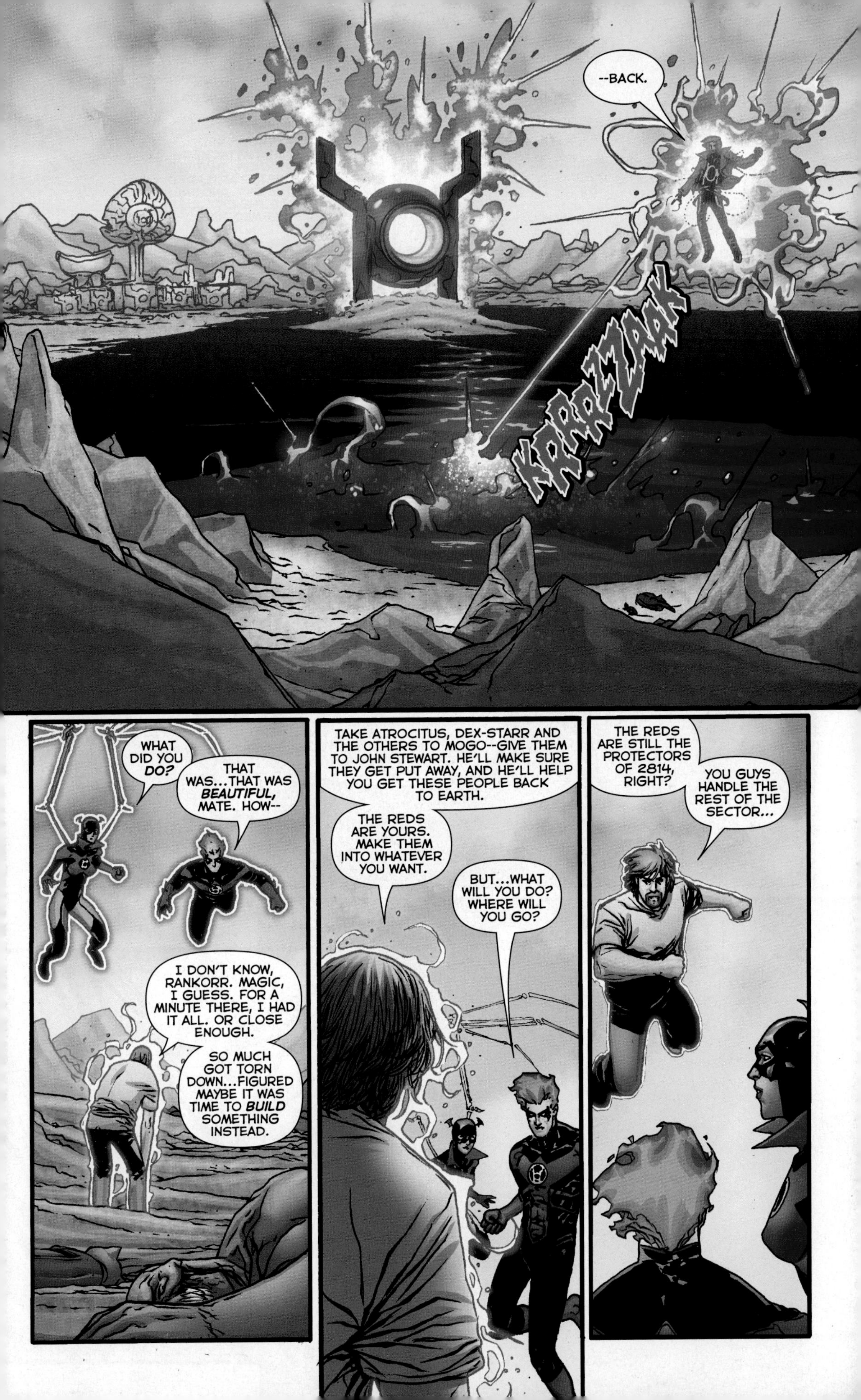
--BACK.
KRRRZZAAK
WHAT DID YOU *DO?*
THAT WAS...THAT WAS *BEAUTIFUL,* MATE. HOW--
I DON'T KNOW, RANKORR. MAGIC, I GUESS. FOR A MINUTE THERE, I HAD IT ALL. OR CLOSE ENOUGH.
SO MUCH GOT TORN DOWN...FIGURED MAYBE IT WAS TIME TO *BUILD* SOMETHING INSTEAD.
TAKE ATROCITUS, DEX-STARR AND THE OTHERS TO MOGO--GIVE THEM TO JOHN STEWART. HE'LL MAKE SURE THEY GET PUT AWAY, AND HE'LL HELP YOU GET THESE PEOPLE BACK TO EARTH.
THE REDS ARE YOURS. MAKE THEM INTO WHATEVER YOU WANT.
BUT...WHAT WILL YOU DO? WHERE WILL YOU GO?
THE REDS ARE STILL THE PROTECTORS OF 2814, RIGHT?
YOU GUYS HANDLE THE REST OF THE SECTOR...

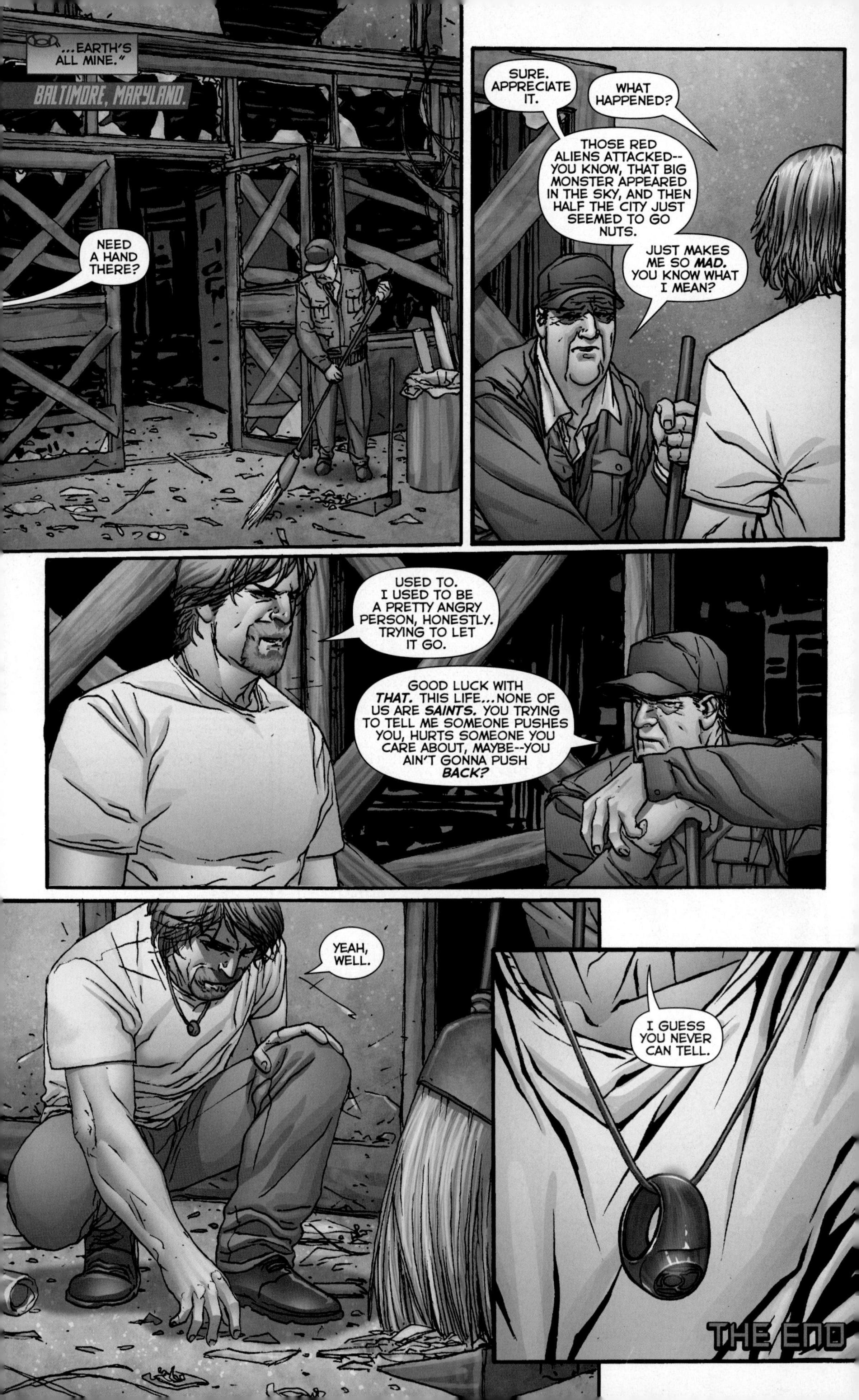

"...EARTH'S ALL MINE."
BALTIMORE, MARYLAND.
NEED A HAND THERE?
SURE. APPRECIATE IT.
WHAT HAPPENED?
THOSE RED ALIENS ATTACKED--YOU KNOW, THAT BIG MONSTER APPEARED IN THE SKY, AND THEN HALF THE CITY JUST SEEMED TO GO NUTS.
JUST MAKES ME SO MAD. YOU KNOW WHAT I MEAN?
USED TO. I USED TO BE A PRETTY ANGRY PERSON, HONESTLY. TRYING TO LET IT GO.
GOOD LUCK WITH THAT. THIS LIFE...NONE OF US ARE SAINTS. YOU TRYING TO TELL ME SOMEONE PUSHES YOU, HURTS SOMEONE YOU CARE ABOUT, MAYBE--YOU AIN'T GONNA PUSH BACK?
YEAH, WELL.
I GUESS YOU NEVER CAN TELL.
THE END

Red Lantern Supergirl design by Kenneth Rocafort

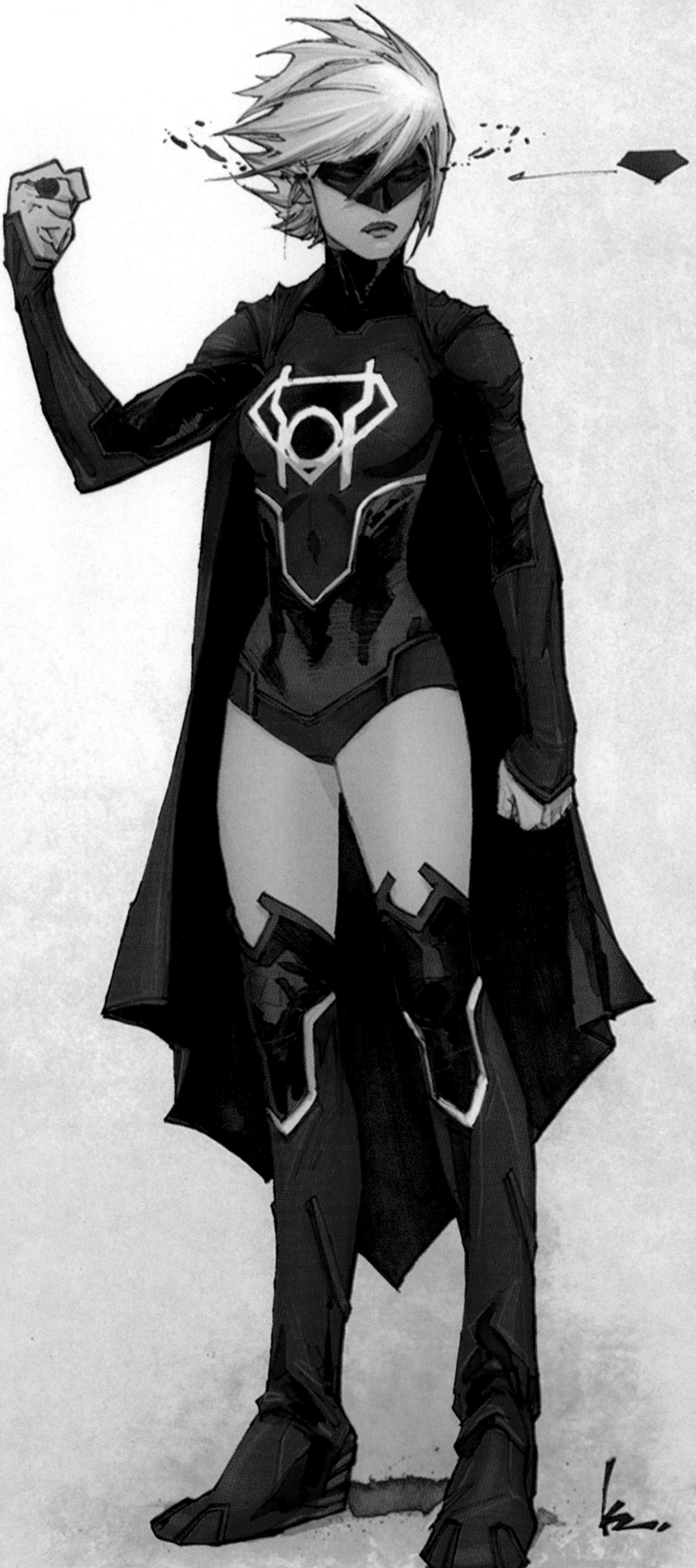

Red Lantern God Guy Gardner designs by Alessandro Vitti

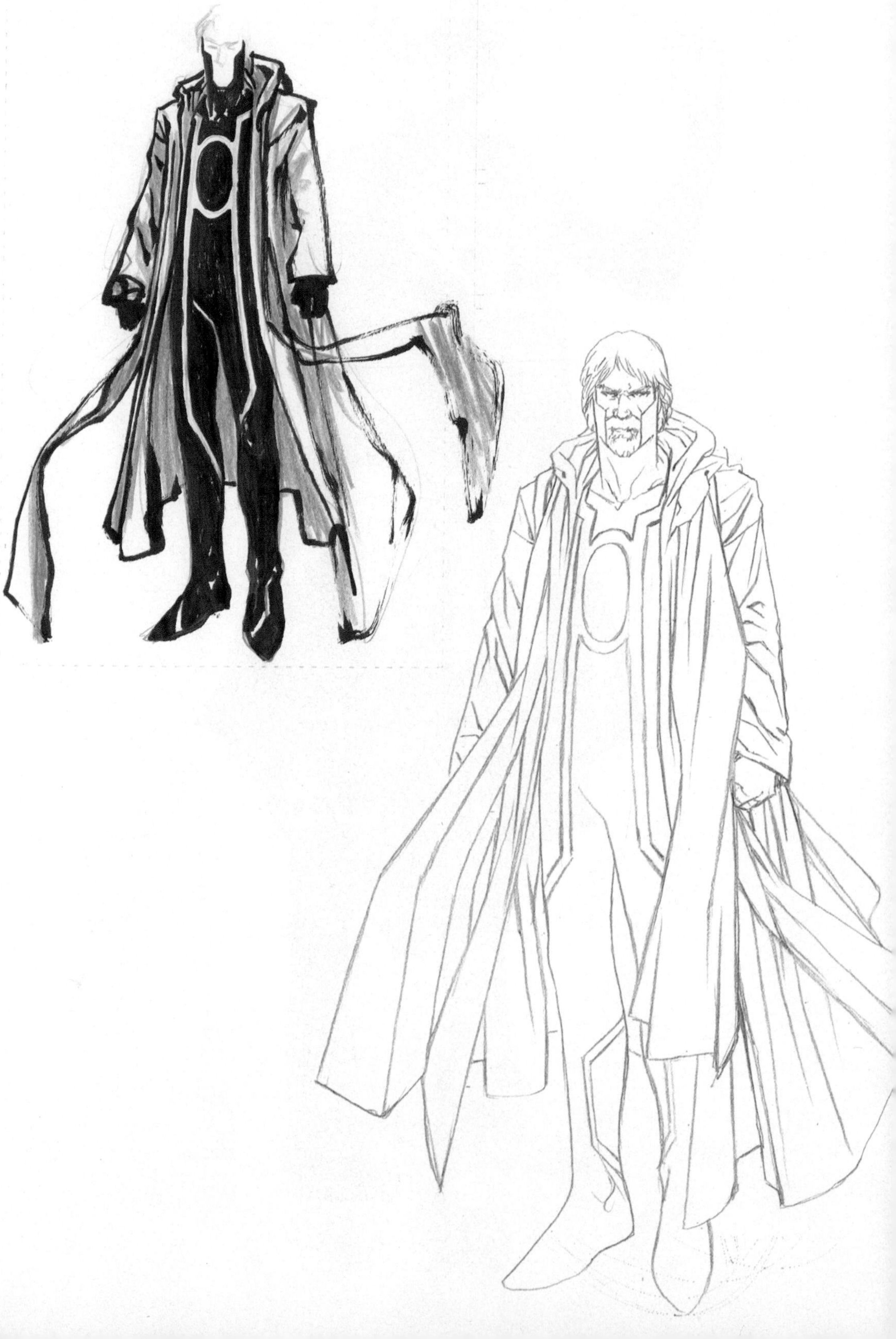

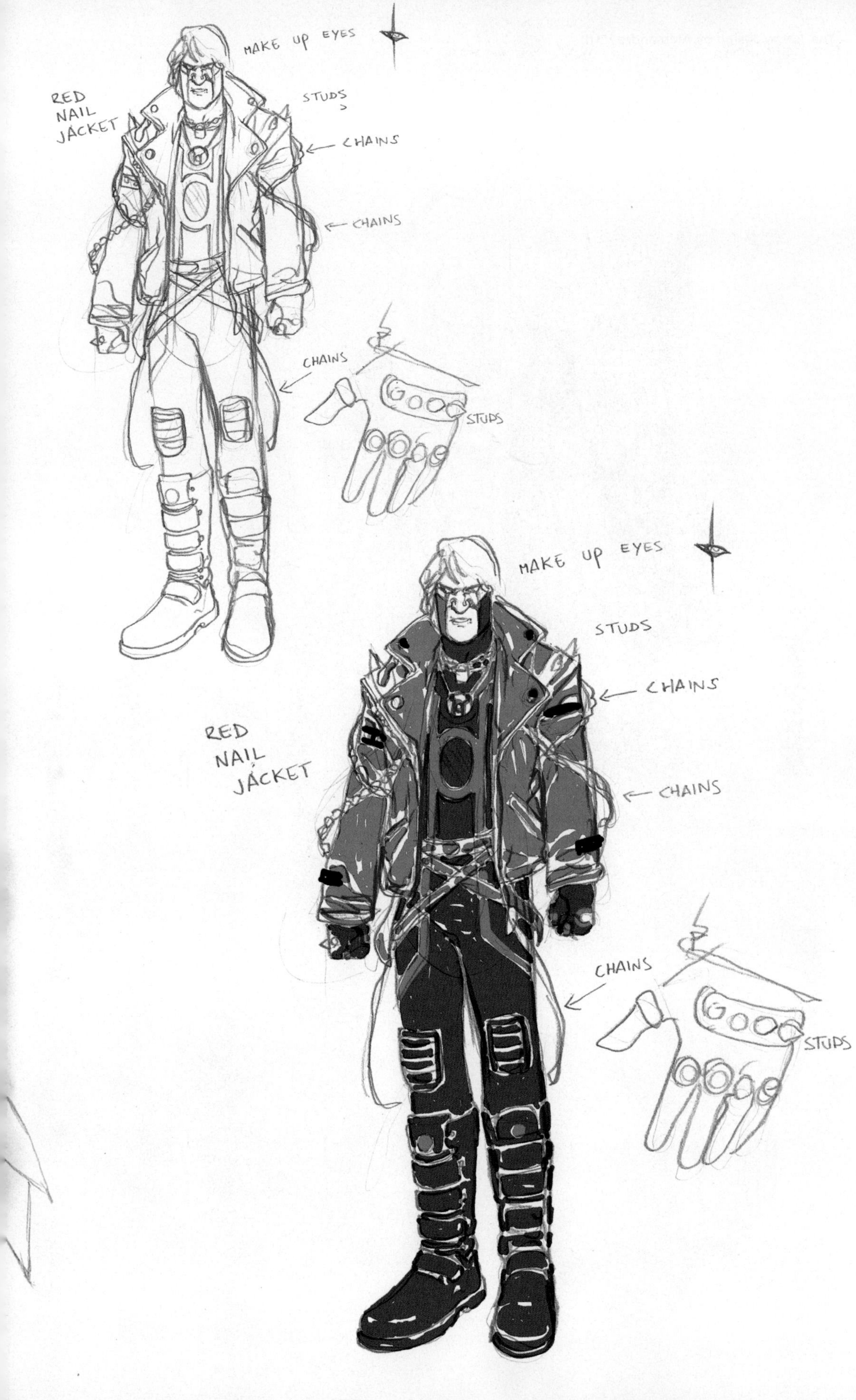
MAKE UP EYES
RED NAIL JACKET
STUDS
CHAINS
CHAINS
CHAINS
STUDS
MAKE UP EYES
STUDS
CHAINS
RED NAIL JACKET
CHAINS
CHAINS
STUDS

The Judge design by Alessandro Vitti

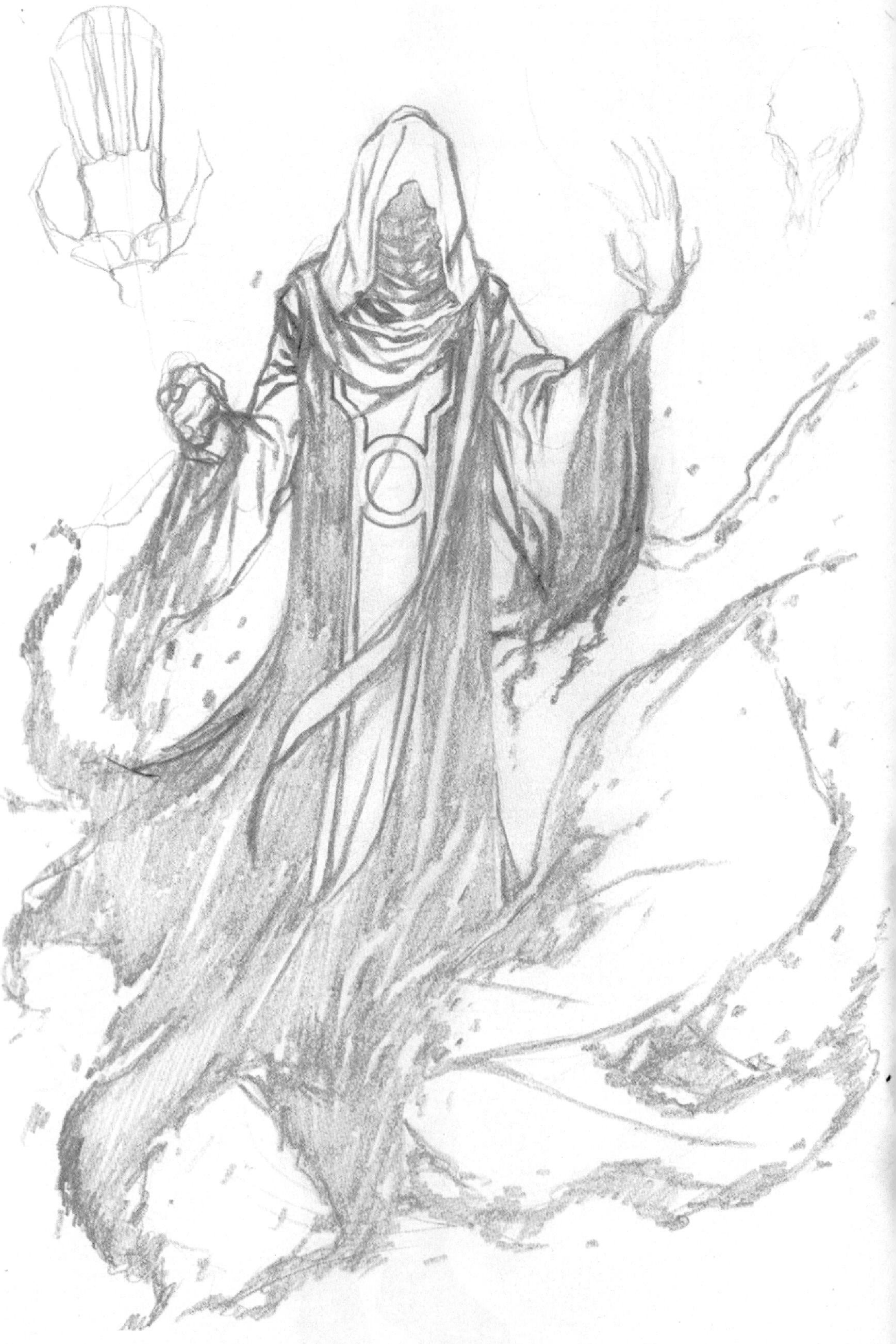

Red Lantern Nayk design by J. Calafiore

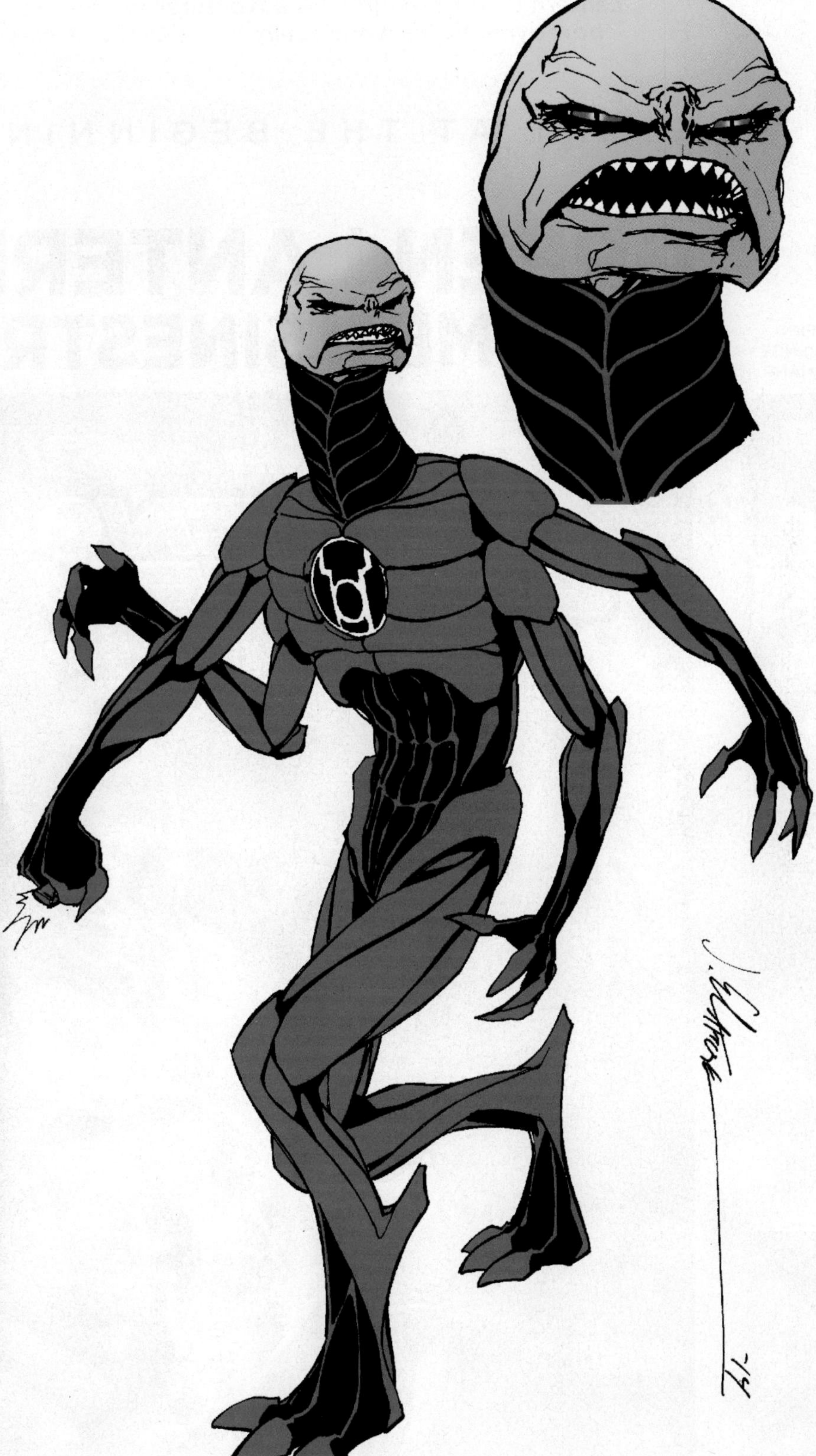

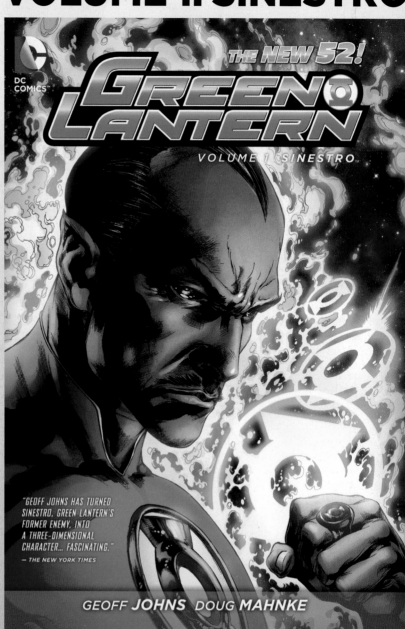